This is a volume in
THE UNIVERSITY OF MICHIGAN HISTORY OF THE MODERN WORLD
Upon completion, the series will consist of the following volumes:

The United States to 1865 *by Michael Kraus*

The United States since 1865 *by Foster Rhea Dulles*

Canada: A Modern History *by John Bartlet Brebner*

Latin America: A Modern History *by J. Fred Rippy*

Great Britain to 1688: A Modern History *by Maurice Ashley*

Great Britain since 1688: A Modern History *by K. B. Smellie*

France: A Modern History *by Albert Guérard*

Germany: A Modern History *by Marshall Dill, Jr.*

Italy: A Modern History *by Denis Mack Smith*

Russia and the Soviet Union: A Modern History *by Warren B. Walsh*

The Near East: A Modern History *by William Yale*

The Far East: A Modern History *by Nathaniel Peffer*

India: A Modern History *by Percival Spear*

The Southwest Pacific to 1900: A Modern History *by C. Hartley Grattan*

The Southwest Pacific since 1900: A Modern History *by C. Hartley Grattan*

Spain: A Modern History *by Rhea Marsh Smith*

Africa to 1875: A Modern History *by Robin Hallett*

Africa since 1875: A Modern History *by Robin Hallett*

Eastern Europe: A Modern History *by John Erickson*

ITALY

A Modern History

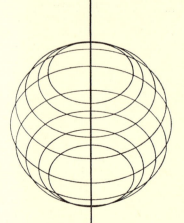

The University of Michigan History of the Modern World

Edited by Allan Nevins and Howard M. Ehrmann

ITALY

A Modern History

BY DENIS MACK SMITH

NEW EDITION
REVISED AND ENLARGED

Ann Arbor : The University of Michigan Press

Copyright © by the University of Michigan 1959, 1969
All rights reserved
Library of Congress Catalog Card No. 69-15851
Published in the United States of America by
the University of Michigan Press and simultaneously
in Don Mills, Canada, by Longmans Canada Limited
Manufactured in the United States of America
by Vail-Ballou Press, Inc., Binghamton, N.Y.

Preface

The best-known histories of modern Italy used to take as their principal theme the making of a new Italian nation in the nineteenth century, but today a quite different emphasis is possible. The *risorgimento* can now be taken not as a central theme but as a starting point, both to trace the consequences of this national movement down to the present, and also to see how the course of later events may throw new light on earlier Italian patriotic feeling. Two world wars were to be fought, both of them severely testing the fabric of Italian society. An empire was also won and was subsequently lost again, as a patriotic movement gradually became imperialistic and then fascist. The careers of Crispi and Mussolini, who were the two chief architects of this particular change, prompt the thought that some flaws must have been embedded in nineteenth-century liberal patriotism and its achievements. For Italy had in 1861 been of all countries the most admired by liberal politicians and historians, and yet it proved to be the first to give way after 1919 before the new dictatorial imperialism. A history of modern Italy must try to account for this fact, as it must further attempt to explain why the fascist dictatorship lasted so long, and why so severe a military defeat was encountered in 1940–43. It must also show how that defeat was to be followed by a vigorous national revival. Finally, it must trace the gradual submergence of the liberals and anticlericals who had triumphed in the *risorgimento,* and their decisive supersession by the Catholics and communists who swept the board in the elections of 1948.

March 1861 has been taken as the starting point of this book, the month in which Count Cavour declared that a kingdom of Italy was born. Institutions and ideas had by that date already begun to develop along lines quite unimagined by the early prophets of Italian nationalism and had acquired a life of their own which down to the present day forms a compact subject of study. Until 1861 there had from the beginning of time been only the history of individual regions, but from that date onward there existed a united kingdom. Cavour in making this united kingdom aimed to create a liberal state, a prosperous state, and a great power; and looking back after nearly a hundred years it is possible for us to assess these sometimes contradictory intentions, to appraise the methods used and the degree of success or failure achieved.

The concluding date of the first edition of this book was 1945, with the death of Mussolini and the end of the war in Europe; but since then a new and much happier chapter of history has been written, and this new edition takes the story to the fall of 1968. Anyone who tries to write on contemporary affairs, or even on the first decades of the present century, will know the impossibility of being perfectly judicial and accurate in a field where tempers have not yet cooled and the pattern of history has not had time to set. Retrospective over-simplification, neglect of the failures and might-have-beens, either of these may easily distort the picture as the price of stressing clarity and noteworthiness and reducing every complex incident to a simple narrative. Often the relevant facts are uncorroborated, unobtainable, or known partly and only by word of mouth. Valuable papers are sometimes inaccessible or missing. Even where the facts are known, they have often not been submitted sufficiently to criticism, elaboration, and synthesis; the true and the false exist together, the important alongside the unimportant, in tendentious personal memoirs, newspaper columns, and the self-justifying chronicle of official reports.

A foreigner has only one advantage over an Italian in this field, namely that he is less involved and so may judge with less passion, but this is not to say that he will be any less prejudiced or opinionated, and he will be especially liable to false perspective and the incomplete comprehension of national character and historical tradition. At every point summary justice must be attempted over bitter political controversies which have produced an exhaustive polemical literature, and the compulsion to take so much on trust often makes it hard to find reliable bearings. Mussolini appointed one of the *quadrumvirs* of his "march on Rome" a director general of historical research, and encouraged professors to earn promotion by discovering the authentic *stile fascista* in the annals alike of Caesar and Garibaldi. Not only the fascists, but the liberals also tried to justify their political faith by historical research, and sometimes twisted the evidence in the opposite direction. Some of these errors are easily exposed, but it is impossible to feel sure of not reproducing a few of the subtler distortions.

This warning may serve as a check upon the sympathies and antipathies which appear in this book. An even more desirable check would have been the provision of footnotes to document the more controversial points, but with some reluctance it was decided that these would not be sufficiently useful unless they became too bulky and complex for a work of this size and aim. No doubt the safer and easier course would therefore have been to play down controversy and avoid all manifest likes and dislikes. Yet he is a coward and a dullard who does not risk some interim judgments on the course of history, even at the peril of either outright misrepresentation or at least of seeming wise after the event.

The principal object has been to reach an understanding of the political problems and achievements of modern Italy. This is a wider aim than it may sound, for the universal themes of liberalism, nationalism, and totalitarianism become properly intelligible only when studied in a living historical context, and modern Italian history is a *locus classicus* for all three. Compressed into a few words, the central thesis is that a great political success in the nineteenth century was followed by collapse and defeat in the twentieth, largely because of mistakes in foreign policy which in turn refer back to constitutional weaknesses in domestic politics. It was these constitutional defects which more than anything else delayed Italy from becoming as liberal and prosperous a nation as some of her founding fathers had intended, and perhaps one can push the story back one stage further still and explain constitutional by social and economic weaknesses.

Nevertheless, underneath the surface of political controversy and social tension, the life of Italy remained animated and robust, for her people proved under severe strain to be among the most resilient as well as among the most civilized and gifted of any in the world. A new constitution was approved in 1947. In the following fifteen years an industrial revolution took place, and a poor nation became, if not rich, at least unrecognizably better off. Inside Italian society, a healthier balance between the classes took away some of the fear and the alienation which had been such a burden on political life. Freed from the fascist incubus, there was a great release of energy, not only in economic development but in culture and the arts. The amenities of civilized living in Europe owe a great deal to what Italians have contributed since 1945. With no aggressive foreign policy, no heavily subsidized armaments industry, no colonies to attract wasteful prestige expenditure, Italy in the last twenty years has done as much to further the cause of international cooperation as she has done to better her own lot.

Contents

1 The "Geographical Expression"

Until 1860 the word *Italy* was used not so much for a nation as for a peninsula, and Metternich wrote disparagingly of this "geographical expression." It is therefore with geography that Italian history must begin. Too often have poverty and political backwardness been blamed on misrule and foreign exploitation, instead of on climate and the lack of natural resources. We need not go so far as to believe that the destinies of a nation are altogether shaped by its wealth and position: a peninsular situation in the Mediterranean may suggest but does not compel a particular choice of allies, the lack of raw materials can make a country either weak or aggressive (or both), an unkind climate may as easily stimulate as depress, and overpopulation can be a military asset as well as an economic liability. But such characteristics are bound to define the scope of a nation within certain limits. It has always been historically important that the Apennines divide Italy from top to bottom and that the Alps cut her off from the rest of Europe; mountains may not be removed, even by faith.

Italy was a territorial unit many centuries before she became a national state—unlike The Netherlands, for instance, which had been politically a state before seeming to be either a nation or a geographical entity. The natural frontiers of Italy are more or less clearly defined, three sides bounded by the sea, and the fourth following the long chain of the Alps. There have been certain ambiguities within these limits. Corsica and Nice have sometimes been claimed from France, Canton Ticino from Switzerland, Malta from Great Britain; and southern Tyrol, Trieste, and Fiume have been disputed with Austria-Hungary and Yugoslavia. Furthermore, the professors have dutifully justified Italian claims to these disputed provinces on grounds of geology, history, and ethnology. Even a physical barrier so formidable as the Alps by no means coincides with the linguistic frontier, and large cisalpine areas are French, German, and Slav by speech.]

Neither the existence of these doubtful frontier provinces nor that of tiny enclaves in San Marino and the Vatican City weakens the compactness of Italy so much as do the differences and sometimes the animosities between its component regions. This parochialism is the product of both geography and history. The various regions still preserve something of their individual customs and literature, their peculiar type of economy and methods of land tenure. Even under the highly centralized government of Mussolini, a fascist party-secretary could arouse keen dislike for being too typically a southerner, and when Marshal Badoglio announced over the radio in 1943 that the fascist regime had collapsed, there were people whose first reaction was to resent his Piedmontese accent. [The natural speech of most Italians has been dialect until quite recently, and most of the dozen or so dialects are largely unintelligible outside their particular district.] Up to 1859 the regions were still politically divided, with different historical traditions of government and law. Weights, measures, and coinage varied everywhere, the ducato of Naples differing from the oncia of Sicily, the papal scudo from the Piedmontese lira. As many as twenty-two different customs barriers existed along the course of the Po—a striking example of that municipalism or *campanilismo* which impeded national unification and the advance of agriculture and industry.

§•

Of all these regions, the matrix of the new Italy was Piedmont in the northwest, with Turin its capital. Piedmont was joined politically with Sardinia and since 1815 also possessed the important shipping center of Genoa which was the great rival of the Austrian-held port of Trieste. Farther east, in the middle of the great plain of Lombardy, was the town of Milan, eventually to become the financial, commercial, and artistic pivot of the new kingdom. Well placed at the intersection of trade routes, Milan was in close touch with the transalpine world. Its people were active and practical, and the Lombard plain was watered by the largest Italian river, the Po, and contained the best and most populous agricultural land in the kingdom. Although Lombardy was wrested from Austria by Piedmont in 1859, it was not until 1866 that Austria surrendered the adjoining region of Venice which she had held for seventy years. Immediately to the south lay the region of Emilia and Romagna, centering around Bologna and Ravenna. Below this were Umbria and the

Marches, conquered in 1860 by Piedmontese troops from the Pope. To the west was Tuscany, which also in 1860 joined this growing nucleus of a united kingdom. Tuscany, a grand duchy with its capital at Florence, had been for centuries the chief cultural focus of the peninsula, and Livorno, known to the English-speaking world as Leghorn, was an important commercial and shipbuilding town. South of Tuscany was the sacrosanct region of Rome, where the Pope ruled over a truncated state until 1870.

The burnt South and the island of Sicily were a region apart by reason of climate and history and by the character of their people. This difference between North and South was fundamental. A peasant from Calabria had little in common with one from Piedmont, and Turin was infinitely more like Paris and London than Naples and Palermo, for these two halves were on quite different levels of civilization. Poets might write of the South as the garden of the world, the land of Sybaris and Capri, and stay-at-home politicians sometimes believed them; but in fact most southerners lived in squalor, afflicted by drought, malaria, and earthquakes. The Bourbon rulers of Naples and Sicily before 1860 had been staunch supporters of a feudal system glamorized by the trappings of a courtly and corrupt society. They had feared the traffic of ideas and had tried to keep their subjects insulated from the agricultural and industrial revolutions of northern Europe. Roads were scanty or nonexistent, and passports necessary even for internal travel. In the *annus mirabilis* of 1860 these backward regions were conquered by Garibaldi and annexed by plebiscite to the North.

In the Mediterranean there has probably not been any drastic change of climate over the centuries, but agricultural conditions have altered for the worse, largely owing to political catastrophes, bad methods of tillage, and neglect of soil conservation and proper rotation of crops. Heavy deforestation has occurred in southern and central Italy, owing to the requirements of shipbuilding, and because of the *carbonari* with their charcoal pits, and the wild goats which crop the young trees. This deforestation has created dustbowl conditions. Agriculture in the South has to reckon not only with less rain than the North, but with more unpredictable rainfall and a worse seasonal distribution. The southern Apennines contain no natural or artificial lakes, and the winter rain pours off them in torrents which dry up in the hot summer and are useless for irrigation. Where no trees remain to hold the moisture, the soil is washed down the mountain slopes, or else avalanches devastate the valleys. Few Italian rivers are useful for navigation. Along the Adriatic, ports have silted up, and Ravenna, once a headquarters of the Roman fleet, has become an inland city. Many large areas have always been subject to floods. The still water of marshland used to breed several deadly species of anopheles mosquito, so that people were driven up into the hill towns, leaving the lowlands untended and desolate. In these conditions nothing like the intensive agricultural system of France was possible, and there was a basic poverty which not even liberal government after 1860 could change.

Comparing favorably with these depressed areas, the northern plain of Lombardy had seen a successful fight against nature. Generations of industrious peasants had turned the northern marshes into paddy fields, and built an extensive and constantly maintained network of waterways. Realizing that prosperity was precarious, and that a few years of neglect would be ruinous, they had developed an advanced community sense: for example, a right of aqueduct, by which water might be carried across other people's property, had long been established by law. Luckily, the River Po relied not on winter rain but on glaciers producing a summer flow. In Lombardy, too, there were flourishing cities and trade centers from which investment capital was always returning to the countryside. This compared well with the predominantly agricultural South, where income was derived almost exclusively from agriculture and barely sufficed for replacement and running expenses.

These facts help to explain the poverty of so much of Italy, and show why so many millions of her people have chosen to emigrate. Italy was a poor and relatively overpopulated country in 1860, a fact which political unification could not change despite many rhetorical promises and extravagant hopes. The country possessed only a fraction of the resources of France and far less cultivable land, yet the population of France, which in 1850 was still one and a half times that of Italy, was to be outpaced by the latter after 1900. In other countries there was an expanding industry which could absorb surplus labor from agriculture, but in Italy the raw materials of industry were lacking. From the time that wood and charcoal gave way to iron and coal, craftsmanship to mass production, Italy was doomed to take a lower place in the economic world, and, as most of her population therefore remained in agriculture, the high proportion of mountainous and barren land was the more disastrous in its effect.

༄

Another important geographical influence is Italy's position on the map. The foreign policy of the united state was bound to be concerned chiefly with those countries along her land frontier, France, Austria, and Serbia. Each of these was potentially dangerous, but each could be played off against the others. The length of her sea coast, about 4,100 miles as against 1,290 miles of northern frontier, not only left her very sensitive toward other Mediterranean powers like France and Britain, but also made her a maritime, and sometimes an imperial, power. Nearly all her imports came by sea. To the east there was the historical memory of Venetian domination over Dalmatia and the Levant. The Balkan mainland is only fifty miles distant from Italy at the narrowest point in the "canal" of Otranto, while North Africa is only three hours distant from Sicily by sea. Not surprisingly, therefore, Cavour and his disciples had occasional "geopolitical" visions, for Italy was the one large European country altogether enclosed in the Mediterranean—a promontory "which links Europe with Africa." Ever since the influence of Turkey and the Barbary corsairs began to decline, and especially when the Suez Canal became a fact, some people could wonder if the old Roman Empire might not be recreated in North Africa.

There were indeed some advantages in being a "geographical expression." Metternich's own Central European empire was not even that, and Austria-Hungary was to be broken in pieces by the new nation states, of which Italy was among the largest and most dangerous.

2 The Idea of National Unity

Italy had always been a unit geographically. In religion, too, she had been practically homogeneous since Gregory the Great, and something of a common Italian language and culture had existed from Dante onward. Until 1861, however, she had never been a political entity, and hardly was one even then. As the Neapolitan historian Luigi Blanch had said ten years before, "the patriotism of the Italians is like that of the ancient Greeks, and is love of a single town, not of a country; it is the feeling of a tribe, not of a nation. Only by foreign conquest have they ever been united. Leave them to themselves and they split into fragments." Some national consciousness had certainly existed on and off for centuries, but it had been vague and tenuous, something manifested only in the wilder speculations of a Dante or Machiavelli, and many had argued on the contrary that national unity would be ruinous rather than profitable, as well as morally wrong. Not much national feeling had in fact existed before the nineteenth century, and even an Italian customs union like the German *Zollverein* was impracticable until Piedmont could impose it. North and south Italy had hardly ever been united under the same rule, but government had for centuries been parceled out between autonomous cities and foreign dynasties, all of whom had an interest in resisting every patriotic movement not led by themselves and suppressing any neighbor who became too important.

Yet in time each invader took on the color of his surroundings and became absorbed by the *genius loci,* until by 1861 these many cities and provinces, only excepting Venice and Rome, stood united in a single state. True enough, there were still important internal divisions, and more than one civil war lay ahead. It is true also that unification was achieved by methods which some Italians detested. Nevertheless, many people would have agreed that the five great powers of Europe had by 1861 become six, and in every free country people looked with warm sympathy and admiration at the rebirth of Italy. The how and why of such an achievement provide one of the fascinating themes of modern history.

Italy of the *risorgimento* was a far cry from the divided Italy of the Renaissance. In the later Middle Ages, Italians made their country the center of European religion, art, and literature, and also of the new capitalist, urban civilization developing around the Italian inventions of banking and credit. Yet, while inhabitants of the medieval Italian communes consciously belonged to a wider community, their loyalty was by no means to a nation, but first to the city and then to Christendom. No threat of invasion by Saracens, Normans, or Germans succeeded in unifying them into a state for mutual aid, and some local rulers always sided with every invader for the sake of their own private advantage. Italy must be the most invaded country in the world, and Lombardy one of the world's great battlefields. Even where temporary leagues of cities could be formed in self-defense, they were never lasting, but melted away with the danger that engendered them or with a new danger which required a new alignment. By 1500, however, the eighty city-states scattered through Italy had been hammered into ten provinces by the more successful and unscrupulous of the local tyrants and civic oligarchies.

Italy in 1500 was about to drift into a period of somnolence during which she lost her commercial and cultural primacy. This was due at least in part to her failure to constitute a national state like contemporary France and Spain. Machiavelli might dream of a more united country, but in practice his ideal prince did not succeed in rallying enough of Italy to combine and play the new game of power politics in Europe. Instead, the French invasion of 1494 from the north, countered at once by that of Spain from the south, opened a new era of civil war and foreign subjection, in which Italy became the cat's-paw, the battlefield, even the private perquisite, of one European nation after another. Once again, one party in every local quarrel was always ready to side with the invader in order to curb a rival faction or a neighboring province. Milan tried and failed to become master of northern Italy. Successive papal families attempted by force of arms to win a temporal hegemony, but Cesare Borgia made too many enemies and so failed to succeed by a narrow margin. Then it was the turn of Venice, only to be crushed by France and a confederacy of other jealous provinces. So strong were these internal jealousies that Florence was left alone to resist the Spanish invasion, while her leading family, the Medici, chose to support the Spanish emperor against their own native city. Florence and Rome were both put to the sack and ruined, and the civilization of the Renaissance was shocked to a standstill.

At the same time the Ottoman Turks and the corsairs of Greece and Africa were obstructing the trade routes which Venice and Genoa had used for their prosperous commerce with the Levant. The commercial centers of Europe were shifting away from the inner Mediterranean to the Atlantic seaboard, where ports looked out to a new world largely discovered by Italians. But Italy herself failed to meet the challenge. Although still the richest country in Europe, although Venice had for centuries sent ships into the Atlantic, and though Genoa was not much further from the Spice Islands than was Amsterdam or London, nevertheless politics did not allow the necessary adjustments to be made. The interests of Italy were subordinated to those of her new Spanish overlords, and the inherited splendor of centuries was dissipated in profitless civil war.

In the two centuries before the *risorgimento,* only the several regions had their individual history, and this was often a pale reflection of transalpine Europe. After the death of Michelangelo in 1564, and from the time when Bruno was burned and Galileo silenced, Italy lived in a backwater. Certain regions managed to retain some political independence, for example, Venice sheltered behind her lagoons and Genoa screened by the Maritime Alps, but only as shadows of what they had once been. Venice indeed, like Ferrara and Palermo, decreased in population between 1500 and 1860. The Venetians failed to retreat in time from the commitments of their Levantine empire; instead of fastening onto the mainland of Italy, they wore themselves out trying to maintain their oversea dominions. The rest of north Italy fell to the Austrian Habsburgs, and southern Italy to Spain and the Bourbons. In between, right across from sea to sea, stretched the states of the Church, where the Pope ruled as a supranational sovereign, a solid barrier against national unification. Spain, France, Austria, and the Pope would scarcely look sympathetically on any movement toward union or independence. Nor was it likely that they would fail to prevent such a movement in any foreseeable circumstances.

It was with the Napoleonic intrusion into Italy, between 1796 and 1814, that the various regions of the peninsula were forced back into the mainstream of European history. Napoleon even created a prototype kingdom of Italy based on Milan. This was an artificial, puppet state, with a population of only six million out of a possible eighteen. But the Napoleonic armies brought with them the germs of liberalism fostered by the French Revolution of 1789, and introduced a minor industrial revolution sufficient at least to provide some of the war equipment required. Experience of Napoleonic rule convinced some people how much Italy stood to gain from strong centralized government, for the French brought more efficient methods of administration and a far more enlightened code of law. Customs barriers were broken down, and the decimal and metric systems of measurement were introduced. The mercantile classes appreciated this, as they appreciated the better roads, the enlarged market, and the destruction of entails which at last made possible the free transfer of land. Fortunes were made on a scale hitherto impossible, and liquid capital suddenly reappeared and sought an outlet in profitable enterprise.

But neither the novelty nor the permanence of Napoleon's contribution must be exaggerated. Some of these reforms had been anticipated in Italy during the Enlightenment, and the rest, once Napoleon had gone, mostly lapsed. The Kingdom of Italy split up again into its constituent elements, and the emperor's laws were usually repealed. Most Italians were glad to be rid of him, less because he was a "foreigner" than because heavy taxes and conscription were obnoxious, and because they hoped that the milder government of pope or duke would be less interfering and easier to disobey. In one real sense, moreover, his legacy was one of division, in that he brought north Italy still further within the economic ambit of France, and his road over the Simplon pass drew Milan nearer to Paris. This notwithstanding, shortly after Napoleon's final defeat the German scholar Niebuhr could write from Rome that Italy was bound to be united in the course of a generation or two, and Stendhal in his diary noted the same trend. That such a revolution was at last conceivable is to be ascribed largely to Napoleon's influence. It is significant that so many leaders of Italian nationalism descended from people who became rich under his regime.

§◆

One cannot give wholly satisfactory reasons for the rise and fall of nations. No simple answer will explain why Spain, whose share in defeating Napoleon was infinitely greater than that of Italy, derived thereby no stimulus to a national rebirth like the *risorgimento,* and received no similar inspiration from the new ideas of nationalism, liberalism, and romanticism. In Italy these ideas caused a ferment compounded of bitter criticism and boundless enthusiasm. Politically, the 1814–15 Restoration might be called a disaster: the Viennese emperor returned to Lombardy, the Bourbons to Naples, the Austrian grand duke to Tuscany; Venice was no longer a free republic but a province of Austria, and Genoa had become a dependency of Piedmont; nor was Piedmont yet a wholly cisalpine and Italian power. Everywhere the aristocracy recovered their privileges and power. But on the nonpolitical plane new forces were at work. There was a feeling of *italianità* which thinkers were beginning to rationalize and statesmen to exploit. There was the liberating wind from the French Revolution blowing freely through the world with its message of political deliverance. There was also an expanding commercial and agricultural middle class with new needs generated by an industrial revolution and by the revival of trade routes in the Mediterranean.

Without these middle classes it is difficult to see how enough backing could have been found for national unification. They found it irksome to have eight separate states in Italy, each with tariff barriers, individual coinage, and measures. Not only the merchants and textile manufacturers of northern Italy, but also some of the landowners who produced grain and wine realized that economic progress presupposed a larger internal market. There was scope for increasing agricultural profits, and some landlords saw the advantages of a centralized government which could build roads and railways, and give them fiscal protection and defend their interests abroad. The commercial classes of Lombardy felt that the Austrian government, for all its relative honesty and enlightenment, exploited their province, and they expected more consideration from a government of Italians.

Economists such as Cavour were at the same time looking forward to a Suez Canal, and calculating that the shortest route from England to India might include the railroad they wanted to build from Turin to Brindisi. The canal was not finished until 1869, but long before then another obstacle disappeared with the destruction of the Barbary pirates. At last it seemed as if the Mediterranean might recover its importance as the main highway of world trade. At a time when Turkish power was declining, it was the more important that a united Italy should be ready to capitalize these potential advantages, for by the 1830's both Greece and Serbia had won their autonomy from Turkey, and Mehemet Ali in Egypt and France in Algeria were altering the Mediterranean balance of power. As things turned out, the canal was in fact to bring few positive advantages to Italy; there was no great influx of trade from the East, and ships did not stop to bunker in a country which lacked the necessary coal. It was none the less important that these changes were, in advance, thought likely to make Italy's fortune if only she were sufficiently united to exploit them.

Quite as impressive as these economic factors, and by and large affecting different people, was the common Italian culture now more in evidence, and the currency being given on a literary and intellectual level to the concept of United Italy. In 1825–27 Alessandro Manzoni published *I promessi sposi,* the most influential novel ever written in Italian. Manzoni was from Lombardy, but the year after publication he visited Florence, and in the next edition fifteen years later he had corrected the style to conform more with the Tuscan dialect. This in the end proved decisive in confirming Tuscan as the classic prose style for Italian literature. The purists objected, but like all masterpieces it carried its own compulsion, and another essential step had been taken toward national consciousness. Meanwhile Grossi and Guerrazzi found the educated public avid for tales of medieval Italian heroes who once beat the French and the Saracens, and Leopardi's patriotic odes had to be confiscated by the Austrian censorship lest they should incite people to revolt. Literature thus helped to reassure Italians that they were not so unfit as some of them imagined for war and politics.

Nor were these littérateurs content with Italy as the legendary land of romance. The Abbé Gioberti in 1843 wrote a celebrated work, *The Moral and Civil Primacy of the Italians,* to show that Italy alone was morally worthy to head a federal Europe. As he said, "a nation cannot hold its due position in the world without first being properly self-confident." His grandiose vision was a compensation for the reality of weakness, a protest against foreigners like Lamartine who called Italy a land of the dead, but it was imaginative and far from real life. The literature of the romantic movement preferred historical legends of past greatness, and gave little thought to the revolution of 1848 or the colorful deeds of Garibaldi. To the romantics, contemporary events seemed cheap and shoddy when compared with their ideal of what Italy ought to be, and perhaps their attitude also betrays a secret shame at their own lack of practical support for Garibaldi and the revolutionaries. Their moral contribution was, however, beyond controversy. National consciousness would never have become practically effective without visionaries and evangelists to implant it by degrees in the minds of those few people who had the strength, the skill, and the courage to act.

3 Mazzini, Garibaldi, and the Revolutionaries

Before this economic and cultural revival could develop into a political *risorgimento,* someone had to transmute ideals into action. Centuries of foreign rule had left Italy not only without a nucleus around which a national movement could gather, but also without experience of free government. Forty years of trial and error were therefore necessary after the Napoleonic period in order to test the various methods and parties which gradually became engaged in the crusade for independence. At one extreme there was the orthodox means of open war and diplomacy; at the other, plotting, piracy, and assassination. Besides conservative monarchists, there were professional anarchists, republican agitators, starving peasants, discontented soldiers and students, all with different aims and methods, but all helping, often unintentionally, to create a united Italy. Of these it was the revolutionary republicans who first persuaded people that unification might be feasible, and who then, by many isolated acts of revolt, forced the conservatives and the lukewarm to join with them in half-unwilling alliance.

Very soon after the Restoration of 1814–15, secret societies became active with the avowed policy of overthrowing the Vienna settlement. In Genoa and Sicily, which had lost their old autonomy to Piedmont and Naples respectively, even conservative aristocrats had an interest in revolt. So had the discharged officers of Napoleon's army and the civil servants who had staffed his government. In 1820–21, therefore, and again in 1831, uprisings took place in several of the larger Italian cities to remedy various local and individual grievances. But they lacked cohesion and co-ordination. Certain towns in Sicily preferred to side with the

Bourbons at Naples against the island capital, Palermo, of whose position they were jealous, and in Bologna the "foreign" refugees from Modena were disarmed even though both cities were fighting Austria.

By 1848, the next year of revolutions, some of the malcontents had realized the need for sacrificing local animosities in a common cause. Soldiers from insurgent Naples joined with Tuscans, Romans, and the Piedmontese army in trying to save the gallant insurrection of Milan, and the Sicilians invited a Piedmontese duke to be their king. Once more, however, all ended in mutual recrimination, Milan accusing Piedmont of treachery and selfish aggrandizement, Piedmont replying that the Milanese were clouding the straight issue of independence with a controversy over republicanism upon which patriots were divided. Province was divided against province, class against class. The poor were not interested in political independence, but only in the price of salt and flour; landowners fell back on the old dynasties rather than countenance the occupation of their land by the peasants in arms; and as for the merchants, they might have wanted freedom, but not at the price of forced loans and inflation. In 1849, therefore, the old regimes were again restored, and although some people had tasted liberty and learned to fight on the barricades, the bitterness of civil war and defeat soured the cause of patriotism.

It is not possible to say exactly who took part in these insurrections. No doubt it was a small minority, for the wars and risings of the *risorgimento* had little effect on ordinary people. If not the intellectuals, it was at least the intelligent, in particular the professional classes, the lawyers, doctors, and shopkeepers who manned the Palermo barricades in 1848 —so observed William Nassau Senior, the economist. Italian lawyers were not as conservative as English lawyers: they were poor in money and esteem, usually excluded from the judicial bench and high society, full of abstract ideas, and hence ready to accept change and revolution. Furthermore, they were a numerous body, for most respectable families were ensnared in hereditary lawsuits, and universities were equipped to teach only medicine and the law. Lawyers were therefore a dangerous element in society.

University students, too, were rebellious by nature. They were the first to join Garibaldi's volunteers, and no university could or would be bold enough to refuse them a degree if some successful patriotic escapade made them miss their examinations. Patriotism offered a glorious relief from the crabbed, patriarchal system which kept them, even after marriage, cooped up in ancestral *palazzi* with generations of relatives. When ruled by austere, authoritarian parents like those of the poet Leopardi, the young were bound to be in revolt. Little travel was possible for them before the age of railroads, and there was no sport except the very necessary art of fencing. In their drab lives a town riot was a tonic and an intoxicant, and in between riots they could show their national enthusiasm by refusing to buy taxed tobacco, by cheering certain arias of Verdi, or by wearing the conical Calabrian hat after its prohibition by the Austrians as a patriotic symbol. The student population of Italy, as of many other countries later, was an ideal revolutionary force. While students had less to lose than men with responsibilities, their education fitted them to understand what they were fighting for, or at least enough about it to make it seem thoroughly glamorous. Besides being persecuted by governments as a source of seditious infection, many of them had small hope of profitable employment in existing society, and all wished to build a brave new world where brains were as important as birth, and where the white-collared man was king.

§❧

The teacher and inspiration of rebellious youth was Giuseppe Mazzini, a republican, a nationalist, and by far the greatest prophet of the *risorgimento*. Mazzini was born at Genoa in 1805, and lived as a revolutionary agitator, sacrificing personal comfort, the company of his family, and the lives of his friends. Exiled from Genoa and Piedmont in 1831, he was then expelled from Switzerland and France, and spent most of his remaining years planning the resurrection of Italy amid the fogs of London. He launched numerous societies and newspapers to convince people that Italy could and must be unified through the exertions of ordinary people. No trust should be placed in princes or in political alliances, he maintained, nor in any appeal to mere self-interest, for the problem was moral more than political, and ordinary citizens must learn that they alone by their own sacrifices could redeem themselves. A nation should be something spiritual; not like America which "is the embodiment, if compared to our own ideal, of the philosophy of mere *rights:* the collective thought is forgotten: the *educational* mission of the state overlooked. It is the negative, individualistic, materialistic school." Mazzini, on the contrary, made national unification a religious duty, and convinced his disciples that it was part of God's providence, in which belief they discovered a quite invaluable sense of inevitability and self-confidence.

Mazzini's practical application of nationalism was by means of continual insurrections, thereby making people conscious of their power and of how to use it in executing God's purpose. He used to visit Piedmont surreptitiously, defying a sentence of death, and frequent uprisings testified to the valor of his lieutenants and to his own fascination. There exists today an edition of his writings in over a hundred volumes, ranging from a manual on guerrilla warfare to the thousands of incendiary letters which kept conspiracy alive. Personally one of the mildest of men, sad, lonely, and affectionate, he thus became one of the most feared and hated personalities in Europe.

It is easy to say with his detractors that Mazzini was a failure. Not only were many of his disciples killed in insurrections which seemed hopeless from the start, but his enemy Cavour was to oust him from the revolutionary leadership, and in 1872 Mazzini died an unhappy and disillusioned fugitive. During the last twenty years of his life he possessed little apparent influence. He had proved impossibly utopian in believing that the populace would rise against tyranny on their own initiative and resolve all the problems of national and class selfishness. When they did rise, it was usually for selfish and non-national reasons of their own, and he found them to be far from the progressive force he had hoped. His disillusionment was profound. "I had thought to evoke the soul of Italy," he said, "but all I find before me is its corpse." The country had turned out to be "rotten with materialism and egoism." Worse still, Mazzini knew that his failure was partly due to his own intractable nature, to his distrust of compromise, and to the temperamental obstinacy which had alienated even his former friend Garibaldi.

Recognition, such as it was, came posthumously, when conservatives and monarchists needed no longer to fear him, and the king could personally unveil a statue in Rome to this republican Apostle of Unity. Mazzini's influence could then be truly appreciated. His theory of popular initiative had been partly vindicated in central and southern Italy during 1859–60. Cavour, the prime minister of Piedmont, would not have conceived it possible that a thousand men, armed only with a few rusty flintlocks, could land in Sicily and conquer a large, disciplined army. But Mazzini had believed in the impossible, and Garibaldi's success in 1860 forced Cavour to defy conservatism, to invade the Papal states and the South, and to proclaim that Rome should one day become the capital of United Italy. Here was Mazzini's revolutionary program almost to the letter, enacted by an orthodox diplomat who had recently called the idea of national unity "silly nonsense." Mazzini's success lay in defining the goal and arousing enthusiasm among more practiced soldiers and statesmen. Cavour as well as Garibaldi was his unacknowledged and ungrateful pupil.

᠙᠀

Italians found their greatest general of modern times in Giuseppe Garibaldi, the inspired leader of guerrillas. Garibaldi was rough and untutored, with little grasp of long-term strategy, but with remarkable flair for irregular warfare. His success with his men, who loved him and believed him invincible, was above all one of character, for he lacked calculation and guile, was unambitious for himself, and devoid of cheap ostentation. He was an honest man with the reputation of being one, whereas Cavour and Mazzini never freed themselves from the suspicion of doubledealing and unscrupulousness. No one could meet Garibaldi without recognizing his single-minded and disinterested love of Italy, and no one failed to be charmed by his courtesy and simplicity of manner, or to be bewitched by his voice. He was temperate even to parsimony, and when his headquarters in 1860 was at the magnificent Palace of Caserta he would still wash his own shirt and sleep on hay with his saddle for a pillow. There was no need in his army for routine discipline, and as he himself was fearless and tireless, so he seemed to turn ordinary men into supermen.

Southern Italians venerated their deliverer as a saint, and in distant countries workmen who had never seen Garibaldi gave up their halfholidays to make arms for him. English dukes begged for his portrait; one of them, himself a cabinet minister, had a son who ran off to join Garibaldi's volunteers; and their wives even raided Caserta to comb out the hairs from his brush for keepsakes. The romancer Dumas followed him around to get copy for novels, and, in return for this privilege, equipped a yacht on which to make red shirts for the revolutionary troops. It was Garibaldi's generous good nature that won over public opinion in Europe to favor the deeds of a buccaneer. From Hungarians to South American Negroes, men of every country joined the bravest of Italian youth in the fantastic army which he could conjure up from nowhere and then as magically disperse again. Chivalrous enthusiasts linked up with charlatans and professional adventurers, for it was not least among Garibaldi's services that, alongside the patriots, he could enroll those social outcasts who are always in the van of any revolution or counterrevolution, the people who thrive on disorder, and who from the *condottieri* to the *carbonari* and the fascist *squadristi* have been among the most combustible and explosive elements in Italian society.

Garibaldi called himself a republican and a socialist. In practice, however, he loyally served the monarchy, and to Mazzini's disgust meekly surrendered to the king the dictatorial powers over the half of Italy which he had conquered in 1860. His confusion of mind helped the process by which most of the republicans and revolutionaries rallied to the throne—a dozen of his famous volunteer Thousand were later to become generals in the regular Italian army, although he himself crumpled up the notice of his own appointment and threw it out of the window. Away from the battlefield, his own political beliefs, for all their honesty, were trite and shallow. He distrusted Mazzini and hated Cavour. As he was quite unable to understand the difficulties of Cavour's position, he blasted him as a coward, a traitor, and a fomenter of civil war. Where Cavour believed in parliaments, Garibaldi was all for a dictatorship modeled on Caesar's, and armed with "fasces." He genuinely believed in what he called liberty, and yet thought that it could and should be forced on people for their own good. Unskilled in public speaking—except from balconies—he had no patience with the talk and the delays of parliamentary government, and so dictatorship was the natural form of government he had chosen for southern Italy in 1860. This would-be republican, anticlerical democrat that he was, had presided from the royal throne during pontifical high mass in the Cathedral of Palermo, claiming the royal rights of apostolic legateship (although a notorious heretic), clad in red shirt and with sword unsheathed as the Gospel was read.

Under all his panache, Garibaldi had neither the ruthlessness nor the ambition and intelligence of Cromwell or Napoleon. He turned up rarely in parliament, sometimes wearing his poncho and red shirt to the dismay of the frock-coated deputies, but he was far happier back on his farm, away from the smart men of politics, awaiting some new call to arms. His real work was finished when Cavour took over the Italian revolution; and like Mazzini he became disillusioned with the Italy which Cavour and the moderates had made. The liberals who came to rule Italy were in their turn to regard him as crude and vulgar, a model *condottiere* and truly great of soul, but a child in politics and slightly ridiculous, a relic from a former age of violence, and now only an embarrassment or an exhibit. Every town had a street or square called after him; the bed on which he died in 1882 was later surrounded by iron railings and a canopy, and was retained even with his most intimate domestic furniture as a national monument. Nevertheless his share in the *risorgimento* was depreciated by officialdom as something of which to be a trifle ashamed.

4 Cavour and the Expansion of Piedmont

Germany and Italy became unified states at much the same time. The methods employed by Italian nationalism were often said to be more liberal than those used in Germany and more diversified, which may suggest one reason why the Italian nation was less firmly established, for liberalism does not always exactly coincide with nationalism. The constituent elements of the new state were embarrassingly variegated. But out of this jumble of regions and parties, Piedmont was eventually to emerge as a nucleus around which the rest of Italy could gather. Until such a center of attraction existed, Mazzini's sermons and Garibaldi's swordplay were in vain. Piedmont and her ambitious, warlike dynasty were needed to put some blood and iron into the movement for independence.

Surprisingly enough, the chosen region was one with no great tradition of *italianità,* but was a partly French-speaking area which straddled the Alps and had existed only on the borderline of Italian history. Rome would have been a more obvious center if only the Romans had showed a glimmer of interest in the prospect. But Rome proved in practice to have either been inured by centuries of clerical despotism, or else to be already satisfied with a position as the capital of a religious empire far larger and grander than Italy. A cynic might say that Roman citizens were content with their virtual monopoly of jobs at the headquarters of the Church, while the poorer classes exploited the pilgrims and the Grand Tour trade, making a passable living out of alms, lodging houses, and religious trinkets. After Rome, Naples was just conceivable as a center of United Italy. Naples was the largest city in the peninsula, capital of the biggest and most populous Italian state. But she was also provincial and retrograde, and ruled by a Spanish dynasty which until the previous century had considered her an appurtenance of Spain.

If prosperity was the criterion, Milan would have been a much more likely capital. The Austrians who ruled Lombardy until 1859 had long since abolished the more abused aristocratic and clerical privileges. Tax farming had been reformed, a census instituted, and the area was being welded into something like an economic unit by the suppression of internal trade barriers. This was way ahead of the rest of Italy. Tuscany, too had an administration under her Austrian grand duke which until the middle of the century was more enlightened than that of Piedmont. The legal and penal system of Tuscany was a model to Europe; its universities gave the best education in Italy; there was less police intrusion than elsewhere, more tolerance of Jews and Protestants, and in general a higher standard of welfare and culture. Many foreigners wintered in Florence and brought with them liberal ideas, so that even its theologians tended toward unorthodoxy. Tuscany, however, was linked to Austria by dynastic ties, and was slow to sense that urge toward political independence which was at the heart of nationalism.

It was political independence which distinguished Piedmont from other regions and enabled the House of Savoy to lead the Italian revolution. This dynasty was the oldest ruling house in Europe. Until the eighteenth century its center of gravity had been on the French and Swiss side of the mountains. The Savoy duchy, a buffer state controlling the Great and Little St. Bernard passes, had been kept alive by the rivalries of France, Spain, and Austria. Through marriage and alliance with these powers in turn, additional territory had spasmodically been incorporated, and, since France formed a strong barrier to the north, expansion was now easier toward Italy. The acquisition of Sardinia early in the eighteenth century brought to the duke of Savoy the title of king; and when by 1748 his land frontier had reached the River Ticino and Lake Maggiore, the new Kingdom of Sardinia at last leaned more heavily on Italian Piedmont than on French Savoy. There was, however, no exclusive feeling for Italy in its almost French rulers, only the dynastic ambition to expand anywhere. They styled themselves "Kings of Sardinia, Cyprus, Jerusalem, etc." But Napoleon's victories temporarily frustrated their ambitions and made Savoy-Piedmont a colony of France for twenty years. Thus, Cavour, Mazzini, and Garibaldi were born subjects of France, and Napoleon's sister stood godmother at Cavour's christening.

Piedmont played no very active part in Napoleon's defeat, but the settlement of 1815 left her well placed for intervention in Italian affairs. Not only was she the Italian region with greatest freedom from Austrian patronage, but in 1815 she was gratuitously presented with Genoa and so obtained one of the four largest ports in the Mediterranean. She thereby also became more markedly an Italian power. The Concert of Europe, moreover, having deliberately recreated this subalpine kingdom as a necessary buffer between France and Austria, would not easily permit its destruction again. Piedmont could therefore follow an audacious foreign policy, knowing that this tacit guarantee gave her everything to gain and little to lose from war. The full implications of this fortunate position were not grasped at once, for Piedmont in 1815 appeared to be merely an appendage of the Holy Alliance, a satisfied and conservative power which, having profited by the treaty, stood to gain by defending rather than attacking it. Not until public opinion had been converted to look upon Austria as the arch-enemy was conservative Piedmont driven to become revolutionary, but Austrian hegemony in the peninsula made this change inevitable sooner or later. After 1815 the balance of power had been upset by the eclipse of France, and this was bound to bring Austria into Italy and hence ultimately into conflict with the Piedmontese, though not until France was strong enough to return into Italian politics could the buffer state again play her accustomed role of *tertius gaudens*. Italian unification in fact required the reappearance of France as a major power, and that meant waiting until Louis Napoleon became emperor in 1851.

A premature attempt was made in 1848, when Milan revolted against Austria and gave King Carlo Alberto of Sardinia his chance to march into Lombardy in support of the rebellion. The result was a disastrous defeat at Custoza in July. Bad tactical direction and inefficient staff work would have been quite enough to ruin the campaign even without tragic political differences with the radical Milanese, for the wars of the *risorgimento* were, one after the other, to show that the Savoy dynasty lacked all the military virtues except courage. Mazzini and the radical republicans also questioned the motive which led Carlo Alberto into the war: they held that it was not fellow feeling for Italians, but just the old selfish dynastic aggressiveness which had always aimed at annexing the fertile grain lands of Lombardy. The radicals ascribed the king's defeat to his greater dislike of Milanese republicanism than of Austrian imperialism, and they fairly concluded that he was putting the interests of monarchy and of himself before national sentiment.

It was, however, significant that other European states would not let Piedmont lose or Austria gain any territory in the peace settlement of 1849, and soon afterward Louis Napoleon restored to Europe a more nicely equivalent balance of power. This momentary equipoise gave just the opportunity needed by a man of Cavour's stamp to establish the fortunes of his country. Fifteen thousand men were thus sent in 1855 to fight the Russians in the Crimea. No great Italian interest was at stake there; rather the reverse, since Russia was a useful check upon Austria, and the very next year Cavour was entreating the Czar to an alliance. But the expedition served to win a seat at the Paris peace congress, and there Cavour took his opportunity to assert in public that Piedmont had as much right as Austria to intervene in the other regions of Italy. Following up this success, in 1859 he carefully and imperturbably provoked a second war against Austria with France as his ally, and so won the long-coveted region of Lombardy. Louis

Napoleon, for his part, welcomed this creation of a compact north Italian state in which French influence would replace Austrian. It was thus by exploiting the rivalries of other European countries that Piedmont compensated for her own weakness and began to annex one province after another, and this set a tradition of foreign policy which Cavour's successors were obliged to follow.

§❧

Count Camillo di Cavour is the most interesting and important figure in modern Italian history. By birth the younger son of an aristocrat, he became an engineer officer in the army, but retired early and took up agriculture. Quite unexpectedly, the events of 1848 drew him by way of newspaper editorship to the forefront of Piedmontese politics. He was a cabinet minister in 1850, prime minister by 1852, and thereafter remained almost continuously at the head of affairs until his death in 1861. Far more amiable and sympathetic than Bismarck, his counterpart in Germany, Cavour was no less sure of touch, no less self-confident, and almost as unscrupulous when occasion demanded.

Like Garibaldi, Cavour had an imperfect knowledge of Italian, and he preferred to write in French. Other people had to revise his newspaper articles, and his secretary found it painful to hear him speak Italian in public. Until quite lately, the Italian language had been unacceptable in Turin society, and Cavour was not untypical in being more at home in French literature and English history than in Italian. He was admirably equipped to interpret to Italy the liberal and industrial revolutions which he had studied in England and France. He was equally fitted, by close study of the national interests of the various powers, to insert the Italian question into the crisscross of European diplomacy. Cavour exploited the rivalries of England and France, France and Austria, Austria and Prussia, and sometimes he thereby managed to give his country a deceptive and counterfeit strength as the makeweight in the balance of power.

Piedmont acquired in Cavour a novel and invaluable spirit of enterprise. A man as great in energy as in vision, he was a gambler who had once lost a substantial fortune by speculating in French securities on a chimerical rumor of war, though he was on the whole a clever and fortunate speculator and was particularly interested in financing banks and railroad development. At times he was audacious in politics to the point of folly, yet this was usually counteracted by common sense, realism, and political tact. He had a remarkable sense of what was possible, and would always compromise with his ideals if that seemed the only way to obtain it, nor was he ever frightened out of changing his mind by the accusation of opportunism.

One is not surprised to find that Bentham was the favorite philosopher of Cavour's youth, and that he once defined Christianity as orthodox utilitarianism. From such a standpoint he was bound to oppose a doctrinaire like Mazzini, for not only was Mazzini adamant upon the utopian dogma of national unity, but Cavour could be made to seem a trimmer, materialistic and irreligious. The conflict of ideas between these two men was as great as the clash of their personalities, and yet it was Cavour's trimming, his materialism, and in part even his irreligion which eventually translated Mazzini's dogma into practical politics.

Between 1850 and 1855 Cavour rendered an indispensable service to Piedmont through his internal reforms. Hitherto the country had been comparatively backward. If the other Italian states did not rush to join Piedmont in the war of 1848–49 as they were to do in 1859–60, the reason was the unenlightenment of her administration quite as much as her deficiency in national consciousness. It is surprising to find that the first Italian steamboat, the first big iron bridge, and the first railroad had appeared not in Piedmont but in Naples under the patronage of the "reactionary" Bourbons, and the first electric telegraph joined Leghorn to Pisa in 1847. There was clearly the need in Piedmont for a strong injection of Adam Smith as well as Bentham, and also of what Cavour himself (aristocrat though he was) called the immortal principles of 1789.

On his farm at Leri, Cavour had already shown himself a bold and successful innovator and had introduced modern accounting methods, crop rotation, experiments in subsoil drainage and livestock breeding, and machinery for making beet sugar and polishing rice. He showed the same spirit when he was a cabinet minister after 1850 and demonstrated that the *risorgimento* was not simply a revolt against foreign oppression, but first of all an internal revolution designed to introduce economic, political, and civil liberty. So doing, he brought Italy into line with the rest of Europe and established Piedmont unquestionably and for the first time as chief among the states of the peninsula.

Cavour's confessed aim was to convince Europe that Italians knew how to govern themselves without Austrian tutelage. He thus consciously compared the role of Piedmont in Italy with that of Prussia in Germany. To assert Piedmontese superiority, the legal codes were reformed and ecclesiastical immunities drastically curtailed. Exiles from other Italian states were liberally welcomed, and it was important that the careers most easily open to these exiles were in the despised and ill-paid though powerful fields of journalism and education where they could instruct public opinion in *italianità*. Some of the more distinguished, Mancini and the economist Francesco Ferrara among them, obtained posts at Turin university; Massari, Bianchi Giovini, and La Farina became editors of important newspapers; while Farini and Minghetti eventually reached cabinet rank. Turin temporarily assumed the leadership in intellectual life hitherto maintained by Florence, and the books published there naturally began to reflect her nationalist ambitions.

No great industrial enterprise had hitherto appeared in Piedmont, but Cavour inaugurated a new bank to provide credit for industry. He reduced tariffs considerably, so that exports and imports tripled in value over the period 1850–59. The railroad network by 1857 stretched from the French to the Swiss and Austrian frontiers, thus facilitating the mobilization and military campaign of 1859. Piedmont, indeed, by 1859 included half the railroad mileage of Italy, and the Mont Cenis tunnel was shortly to bring Paris within one day's journey. Cavour also laid the foundations of an armament industry, sending engineers to learn in England how to make naval engines, armor plate, and rifled cannon. In 1857 a start was made on the famous Cavour canal, which was to irrigate a large area around Vercelli and Novara and make it some of the most fertile land in the country. An important effect of such enterprise was that Rothschild of Paris and Baring and Hambro of London put their money into these developments and so obtained an interest in Piedmontese advancement.

In carrying through such reforms Cavour was by no means altogether typical of his colleagues and fellow citizens, but his own expansive character created the impression that Piedmont was more enlightened and liberal than was really so. Although its center of gravity had shifted from Chambéry in Savoy to the less illiberal milieu of Turin, the Court was still full of reactionary Savoyard generals from across the Alps. With clericals and reactionaries under Solaro della Margherita on one wing, and, on the other, radicals such as Depretis who were tinged with Jacobinism, Cavour had no easy passage for his favorite doctrine of the golden mean in everything.

In the end his good sense was invincible. "You will see, gentlemen," he had told parliament in March 1850, "how reforms carried out in time, instead of weakening authority, reinforce it; instead of precipitating revolution, they prevent it." He contended that the only real progress was slow and wisely ordered, and that by social reforms alone could socialism be resisted. He was no democrat, but he realized that, for better or worse, democracy was in the long run irresistible; while he would concede no natural right of participation in government, he was ready to extend the suffrage to all who accepted existing institutions. This was his customary pragmatic approach. All governments, he saw, now rested either tacitly or explicitly on public support. At a time when his protector Louis Napoleon was establishing plebiscitary dictatorship in France, Cavour was prudent enough to foster constitutional monarchy as "the only type of government which can reconcile liberty with order." Public opinion as revealed in parliament showed him the direction of popular sympathies, and out of the free conflict of ideas he would choose the policy which had most support. "I have no faith in dictatorships, especially civilian dictatorships," he wrote. "I think one can do many things with a parliament that would be impossible with absolute power . . . and I never feel so weak as when the House is shut."

Although Cavour expressed the hope that Italy could be created without a Cromwell, his actions were sometimes less liberal than his theories. This was important, because Cavour was to earn the reputation of being the one really successful Italian politician, and it was his practice which set the tone for political life after 1861. A shrewd fellow deputy called him a cross between Robert Peel and Machiavelli, and some later Italians were even to claim him as the great authoritarian. If he avoided repressive measures where possible, this seems to have been not so much because they were inherently bad, as because he knew that repression often defeated its own purposes. While he was sincere in his liberal beliefs, he was too practical a person to be doctrinaire and unyielding about them. The liberal method was good because "free institutions tend to make people richer," and it was this practical test of success which would justify any means so long as the end were good. Thus corruption in politics might well be legitimate, and in any case public and private life each had their separate code of morals: "If you must resort to extraordinary means, then adopt them as energetically as possible, so that the grandeur of your aim may make up for the hateful methods you employ, and so that your government will not appear ridiculous as well as odious."

Cavour appreciated the value of the free conflict of ideas; yet though he wrote that he felt weaker when parliament was shut, in practice he was glad to rule without it when he most needed to feel strong. In theory he claimed to admit that the Mazzinians were less dangerous inside than outside parliament, yet in practice he drove the extremists into clandestine conspiracy by preventing the free expression of their opinions. When the last surviving republican paper was studiously careful not to give him legal grounds for suppression, he first tried to bribe the printer to cease publication and then ordered the Genoese authorities to compel the editor into bankruptcy by "frequent and almost daily sequestrations, legal or illegal." The Mazzinians said that they wanted national unity far more than they wanted a republic, but Cavour on the contrary said that he would refuse an alliance with them even if it meant Italy remaining divided. Sometimes he connived at their insurrections, sometimes he went to the other extreme and warned Austria or her satellites of Mazzini's plans. At all costs, however, the revolutionaries had to be kept powerless and discredited, and used merely to frighten Europe into tolerating his own mild revolution in preference.

§

Cavour's theoretical liberalism and practical Machiavellism both helped in realizing national unification. For many years he had believed that Italy might in the distant future become an independent nation, but in practice his own immediate plans were for a kingdom of northern Italy, linked by alliance with other Italian states. The fact was that he disliked revolutionary republicanism as much if not more than he loved national unity, and he feared that Mazzini's insurrections would embroil him with France and undermine the predominance of Piedmont which depended on French support. Luckily he was met halfway by some of the more practical revolutionaries who had abandoned Mazzini's utopianism. Futile republican uprisings, for instance those of the Bandiera brothers in 1844 and Pisacane in 1857, convinced radicals like Manin and La Farina that a national revolution could succeed only if supported by the Piedmontese army, and accordingly they placed their hopes on convincing Cavour that public opinion was now ready for a unified Italian kingdom. It was Garibaldi's conquest of Sicily in 1860 which finally persuaded him that Manin was right.

Cavour at first did all he dared to stop Garibaldi from sailing on this madcap venture, and even after the landing in Sicily he remained for a while unhelpful and skeptical. But, as always, he was clever enough to let events take their course without implicating himself too far, and, while fully prepared to disown the revolutionaries if necessary, he was equally ready to lend a hand and reassert his influence should they prove victorious. His diplomatic tact had already been shown earlier in 1860, for against much opposition he had sacrificed the two northeastern provinces of Savoy and Nice to France, and so won Louis Napoleon for an accomplice in the acquisition of central Italy as a *quid pro quo*. Plebiscites had then been held in Tuscany and Emilia to confirm their annexation. And not content with this, Cavour then suggested to Britain that, while France wanted no more than a state of northern Italy as a check upon Austria, it might be a British interest that an even larger Italy should emerge as a counterpoise to France in the Mediterranean. It was at this point that Garibaldi evaded the Piedmontese and Neapolitan fleets and landed in Sicily.

The sudden news of Garibaldi's overwhelming success made Cavour decide that the best chance of controlling the revolutionaries was to outdo them at their own game. While still pretending to treat with the Bourbons, he sent secret agents to try to forestall Garibaldi with a more conservative insurrection at Naples, offering promotion to officers in the Neapolitan army and seducing politicians from their loyalty. When Garibaldi arrived at Naples first, Cavour was still not to be out-done. He quickly engineered popular uprisings in the Papal states as a pretext to invade Umbria and the Marches, and annexed most papal territory except the area around Rome. He was then able to advance southward and force Garibaldi by the threat of civil war to yield Naples and Sicily as well.

Legitimists and Catholics everywhere were profoundly disturbed by this invasion of the Papal states, but Cavour gave the ingenious excuse that only thus could the anticlerical Garibaldi be prevented from overthrowing the government of Rome itself. "The aim," he said, "has been holy, and perhaps this will justify any irregularities in the means which we have had to use." Almost before people could see what he was about, Cavour had unified most of Italy and held the usual rigged plebiscites to regularize the fact. When parliament met early in 1861, a new kingdom of twenty-two million people could be officially declared in existence. Only Rome with its French garrison, and Venice under Austrian rule, remained outside.

5 The Constitution, The King, and Parliament

The constitution of Italy was to remain that granted by Carlo Alberto to his Kingdom of Sardinia in 1848. There was some agitation in 1860–61 for a constituent assembly to draw up a new scheme of government for the united kingdom, but Cavour was particularly anxious not to have a complete breach with tradition, and he feared what would happen once basic institutions were called in question.

The *statuto* of 1848 therefore constituted the fundamental law of the realm for a hundred years to come. Despite the claim in its preamble to irrevocability, the details and the spirit were in fact altered, first in a liberal, later in an authoritarian sense. Specific articles guaranteed a right of public assembly, and a right to freedom of expression in the press, though in practice even under Cavour himself such liberties were not inviolate. Ministers were technically responsible to the king and not to parliament, but in practice this merely "constitutional government" based on royal power was already giving way to "parliamentary government" based on the cabinet. Such flexibility could work either way, and all depended on the character of the sovereign and his ministers.

Vittorio Emanuele II, while less powerful than the rulers of Prussia, had more authority than most constitutional monarchs. Article 65 of the *statuto* laid down that "the king nominates and dismisses his ministers"; he was under no obligation to follow their advice, and the constitution contained only the vaguest generalities about ministerial power. By not being too definite about who had the chief initiative in legislation, the path was left open for an empirical development of constitutional conventions. The king developed the power of issuing proclamations having the force of law. He appointed all members of the Senate. The king summoned and dissolved parliament, and in early years even presided at cabinet meetings. Article 5 provided that:

The king alone has the executive power. He is the supreme head of the state, commands all the armed forces by sea and land, declares war, makes treaties of peace, of alliance, of commerce, but giving notice of them to the two Houses as far as security and national interest permit. Treaties which demand any financial burden, or which would alter the territorial boundaries of the state, shall not have any effect until after the two Houses have consented to them.

Although most treaties were put before parliament, the king retained a dominating influence in foreign affairs: the foreign minister was usually his personal nominee, and sometimes he conducted a private policy which was independent of or even contrary to that of his prime minister.

A further channel of royal influence was the Court party, with whose help the king could resume a personal direction of government in moments of crisis. After the Treaty of Villafranca in 1859, after the Turin riots of September 1864, in 1867, 1896, 1898, and 1943, the king at critical moments handed over government to one of the army command-ders. Until the twentieth century, moreover, the ministers of war and of the navy were invariably generals and admirals, people who had sworn a military oath to obey the king and so were in a special way his servants. These military officers commonly remained in office from one ministry to the next, as placemen of the crown.

The monarch was always surrounded by army officers, and it is rare to find a picture of him in civilian clothes. The Court was not un-like a military encampment, and the heir to the throne was educated under martial discipline. Instructed in spartan habits, successive kings were men of simple and modest tastes, but this military atmosphere bred in them the morals and politics of an army clique and a barrack-room language and behavior. It also perpetuated the absurd and dangerous notion that war was a gentlemanly and desirable occupation. The national economy was to be crushed by ruinous expenditure on army and navy, sometimes without parliamentary sanction, and wars were lightheartedly provoked when Italy was in no position to fight.

Vittorio Emanuele became King of Sardinia in 1849, and King of Italy in 1861. He died in 1878. Because of the challenge of republicanism and the need to overshadow Garibaldi in popular esteem, an official apologetic and panegyric was developed to inflate his reputation. The true picture behind these clouds of incense is of a puny and usually insignificant man, good-natured and shrewd, but superstitious and ill-educated, possessing a rough hewn and by no means despicable character but little of the luster and aureole of majesty. His own enthusiasm was chiefly reserved for women, horses, and hunting. When his ancestral province of Savoy had to be ceded to France, his first anxiety was the loss of his hunting grounds. Like his forebears and his son he publicly maintained a mistress and illegitimate children, and seemed to think that this conduct was expected of a real king. He used to tell his friends the unlikely story of how Queen Victoria's daughter fell in love with him, but knew too much Greek and Latin for his tastes. His own preferences were more rude and proletarian—"too much the father of his people," said the wags.

There were obvious weaknesses in his position after 1861. He was resented by adherents of other Italian dynasties which he had displaced. A long tradition of republicanism existed in some areas, and only Piedmont and Naples were strongly monarchist. Divine right was no longer what it had been in his father's time, and after the plebiscites the king technically held office by will of the nation as well as by the grace of God. He did not possess those natural allies of monarchs, a strong aristocracy and a royalist priesthood, especially once the Church had excommunicated the violators of the Papal states.

Vittorio Emanuele's chief strength lay in the guarantee of political stability which he afforded. Opposition from the radical Left was reduced by Garibaldi's fortunate belief that the king was a God-given instrument to end the temporal power of the Papacy. Opposition from the clericals of the Right was partly neutralized by the monarch's sincere but not very energetic attempt to behave as a good Catholic. Cavour skillfully used this counteraction between the two extremes to make the king rely more on the liberals of the Center. The king was never very friendly with Cavour: they came to an open breach over foreign policy, and again when the royal mistress and Cavour unsuccessfully tried to exclude each other from their respective offices. But although the king's temperament repeatedly led him into sudden personal interventions in government, for the most part he kept fairly narrowly within constitutional bounds, and in his attitude toward Mazzini and Garibaldi he showed more tolerance and sometimes more common sense than Cavour himself.

૬ၹ

A special instrument for the exercise of royal influence was the Senate. Chosen by the king, it was a conservative body made up of ex-deputies and other prominent citizens, and, as only the elderly and moderate were chosen, it lacked liveliness and the stimulus of sharp conflict. Financial measures had to be first introduced in the Lower House, and though otherwise both Houses were equal in status, this financial initiative soon gave the Chamber a distinct primacy. A Senate vote of no confidence did not compel resignation. Cavour, who would have preferred an elected Senate, several times led the Chamber in collision with the Upper House, and when he died in 1861 the latter body evidently possessed little more than a delaying power. Out of thirty subsequent prime ministers, only Menabrea in 1867–69, Pelloux and Saracco in 1899–1901, and Badoglio in 1943–44 were senators.

Ministers of the crown could speak in either House, but could vote only in that to which they properly belonged. Ministers were selected by the king and in theory were responsible to him alone, but parliament developed some control by interrogating them in "interpellations," and by votes of no confidence and general debates on finance. The prime ministership was an office not mentioned in the constitution, but Cavour made it all-important. The prime minister usually came to hold executive responsibility by also taking a powerful departmental post, either finance or the interior. Collective cabinet responsibility was not thought essential; an individual minister might resign if his department was censured and the prime minister could then reform his cabinet in a *rimpasto*. Lowell said that each single minister was less a member of a group than a free lance fighting on his own behalf at the head of his retainers. This made governments highly unstable, and altogether there were thirty-three different cabinets in the thirty-five years between 1861 and 1896.

Parliament itself had respectable medieval progenitors, but its roots in history had withered, and the strongest national traditions were those of paternal monarchy. Cavour had a great gift for parliamentary government and had closely studied constitutional practice abroad. He worked to increase the power and responsibility of the Chamber, for he recognized it to be his main check on the king and on his chief enemies, Mazzini, Garibaldi, and the clericals. By 1861, therefore, convention had settled that the ministers should normally be the expression of a majority in the House.

Parliamentary life in 1861 and after was strongly influenced by the alliance of Right Center with Left Center upon which Cavour had first embarked nine years earlier. His opponents in 1852 had called his action an unscrupulous intrigue for power, and there is no doubt that he had made this alliance behind the back of his cabinet colleagues and in order to supplant D'Azeglio in the premiership. But Cavour himself claimed this *connubio* as his political masterpiece, since it consolidated the constitution by allying the Center groups against both extremes. This made for moderation and the golden mean in everything. It also set the fashion for basing power on mutable alliances within an amorphous government majority, rather than on a single party with a tight and consistent program. Instead of resigning if their policy failed to gain support, prime ministers tended to change that policy and try to build another compromise coalition. Cavour's shifting majority thus comprised many shades of opinion: it contained centralizers like Ricasoli and Spaventa, together with decentralizers like Farini and Minghetti; Jacini of the Catholic Right, and Rattazzi of the anticlerical Left; Sella who wanted state control over the Church, and Lanza who wanted a free church in a free state. One result of this was to inhibit the growth of a clear-cut party system and an organized opposition.

Cavour was not a party man, but rather an opportunist who took care never to be very far behind or ahead of public opinion. If no well-articulated parties were to appear before the time of socialism and fascism, this was largely because differences of principle were thus discounted and fluctuations deliberately encouraged with the idea of putting national before sectional interests. Any group not adopting these coalition tactics was out of the game, and any major challenge of principle was thus rendered impotent. The clericals, for instance, when they tried to take part in parliamentary politics, were not encouraged to do so but were treated as traitors who had to repudiate opposition or else stand aside. Similarly the republicans and autonomists were muzzled, and their views kept as far as possible from public scrutiny. Coalition government was in practice aided by the fact that, out of a population of twenty-two million, there was an electorate of only half a million, of whom only 300,000 voted, and these constituted a narrow class which did not often contain strong divergencies of view. Instead of a two-party system, therefore, moderates of both the so-called Right and Left used to combine in every cabinet, and the government majority was perpetually being modified as the many small groups rallied for tactical reasons around one strong personality after another.

The philosopher Croce and others were to justify this practice as an admirable and peculiarly Italian type of parliamentary government. Nevertheless, quite apart from causing extreme political instability, it also left governments sometimes dangerously free from opposition and criticism. There seldom existed any alternative government ready to take office with a completely different composition and policy. Parties were merely clusters of clients around their patrons, and both policy and tactics were altered *en passant*. Political life therefore revolved less around principles than around persons, and parliamentary history was a tale of shifting loyalties, not of party conflict. Major oppositions of principle could thus be buried altogether, with surprising results, and though many politicians of both Right and Left regarded this as unsatisfactory, still they could do nothing to alter the fact.

§❧

Right and Left are generalized categories which mark the rough division of deputies into conservative-liberal and radical-democrat, and frequent coalitions between the two must not be allowed to conceal the basic distinction. The patriots were polarized into two wings, liberal and radical, which represent a fairly clear division in Italian history. The liberals after 1815 had made a temporary and uneasy alliance with the radical revolutionaries against the unenlightened despotism of the *ancien régime;* but then, after the autocrats had disappeared in 1859–60, the liberals were revealed as the chief beneficiaries under the revolution, and became increasingly conservative of results achieved. The radicals, on the other hand, were more democratic and believed in equal rights for all, especially as they themselves had been edged out of some positions of power. They thought that, if economic matters were left unregulated as the liberals taught, progress would be too slow to be sure. They looked all the time to reforms in the future, while the others were more conscious of history and tradition.

Conservative-liberals such as Minghetti had been slow to accept Mazzini's ideas of national unity, and D'Azeglio would have preferred to stop short of annexing Rome and the South. While they had taken a most necessary share in the Italian revolution, these liberals had been less single-minded in their revolutionism, and had sometimes repudiated the liberal cause when straight political issues were confused by social revolution. Nevertheless, it was upon the conservative-liberals that success eventually depended, for they represented the cautious trimmers who made up "public opinion" in Italy. Cavour and Ricasoli were safer and more realistic than Mazzini and Cattaneo: they knew how to husband resources, and how to wait for the moment when Italy could profitably intervene in the crosscurrents of European diplomacy. Although not the people to initiate a revolt, they alone could make it succeed and then ligature the wound it left.

§❧

Cavour's majority after the elections of January 1861 was very substantial, and its focus was somewhere a little to the right of center. The "opposition" was small and various. On the extreme right-wing benches were about twenty illiberal reactionaries, or "ultras," representing those few adherents of the pre-1860 dynasties who had not gone off into quietist abstention. Among them were some Piedmontese disciples of Solaro della Margherita who were more monarchical than the king. They had deplored their divinely appointed ruler stooping to accept a revolutionary and popular resettlement of Italy; they resented the plebiscites, and could hardly bear to see the Turin parliament invaded by "Italians." It was perhaps unfortunate that the extreme Right was so doctrinaire and ineffective. Still worse, the Catholics were boycotting politics, because the Pope refused to recognize a state which had filched two-thirds of his domain; and Cavour himself, in a misguided fear of opposition, had once persuaded parliament to annul the election of extreme Catholic deputies. Italy therefore lacked a strictly conservative party. Equally important, this meant that a quite inadequate representation was accorded those Italians whose political heirs under universal suffrage in 1948 were to give an overwhelming vote to a Catholic party. Politics in Italy remained to this extent unrepresentative and "undemocratic." In France, by contrast, the liberals were forced closer together by the presence of a "reactionary" opposition, but in Italy the weakness of such opposition allowed the many fractional center groups to retain their individual loyalties, and thereby made the government coalition often characterless and always liable to disintegration.

Rattazzi and Depretis were the principal leaders of the Left Center. They were liberal before they were radical, and always within or near the borders of Cavour's coalition. Beyond them were the groups of the extreme Left, comprising fifty ill-assorted federalists, Garibaldians, and semirepublicans, the radical democrats of Tuscany under Guerrazzi, those of Piedmont under Brofferio, and a handful of Sicilians around Crispi. The loyalties of these groups were sometimes as much regional as political. Mazzini himself was still in exile, an outlaw under sentence of death. His republican followers were no longer a force to be feared, although Cavour continued to persecute them.

Garibaldi in April 1861 turned up in parliament flaunting his red shirt and caused an uproar by accusing Cavour of dividing the country and threatening it with civil war. This outburst was in character, and it reflected the irresponsibility and frustration of those outside the government coalition. Garibaldi's lack of political tact threatened to carry Italy into dangerous revolutionary waters, for he still meant to capture Venice and Rome. Cavour and subsequent prime ministers, in their dealings with Garibaldi, showed equal tactlessness and incomprehension. The ex-Dictator of the Two Sicilies therefore resigned from parliament where, as he said, intrigue and talk were substitutes for action. He retired to write an autobiographical poem and to campaign for universal peace and a world state, his followers distributing themselves over the political spectrum.

This miscellaneous left-wing opposition was hamstrung by Cavour's able parliamentary maneuvers. Its leaders had served well enough on the battlefield, but their political energies had been perverted by years of conspiracy, exile, and imprisonment. Their good qualities were moral rather than political, and although full of fine intentions and popular appeal, they lacked the moderation and skill for parliamentary business. Italian politics thus lacked a strong Left as well as a strong Right, and opposition from either quarter tended to be irresponsible and utopian. The radical democrats were generals without an army, and had no possibility of organizing a strong national party. Their program consisted of various paper schemes for universal suffrage, compulsory education, a progressive income tax, but otherwise a general minimization of state action.

Not only was this extreme Left inherently weak in both numbers and leadership, but Cavour and his successors freely used local-government machinery to rig elections and defeat them. The Left complained that a quarter of the electorate were in one sense or another government pensioners and amenable to official direction. When, despite this, Mazzini was repeatedly elected *in absentia* at Messina, the safe majority of official placemen could be relied on to expel him from parliament. Bribery and intimidation of the press was another weapon. Dumas *père* accepted a monthly subsidy from the government, although he claimed to be a republican and his Neapolitan paper called itself *L'Indipendente*. Cavour did his best to do without martial law, but he could not avoid it at Naples in 1861, and police regulations were enforced harshly when men such as Spaventa and Nicotera succeeded him as minister of the interior. Arbitrary government was made necessary by the unfriendliness of the countryside, and was defended by politicians who knew that, had the will of the people prevailed, there might have been no *risorgimento* at all.

ം

It was this general hostility or indifference of the masses which precluded any extension of the suffrage. Even among the enfranchised 2 per cent, public spirit was weak. There had been no political education and no training in responsibility under the Habsburgs in Lombardy or the Bourbons of Naples, and even in Piedmont there existed no solid basis of local self-government to educate people in applied liberalism.

Without a widespread class of independent smallholders, another prerequisite of liberal parliamentary government was lacking. In the North,
public-spirited landowners like Cavour and Minghetti lamented that the
facility with which real property could be conveyed and divided among
heirs prevented the formation of a stable class of rich landlords trained
to carry out the tasks of public life. In the South, there was rich land-
lordism in plenty but little social or political conscience. Local government was there exploited by cliques who created jobs for their relatives,
managed the communal lands and charities in their own interests, and
built roads at public cost for their private benefit. Those who ran municipal administration regularly arranged that taxes were levied chiefly on
basic foodstuffs and so fell principally on the poor.

In all classes the absence of a community sense resulted from a habit
of insubordination learned in centuries of despotism. Even the nobles had
become accustomed to obstruction, and thought that governments could
be fairly cheated without moral obliquity so long as the cheating were
successful. In December 1861 a special warning had to be issued against
the private agencies which claimed to help people influence government
departments. Instead of recognizing that taxes had to be paid, the attitude was rather that if one group of people had discovered a profitable
evasion, then other groups had better look to their own interests. Each
province, each class, each industry thus endeavored to gain at the expense of the community. Before such traditional habits of mind could
be changed, a slow and costly course of political education was necessary
for both rulers and ruled.

6 The Social Hierarchy

The cause of national independence in Italy was associated with the liberalizing of government; it was also connected with the rise of towns, and with a social transformation in which new classes broke through a hitherto stifling political and social system. Before the *risorgimento,* the ruling classes had consisted of a landowning aristocracy in alliance with the Church, whereas by 1861 a professional and mercantile element, allied to a new middle class of landed gentry, was much more prominent.

The *bourgeoisie* had hardly appeared as a force in politics before the Napoleonic period, but they were bound to discern in nationalism and liberalism an attractive ideology which would justify their advance toward prosperity and power. Lombard merchants had been cut off by Austria from their southern outlet in Genoa, and toward the north met a discrimination in favor of, for instance, the textiles of Bohemia. Nationalism therefore had a special advantage for them in combating restrictive monopolies and unenlightened protection. For the newly rich it meant expropriating the huge domains of the Church and purchasing them cheaply in a buyers' market: this was particularly true in Sicily, where neither Napoleon nor the principles of 1789 had ever reached, and where ecclesiastical land held in mortmain amounted to a tenth of all cultivable ground. Similarly with the common lands in each village, the more enterprising landowners wanted an "enlightened" government which would let them enclose the commons. Whereas the Bourbons had favored the poor against the middle classes—for example by forbidding the export of grain in order to keep bread cheap—after 1861 a free market was created which allowed agricultural prices to rise. Economic progress certainly demanded that free trade should thus succeed paternalism, but the change-over was effected in a way which was as harsh on the underprivileged as it was agreeable to many of their betters.

The *risorgimento* was, as one would expect, a movement not of the populace but of an elite. In Garibaldi's Thousand there were no peasants, but rather students, independent craftsmen, and *litterati.* The backbone of the national revolution was made up of ex-officers such as Cavour and Pisacane, sailors such as Bixio and Garibaldi, doctors such as Bertani and Farini, lawyers like Crispi and Rattazzi, writers and scholars like Amari and De Sanctis. On the other hand few men of great possessions were listed in the secret societies, because the *risorgimento,* while anything but popular, was a revolution of the disinherited, of the starry-eyed. The educated unemployed and underemployed were one of its chief driving forces, the same class of people who later supplied a significant element in the triumph of Mussolini.

§❧

The nobles in Italy had little political importance as a group, not possessing the same feudal or military privileges as their equivalents in Germany, nor the habit of government as in England. Nobility did not imply wealth or power, and certainly there was nothing of a standardized aristocratic caste. Count Cavour, as a younger son, had to carve out his own fortune in finance and agriculture. The Marquis d'Azeglio, his predecessor as prime minister, was a successful painter and novelist. At Rome, the first of the princely Torlonia family had begun by selling castoff clothes in the city before he advanced to management of the lucrative salt and tobacco monopolies and ultimately became a millionaire. In Sicily alone there were sixty dukes, a hundred princes, and innumerable barons and marquises, many of them as illiterate as their grooms. In each province the nobility had a different character, and so it never formed a caste barrier against the advance of democracy. In Piedmont or Tuscany it was often liberal, just as it was clerical in Rome and feudal in Naples.

Far from having common interests with their counterparts in Piedmont, the titled families of Milan and Naples resented the surrender to Turin of the offices and patronage which before 1860 they had enjoyed in their provincial capitals. The multiplication of titles after 1861 also helped to break any remaining caste feeling. As the king once said, he could never refuse a cigar or a title to a gentleman—and the cynics added that he was not always too careful about their being gentlemen. Cavour recognized that the ineffectiveness of the Italian aristocracy ruled out any House of Lords, and there was never any suggestion that hereditary peers should sit in the Senate by right. The only titled prime ministers after Cavour himself were the Savoyard Menabrea, the Tuscan barons Ricasoli and Sonnino, and the Sicilian Marquis di Rudinì.

Economically as well as politically the old families were in decline. They did not readily enter commerce or industry, because they were, as Cattaneo said, rooted in the soil like an old plant which desires only a comfortable immobility; and there was little incentive even to mechanize farms when labor was so plentiful and cheap. They were therefore increasingly left behind by new men, such as Pirelli, Orlando, and Breda, who rose through industrial enterprise to the dignity of the Senate. After

1815, Piedmont and Naples had tried to rehabilitate the landed aristocracy by restoring entails and primogeniture, but the wars and the subsequent depression left most of the big estates heavily mortgaged. Their owners had seldom been enterprising landlords, nor had they ploughed enough of their profits back into the land. After 1815 they partly won back their social position, but their economic power was waning. Few Roman aristocratic families except the Colonna and Doria retained their former affluence. Many of the others had wasted their fortunes at faro or *trente et quarante,* trusting that the papal government would save them from bankruptcy. The princely families who owned the Campagna lived at Rome and farmed out their estates to the wealthy *mercanti di campagna,* who in their turn, if they ended by owning property, made it a point of honor and social prestige to hire out the management to others.

The middle classes worked far harder than the nobles. An American diplomat in 1860 specially noted the contempt with which practical agricultural pursuits were regarded by the Neapolitan nobility. The Sicilian aristocracy, like the Spanish dons from whom many of them descended, would not stoop to the professions or even the Church, let alone to trade. They had led the feudal revolution of 1812, but the succeeding revolutions of 1848 and 1860 found the professional middle classes more in command. Between 1820 and 1860, according to the British consul Goodwin, the number of landowning families in Sicily had risen from two thousand to twenty thousand, and the size of estates was smaller in proportion. What was happening here was happening elsewhere, and whether in the army, or in administration and diplomacy, the middle classes were assuming the position to which their numbers, enterprise, and ability entitled them.

A decayed social status alone was left to the nobility. If too poor to own a carriage or a gondola, they would hire one for the afternoon *passeggiata,* and affix their own special door or emblem bearing the family coat of arms. In the North they were merging rapidly into the rest of society. In the South they were often lazy, corrupt, and ignorant good-for-nothings, who on rare visits to their estates played the *gran signore* in a fortress surrounded by armed retainers. Thus Goodwin described them in 1860:

The Sicilian nobleman, brought up at home by a priest and allowed to herd with menials, has no companion among his equals. Thrown into the hands of a pedagogue, he merely learns to read and write, then passes into the care of a friar who teaches him his catechism and the rudiments of Latin, and he finally goes to a school of nobles, where he obtains a mere smattering of *Belles Lettres.* Then his education finishes. Coming home at 16 or 17, he throws aside his classics, betakes himself to novel reading, and sets up as a man about town. Prevented by class prejudice from entering the army or navy, he learns neither to command or obey; and excluded as he is from the magistracy by his legal ignorance, he neither administers justice nor enforces the laws. None of the nobility live on their estates. Most of the Sicilian towns serve for the residence of the neighbouring landlords on whose scanty outlay they depend for their subsistence. The family mansion standing on the deserted market place shows traces of former splendour in painted ceilings, gilt doors and embossed furniture. Here lost in space dwell the present possessors, ignorant of what is going on in the political world, falling gradually to the lowest level. They are destined to be supplanted by men of business and industry on a not distant day.

These men still considered local government their perquisite, "like so many Machiavellis or Palmerstons," as one Sicilian paper wrote in 1860, but they were not of the caliber to influence national politics.

§❧

Because the *risorgimento* was a civil war between the old and new ruling classes, the peasants were neutral except in so far as their own perennial social war became accidentally involved. They certainly had no love for United Italy, and probably no idea what the term signified until it came home to them in higher prices, taxes, and conscription. Their natural tendency was to oppose any invading army which requisitioned their scanty food supplies, and hence they were a counterrevolutionary force in politics. In 1848 the Lombard peasants had opened the dikes against the invading Piedmontese. In 1849, as in 1799, they had fought for the old dynasties in both North and South, because their dislike of royal tyranny was less than their hatred of the local lawyer, the usurer, and the factor who managed the lord's estate, all of whom represented a more immediate and more effective oppression. Pisacane, the nationalist, had been killed in 1857 by the very peasants he had hoped to liberate, the same rustic churls who sometimes hindered Garibaldi and who stripped and robbed the fallen soldiers of both sides on every battlefield.

Since Italy was a land of agriculture, peasants made up the great bulk of the population—national figures like Verdi, Pius X, and Mussolini never quite threw off their humble origins, and Garibaldi and even the king had more in common with rustic plebeians than with intellectual landowners such as Cavour. During long periods of the year, most agricultural workers were unemployed, and overpopulation kept their wages at a mere subsistence level. Though legally they were emancipated from feudalism, they had lost rights as well as duties thereby, because feudal landlords had also assumed obligations and responsibilities which now lapsed. The compulsion to grind grain at their lord's mill and bake at his oven disappeared in theory, but increased taxation forced poorer farmers to give up subsistence farming in favor of cash crops, and this introduced the extra hazard of market conditions. They had the worst of both worlds: whatever the law might say, the peasant still labored at the *corvée;* his family could still be the virtual property of the landlord, kept in a state of personal dependence by armed *campieri* and *mazzieri* who wore their lord's livery. The laborer who lacked animals and tools was also at the mercy of the richer peasant, and in a year of bad harvest only the moneylender stood between him and starvation.

Sonnino in 1877 described how peasants in the lower Po Valley ate corn almost exclusively, because it was cheaper and gave more sense of repletion than other foods. In Apulia the day laborers consumed little but black barley bread baked two or three times a year. Since they could not buy, industry was deprived of a potential market, and industrial development was consequently retarded. Thus, there was no outlet for the surplus labor which impoverished the countryside. Only a few philanthropists concerned themselves with the submerged nine-tenths of Italian society. It was not easy for the doctors to connect pellagra with consumption of corn, nor did they understand what caused the malaria which infected several million Italians with chronic tertian and quartan fevers, and kept perhaps four million acres uncultivable. Hundreds of thousands of people lived in caves, or in windowless wattle-and-daub huts, or in the damp cellars of the Neapolitan *fondaci,* and figures given to parliament in 1879 imply that many working-class areas in Rome had a population density of ten people per room.

In the southern agricultural regions nearly everyone was illiterate. The saying went there that a donkey cost more to maintain than a man, and Garibaldi's town-bred Thousand were astonished to find shepherds clad only in goat skins. Roads were nonexistent even between some of the chief cities; there was little commerce, only sparse cultivation, the surrounding sea was a highway for pirates, and the land resembled North Africa more than north Italy. The combination of malaria, brigands, and lack of water forced people to cluster in large villages perhaps as much as a dozen miles' walk from where they worked. Parts of the South in 1861 still possessed an economy where money was unessential. Rent, the services of the priest, the "protection" given by the lords' *campieri,* and the interest due to usurers, could all be paid in kind. Feudal conditions easily survived in such an environment; there was great inequality of wealth, and little pretense of equality before the law. It was a Counter Reformation world where the clergy had great influence over a hand-kissing population of serfs, where people learned their scanty morals and politics in church, and avoided sending their children to school. Conditions of life and work reduced the peasants permanently to the verge of revolt, and no political upheaval occurred but they rose to exploit it in an insurrection of hideous cruelty.

However unsympathetic these peasants were toward the political aspirations of liberalism, without their unintended help the political revolution itself might have failed. In their eyes, insurrection meant a chance for sack and arson, an opportunity to attack their lord's bailiff and the police, to burn the town hall with its tax rolls and title deeds, to occupy their lord's land and divert water from his mill. Sometimes, driven by hunger, they thus ignited the first spark of what later became political rebellion, for they alone had everything to gain and little to lose by open class war. The driving force of the *risorgimento* was therefore by no means just the heroism of Garibaldi and the brains of Cavour; it was also family and personal vendettas, and the lust for loot and rapine. Every ten years there was a major peasant revolt, and the terror they inspired went deep into the collective subconscious.

Both the peasants and the city intellectuals thus had an interest in starting a revolution, the one with a social, the other with a political objective. Once insurrections had begun, however, the success of one class spelled ruin for the other. The rebellions of 1820–21 and 1848–49 had failed principally because the middle classes had not completed their political revolution before the peasants, profiting from the ensuing anarchy, started a separate grudge war of their own. Liberal landowners had therefore been forced to change sides and hope that the Bourbons would succeed in repressing social disorder. It was fortunate for them and for Italy that circumstances were different in 1859–60.

The 1860 revolt in southern Italy is of great interest for its illustration of the attitude and the importance of the peasants. A combination of urban unemployment riots with anarchical *jacqueries* disintegrated local government and forced the terrified Bourbon police to run for their lives. This was an unintended but indispensable condition for the success of Garibaldi's invasion. A few days of rick burning, cattle stealing, land occupation, assassination, and even cannibalism followed, but this outraged all owners of property, even those who were liberals and nationalists. As was said of the Catanians at the time: "They wanted liberty, but only if it could be won without sacrifice or inconvenience to themselves, and without any social insurrection that might expose their houses to robbery." Garibaldi had at first played for peasant support, and his early decrees cleverly promised land distribution and cheaper food. But he soon found that his sole chance of permanent political victory lay in the support of the landlords who alone were interested in enforcing law and order, and many of whom by this time were interested in little else. So he altered course and executed the "communists" on the Nelson estates at Bronte. This was the price the landowners demanded in exchange for backing the nationalist revolution.

The peasants were thus not only instrumental in undermining the Bourbons at a decisive moment, but also in compelling some of the old ruling classes to turn toward victorious Piedmont as the defender of social order against their serfs. These peasants soon realized that Garibaldi was no longer a rebel on their side, but rather represented a new and yet more oppressive government. By that time, however, the forces of order were back in control. The middle classes, whether conservative or radical in politics, were at one on the social question. Cavour had correctly analyzed this: "In Italy a democratic revolution has little chance of success. To appreciate this it is enough to examine the elements making up the party which wants political change. This party meets with little sympathy among the masses which, except for one or two sections in the towns, are generally attached to the old institutions of the country. Its main strength resides almost exclusively in the middle and a part of the upper classes. And both of these have many interests to defend. Property, thank heaven, is not in Italy the exclusive privilege of any one class. If social order were really threatened, if the great principles on which society reposes were challenged, I am sure that we should find even the most extreme republicans in the forefront of the conservative party."

By its own logic, therefore, a movement which had grown out of peasants rebelling against landowners ended up on the side of the landowners against their peasants—indeed this was one important reason for its success. The common people were otherwise irrelevant to nationalism, and this helps to explain why so little trouble was taken by any national leader to win them over. Cavour, in his early days at least, had spoken of competing with the socialists in offering social reform, but he confined himself to vague admonitions. Mazzini, too, was content with sincere but noncommittal statements, as that liberty implied equality, and political revolution implied social revolution. Except for Pisacane and Garibaldi, the early radicals paid little attention to social reform and the condition of the poor.

For some time after 1860 social problems remained in the background. The middle classes had, as it were, gained a premature victory over the feudal landlords. Feudalism had been destroyed before its successor, capitalism, was ready to take over the management of society, and before labor was sufficiently articulate to state its needs. According to Sonnino, the only social legislation in the first decades of United Italy was a measure on postal savings banks in 1870, and an ineffective act of 1873 about child employment in industry. So far as one can see, the general standard of living showed little or no improvement for some time. Insufficient money was spent on public works, and political instability discouraged any detached study of social and economic problems. Deeper still lay a dangerous cast of mind which associated liberalism with the interests of the rich. History was to show, for instance, that night work in the textile industry was to be prohibited only when overproduction gave factory owners a real interest in reducing output.

To become an inherent part of Italian life and consciousness, the political *risorgimento* required a supplementary social revolution, one which could attract popular sympathy to the government and convince the ruling classes that social remedies might be a prerequisite of political stability. To complete the process of unification, the common people had to be brought into the mainstream of national life. This was a lesson to be learned, and reluctance to learn it was to bring severe trials upon Italy in the next ninety years.

7 Agriculture and Industry

The great majority of Italians lived by argiculture, yet Italy was not self-sufficient in food; the basic cause of this was the scarcity and misuse of capital. Rather than improve existing possessions, wealthy proprietors preferred to extend them or buy titles, for this was the best way to purchase social esteem. Savings disappeared in interest on mortgages, which in 1860 was thought to consume as much as one-third of the revenue from the soil, and this misuse of credit in the past was a crippling burden on the major national industry. The most popular types of cultivation were not always the most profitable, for the crops that paid more needed a greater outlay than the average farmer could afford—vines, olives, and almonds, for instance, all took ten years or more to mature. In some areas there was no money to build roads to the local market, and transportation difficulties added to the cost of marketing. Although labor was cheap, money could be borrowed only at 6 to 8 per cent, and people often lacked the resources or the will to cultivate their land with more than moderate efficiency. Rivers were left without embankments because it paid no one to build and maintain them, and large areas which might have absorbed the surplus agricultural population were abandoned to malarial marsh and swamp. After two or three crops had been extravagantly raised on recently cleared land, it might be deserted, its owner preferring to exploit other virgin soil rather than stay and pay his quota of land tax.

A prerequisite of improvement was a new attitude as much as new capital. Certainly state help was required wherever land reclamation was beyond the capacity of individual proprietors. Great areas would have to be drained or irrigated, water supplies regulated, and mountains saved from erosion by tree planting. More important was a change of outlook among the cultivators themselves. The Italian laborer was one of the hardest working in the world, and when employment was insufficient at home he made seasonal expeditions abroad to build the Suez Canal, the Forth Bridge, the railroads of America, the Alpine tunnels, and the harbors of Calais and Marseille. No permanent improvement was likely at home, however, until domestic agriculture was made more efficient and enterprising and more able to provide for an industrial population.

Peasant families still spun and wove their clothes from home-grown hemp and flax. Subsistence agriculture had to cover almost all their needs, and this restricted the possibilities of improvement. Even on the big farms of Lombardy after 1860 the wooden plough and the hand flail were in general use. A Sicilian nobleman who imported subsoil ploughs found that his workers broke them to escape the extra labor involved, and well into the next century sowing and reaping were done by hand. The southern peasant distrusted innovations, often believing, for instance, that machine-made cloth could not be durable. He still prayed to one saint against hail, to another against drought, to St. Cataldo before threshing, to St. Erasmo if his ass were ailing. Even in the twentieth century, villages have been known to change their patron saint if they received less rain than other nearby districts. This psychological conservatism and technical ignorance were other factors which limited any advance in agricultural efficiency and standards of life.

Among methods of land tenure, the extensive farm or *latifondo* of the South had survived two thousand years of war and revolution, despite frequent changes of ownership and much hostile legislation. The legal abolition of feudalism by Napoleon had temporarily broken up some of these *latifondi,* but intensive agriculture was precluded by natural conditions. Hence, as before and since, they reappeared around the only people who had capital. Where three harvests regularly failed out of ten, the peasant had insufficient reserves to work on his own; a balanced farm unit would have been too large for his resources, and it was difficult on small holdings to rotate crops efficiently or to grow enough fodder for the necessary oxen. Napoleon's government had therefore been unable to prevent people selling back their parcels of land once the estates had been divided. Common land belonging to the village, wherever it was distributed in lots to the peasants, likewise passed straight to the land speculators who had ready cash, or else the landowners simply used their control of local government to enclose the commons without any pretense of equity. The large estates increased in size, while the peasants lost rights of grazing and wood collecting on the common land which had been important in their economy.

Only a small proportion of Italians owned property more extensive than a hovel and a back yard, and many more were casual day laborers whose lot was miserable. In Tuscany and elsewhere a beneficial system of *métayage* or *mezzadria* had been developed, by which the owner gave the seed, vines, and olive trees, perhaps the cattle, and would pay all rates and taxes, while the tenant supplied tools and labor. No money rent was involved, but the profits were divided half and half, or more favorably to the landlord. This sharecropping hardly encouraged investment in land, since either party knew that the other would gain half of the return on any improvement. In compensation it certainly made for social stability, and it was often therefore called an ideal type of collaboration. But as markets became wider and tools more expensive, the security of tenure given by the *mezzadria* did not compensate for the low output per unit of land. It usually meant that crops were grown for subsistence alone, vegetables indiscriminately among the vines, without incentive to specialization.

The principal crops in Italy were cereals and grapes. Cereals, needing little capital outlay, were grown even in areas which were thoroughly unsuitable, and took up nearly half the country's productive acreage. Nassau Senior in 1851 found that in Sicily sixteen bushels of wheat to the acre were produced every other year, the land laying fallow the next, and he commented that this was no more than in the time of Cicero. Except on the great northern plain, vines, olives, and fruit trees were more suited to the prevalent conditions of scanty and uncertain rainfall. In some years more wine was exported from Italy than from France, although Italy suffered from the bad organization and insufficient skill of growers and manufacturers. There was little selection of vines, and because of the fear of theft and hail the grapes were often harvested too early. Types of wine varied too much from year to year, and there was little attempt to study foreign taste. The other chief export products of Italian agriculture were oil, fruit, and cheese. Hemp and flax were grown in considerable quantities, and there was a momentary boom in cotton when the American Civil War created the illusion that Sicily and Sardinia could supply the north Italian textile industries.

§❧

Before 1860, Italy had hardly begun to share in the industrial revolution. The country was deficient in raw materials, and, though labor was abundant, skilled technicians were rare, for the worst-paid lawyer or white-collar worker thought himself far above the most skilled artisan. The progressive industrialist who brought over machines from England might find no one to assemble or maintain them, and a surplus of ordinary manpower lessened the incentive to mechanization. In any case power was lacking, and machinery from abroad was expensive.

The mental attitude of both rich and poor was unfavorable to great industrial development. As Cavour complained, too much investment had been diverted from industry to real property. People brought up under the *ancien régime* had been taught to think speculation improper and credit something uncanny or unholy—King Ferdinando of Naples had been irritated by the very mention of bills of exchange. Paper money continued to be distrusted and coins hoarded long after 1860; cattle and farm produce went on being exchanged by barter; over fifty different coins continued in occasional use—ducat, piastre, oncia, scudo, lira, marengo, and florin. Alongside the new decimal and metric systems, the old illegal weights and measures survived in country districts until the end of the century.

Such industry as existed was never far removed from agriculture. Town dwellers continued to own small holdings outside the city walls, and agricultural laborers during winter might seek part-time employment in the towns. Quarrying and mining were generally undertaken by part-time farmers, and the Lombard silk industry was largely operated by women who worked for much of the year in the fields. Even when cottage industries gave way to a factory system using power looms, silk throwing remained a seasonal occupation for agricultural workers. The 1861 census recorded nearly eight million agriculturists, but only three million workers engaged in craftsmanship and manufacture, and of these three million most were women working part-time. Ellena calculated in 1880 that only 20 per cent of industrial workers were adult males. For some years after 1861, the number of textile workers doing piecework in their homes must actually have grown. The workers were the first to protest against factory employment, because auxiliary domestic jobs were precious to a farming family which had to reckon with seasonal unemployment, and they were also afraid of losing independence and security in factory life. They could not see that factories held out the potential benefit of combination in trade unions, whereas in cottage industry their wages would be tied to the rates prevailing in agriculture.

The money which might have promoted an industrial revolution had for centuries been hidden in the countryside, often unproductively. Potential investors had been deterred by the unsympathetic attitude of the pre-1860 regimes and by the wars and unrest of the *risorgimento*. In Lombardy, the only region which had a regular surplus of exports over imports, Cattaneo estimated that in 1850 there was five times as much investment in agriculture as in industry. Three out of the four big Italian railroad companies were to be completely financed from abroad, and the fourth largely so; the first installations of gas in Italy were the product of foreign enterprise, and foreign houses owned much of the textile and shipping industries. English capital was sunk in the sulphur, wine, and essential-oil trades of Sicily, as well as in Venetian hotels and glass. French investment was directed mainly to Piedmont and Naples, German and Swiss to Lombardy, in a process which incidentally had the not unimportant effect of binding to the fortunes of Italy some of the chief banking houses and capitalists of Europe.

Cavour constantly complained that there was so little domestic enterprise. He pointed out that the national debt and property mortgages absorbed savings that should have gone into agriculture and industry. Government stock and the purchase of land were thought safer, and ironically enough the desire for safety also caused Italian money to flow abroad into French bonds. Cavour himself was partly responsible, for in a sense this fact was part of the cost of the *risorgimento*. Cavour had created the national debt; he had set the fashion of consuming too much, and of immobilizing so much of the national wealth in unproductive military expenditure. As there was never enough capital invested in production, there was never enough employment, salaries were too low and the rate of interest too high.

In an age of iron and steel, Italy suffered, and her few natural resources could not be properly exploited until hydroelectric power became cheap. The situation was not improved by the governmental protection given before 1860 in the South to inefficient methods and industries. Cavour in Piedmont had set a different example by freeing trade and giving encouragement only to a few selected industries. When this policy was applied to the rest of Italy after 1860, inefficient concerns were ruined, and the industrial life of the country was concentrated in the triangle between Milan, Turin, and Genoa. Water power was more accessible in this northern area, transport easier, and markets nearer. The North had more industrial tradition than elsewhere, more financial experience, and more readiness to speculate and improve.

A good example is provided by the history of the Orlando family, who began making agricultural machinery in Sicily, but soon moved to Genoa where the government was less restrictive and the market more attractive. There the Orlandos deliberately set themselves to prove that Italians, as well as forming a nation, possessed industrial skill and enterprise, and could produce textile machinery, marine engines, and armaments equal to the best anywhere. The cause of nationalism naturally found them enthusiastic. Cavour at once saw their value, and though they were tainted politically with Mazzinianism, he set them to dredge ports and reorganize the Ansaldo engineering works. Luigi Orlando, who in 1848 had aided insurrection by constructing prefabricated movable barricades and iron-ringed wooden cannon, in 1855 was experimenting with ironclads, and the next year made Garibaldi captain of the first Italian screw-propelled ship. By 1860 he was already employing a thousand workers, and was able to equip the Thousand with arms made secretly and largely at his own expense. His brother, Giuseppe, was chief engineer on one of the two paddle steamers which carried Garibaldi's troops to Sicily. Constantly fed by government orders, the Orlando workshops became the most important factory for armaments and locomotives in Italy.

Textiles were, however, of more importance in the Italian economy. From 1816 onward, jennies driven by water power were being used, and the industry spread in small rural townships where fast-flowing rivers and part-time female labor were available. The creation of a larger domestic market and the appearance later of steam-driven looms then made big urban factories more economic. The woolen industry was most prosperous in Piedmont, and here an important stimulus was the need for uniforms during the Crimean war of 1855 and the Austrian war of 1859. More important was silk manufacture, which was found all over Italy but particularly in Lombardy and Piedmont. In the days of government protection the export of raw silk had been prohibited, as a result of which Lyons had become the European center of silk manufacture, but in an age of freer trade, raw and manufactured silk again became the chief Italian export.

Italy's second export industry was the sulphur mining of Sicily, in which ten thousand workers were engaged about 1861, half of them young boys. This sulphur industry lacked an adequate incentive to greater efficiency until it met competition from the United States about 1900. The ore was extracted by methods which wasted one-third, and there was little attempt to regulate supply with demand. No advantage, moreover, had been taken of Sicily's monopoly position to set up refineries or capacity for sulphuric acid manufacture on the spot. Another mining industry which enjoyed a quasi-monopoly was that of marble. Deposits of coal were negligible, and though a little iron was found in Sardinia, Elba, and the Val d'Aosta, before long the mines were going to need protective duties which raised the price of the raw material at the expense of the Italian consumer.

$ஒ

The impact of unification on the Italian economy disappointed some people who had been led by the romantic and heroic aspects of the *risorgimento* to hope for too much. There had been a popular illusion that independence would automatically bring more pay and a lower cost of living, perhaps even less work and lighter taxes. The abolition of internal customs barriers and the reduction of tariffs were undoubtedly advantageous, as were decimal measurements and a uniform currency. Yet long-term benefits had to be purchased by short-term losses.

For example Naples, like Florence and Milan, felt the pinch at once, and with the disappearance of its royal court lost many of the public services, building contracts, and bureaucratic appointments which had formerly provided an artificial prosperity. Naples was the largest town in Europe after London, Paris, and St. Petersburg, and before 1861 had been the capital city of a kingdom of eight million people. This Neapolitan kingdom had possessed four times the merchant shipping of Piedmont, and a considerably larger navy. But owing to the unenlightened protection enjoyed by Neapolitan industry before 1861, severe losses were sustained when the new Italy eliminated marginally productive industries by allowing free competition from the North. Some of the southern textile producers had been accustomed to 100 per cent protection, whereas Piedmont by 1860 had reduced her duties to about 10 per cent by value.

The prevailing school of economists in the North believed wholeheartedly in free trade. Under their influence the liberal fiscal system of Piedmont, designed to suit a prosperous community, was extended after 1861 to more backward areas. The other regional banks successfully fought against the Bank of Turin having a monopoly of note issue, but southern industrialists were not united enough to press their common interests in parliament. Northern industries, already accustomed to freer trade, were in a fine competitive position when other provinces had to reduce their tariff on iron from twenty or thirty lire a kilogram to three. It was even said that the general application of the low Piedmontese tariff was intentionally designed to sweeten the pill of unity for the North, which now obtained a new and defenseless market.

Competition thus drove out of circulation many local products in the South, and even in some of the lately annexed northern towns, Modena and Parma for example, native industry proved too fragile. It is true that for a short while the cheapness of northern goods was partly offset by high freight charges, and as late as 1872 cotton manufacturers in the North could still tell a commission of inquiry that unification had not yet improved their sales. But gradually the "conquest" of the South by northern industry and finance was creating the unified market upon which general prosperity depended. Milan and Turin were bound to prevail in the end. Protection was introduced again during the eighties, but, like free trade in the sixties, this was again designed to aid the richest and most powerful regions of the country at the expense of the poorest.

In agriculture, though output increased and prices rose after 1861, improvement was not unqualified. The great number of ecclesiastical estates thrown cheaply upon the market encouraged farmers to go for quick returns irrespective of damage done to the land. Contact with a wider world progressively exposed southern agriculturists to world economic crises. Cotton was ill-advisedly planted during the American Civil War, and a vast acreage in the South was given over to vineyards when phylloxera ravaged those of France. In each case the change was temporary, and valuable long-term investments in olives and fruit trees were sacrificed to meet these momentary changes in world demand. This was part of the price paid for greater economic unification of the peninsula.

It was a price which in the long run was well worth paying when the benefits of improved communications were felt. Italy had missed the canal age, because of its mountains and because irrigation had a prior claim on water supplies. This made it the more deplorable that land communications were so poor. In the Kingdom of Naples about 1860, according to Nisco, 1,621 out of 1,848 villages had no roads at all, and there were only a hundred miles of railroad, with no services operating on saints' days or in Holy Week, and no tunnels lest public morality should suffer. The railroad track from Milan to central Italy stopped at Bologna. Venice was still cut off from Emilia. The Tuscan network was isolated both to north and south, and a journey southward to Rome still involved travel by ship or post chaise. In Sicily and Sardinia there were no railroads at all. Not until railroad construction proved a less risky investment did Italian capitalists budge from what Cavour called "culpable apathy" in this matter.

Not only prosperity, but also the free commerce of ideas and the moral gain of feeling really united were dependent on these developments, and after 1861 a general railroad boom gradually overcame many forces making for inertia. Brigands saw their livelihood threatened and tore up the track. Contractors exploited bureaucratic ignorance and built badly. Parliamentarians courted powerful electors by arranging uneconomic branch lines in their constituencies. Local authorities undermined each others' projects in the competition to secure a place on the main lines. But the tracks were laid. Most of the money came from abroad, most of the companies engaged went bankrupt, and the return per mile progressively declined. But in the last resort the state paid rather than let a line stop short. The building of the Mont Cenis tunnel at government expense between 1857 and 1871 linked the Italian with the French system; the St. Gotthard between 1872 and 1882 joined Italy to Central Europe; and when the Simplon tunnel was built in the years 1898–1906, the network was substantially complete.

8 Immediate Political Problems

On February 18, 1861, a parliament representing all the recently united provinces met at Turin. A month later, with no dissentient voice, it officially conferred on Vittorio Emanuele the new title of King of Italy by grace of God and will of the people, and it was declared that Rome should one day become the national capital.

Cavour's first difficulty was the dearth of good subordinates. Lieutenants had to be promoted into colonels almost overnight, junior teachers into headmasters, small-time lawyers and professors into cabinet ministers. For the *risorgimento* had not thrown up enough leaders of first-class caliber, and those who had not been killed had sometimes been soured in frustrating conspiracy and exile. It may have been that too little of their success had been due to the Italians themselves, and too much to a fortunate international situation, so that they lacked enough practical experience of administration and statesmanship. Cavour himself did not have the time or the skill to educate a new class of governors, preferring to concentrate power and take three or more portfolios in his own direct control. He had broken successively with D'Azeglio, Rattazzi, and Ricasoli, and could not abide the men of the future such as Depretis and Crispi. When he went over the names for his new cabinet he lamented to the British ambassador that there was not a single Lombard or southerner who was both reputable and pliant enough for his needs.

Cavour himself in 1861 was worn out with playing Atlas, and less fertile in the expedients for which he had been renowned. The other leaders of the *risorgimento,* men like Garibaldi and Mazzini, were becoming old and embittered, and there were few new figures to catch the enthusiasm of a younger generation and solve the many problems attending the birth of a new state. Cavour's sudden death in June 1861 was for this reason a shattering blow—Bismarck, who was only five years younger, still had thirty years of power ahead of him. The making of Italy was due in great measure to Cavour's personal skill, and he alone among Italian statesmen comprehended most of the difficulties of resettlement. He may have died opportunely for his own reputation, but for Italy his loss was irreparable.

≶●

Cavour left his successors no stable majority, for much of his following had been personal. Until 1876 governments went on chiefly being formed from his own group of liberal conservatives on the political Right. These men, though they had used revolutionary and conspiratorial means to overthrow the old regime, were determined to allow no further revolution against themselves, and despite appeals from Verdi among others, Mazzini remained an outlaw and threatened with execution if he should be caught. The governmental *consorteria* (as it was called) was a loose union of interests. In its fifteen years of rule, cabinets were to be constantly overthrown by internal quarrels, and repeated attempts were made by one subgroup or another to break loose and form another *connubio.* No single leader, however, possessed Cavour's charm and fascination, his sense of the practicable, and his ingenuity in compromise and timing. They were honest, hard-working men, who set an invaluable example of loyal service and probity, but on the whole they were narrow and unimaginative, and their personal rivalries caused a confusion of political issues which did not help the emergence of healthy parliamentary conflict. The extreme Right and the extreme Left occasionally united in common opposition, and whenever these were joined by a secession from the government majority, the cabinet was likely to fall.

Cavour had not belittled such problems as reconciliation with the Church, the annexation of Venice and Rome, and the fusion of North and South, but he had no time to prepare a comprehensive and effective policy. Personally, he knew far more about agricultural conditions in Ireland than about those in Sicily or Sardinia, and far more about Paris than Rome. Had he lived he would perhaps have learned to improvise as successfully in domestic as in foreign policy. But his successors neither improvised well nor gave much evidence of a sense of considered purpose. The very existence of a "southern problem" was denied. It was recognized that Rome must be won, but no plan was laid, and relations with the Church were allowed to drift from bad to worse. Though professedly Catholic, the new state began its career under what was almost an interdict, and the friar who kept his promise by attending Cavour's deathbed was punished for this action by his superiors.

Faced by parliamentary indiscipline, with vested interests ready to resent any preferential treatment of others, commitment to a definite policy was difficult. Seven different financial systems had to be unified; some of them were quite chaotic and they possessed different tax structures and methods of accounting. Care had to be taken to divide the jobs, decorations, and contracts not too unfairly between the different provinces. The petitions placed before parliament show the strength and variety of these sectional interests. Many towns and regions were squabbling about who should have the railroads; Syracuse was claiming recognition against Noto as the leading town of its province; and the Calabrians requested that ships on the Genoa-Messina route should touch at Reggio. At Naples, Nigra thus described what he found on his arrival as governor in 1861:

There is a continual clamor: "Simplify, improve, moralize the administration, dismiss Bourbon employees, replace them with the victims of Bourbon tyranny, give the people work and bread, give us roads, schools, industry, and commerce, repress the hostility of the clergy, organize the municipalities, give arms to the National Guard, send us troops and gendarmes." One side cries, "Hurry up with unification, destroy every vestige of autonomy, give the central government entire responsibility for local affairs." The other side replies, "Respect the traditions and institutions already in existence, keep all that is good in local administration, and do not turn away destitute all the old servants of the Bourbons."

Nigra's comment was that

. . . one cannot improvize in a few months a whole system of railroads; one cannot create schools without schoolmasters; one cannot base industry and commerce on anything but general confidence and the slow but sure action of free institutions; one cannot change in one moment a people who have been for ages subjected to slavery and ignorance, nor suddenly make them civilized and cultured; public opinion can only be built up gradually by the exercise of freedom.

In all the newly annexed provinces many interests had been damaged by the revolution. Local oligarchs had been displaced by rival families who had been quicker to turn their coat, and great numbers of public servants had been abruptly discharged. When former political prisoners were clamoring for jobs, it was a delicate question whether to appoint new and inexperienced officials instead of the trained employees of corrupt and despotic dynasties. Time was needed before former judges and ministers could sit in the same courtroom or cabinet with people they had once condemned to torture and the galleys. The lawyers were disgruntled at having to use an unfamiliar code of law; local officials were discomfited by dependence on far-off Turin; while at Turin itself the central departments were quite bewildered by so many diverse problems and local circumstances. Landowners sometimes found their estates occupied by their own hired men, and they resented being ruled by lawyers instead of representatives of their own privileged class.

No government could have appeased so many various interests, nor was there time to be entirely consistent. Promises were made of decentralization, and at the same time many steps had to be taken toward greater centralization. The civil servants of both Francesco di Borbone and Garibaldi often had to be retained simultaneously in lieu of granting unemployment relief, despite the cost and the dangerous multiplication of officialdom. Senatorial and ministerial posts were distributed geographically, and higher administrative officials too were chosen less for their competence than so as not to offend regional susceptibilities. The poor *lazzaroni* were set to work building railroads, and the rich *latifondisti* kept quiet by the cheap sale of ecclesiastical estates. But placating all parties was a complicated business and sometimes proved self-defeating as well as inconsistent.

One especially embarrassing problem was the amalgamation of the old provincial armies into a new Italian army along with Garibaldi's volunteers. When Cavour halted Garibaldi at Naples in 1860, one avowed reason had been his fear that the prestige of the monarchy and the regular troops might suffer if these irregulars and near-republicans were too successful. The government, therefore, not only tried to deflate Garibaldi's prestige, but disowned him in front of Europe and even hinted that a civil war against him was not out of the question. Although the volunteers had conquered half the peninsula for the king, the defeated Neapolitan army was treated better, because the Piedmontese generals were jealous of the much greater contributions of these irregular troops, and preferred to amalgamate with regular soldiers who were officers and gentlemen and had been through the orthodox military academies. The Neapolitan Nunziante was thus made a general in the Italian army, despite the fact that much of his life had been spent repressing liberalism, and despite his last-minute betrayal of his king and his military oath when he deserted to join the victors. Garibaldi's guerrillas, on the other hand, had to submit to rigorous screening, which, while no doubt useful for excluding undesirables, drove many excellent men to despair.

The nation was to thrive on the store of energy and healthy rivalry produced by regional divisions; nevertheless, especially in these early years, the old traditions of municipalism threatened to disintegrate society. It is noteworthy and paradoxical that so many among the motives which brought about national unity were non-national in origin. The overmastering urge of Sicily to break free of Naples had enormously helped Garibaldi in 1860, and Garibaldi's own animosity—as a Niçois and a convicted felon—against the Piedmontese government lay behind his breach with Cavour and the saga of the Thousand. This pervasive regionalism and individualism soon became restive when the result of the national revolution was revealed to be so large an increase in centralized government. Some of the regions were made to feel conquered and exploited and were not happy in subordination to Turin. It was easy for them to doubt the adequacy of a single administrative system in a country containing such diverse traditions and levels of social development.

The backwardness of the South illustrated this difficulty of applying uniform laws. Virtually the whole southern agricultural population was illiterate, as compared with 78 per cent for Italy as a whole. It was quite impossible to extend the Casati law of 1859 which had specified two years' compulsory education, for parents would not have co-operated even if the teachers and schools could have been found. Indeed, in defiance of subsequent regulations, forty-five years later almost one-quarter of the children of Italy were still not attending school, because education was made a charge upon the villages, and the village taxpayers often neither wanted it, nor could afford it, nor were they equipped to face the effort of organization required.

Political education, too, was rudimentary in direct proportion as the standard of living was low. Maxime du Camp at Naples in 1860 heard people in the streets shout "long live Italy" and then ask their neighbor what the word "Italy" meant. Another observer heard people join in the cry of "long live the king and the constitution," but what they were saying proved to be "long live the king and his uniform." The introduction of the jury system was especially difficult in backward areas. Very often no witnesses could be found, let alone jurymen to convict, because private vengeance against witnesses was more fearful and more certain than the legal penalties for crime. Even in the North, Cavour found that the jury system did not work properly. The situation was much worse in the South, where "livery and maintenance" was a deplorable relic of the Middle Ages.

It was understandable that the government should wish to centralize and standardize administration more quickly than was expedient, for these internal divisions were potentially dangerous, and national consciousness was still surprisingly weak. Even many educated Italians knew little of their country except from books. There was still no standard language that was fully intelligible to the majority. Manzoni had spent a month as far south as Florence, and Cavour several days there, but neither of them ever went to Rome or Naples, let alone Sicily, Calabria, or Apulia, and both of them would have felt infinitely more at home in Paris than anywhere south of the Apennines. Some Italians, and especially Piedmontese, therefore tried to impose national feeling from the north through a centralized administration and uniform laws.

The Lombard radical, Cattaneo, on the other hand, advocated a federal constitution with regional autonomy as a more realistic and a more liberal plan. He prophesied—and Gladstone and Lord John Russell were privately saying much the same—that a centralized Italian state would tend to put national power before personal freedom, and that foreign wars might then lead to the militarization of society. Cattaneo's analysis was often profound and farsighted, and it is a reminder that other solutions were proposed to the Italian question than those of the republican unitarists or the royalist Piedmontese. But in practice federalism remained an intellectual concept only, and, after the conversion of former enthusiasts such as Balbo and Gioberti, had little influence on politics. Cavour himself toyed with federalism as late as 1859, but the events of 1859–61 settled that Italy was to be a centralized monarchical state instead of a federal republic.

§◆

The new government of Italy countered these deep-rooted regional sentiments by an administrative centralization which perhaps exceeded in the urgency of the moment what was justified or wise. Already, in November 1859, without waiting for any parliamentary debate to justify such an arbitrary act, Piedmontese laws had been hastily applied to Lombardy in the teeth of local opposition, and other regions were similarly treated after 1860. The Piedmontese administrative and judicial systems, copied from France, had proved adequate enough, and it was thought undesirable to waste time in comparative study of other systems in the peninsula. Local separatism and municipalism had to be soundly beaten, and a centralized, even autocratic control was needed in combating the brigandage and disaffection rife in the South. The Franco-Piedmontese system of departments could also be superimposed across former regional boundaries and had the advantage of creating novel territorial units devoid of traditional sentiment.

Even where the arguments for regional devolution were intellectually accepted, the argument from convenience and speed still told decisively against them. In the case of education, for example, administrative convenience made it desirable for the universities to adopt uniform courses, to restrict optional subjects and lectures, and to make professors into state officials who were centrally appointed and who swore to obey the king. In those few educational matters where initiative was left to the localities, the larger regions were suspect; responsibility for primary education, as for provision of local roads under the law of 1865, was therefore put upon poor villages whose first anxiety was to keep down the rates.

This failure to develop a vital local self-government stifled local initiative and was to hinder the growth of parliamentary democracy, while the government-controlled prefect was said by many Italian liberals to be incompatible with true liberalism. It also meant that much parliamentary time was wasted on parochial matters. But the chief objection raised by opponents of centralization was that theory and logic were allowed to prevail over local custom and a more empirical approach, and this made the national movement dangerously rootless and revolutionary.

Cavour's views here are uncertain, for like a true empiricist he was hesitant to commit himself publicly and irrevocably. Having cleverly hinted to waverers in the South that he would allow considerable local autonomy if only they joined United Italy, he then was caught off balance by the suddenness of success and changed his mind once the union was achieved. He knew that some Piedmontese would support the *risorgimento* only on condition that the primacy of their own laws and traditions was clearly recognized. Farini and Minghetti, two leading members of his cabinet, neither of them Piedmontese by origin, had prepared in 1860 a project for administrative devolution. This was based on six regions "which represented the old autonomous states of Italy." But the scheme was dropped the following year. One reason was that some people associated regional autonomy with national disintegration. Another was the fear that local self-government would play into the hands of corrupt local cliques who coveted the patronage involved in the multiplication of minor offices. Individual communes, too, saw that they would retain more independence of Florence, Naples, and the other provincial capitals if power lay not in the regions but in a central government. A royal decree of 1861 therefore changed the old intendants into prefects, and—apparently against cabinet advice—abolished the last relics of autonomy in Naples and Tuscany.

This imposition of the Piedmontese administrative system reinforced the impression that one region had virtually conquered the rest. The

Milanese federalist, Ferrari, acidly called what had happened the last of the barbarian invasions. Jurists confirmed that the Kingdom of Italy in 1861 was legally not a new state, but merely an extension of the Kingdom of Sardinia. In deference to dynastic vanity the Italian constitution remained exactly that granted to the Piedmontese in 1848, and the parliament of 1861 was the eighth not the first by official reckoning. The king also continued to style himself Vittorio Emanuele *the Second,* and kept his jubilee in 1874, though critics pointed out that James VI of Scotland had been gracious enough to call himself James the First of England, and that Henry III of Navarre became Henry IV of France.

Outside Piedmont this was not always popular. Cavour's successor, Baron Ricasoli, regretted that his fellow Tuscans were heavily outnumbered on the commissions set up to study the new administrative and legal changes, and he found that the Piedmontese only understood French things and so talked a different language. At Milan, the historian Cantù noted that the Piedmontese and Lombards did not mix in society. At Bologna, thirty-five professors refused to take an oath of loyalty to the new government, and were dismissed from their posts. As for Neapolitans, they would allow no other city to precede Naples except Rome, and many books and pamphlets were written to show that Turin was of all cities the least Italian in history and character. Crispi, the future prime minister, claimed that the southern provinces were ahead of the North as regards their legal codes and administration. Everywhere there were grumbles that Piedmont received too many government contracts, that the South paid more than its fair share of taxation, and that all local institutions and customs were being brushed aside in the interests of uniformity. The very process of "piedmontization" thus provoked a revival of local sentiment, and Cavour's attempt to replace the Bank of Naples failed completely, for southerners refused to use northern banknotes, and southern branches of the Turin bank soon began to run at a loss.

Some of the critics later admitted that Piedmont had behaved much better than report said, and they could not deny that the North had a great deal to offer the South. Though the Piedmontese administration was uninspiring and unimaginative, it was comparatively honest, reasonably efficient, and in most cases stood for a moderate and tolerant ideal of civil and economic liberty. Though her legal codes may have been less finished and somewhat less humane than the Tuscan, a free press and a jury system was a novelty for some of the regions, even if an illiterate population made juries unworkable in any liberal sense. The king, too, made a slight effort to italianize his family. At least he arranged for his grandson to be born at Naples and to be given among many other names that of the local saint, Gennaro, and instructors were later brought from

Tuscany to correct the worst asperities of the prince's thick northern accent. Although Savoyards and Piedmontese predominated in Court circles, the king used to go on circuit and stay part of the year hunting in the several provinces.

As may well be imagined, this could not prevent a burden of misunderstanding and recrimination between North and South accumulating for the future, and there continued to exist a tense rivalry between the center and the localities which was a mixed blessing and curse. The Neapolitan historian, De Ruggiero, was still able to conclude in the next century that, after more than sixty years of existence as a single state, the Italian people were not yet an organic unity. After so many centuries of division, this was hardly surprising, nor was it essentially unhealthy, but it is a fact which is easily forgotten, and without which an understanding of modern Italy is impossible.

9 Ricasoli, Rattazzi, and Minghetti, 1861-1865

Bettino Ricasoli, who became prime minister in June 1861, was like Cavour a notable agriculturist—his castle of Brolio gave its name to one of the most famous wines of Chianti. Unlike Cavour, he was a deeply religious man who would even preach to his peasants, and he was a radical tory with less of his predecessor's whig intolerance of Mazzini. Ricasoli, indeed, might have been the person to attract both radicals and clericals into parliamentary politics. His concern for the welfare of the poor, as well as his sincere intention to bring Mazzini back from exile, earned him some support on the Left, and as a Tuscan he stood for those who were irked by Piedmontese domination.

Ricasoli copied Cavour in seeking support from both Right and Left, and this deprived him of a secure basis in policy and principle. The "Iron Baron" lacked Cavour's parliamentary experience and *tact des choses possibles;* integrity by itself was insufficient, and more finesse and subtlety were required in order to make this type of coalition work. Cavour had sharply criticized his conduct as governor of Tuscany in 1860, and now in 1861 Ricasoli was to prove too rigid a statesman to maintain such a broad government majority.

In 1861 this Tuscan aristocrat formed the first of a series of short and unstable cabinets, and it soon appeared likely that he would fall between two stools, king and parliament, being too proud for the one, too inflexible for the other. He treated the libertine king with an air of superiority and moral condescension, and publicly boasted that his ancestry was longer and—by implication—better than the House of Savoy.

He neglected to comply when the king asked him to wear the customary ministerial uniform, saying that his forebears had never worn anyone's livery. Out of the same pride he refused to take his salary or even to use the free railroad tickets which he was allowed.

Vittorio Emanuele was soon plotting to overthrow a prime minister who treated him with such disrespect and who tried to confine him so rigidly within constitutional bounds. Court circles preferred Rattazzi, who though a self-styled radical was at least a courtier and a Piedmontese. Before long the king was actively intervening to break up Ricasoli's coalition, and reports of cabinet meetings were even communicated surreptitiously to the palace by one of the junior ministers. This alliance of the Court with Rattazzi was welcomed by those Piedmontese deputies who did not like government by a Tuscan. The clericals also began to think that Ricasoli's religious enthusiasm verged on the Jansenist heresy, while other conservatives feared his coquetting with the Left and his refusal to break up democratic meetings. It was not in Ricasoli's nature to chase popularity, and despite a large majority vote in the Chamber, he chose to resign in February 1862. Ferrari in parliament called this a royal *coup d'état,* and such in effect it was.

§⋙

Urbano Rattazzi, who followed, was a man much distrusted. The British ambassador thought him a "cunning, scheming, low political attorney." Cavour had for five years made Rattazzi his chief lieutenant, but believed him devoid of principles and firmness of direction. "Rattazzi exaggerated the parliamentary system, so that deputies won too much influence in administrative matters. . . . Though he has singular qualities of mind and heart, he entirely lacks initiative. He would be an admirable legal or political adviser, indeed the best I know, but he cannot run an important department of state."

The new premier inherited plenty of Cavour's ingenuity in forming coalitions, and his cabinet included Sella from the Right and Depretis from the Left, but once again, and not for the last time, this confusion of principles and programs led to disaster. Rattazzi's aims are still obscure, but his administration was a byword for what Sir James Lacaita termed "corruption, jobbery, and intrigue unprecedented in the parliamentary history of Piedmont." Lacaita continued: "In every principal Italian city he sought supporters amongst the worst and most disreputable set of politicians and demagogues. Public money has been squandered in the most scandalous manner. Had I not been here and ascertained many facts, I would never have believed them. The moral sense of the

Nation was roused against him, and he has fallen under the pressure of public morality."

Rattazzi's fall resulted from his complete mismanagement of another Garibaldian insurrection for the capture of Rome. The responsibility for this insurrection and its failure are still in dispute, but undoubtedly Rattazzi and the king connived at it, and exposure of this fact was a blow to the regime. Garibaldi had always claimed—and Cavour tacitly allowed—that when the government could not take the next step toward national unification, the volunteers had a right to act on their own. In 1862 he was permitted to go on thinking that the same implicit arrangement still held good by which the government would deny him openly, yet secretly would hope for and perhaps even help his success.

Rattazzi, like Cavour, found it useful to keep Garibaldi on the point of insurrection. The prime minister hoped thereby to convince Napoleon III that France should let the Italians occupy Rome, for otherwise the radicals would capture it by force of arms and push Italy leftward in the process. Garibaldi was therefore given secret hints of support which he misinterpreted. The tragedy of Aspromonte came about through deliberate governmental equivocation. The ministry incited Garibaldi to action (the king confessed as much to foreign diplomats), and was determined either to appropriate his success or to disclaim and punish his failure.

When Garibaldi sailed for Sicily in June 1862, some politicians realized what might happen if he were not distinctly told where he must stop. Instead, the military and naval authorities were given the impression that he was under secret orders from the king. Many responsible officials were on vacation, and there was a noticeable lack of co-ordination between Palermo and Turin. Partly by error, partly on purpose, the government postponed action until all control over events had been lost.

When, in July, Garibaldi reviewed the National Guard at Palermo, he still had no revolutionary program. Only when a voice from the crowd cried "Rome or death" was he intoxicated by the exciting atmosphere, and he adopted this exclamation as a war cry and a policy. There were at this time about sixty battalions of infantry in the South. Yet, although Garibaldi's intentions were now public, no action was taken to prevent him from recruiting and drilling volunteers, and several merchant ships were captured under the very eyes of the navy. Parliamentary deputies were informed by the naval command that no orders had been sent to stop him, and he was therefore able to embark three thousand men in front of cheering crowds at Catania, while two warships stood off the port in idle and purposeless expectation. Rattazzi later explained how he himself had assumed that the fleet had instructions to arrest Garibaldi, but the order in fact given by Vice-Admiral Persano seemed deliberately ambiguous: "Take any steps which may be necessary, but always remember to put king and country first." Persano was a minister in the cabinet; he later put the blame on the two unfortunate captains and dismissed them for their inaction.

When Garibaldi landed his force in Calabria, Rattazzi was reluctantly forced either to brand him as a rebel or to brave the French and take responsibility for the march on Rome. However unpleasant the alternative, only one choice could be made, and Cialdini's troops advanced to disperse the volunteers. The two forces met at Aspromonte. Heavily outnumbered, and astonished by what he took to be a breach of faith, Garibaldi told his men not to return Cialdini's fire, and although badly wounded himself he took off his hat to cry *"viva l'Italia"* before lighting a cigar and yielding himself a prisoner. The regular troops shamelessly pretended that there had been a real battle, though only a dozen men had been killed in this one-sided affray. One officer was promoted to general on the spot in reward for his magnificent services, and seventy-six medals were bestowed on the victors for military valor. Garibaldi himself was imprisoned, and some of those who had deserted the army to join him were summarily executed—although two years earlier in similar circumstances the government had rewarded deserters very differently. The world-wide sympathy for Garibaldi was a tacit condemnation of Italian action in this sorry affair, and the king took the first occasion to grant a partial amnesty to the volunteers when his daughter married the King of Portugal.

As a result of Aspromonte, the king sacrificed Rattazzi as easily as he had done Ricasoli. Prime ministers had to learn that the dynasty must be served even in its own despite, and that the king's responsible ministers must take the blame loyally for the king's own irresponsible actions. The next premier, for want of anyone else, was Farini, a safe man and one of Cavour's liberal-conservative disciples. This was the first of a number of occasions when the absence of party organization enabled the sovereign to choose a weak stopgap minister and avoid dependence on the more powerful parliamentary leaders. Farini had contributed signally to the *risorgimento* both as writer and politician, and now he became prime minister for three months. It soon became clear, however, that he was in an advanced state of mental derangement, and cabinet meetings became a tragic farce, though the pretense had to continue for a while so as not to alarm the financiers who were being approached by the government for a loan. But when Farini threatened the king with a knife to force a declaration of war on Russia, he was hastily persuaded to resign. He was voted a state pension, and died shortly afterward.

Marco Minghetti, his successor, was another of those moderates who had been unenthusiastic for national unity until Cavour made nationalism socially conservative. He was a cultured, traveled man who was said to know his Dante by heart. Compared with Rattazzi he was politically well to the Right, and, though usually tolerant and easygoing, after sharp words in parliament in June 1863 he wounded Rattazzi in a duel. A native of Bologna, Minghetti sympathized with the idea of regional devolution, and this challenge to Piedmontese supremacy was not easily forgiven. The Piedmontese profited from Turin being the seat of government; they also possessed the unconcealed favor of the king, and had more experience than others of parliamentary rule and procedure. On the other hand, certain Tuscan deputies led by Peruzzi were openly saying that the capital should be moved to somewhere more central and more Italian. Minghetti agreed with them.

The growth of this feeling led in September 1864 to a convention with France by which Napoleon III promised to withdraw his troops from Rome within two years if Italy would transfer her capital to Florence. The French had been garrisoning Rome to protect the Holy Father from invasion, but England was suspicious of this occupation, especially when the Mexican expedition revealed the wide-ranging ambitious nature of Louis Napoleon. For this reason, and because Napoleon wanted both French Catholic support and the friendship of Italy as a client state, the emperor now proposed to withdraw his troops. He insisted, however, on the humiliating condition that Italy should promise never to attack papal territory, and even that she should bind herself to defend it against Garibaldi or any other aggressor. He also insisted on the change of capital as a pledge that Italy had given up her ambitions on Rome. Napoleon could not know that Minghetti, in bad faith, merely wanted the French out of the way so that the rest of the Papal states could be annexed at leisure.

Cavour had half admitted that Turin was geographically and temperamentally too close to France, and that it possessed too few romantic and historic associations to be the national capital, but he himself had no wish to move from his home town, and he confessed to private doubts about transferring to the corrupt atmosphere of Rome. Minghetti, Peruzzi, and other non-Piedmontese ministers would have been content with the capital at Naples, but Amari contended that Sicily would not abide Neapolitan domination. Florence was therefore the obvious choice.

Minghetti's embarrassment was indicated by the fact that, until negotiations were complete, he told neither the king nor apparently the full cabinet what was being arranged. In the end Rattazzi voted for this convention, but it was bitterly resented by other deputies on the Left as an apparent surrender of national claims to Rome. The Piedmontese were even more disgusted, for different reasons; now that they were called upon to sacrifice their own pre-eminent position, Left and Right in Piedmont were at one. Turin was faced with a catastrophic drop in property values as well as a blow to her regional superiority complex, and in two days of quite unexpected civic rioting, twenty-three people were killed and hundreds wounded. Piedmontese deputies broke from the *consorteria* to form a federation of groups known as the *permanente,* a secession which weakened the government and again exemplified regional loyalties cutting across differences of political principle. The king abruptly dismissed Minghetti by telegram, just as if parliament were irrelevant. He was particularly angry that his Court ball was hissed by the irate townspeople and his guests manhandled as they arrived.

The next prime minister was an army officer of the Court party. General Lamarmora, as a Piedmontese, disliked the change of capital—he was one of the last Italian statesmen to have to learn Italian almost as a new language. But he was a loyal servant of the crown and dutifully accepted the move, because it was imperative that France should not be offended and that Rome should be liberated of her French garrison. Lamarmora managed to find new accommodation at Florence, and effected the removal of all government staff and papers in six months. Administratively as well as politically it was a formidable undertaking, carried out with efficiency and skill.

§❧

The abandonment of Turin severed one more link with the past and weakened the stabilizing force of tradition. The new kingdom was not making a very strong start. In four years there had been no striking success except the grim farce of a civil war against Garibaldi. The disaffection in some southern provinces still necessitated the presence there of an army of occupation—90,000 troops was the figure given by the minister in November 1862. Unity and independence sometimes appeared to be only what Gladstone called the "upthrow of a political movement which some following convulsion may displace," rather than, as he later believed, "the long prepared and definitive results of causes permanent in their nature." Disaster occasionally seemed so imminent that the king's abdication was sometimes expected.

As the monarch claimed to hold his new office "by will of the people," this disaffection seemed to throw doubt on Italy's right to exist. The provincial plebiscites of 1859–60 had always given a 99 per cent majority

for "Italy one and indivisible," but it was suspicious that so few constituencies had recorded any negative votes. Often there had been no
properly drawn up electoral registers, so that people of any age, sex, or
country could and did vote. Opposition newspapers had been muzzled,
and as the ballot was public and most voters could not so much as read
their voting papers, influence was easily exercised by presiding authorities who had already taken an oath of loyalty to Vittorio Emanuele and
made not the slightest pretense of impartiality. The landowners and the
National Guard officers often marched their men to vote en bloc, as
Ricasoli himself had done. Some foreign observers thought that most
southerners who could understand the issues had wanted local autonomy,
but that the wording and manner of the vote had left them quite unable
to state their true wishes. The Sicilian peasants had sometimes simply
fled into the hills on polling day, as this strange new device looked to
them like a novel method of tax collection.

Not only was the very constituent act of the new kingdom called in
question, but the Italy resulting from these plebiscites seemed artificial
and deficient in national character. Italian culture still lacked a complete
identity of its own: the intellectual classes looked to France for their
lead, and the liberal aristocracy to England. Regional self-sufficiency
could not be broken down in a day, and there had been no social revolution to convince the peasants that they were participants in, not victims
of, the new order. The great southern liberal, Giustino Fortunato, lamented that Italy was several centuries behind other civilized nations,
and that the speed of her national revolution had allowed it to penetrate
only skin-deep; unification had been "improvised," it had been a "mira-
cle" going against both history and geography, and for the next fifty years
he went on expecting that the new nation might break up again. As
D'Azeglio indicated, though Italy was made, it was now necessary to
make the Italians. To such men the new state was scarcely stable and
permanent, and they were almost frightened of what they had done and
of what Europe might think. D'Azeglio on the Right and Ferrari on the
left hoped fervently that Rome might be left independent, and some
wanted the whole South to be abandoned. Quite apart from the clericals
who opposed on principle, many moderate conservatives were ashamed
of Cavour's deceitful methods, and from the other extreme, Mazzini and
Garibaldi, though now representing only an unimportant fringe, were in
open opposition to the movement which they themselves had initiated.

As the *risorgimento* had aroused too many hopes, this disillusionment
was inescapable. After the civil wars of 1860, the defeated parties,
whether autonomists, federalists, republicans, Garibaldians, Catholics,
or Bourbonists, all nursed varying degrees of indignation. National unity

had cost the savings of more than one generation. The naïve expectation had been that political change would suddenly release a great store of hidden wealth, but in fact it had only accustomed Italians to spending more than they could afford. Meanwhile, the nation appeared ineffective except as a French satellite, and it suffered mortification in having to tolerate the French in Rome and Austrian rule at Venice. As achievement fell short of hopes, the essential weakness of the country disillusioned those who had grown up on the heroic national myths.

Typical of this protest against the prosaic outcome of the glorious revolution was the early poetry of Giosuè Carducci. This man had grown up amid republican fervor, but he now feared that heroism had been almost in vain, bringing forth only a ridiculous mouse. It was a misfortune that the first great national poet should have given expression to such a disillusioned mood. Apparently, the birth of a nation was not portentous enough to evoke great art or literature, or at any rate the Italian creative genius was not rising to the occasion. Manzoni wrote surprisingly little between 1827 and his death in 1873; just as Rossini likewise produced almost nothing after *William Tell* in 1829, and until he died in 1868 spent empty years in Paris. Even Verdi, though he was idolized as a national hero, stood outside politics; he was elected a deputy, but resigned after several weeks, and never carried out his duties as a senator. Through literature and the arts, some of the infelicities, egoisms, and disappointments which were bound to accompany such a revolution might have been purged or idealized. Unhappily, the person of Vittorio Emanuele hardly caught the imagination except on the crudest level. It was possible to think that his principal motive had been dynastic ambition, and certainly he had been placed on his new throne less through his own merits than by the efforts of Louis Napoleon and Garibaldi, to whom he was thus beholden. Carducci's acid reference to such awkward points was to earn temporary suspension from his professorial chair in 1867.

To many people it was a bitter thought that the *risorgimento* had "cost more in money than in blood," and they compensated for this with a hagiology which described the national heroes as prodigies of valor and wisdom. History was falsified to prove that the revolution had been a purely liberal and liberating movement and that Italy was by natural endowment a great power. This myth overemphasized the heroism, just as the pessimists exaggerated the humdrum qualities of the new state. Sonnino could write in 1880 that if only the liberals had known the country better they might not have found the courage to unite Italy, but this was an unverifiable guess at the other extreme. The simple truth was that political unification did not complete, nor could it have completed, the *risorgimento*. A stupendous and slow task of reconstruction still lay ahead, the forging of a national consciousness, the discovery and fostering of national interests abroad, and raising standards of living at home. Such activity did not always lend itself to poetry or heroics.

And yet, after discounting exaggerated hopes and fears, the nation already justified itself. Italy was regarded elsewhere as a textbook liberal creation, and liberalism in Europe seemed to stand or fall by her success. Gladstone, for one, recognized the initial difficulties and achievements. "May God prosper and bless the work," was his comment in 1862; "seldom, I believe, has there been one in the sphere of politics charged with deeper interest to his creatures."

10 Counterrevolution and Brigandage, 1860-1865

The first important threat to the stability of the new regime came from the South. In 1860, Francesco the ex-king of Naples had fled with his numerous brothers and uncles to seek sanctuary in Rome, where an observer inside St. Peter's likened them to a little heap of withered leaves. From there they made one last effort at counterrevolution, relying on open or covert support among both the aristocracy and the peasants in their former kingdom.

Cavour had chosen rashly when in October 1860 he sent the ailing and unstable Farini to Naples to crush the Garibaldians and Bourbonists. Garibaldi had hoped to continue as royal vicegerent in southern Italy until the time came to march on Rome, but Cavour had many personal and political reasons for preventing this. His first concern was to subdue Garibaldi and to merge the administration of South and North, if necessary overriding any opposition from the radical democrats or from local sentiment. He and Farini were well aware that the governments of Europe, as well as potential investors and railroad contractors, were waiting to see how Italy dealt with her first really vital problem, and they decided that firmness alone would succeed.

Cavour had thus told Farini to use the army at the least sign of unrest and to close down the advisory Chamber at Naples which Garibaldi had established. Military government alone was thought to be adequate for what Cavour called "the weakest and most corrupt part of Italy," and instructions came from Turin that the local press should be curbed, and "that some rough military treatment would be a salutary medicine." In the long run Naples was to benefit much from the honesty and efficiency of her new administrators, but, while Silvio Spaventa was in charge of the Neapolitan police, painful memories of his own detention on the penal isles made his rule as rigorous and almost as illiberal as that of the Bourbons.

Local opposition was bound to ensue. Although Naples had taken very little share indeed in its own military liberation, there was shocked alarm when the province found itself treated as a conquest of Piedmont. Garibaldi's advisory Chamber of Neapolitans had recommended that the South should be given some local autonomy, but Farini introduced northern laws and administration as fast as possible so that parliament could be presented with a *fait accompli*. The northern carpetbaggers therefore had themselves to thank when they became highly unpopular, and it was perhaps in part their own fault that, as they themselves had to recognize, the majority of Neapolitans had little interest in Italy. Newspaper correspondents wrote as if another movement for independence might break out at any moment. Sir James Lacaita—who despite his British title was a landowner from Apulia—wrote Cavour in December 1860 that "the friends of annexation are in a very small minority; you must not be deceived by the results of the recent plebiscite, which were due to the general abomination of the perjured dynasty, the aversion to Mazzinianism . . . and in some part also to intimidation. . . . Farini's misgovernment, which has split the Liberal party, has accentuated the anarchy of the provinces, and brought the annexation into ridicule and contempt." Another liberal Neapolitan, Fortunato, concluded that not even the middle classes of the South could have really desired unity, and that the *risorgimento* had been due less to popular feeling than to intellectual influences and a fortunate alignment in European diplomatic relations.

The South had originally turned against the Bourbons on the grounds of misgovernment. When the same symptoms of apparent misgovernment persisted after 1861, it became clear that they derived rather from something intractable about the South and its inhabitants. Too late did these people discover that they had misconceived their wishes and wanted not better government but less government and still lower taxes. Hence the derisory comment that this incursion of northerners was another barbarian invasion; hence the dislike of Piedmont, much as some southern Germans disliked Prussia. When a big scandal was unearthed in 1864 over railroad contracts in the South, it was noteworthy that none of the five deputies who had to resign was a southerner (though Count Bastogi for one had been in Cavour's cabinet), and the opinion gained ground that the North was battening corruptly on this defenseless area. The accusation was much exaggerated. A more just criticism was that the ministers and advisers whom Cavour chose from the South, De Sanctis, Amari, Massari, Spaventa, and Scialoia, had been cut off from their home provinces in long years of exile, and had learned to despise their fellow Neapolitans. Another factor in the breach was a tactless letter written in August 1861 by the former Piedmontese prime minister, D'Azeglio, which received wide publicity as a statement of the leading liberal conservative in the North. D'Azeglio had written: "At Naples we overthrew a sovereign in order to set up a government based on universal suffrage. And yet we still today need sixty battalions of soldiers to hold the people down, or even more, since these are not enough; whereas in other provinces of Italy nothing of the sort is necessary. One must therefore conclude that there was some mistake about the plebiscite. We must ask the Neapolitans once again whether they want the Piedmontese or no." The South was thus becoming the scene of a civil war on the Irish pattern, and for a number of years had to support a virtual army of occupation.

༄

Political issues fomented but did not create the age-old social phenomenon of brigandage. During the Napoleonic wars the English, with political intent, had encouraged the Neapolitan brigands against the French, and the Bourbons later had had to treat with Fra Diavolo as with a sovereign power. Now the exiled King Francesco exploited banditry as a weapon of political counterrevolution, and relentlessly stirred up a class war against the rich. The brigands in their turn exploited Francesco, taking his money and enjoying the political sanctuary offered across the papal frontier. The Pope understandably regarded the Piedmontese as the real brigands, since they had recently stolen most of his dominions by shameless aggression. False money was therefore coined at Rome in the name of Francesco, and men were enrolled in his legitimist army from the migrant workmen who crossed the frontier for seasonal employment in the Agro Romano.

The most notable leader, Borjès the Spaniard, who had fought on the Carlist side in the Spanish civil war, was enlisted abroad by royalist agents, made a general, and authorized by the ex-king to appropriate public funds in any Neapolitan town. For three months he marched the length and breadth of the South, meeting other brigand bands but discovering very few people motivated by true royalist sentiments, and receiving the ridicule of straightforward professional brigands like Crocco. Nevertheless, any rebel could rely on the anarchic sentiments which set village against village, country against town, Church against state, taxpayer against tax collector. Some support was forthcoming in the last flickering of feudal and separatist reaction against the nation state, and the memory of successful counterrevolutions in 1799 and 1849 made some people afraid to adopt the nationalist cause too quickly. The result may properly be called a minor civil war, and it helped to perpetuate the unfortunate impression that Italy might collapse at any moment.

Much more than a political rising, it was a product of unemployment and of a tradition of highway robbery activated by a revolt of the plebs. Many brigands had first adopted their métier in order to settle accounts with some local enemy, and had then fled from justice to the mountains. There were men such as Carmine Donatello, galley slave and murderer, who for a time in 1860 had helped Garibaldi, hoping for pardon and reward; there were renegade priests who celebrated clandestine mass in the woods; there were revengeful peasants who found banditry more rewarding than toiling for a pittance on other people's land. Most of them were merely seasonal brigands, who took to the *maquis* in the months when agriculture offered scanty employment. There were also the unemployed ex-Bourbon soldiers, together with deserters and fugitives from conscription, jail breakers, and those enticed by the lure of booty.

Many ordinary citizens, while not active themselves, regarded the brigands as legitimate combatants in the ceaseless war against landlords and an impossibly remote, almost foreign government. Amid all the excesses and hatreds of this futile fight, some believed that the rebels were fighting for the Church and the legitimate dynasty. The Piedmontese were excommunicate; they had arbitrarily introduced their own secularist legislation into the South; and they persecuted the clergy, the sole friends of the poor. The nationalists affected a pious abhorrence at the Church encouraging brigandage, but it was naïve to imagine that they could despoil the clergy without the latter resisting.

Massari described the peasants "to whose admiring eyes the brigand becomes something different, a fantastic being, a symbol of their frustrated aspirations, the vindicator of their wrongs. He is no longer the assassin, the thief, the man of sack and rapine, but the person whose own powers suffice to get for himself and for others the justice which the law fails to give. And the man who protects him becomes a hero." To further his revenge on society, the peasant would readily give food, information, and shelter to such men. When soldiers came in sight, malefactors would put their rifles behind a hedge and take up hoes with other workers in the field. Not until a sense of security and a fear of justice could be instilled would country folk co-operate effectively with the government; until that moment, fear, honor, and sympathy restrained them.

The ferocity of this kind of war knows no bounds. When the Piedmontese entered Neapolitan territory in October 1860, one of the first actions of General Cialdini was to shoot every peasant found carrying arms. This was a ruthless declaration of war on people who had no other means of defense, and it reaped the whirlwind. Captured soldiers were sometimes tied to trees and burned alive; others were crucified and mutilated. Times had not changed much since the days of the brigand Mammone, who had been wont to drink out of a human skull, and never to dine without a freshly severed human head decorating his table. The law of the jungle prevailed, and the soldiers were stirred to excesses in retaliation. No quarter was given, but terror was used against terror. Men were shot on suspicion, whole families were punished for the actions of one of their number, and villages were sacked and burned for sheltering bandits.

Successive viceroys from Farini onward, before dealing with this social war in the provinces, first had to control the city of Naples itself. There they tried every policy, siding first with the aristocratic party, and then with the radicals; they attempted to suppress the secret society known as the *camorra,* and then tried handing over to this nefarious body the duties of the police. Before long, petitions were pouring in from the provinces to say that the chief result of annexation was the disintegration of society. This was not an easy challenge to accept, but in the middle of 1861 the secret political funds which Garibaldi had abolished were restored to the prefects, and a more conciliatory attitude was adopted toward the clergy. The government even had to open a public subscription list to help pay for a more rigorous policy, and the dangerous expedient was adopted of encouraging the landowners to form private armies. At the beginning of 1862, according to papers captured on an English adventurer, there was an organization of 80,702 rebels in the Neapolitan provinces. Against these men total war was declared and fought with great loss of life and reputation. Police figures in 1863 showed that, after one and a half years, 1,038 men had been caught in possession of arms and summarily shot, 2,413 had been killed fighting, and 2,768 imprisoned.

§●

In January 1863, a parliamentary commission of inquiry under Massari left Genoa for Naples. Its report, read in secret session to parliament, is an invaluable document about conditions in the South. Among many interesting conclusions, the commission established that brigandage was weakest where relations between worker and employer were satisfactory, as around the relatively wealthy port of Reggio Calabria, or wherever the *mezzadria* system of land tenure was established and the laborers were not nomadic but bound to the soil by ties of interest:

> But wherever large estates are the rule, the proletariat is very numerous . . . and many people are at their wits' end to make a bare living. . . . The existence of a bandit has many attractions there for the poor laborer . . . and brigandage becomes a savage protest against centuries of injustice by men reduced to the utmost poverty. With such people there is an absolute lack of confidence in the law and the exercise of justice. . . . Corruption in communal and provincial administration, justice not always honestly administered, and the hopeless inadequacy of the local police, are new and powerful contributions to the spread of brigandage. . . . The barons and their retainers have set the example of lawlessness, and now people have learned to reserve their greatest respect for men who have committed the worst crimes and atrocities.

The report was quite clear that the papal government had helped the brigands with money and recruitment from Rome, and had used the Neapolitan episcopate for transmitting instructions.

Massari's report suggested that long-term remedies be at once applied, for people must be shown the unmistakable advantages of liberty and be convinced that it would bring eventual prosperity and employment:

> You must extend education and see to a fairer distribution of the land. Roads must be built, marshes reclaimed, public works begun, the forests looked after. . . . It is absolutely necessary that the old customary laws should be repealed, and large areas of common domain such as the Tavoliere di Puglia be broken up into small holdings. . . . Freeing the land from such primitive communal restrictions would help to eradicate the savage proletariat who are driven by hunger to know no law but that of rapine. It is also indispensable to settle the disputes about communal land which for so long have divided every village against itself.

Property held in mortmain had to be broken up so that landless highwaymen could become peasant cultivators. The police profession had to be raised in public esteem and put more on a par with that in England. Communications would have to be vastly improved, "for you know, gentlemen, how Scotland after its union with England was similarly given over to brigandage until roads were built."

Above all, the government must provide security and prove that there was neither fear nor hope of a Bourbon restoration, for without this conviction people were too fearful of reprisals to organize communal action against banditry. Prison reform was indispensable "from the moral and hygienic point of view, but also from that of security, since the ease of escaping is a great source of recruitment to brigandage." Jailers were miserably paid and often no less criminal than their prisoners. The report added that they had found people kept in prison at Naples for three years without trial, even when this period was longer than the maximum sentence for the crime of which they had been accused. Not only had government to be efficient, but justice had to be done and be seen to be done, or else people would continue to look on the government as an enemy instead of a friend.

These were long-term measures, and until they could take effect martial law was indispensable; money should be made available for espionage and bribery, and the normal rules of war disregarded. Short-term severity was something more obviously urgent and more easily understood in distant Turin. As a result, the Pica law was passed, which made harsh repression not something exceptional but a measure on the statute book.

The government shall be empowered to confine under house arrest for anything up to a year any vagabond or unemployed person, or anyone suspected of belonging to the *camorra* or harboring brigands. . . . In those provinces declared by royal decree to be infested with brigands, any armed band of over three persons organized for criminal purposes and their accomplices shall be punishable by a military court.

This suspension of constitutional liberties was passed after very little debate, for the deputies were impatient for their summer vacation. There were soon 120,000 soldiers concentrated in Sicily and the South, almost half the national army.

By 1865 the war was virtually over. Crocco had fled to the Papal states leaving his bands leaderless, and the foreign adventurers who had fought in misguided enthusiasm for Francesco had melted away. Local highway robbery remained a widespread feature of the South, and Turiello in 1882 wrote that not only were escorts necessary for travel, but the roads were more dangerous than before 1860. Yet landowners could collect their rents once more; men could report evil deeds and bear witness without a certainty of reprisal; it was no longer necessary to take hostages, to evacuate whole villages, or to expose the heads of criminals at the crossroads.

The North had outwardly pacified the South, and yet the underlying regional animosity was intensified by the clash. A civil war is the cruelest thing that can happen to a country, and the *risorgimento* had been a succession of civil wars of which this was the most cruel, the most protracted and costly. Among the casualties of this simple fight against brigandage, there were more regular soldiers who died from malaria alone than were killed in all the campaigns of 1860, and more people perished in it than were killed in all the other wars of the *risorgimento* put together.

11 The War for Venice, 1866

From 1861 onward, Italian foreign policy never left Venice and Rome far out of sight, and the only doubt was how long a wait would be necessary before the third war of liberation was fought against Austria. There was no easy passage to great-power status. Cavour had longed for a major European war which would give scope for his own diplomatic skill and allow Italy to count for something in the balance of power. During the last few months of his life he had been intriguing with Kossuth and Klapka to stir Hungary into insurrection against Austria, and had employed the Italian diplomatic service to smuggle cargoes of arms into the Balkans. When found out, he denied all knowledge of this illicit traffic and tried to blame Garibaldi, but unfortunately the captured crates of munitions were all clearly labeled as special consignments from the royal arsenal at Genoa. Cavour had usually known how to couple audacity with caution. He did not flinch at the thought of taking on Austria single-handed, since he calculated that Italy had more to gain than Europe could afford to let her lose. "We have conquered the world before now," he once said in an unguarded moment, "and shall do so again." On one desperate occasion he even spoke of allying with the United States and proceeding to defeat Britain as well.

After Cavour's death Italian foreign policy became far more timid. French backing was less substantial, for Louis Napoleon was becoming respectable, and Italy was already large enough for France to feel slightly apprehensive. The king, with Rattazzi's encouragement, continued to push his dynastic claims in the Iberian Peninsula, and tried to replace King Otto in Greece by the Prince of Carignano or the Duke of Aosta. He also thought of persuading England to cede Malta, as she was giving the Ionian Islands to Greece. But for Italians generally, the conquest of Venetia was the one thing necessary for self-respect.

Mazzini and Garibaldi urged the king to march directly on Venice, threatening to resume their republican propaganda if he delayed. Mazzini argued that Austria was in grave financial difficulties, and that Slav and Hungarian disaffection was such that Austria would be outnumbered by Italian troops on her southern frontier. Half-persuaded, the king in 1863–

64 entered into secret communication with Mazzini himself. His ministers knew nothing of this, but were unscrupulously trying to goad the Western powers into a war against Russia from which Italy could perhaps snatch some advantage during the general confusion. Opinion hardened still further against Austria when the elections of 1865, reflecting a disillusionment with the *consorteria,* reinforced the radical Left.

§●

The king, who like his father had married an Austrian archduchess, first demanded that Austria be sounded by negotiation. He knew that the British believed in a strong Austria for maintaining the stability of Europe, and hence a war might not be easy. Some farsighted Austrian statesmen and financiers also realized that the Prussian threat and a financial crisis together made it advisable to placate Italy. As the two countries were not yet on diplomatic terms, negotiations were opened through private individuals, but the talks broke down, because Italy preferred war to anything less than complete Austrian surrender. Lamarmora was engaged in simultaneous discussions with Prussia, a fact which Austria knew full well from intercepted messages, and he was already sending officers in disguise over the Austrian frontier in order to prepare for hostilities.

From Bismarck's point of view, an Italian alliance would be useful in establishing Prussian hegemony in Germany. The two countries had a common enemy, and as yet no conflicting interests. Cavour and Mazzini had both appreciated the value of a Prussian alliance. Bismarck for his part kept in close touch both with the official government of Italy and with the Mazzinians, and while paying Italian agitators to stir up trouble, he made doubly sure by negotiating privately with the king behind the prime minister's back.

Italy's mistake in treating simultaneously with Austria and Prussia was underlined when Austria at the last moment offered to cede Venice peacefully in exchange for Italian neutrality. The prime minister, General Lamarmora, had to refuse this sensible and generous offer because he held that Italian honor was by then pledged to aid Prussia in war. As a soldier, the idea of simple barter was unwelcome to him, and he also miscalculated that, with Prussian aid, a war would win the Trentino as well as Venice. He was well aware of the sentiment which Gregorovius had lately expressed at Rome in his diary, that not until the Italian revolution had achieved a great victory would the disreputable means used to attain it be forgotten. Military victory would be a tonic to Italy, and a demonstration of strength to the world at large.

A secret alliance was therefore signed with Prussia in April 1866, by which Italy obtained a good hope of annexing Venice, though unfortunately Bismarck excluded the Trentino on the grounds that it was German territory. Lamarmora meant to fight his own war, and turned down the suggestion that he should also sign a military convention and collaborate in the Prussian strategic plan. Bismarck was known to agree with Garibaldi in wanting the Italians to cross the Adriatic to raise Hungary and the Slavs in rebellion. Lamarmora, however, was a narrow product of the Turin Military Academy; not only did he intend to organize his own campaign, but the fomentation of rebellion was objectionable on "every principle of humanity, morality, and sound policy." He vetoed outright General Türr's mission in Serbia and Croatia which Bismarck and Vittorio Emanuele had actively promoted. Thus false pride was to prevent Italy from deriving the full military benefit from her Prussian alliance.

Lamarmora deceived himself into overestimating Italian military power. In five years the army had more than doubled and was now nearly 400,000 strong. This was considerably larger than the forces of the whole British Empire, and certainly larger than the industrial potential of Italy warranted. It considerably outnumbered the forces which Austria could oppose to it, and the Italian fleet was twice as large as the Austrian. Yet there were serious weaknesses in organization and morale. The component regional elements had been intermingled in the army, but the new units were not yet properly fused; they lacked *esprit de corps* as well as adequate equipment and experienced generals. The Piedmontese and Neapolitan armies had too recently been fighting each other for a proper harmony of sentiment, and both of them disliked the Garibaldians for their unorthodoxy, their political unreliability, their popularity and success. Soldiers were looked upon as a caste apart in society, and had not yet become the civilian army that popular imagination seized on after De Amicis wrote his *Vita militare* in 1868. They were regarded less as defenders of the nation than as a hated army of occupation and the executors of martial law. Almost half of the Sicilians drafted for military service regularly took to the hills, while in the Basilicata the proportion was nearer three-quarters (even fifty years later it was still one-fifth in these unreconciled southern provinces). Italians themselves began to wonder whether since Roman times their military qualities had not been sapped.

§◆

General Lamarmora was a fine man but an indifferent commander, and he plunged headlong into war without any of the requisite preliminaries. Supply was mismanaged, and the staff's preparatory planning was wholly insufficient. Disregarding the lessons of 1848 and 1859, the Italians again chose direct attack against the quadrilateral of fortress cities upon which the Austrian defense system in north Italy was based. With false confidence, and a vain idea of economy, the annual draft had also been delayed in order to improve the budget figures. Such was the mutual jealousy of the generals that the prime minister had to become chief of staff himself after General Cialdini vetoed the obvious candidate. Moreover, Cialdini agreed with Bismarck in opposing the plan for a direct attack, and was therefore given a practically independent command on the Po, while the king and Lamarmora led the main forces on the River Mincio. The king was commander in chief under the terms of the constitution and was thus able to intervene in strategic decisions without having immediate responsibility for their execution. The generals were alarmed, for they knew that the king had no military talent or experience; yet political and dynastic reasons demanded that he should figure prominently in the campaign.

At the last minute the Italian intrigue for war was nearly wrecked when Napoleon III proposed to settle the dispute by discussion, but the military element in Viennese court circles had momentarily returned to power, and a stupid reply lost Austria her last hope of a peaceful settlement. Hostilities began in the middle of June. Lamarmora began his frontal advance without waiting either for Cialdini or for information about the Austrian dispositions. A few days after the declaration of war a battle was fought near the village of Custoza, in which the Archduke Albert with half the number of troops succeeded in defeating Lamarmora's advance guard. The Italian high command was unrealistic enough to think that this small encounter, in which fewer than 750 Italians were killed, was a major defeat. Lamarmora fell back behind the Mincio, and Cialdini, against Lamarmora's express injunctions, also began a retreat without even going into action.

There was no further big engagement, for it took a month to reorganize the army, and only the old Bourbonist general Pianell survived without loss to his reputation. Cialdini showed himself proud, arrogant, and intractable, and quite ready to disobey orders alike from king and government. Had he crossed the Po at the right moment, as the king desired, he might yet have threatened the Austrians and allowed Italian numerical superiority to prevail, but he chose to give the war up for lost, and petulantly criticized royal intervention as the cause of defeat. The Austrians could not follow up their success, but entrained many of their men for the north where Prussia, though a smaller country than Italy, won a crushing victory at Sadowa on July 3. Bismarck had some excuse for deriding the retreat of his Italian allies and their exaggeratedly fearful communiqués.

The nation had clamored from the first for Garibaldi to take a prominent part in the war, but the army and the king begrudged him his share of the limelight, and only a few of his volunteers were allowed to take the field. For as long as possible they were kept in the distant South. They were then belatedly concentrated on a subordinate front in the South Tyrol, where they kept up a slow but steady advance through the mountains, and once more showed that, while they lacked the discipline of a regular corps, they compensated for this by dash and enterprise. These Garibaldians in the Trentino included some of the finest and most enthusiastic of the younger generation, people such as Boito the composer, later the librettist of Verdi's *Otello* and *Falstaff,* and Pirelli, soon to become world-famous in the Italian industrial revolution. Once again Garibaldi's men came off more honorably than the regular army, and when finally given the order to fall back were at the gates of Trent itself.

After Custoza the navy was ordered to provoke an action with its superior forces, for the Prussians were winning and it was important for Italy to claim some kind of success before the armistice. Unfortunately, Admiral Persano was much distrusted by other naval officers, and with reason. He owed his position to favoritism more than merit, and had once wrecked a warship with the royal family on board. As minister of marine he had paid small regard to parliament, and as admiral in chief he had prepared not the least plan for offensive action against Austria in the Adriatic. The Austrian vice-admiral Tegetthoff was more than ready, and his ships, though lighter and slower, appeared before Ancona where Persano's fleet was lying. But the Austrian fire was not even returned, Persano pleading trouble among his engineers and insufficient coal. The crews rapidly lost their enthusiasm through this inaction, and the admiral was accused of cowardice. Driven on by government reproaches, Persano finally left port, still manifestly trying to avoid contact with the enemy. When he returned to Ancona he received peremptory instructions from Lamarmora and a threat of dismissal, and so set out once more, without plan or even accurate maps, to meet defeat off the island of Lissa on July 20.

This was the first large engagement ever fought between ironclad steam fleets. The Austrians had only seven ironclads against twice as many, but their gunnery and tactics were greatly superior. Persano had placed his ships in a single line, and allowed the Austrians to choose several concentrated points of attack. The admiral, who had contrived not to be on his flagship when it was rammed and sunk, dared not then risk the further action which some of his captains urged. Public opinion was quite dumbfounded, for the government had earlier put out a falsely triumphant report, and matters were not improved when Persano began blaming his subordinates in public. When the Senate, acting as a court of justice, dismissed him from the service with loss of pension and decorations, Italy's discomfiture was complete.

§❧

Bismarck's policy for the future demanded Austrian friendship, and he therefore did not press his victory. After Sadowa, unknown to his ally, he made approaches for peace, realizing that Italy must accept whatever terms he concluded. It was agreed that Austria should surrender Venice, but to France and not directly to her defeated enemy. This horrified Lamarmora. It would be dishonorable, he said, to receive Venice as a gift from France, for the country would become ungovernable, and the army would lose all its prestige. But the Austrians were able to dispatch more troops to their southern sector and compel Italy to accept an armistice at the end of July. Venetia was to be Italian, but only that part of it which had constituted the Austrian administrative province. Austria retained the Trentino, and Garibaldi therefore had to withdraw from territory he had already conquered. The northeastern frontier of Italy was still exposed and vulnerable. What was worse, people had grotesquely looked upon war as a test of progress and civilization, and there was a grave loss of morale when it appeared that other countries made better weapons and knew better how to use them.

Italy was fortunate to gain as much from the treaty as she did. Austria at last recognized the new kingdom, Venice was won, and the "quadrilateral" was no longer in foreign hands. Yet military defeat had shaken confidence in the armed forces and in the king himself, especially as it was followed by an undignified and public wrangle among various generals and admirals, each trying to blame the other. Italy secured little glory out of Prussia's success, and could not even point to that "heroism in defeat" which had illumined earlier pages of the *risorgimento*.

Some writers, for example Villari, were to lament that the war had not lasted longer and so toughened and inured the national character. Garibaldi was outraged that the Venetians had not risen of their own accord, not even in the countryside where it would have been easy, but had waited passively for deliverance, and he noted how "Italians" from the Trentino had actually fought against Italy. Garibaldi looked back over his experience since 1848 and reflected that only in Sicily and Calabria had the peasants backed Italian patriotism, and even there they had been moved by social and regional more than by national feeling. Elsewhere they had usually been the enemies and not the friends of unification. He had seen with his own eyes how they rejoiced at the return of the Austrians after a short interval of national "liberation," and how they deserted from the army as soon as a war began to go badly. Italy in their eyes too often meant just the landlords and the boss. They possessed little in common with the upper classes who had a mercantile grievance against Austria, and even less with the intellectuals who manufactured the patriotic myths which in retrospect softened and justified the movement for national liberation. Unfortunately, moreover, these peasants represented an overwhelming majority of the Italian nation.

Italy was now one step further on the way to her "natural frontiers," but the war had not gone down deeply enough to create a firmer national consciousness. Verga has a story about a Sicilian fisherman who lost his son at the battle of Lissa without being able to understand where or why this had happened. Ordinary citizens were not greatly enthusiastic when, after peace was signed in October 1866, Austria presented Venice to a French commissioner, and the inevitable plebiscite was taken which showed 641,000 votes for and only sixty-nine against union with Italy.

12 Financial and Other Problems, 1866-1867

At the end of the war, events led to a rebellion at Palermo which bore some resemblance to earlier Sicilian outbreaks in 1820, 1848, and 1860. Very soon after 1860 the same bands of irregulars, which formerly had helped Garibaldi, re-emerged as if to undo his work, for in their eyes all governments were tarred with the same brush. Already in 1861 the first parliamentary elections provided ominous examples of bloodshed in Sicily. Administrators who came from the north reported that three-quarters of the population was semibarbarous, and that nearly everyone was estranged from the government of Turin. Lack of roads put large areas of the island beyond easy reach of the law, and people still customarily traveled in caravans for safety. Tens of thousands of deserters were at large, and the mafia continued to organize resistance and a system of private justice against Vittorio Emanuele's government, just as it had against the Bourbons. The legend grew that Sicily was quite ungovernable, and successive administrations had to enter into collusion with the *mala vita* as their sole means of exercising sufficient authority.

In 1863 the army was forced to take the field against this disorder simultaneously with its campaign against brigandage in Naples. General Govone was a young Piedmontese who had learned on the mainland that severity and even cruelty might be required, and Sicily therefore had to endure six months of large-scale military operations. Families and villages were held hostage and subjected to dragonnades. Govone was accused in parliament of having cut off water from villages in the middle of the Sicilian heat, of using torture to exact information, and even of burning people alive in their houses. Matters only became worse when he explained publicly in his defense that Sicilians were barbarous and uncivilized and so had to be treated roughly.

The result of these operations was the capture of four thousand out of the twenty-five thousand refugees dodging military service. Eight thousand people were also found wrongly inscribed on the electoral lists, and a substantial sum was collected in tax arrears. This achievement, and even more the methods used, added fuel to the mounting feud against the mainland. Martial law and the enforced exile of hundreds of Sicilians seemed to belie the promise of a liberal constitution. Few people in the North had the least idea of the social and economic derangement which unification had brought to the South, and when feelings of revolt became more and more intense, this was treated as just simple lawlessness calling for straightforward police repression.

The end of the Austrian war in 1866 came only just in time for more troops to be transferred south. In September there was a "march on Palermo," when numerous armed bands from the hills erupted into the city and overcame the garrison of three thousand just as Garibaldi had done in May 1860. This time, however, they acknowledged no single leader and had but the vaguest intentions; there was only a sullen hatred against the government, against its taxes, its attempt to dissolve the monasteries, its remoteness and severity. Escaped prisoners, deserters, dismissed Bourbon employees, autonomists, even the Mazzinians and the dispossessed clergy raised their several cries of *"viva Francesco secondo,"* *"viva la repubblica," "viva Santa Rosalia."* Manifestos reviling "the gang of thieves which has been ruling Italy for six years" incited the populace to assault police stations, arms magazines, and customs houses.

The government was caught by surprise, and the National Guard, immobilized by fear, in many places surrendered their weapons. Some of the wealthier citizens seem to have been sympathetic at first but to have reversed their views when the elements of class war became more pronounced, especially when forced to pay heavy protection money to the various gangs. The rebels set up a provisional government, in which six princes, two barons, and one *monsignore* were induced to sit. Only the port, the palace, and the prison were still held by the twenty-seven-year-old Marquis di Rudinì who was then mayor.

Finally, a special expeditionary force was dispatched from Genoa and Leghorn under General Cadorna to put down the revolt, a surrender being negotiated through the French consul. The government found it prudent not to probe too deeply into the causes of the revolution, which were therefore neither remedied nor even properly understood. Di Rudinì said that he had to deal with the most corrupt people in all Italy, and so he was none too scrupulous in his repressive measures. Many thousands were kept in prison under suspicion. The Archbishop of Monreale and many other churchmen were arrested, and several hundred friars were exiled to Genoa. Worse still, cholera came in with the troops and killed 7,800 people in Palermo alone—the superstitious citizenry said that this infection was introduced of malice and on purpose.

§❧

The prime minister in office was Ricasoli, who had returned to succeed Lamarmora in June 1866 when the latter became chief of staff. The events in Sicily lost Ricasoli much good will, and when the elections of March 1867 depleted his coalition, he resigned. This brought back Rattazzi and the constitutional Left to office for a few months, because personal squabbles divided Minghetti, Lanza, Sella, and the other leaders of the *consorteria.*

Although Rattazzi's former governments had coincided with the two national calamities of Novara in 1849 and Aspromonte in 1862, he had done the state some service by educating the Left in the theory and practice of constitutional government. While keeping clear of the extreme radicals, he had entered into the group system and—when he could—into the government majority. The extreme Left disapproved of such a transparent political maneuver, but these irreconcilables had lost their *raison d'être* along with their monopoly of the national unification program. They were bound to fall behind when new weapons and military techniques ended the age of barricades and guerrilla leaders. Garibaldi himself ostentatiously resigned from parliament in disgust at the harsh treatment given to Sicily, and this was a sign that he realized his own ineffectiveness there.

Mazzini, repeatedly elected, was again deprived of his parliamentary seat, being still under sentence of execution, and he therefore returned to the political sterility of uncompromising republicanism. At Italian request he had been extradited from one country after another, and in 1870 he was at long last caught and imprisoned after a final attempt at insurrection in Sicily. Two years later he died, a lonely, disappointed man. By that time only a few of his old followers such as Mario and Quadrio continued unrepentant in their republicanism, because the rest had been absorbed by Rattazzi and Depretis into the *juste milieu* prescribed by Cavour as the golden rule of politics.

§

Neither Right nor Left could differ much over the really urgent questions of national finance. The Austrian war of 1848–49 had cost some 200 million lire, the Crimean war 50 million, the war of 1859 250 million, and that of 1866 nearly 800 million. Against this, the annual revenue of the state had remained stationary for three years at about 480 million, but rose to 600 million by 1866. Cavour had once confessed that finance was more important even than foreign policy. He knew how to be enterprisingly spendthrift on occasion, in building the Fréjus tunnel, the Cavour canal, or the new naval port at Spezia, but Piedmont had bankrupted itself in achieving unification, and now Cavour's successors, with less financial acumen, had to meet expenses many times the sum of those paid by all the individual states together before 1860.

Italy was determined to justify her position as a great power, and therefore the public debt, which in 1861 stood at 2,450 million lire, had more than doubled four years later. But while human decision could make expenses grow out of all measure, revenue was more intractable. One-third of this revenue went in servicing the national debt, and more than a quarter on the armed forces. The deficit between 1861 and 1864 was as much as 47 per cent of the total state expenditure, and in 1866 was well over 60 per cent. Since the national credit was not buoyant, loans paid up to 8 per cent interest and had to be offered at 70 per cent or less of their par value.

Quintino Sella, who was finance minister in 1862 and 1864, was perhaps the most able of Cavour's disciples. He was a mining engineer and mineralogist rather than a financier, but he was the first to realize what sacrifices and economies would be necessary to pay for the making of Italy. Sella was an excellent example of the honest, hard-working middle classes, with a high sense of public service and a carelessness about unpopularity in their insistence upon efficient administration. But Rattazzi's ministry of 1862 had fallen before Sella could try out his economies or his scheme to stop tax avoidance. This was one of the tragedies of the Italian political system, that a minister was seldom in office long enough to plan and carry out a reform. The next finance minister, Minghetti, though apt enough in circumventing individual problems, was not forceful enough in character to propose a comprehensive remedy and brave the consequences.

This was another of the vices of Italy, that the greatest beneficiaries of the *risorgimento* were unwilling to pay for it. The rich who monopolized politics found it easy to put the greater burden of taxation on the poor who had gained less from the national revolution. Italy could boast almost the lowest wages in Europe, along with about the highest indirect dues payable on food, and the reformers all agreed that taxes fell disproportionately on consumption rather than on income or property. Even some conservatives confessed that the less a man owned the more he seemed to pay, and Sonnino admitted in the Chamber that the tax collector and the policeman were the only contact the brutish peasantry had with the state, whereas the rich could bribe impoverished revenue officers and rely on the inefficient system of checking tax returns.

Instead of devising a more rational plan of assessment and collection, the state simply recouped some of its losses with yet more numerous taxes, and so made legislation more complex. New taxes often overlapped the old, and were based on so many varying systems that they were wasteful as well as exorbitant. The uneven efficiency of local offices made for variation in yield, and as so much depended on the arbitrary assessment of some ignorant official, uncertainty was added to unfairness. Later in the century, Fortunato computed that over 30 per cent of individual incomes went in taxation—probably a higher proportion than anywhere else in the world.

An economic crisis was not long in coming after 1861. Railroad building, the brigandage campaign, transferring the capital to Florence, the war of 1866, all these caused exorbitant expenditure. The Anglo-Italian Bank, of which Ricasoli himself was president, collapsed. Reconstruction loans became increasingly expensive as European banking houses shied away from them, and government stock after Lissa was down to 37. Confidence could only be restored by bringing a better balance into the government accounts, but it was not easy to see how. An increased land tax would meet fierce resistance, and in any case would require a lengthy new cadastral survey. Free-trade principles ruled out any rise in customs revenue. There had already been a great leveling upward of taxation to Piedmontese standards, and this had aroused fury in other provinces. An attempt to raise the tax on salt and tobacco led only to a decrease in sale.

Sella ultimately decided, against Lanza's advice and tremendous left-wing opposition, to restore the hated tax on the grinding of wheat and corn. This had been the cause of many rebellions before 1860, and it had been abolished by the national state as an earnest of future prosperity.

But it had the great advantage of being easy to impose and difficult to evade. Sella expected to obtain from it a hundred million lire a year, and this was not a great exaggeration. Where he went wrong was in his confident prophecy that the tax would not cause hunger. The middle classes, having won their own freedom from feudalism, were hardly aware that a social question existed, and were quite ignorant about the common people who lived on bread, *pasta,* and *polenta.*

The grist tax was approved by 182 votes against 164, and came into force in January 1869. At once rioting began, and after two weeks there had been 250 deaths, 1,000 people wounded, and 4,000 rioters were in prison. Cries were heard of "long live the Pope and the Austrians." Country vicars and newspaper editors were among those arrested for showing sympathy with the rebellion, and an army corps under General Cadorna had to be mobilized in Emilia. But the tax went on being collected. It was coupled with the farming out of the tobacco monopoly at what seemed very unrewarding terms to the state, but the private company which exploited this monopoly did at least expose some of the ineffective methods of government administration hitherto.

The chief financial result of the 1866 war was the large-scale resort to credit. Scialoia had to issue 650 million lire worth of paper money and compel acceptance of nonconvertible notes of the Banca Nazionale. Four-fifths of the money hitherto in circulation had been coin, and this new temporary measure did at least result in making paper money more acceptable. It also made obtaining foreign loans still harder, and this emphasized the need to balance income with expenditure and borrow more at home. As an immediate result, money lost much of its value, and the "forced currency" further lowered national credit. The bank gained handsomely, but coin left for France at an alarming rate, and the inflationary effect of a fall in money values reduced the real wages of the people. Although the salaries of king and ministers were cut to show their good intentions, this was small consolation to the genuinely poor.

༄

Another governmental money-making device was the sale of ecclesiastical property. Much agricultural land had accumulated in mortmain through possession by ecclesiastical bodies and charitable trusts. The breaking up of such estates, it was now argued, would benefit agriculture, and lawyers decided that the state might properly requisition such a national asset to meet the capital expense of a national war. An act was therefore passed to this effect in 1867, and the land thrown on the market, but in such quantity that land values fell and the proceeds were less than expected. By 1880 over a million acres had been alienated in this way, and the state had realized and irretrievably spent its most lucrative capital gain.

These ecclesiastical estates had by law to be sold in small lots, if necessary with deferred payments so that poorer farmers could buy. But in practice the ruling consideration was fiscal and the land went chiefly to speculators and existing landowners. Peasants found it difficult to borrow money for their purchases, since moneylenders discovered a far better investment in direct acquisition of real estate at this price. Often the auctions were openly rigged. Even when the small farmer was successful in purchasing a plot of land, he possessed little capital for running expenses and so might have to sell out after the first poor harvest. His discomfiture was the greater in that the commons, which had furnished him hitherto with pasture and firewood, were now being enclosed as private property, and in addition, instead of paying rent to the Church, he now had to reckon with more businesslike and exorbitant owners.

It was not the old families any more than the peasant who gained from this land distribution, nor even the parish priest whose meager stipend was to have been augmented out of the proceeds, but rather the financiers and middle-class businessmen who regarded cheap land as a hedge against inflation and a means of social climbing. Since prestige was conferred more by broader acres than by improvement of existing estates, the result was to increase the extent of the *latifondi* and to divert money away from more useful work. In a country where there was little saving and where savers were timid, this was serious. Purchase money had to be borrowed at 6 per cent or more, and this payable interest was often higher than the gross income from the land; at least it never left much margin for settling the debt.

13 The Capture of Rome

By express provision of the constitution "the Catholic, Apostolic, and Roman religion is the sole religion of the state," and yet the *risorgimento* passed for an anticlerical movement. Even the devout Catholics of Ricasoli's circle wanted a reform in the Church, and most other nationalist leaders were heretics, deists, or skeptics. Nationalism stood for secularization of the state as well as for destruction of the Pope's temporal power. By 1860, therefore, patriotic Italians found themselves under a kind of collective excommunication, theoretically barred from the sacraments and religious burial, and until 1929 the Vatican refused to recognize the existence of Italy.

Cavour shrewdly and correctly foresaw that lay Catholics and even the lower clergy would pay little mind if the Holy See condemned nationalism. He himself was not a good practicing Catholic. Believing that the contemplative religious orders were now "useless and even harmful," he had already gone far toward secularizing Piedmont before 1860, dissolving the monasteries and abolishing clerical privileges at law. He sharply cautioned the clergy that civil war might follow if they intruded into secular politics. Personally, he was ready to give up the old jurisdictional claim to intervene in episcopal appointments, but he stipulated in return that lay Italy should be the master. Mistakenly thinking that he held all the cards, he confiscated papal territory and killed the Pope's subjects when they tried to defend themselves, yet still apparently thought that Catholics would accept the triumph of liberalism and his formula of "a free Church in a free state."

Garibaldi and Mazzini had realized the inherent incompatibility from the first. They were both perhaps more naturally religious and yet more anticlerical than was Cavour. Garibaldi used to call the priests wolves and assassins and the Pope not a true Christian. He blamed the national backwardness on clerical ascendancy in the schools and the consequent predominance of classical and rhetorical studies over technical and physical education. At Naples in 1860 Garibaldi had shocked the faithful by allowing the importation of Bibles and the construction of evangelical churches, and in the North he had even baptized children with his own hands. Crispi and Bixio kept up his cry in parliament that Rome be invaded and the cardinals thrown into the Tiber, while the young poet,

Carducci, wrote a *Hymn to Satan,* in which the Church was the great enemy, and patriots were pictured as fighting not only against the Papal states but against religion itself.

Unification brought the extension of Piedmontese secularist laws to the newly annexed provinces. Without waiting even so much as to consult parliament, the new northern proconsuls unilaterally denounced the Neapolitan concordat, and within a few months sixty-six bishops had been arrested in these southern provinces alone. Many more ecclesiastics had to wait years without receiving the royal exequatur permitting them to enter upon their office, and the revenue of their sees was thus forfeit. Don Bosco, soon to be beatified, was held by the police for questioning, and five cardinals were prosecuted in as many years. Ricasoli ordered the Cardinal of Pisa to celebrate independence day with a solemn *Te Deum,* and when the cardinal barred his cathedral in protest, the chancel was forced and the service sung without him. Then he himself was taken under arrest to Turin.

Such actions did not assist the successive attempts to negotiate with the Pope, and the simple confiscation of Church property was a poor advertisement for liberalism. Many Catholics realized that reforms in the relation between Church and state were overdue, but injustice was bound to be caused by so sudden and severe a secularization in a land of so many clergy, and especially when such changes were effected by unilateral action.

Cavour secretly sent considerable sums to Rome for bribing the ecclesiastical authorities, and his personal agent, the Jesuit priest Passaglia, at one point opened negotiations with the papal secretary of state himself, the affluent and more than disreputable Cardinal Antonelli. Antonelli's sincerity or otherwise in these talks cannot be proved until the Vatican archives are opened, but some prelates were favorable to a negotiated solution of the "Roman question," among them the theologian Cardinal Santucci. The Pope, however, remained adamant on retaining his temporal power, even though this was not declared an article of faith. The Church after 1848 had entered a conservative phase in both politics and religion, and the age of liberal Catholicism had passed away with Rosmini and Gioberti.

In December 1864 the papal encyclical *Quanta cura* appeared, together with a syllabus of errors including all the major principles of liberalism. Among the eighty propositions advanced, number 79 suggested that freedom of discussion might corrupt the soul; and number 32 hinted that the clergy had a natural right to avoid military service. Religious toleration, freedom of conscience and the press, the validity of secularist legislation, were all challenged, along with socialism, rationalism, and Bible societies, and it was denied that the Pope either could or should come to terms with "progress, liberalism, and modern civilization."

This syllabus aroused great indignation. Although the less illiberal churchmen quickly threw doubt on both its significance and its authority, most of the hierarchy took it as an infallible pronouncement. Subsequent apologists managed to explain that it did not prevent a Catholic styling himself a liberal in politics. Indeed, since the condemned propositions were spreading fast, the Church was likely to have to change tack and come to terms with liberalism and modern civilization before very long. Its original publication, however, seemed a blow to compromise and provoked an outburst of anticlericalism. Crispi pedantically told parliament that Christianity must be purged of the vices of the Roman Church or else it would perish. Successive conservative governments proposed that seminaries should be under government inspection, that prefects might interfere even in ritual if necessary, and that priests could be indicted for refusing absolution to those excommunicated for political offences.

A law of 1866 then declared that almost all the religious orders and congregations should have their houses dissolved and their goods confiscated. Some thirteen thousand ecclesiastical bodies had already been suppressed, and under this ruling another twenty-five thousand followed. It was explained in justification that some Church endowments ought to pass to the state now that the latter intended to assume responsibility for education and charity. Parish revenues were left intact, but cathedral chapters and bishops were compelled to follow the monasteries in surrendering their capital to the state, receiving 5 per cent in return (after three-tenths of the capital had first been deducted for educational and charitable purposes). Now that the regular clergy had been pensioned off, many of the seculars followed them in becoming as it were salaried officials of the state. Seminarists were also made liable to military service, and the new civil code denied legal sanction to such marriages as were not performed by a civil ceremony.

§❧

This still did not solve the Roman question. Cavour had publicly stated his intention of making Rome the future capital of Italy, but the convention of 1864 with France seemed to carry a moral obligation to renounce this aim. The more religious-minded among the liberals, Jacini for instance, agreed with the more anticlerical such as D'Azeglio, and disliked the whole idea of Rome as a capital. The project seemed to give undue weight to sentimental and historical as against cultural and economic arguments. "Thank God, this will rid us of Rome," had been the reaction of the Catholic Count Pasolini to the convention. On the other hand the doctrinaire nationalists had always insisted that Italy without Rome was no true nation, and Bismarck actively abetted them so as to create a diversion and prevent anticlerical Italy from joining with Catholic Austria and France against him. A man such as Cavour might easily have used this split between Bismarck and Louis Napoleon to denounce the September convention and annex Rome, and Rattazzi the new prime minister knew as much, but did not understand how to work the charm himself.

Apart from Rattazzi's hesitancy, the main reason for Garibaldi's defeat in his third attempt to march on Rome was the indifference of the Roman citizens, and the fact that their faith and their interest kept them loyal to Pius IX. Even some of the lukewarm nationalists in Rome were so fearful of social revolution that they split away from the adherents of Mazzini and Garibaldi, and on occasion delated them to the police. Rome was still the "parasite city" of clerics, hotelkeepers, and beggars. Half its population virtually existed on official alms, and the governing classes of clergy exempted themselves from taxes and had a highly privileged position to defend. Had there been a stronger lay middle class, or even had the moderates and radicals been more in agreement, Garibaldi might not have failed so dismally.

It is almost incredible that a catastrophe similar to that of Aspromonte should have been allowed to happen again in 1867. Rattazzi was in office on both occasions. Once again he hoped that Rome would rise of its own accord and declare itself annexed with a mock plebiscite, and at least he must have hoped to let things go so far as to persuade Louis Napoleon that Garibaldi would become ungovernable if the popular demand for Rome went unsatisfied. But his chief desire was that of not compromising himself irretrievably either way, and so once again he failed, neither convincing Europe that Italian eagerness for Rome was irresistible, nor demonstrating that Italy could control her own revolutionaries without foreign interference. He thus permitted the "spontaneous" enrollment of volunteers, with arms sometimes officially provided. Garibaldi's story was that the government even incited him to invade the Papal states as a pretext for the national troops to move in and "restore order." Rattazzi denied this story, but the king's statements to the French and British ministers confirm it in detail and add the refinement that the king intended to use this excuse to "massacre" the Garibaldians as well as defeat the papal mercenaries. The memoirs of Finali confirm authoritatively that the secret service funds were used to stir up the rising which was to give the excuse for this operation.

Humiliated by the vicarious acquisition of Venice, the ingenuous but noblehearted Garibaldi had been anxious to show that the voluntary initiative of the Italian people could complete the work of national unification. Urged on by the government, bands of volunteers therefore collected on the papal frontier in the late summer of 1867. Mazzini did not usually err on the side of caution, but for once he counseled Garibaldi to stay quiet, because he saw that Rattazzi, like Cavour, would disown the rebels if they failed and merely exploit and then crush them if they won. In September the government arrested Garibaldi, and sent him back home to Caprera, but as he was not put in strict custody, and as the volunteers remained on the frontier, this was again considered a ruse to deceive foreign diplomats.

Rattazzi may have hoped in this way to make time for the Romans to rise and give him an excuse for intervention. The liberals in Rome, however, did not stir, and Napoleon III reluctantly deferred to French public opinion and sent back to the Holy City the armies he had withdrawn after the convention of 1864. If the Italians were not going to keep their word and defend the Papal states, then he must do it again himself. The possibility of French intervention does not even seem to have occurred to the king or his government. Rattazzi had thought that he was still in charge of the situation, and realized too late that he had gone either too far or not far enough. When confronted with the choice of arresting the volunteers, or invading the Papal states himself before the French could arrive, he panicked, and resigned office in October after hard words with the king.

At this point Garibaldi suddenly reappeared on the mainland and ordered his bands to advance. So free were his movements that they seemed to have official blessing, and the king in fact was still guardedly weighing his chances. But the people under papal rule evidently did not want "deliverance," since the peasants remained sullen and reluctant to give help or information to Garibaldi. Gregorovius, the German historian then living at Rome, wrote in his diary: "It is a fact that no rising has anywhere occurred in the provinces. No one will compromise himself. Rome remains entirely quiet. . . . The tumult that was expected to break out yesterday evening, and which had been announced the day before, was, it is said, put off on account of the rain. Two young men asserted that the rising would break out in an hour, since something must necessarily take place to redeem the Romans from the charge of cowardice . . . but the night passed quietly; the great deed of heroism remained unperformed." In contrast to this apathy, the invaders performed many deeds of individual courage, and two of the brothers Cairoli became a national legend when one was killed and the other very badly wounded trying to run guns into the city; but on the whole the volunteers this time fought poorly, and many deserted.

When Louis Napoleon finally embarked French troops for Civitavecchia, Vittorio Emanuele inexpertly tried to save appearances at the eleventh hour by ordering his troops to march against Garibaldi, and calling the French his good allies. General Cialdini crossed the frontier in pursuit of the "rebels," only to be peremptorily ordered back by the French, and on November 3 the volunteers were defeated by De Failly at Mentana. The French were back in Rome, and the chances of Italian occupation seemed infinitely reduced. Political cleavages in Italy had been sharpened. Furthermore, the *papalini* could now argue plausibly that the Romans evidently had little wish for union with Italy and hence that the liberal justification for nationalism was merely a blind for something much less creditable.

§❧

This catastrophe had forced Rattazzi out of politics, though his three-day speech in self-defense was long remembered for its eloquence. In the emergency the king turned to another general, the Savoyard senator Menabrea. The shock of Mentana, coming after Custoza and Lissa, had compromised the dynasty, and the king looked to the Court party to tide him over some awkward parliamentary debates. Menabrea himself and several of his cabinet were former officials of the royal household, and yet, although some people demanded suspension of the constitution, the king himself was not thinking of restoring absolutism. On the contrary, while decree laws now became less frequent, parliamentary sessions became more so, and in 1869, Lanza and Sella were allowed to overthrow the government of this royal aide-de-camp. Here was an auspicious symptom of growth in parliamentary experience.

The king was opposed to any further move toward winning Rome, for Garibaldi's failure had seriously embarrassed his alliance with France. He also had an affectionate regard *"pour ce pauvre diable de Saint Père,"* and when gravely ill in 1869 he very properly married his mistress and plied Rome with telegrams for papal benediction. As a Catholic, as a Piedmontese, as a loyal vassal of Napoleon III, he had eventually turned against Garibaldi's invasion in 1867, and in 1869 he was still trying to negotiate a more formal alliance with France which, if successful, would have excluded him specifically from acquisition of the Holy City. Even after the outbreak of the Franco-Prussian war in 1870, the king and most of the cabinet momentarily agreed on what might have proved a fatal policy of declaring war for France against Prussia. In the Senate, moreover, Cialdini spoke for the Court party in terms which seemed to challenge parliamentary government itself. Lanza told Rattazzi that the king's ideas about foreign policy were threatening to prove a disaster: "The king is in practice his own minister of foreign affairs, and in order to form his policy he keeps up a secret and direct correspondence of his own with our ambassadors and with Louis Napoleon. This may not be constitutional, but it is unfortunately a fact."

Throughout August 1870 the French troops were leaving Rome again, this time because they were needed on the Rhine front, but still the king taunted his ministers with cowardice because they tried to prevent him fighting against his late ally, Prussia. For he was banking on a French victory, and hoped once again to be on the winning side in a European war. Indeed, only the news of Louis Napoleon's crushing defeat at Sedan suddenly forced upon him a more realistic view. Sella threatened to resign if this heaven-sent chance to defy the French and occupy Rome were not seized. Ominous threats also came in from the prefects about possible revolution, and the Left hinted that they might abandon parliament altogether. Manifestly, the French alliance was now a double handicap, so the king nimbly changed sides, taking care to explain to the Pope how he was being forced into annexing Rome against his own better judgment. Lanza's letters show that once again the secret service funds were used for an uprising which would give a pretext for having "to restore law and order," but no more than before did the Romans rise. Instead, another excuse for invasion had to be found, and townships inside the papal frontier were urged to petition Turin for protection against anarchy. A brief clash, a breach in the walls, and the Holy City had fallen to the last in a long line of covetous enemies, the papalists losing nineteen men and the Italians forty-nine.

Italy thus casually gained Rome after Sedan as just another by-product of Prussian victory. The nationalists were genuinely surprised at the manner of this success. They could not understand why Aspromonte, Mentana, and the bombardment of the Porta Pia had successively passed without any spontaneous upsurge of the Roman people, and it all seemed a most unsatisfactory ending to the wars of liberation. Pelloux, a future premier, was awarded a military cross for opening up the walls with his batteries, but there could be no real glory in defeating the merely token resistance of this tiny papal army. Once again, too much had been due to fortune and foreigners, and the national energy expended seemed almost disproportionately small.

Whatever the expense, Italy was at last substantially united and complete. Mrs. Cobbe calculated the cost of unification as forty million pounds sterling; Fortunato on the basis of official figures put it altogether at the astonishingly low figure of six thousand dead and less than twenty thousand wounded between 1848 and 1870—the Germans lost more in one day of August 1870. But the result was indisputable. A new nation of twenty-seven million people had appeared, alongside Britain with thirty-two million, France with thirty-six, and Germany with forty-one. It remained to be seen what would be the effect on international politics.

§❧

The destruction of the temporal power of the Papacy was the climax of the *risorgimento* and perhaps its most important achievement. Ever since the time of Petrarch, Italians had looked on Rome not only as the center of the world and of true religion, but as the heart of Italy. Machiavelli had reviled the temporal power of the Church as the greatest obstacle to national unity. But when the Papacy finally fell in 1870, patriots like Jacini and Capponi could still dislike the bullying tone given to this nationalist triumph by the bombardment of Rome. When the Pope refused to hand over the keys of the Quirinal and fulminated against the king as a new Attila, the government had to break open the palace and confiscate newspapers which printed the papal decree. In October, however, another plebiscite gave an inevitable endorsement of the invasion, and out of a population of 220,000 there were 167,000 eligible voters, of whom 133,000 approved and only 1,500 disapproved. Those who believed in plebiscites could now feel happier.

It was not wholly by chance that temporal defeat for the Pope came simultaneously with the proclamation of papal infallibility as a dogma. In the first place, the meeting of the Vatican Council at the end of 1869 frightened even Catholic Europe with the specter of ultramontanism, and so let Italy take Rome without active opposition from the other Catholic powers. In the second place, the loss of territorial power left the Pope with less need to temporize and greater freedom to speak the truth as he saw it. By 1870 the strongest current of opinion in the Church was that of the Jesuits in favor of increased centralization and clericalism, and a declaration about papal infallibility was the natural upshot. The new dogma did not produce any schism of importance in Italy as it did in Germany, though many liberal conservatives like Sella, Bonghi, and Acton's friend Minghetti sympathized with those bishops who constituted the dissentient minority.

A special law was passed by the state to regularize the Pope's position in a Rome over which he no longer ruled. His person was declared inviolable. He was to have all the honors due a king, free communication with Catholics throughout the world, and diplomatic immunities for foreign ministers attached to the Vatican. An income of over three million lire per annum was assigned him in perpetuity. The state also gave up most (but not all) of its restrictive controls over Church action, and renounced the hereditary apostolic legateship which the king had claimed to exercise in Sicily. State and Church were to exist separately. Church property was to be secularized, and ecclesiastical salaries paid (after deduction of fairly heavy expenses) out of a nationalized *fondo per il culto.*

Successive Popes, however, utterly repudiated this settlement. They could not take a pension from Italy without appearing to be her lackey, or without seeming to sanction this violation of the sanctuary. Not having been consulted, Pius IX preferred the role of an invaded and aggrieved party, as "the prisoner of the Vatican." On the other hand, not only Crispi and the Left, but Sella and many others feared that the Pope had been granted too much by this offer of exemption from ordinary Italian law, and that the new clerical liberties were an unjustified diminution of national sovereignty. When the Pope rejected the Law of Guarantees, they welcomed this fact as a release from further obligation.

A *modus vivendi* was gradually worked out, papal honor being satisfied by absolute refusal to recognize the new kingdom, while the Church continued in practice to enjoy protection and a usually benevolent interpretation of existing laws. Legal fictions circumvented the prohibition against religious orders holding property, and an increase in the wealth of these orders was one sign of a new flowering of religion. Deprivation of temporal power was proving, as Cavour had foretold in the teeth of clerical opposition, to be a help and not a hindrance to propagation of the faith.

§❧

The Church meanwhile boycotted domestic Italian politics with resolution and tried hard to prohibit Catholics from sharing the full duties of citizenship. The Abbé Gioberti had vainly hoped that the Church would once more stand actively in politics for popular welfare and against tyranny, and Jacini had sought, also in vain, to find in Catholicism the basis for an active conservative party. Cavour himself had, theoretically, welcomed clerical participation in elections as a sign that the Church was coming inside the orbit of parliamentary government where it would assimilate liberal precept and practice. But when in 1858 he vitiated this theory by annulling the election of certain Catholic deputies, the latter understandably decided that their protest would be more effective outside parliament. The editor of the leading Catholic paper in Turin, Don Margotti, coined the phrase "neither electors nor elected," which later became an official prohibition against Catholics intervening in national politics. If clerical deputies entered parliament, so the argument went, they would have to swear loyalty to the conquerors of papal territory; tenure of any office in the state might likewise involve them in excommunication, and even as mayors of villages they would have to marry people by a civil ceremony which the Church did not recognize. In 1866 the Sacred Penitentiary conceded that a Catholic might sit in parliament if he added to his oath the words "so far as divine and ecclesiastical law allow," but when the following year Count Crotti tried to use this formula, he spoke too loudly and pandemonium broke out. His oath was disallowed and he was expelled from the Chamber.

It cannot, therefore, be wholly blamed upon the Church that Catholics remained aloof, for the state was the aggressor in this particular war, and indeed some cabinet ministers thought that practicing believers should be excluded from all public office. In the elections of 1874 the Vatican declared it "inexpedient" for Catholics to vote at all, and this *non expedit* later became a formal prohibition, despite the fact that many of the faithful continued to disobey. About 60 per cent of the whole electorate usually voted, and this percentage was not materially increased when the ban was lifted. Much the same proportion also held good for local elections where there was no veto at all.

The veto was sterile in fact but quite valid in theory. The Church had to protest against injustice, especially as she continued to assume that the Italian occupation was temporary and God would yet restore his own. She could not refrain from censure when a Protestant church was built in Rome in 1873 and a Masonic temple two years later. In his pose as a prisoner, the Pope did not stir from the Vatican, and he admitted no good-will envoys from the king. The last official act of Pius IX was a defiant protest. Leo XIII, who was Pope from 1878 to 1903, protested over sixty times, and on at least four occasions allowed a rumor to spread that he might remove from Rome to a new Avignon. Up to 1929 this formal protest was maintained and the very suggestion of compromise repudiated. When the celebrated Jesuit, Padre Curci, changed from attacking Italy to defending it, he was straightway expelled by his order.

Lay statesmen called the Pope's attitude merely the melodramatic pose of a would-be martyr, especially since both sides in practice dropped their condemnations and co-operated in many matters. Practicing Catholics were partly cut off from the rest of the nation, with separate schools, a distinct social life, and without full exercise of their rights and duties as citizens. A disaster for the state, this was even more a disaster for the Church. Yet the novels of the Catholic Fogazzaro show how easy it was for clerical influence to remain important in local politics. Complete nonco-operation would have been disastrous: on the one hand it would have given the anticlericals free rein, and on the other the nation would have been divided against itself. Even the majority of anticlericals were proud of having the Pope in Rome, and abated their reforming zeal when he threatened to leave.

14 The Last Years
of the Right, 1870-1876

The elevation of Rome into a national capital created special problems. The city was divided into "blacks" and "whites" as in the time of Guelphs and Ghibellines, family rivalries here mixing with religious feeling. The "black" aristocracy, which had done little enough to defend the Pope, now compensated by holding aloof from the royal Court, and the Quirinal palace and its chapel were placed under interdict. The families of the Orsini and Colonna were internally divided, but the Chigi, Borghese, and Barberini, which had thrived under papal nepotism, solidly put their religious before their civil allegiance. The fabulously rich Prince Torlonia changed the livery of his household so as not to resemble the royal colors, and "black" ladies paraded their carriages along the Corso only in the summer months when good royalists were away in the country. Of all the Roman nobility, the Duke of Sermoneta alone had been a confessed liberal before 1870. From then onward there was to be a gradual process of conversion, but for many years there were two distinct social sets as well as two Courts and two *corps diplomatiques.*

Vittorio Emanuele was too simple and unsociable to cut much of a figure among these grandees. He suffered from being morganatically married to a commoner, as well as from his temperamental lack of grace and glitter. Even more he suffered from having declared war on the Pope while trying to have it both ways by posing as a humble churchman. He had been brazenly aggressive; he seemed a bully for attacking the weak and a coward for waiting before doing so until France was in desperate difficulties. His conquest was in any case legally and morally indefensible, for in 1864 he had undertaken in a treaty to defend the papal frontier against all comers.

Successive governments nevertheless tried hard to catch the imagination and sympathy of the common people in the capital. Great sums of money were spent on spectacular buildings to give employment and gild the pill of northern occupation. Forty thousand state officials had somehow to be housed, and a consequent attempt to modernize the old city started a wave of speculation in land. Romans soon found that their taxes had increased from 64 to 145 lire a head, and the rates were over five times as high as before 1870. Cardinals and princes competed to buy up the large private gardens on the Quirinal and Esquiline hills, and then sold them profitably for building. The results were effective, if not always in good taste: *palazzi* were converted into government departments, the flora of the Coliseum (on which an Englishman had written a whole book) was stripped off, and excavations began on the site of the forums. Augustus Hare was later to write that a few years of Italian rule had done more to destroy Rome than the Goths and Vandals together.

But attempts to make Rome a capital in the style of Paris were to fail, for the rival allegiance to the Vatican was an almost insuperable difficulty. Strong regional sentiment still left Turin and Milan almost equally important as centers of national life. Rome lacked the resources to become industrial and remained provincial in culture. Its university had never been of much note, and the city never became the national center for books and newspapers. Its climate and geographical situation were poor, and though it was the seat of parliament, parliament itself was in a sense cut off from the real life of Italy. Rome remained a city of the past— ancient, medieval, or baroque. It was not a town of theaters and banks, but of churches, palaces, and monuments. Some people called it too southern, others too international, others too corrupt, and it soon became fashionable to lament that the capital was not somewhere else.

ဇ

Fortunately, the surface of politics remained tranquil during these years. Lanza succeeded Menabrea in office for an unusually long period, from 1869 to 1873, and fell only when Depretis of the Left joined Minghetti in voting to multiply fourfold the grant proposed for the new naval dockyard at Taranto. Minghetti, who followed Lanza, also remained in power for the uncommon duration of three years. The Right, however, was not a compact body, and though arbitrary government influence was used even more than usual in the elections of 1874, the potential opposition increased by about 30 seats, thus commanding about

233 votes in the Chamber against 275. After this, Minghetti survived precariously in the fear of a defection by some of his supporters.

The Right always had a tendency to dissolve into regional elements. One dissident element was the Piedmontese *permanente,* which had broken away after the abandonment of Turin and never returned to a more than lukewarm support. Another rebellious group, larger and more discontented, was formed by those southern deputies who were disillusioned by the steeply increased taxation and the small economic gain which union had meant for the South. A Tuscan group under Peruzzi made a further grievance out of the removal of the capital to Rome, and demanded compensation for the many Florentine speculators who had suffered by the transfer. Florentine lawyers had lost a valuable legal practice, and their city forfeited many indirect sources of revenue. When Minghetti's minister of public works, Spaventa, proposed to nationalize the railroads, this threatened the investments in railroad construction of the Tuscan banking houses. Influential financiers like Bastogi feared that Spaventa was attacking their monopoly of railroad development in southern Italy, just as Correnti and the Lombard merchants feared that this nationalization presaged a general departure from the best free-trade principles.

Despite these grievances, the statesmen of the Right, whose term of office was now drawing to its close, had set a great example of patriotism and political skill. During these early difficult years they had done what they could to create traditions of parliamentary government and political rectitude. Seldom in Italian history has the country possessed rulers so talented and incorruptible as the agriculturist Ricasoli, the doctors of medicine Farini and Lanza, Sella the geologist, and Ferrara the professor of economics. Not often did prime ministers hand over to their successors such a large balance in the secret service fund as did Lanza, although he was under no obligation to account for his expenditure. He was as thrifty with the state's finances as with his own, and he lived modestly and left office a poor man. "This spiritual aristocracy of upright and loyal gentlemen," as Croce called them, never sought cheap popularity, but remained courageously disinterested in their conduct of public affairs, even at the price of losing office.

It would be incorrect to label these men as unqualified conservatives. The national movement had been so revolutionary that to call oneself conservative was to invite political failure, and deputies therefore used to compete for seats near the center of the Chamber. The old aristocracy had either become liberal or else was unimportant in politics. The new industrialists could not be conservative, at least not yet, for they were still in the process of overthrowing feudal and aristocratic Italy, and were not yet entrenched in established industries under state protection. The Right was in fact composed of people who were liberal before they were conservative. True enough, they had little notion of the needs and interests of ordinary citizens. They were invariably moderate, prudent, and fearful of change, but some were more "progressive" than the so-called Left, as Cavour had been more "revolutionary" than Rattazzi. Spaventa tried to nationalize the railroads despite radical opposition, and Scialoia in 1874 tried to make elementary education compulsory. Minghetti was taxed by the radical anticlericals with "Vaticanism," but was able to reply that, of 94 requests by bishops for the royal exequatur, he had granted only 28, and shortly afterward he expelled 33 prelates from their sees for failing to secure such permission.

This necessity to be at once revolutionary and conservative had its disadvantages. It meant that the issues in politics remained blurred, and that the electorate could hardly ever choose between a clear juxtaposition of alternative policies. It meant also that the Right had no very deep or firm basis in ideology and was thus peculiarly brittle. Some of its constituent groups were permeated with Hegelianism and so they were not all equally concerned to defend the individual against excessive claims by the state. Some had already abjured the free-trade tradition stemming from Cavour, as others ignored his injunctions against administrative centralization and rejected his "free Church in a free state." In consequence, when the Right fell from power in 1876, it found itself without a coherent program, and simply disintegrated.

Italian parliamentary life was in fact continuing to develop a special character in which the government majority included many diverse groups held together by loose and evanescent ties. The leading politicians were too independent in their views for a strict party system. Lanza had sat on the Left when first elected to parliament, and Sella was close to the Left on Church policy and on franchise reform. Yet, at the same time, Sella was well over to the Right on matters of finance and the grist tax. Minghetti, on the other hand, was ready to abolish the grist tax, and was divided from most of the others by his leaning toward the idea of partially autonomous regions. Sella and Minghetti never sat in the same cabinet because there were also personal differences between them. Such a situation, in which private relations counted for more than policy, was typical; the groups inside the Right were kept from open breach only by their common distrust of Depretis and his still more radical associates.

The Right had many achievements to its credit: the annexation of Venice and Rome rounded off the united kingdom, an industrial and agricultural revolution had been initiated, in fifteen years the revenue had been tripled, and at last in 1876 the budget could be given the appearance of balancing.

Against these achievements must be set the fact that the country was more stringently taxed than any in Europe, and taxed with less concern for general economic welfare. By now most of the domanial and ecclesiastical lands were sold, and yet a huge debt had accumulated which drained away more and more money from land improvement and industry. Francesco Ferrara, the greatest economist of the time, lamented that there was no sign in the economic life of the country to suggest that the nation had been finally unified. The conservative Villari painted a much blacker picture. In science, letters, industry, commerce, and education, Italy was lagging behind the other civilized powers, yet still (so he said) thought that she was better than them all. Armaments, ships, and engineers had to be imported from abroad. Italian books were not read beyond the Alps, Villari complained. Italy's generals were incompetent, her administrators were appointed by favor or nepotism. Another pessimistic statement came from Rattazzi in 1873 just before he died, when describing to parliament what remained to be done: "In ten years we have spent thirteen billions and we have still not built an adequate army or fleet, nor have we obtained public security at home, nor are our frontiers in a proper state of defense, nor above all have we enough schools. . . . No one in Europe regards us as a great power. . . . Our magistrates are intellectually despicable, and their moral standards deplorable. And Austria has beaten us by sea and land."

Apart from internal divisions, another reason for the weakness of the Right was its haughty condescension toward the radicals as uneducated and socially impossible, and its unwillingness or inability to entice them inside the government majority. The system of coalitions depended for its success on a proper "circulation of elites," but Lanza made no overtures to the Left comparable with those made to him by Cavour. The radical-democrats therefore remained as a factious and irresponsible opposition, while the liberal-conservatives continued self-righteously to profess a monopoly of patriotic fervor. Garibaldi was becoming a frustrated, gouty, and silly old man. In 1870 he wrote to offer "what is left of me" to the French Republic against Germany and acquitted himself well, for which service he was elected to the French Assembly. But at home, apart from a mild flirtation with socialism, he passed the time tending his bees and beans on Caprera, or campaigning for some lost cause like the diversion of the Tiber.

Most of Mazzini's followers had by now been realistic enough to renounce their republicanism and swear the oath of loyalty as deputies.

Crispi and Bertani of the radical *estrema* were fighting inside the Chamber for increased democracy in the state. Another future leader of the extreme democrats, Cavallotti, accepted the oath in 1873, adding the rider that he looked upon it as null and an infringement of popular sovereignty. Such radical thinkers found much sympathy among young men excluded from the closed shop of politics.

Other miscellaneous symptoms of discontent could be found. Many independent liberals, especially those infected with Freemasonry, envied the process of parliamentary reform in Britain, and some of them believed that the greatness and prosperity of their own nation needed more active participation by the working classes in government. Meanwhile the protest of the *avant garde* helped to diffuse a sense of bitterness and frustration among the intellectuals. Cavour's last minister of education, Professor De Sanctis, had already deserted the government majority, and proclaiming the necessity of a two-party system he had ranged with the left-wing opposition from about 1865. Another observer on the Right, Sidney Sonnino, echoed Rattazzi's indictment of the government when he wrote in 1872 that political education was actually diminishing rather than increasing; there was an indifference to everything that related to representative government and the exercise of a citizen's rights; there was a confusion in parties, an instability and weakness in the government, and a general loss of confidence. This apparently was the result of ten years of parliamentary rule. Sonnino also observed that in the lowest and most populous section of society there existed an accumulation of discontents and hatreds which had to be taken into account if it was intended to give a secure basis to parliamentary institutions. Even Sonnino had to admit that Depretis and the politicians of the Left were temperamentally more fitted to understand these popular discontents.

The tactics of coalition government should have suggested a more imaginative program to a prime minister in this situation. But Minghetti remained strict and unyielding, and instead of adapting his tactics to win over the more moderate of his opponents, made only a halfhearted approach toward the Left. On the other hand a notorious incident took place at the Villa Ruffi near Rimini, when a number of people were arrested on the quite unjustified suspicion of plotting a republican revolt. They included Fortis, a future prime minister, and Saffi, one of the triumvirs who had governed the Roman republic in 1849. After a panic decision for their arrest, they were hustled handcuffed into a crowded railroad compartment and spent the night on straw. It was a severe setback for the government when after some months in prison they were acquitted.

In 1875, Depretis, who had succeeded Rattazzi as leader of the constitutional Left, laid down a challenging program in a famous speech at Stradella. Among other things he claimed to stand for free and compulsory education, an extension of the suffrage, decentralization of administration, and more local self-government. This obtained a good press, and as the speech betrayed the slightly vaporous language of Correnti, it suggested that certain group leaders on the Center Right were wavering in their allegiance. A temporary coalition was forming of Left, Right, and Center deputies such as had overturned Menabrea in 1869 and Lanza in 1873. Matters were working toward a climax when, in March 1876, Minghetti was defeated over the *macinato* tax and his project of railroad nationalization. Ironically, this defeat came just after his greatest success in announcing that for the first time expenditure was less than revenue. The Right had completed their task of tightfisted and unspectacular administration. New times called for new men.

15 Depretis and Transformism, 1870-1880

The accession to power of the Left was a healthy sign for constitutional development. Technically, there was no obligation under the 1848 *statuto* for governments to hold themselves responsible to parliament, but the king shrewdly recognized the advantages of broadening the basis of the political class. He privately reassured his friends that he would still keep a hand on the reins himself, so they need not be frightened of Depretis in power.

The center of gravity of the state therefore shifted a little. Some of the more obstreperous radicals such as Nicotera and Crispi were at last enticed inside the governing classes, and in particular the South gained far greater representation in the government. Certain important sectional groups thus moved over to defend the new order instead of wasting themselves in factious opposition, and an avenue for legitimate ambition was opened for younger men. Most of the new cabinet had never held ministerial rank before, and the practice of the spoils system now advanced many other new people to minor office. With Agostino Depretis as premier there was little danger of another *consorteria* being formed, since, far from being rigid and exclusive, he went to the other extreme of promoting too easy an amalgamation among all manner of groups and interests. The Left soon revealed itself even more than the Right as a political party without fixed composition and policy.

Among the many worthy men who took office with Depretis were Zanardelli at the ministry of public works, the Neapolitan jurist Mancini at the ministry of justice, Professor Coppino at the ministry of education, and the Piedmontese Admiral Brin in the admiralty. Depretis personally was one of the most respectable men in modern Italian history. Even when prime minister he continued to live in a top-floor apartment one hundred and twenty steps up. Compared with the doctrinaires and ideologues on both extremes he was always sensible and matter-of-fact, and his approach to every problem was calm, self-possessed, and usually over-cautious. Experience of administration as an official in various departments had taught him much. He was not a great man—and Italy needed a great man at this moment—but he was adroit in maneuver, fertile in expedients, and always moderate enough not to do much positive harm. Depretis gained as well as lost from his habitual attempt to circumnavigate a problem rather than face it squarely. He possessed few strong opinions of his own, and people usually left his presence with the impression that he agreed with them. Pareto wrote of him as someone with a skeptical turn of mind, who never embarrassed himself with principles or convictions and never bothered much about the truth. Always ready to follow any route which would assure him of a majority, he enjoyed in the later years of his life what Pareto called the most absolute dictatorship possible under a parliamentary regime. These comments were intended as criticism, but they might easily have been said of Cavour by some of his admirers.

§⁂

While in opposition, the Left had possessed not so much a program as an accumulation of grudges—at least, ever since their anticlericalism and enthusiasm for unification had been taken over by Cavour and the liberal conservatives. In foreign affairs the Left in office had not much room nor much reason to depart very far from traditional policies. At home Depretis had vaguely projected certain democratic reforms, and the more rash and forthright Crispi had called for universal suffrage as well as for an elected Senate and elected judges. Abolition of the grist tax and increased expenditure on public works had often been demanded from the radical benches, and also a diminution of state controls. The state should be "felt and seen as little as possible," said Crispi against those of the Right who had recently begun to talk about the nationalization of private enterprise.

Once in office, the Left, which had risen to power only with help from dissident groups inside the Right, found reform harder to practice than to preach. The king's opening message to parliament in November 1876 spoke once more of administrative decentralization, but this was only talk. Depretis tried hard to make his ministry look more progressive than its predecessor, yet he could do little more than promise to study possible reforms and to use less authoritarian methods of law enforcement. Nor was this last promise kept. Undoubtedly, under his administration Italy became a more democratic society, but this tendency was independent of official policy, as Cavour and others had realized. After the Law of Guarantees, the Left was hardly more anticlerical than the Right; indeed the fact that the Left and the clericals had sometimes combined when in opposition made it plausible to accuse Depretis of making undue concessions to the Vatican. The doctrine of coalition government, the same which had caused Cavour to move leftward and take over the policy of national unity from the democrats, now made Depretis move the other way and borrow from the Right.

When in opposition, Depretis had condemned the use of government "influence" at election time, but in the six months before November 1876 the prefects were strictly enjoined to use their administrative authority to manipulate or "make" the elections. Recalcitrant local government officials were transferred to less pleasant regions, or were reduced to conformity by the threat of such transfer and its hampering effect on their future careers. In the key centers of Rome, Naples, Palermo, Milan, Bologna, Turin, and Genoa, the prefects were changed at once. It was intimated that special favor in the matter of schools, railroad concessions, and other government contracts would be shown to those constituencies which voted the right way. The minister of the interior, Nicotera, left nothing to chance, and so won for his friends an overwhelming majority of about 380 deputies against 130. Many leaders of the Right, including Bonghi, Spaventa, and Massari, failed to be returned, and in southern Italy, where corrupt influence was most easily wielded, only four deputies of the Right were elected. It soon appeared, indeed, that victory had been too complete, for the lack of an effective conservative party impaired the political education of both sides. The absence of opposition and the presence of so many inexperienced deputies left this great majority exposed to the same internal disintegration which has sapped so many other ministries in Italian history.

The complete reconstitution of the Lower House brought with it some decline in quality among the deputies. The conservatives used to say, spitefully but not altogether untruthfully, that this triumph of the Left introduced nothing into politics except intrigue, corruption, and a moral vacuum. During almost sixteen years of opposition, Depretis had become accustomed to seek allies indiscriminately, and to promise too much to too many. His chief strength lay in southern Italy, where political life had always been unhealthy, where men had learned their politics in the school of conspiracy or else by cringing under a corrupt Bourbon despotism. His electoral success was incontestable, but instead of expressing a general reaction against the *consorteria,* it rather reflected a marriage of expediency between Nicotera and the bosses who dominated local government. Deputies henceforward were too frequently in the pay of local concerns, and were the mouthpieces of parish-pump politics; they would trade their votes to each ministry in turn so long as certain private interests were placated. Depretis persuaded parliament to vote en bloc for building two thousand kilometers of railroad, which he then parceled out, it was said, in return for votes. Another of his first measures was to increase the sugar tax, a few days after which some seventy deputies were raised to the dignity of *commendatore* or *cavaliere:* the connection seemed obvious. Depretis perhaps used no more violent pressure than Farini had done in 1861 or Minghetti in 1874. But he created an electoral machine which henceforward hardly ever failed to register the desired result.

If the use of government influence in elections was the first principle of Depretis's administration, the second was the formation of a parliamentary majority by "transforming" the old groups into a new government coalition. In an election speech of October 1876 he said: "I hope my words will help bring about the fertile transformation of parties, and the unification of all shades of liberal in parliament, in exchange for those old party labels so often abused and so often decided only by the topography of the Chamber." Here again Depretis was exploiting a trend which already existed, and the word *trasformismo* was coined merely to express that absence of party coherence and organization which had itself brought about the fall of the Right. Transformism was only the rationalization of Cavour's practice. None of the prime ministers since 1852 had been strictly party men, and all of them had been willing to accept support from anywhere except the two extremes.

Each prime minister in turn had the same problem of creating a government coalition which would be both liberal and conservative, and the differences among them therefore lay mostly just in emphasis. One reason put forward to explain these inevitable coalitions is the absence from parliament of the extreme clericals and Mazzinians, the most powerful catalysts available. The need to keep these extremes out of politics drove all varieties of progressive-liberal and conservative-liberal into a common refuge where they laid aside their internal quarrels and joined in parceling out power and jobbery. The self-confidence of strong men like Cavour and Depretis aided this process, for their domination of the political scene was connected with the elasticity of these center groups and the refusal by all politicians to stand too much on principle. Even Minghetti, who believed theoretically in a two-party system, thought strong government to be of overriding importance, and rallied many conservatives behind Depretis in their common fear of radicals and clericals.

Whatever the reason, political controversies were quite clearly not taking the form of party conflict. De Sanctis was another of Cavour's ex-colleagues who deplored this fact. In 1877 he wrote: "We have now reached the point where there are no solidly built parties in Italy except those based on either regional differences or the personal relation of client to patron; and these are the twin plagues of Italy." Existing groups were composed of men who might change their ideas and their allegiance as occasion demanded, a fact which made election results unreliable for both politician and historian. Depretis nevertheless argued that this was quite proper, and that the existence of a well-organized opposition would only slow up governmental activity and divide the best elements of the nation into two ineffective halves.

Transformism is one method of parliamentary government, and this kind of constant Center coalition undoubtedly tended to make politics less controversial and more moderate. But occasionally some of the liberals recognized that, as De Sanctis and Croce taught in the different fields of literature and aesthetics, the lack of clear controversy was deadening and stultifying. Cavour had been blamed for purposely splitting up existing parties as a means of increasing his own power, and Menabrea and Saracco, for instance, had from two quite different angles criticized his eclectic policy and his "game of political seesaw." Now Zanardelli accused Depretis of "confounding political parties which are necessary to our national greatness, and exhausting the political passions which are the lifeblood of free government." Transformism was attacked for degrading the practice of compromise, because what had been a patriotic duty in the common struggle against Austria was now being debased into a mere political habit to cover an absence of conviction. Spaventa and Di Rudinì of the defeated Right made much of this charge, and began to pay unaccustomed compliments to the two-party method of government.

Giolitti added to this that what had begun as a laudable attempt to create a coalition of moderates soon deteriorated into a mere instrument of ambition for Depretis. Crispi, too, began attacking *trasformismo* on the same grounds, only to adopt the technique himself when he succeeded to power on Depretis's death in 1887. Depretis, Crispi, and then Giolitti himself, all in turn had recourse to this method to prevent the growth of an organized opposition, for in an emergency a prime minister would be tempted to reinforce his supporters by a *combinazione* with some of the potential dissidents. This absence of any well-articulated opposition sometimes had unfortunate effects in Italian constitutional history, and so did the quick succession of cabinets which resulted, for an apparently solid majority was sometimes dispersed almost overnight.

The primary intention of Depretis was to recreate the benevolent "parliamentary dictatorship" which Italy had known under Cavour, and in this he partly succeeded. A decree of July 1876 for the first time accorded legal status to the President of the Council, who now became more of a prime minister than his counterpart in England or France, receiving special responsibility for cabinet decisions and the execution of government policy. Depretis then announced his technique of government—perhaps realizing that these were almost the very words of Cavour himself: "Whereas it used to be said that the government represented a party, we intend to rule in the interests of everyone . . . and will accept the help of all honest and loyal men of whatsoever group." Accordingly, while Depretis's coalition extended leftward almost as far as Bertani, he also approached Peruzzi and the dissident Tuscans who had helped unseat their former colleagues on the Right. Twenty-five years earlier Depretis had deplored Cavour's *connubio* with Rattazzi; to reproach him now with inconsistency would be irrelevant, for at last power was within his grasp and he believed he could use it in this way to Italy's advantage.

Indubitably, this imparted an element of peacefulness to parliamentary life. Depretis's temperament inclined him to soft-pedal personal feuds and shun the clash of rival theories. He was above all an administrator, who preferred always to establish the admitted facts of a case, and then to try empirically to secure broad agreement on the basis of these facts without allowing preconceived ideas to influence the decision. Effective though this was, by avoiding conflict and opposition he deprived government of a desirable check, and often confused principles and destroyed clear thinking as well. He did indeed have more chance of remaining in power if he could cloud the issues and seem to agree with everyone, but in the effort to soften discord and polemics he sometimes suffocated all idealism. Like Cavour, he shied away from formulating a rigid policy which could be voted down, and preferred expedients which might be abandoned at will by simply dropping an unpopular minister and reforming his cabinet. Small wonder that Depretis was called the wizard of Stradella and the Robert Walpole of Italy.

§≫

For a time the leaders of the Right held out against the transformation of political groups which Depretis was effecting. They could not yet believe that the elections of 1876 represented a final loss of power. But under Minghetti and Sella the hundred-odd deputies of this right-wing opposition never became a well-constituted body. In the Senate they still had a majority, yet instead of redoubling their efforts, the senators of the Right tended to absent themselves from parliament, while Depretis gradually used the powers of royal nomination to pack the House. Now that the hope of spoils and perquisites was diminished for right-wing deputies, their abstention indicated that many people had considered politics as no more than a perquisite for those in power, and hence saw little point in mere opposition. This defeatism was the more easily exploited by Depretis because Sella, Minghetti, Spaventa, Bonghi, Sonnino, and Villari had so little in common. Once he was clearly the master in parliament, some of these conservatives were always ready to accept a coalition. Of the rest, a good number retired to continue their criticism on a purely academic level. They would write articles for magazines like the *Rassegna Settimanale,* or for the *Corriere della Sera*—that great achievement of Italian journalism which was launched by a group of Milanese industrialists in 1876.

The radicals to the left of Depretis were no longer formidable now that Rome was won and the monarchy settled in the Quirinal. The two southerners Nicotera and Crispi, who had once endured exile for their republican faith, were appointed ministers of the crown in 1876 and 1877, respectively. Former conspirators such as General Medici and Visconti-Venosta had become respectable marquises, and Carducci, another notable ex-republican, began to write odes of humble loyalty to the royal house. Garibaldi himself, since his friends were in office, hastened to accept what he had hitherto refused, a substantial sum of money from the state for his former services.

There were still some elements of the extreme Left who, while agreeing to sit in parliament, stood aloof from the process of transformism. Bertani in eight successive parliaments and later Cavallotti in others tried to give some coherence to these democrats who made up what was called the *estrema.* Their task was to goad the government into fulfilling its early program of social reform. Though they had little corporate discipline, they included some of the most forthright and attractive Italian

politicians, and these radicals, republicans, and (later) socialists constituted a pressure group more powerful than their numbers might suggest.

ॶ

It was in part due to the stimulus of the *estrema* that Depretis at the
beginning of 1877 introduced a measure to abolish arrest for debt, and
set up at Bertani's request a special committee to inquire into agricultural
conditions. Another noteworthy reform was the Coppino law which made
education free and compulsory for children between the ages of six and
nine. Only twenty deputies voted against this law, but its negligent enforcement enabled the critics to say that Depretis was trying to acquire
the fame of a progressive liberal without being one in fact. The Catholics
demurred at the spread of lay education as a possible threat to the faith,
especially as this law abolished compulsory religious teaching in elementary schools. But there was also a general inertia among local authorities
which made the bill only partly effective.

The liberal spirit behind these measures was contradicted by the harsh
methods of Baron Nicotera, the minister of the interior. His overbearing
conduct antagonized moderate members of the Left like Cairoli, and
convinced Spaventa that standards were daily sinking further below the
level maintained by other governments of civilized Europe. Nicotera
arbitrarily prohibited or dissolved public meetings, whether socialist or
Catholic. When a meeting of protest against the grist tax was announced,
he forbade it on the grounds that public order might be endangered, and
then asked parliament to absolve him for thus infringing the constitution.
In December 1876 he explained and defended in parliament his system
of *domicilio coatto,* a form of internal exile which he had taken over
from his predecessors and employed widely in some provinces. He sent
labor agitators to the penal islands. He also banned some newspapers,
forbade employees of his ministry to read others, and bought the favor
of opposition journals with the secret funds of his department.

This policy was all too reminiscent of that once followed by Spaventa
himself, and it confirmed what many intelligent men had prophesied,
namely that the Left in power, despite their paper policy of reform, would
prove no more liberal than the Right. From the common people's view-
point, it strengthened the impression that the government of United Italy
was still the same oppressive conspiracy of the powerful against the
weak, of the rich against the poor, and that the police, far from being
defenders of society, were sometimes almost its enemies.

As soon as this authoritarian attitude began to weaken the ministry
in public opinion, Depretis in December 1877 replaced the unpopular
Nicotera by Crispi, taking as his pretext the scandalous revelation that

the former had been tapping private telegraph messages. Crispi had until now condemned the "parliamentary incest" by which the radical Nicotera had been transformed into a pillar of conservative government. But Depretis knew his man, and Crispi surrendered to transformism quite as easily, not even protesting when the cabinet was eventually completed with General Bertolé-Viale from the Right. Nicotera took his revenge by showing that Crispi had gone through a mock marriage under a forged signature with a lady whom he had then left after twenty years in order to legitimize his daughter by another woman. Accused of bigamy, Crispi had to resign until people could forget this peccadillo.

Such animosities soon broke up the false majority of the Left into its component groups, especially as the opposition deputies were too few and too disorganized to weld together the rank and file of government supporters. Every suggested reform merely created fresh political divisions. In 1877 Garibaldi was already accusing Depretis of preferring wasteful expenditure on a large army to aiding the poor in winning a decent livelihood. In November, Zanardelli resigned from the cabinet as a protest against extravagance in apportioning railroad contracts. A group of about eighty deputies began to form around Benedetto Cairoli and to move away from Depretis and toward the twenty other deputies composing the *estrema*. Later on, the finance minister, Grimaldi, resigned in 1879 when the grist tax was finally abolished, because he maintained that this put politics before finance. There was tension between laissez-faire liberals such as Zanardelli and the authoritarian Nicotera. Personal disagreements separated Crispi from Cairoli, yet both of them favored a much larger extension of the suffrage than Depretis and Nicotera would have tolerated. The two leading writers on the Left, Carducci and the great literary critic De Sanctis, both castigated Depretis for his lack of idealism and his policy of expedients. Owing to these divisions, instead of transformism bringing stability, one cabinet quickly followed another, and each ex-minister became the leader of a group potentially hostile to his successor. Collective cabinet responsibility was even weaker than before, and although Zanardelli had been in the same cabinet as Nicotera in 1877, a few months later he entirely reversed Nicotera's policy.

No obvious political crisis had brought the Left to power, nor was it over any clear issues of policy that five separate ministries fell in less than two years. The second ministry of Depretis, formed in December 1877, resigned after four months when his candidate for the post of Speaker in the Chamber was not approved. Cairoli then took office in March 1878, along with Zanardelli and De Sanctis. On Cairoli's resignation, Depretis took over at the end of the year; then there were two more Cairoli ministries in 1879, one of which included Depretis as minister of the interior. These unstable cabinets caused great scandal among the main body of liberals, especially as there was so little connection between their formation and any vote of parliament. There was little to distinguish them from one another, or even from their predecessors before 1876. Despite election promises, the Left went on with the policy of centralization and the practice of decree laws, and interfered quite as much with the press and with personal liberty. Though the grist tax was abolished, the price of bread continued to rise, and there was no appreciable fall in taxation. Turiello was not alone in concluding that the Left was more conservative and less revolutionary than the old Right.

It would be more accurate to say simply that the Left leaders in office became more pragmatic and less irresponsible. At the other wing of the Chamber, Spaventa and Bonghi, who had once opposed any extension of the suffrage, were now ready to accept moderate reform proposals. Both Right and Left depended in fact on the same class of people, and had common interests against clericals and reactionaries on the one hand, and radicals and socialists on the other. Every prime minister in turn depended on this fact for his power, until Mussolini altered the rules of the game, and such differences of opinion as remained were purposely minimized by Depretis and the rest in their effort to build up a liberal coalition of the Center.

§◆

One sign of a new age in 1878 was the accession of two new potentates in Italy, King Umberto and Pope Leo XIII. Vittorio Emanuele had died of malaria, a symptom of the unhealthiness of his new capital amid the marshes. Special permission was given by Pius IX for him to receive the last sacraments and for ecclesiastical censures to be momentarily lifted, and the whole Court by custom filed before his bed as he lay dying. The new king was more dutiful and dignified than his father, and less original in his notion of kingship. On Crispi's insistence he took the title of Umberto *the First,* instead of carrying on the numeration of the Savoy dynasty.

Umberto had made a dynastic and loveless marriage with his cousin Margherita, a proud and beautiful woman who lived long enough to back Mussolini. Margherita had hard words for parliament, and was religious to the point of bigotry. She also became a fervent nationalist, and used to write longingly to her favorite Minghetti of the day when Italy would be feared in the world. But she charmed such ex-republicans as Carducci and Crispi, and at the Court ball in 1875 she inaugurated a new epoch by dancing the first quadrille with Nicotera—though it remained her grumble that the leaders of the Left were inexpert dancers. Rosina, the second wife of Vittorio Emanuele, had been a coarse *popolana,* daughter of a sergeant in the army, but the new royal consort was a queen to her fingertips, and a leader of fashion whose toilettes were copied assiduously.

Umberto and Margherita set up an impressive royal household at Rome which tried to rival that of the Vatican. Three deep bows before the king, and walking backward out of his presence, were *de rigueur.* Fox-hunting parties in the English manner were made fashionable, with red coats and sandwich lunches, and were much followed by the French and other ambassadors as a means of diplomatic contact. Together the royal couple tried to win over both the "blacks" on the Right and the "reds" on the Left and to reconcile Roman society to the national revolution.

16 Foreign Policy, 1860-1882

The near identity of views among Italian politicians about foreign affairs is explained by certain compelling facts. That Austria owned Italian territory and was Italy's traditional enemy constituted one such fact. The general benevolence of most other European countries toward Italy was another. Unification had become possible only because France, Britain, and Prussia had competed in favoring Italy through their own mutual fears and jealousy. When Queen Victoria inveighed against Lord John Russell's sympathy for "this *really bad,* unscrupulous Sardinian government," he retorted that either Italy would have to be Italian or it would again become Austrian or French. British statesmen were satisfied that "another Prussia has arisen in the South of Europe, which will in all probability be a new guarantee for the Balance of Power." This sounds odd today, but at the time seemed true enough.

The sympathy of Europe had given Italy a false advantage, and led her statesmen to plan policy on two mistaken assumptions: that their country was strong, and that other nations would continue to find their interests promoted by the welfare and expansion of Italy. At first she was able to run risks in the confidence of being considered a natural ally by both France and Britain, and when this advantage ceased to apply she thought herself harshly used. In such artificially favorable circumstances it was difficult to take proper stock of her interests and responsibilities, and the temptation was to devise a foreign policy involving risks too great for her strength. She also had to discover which of the powers was her most likely ally, or whether indeed she had any natural ally. Possibly, she would have to continue the traditionally fickle policy of the House of Savoy if she wished to carry more influence than her capabilities warranted.

Up to 1870 Italy continued to be a modest hanger-on of Napoleon III. She shared with France the enmity of Austria, and a kinship in Romance culture and language. More tangibly, in her legal code, her metric system of measurements, even in her tricolor flag and her fashions of dress and behavior, Italy showed a marked tendency to imitate her sister country. The royalties of French authors in Italy were large, and as late as 1900 there was a prime minister whose native language was French and who spoke Italian with a foreign accent. The military aid of France had been indispensable for the conquest of Lombardy in 1859, and the king obstinately maintained his entente with France until Louis Napoleon's defeat in 1870.

Almost as necessary was the friendship of England. Not until 1935 did an understanding with England cease to be a more or less fixed point in Italian foreign policy. Since Italy was highly sensitive to invasion or blockade by sea, and because most of her imports came through channels dominated by the British navy, she was particularly anxious not to challenge this power. The generation of Cavour had a great admiration for England. From the very beginning of his political career, according to his secretary Artom, Cavour tried to model Piedmont upon English institutions. This admiration and good will waned slightly with the years. None the less it was reciprocated in Britain, even though fear of Russia and France forced the British into an Austrian alliance which made a complete understanding with Italy impossible. Italy was valued by Great Britain as another potential check upon France. The tory Clarendon had agreed with the whig Russell in 1860 that the time was ripe for Italy's annexation of Venice, and as early as 1861 the Italian ambassador had been told that Rome could be occupied at once as far as Great Britain was concerned. Unofficial opinion in England as in America was wildly enthusiastic over the achievement of Italian independence, and half a million Londoners lined the streets to cheer Garibaldi when the *invitto Duce* paid a visit in 1864; probably no one else in history before that moment had ever received such a welcome.

§●

By 1866, when the backing of Prussia was added to that of France and Britain, Italians were no longer content with the prospect of a neutral position in Europe like that of Belgium or Switzerland, and in their consciousness of being a great power their foreign policy became more pugnacious. Some of their leaders became oversensitive about whether Italy was receiving due admiration and respect, and not only resented criticism but imagined it where it did not exist. They were incensed by the thought that their country was looked upon as a museum of ruins, as a tourist paradise, a country of opera singers, organ-grinders, ice-cream vendors, beggars, and touts; and in an endeavor to dispel this patronizing attitude, Italian politicians tended to become adventurous and bellicose. One of the arguments for intervention in the Crimean War had been the necessity of demonstrating Italian fighting qualities, and Cavour had preached the dangerous and false doctrine that seldom was anything gained by neutrality. Vittorio Emanuele issued the ominous pronouncement, heartily echoed by Umberto and Margherita, that "Italy must not only be respected, she must make herself feared."

This attitude was comprehensible, but it led to a forward and forceful foreign policy which proved an expensive habit. Former allies became more grudging of their assistance than when Italy had been relatively powerless; hitherto she had always been able to retreat if conflict with another country threatened, but as soon as she pretended to greatness her honor was at stake and withdrawal was less easy. Some detached and careful observers perceived this trend. Fortunato was brave enough to say that Italy was at fault in her vanity, in her desire to cut a figure, and in the absurd belief that she was potentially rich and powerful. In 1900 he pointed out that 21 per cent of government expenditure was military supply compared with 17 per cent in Germany, that 33 per cent of Italy's budget went on debt service compared with 20 per cent of Germany's, and that the national income was only a third of the French. He therefore tried to make parliament spend less on the army and navy, showing how absurd it was to claim parity with France and Germany. Garibaldi, too, toyed with pacifism and internationalism in his old age, even arguing that the army took too many peasants away from the fields and so actually weakened Italy by making her dependent on foreign food. On the other hand, General Cialdini resigned in protest against economies in army expenditure, and called them a monument of political incompetence.

Successive governments tended to support Cialdini. Under an illusion about her own wealth and power, Italy was launched into the general race for armaments. After 1870 General Ricotti reorganized the army on the Prussian model, and extended conscription to all able-bodied men without allowing the purchase of exemption. On German advice he decided that Italy could not be defended easily, and hence needed to be able to attack, notwithstanding the expense. Naval construction was based on holding a decisive superiority over Austria-Hungary. It was never seriously debated whether Italy could afford simultaneously a front-rank army and navy. Neither was it foreseen that every new technical invention and development would progressively exhaust a country which lacked iron and fuel, nor that each increase in armaments would involve her prestige more deeply. An army would not remain unused for long, and as the illusion of national strength grew, legitimate patriotism eventually developed into aggressive nationalism. Well over a third of state expenditure was to be allocated to provision for war between 1860 and 1940.

The French alliance was wearing thin by the time Italy made her treaty with Prussia in 1866, although there was no open breach for another fifteen years. Ill-feeling grew after the return of French troops to Rome in 1867 and the victory of the *chassepots* over Garibaldi at Mentana. A sense of rivalry with France began to show itself in North Africa, and economists also feared that Italy's dependence upon French investment and the French market was too exclusive. Prussia, on the other hand, was not a Mediterranean power, and had no common frontier with Italy over which friction could arise. She was also a rapidly growing nation and determined to upset what was left of the Vienna settlement. When the Prussian minister expressed doubts about Cavour's invasion of the Papal states in 1860, the latter replied that Prussia was similarly situated and might one day thank Piedmont for this example of national unification. Out of this community of sentiment emerged the alliance which defeated Austria in 1866, an alliance which Louis Napoleon in his foolishness actually approved.

Italy thus returned to the situation which Piedmont had always sought in the distant past, where her own support, if judiciously marketed between the two titans, France and Germany, might be priced above its real worth. From the War of the Spanish Succession to the Triple Alliance and beyond she proved remarkably adroit in knowing when to change her allegiance in order to end up on the winning side. But this was a dangerous game, and when the balance of Europe tipped too heavily, as it did after 1870 against France and after 1918 and 1945 against Germany, Italy's illusion of strength was dissipated. Her most successful foreign ministers were those who recognized her essential limitations and were not lured by ambition to attempt more than preserving the balance or righting it when upset. The fascists held such unheroic behavior up to shame, but in fact it met with success, whereas Mussolini, like Crispi before him, led his country into disastrous defeat.

Before the time of Crispi, both Right and Left were generally agreed in playing safe. Visconti-Venosta, the foreign minister of the Right, insisted that Italy should be "unadventurous"; Cairoli of the Left believed in a policy of "freedom from ties and commitments"; Depretis thought foreign affairs a bore, and ranked diplomats with professors as the people he liked least. The older men of the Right tended toward the francophile tradition of Cavour, while the younger radicals welcomed Bismarck as an anticlerical and an exponent of state socialism. But this difference was not pushed very far.

Continuity in foreign policy was greatly assisted by the fact that the king kept a special prerogative of supervision in this field. The foreign minister was generally a royal nominee, or else the sovereign might carry out a personal policy by corresponding with ambassadors without his ministers' knowledge. Either way the cabinet as a whole was as a rule unconsulted and uninformed, and Cavour had shown that in practice this could work satisfactorily. Vittorio Emanuele was not unmindful of what he thought were the true interests of the nation, and usually proved to be too "correct" and too indolent to object when the diplomats of the Palazzo della Consulta developed ideas of their own. Purely dynastic ambitions did, however, continue to weigh with him. His daughter Clotilde was married to the rakish Prince Napoleon, Maria Pia to the King of Portugal; and his second son Amedeo accepted an invitation to become King of Spain in 1870, and reigned until forced to abdicate in 1873.

Perhaps the king's own first marriage had helped predispose him to a partial reconciliation with Austria-Hungary, but there were also more solid reasons for not pressing this traditional animosity too far. Whereas France after 1870 was a defeated republic and so doubly undesirable as an ally, Germany and Austria were both ruled by successful conservative monarchs, one of whom had Bismarck, the master of Europe, behind him. In 1873 Vittorio Emanuele made a state appearance in Vienna and Berlin, and, when in 1875 Franz Joseph responded by visiting the former Austrian possession of Venice, his action was hailed as recognition that the hard feelings of the war of 1866 were dead. Even though Austria still ruled the "unredeemed lands" of Trent and Trieste, King Vittorio's speech to parliament in 1876 mentioned "the cordial friendship and sympathy between our two peoples," and privately he told the emperor that Italian irredentist claims would be dropped.

This *rapprochement* with Austria took place under Minghetti before the Left came into power. Not everyone approved of it, and though it continued on paper for forty years, there were always independent and opposite forces working in other directions. The European balance of power had swung heavily toward Germany in 1870, and some people thought that Italy should try to redress this swing rather than join with the dominant power. Other politicians would have preferred a war to annex Trieste and the Trentino, and could not willingly ally with the hereditary foe while these *terre irredente* were still in foreign hands. In 1877 Crispi, for instance, went to see Bismarck and tried to embroil Germany against Austria, but without success.

The influence of this Sicilian radical, Francesco Crispi, was to be ruinous for Italy. He was one of a new generation of lawyer-politicians, blustering, assertive, often impetuous, men whose reasoning was often more juridical than political. They had not the educational advantages of Minghetti and his friends on the Right, nor their wide European outlook. Even before Crispi obtained office he was agitating for an aggressive policy. In 1877 he urged Depretis that "it is of paramount importance that Europe should esteem us as sufficiently powerful to make our strength felt should complications result from the war in the East. . . . At no matter what cost Italy must complete her armament. . . . My regret is profound when I reflect that as far back as 1870 the ministry of the Right turned a deaf ear to my petition to arm the country in anticipation of mighty events." After a talk with Vittorio Emanuele, Crispi wrote to tell the prime minister how "the king feels the need of crowning his lifework with a victory which shall give our army the power and prestige it now lacks in the eyes of the world."

Crispi was already ambitious to be a man of destiny, and his grand designs were not unwelcome at Court. Unfortunately for him, Bismarck had chosen to side with Austria-Hungary. One result of the overwhelming Prussian victories of 1866 and 1870 was that Italians could no longer play off Germany against Austria or France against Germany, and Crispi's mission to Friedrichsruh therefore ended with the single result that Crispi himself came dangerously under Bismarck's fascination. When the Congress of Berlin met in 1878, Italy was unable to make her influence felt there, for she had neither an ally to support her nor scope for maneuver. In any case the Italian parliamentary system was such that no cabinet remained in office long enough to develop a special policy of its own.

The Congress of Berlin took place when Cairoli was prime minister, and he appointed his schoolfriend Count Corti to be foreign minister for six months. Corti arrived at the Congress unbriefed on the various problems for consideration. As a result, while Austria won a protectorate over Bosnia and Herzegovina, while Britain acquired Cyprus, and France secured recognition of claims on North Africa, Italy left with clean but empty hands. A tentative demand was made for the Trentino, but this only provoked Gortchakov's jibe that Italy must have lost another battle if she was asking to annex another province. Bismarck suggested that she might compensate herself in Albania; Britain cynically proffered the alternative of Tunis. But Cairoli, who had once fought among Garibaldi's volunteers, made a poor diplomat, and was too simple and generous to stoop to the barter of territories and the sharing of "compensation" in secret treaties. His was a good-natured and praiseworthy idealism, but this did not make for worldly success.

Failure to assert the national interests left Italians feeling touchily aggrieved, for not many of them approved Cairoli's policy of "clean hands." It was not sufficiently appreciated that at Berlin their country was sitting for the first time as an acknowledged power in the Concert of Europe. Nor did they recognize that, as Italy had not been involved in the Eastern crisis which had led to the Congress, it was hardly a defeat if she not emerge with large gains. Failure lay not so much in empty-handedness abroad, but rather in the inability at home to recognize Italy's true interests, and in the belief that more expenditure on armaments was an easy and sure path to great victories. Crispi's criticism of Cairoli merely fostered the suspicion that his countrymen had suffered a diplomatic reverse, and when this was confirmed by a second defeat over the French occupation of Tunis in 1881, Italy abandoned her policy of "no commitments" and unadventurousness. She committed herself to Bismarck, and in May 1882 became a very junior partner in the Triple Alliance.

§⁕

By joining Germany and Austria, Italy hoped to secure her back door while she fished for colonies and improved her international position. There was some truth in Goluchowski's statement that between Italy and Austria the only possible relations were either alliance or war. As the rest of Europe was not yet ready to satisfy Italian hopes for Trent and Trieste, the next best thing was to shelve them in exchange for a guarantee by Catholic Austria against a resumption of papal sovereignty in Rome. Another motive for the alliance was pique at being forestalled in Tunis, and the determination to wound France even at the cost of upsetting the equilibrium of Europe. The politicians of the Left were severely shaken by this French colonial victory, and needed some counterbalancing success to underwrite their parliamentary position. It was said that Italy needed to emerge from diplomatic isolation, and, this being so, the king had special reasons for preferring monarchical and militarist Germany to republican France.

Crispi and his friends later claimed credit for this new policy of direct alignment with Germany against France, but the foreign minister in fact responsible was Mancini, and it was largely due to Baron Blanc and his permanent officials at the Consulta. Depretis himself entered into the *Triplice* somewhat reluctantly, and tried to conceal its existence lest France should take alarm. The treaty was not officially admitted until some years later, and the actual text was not published until the next century.

By express intention the pact was a guarantee against French aggression. With the amplifications subsequently added during its thirty-three years of life, military aid was promised if one signatory through no fault of its own were attacked by other powers, and benevolent neutrality if one were forced to initiate a war. A particular importance was to attach to what later became Article 7:

> Austria-Hungary and Italy undertake to use their influence to prevent all territorial changes which might be disadvantageous to one or the other signatory power. To this end they agree to interchange all information throwing light on their own intentions. If, however, Austria-Hungary or Italy should be compelled to alter the *status quo* in the Balkans, whether by a temporary or by a permanent occupation, such occupation shall not take place without previous agreement between the two powers based on the principle of reciprocal compensation for every advantage, territorial, or otherwise.

Apart from this, there was nothing very radical or menacing about its provisions. Mancini easily defeated Kálnocky's attempt to introduce a clause reminiscent of the Holy Alliance which would have imposed a common conservative internal policy on each signatory, and by mutual agreement the treaty was stated to be in no way directed against Great Britain.

Quite obviously such an engagement would favor Germany more than Italy, for while France might try to reconquer Alsace-Lorraine, a French invasion of Italy was hardly credible except to Crispi's torrid imagination. Italy might thus have to fight for Germany, but not

Germany for Italy. In return for very doubtful gains, Italians had to renounce their irredentist claims on Austria. Although Beust had once hinted that Austria might possibly cede the Trentino as compensation for being allowed to annex Bosnia, after 1882 Italy was less strongly placed for pressing any such suggestion. This was an important disadvantage of the *Triplice*. Another was that, though ostensibly a measure for peace, its effect was to increase tension and enlarge military expenditure. Italy's real interest in peace was buried by Crispi's magniloquent insistence on prestige and by the military obsessions of the Court. The king had come back from Berlin an enthusiast for the German war machine, and one of his retinue heard him grumble that the worst soldier in the Thirteenth Hussars looked better than the best soldier in the whole Italian army. The Italian taxpayer had to make good this deficiency.

Above all, the Triple Alliance curtailed the freedom of action which was one of Italy's chief assets, for in alienating France she lost her ability to treat with both sides. Instead of striving to preserve a general equilibrium, she was helping to overturn it, and while this may have made her more feared, it also earned her a reputation for untrustworthiness. Other nations were not easily persuaded that an alliance formed by Bismarck had no aggressive purpose, and they hardly thought that Italy would have given up her demands upon Austria without the hope of fairly sizable compensation to be wrested from France.

Depretis was, of course, in a poor bargaining position. He had to rest content with the feeling of security conveyed by the alliance, and with its comfortable acknowledgement that the temporal power of the Papacy had now probably gone for good. Some Italians hoped that, if not offensive in intention as yet, the alliance would soon become so, with Austria advancing into the Balkans in return for adjustment of Italy's northeastern frontier. Others supported the treaty on the quite different grounds that it deterred France and Russia from breaking the peace. Another claim was that it brought economic advantages, for while the previous alliance with France had connected two predominantly agricultural states, henceforward Italy would have an outlet in Central Europe for her agricultural products, and receive manufactured goods in exchange. There was some truth in this contention, but not much, for trade with France had been substantial, whereas, apart from timber and horses, Italy was to receive unexpectedly little from Austria, and the influx of capital and industrial goods from northern Germany was not without its economic and political dangers.

The Triple Alliance gave a moral boost to Italy, but it seldom had much influence on the actions of its signatories. It was never an unlimited pact, but only contemplated certain well-defined contingencies which were not very likely to arise. The chief satisfaction which it bestowed on Italy was the recognition by the great powers that she was of their number. This desire for prestige was a sentimental and not a material consideration, and, though natural enough, was to bulk far too large in Italian foreign and colonial policy.

17 Colonial Enterprise, 1860-1882

As soon as United Italy became self-conscious, ancestral memories of earlier colonial expansion were revived to support the argument that prestige demanded active emulation of the past. Rome had conquered Hannibal and Jugurtha, and medieval communes had fought against Saracens and Barbary pirates along the North African coast. The empire of Venice had stretched through Greece to Constantinople and the Levant, while the discoveries of Columbus and Vespucci gave some Italian historians an almost proprietary feeling about the New World.

The nineteenth century found these past memories very much alive. Large Italian settlements still flourished at Cairo, Alexandria, and Tunis. The tradition of maritime enterprise was upheld by Garibaldi, who as a ship's captain had cruised to Newcastle and Constantinople, to China and Peru, and who had lived for many years in North and South America and North Africa. The Mediterranean had seemingly become a backwater at the beginning of modern times, but the new generation intended to restore its importance. Moreover, Spain and Turkey, which had once invaded the Italian peninsula and captured its oversea possessions, were now in full decline, and this left a gap which a rising nation might fill. On the other hand, the Italian language, once a lingua franca throughout the Mediterranean, was being displaced in the Levant by French, in Malta by English and Maltese; and the political expansion of France into Algeria and beyond was another trend which had to be resisted if resurgent Italy were to receive what was thought to be its due. The nation which, geopolitically speaking, seemed best placed to predominate in the Mediterranean, found its three outlets, Gibraltar, the Bosporus, and Suez, all controlled by outsiders.

Italians in the eighteenth century had recognized the importance of Malta and Tunis, but it remained for Cesare Balbo and Gioberti to argue that geography and history alike offered Italy a natural leadership in the Mediterranean. In the 1830's Italian missionaries such as the Lazzarist Sapeto were established at Massawa on the Red Sea. Padre Massaia penetrated into Ethiopia, and at Cavour's wish established friendly relations with local chieftains. Cavour was often farsighted in initiating small measures which might one day turn out profitably. In the early 1850's he subsidized the Rubattino shipping company, and even lent it naval vessels to inaugurate a shipping service from Genoa to Tunis. Less wisely, he set up a government-subsidized transatlantic shipping service which quickly went bankrupt. He was similarly conscious of Italian interests on the Austrian coast of the Adriatic, and his participation in the Crimean War was partly planned as a move in a larger Mediterranean policy toward which he was groping.

For a long time after Cavour, governments almost lost interest in colonialism, in part perhaps because unification was the work of landbound Piedmont which had no seafaring tradition and so depreciated the value of colonies and sea power. Desultory negotiations began with Portugal for concessions in Angola and Mozambique, with Britain for the Falklands and for a station in Nigeria, with Denmark and Russia for a share in the Nicobar Islands, the Antilles, and the Aleutians. Menabrea mildly encouraged the traveler Cerruti to seek out possible spheres of influence in the Indian and Pacific oceans. Private individuals were active, and explorers and missionaries from Italy did important work between 1860 and 1875 in Burma, Siam, Borneo, and New Guinea. A certain Moreno in 1867 even had the idea of presenting Italy with sovereign rights in Sumatra which he claimed to have acquired through marriage with several local princesses. More realistically in the same year an African society was founded at Naples, and a number of explorers were sent out to trace the sources of the Nile. Through the activity of these private individuals public opinion was aroused about Africa, thus creating the interest which was a prerequisite for colonial enterprise.

The beginning of work on the Suez Canal gave a strong impetus to colonialization, and Cavour intended that the Italian merchant marine should be in the van of opening up this passage to the East. Some Italian historians even state that the most important contribution of all toward the canal was made by Italians. But although Italian labor was largely employed, there was comparatively little Italian capital or initiative in the venture. Negrelli, who did so much to further it, was despite his name a loyal Austrian subject and director of the Austrian railroads, and his object was to create a trade outlet from Central Europe through Trieste. When after fifteen years' work the canal was finally opened, it did not in fact do nearly so much for the advancement of Italy as Cavour had hoped. Perhaps Cavour's policy of giving interest-free loans to shipping companies left them too comfortably subsidized to bother. In 1870 only 1.3 per cent of the tonnage going through the canal was Italian, and in the year 1913 only 101 Italian ships used this route as compared with nearly three thousand British vessels.

The missionaries, however, supported the chamber of commerce at Genoa in encouraging the government to set up trading and refueling stations in the Red Sea. Sapeto was allowed to make a reconnaissance in a naval ship with Vice-Admiral Acton as his technical adviser, ostensibly on behalf of the patriotic Genoese shipbuilder and ship-owner, Rubattino. They sailed in one of the first vessels to pass through the canal and finally chose the Bay of Assab as the most promising station for a service between Genoa and the Indies. Rubattino promptly purchased a concession of land in the bay, as the government expected less diplomatic difficulty if this private company appeared to be working on its own. But almost at once Egypt protested, and the Italian government was forced to show its hand and make Egyptian troops withdraw from the area. Thus before politicians had finally decided whether colonization was wise, and if so whether Assab was the best place to begin, the Italian flag was committed and retreat was impossible without loss of face. As soon as a few marines were killed there, the government would have to buy up the rights of Rubattino and proclaim Italian sovereignty. This was to be a familiar story.

§❧

There was no lack of partisans to justify such casually incurred obligations, for already the imperialists were arguing in terms of surplus population and living space, and there were missionaries and philanthropists wanting to civilize backward races. The usual adventurers rushed forward; scientists were excited by the search for new lands, and some jurists wanted penal settlements for captured brigands, especially when the death penalty was abolished. It was said with some rhetorical exaggeration that Italy had to be "either the prisoner of the Mediterranean or its conqueror" and that she should not remain the only Mediterranean country with no bases outside her own mainland territory.

Other leaders, no less patriotic, argued strongly against any such extension of national commitments. As soon as traders and missionaries began to involve Italian prestige with native tribes, and to collide with other foreign expeditions, national feeling was likely to be dangerously aroused, even to the pitch of war. Available military resources might be better occupied in preparing for the inevitable rectification of the northern frontier. Financial difficulties in any case made it impossible to invest enough in colonies to ensure a sufficient return, for Italy lacked certain prerequisites of expansion; her industry was not adequate even for the domestic market, and was quite unable to compete with that of Britain, while the British also had enough surplus production to make colonies less a luxury than an economic requirement. Italy had no comparable need yet for new markets or fields for foreign investment, and indeed she was hardly able to absorb the raw materials which colonies might supply. Whereas elsewhere colonialism was a product of riches, in Italy it grew out of poverty and from the illusion that here was a quick way to get rich.

Ricasoli had warned his countrymen in 1864 that they were already spending too much on luxuries, and he mentioned the San Carlo theater at Naples. Rattazzi agreed with him that prestige ventures abroad were less important than raising the standard of living in the South. Garibaldi also insisted that the *latifondi* and marshlands of Italy were the first areas in need of colonization, and he reiterated that colonialism put prestige before welfare, and would mean increased expenditure on army and navy and a continual risk of war. The settlement of Assab therefore found public opinion at first largely indifferent or hostile. Responsible statesmen like Sella and Minghetti became restive as one commitment led to another, and rightly prophesied that additional taxes which the country could not afford and would not tolerate must follow. A special commission under Negri discussed the whole colonial question for sixteen months in 1871–72, but its members could not agree one way or the other and the advocates of expansion again took heart.

§🐘

On strategic and sentimental grounds, Tunisia was much more important than Assab. Cape Bon jutted out from Africa almost within sight of Sicily. Many Sicilians had settled there, and in a parliamentary debate of 1864 one speaker called it "a branch of Italy." There was a proposal in that year for a partition of Tunis between France and Italy, to which the government at first gave favorable consideration, but after pondering the costly colonial war to which France was committed in Algeria, Visconti-Venosta backed down. Instead he decided on economic penetration, and in 1868 a treaty was signed between Italy and the Bey of Tunis, followed by attempts to obtain fishing and tobacco-growing rights there. But this was to reckon without France. It was not appreciated that, even if Italian settlers were more numerous, France had far more investments to defend in Tunisia, and a political interest arising out of the need to control her restless subjects in neighboring Algeria.

In 1876 Austria tried to embroil Italy with France by suggesting that she might declare a protectorate over Tunis, and the Austrians also may have hoped that this would fend off any Italian request to be compensated in the Trentino for Austrian expansion into Bosnia. In the next year, Russia and Britain made much the same suggestion, so as to compensate Italy in advance for their own forward policy in the disintegrating Ottoman empire. But Italian policy was momentarily fixed on the acquisition of Trent and Trieste instead of on a costly colonial enterprise. Depretis and Cairoli refused even to discuss Mediterranean affairs in the preliminary talks before the Congress of Berlin, and then neglected to profit from the hard bargaining which accompanied the Congress. In Cairoli's famous comment to the Austrian ambassador, "Italy will go to Berlin with her hands free, and wishes to leave it with her hands clean."

To Crispi and the imperialists this attitude was a scandal. Crispi would probably have liked to profit from the French defeat in 1870 to assert Italian claims in North Africa, but the other leaders of the Left feared an economic struggle with France, and still preferred the policy of winning French support to make Austria yield the *terre irredente*. Not until 1882 did they abandon irredentism for a time to line up with the Central Powers, and, in the intervening years before then, France was free to establish her protectorate over Tunis.

Cairoli's first mistake in 1878 was to imagine that Italian and French interests could for long coexist without friction. Then he allowed France to state unilaterally through her ambassador at Rome that she would never allow any country but herself to establish a protectorate in the Regency. If Italy had made a similar declaration, the position might yet have been retrieved, but nothing was said, and England and Germany, having received no response to their previous suggestions to Italy, had meanwhile reconciled themselves to the French occupation. Cairoli said nothing: either he had been inexcusably ignorant of the aims of French policy, or else he was afraid to confess in public how he had failed to nurse Italian interests in North Africa.

When, too late, he realized the turn events were taking, he sent a consul and an armed guard of marines with orders to push Italian interests in Tunis to the limit. The French consul was then given similar instructions by his government, and direct conflict was only just avoided.

An English company which owned a railroad in Tunis was agreeably surprised to encounter a prestige competition for its purchase: the French bid was first accepted, at a price far above its real worth, but then Cairoli had the contract declared invalid by the English courts. A small mishandled colonial squabble was thus turning into a direct threat to peace. Although the succession of the more unemotional Depretis brought a relaxation of tension, Italy now felt herself irretrievably pledged to the drive for Tunis, and yet the government had neither the means nor apparently the resolve to follow economic with politicial penetration.

Understandably enough, France decided to put an end to this dubious and dangerous situation, and the railroad dispute gave her the excuse she needed. Her intention was to declare a protectorate over Tunis while Italy still lacked a powerful ally in Europe, guessing that Depretis and Cairoli dare not push matters anywhere near the verge of war. Profiting therefore by incidents on the doubtful frontier between Tunis and Algeria, she landed troops, and in May 1881 won recognition of her claims from the Bey by the Treaty of Bardo. Cairoli, now back in office, protested, but he was assured that there was no idea of permanent occupation, so he had to try to convince himself, and parliament, that no alteration had been made in the Mediterranean *status quo*. The *Rassegna Settimanale,* on the contrary, declared that "the subjection of the north coast of Africa to France will bring with it as a necessary consequence the destruction of Italy's future as a great power." This feeling of helplessness, exacerbated by the public affront, helped to clinch the German alliance in the following year. Not until 1896 was recognition given to the French protectorate in Tunis, and some Italians continued to claim that the colony was still theirs by right.

Egypt was the other country in North Africa in which there were substantial Italian settlements and financial interests. Important public men, the writers Marinetti and Ungaretti among them, were born in Alexandria, and one prominent politician, Scialoia, left Italy to become servants of the khedive. When after 1876 England gradually intruded into Egyptian affairs, Italy kept in close touch with the local nationalists. After his deposition in 1879, Khedive Ismail fled to Italy, and Arabi Bey then became for the Italian press a sort of Egyptian Garibaldi, as was the Mahdi in the Sudan.

This helps to explain why Mancini in July 1882 refused a British proposal for joint military intervention in Egypt. Crispi, Minghetti, Sonnino, and Visconti-Venosta from their various standpoints disapproved of this refusal, and called it one of the greatest failures in Italian foreign policy, but Mancini knew that he had neither troops nor money to spare for the scramble after colonies. Only when Britain emerged easily and unexpectedly successful in Egypt did he let it be known at London that his earlier refusal no longer stood. Britain, however, was in no mood to share her responsibilities after she had borne the risk and expenses of the campaign alone.

Once again, by refusing a second British offer to help offset the growing power of France in North Africa, Italy had to stand by and watch the balance of the Mediterranean weighted against her. The paramount position in that sea which Gioberti had prophesied for his country was far from becoming a reality. Parliament on this occasion gave Mancini a vote of confidence, but the debate indicated that the younger generation was beginning to think along more aggressive lines on the subject of colonial aggrandizement.

18 Depretis and Crispi, 1880-1890

The Left majority in parliament was weakened by the elections of 1880. Its somewhat unreliable radical wing around Nicotera and Crispi won more than a hundred seats between them, and at the other extreme the old Right increased their representation to about 170. Against this, the Center groups around Cairoli and Depretis mustered some 220 deputies. So confused were the issues of politics that in constituencies where no candidate had an absolute majority the two extremes sometimes voted together in the second ballot.

This partial victory of the Left was, however, taken to confirm their original mandate for electoral reform. So restricted was the parliamentary suffrage that in some constituencies the poll was a hundred votes or less—Cavour had even once referred to deputies being returned by only five or six votes in all. On the other hand the plebiscites of 1860, 1866, and 1870 had exemplified the successful working of universal manhood suffrage. Cavour had given his authority in favor of a progressive widening of the franchise, provided that voters had enough education to be independent and enough income to be interested in preserving social order. Cavour had argued on behalf of a wider suffrage that it would give citizens a moral dignity and sense of responsibility, and some of the conservatives such as Bonghi followed Cavour's precept and supported the moderate measure of reform which Depretis now proposed.

The project which became law in 1882 raised the number of voters from half a million to something over two million. The taxpaying qualification was reduced from forty lire a year to nineteen, the age qualification from twenty-five to twenty-one, and the educational qualification to knowing how to read and write; in other words it enfranchised the petty bourgeois and the intelligent artisan. A halfhearted attempt was simultaneously made to diminish governmental influence in elections through a new procedure for registering voters and securing the secrecy of the ballot. The method of *scrutinio di lista* was introduced to replace that of small constituencies, and it was hoped thereby to reduce the power of questionable local interests. The resultant enlargement of electoral districts was also accompanied by provisions to secure a more just representation for minorities.

Among the disadvantages of this electoral law, the increased representation of minority groups aggravated some of the worst features of transformism, for it gave a far bigger opening to parliamentary manipulation. No doubt Depretis had intended as much. Over a third of the deputies returned in 1882 had never sat before, and the old party labels lay lightly on them. On general grounds it might have been thought satisfactory that 7 per cent instead of 2 per cent of Italians now had the vote, but the pessimists saw in this only more room for demagogues and pressure groups. The history of Italy, like that of Germany, was to prove that a broadening of the electorate could be harnessed to the cause of the strong state and in itself signified no necessary advance in liberalism. Another dubious result of this reform was to enfranchise the cities more than the countryside, the North rather than the South, and this dangerously worsened an existing differentiation, for example making it easier to neglect the interests of southern agriculture when the time came for tariff reforms. Some of its provisions proved less satisfactory in practice than in theory, and the system of *scrutinio di lista* was repealed in 1891. But as literacy spread, so the suffrage continued automatically to widen until Giolitti made it general in 1912. The advent of mass democracy, however unwelcome to some of the liberals, was proving irresistible.

§🍎

One symptom of transformism was that some leaders of the old Right, for instance Sonnino and Professor Villari, lined up with the radicals in wanting even more suffrage concessions than Depretis was ready to allow. The influential *Rassegna Nazionale* at Florence, a paper for "conservatives who are yet friends of progress," showed that some of the Catholics too supported political reform. Villari's famous *Letters from the South* voiced a new spirit of realistic appraisal and self-criticism: "When I think what conservatives have done in England on behalf of the poor and of agriculture, I blush with shame. . . . It is high time that Italy began to realize that she has inside herself an enemy which is stronger than Austria. Somehow we must face up to our multitude of illiterates, the ineptitude of our bureaucratic machine, the ignorance of our professors, the existence of people who in politics are mere children, the incapacity of our diplomats and generals, the lack of skill in our workers, our patriarchal system of agriculture, and on top of all, the rhetoric which gnaws our very bones. It is not the quadrilateral of fortresses at Mantua and Verona which has arrested our path, but the quadrilateral of seventeen million illiterates." Not even Depretis himself showed so much reforming zeal as this. His promises of decentralization, government economy, and cheaper food had sounded impressive but were simply not being kept, and any public references he made to carrying out his 1875 "program of Stradella" were usually greeted with ironic mirth.

The fact that moderate reform found apologists on either side of the House indicates that transformism was no mere machination of Depretis, but something rooted in the structure of the Italian parliament or in the nature of Italians. Depretis said, and with some justification, that the former differences between Left and Right were settled by the time of the 1882 elections; what this statement tried to conceal was that his support now came from the Center and the Right. The first socialist was already in parliament, and the various bourgeois groups therefore had a joint interest in making common cause. Speeches by Depretis at Stradella and by Minghetti at Legnano implied that their respective parliamentary groups had been transformed into a new government majority. From both sides came the suggestion that moderates on either side should merge during a transitional period, until new issues had arisen and a "normal opposition" could be restored.

Other people were more doubtful, and while agreeing that transformism might help by shuffling the old parties which had lost their reason for existence, yet deplored that no new parties were arising to replace them. But even Fortunato who took this view could not say where these new parties ought to be found, and the parliamentary situation of an amorphous government coalition of *ministeriali* opposed by a few miscellaneous *anti-ministeriali* was soon so generally accepted that the word transformism lost some of its pejorative significance. In a speech to parliament in 1883, the conservative Serena said that *trasformismo* had destroyed the Left; at which Crispi contradicted him and said that it had rather destroyed the Right; and the parliamentary records mention that an anonymous voice, which may serve for that of Clio herself, interposed that it had killed them both.

Depretis's tactical alliance with Minghetti alienated many of his left-wing colleagues, and Zanardelli and Baccarini led those who blamed him for abandoning the principles and the party by which he had risen to power. They contended that he was confusing issues simply in order to retain office, and thereby retarding the nation's political education. Depretis replied that he had not altered his views in the least, but that he had to accept the alliance of those members of the Right who came over to adopt his program. For good measure he added that he would never "make a criterion of government out of the topography of the Chamber," and that the word "Left" was now an archaism which had lost its meaning. Zanardelli and Baccarini therefore resigned from the government in May 1883, and joined with the "historic Left" of Crispi, Nicotera, and Cairoli to form what was called in jest the Pentarchy.

It was the failure of this Pentarchy to make good its high-sounding principles which did most to substantiate the attitude of Depretis. The irascible and ambitious Nicotera fell in public esteem when for an imaginary offence he spat on a junior minister and forced him to a duel behind the Castel Sant'Angelo, a barbarous as well as an illegal occasion. Nicotera was to show himself quite ready to treat with the conservatives Sella and Di Rudinì if he could thus reach office, and Crispi too, who while in opposition had insisted that parties should not be confused, was shortly to make confusion worse confounded. Crispi used these words in parliament when criticizing the transformism of Depretis: "Since 1878 we have had no political parties in Italy . . . only political men and groups, and each group, instead of comprehending an order of ideas, has been just an association of individuals whose opinions have constantly changed. This state of affairs has been actively encouraged by the government. In the meantime I stood apart, with a few friends and firmly held beliefs which were not just personal to myself. With the elections of 1882, the disorders of the Chamber penetrated into the country at large. The candidates did not form up in parties with definite programs, since they had no principles to defend, but were possessed only of the intention to re-enter parliament."

Crispi was unconsciously criticizing himself, for in his turn he separated from Nicotera, Cairoli, and Depretis despite the fact that he had lately been their colleague and was to join Depretis again in 1887. The wizard of Stradella had so melted all existing groups that Crispi, as soon as he found it a hindrance to advancement, gave up trying to reconstitute the historic Left. Only the twenty deputies of the *estrema sinistra* under Bertani, and after Bertani's death in 1886 under Cavallotti, had no intention of compromising with this parliamentary game of ins and outs.

Of the old Right, the major part under Minghetti had associated with the government coalition in 1882. A somewhat more extreme group under Bonghi and Spaventa was still independent, and so was a faction of the Center Right under Di Rudinì, which included Pelloux, Sonnino, Giolitti, and some forty others. This latter group opened negotiation with the Pentarchy, making the condition that Cairoli with his foreign policy of "clean hands" should be replaced by the more assertive Crispi in its leadership. Not that there was any point of principle upon which they disagreed with Depretis—unless it were the dubious expedients used by the minister of finance, Magliani, to cover his losses. Since the grist tax had gone and expenditure had by no means been lowered to balance this loss, Magliani tried to conceal some expenses under the heading of capital investment. *Finanza alla Magliani* became a byword, and critics here had a target which it was hard to miss.

Depretis in the eleven years after 1876 showed himself a master of tactics and expedients, placid, subtle, with an infinite capacity for assimilating other political groups, able to mold parliament almost at will. Nothing had been seen like this since the death of that other great Piedmontese statesman, Cavour. The chief gift of Depretis to Italy was efficient administration, under which some liberal reforms were unobtrusively carried out without the surface of politics being ruffled by too much violent controversy. In foreign as in domestic policy his natural instinct was, as he put it, to open his umbrella when he saw a cloud on the horizon, and wait till it had passed. He developed the tactic of forestalling parliamentary defeat by timely resignation, and successively in 1883, 1884, 1885, and 1887 resigned so as to leave himself free to change direction and remold his coalition. In one such *rimpasto* he readily accepted as a minister General Ricotti, who had been last in office with the Right. When he formed his eighth and final cabinet in April 1887, he dropped Generals di Robilant and Ricotti of the Right and took on Crispi and Zanardelli of the Left. Crispi in opposition had not stinted his criticisms of Magliani, but now had no qualms about becoming his colleague, and the other deputies had lost their capacity for surprise at this sort of tergiversation. By collaborating again with the foxy Depretis after ten years out of office, Crispi abandoned the independent Left and entered the system of *trasformismo,* and he thus marked himself out as the successor to Depretis when the latter died later in the year.

༄

In August 1887, at the age of sixty-seven, this extraordinary man became prime minister at last. Crispi belonged to an Albanian family which had long since emigrated to Sicily, and his grandfather had been a priest in the Greek Orthodox Church. Admirers claimed he was a sincere, high-minded politician, and certainly he was a hero to men as diverse as Carducci, King Umberto, and Mussolini. He was undeniably a great patriot who had served his country in bitter years of conspiracy and exile.

It was nevertheless Crispi's misfortune to be governed too exclusively by motives of personal and national dignity. He lacked balance and serenity, and was moody, secluded, and taciturn, as well as fiery and quick to anger. Like many Sicilians he was proud and oversensitive to criticism. He could be grossly discourteous, not only to the press and to parliamentary opponents, but to foreign statesmen, and his rudeness and indifference to other people helped to make him a thoroughly bad influence in foreign affairs. He was also simple-minded to a degree, and could be provoked to action by the improbable suspicion that the Sicilian socialists were in alliance with Czarist Russia, or that France planned a surprise attack on Genoa. It must be added that well-founded charges of political corruption and personal immorality were made against him. A notorious scandal developed when he abandoned his former mistress Rosalia Montmasson who had sailed with him among Garibaldi's famous Thousand, and on this and other matters he received much abuse and denigration from his many personal enemies. But his force of character was such that he went from strength to strength until a disastrous military defeat in Ethiopia caused his ignominious disappearance from public life in 1896.

Crispi's politics were nothing if not personal to himself. When asked in the 1860's whether he was a Mazzinian or a Garibaldian, he had replied, "Neither, I am Crispi." He it was who had led the retreat from republicanism with the much-quoted slogan that "the monarchy unites us, the republic would divide us." Out of office he at first sat well over to the Left in parliament, and on many points saw eye to eye with the *estrema,* since along with Nicotera and Cairoli he had both a Garibaldian and even a Mazzinian past. Like the much more ingratiating and persuasive Cavallotti, he remained radical and anticlerical, however much he differed from other radicals over foreign policy and social reform. Crispi in his time had fought for internal liberties against the omnipotence of the state and had campaigned for an elective Senate and universal suffrage. He was, indeed, always to remain a volcanic revolutionary by temperament, but he partly matured into a political conservative once he had to defend the position which his great talents and energy had won him.

Although theoretically he had believed in freedom and the alternation of well-defined parties after the English model, Crispi in practice used dictatorial means to reform his country at home and to strengthen it abroad. Full of admiration for Bismarck, he became a confirmed believer in paternal government, anxious to increase the power of the throne "lest parliament should become a tyrant and the cabinet its slave." This ex-republican thus began to apotheosize the monarchy, and he had grandiose ideas about building a splendid royal palace in Rome. But before long the real tyrant was clearly none other than Crispi himself, who would lightly dispatch troops to quell labor unrest, or rudely suspend Prince Torlonia from the mayoralty of Rome for daring to congratulate the Pope on his jubilee. It was typical of him that, like Cavour, he gave little power and responsibility to his subordinates: when over seventy he still ran three major departmental ministries as well as the premiership, and his colleagues have described how he bullied his cabinets. Though he had condemned transformism as the ruin of parliament, in 1888 he dismissed his minister of education, Coppino, in favor of Boselli from the old Right. He lavishly purchased the support of the press, paying particular attention to the Stefani news agency, and this same habit of mind led him to explain English unfriendliness by the supposition that he must have spent too little on bribing the *Times*.

Nevertheless, during this first spell of three and a half years in office, Crispi went only part of the way toward setting up a Bismarckian chancellorship. Though he became more and more autocratic in practice, at heart he believed in his own form of liberalism. He had probably been sincere in his reply of November 1877 to an accusation of dictatorialism: "Italy is a country with too solid a foundation of liberty to tolerate a dictatorship, and whoever might dare to attack her liberties, whether from the Right or the Left, would meet a resistance from the great majority of Italians such as would foil all his attempts." Gradually, however, he was to come around to Garibaldi's view that only strong action would hustle a corrupt and ineffective parliament along the path of reform.

Crispi's government introduced many liberal measures. There was the Public Health Act of 1888, a long-overdue prison reform, and the further extension into local government of the elective principle. In 1889 Zanardelli's civil code of law supplemented the penal code of 1865, and among other things set up special tribunals for redress against abuses by the administration, and at last allowed a limited right to strike—this new legal code was not replaced until the 1930's. Crispi also reformed the numerous charitable institutions run by the Church. He himself, like so many of the liberals, was a freethinker who died unreconciled to the Church, but he firmly believed in the "usefulness" of religion among the people, and made greater efforts than some Christians to solve the impasse with the Vatican. Perhaps these various reforms, the parliamentary situation being what it was, might not have been so easily effected without someone of Crispi's mettle to force them through.

If his ideas were liberal but his methods violent, if finally he came to rule by martial law, the explanation is partly that he was corrupted by power, partly that he became more cynical about his fellow citizens, partly that people suddenly recognized in him an agent for releasing certain of their own subconscious desires. According to Fortunato's melancholy dictum: "We Italians are authoritarian to the very marrow of our bones, and by tradition, habit, and education we have become conditioned either to command too much or to obey too much. We may learn from books and from foreigners that liberty is something to be desired for its own sake, but we never, absolutely never, feel that this is true deep down in our hearts." The new criminal code was thus never submitted to parliament in its final text, but the government was simply empowered to draft and promulgate it by royal decree. Parliament likewise gave Crispi the authority to determine by decree what were the powers of the prime minister, and how many other ministers there should be. He was allowed to raise taxes by decree, and have them retrospectively confirmed by statute, and his successor had to ask for a bill of indemnity to cover expenditure incurred by Crispi without warrant.

This was the very pattern of Italian parliamentary dictatorship, and it differed only in degree whether under Cavour, Depretis, Crispi, or Giolitti, or even under Mussolini during his first years of power. The deputies themselves were usually grateful when a man of action cut through their interminable debates, arbitrated their conflicting views, and relieved them of responsibility for unpopular decisions.

19 Irredentism and Nationalist Fervor

A man of Crispi's vanity and energy could do particular damage in foreign relations, and his germanophile sentiments did not pass long without criticism. Those who had fought three wars of independence against the Habsburgs sharply protested when the king exchanged courtesies and decorations with the enemy, and was even seen garbed as an Austrian colonel in Vienna. Right-wing newspapers attacked the Triple Alliance as a breach of tradition and a bar to Italy's freedom of movement, while on the Left Zanardelli was not alone in preferring liberal England and republican France to militarist Germany.

Crispi's rejoinder was to call public opinion a poor judge of foreign policy. This was true enough, and yet any foreign policy inevitably lost something in strength if unsupported by popular opinion. The public was largely uninstructed in foreign affairs: occasional Green Books were published, but, as Petruccelli said, one might understand more before reading a Green Book than after, so deeply buried was the relevant information under insignificant dispatches. Moreover, parliament was asked to comment only after treaty commitments had already been made by the king and his government.

༄

The revolt against the Austrian alliance received special support from those bent on the acquisition of Trent and Trieste, and in 1882, the very year of the *Triplice,* the martyrdom of Oberdan gave a great fillip to these irredentists. Oberdan was a republican from Trieste, who had deserted from the Austrian army and taken refuge in Italy. In September 1882 he went back to try to assassinate the Emperor Franz Joseph, believing that the cause of Trieste needed a martyr, and hoping that his attempt might ruin the treaty which King Umberto, "the Austrian colonel," had just signed. Before he could carry out his horrible design he was arrested and executed, but, so sensitive was public feeling, this would-be assassin became a legend and a symbol, and his action took its place in Italian history books as an admirable deed of patriotism.

Certainly, the attempt put Trieste on the map for many of Oberdan's countrymen who hitherto had not heard of it. Most people would have assumed that the absorption of Rome in 1870 had completed Italian unification, not foreseeing that this very act might generate an appetite for still further aggrandizement. Sonnino in the *Rassegna Settimanale* of May 1881 had denied that Italy possessed any serious claims on Trent or Trieste. But a new generation was witnessing patriotic sentiment almost imperceptibly developing into nationalism and imperialism. Not long after 1870, deputies were saying publicly that Italians would shortly find other provinces worthy of redemption, and the ex-Garibaldian, Imbriani, popularized the phrase *"terre irredente."*

There was no doubt that the war of 1866 had left the northeastern frontier strategically and ethnically defective. The Trentino was a large Austrian wedge driven southward through the Dolomites, and this exposed the peninsula to invasion. Most inhabitants of this wedge spoke Italian and recognized their close links with Italy; yet their separation from Venice in 1866 left them too weak numerically to stop Austria progressively Germanizing the province. The Brenner railroad, the Alpine mountaineering clubs, and the *Volksbund* all helped to foster Austrian influence there, and German language, education, and trade were on the increase. To the countrymen of Goethe and Wagner, the *lago di Garda* was the *Gardasee.* None too soon, rival Alpine societies were established in the Italian interest, with rival guides and alternative mountain refuges to keep the Italian element organized and self-conscious. When the German element in 1891 erected a bronze statue of Walther von der Vogelweide in Bozen (Bolzano), the Italians responded with a monument in Trent to Dante. Battisti—as later the young De Gasperi—represented the province in the imperial parliament of Vienna, and voiced the desire to separate Trent from the rest of the Austrian Tyrol. But this separatist movement was checked by the Triple Alliance, and had to wait until Austria became the national enemy again in the different circumstances of 1915.

Agitation was as yet even less strong for Trieste and the Istrian Peninsula, and still less for Fiume or the rest of the Dalmatian coast along which the medieval Venetian settlements had implanted strong traditions of Italian culture. On ethnic and historical grounds Italy had much the same right to Trieste as to Trent, but strategically it was less urgent, and only when Austria had made Trieste into a great emporium of commerce did it become desirable in itself and a threat to the trade of Venice. Mazzini and Cavour had agreed in hoping that one day Trieste would be Italian, but the paramount obstacles were first that Trieste was an Italian town in the middle of a Slav countryside, and second that Greater Germany found it her best outlet to the Mediterranean. Not only was Trieste the only port in the Austrian empire with a big export trade, but it was a center of finance and banking, and an excellent base for any advance into the Balkans. Thus, there was a determined refusal by Austrians to recognize the predominant Italian element in Trieste, and an attempt to increase the German and subsequently the Slav elements in its population.

Since their naval defeat at Lissa in 1866, Italians had been very sensitive in the northern Adriatic, and though Crispi tried to divert attention from this danger area, the wave of nationalism which accompanied his premiership carried a momentum which he could do little to control. Lissa also marked a stage in the southward advance of Germanism, and yet the Slavs were bound to be more of a danger in the long run. The urban pockets of *italianità* in Trieste, Fiume, Gorizia, and Pola were gradually becoming submerged, as the advance of democracy and national consciousness told in favor of the Serbs and Croats. Italians had long dominated the area, being rich and owning the land, but the Slav middle classes were increasing all the time, and even some of the peasants were beginning to become literate. Slav schoolmasters were an important force and were often allied with the Church. More and more town councils gave up Italian as their official language, and after 1870 no longer could one be sure that most newspapers in Trieste and Ragusa (Dubrovnik) would remain Italian. Italians were edged out of the best jobs, and they were meeting this challenge by learning Croat and becoming slavized themselves. The process was natural enough, but it produced an understandable bellicosity and touchiness on both sides.

The activities of Battisti in the southern Tyrol, and of Oberdan and Barzilai at Trieste, were the most striking signs of a new outward-turning nationalism after 1880. Advocates of the Austrian alliance tried to divert this nationalism into colonial wars, or into the more remote claims which could be made upon Corsica, Nice, and Malta. The use of Italian in the law courts of Malta was a privilege jealously watched, though it was manifestly weakening with the passage of time. Even in the Swiss Canton Ticino, Italian culture was carefully tended, and schools and newspapers preserved against the possible day when Switzerland might break up. In these and other marginal areas, irredentist movements were kept alive among discontented elements in the population.

There was no general doctrine of irredentism, but *ad hoc* arguments were devised to serve each immediate political purpose. The geographical argument of natural frontiers was advanced for Southern Tyrol, and held to outweigh the fact that so many of the inhabitants of this area were German by speech and historical tradition. In Dalmatia the very opposite proposition was used, namely that Italian communities must be absorbed wherever they were, despite all geographical difficulties.

Corsica and Nice were claimed on the historical ground that they had recently belonged to Italy, while with Trent and Malta such historical arguments were deliberately and understandably rejected. None of the irredentists showed any comprehension of the German claim to Trieste or the Slav interest in Fiume and Dalmatia. They preferred to assume that the Italian interest was incontestably superior.

§●

The realist Depretis, who looked upon these irredentist fancies as merely *"des vieux cancans,"* had formally renewed the Triple Alliance just before his death. Italy was then in a good bargaining position, what with the existing unfriendliness between Russia and Austria and between Germany and France. In fact Bismarck was so concerned over General Boulanger and French nationalism that he himself had opened discussions for renewing the alliance. Profiting from this, Italy obtained special assurances that she would receive full compensation if Austria advanced in the Balkans. The Catholic emperor in Vienna also undertook not to play off the Pope against Italy, and Depretis received the promise of German support if France ever tried to extend her dominion in the Mediterranean through Morocco and Tripoli. But the treaty remained defensive only, and those Italians were in error who subsequently claimed that Germany had accepted an obligation to back Italy's policy of conquest in Africa.

Crispi was far more of a "triplicist" than Depretis, and in general he had more interest in foreign policy than any politician since Cavour. When he became prime minister in 1887 he also took over in person the foreign office as well as the home office, and within two months was visiting Bismarck. He had the effrontery to assure the German chancellor that an Italian expeditionary force was ready for war with France, and that (so runs his diary) by April he would be able to put half a million men into the field, not counting reserves and the militia. His conversion from irredentism seemed to be complete, since he added that he considered Austria's existence necessary for the balance of power, and he was sure that Italy would prove a faithful ally to her.

Within a year Crispi was once more at Friedrichsruh. Like Mussolini later, he built his policy on German restlessness and the Germany army, hoping that Italy would gain from any revision on the map of Europe which Bismarck might make. In 1888 he presented to parliament a request for emergency expenditure on army and navy, and partly as a result the fiscal year 1888–89 was the worst for Italian finances since 1870. He contemplated a joint penetration of the Balkans against the

Slavs, and in 1889, to curry favor with Austria, he dissolved the Roman "Committee for Trent and Trieste." The following year, when his colleague, Seismit-Doda, failed to protest against an irredentist speech made during a banquet he was attending, Crispi first tried to make the offending minister resign, and then simply dismissed him by telegram. Yet Crispi did not stop subsidizing the irredentists on the secret service account. Privately, he hoped that the Austro-Hungarian empire would one day break up, to Italy's profit, but he did not believe she should anticipate that event. Meanwhile, as he added in an angry oration at Florence in October 1890, irredentism was the enemy of the unity that Italians had so far achieved; nationalism should not be taken too far as a rule of politics, or else Austria, France, England, Switzerland, all the countries who possessed Italian minorities, would be forced to retort in self-defense.

What chiefly mattered to him in foreign policy was prestige. He proudly claimed of himself at the end of 1888 that "a man has appeared who considers Italy the equal of any other nation, and intends to see that her voice shall be heard and respected." This pose as the leader of a great and powerful country in the end deceived even himself into thinking that it was the truth. In 1889 he fabricated an imaginary war scare against France, and was ingenuous enough to inform England that the French navy was moving on Spezia. A British admiral was at once dispatched with his fleet to Genoa, and on arrival found that Crispi had acted on an unsubstantiated rumor from a secret agent in the Vatican. He had simply imagined the French threat, and perhaps he was trying to make the world believe that his disastrous denunciation of the French commercial treaty had been justified after all.

Crispi's irritability and alarmism kept the whole country tense and were to end in personal and national tragedy. The explanation is in part that he needed to divert attention from unrest in Sicily and some notorious bank scandals at Rome. As these were endangering his majority, he tried to consolidate his coalition by pretending that the country was in danger. In meeting these imaginary threats he had few scruples about the use of martial law, and maintained that opposition by the very fact of being opposition must be factious and unpatriotic. Every means would be legitimate provided he could give Italians the reality or the illusion of national greatness. As he told parliament, "for twenty years we have gone on merely debating, Left against Right, and forgetting the really important questions which if solved would give to our nation not only power but the reputation and consequences of power." Loud cries of *"bravo, benissimo"* greeted this statement.

In fulfillment of his warlike intentions, Crispi did not confine himself to picking a quarrel with France. The very first month of his premiership he made overtures in London for a military convention against Russia. He might have known the almost insuperable difficulty of making Britain commit herself on the Continent, but he seemed determined to fight a war somewhere and be on the winning side. He began to talk of frontier rectifications, of "Italian rights in the Mediterranean," of "the necessity to expand," and after much rhetorical repetition he managed to indoctrinate the ruling elite with the glamor of imperialism. It was a lesson which Mussolini learned from him later, and it was Mussolini who dubbed Crispi the forerunner of resurgent fascist Italy.

The imperialists argued that Italy was compelled into a more active foreign policy by the French advance in Algeria and Tunis, by the British in Cyprus and Egypt, and the Austrian in Bosnia, for the distribution of power in the Mediterranean was being altered against her. It was unfortunate that Italy and Germany emerged as nation states just when an industrial revolution, accompanied by an enormous development in communications and popular education, put unprecedented power at the service of aggravated feelings of national self-sufficiency and self-worship. The capture of Rome, moreover, had awakened memories of imperial expansion. Despite her astonishingly successful career of advancement, the new Italy very soon began to conceive of herself as a have-not power, and a nation of her quality was said to need colonies if she were to keep up appearances. Her old war cry for "the liberation of subject peoples" might still apply to border zones like Trieste or Trent, but it was inapposite in the case of Ethiopia or Albania, where something more exalted and virile seemed to be required.

The Triple Alliance, the penetration of Eritrea, the tariff war with France after 1887, all reflected the belief that Italy should play the great power. In fairness to Crispi it must be recognized that others were here ahead of him. Pasquale Turiello, for instance, was arguing that, since the fact of unification had not yet sunk deeply into popular consciousness, military enterprise abroad should be encouraged in order to bind the country more firmly and reinvigorate the national character. One of Turiello's books was significantly entitled *National Virility and the Colonies*. In others he described the ruthless and inevitable fight for existence between nations, and demonstrated to his own satisfaction that peace and international concord were as illusory as democracy and representative government. The weak not only did but should go to the wall, since the future was to the strong. Nations had to find colonies and pervade large areas with their language and culture, or else they would disappear in the struggle for life.

Another writer who carried weight with the new generation was the brilliant but corrupt and unstable Rocco de Zerbi. He, too, was a man of the Right and an advocate of Italian imperialism. He also was the deputy who was most immediately implicated in the bank scandals. De Zerbi had written: "I speak of my own country in bitterness, for I do not see her eager to carry herself forward to power, but only content with her own smallness. She does not know what she wants, or, if ever she does, she has no idea how to subordinate everything to that end." It was De Zerbi who developed the theory that Italy needed purging and rejuvenation in what he termed a "bath of blood."

§❧

It was to be expected that many people would react strongly against this aggressive rhetorical nationalism, and against Crispi its representative. The more respectable conservatives, for example that other Sicilian the Marquis di Rudinì, feared and despised Crispi as a conspirator and a mischief-maker. Others objected to his anticlericalism, and Prinetti and Colombo, the political representatives of Milanese industry, were aghast at his lavish expenditure on the army and colonies. Meanwhile, his own former friends on the Left had been shattered by personal and ideological differences into a confusion of splinter groups. Crispi's coalition was therefore vulnerable on both its wings, and this helped to counteract his extremist policy of repression at home and conquest abroad.

The weakness of this coalition, as also had been true of Cavour's, was that it was a personal majority, heterogeneous, with no basic agreement on policy. When Left and Right combined against him, Crispi began to talk of trying to build or rebuild a party system and so to recreate a firm and principled opposition. Yet he believed to the last that he would go on being accepted as the necessary man, and in practice continued to manipulate groups in a personal coalition revolving around "the minister's friends." This earned him more criticism from Bonghi and others who had supported transformism as a temporary tactic but who found it intolerable as an end in itself.

Despite a considerable victory in the elections of November 1890, Crispi tripped up when in January 1891 he rashly upbraided the conservatives in parliament with having left Italy disarmed before 1876. He even accused them of having compelled the country to follow "a policy of servility to the foreigner." This was one of those positive and

unequivocal statements which were illegitimate in a transformist political system depending on delicate finesse and compromise coalitions. It
shows how Crispi's tactlessness made him at best a mediocre politician
in this milieu, for he could not avoid showing resentment, nor could he
restrain his desire to wound and taunt.

On this occasion, so unworthy was his remark that one of his own
ministers walked straight out of the Chamber, and Crispi was challenged
by a surprise motion of no confidence. He thought fit to warn the deputies that "your vote will decide whether Italy desires a strong government, or whether she intends to return to the kind of cabinet which has
brought discredit on our country by its hesitation and inconsistencies."
To his astonishment, parliament and Italy did not agree with his own
opinion of himself, and despite his large majority in the recent election,
he had to resign in favor of Di Rudinì. For several years he remained
out of power.

20 Agriculture and Industry about 1880

Some of the finer and more disinterested minds in Italy were deeply
disturbed by the excessive concentration of politicians upon problems
of foreign policy and parliamentary tactics. Jacini, for instance, repeatedly reminded parliament that agriculture provided by far the most
urgent questions for a nation like Italy, and Sonnino insisted that the
moral and physical welfare of the common people should be the first
concern of the privileged classes, even if this meant spending on their
peasants money which could have bought an extra carriage for their
wives or hired a box at La Scala. Sonnino made practical suggestions
about forming peasant co-operatives, and he hoped that local administration could be reformed to ensure that the interests of the whole community and not of a single class should prevail.

These conservative reformers were thus in agreement with Bertani
and the other radicals who agitated for a parliamentary investigation
into agriculture. Bertani's speech on this topic in 1872 had shocked the
deputies by describing how, almost within sight of Rome, fifteen thou-

sand people were living in caves like Stone Age lake dwellers. But neither the commission then appointed, nor individual investigators like Sonnino, Franchetti, and Fortunato, met with much enthusiasm during their inquiries, because the conscience of the nation was as yet barely touched, and farmers generally were afraid to give accurate evidence about agricultural conditions lest this should be designed to raise their tax liability.

The parliamentary commission began work in 1877. Its report in fifteen volumes was presented in 1885, and painted a depressing picture. Agriculture was at a standstill. Landowners were consuming their entire revenue and had little margin of profit for emergency reserves or for new capital to put back into the land. Even the extinction of communal rights of pasture and wood gathering, and of the rights of way for the long-distance migration of herds—an extinction economically justified—momentarily took away the livelihood of many people. The breaking up of communal lands and of the estates held by ecclesiastical and charitable trusts had not produced a stabilizing class of peasant proprietors, but had rather benefited existing landlords. Local authorities had habitually defied the law and allowed the commons to be enclosed by landowners who then would pay a merely nominal rent. In fact the number of people owning land declined substantially between the censuses of 1861 and 1901.

Agricultural strikes and the forcible occupation of land by the peasants continued spasmodically, and kept alive an ominous sense of alarm. There was doubtless a crying need to improve conditions of work and living, and yet the remedy proposed by the radicals of distributing land among the peasants was hardly economic, because modern methods of reaping, threshing, and making oil and wine needed ever greater resources of capital. Those who, by force or consent, got possession of some small plot, frequently had to surrender it again since they could not afford the expenses of farming, and even the system of *mezzadria* or sharecropping began to fail now that an ever-increasing amount of capital and tools was required.

When times were so hard for the more prosperous peasants, not even a well-intentioned parliamentary commission could suggest an alternative remedy for the landless poor. Corbino discovered from the census returns of 1881 that out of every thousand inhabitants there were only forty-six *mezzadri* and fifty-nine peasant proprietors. The majority were simple laborers, with luck employed for half the year, whose standard of living was minimal, and who gained nothing when higher prices later brought prosperity to those who owned land. There was no public maintenance for those unable to labor, no public provision for the able-bodied poor, while the nationalization of ecclesiastical charities meant that more money was spent on their administration and less on actual relief than the Church had formerly spent.

Bertani said that there were two races of human beings in Italy, those who ate white bread and those who ate black. Most of the peasants rarely if ever had meat; their food often consisted entirely of rice, beans, bread, *pasta,* and polenta made from corn. Imbriani drew attention to the fact that only 203 out of the 3,672 Sicilian sulphur miners drafted for military service in 1881–84 were fit enough for acceptance, and much the same proportion might have been found among the grotto dwellers of the Agro Romano, almost all of whom suffered from chronic malaria.

This disease continued to spread rapidly after 1860, as deforestation encouraged the breeding of mosquitoes, and regular fevers were still thought inevitable and natural. Only at the end of the century was malaria found to be curable and controllable. Another plague on the increase was pellagra, a deficiency disease caused by a starchy diet, of which there were over a hundred thousand reported cases in 1881. Cholera epidemics killed 55,000 people between 1884 and 1887, and only then did people discover that they sprang directly from slum conditions. A belated start was made with the *sventramento* or gutting of the old city of Naples, and giving it adequate drains and water. But Sonnino was able to show that the state loan made for this purpose was perverted by speculators, so that behind the fine and showy main streets new slums were built and a larger number of people fitted into the same disease-ridden area.

§❧

One of the chief obstacles to progress in agriculture was the heavy indebtedness of the state and the consequently high taxation. Minghetti in 1876 had at last given the national accounts an illusion of balancing, though only by excluding expenditure on railroad construction; yet it was said at the time that this surplus on revenue had ruined the country by the excessive taxation which it implied. The wars of the *risorgimento* had not been paid for. The vast deficits of the years 1861–76 still encumbered the national revenue, and the confiscated ecclesiastical lands had by now been sold with little to show for them. Railways, roads, ships, armaments, and schools, all had to be provided in excess of current ability to pay, and it was hard to know the exact point where this became too risky to be advisable.

When the Left came to power in 1876, balancing the budget was given a much lower priority. New expenditure was taken on lightly under an excessive illusion about national strength, and yet Cairoli attempted to repeal the grist tax and so diminish revenue. This levy on the grinding of wheat had been deliberately aimed at the poor, who both consumed more bread than the rich and also spent a far higher proportion of their income on farinaceous foods. Financially this tax was so necessary that the Senate at first refused to allow its repeal, but the government showed resolution in naming over fifty new senators, and it was allowed to pass when the elections of 1880 confirmed the Left in office. Without sixty million lire a year from the grist tax, however, and with a reduced tax on salt, the state would again be running at a loss, and the minister of finance, Grimaldi, resigned in protest.

Unfortunately, almost without a break between 1878 and 1888, the treasury was controlled by Magliani who allowed Depretis carelessly to take on new expenditure without balancing this by more taxation. Magliani was the author of a book on monetary theory, and a professional illusionist with figures. Closely connected with Hambro and Rothschild, he helped restore Italian credit abroad, but could not entirely conceal the annual deficit which began again in 1885 and by 1889 was 238 million lire a year. Finally, in 1888 Magliani made some effort to raise taxes so as to meet the deficit, but this would have lost the Left too much popularity, and rather than force the issue he resigned. Agriculture suffered indirectly from this deficit, for, as the wealth of the country lay predominantly in land, it was assumed that the land tax could remain indefinitely at its high level. In 1883 Magliani also allowed the banks to resume payment in specie, and this had hit farmers by sending up the value of the lira, cheapening agricultural imports still further and discouraging exports.

§❧

But the agricultural slump was due only in part to government action or inaction. Its fundamental cause was the lack of capital which was needed for effecting the switch from subsistence farming to production for an international market. As railroad routes through the Mont Cenis and Brenner passes opened Italy to foreign competition and wider price fluctuations, the more backward parts of the country lost the artificial protection which had insulated them. Contacts with the wider world brought land into production during the American Civil War and afterward which was only profitable at scarcity prices, and severe losses were caused when peace caused another contraction of demand. Again, the new Suez Canal brought an influx of rice and silk from the East which undercut two staple domestic products.

When steam navigation made cargo shipping cheaper during the

1880's, freight charges fell by over 60 per cent, and the cheap cereals which flooded into Europe caused the most severe crisis of all. From 30 lire a quintal in January 1880, the price of wheat fell in several years to 22 lire. The acreage under cereals had been too large, and although poverty made Italians consume more flour than any other country, the yield per acre was little more than a third of that in England. America and Russia produced grain far more cheaply, and as with cotton, flax, and vegetable dyes, this foreign competition ruined many domestic growers. Imports made food cheaper, and in the long run forced Italian farming to become more efficient, but the immediate effect was catastrophic.

It was not an unmixed blessing that the vine disease of phylloxera in France simultaneously put an artificial premium on Italian grapes and made Italy for a while the chief wine-producing country in Europe. Between 1874 and 1883 the area under vines increased from five to over seven million acres, displacing fruit trees, walnuts, and chestnuts, and even century-old olive plantations in Apulia and Sicily. Annual production of wine went up in this period from 27 to 36 million hectoliters, and there was a great increase in export to France, where the strength and color of Italian wines made them suitable *vins de coupage* for blending.

Then in 1888 a commercial rupture with France suddenly reversed this trend and caused a crisis of overproduction. Southern Italy was especially vulnerable, where the strong sun and cheap labor had made new vineyards particularly extensive. As the expansion had been paid for by expensive borrowing, and had often meant the destruction of olive groves and other long-term investments, an explosive situation was generated. The diseased French vineyards had now been restocked with hardier American varieties, and the Algerian vineyards also came into heavy production just when Italy herself fell a victim to phylloxera. The new plantations had not been accompanied by improvements in wine manufacture and the cultivation of reliable markets. Too late it was found that the manufacture of wine for export was becoming too technical a process for small growers who knew nothing of foreign tastes or of how to maintain a constant standard. As a result, prices fell abruptly and there were numerous bankruptcies all over the South.

Similar difficulties were met with olives and citrus fruit. The yield of olive plantations was irregular, partly owing to ignorance about pruning: trees were often pruned only every third year, mainly as a way of gathering firewood. The oil produced was known to be too heavy for most tastes, yet nothing was done to change it. The difficulties which then ensued from the increasing competition of seed oils were also felt more particularly in the South. Seventy per cent of Italy's oranges and lemons came from Sicily, and it was therefore again in the South that a threefold increase in output of citrus fruits between 1885 and 1905 left Italy with an unsalable surplus. Growers in California had better fruit, better sales organizations, and more scientific methods of transportation. Italy as a backward country, and in particular its more backward provinces, was bound to suffer when measured against more progressive and more favored nations overseas, and the slump which followed this agricultural crisis was to have important political repercussions.

The political troubles of the 1890's were partly connected also with the development of Italian industry. Here it is difficult to find convincing statistics, whether for production, consumption of raw materials, the amount of mechanization, or the number of operatives employed. Facts were sometimes falsified to obtain increased state protection, or to avoid a feared increase in ratable value. There was a national census every ten years, but the different criteria employed each time often make the figures incomparable. The census sometimes included under "productive population" people over the age of eleven, sometimes those over nine; some regions reported women working part-time in the fields as productive, others not; peasant families engaged in both farming and weaving could be either agricultural or industrial. Even the official estimates of the actual area of Italy varied.

Up to and beyond the imposition of national tariffs in 1878 and 1887, industry was still largely built on independent craftsmen working in their own homes. Even in the North there was perhaps no single region which could have been called predominantly industrial, and many or most industrial workers spent much of their time on the land. In the language of the people, *industria* had rather the meaning of ploughing or cheese making, and an *industriale* was a workman engaged in these occupations.

The railroad network did not create what could be called a nationwide market until the late 1870's. Only then was there appearing a demand for industrial goods and a possibility of local specialization, though the anomalous "medieval" immunities had still not been abolished in the free ports of Leghorn, Ancona, Venice, and Messina. The most consistent grievance presented to the Royal Commission on Industry in 1871–72 was that the municipal octrois or duties on consumption hindered internal trade. These local tariffs were unfortunately the chief item in the revenue of each commune, and they took the place of the restrictive regional customs barriers, which had rightly been abolished in 1859–61. For example, at Iglesias in Sardinia the commune took 15 per cent of the value of all local coal, and so made the smelting industry of the district unduly expensive.

One other complaint made in 1872 was that foreign industry had gained more than Italian from national unification. Of the locomotives in use in north Italy in 1878, 702 had been made abroad, and only 39 in Italy by the Ansaldo company. The railroad track was almost all imported, because the native steel industry was frail and diminutive, and competition on anything like equal terms was unthinkable. Raw materials and machinery were dearer in Italy than elsewhere, and labor, though much cheaper, was inexperienced and uneducated. A period of foreign tutelage was inevitable, and in the long run was highly beneficial, but it was frustrating to find that managers and foremen were sometimes Germans, Swiss, or Scotsmen.

The common people of Italy were too poor for there to be much effective demand for industrial products, and though peasants were beginning to sell increasingly in a cash market, too much of their earnings went to pay taxes and the interest on loans. Many town families lived on food which they themselves produced outside the city walls; bread was baked at home, and the spread of specialist retailers was still to come. The artisan was cushioned against industrial crises by his part-time employment in agriculture, and not until he was ready to forego this luxury were large factories possible. Yet another prerequisite of progress was a change in social habits, for the middle classes still thought the learned professions and clerical work to be far more estimable than commerce and industry.

The great advance in industry began somewhere around 1879. One sign is that in the following six years coal imports nearly doubled, until they stood at about three million tons annually. Giovanni Pirelli, the ex-Garibaldian volunteer, was beginning to create the rubber industry that still carries his name, and his first factory was built in 1872 at Milan. The railroad builder, Breda of Padua, set up the famous steelworks of Terni. In textiles there were Tosi of Legnano and the wool-masters of Vicenza and Biella, these industries being the first to gain from the tariff of 1878. Silk manufacture in particular, which had had a long history in Italy, already possessed the requisite skills and techniques and had its machines made at home.

The heavier industries grew up either near what few iron mines there were in Elba and the Val d'Aosta, or in later years where hydroelectric energy was easily obtained, as at Terni, or else where the proximity of seaports and ancillary mechanical industries offered special attractions as at Savona and Sestri in Liguria. Since the old iron foundries of Lombardy were being driven out of existence by foreign competitors, and as the existing ordnance factories at Brescia and Turin were too near the frontier for security, Admiral Brin had called on Breda to create a new armament industry at Terni. The chosen site was securely placed in Umbria, much nearer the new capital at Rome, and well supplied with water power from a tributary of the Tiber. Fitted out with the most modern equipment, this large complex of factories was much more able to compete with foreign production, even though it was only enabled to exist by generous and not always discriminating state patronage, and by heavy tariffs on imported pig iron.

The Terni steelworks were in production by 1886, a year after Depretis had persuaded the British firm of Armstrong to open a naval shipyard and cannon foundry at Pozzuoli. Only the hypothesis of war justified these armament works, and it soon became clear that efficiency and economy of production had been sacrificed to military requirements and the goal of self-sufficiency. A parasite industry had been conjured up at the expense of domestic consumers, and so irrational were the tariffs protecting it that (people used to say) metal was deliberately produced as scrap by foreign foundries for sale in Italy. As the industry in fact depended altogether on the state for its prosperity, it was from the first a corrupting influence, and it financed newspapers, deputies, and high-ranking officials in order to persuade the government that such a costly, artificial industry was necessary for the country's greatness and should be protected to the limit.

The liberal economists protested. So did those who wanted to imitate eighteenth-century Tuscany and renounce such disproportionate military expenditure. Many people felt that what Italy could afford would never be quite sufficient to guarantee her frontiers, and that her prestige in the world would not be the less for having fewer military pretensions. But though the industrialist Colombo in 1896 resigned from the cabinet rather than sanction extra military expenditure, it was politicians like Crispi with exaggerated notions of military greatness who were now in charge, and they were easily prevailed on by other less worthy industrialists who wanted the state to underwrite their rickety concerns and keep the armament industry employed.

୫୭

Similar reasons induced the government to subsidize the shipping industry, with much the same results. Steamships had in general begun to oust sail by 1860, in which year Garibaldi used paddle steamers for his

Sicilian venture. But although the Orlando brothers were then trying out the first Italian-built marine engine and experimenting with metal hulls, Italy owned the raw materials for wooden ships only, and therefore had to depend largely on foreign construction for ironclads. Italian shipyards still confined themselves almost exclusively to sailing ships, although iron steamers were bigger, faster, and more reliable. The merchant marine in 1871 had a million tons of sail, but only 32,000 tons of steam, and even the larger shipping companies could not afford the more expensive methods of construction. By 1880 there were still only 77,000 tons of steam navigation, and Italy had fallen to fifth place in Europe for gross tonnage. By the end of the century, says Volpe, 85 per cent of Italian imports and 70 per cent of her exports still traveled in foreign vessels, and her own ships were mostly bought secondhand from foreign companies.

The two biggest Italian shipping companies, Rubattino and Florio, were given subsidized government contracts in 1862, and in 1881 they were fused to form the *Navigazione Generale Italiana* which was to dominate Italian shipping for many years. In the same year a commission was appointed under Boselli to inquire into the state of the merchant marine, and on its recommendation the government in 1885 gave fifty-three million lire to subsidize shipbuilding, together with many tax exemptions. Half this sum was allocated to building sailing ships, since the industry was pressing hard to be preserved from the full blast of free competition. Steam finally overtook sail quantitatively in 1905, although most Italian steamships continued to be built in Great Britain. These bounties and subsidies were incidentally helping to keep inefficient techniques and practices alive.

It was different with the navy. For a time the Italian navy ranked third in the world by tonnage, and it was always the most efficient of the Italian fighting services. Cavour had been an enthusiastic naval minister, yet in 1861 the Italian navy consisted of only 117,000 tons all told, the largest ship being 3,800 tons. But the first two armor-plated ships for the navy were already being laid down in France. Perhaps not one of the capital ships engaged at Lissa had been built in Italy, but, with the construction of the *Duilio* and *Dandolo,* Italy by 1878 took the lead in developing naval ironclads—they were over 11,000 tons apiece and sailed at fifteen knots.

This was largely the work of Admiral Brin, minister of the navy under Depretis and Cairoli, and then again under Crispi and Di Rudinì. Brin's policy of increased expenditure on armaments met with wide approval, even though he did not always work through the normal parliamentary channels. There were only a few cynics who doubted the usefulness of this fine navy and stressed its huge cost. Nevertheless, as armor plate continued to become thicker, Italy's limited resources put her at an increasing disadvantage with other powers. The effort to hold her place was likely one day to prove too costly, as it also made war more probable and an expensive foreign policy less easy to avoid.

21 The Tariff War with France, 1887-1892

On top of all the other inherent difficulties of adjustment, the agricultural community was involved by the government in an extraneous tariff war with France, their chief customer. The revised Italian tariff of 1886–87, and the consequent repudiation of the French commercial treaty, precipitated the economic depression of 1887–90, and this was to trigger off a Sicilian revolution and a banking crisis which together shook Italian society to its foundations.

The north of Italy had gained considerably from Cavour's heavy reduction of customs duties. Inefficient industries had been weeded out, prices kept low, and commerce generally had prospered. There had been in 1878 a small increase in duties, but not enough to increase the cost of living very much. Depretis had at that moment been trying to reduce the price of bread by abolishing the grist tax, and did not wish to nullify this by putting additional import dues on foreign grain. He was not himself a champion of the doctrine that the national wealth could be increased by introducing protection, and he claimed that the 1878 tariff was in fact imposed only to augment the revenue.

And yet the free traders had opened the door against themselves by allowing this partial tariff. The government saw that a further increment in duties, as well as constituting a useful source of revenue, would provide a bargaining counter against foreign nations. Industrialists were increasingly sensitive to the pinch of competition, now made more acute by cheaper transportation, and as foreign markets were difficult to find, they wished at least to make a hedge around the domestic market as more of a monopoly for themselves.

A report on the great Milanese industrial fair of 1881 makes it clear that hardly one industry was without some claim for protection. No sooner had Cavour left the political scene than the silk manufacturers of Lombardy began a campaign for government assistance. The growing steel interests pointed to the existing French commercial treaties as the prime obstacle to their prosperity, and they received ample support from people who, out of misguided patriotism, wished to make the country more independent of foreign supplies. Some financiers with less worthy motives were ready to use tariffs for the purpose of speculation; other industrialists wanted protection simply because their industries were uneconomic, and either could not be made more competitive at all, or else could be improved only at a cost they would rather not pay. Soon the question was intricately involved with parliamentary politics, and by 1886 Depretis was forced to think that concession of higher duties might be the only way to maintain his majority. Pareto commented that the new scale of duties was designed less to build up strong industries than to reward the power groups which had supported or would support the government. Above all, this meant the steel industry, and hence placed a heavy burden on the Italian economy for many decades. It meant high coal imports which the country could ill afford, whereas the low-coal-using mechanical industries not only received less protection but now had to pay an uncompetitively high price for their iron and steel.

Among the groups thus seeking to make individual capital out of the community were those agriculturists hit by the depression or threatened in their domination over the home market. Producers of oil, wine, raw silk, fruit, and vegetables were on the whole anxious to have no import duties, because they had little competition to fear inside Italy, and yet liked to be able to export, so that they did not want to provoke foreigners to discriminate against Italian goods. But the big grain producers were a good deal more easily organized than other farmers and carried greater weight with the government because of their social position. According to the parliamentary discussions of 1885–86, the experts were agreed that agriculture generally would suffer from protection; yet many of the big landowners thought otherwise. They wanted protection for themselves, and were ready to support protection for industrialists too in a compact for mutual profit. This was an unholy and unwholesome alliance.

Among the specious arguments advanced was that any increase in duties could be rescinded when wheat prices returned to normal, and meanwhile agricultural protection would compensate the South for the higher prices of manufactured goods consequent upon the industrial protection conceded to the North. In fact, however, of the agricultural products to be given protection, rice, sugar, and hemp came almost entirely from northern Italy, whereas such wheat as was grown in the South was more for subsistence than for sale. The cereal growers who produced for a market came mostly from the North and Center, and these were the people who profited. Those who lost were consumers everywhere; those who gained were the owners of large farms where the soil was good and yield was high. An increase in duty from three to five lire a quintal meant a small fortune for such people, and although the more enlightened southern land-owners—the Calabrian Fortunato, for instance—spoke strongly against it, the pressure groups at Rome were too powerful.

Economists were not lacking to justify the revision of tariffs. Magliani at first opposed it but was won over. Most of the younger economists were now no longer trained in the English school, as Cavour and Minghetti had been, but in Germany, whence they came back imbued with protectionist and authoritarian principles. From 1875 onward, Luzzatti and others of this new school put forward their ideas in the *Giornale degli Economisti* at Padua. In opposition to them the classical school of economists, represented by Bastogi and Ferrara, formed the Adam Smith Society and published the *Economista*. But this latter group became increasingly remote and ineffective: they were even extreme enough to be doubtful about postal savings banks and about appointing a commission of inquiry on women and children in factories. To some of them even the coining of money by the state was the wedge of governmental interference with private enterprise.

The tide in favor of protection rose so high in the years 1886–88 that government and parliament outdid each other in advocating a general increase in duties, regardless of the current commercial treaty with France. Few people stopped to consider the political implications of this move and the disorder it might bring into the national economy. Prohibitive duties on French goods naturally provoked retaliation, so that 40 per cent of Italian exports were dammed up. The figures of annual exports to France dropped suddenly from a valuation of 500 million lire to one of 167 million, and imports from France dropped from 366 million to 164 million in value. This hit the South particularly, and hence one direct result of the new duties was to take capital away from southern agriculture and put it into the North and into industry. Grain prices of course improved, but this harmed those peasants who suffered as consumers and did not gain as producers. Bread prices rose proportionately, and the grist tax had simply come back in disguise, except that this time the profit went to the landowners rather than to the state. Sugar beet was henceforward so heavily protected that sugar was quite beyond the pocketbook of half the population, but the sugar interest flourished exceedingly, and soon claimed to own newspapers and deputies and to wield considerable influence in the affairs of state.

§∾

Abrogation of the French commercial treaty had been an incidental but deliberate object of the more extreme protectionists. This treaty had been voluntarily renewed in 1881, but was now declared to discriminate unfairly against Italian economic interests. The advent of Crispi to power in 1887, first as minister of the interior and then also prime minister (and foreign minister), brought anti-French opinion to the fore. Crispi held that Italy had depended too much on France for her trade and capital investment and had been unduly submissive to the political dependence which this implied: "France must now forget the history of the supremacy and influence which she once possessed on this side of the Alps; she should recognize that the Italian nation is as good as herself and must now be allowed to enjoy its independence and profit from it." Gratitude to France for her assistance in creating this Italian nation was no longer an operative force in politics. The French chargé d'affaires in Rome was shocked to find several Italian children who assured him that the battle of Solferino in 1859 had been won by the Italians fighting against the French, and who had been taught at school that Nice, Corsica, and Savoy were Italian. Crispi's own persecution mania, furthermore, made him think that France was in any case seeking a pretext to quarrel, and that she intended to spite him personally.

The unilateral denunciation of the treaty in 1888 was accompanied by the statement that it was hoped to negotiate a new agreement more considerate of Italian economic interests, but when France asked that any negotiations should be based on the old treaty and not on the new Italian tariff of 1887, Crispi simply assumed that France was thereby putting herself morally in the wrong. This allowed him to break off negotiations, and he now thought that he could line up his country alongside Germany with right on his side. Crispi hoped to use the campaign for protection in order to reinforce the Triple Alliance against France, and he justified this pro-German policy by the remarkable assumption that the commercial breach had merely forestalled a French move in the same direction. He was convinced that Italy was strong enough to force the acceptance of her conditions, and that France would not be able to do without Italian silk and wine. He said as much in parliament.

The obvious fact was, however, that Italy was far more vulnerable than France and already had a large adverse balance of trade. Only the attempt to base policy on considerations of sentiment and prestige can have blinded Crispi to this simple truth. Pantaleoni, the economist, estimated in 1884 that the Italian national income was only a quarter of the French, and France therefore suffered less from the breach, just as she was well able to turn to Algeria for wine and to the East for silk. Even though some of the industries in northern Italy gained from the war of reprisals, and urged the government to continue it, great damage was done to the raw and spun silk of Lombardy, Venice, and Piedmont, and there was a fall in the export of rice, cattle, and cheese which also came mainly from the North. The vineyards of Apulia and Sicily, however, felt the effects of the breach most severely of all, for there people had lately made heavy investments in wine for export. The economy of these provinces was less diversified than that of the North, and a rupture with France meant ruin to them.

Another harmful result was that the French began to sell their Italian securities, and the great number of bank failures in 1889–90 was partly due to this withdrawal of French capital. Though Germany supported her ally by buying on the Paris bourse to restore confidence, it was not enough and not in time to avert catastrophe. For the agricultural depression led naturally to a drop in the consumption of manufactured goods, and many speculative ventures built on an unwise use of credit began to fail. All this was shortly going to have important political results.

Crispi was finally forced in 1890 to admit defeat, and to surrender some of the heavier duties he had imposed on French produce. His own failures of character and of political sense had been ruinous, and now it seemed that the sufferings of so many Italians had been to no purpose whatever. A modified trade war continued, though reduced in scale, until a year or so later when alternative outlets were opened through commercial treaties with Austria, Switzerland, and Germany. These helped to repair some of the damage done by this irresponsible and ill-prepared essay in government protection.

But the duties on cereals remained, and an agrarian group, or *partito degli agrari,* was formed which used its great influence in politics to increase this protection still higher as a *quid pro quo* for the subsidization of merchant shipping. For landowners, the tax of 7.5 lire per quintal on imported grain constituted in effect a partial reimbursement of the land tax about which they grumbled so much, but for the poor who lived mostly off cereals it spelled hunger and disease. Economists pointed out how this duty made agriculture progressively uneconomic, by forcing poor land into inefficient use and exonerating producers from seeking out better techniques in the face of growing world competition. And a report by De Johannis on the position at the turn of the century even advised against investing further in agricultural improvements, just because experience suggested that it would be money wasted.

The results of this state of affairs were to be seen in the Sicilian rebellion of 1892–93, in the general exodus from the land to the towns, and the great wave of emigration overseas which now became a flood. A predominantly peasant society was being brutally disrupted, and revolutionary forces were being built up which had to find some outlet at home or abroad.

22 Corruption
and the Banks, 1889-1893

Between 1889 and 1893 the failure of certain important banks developed into a full-scale crisis of political morality, which had something like the effect of the Panama scandal in France, and came near to ruining Crispi and blighting Giolitti's political career before it had really begun.

Political corruption had flourished under the pre-1860 despotisms, and the habit could hardly be cured overnight. Northerners, not without some reason, thought it specially typical of the South. Cavour's friend, the British ambassador Sir James Hudson, had unctuously written in 1860 that "the Neapolitans are too corrupt, and the entire Civil and Military administration is so abominable that their junction with Northern Italy (where honesty is the rule in the Public Offices) would merely produce a social decomposition, and then a political putrefaction." His prophecy was exaggerated but not beside the point. The deputies at Turin affected a shocked surprise when Massari told how "at Naples there exists a class of person who comes between the administration and interested parties and knows how to bribe government officials." But Ricasoli's government soon had to deal with the same contact men in the North. Politicians lacked the financial resources for organization and propaganda, not having large parties behind them, and banks and industrial firms therefore put money at the disposal of small groups and individuals in return for services rendered.

People at first ascribed this simply to defective political habits which national unification would alter, yet the passing of years brought no great improvement. In 1875 the deputy Tajani revealed to parliament how the police in Sicily connived at the crimes of the mafia and protected the *mafiosi* from justice. The following year a parliamentary commission on Sicily reported that this underworld life was not peculiar to the South, and instanced the *squadracce* of Ravenna and Bologna, the *pugnalatori* of Parma, the *cocca* of Turin, and the *sicari* of Rome. Such disreputable gangs could be found in most other countries too; what typified Italy was not this professional crime but the universal mistrust and unco-operativeness of people in every social class toward the government. In some areas 20 per cent of the annual draft contrived to disappear altogether. The unscrupulous rich found it relatively easy to pay hush money to the tax collectors, and it was estimated that at some moments only one-tenth of the taxes due was reaching the Treasury. Scandals over the construction of railroads, which had once ruined the ministerial career of Count Bastogi, came close to tumbling Vincenzo Breda himself, and with the enormous expansion of state expenditure and patronage after the 1880's, corrupt practices over government contracts became a byword.

The particular bank scandals of 1889–93 were given unfortunate publicity, but Italy profited from the exposure, painful though it was at the time. The financial crash of 1889 was immediately due to an overexpansion of the building industry for which the banks had allowed far too much credit. This building craze had begun with the new government offices at Rome, and had continued with the rebuilding of the old insanitary parts of Naples. Rome itself, with a population of 220,000 in 1870, nearly doubled in size during the next twenty years, and became a mecca for every kind of adventurer. The banks of Turin had thrown over all good financial doctrine when they saw the great profits realized from speculation in land and building, and far too much of the capital which should have gone into agriculture or industry was diverted into this deceptively profitable investment. The Banca Nazionale increased its note circulation from 462 million lire in 1883 to 611 million by the end of 1886, and reserves in bullion dropped from a half to one-third of the total. Crispi then helped this process by lifting certain legal restrictions on credit, for the profiteers evidently wielded considerable influence in government circles.

At the beginning of 1889 one or two banks began to suspend payment. Once again Crispi intervened unobtrusively and persuaded the larger financial houses to cover the failing Banca Tiberina with a loan of forty-five million lire so that it might complete its contracts for public works. A small slump in the Roman building trade had already caused minor riots of unemployed men plundering the shops of the capital, and Crispi feared what would happen if the bubble really burst. It was also said, maliciously but not implausibly, that he had the interests of certain influential financiers very close at heart. But his action led to a further inflation of credit and made the collapse worse when it came, for loans from the Banca Nazionale could not sustain this inflation indefinitely. Meanwhile, the other banks followed his lead, and backed up semibankrupt enterprises which would better have been allowed to collapse.

The various regions of Italy still jealously guarded their right to a bank of issue. The governor of the Banca Romana, one of the six such banks, was a certain Tanlongo. He had begun his career as a factor on one of the large estates of the Roman Campagna, and had gradually built up estates of his own. Cavour had employed him in the attempt to bribe officials in the papal curia. A none too scrupulous career had finally brought this half-illiterate but skillful and audacious man to the point of giving financial advice to a succession of premiers, as well as to cardinals, to the Jesuits, and the king himself, and handsome loans sometimes accompanied this "advice." Tanlongo was one of the quickest to profit from the wave of land speculation which was swamping baroque Rome under a new Humbertine city. He had had the paper notes of the Banca Romana printed in England, and without any reference to the government he had been able to order any quantity—"just like a barrel of beer," said Giolitti. The circulation of his bank was thus sixty million lire in excess of the legal limit, and there were at least forty million in false notes which had been issued as a duplicate series.

When the bank failures of 1889 allowed these financial irregularities to leak out, it also became known that a good deal of this surplus had been spent on interest-free "loans" to deputies and ministers. The banks of issue had come to wield considerable political pressure, and deputies were shy of any proposal to control them because it might have exposed the existence of these "loans." The Banca di Napoli, while its circulation was more or less correct, turned out to have incurred debts of some twenty million, much of which had been accumulated in this concealed political bribery. Its director, when accused of peculation, implicated

Crispi himself, and it was established that Crispi had at least counter-manded an inquiry which should have been made into the state of this bank. Even if he personally did not profit from these malpractices, Crispi was not so simple-minded as not to have known what was afoot. His many enemies connected this with his sudden appointment of eighty-four new men to the Senate, among them many titled names, and the cap-tains of industry, Breda, Bastogi, and Orlando.

When the purely financial crisis reached a point where no further postponement of the reckoning seemed possible, the minister Miceli, at the end of 1889, appointed a private commission of inquiry to see if the banks were exceeding their reserves. This commission under Senator Alvisi drew attention to many serious irregularities, but their report was not published and Alvisi's attempt to raise the matter in parliament was ruled out of order. Several ministers later pretended that they did not even read the Alvisi report, but had been content with assurances that everything could be hushed up and rectified without public scandal. For several years the matter was allowed to lie dormant, and the fact that so many people kept silent was a poor commentary on the health of Italian public institutions.

୨ல

The administration led by Crispi resigned early in 1891 after three and a half years of power. Di Rudinì, the wealthy Sicilian *gran signore* with the monocle and long red beard who then succeeded as prime minister, had been leader of the Right since Minghetti's death in 1886; nevertheless he made the radical Nicotera his minister of the interior. Whereas Crispi's two ministries had shown transformism on the Left, Di Rudinì, who when out of office had objected to this process, now himself applied it the other way around. Though basing his government on the Right Center, he gave the most important of all offices to the architect of the sweeping Left victory of 1876. Transformism on this occasion showed itself to be a moderating even if a confusing force. The new gov-ernment was less anticlerical than its predecessor, more eager for a balanced budget, especially anxious for reduced military expenditure, and less authoritarian in its domestic policy.

Abroad, Di Rudinì was all for economy, for peace and quiet and the restoration of good relations with France. He hoped that commerce and industry might prosper unhindered either by war scares or by the irre-sponsible breach of trade relations with neighboring countries upon whom Italy's prosperity depended. He cut the funds of Italian schools abroad which Crispi's patriotism had heavily endowed, and in general played down jingoism and put Italian foreign policy back more in the middle of the road. As Jacini wrote just before his death in 1891: "It was the mania of aggrandizement that led us to ally with the Central Powers, and the Triple Alliance now imposes on us an enormous armament quite disproportionate to our economic resources. . . . The high taxes which inevitably follow are drying up our capacity for production, especially in agriculture." To let the Triple Alliance lapse entirely, on the other hand, would have meant diplomatic isolation again, and so in 1891, without consulting the cabinet, it was renewed. Yet counterbalancing it was the fact that irredentism was now infecting the Right as well as the extreme Left, and when the irredentist Dante Alighieri Society was founded in 1889, its name was suggested by the radical Carducci, but its first president was the conservative Bonghi.

Crispi could not abide the greater friendliness with France which followed this renunciation of his policy, and protested to the king that Italian strength and reputation were being thrown away wantonly by his successor. Better that Italy should not have been made at all, he said, than reconcile herself to being a second-class power. What was wanted, so Crispi privately told the king, was a strong man as premier who would not hesitate if necessary to govern against parliament and who could impose an uncompromisingly nationalist and authoritarian policy.

Di Rudinì did not fit this definition, nor was he even one of those statesmen who by patience and intrigue could build up a firm majority. When his coalition dissolved in May 1892, he was succeeded by Giovanni Giolitti, another personal enemy of Crispi's but a far more capable tactician. Giolitti was a man of the Center, with the reputation of being a safe man who would do nothing rash, a liberal who yet had no advanced ideas. Indeed, having almost no fixed ideas of any kind, he was the obvious man to come to the top under such a system of broad coalition. In particular he was *bien vu* by the Court party who welcomed a Piedmontese after two Sicilians. The king's adviser on this occasion was the younger Rattazzi, who, following his more famous uncle, had been taken into Court administration and had become Minister of the Royal House. For a short time Rattazzi seems to have played at being a Grey Eminence. Although the scope of his activities is still obscure, it seems that he used the civil list, his influence with the banks, and the gift of minor offices in his patronage to keep Giolitti in power.

Giolitti was determined to give himself a firmer basis of support, and so dissolved parliament at the end of 1892. For the new elections he made free use of government influence, even more than Minghetti and Depretis before him. He took the precaution of dismissing or transferring forty-nine out of sixty-nine prefects, and also freely dissolved communal

administrations. Help was purchased by the offer of senatorial appointments. It was noted that the widening of the suffrage and the recent return to single-member constituencies made electoral corruption easier.
Very few constituencies in all Italy, said Luzzatti, were free from such
corruption in 1892. But Giolitti argued that, if the government did not
use these somewhat dubious methods, the elections would merely be
managed by local cliques of *camorristi* with methods which were even
worse. He thus began to construct the electoral machine which, by the
beginning of the new century, was to make him the arbiter of Italian
politics. This time it secured the election of what were estimated to be
380 ministerial deputies out of a total of 508.

For the moment, however, Giolitti had neither the experience nor the
necessary power to weld his majority together. Managed elections of this
kind were fought on no clear issue of principle, so that the resultant
majority had little cohesion; weakened by the absence of exact party
allegiance, that majority could evaporate at a very moderate temperature. Giolitti, moreover, had not yet perfected the technique of running
miscellaneous groups in common harness, for his ministry was weighted
to the Left, and he failed to offer enough inducements to the other wing
of the inevitable coalition. Four ministers of justice and three of finance
followed each other in the space of eighteen months. The Senate resented the inclusion of only one senator in his cabinet, and was also
shocked by his nomination to the Upper House of so many people, some
of them doubtful characters such as Tanlongo. The influence of Queen
Margherita was used to back the reactionaries; while of the king's two
known mistresses, the Countess of Santafiora favored Crispi, and the
Duchess Litta was for Di Rudinì. The re-emergence of the bank question sealed Giolitti's fate, and then Rattazzi was overturned by another
faction at Court under Domenico Farini.

୨🍂

Rumors of continued malversation had not been appeased by an
official statement in June 1891 that the national interests forbade the
publication of Alvisi's report. Then in November 1892 came the nomination of Tanlongo to the Senate for services rendered, an appointment
published, significantly enough, a few days before Giolitti's first experiment in "making" the elections. Several months after this nomination,
Tanlongo was in prison. For quite unexpectedly, in December 1892, the
deputy Colajanni had reopened the whole issue by discovering and publishing Alvisi's conclusions. The faithful deputies duly voted by 316 to
27 to bury the whole matter again, but the newspapers bit deep into the
scandal and concealment became impossible. Behind Colajanni there

was clearly a concerted political move, and Farini's diary implicates Di Rudinì, Pareto, and Pantaleoni among others.

Giolitti put himself still further in the wrong by refusing a request for a parliamentary inquiry on the banks. It is interesting that Crispi spoke from the opposition benches in Giolitti's support, saying that a parliamentary investigation would be unpatriotic, and would damage Italian credit abroad, but later it turned out that Crispi was himself still borrowing from the banks far beyond his capacity to repay. Instead of a parliamentary inquiry, a governmental commission was appointed under Finali, and the House approved this appointment by an almost unanimous vote. The Banca Romana spent some hasty days correcting its books, but even so the Finali report indicated that its note circulation was twice that allowed by law, and that up to fifty million lire had been lost through unwise speculations, malversation, and bribery.

In the same year one of the largest credit institutions in the country, the Credito Mobiliare, had to suspend payments since speculative investing had heavily depreciated its capital. Building enterprises and industrial shares at once began to reflect a general loss of confidence. Deputies were being publicly implicated by name, and the popular hero De Zerbi, a champion of the bank in parliament and who owed it half a million, died from "shock." A former director of the Bank of Sicily was brutally murdered in a railroad car as he returned to Palermo. A director of the Bank of Naples disappeared and was arrested attempting to take poison when disguised as a priest. Finally, in March 1893, Giolitti had to let parliament appoint a third committee under Mordini to consider the political implications of what had been revealed.

Eight months of tension went by before the report of this committee was presented in November. Although it added little that was new in the way of facts, and though it had without doubt been inspired by the desire to play the whole matter down, the air was effectively cleared. A number of deputies were blamed by name because they and their friends were on the payroll of the bank, and many more were implicated less directly. As for Giolitti, his own personal memoirs were to protest his complete innocence, but the committee decided that he knew the true condition of the Banca Romana yet continued to have financial dealings with it, and in return for its help had made its president a senator. These were gigantic political errors, for he had known perfectly well the suspicion attached to Tanlongo's name. Giolitti's direct transactions concerned no more than sixty thousand lire which he had borrowed from the bank, probably for bribing the French press to favor the Columbus festival of 1892, and this sum had been duly repaid. As for the accusation that he had had an additional sum for electoral ex-

penses, this was "not proven," but the records of the bank must have
been in a poor state if it could not be decided one way or the other. Although still undefeated in parliament, he now chose to resign, and a subsequent disappearance abroad made some people suspect the worst.

Crispi was far more closely implicated having been prime minister
during the original Alvisi inquiry. As he had used his political position
to draw on the bank, his refusal to act on Alvisi's report was highly
discreditable to say the least. Now that the pact of secrecy about these
political loans was broken, Crispi, resenting the accession to power of
this young upstart from the North, tried to throw all the blame on Giolitti, but his accusations rebounded, for he and his wife owed the bank
over twenty times his premier's salary and he had without doubt sold an
occasional title to international financiers of scandalous reputation. Admittedly, Crispi left public life in 1896 a poor man, whereas (some
historians have suggested) he could easily have used the secret service
fund to pay his debts. On the other hand he required heavy subventions
for his own paper La Riforma, and his general attitude to the press
as a purchasable commodity had also cost money. Even so he had
enough rich backers not to have need for recourse to more shady means
of finance. What political influence these financiers managed to wield
through their activities must be purely conjectural. But Crispi at least
showed poor judgment in not breaking off from the bank at the first
hint of embezzlement, and his effort at concealment made the scandal
seem worse than it was.

§❧

Italy emerged from this inquiry with a cleaner bill than some had
feared. Reforms were introduced to reduce the number of banks and
bring note circulation under stricter state control, and deputies and
senators were henceforth forbidden to become directors of the note-
issuing banks. Giolitti had to resign as prime minister, but he did not
challenge a parliamentary vote, and the king was therefore able to
choose a successor where he liked. Zanardelli was first asked to form a
ministry, because here was a man respected by all for his integrity, a
politician who would help to restore confidence in parliamentary government. But when Zanardelli submitted the name of General Baratieri as
foreign minister, the king vetoed the suggestion in compliance with a
warning from Austria, since Baratieri came from the Austrian province
of Trentino. Zanardelli would not accept this veto, and Crispi of all
people was invited to replace him.

Inculpated himself, Crispi was hardly the man to reassure the country, but another dangerous revolt was brewing among the peasants of

Sicily, and many propertied men were prepared (as again in 1922) to sacrifice liberal government if that were the price for having a strong man at the helm. To them Giolitti and Zanardelli were radical reformers, for in October 1893 Giolitti had even advocated a progressive income tax, and he had refused to dissolve the Sicilian workers' unions. Crispi agreed with those many people who wanted to forget the unsavory bank episode, and he was especially welcome for wanting also to enlarge and strengthen the army. He told parliament that no party considerations would influence the forming of his emergency government: "When the fortunes of the country have been restored then we can go back to normal again; but to continue with our personal squabbles now would be a crime. When in danger we must all unite in common defense."

The danger which Crispi referred to was socialism, and against this growing menace he intended to play the strong man and the delivering hero. He took office only on condition that he could dissolve the Chamber if necessary, and as the Giolittian majority knew what would happen if he managed the next elections, they dutifully allowed him to govern as he chose. Social disorder had momentarily restored a rough political consensus among the ruling elite, and events in Sicily and Ethiopia conveniently changed the subject and prevented an adequate debate on Mordini's report.

COLONIAL DEFEAT
AND POLITICAL REACTION,
1893–1900

23 Social Unrest
and Crispi's Last Ministry

Socialism was now a force to be reckoned with, and the fear which it inspired helped Crispi into power for his last fatal ministry. Many diverse strands had come together in Italian socialism: the simple enthusiasm for social justice of Garibaldi, the republicanism of Mazzini, the anarchism of Bakunin, the Marxism of Antonio Labriola, and the rough force of the nameless, disorganized agrarian revolts which erupted spontaneously all over the country long before there was any doctrine to give them reason and pattern. The peasants were potentially the most rebellious element in Italian society, but hardly yet the target for propaganda from the socialist intellectuals. In their animosity toward the new middle-class state, these peasants discovered an ally in the Church, and it was the clericals even more than the socialists who stirred up class war.

Alongside the peasants, but with quite different interests and outlook, were the industrial artisans. At first only the printing trade seems to have had a workers' organization, and this looked back to the medieval *compagnonnages* rather than forward to trade unionism. Isolated events, however, pointed toward the future. Thus in 1862, at Intra on Lake Maggiore, the hat-makers met to discuss how they could fight the machines threatening to challenge their livelihood. In 1865 the unemployed wool workers at Arpino invaded one of the new factories to break up the textile machinery which was depriving them of work. During these early years the workers engaged in railroad construction were particularly difficult to manage, especially in the South and on the forgotten island of Sardinia. But such local protest movements were less organized strikes than the natural reaction of semiagricultural workers against the new and insecure conditions of an industrial revolution. The Sardinian peasants even attacked and demolished one of the first railroad stations, symbolic to them of a new bondage.

The habit of organization developed naturally out of innumerable secret societies and mutual-aid fraternities. Employees in the Sicilian flour mills had an embryonic kind of union known as the P.O.S.A., and paid a subscription to a fund for sickness, old age, and military service. As with the dreaded mafia, it prescribed penal sanctions and even death for millowners who did not employ its members, and as with the Venetian gondoliers, members were expected not to compete with or undercut each other. In Sicily and Naples, the mafia and camorra could carry considerable influence, and employers might have to give in to their demands or purchase their good will. In the North, the employers were better placed, and when the first Chambers of Labor were formed, they were sometimes dissolved and their leaders put on trial. The right of free association, though implicit in the constitution, was first curtailed, and then specifically repudiated by parliament in April 1886. Socialism was already something to be feared and suppressed.

Garibaldi was by temperament a man of the extreme Left and naturally ranged himself with the socialists. He even adhered to the International and appeared at one of its meetings. Though he repudiated the socialist doctrine which called property or inheritance theft, he believed in minimizing all social privilege. He wanted a United States of Europe where wars and armies would be impossible, and he preached the brotherhood of all men whatever their color or nationality. He even regretted that he had not fought for the workers of Paris during the commune of 1870. In the following year he wrote that a fourth estate was appearing which would one day include all the workers in town and country and then carry all before it. No wonder that, to the common people, Garibaldi symbolized the underdog. To them he was the man who, though unprivileged and self-educated, had risen to be on speaking terms with princes, and his picture decorated the humblest cottages as frequently as did portraits of Pope and king.

Mazzini, too, for several years was a friend of the International, and always believed in vague projects for social regeneration. Most of the early socialists first became politically conscious as republicans under the inspiration of Mazzini. Many of his followers were able to believe that he had abandoned his own doctrines when he condemned the Paris commune, and some argued that socialism did not contradict Mazzini's doctrine but rather evolved from it—in spite of the fact that socialists put class and economic problems first, while Mazzini believed in a national and classless society. Some socialists recognized the latent incompatibility here, and had thus, like Proudhon, opposed the unification of Italy as a dangerous piece of bourgeois deception. To Mazzini, however, national unification was a religious duty, whereas class struggle was something materialistic and irrelevant. Too religious and mystical for the new revolutionaries, Mazzini was already out of fashion by 1870. Once the nation was in existence he had nothing to say, and what was revolutionary in his creed had been absorbed by others.

Alone among the early Italian radicals, Pisacane was claimed by the socialists as a serious forerunner, and he was an isolated figure who died young and with few followers. Not until Bakunin were the republicans displaced from their position as the most combative and the most extreme-Left group in politics. The Russian anarchist Bakunin came into Italian life almost on Mazzini's introduction, and some years passed before he was a distinct political force of his own. Like that of Pisacane, Bakunin's socialism was atheistic and materialistic. He believed in social revolution, as Mazzini had never done, and welcomed the starving peasantry as a revolutionary force. Even though Bakunin was expelled by the Marxists from the socialist International for being too independent and too liberal, his brand of revolutionary anarchism continued until after 1880 to attract some of the extremists.

In 1874 Bakunin had instigated an abortive rising at Bologna, which became the subject of a famous historical novel by Riccardo Bacchelli. Involved in this rising was Andrea Costa, a fiery Romagnol who had seen the inside of French and Italian prisons and was soon afterward to help found Italian socialism. Costa's artisan friends in 1882 began a "Workers Party" at Milan, distinct from the disciples of Mazzini and Bakunin. This party was unrealistic and utopian, advocating abolition of the bureaucracy and a foreign policy of universal freedom and brotherhood: it remained for Marxism to put some backbone into the socialist movement. But Costa was persuaded by Depretis's extension of the franchise that parliamentary government might be workable, and in the elections of 1882 at Ravenna he became the first socialist deputy.

§◆

Republicanism and anarchism were strongest in Emilia, and Italian Marxism was to center on Milan. But the most revolutionary part of the kingdom was Sicily. Those few Sicilian deputies who moved among the rural poor knew that they were living on top of a volcano. Blind opposition to the tyranny of absentee landlords was superimposed on anarchic resentment against all government and an insular protest against a mainland which seemed to exploit Sicily as a conquered possession. The politicians in distant Rome, by their irresponsible breach with France, had ruined thousands of southern families whose savings had gone into plantations for the export trade. Wine, fruit, and sulphur, the chief exports of Sicily, were all gravely damaged. The sulphur industry was being defeated by American competition and by a new synthetic process for the manufacture of sulphuric acid. More than a hundred thousand people received their living from the mines, and when the price of sulphur fell from 140 to 60 lire a ton, many of these were turned out to compete for agricultural employment in an already overpopulated countryside.

The gradual advance of education and civilization simultaneously contributed to making the rural South disaffected. As railways and roads brought them more into touch with the towns, the peasants became more conscious of their poverty, and their sons who returned from military service had learned elsewhere about higher standards of living. Then came the agricultural depression of the 1880's which forced some of them to the point of starvation, and henceforward there were some who had nothing more to lose by revolt. Agrarian strikes spread after 1890 and began to cause violence and bloodshed.

The socialists were as little prepared for this peasant revolt as anyone else. They were mostly middle-class intellectuals, and were hardly convinced yet of the need to win over the agricultural masses. Indeed they had some reason to fear the conservatism of the *contadini*. Naturally, they associated themselves with the Sicilian revolt once it had broken out and tried to explain it in their own terms, but Crispi was quite wrong in ascribing this outbreak to socialist initiative. Workers' groups or *fasci* had existed spontaneously in the island for some years, and they had no need of socialist doctrine or organization to make them rise in a hunger rebellion to reoccupy the communal lands which had been usurped from them.

Giolitti realized as much. He commented in his memoirs that the movement was much less serious than other subsequent outbreaks, but the wealthy classes were not yet accustomed to this kind of struggle and mistook economic agitation for social revolution. The proprietors had the ear of the government and were far more easily organized than the peasantry. Their traditional remedy for agrarian unrest was exemplary repression, and a meeting of landowners at Caltagirone even decided that popular education should be prohibited because it clearly left the poor dissatisfied with their inferior status. As Crispi himself was to find, the one policy they would resist by every legal or illegal means was the reform of the *latifondi*. They first tried to combine in refusing to employ members of the *fasci,* and then persuaded the local magistrates that a strike was tantamount to a violent breach of the peace. Meanwhile, notifications came in of refusal to pay excise duties, of telegraph wires cut, of attacks on town halls and customs houses, and in one tragic episode the troops opened fire and ninety-two peasants and one soldier were killed. Politicians in Rome began to fear that an organized socialist revolution had broken out, and Crispi encouraged this illusion as an excuse to justify his return to power.

The Sicilian writers, Pirandello and Verga, showed more sympathy and understanding for the troubles of this unhappy island than did the Sicilian politicians, Crispi and Di Rudinì. Pirandello wrote of a peasant from his native Girgenti who, perhaps like many others in actual life, was quite unable to grasp the significance of the *fasci:* thinking only that they must be enemies of the community, he took arms against them, and was killed by the very soldiers who arrived to suppress the movement. The novelist Verga knew even better at first hand the rustic Sicilians for whom the state meant little but oppression, yet for whom socialism would have been unintelligible and irrelevant.

❧

The bloody outcome of this unrest led to questions in parliament, and helped to upset Giolitti's ministry in November 1893. Giolitti had tried to keep order, but recognized the right to strike and hoped things would settle down of their own accord. But this was not good enough for the Sicilian landowners, and in Crispi they found a man who was on tiptoe for just such an occasion in order to pose as the national deliverer and divert attention from the general exposure of fraudulence in high finance and politics. A dangerous run on the savings banks made a strong hand even more necessary.

Radical though in some ways he remained, Crispi was unable to envisage that the origin of the rising might be found not in some contrived plot but in economic despair. Unlike Giolitti, he never came near to understanding socialism, and while he exaggerated its dangers he was equally mistaken in believing that repressive measures by themselves would prevail against it. He told parliament that socialism was unpatriotic, indistinguishable from anarchism, and signified the end of all liberty, adding that the common people were "corrupted by ignorance, gnawed by envy and ingratitude, and should not be allowed any say in politics." When in opposition, Crispi had censured Depretis for inhibiting the growth of party politics, but now that he was himself in power he claimed to speak for the whole nation and the General Will, and condemned socialism for being a sectional party. He was credulous enough to believe that the Sicilian revolutionaries, as well as receiving money from the American consul, had a secret treaty with a Russian grand duke and were in league with France and the Vatican, and hence that the request for local self-government in the island was an unscrupulous intrigue to be resisted at all costs.

Such was the general panic that Crispi, in spite of his own implication in the bank frauds, despite even the recent elections which had returned a large Giolittian majority, obtained an overwhelming vote of confidence from the Chamber by 342 votes to 45. These disorders had come opportunely to rescue his reputation and give him supreme power. Farini was now genuinely convinced that this man was "the one moral force left in Italy," and when Crispi was told as much it went to his head. He replied that he was quite ready to rule without parliament if necessary; and hence the deputies, faced with such determination, meekly did as they were bid. A new class of reservists was called up and fifty thousand soldiers were sent to Sicily, martial law and a state of siege being proclaimed as though a civil war were raging. Military tribunals were installed and given retrospective cognizance of offences committed over the previous year. When in January 1894 the marble workers of Massa and Carrara in the North rose and attacked the local barracks, martial law was proclaimed there also.

For seven months these emergency regulations continued, and eventually a thousand Sicilians were on the penal islands. It did not increase people's respect for Italian justice that the courts in July 1894 finally absolved those accused in the bank scandals, even people who had made a public confession of theft, whereas Sicilians were being imprisoned on mere suspicion and harshly sentenced. De Felice, a personal opponent of Crispi who had been elected in 1892 by a heavy majority, was given a severe sentence despite his parliamentary privilege. Crispi was also allowed exceptional powers to control the press and confine political suspects in *domicilio coatto,* and believing that socialism was the chief enemy he used these powers to dissolve the socialist party and prosecute its leaders. At his request a hundred thousand people were disenfranchised on the grounds of being improperly inscribed on the electoral roll. His policy, indeed, seemed thoroughly illiberal and provocative, and his former friends of the *estrema* were dumbfounded that he had so far forgotten his own persecution before 1860 at the hands of another arbitrary government.

To rally support against this man, a "League for the Defense of Liberty" was formed at Milan, in which socialists, radicals, and even left-wing liberals tried to forget their differences and stand, as Crispi himself had once stood, for liberty against oppression. This drove him still further to the Right. He even made some efforts to renounce his Masonic friends and anticlerical past in order to win clerical support, but the Vatican turned down his approach with scorn. Crispi, like Mussolini, was to learn that a strong man was welcome only while there was immediate peril of revolution, or while he was surrounded by the prestige of success. His cry of "the country in danger" could not continue forever as a substitute for a constructive policy.

§❧

In December 1894, several months after Crispi's dissolution of the socialist party, there came the last flicker of the bank scandals, when Giolitti tried to stage a comeback by laying before parliament his famous *plico,* or bundle of incriminating letters, to prove Crispi's involvement. It was an unfortunate practice of Italian ministers to appropriate official documents when they left office, and Giolitti in particular seems to have carried off many personal details about other politicians whom he could then perhaps influence by the threat of exposure. This *plico* included letters from ministerial files, but also many of a personal nature which suggested that Crispi's private life had been under secret surveillance. For instance, there were a hundred letters from Signora Crispi, as well as some correspondence with Tanlongo, and references to large sums which Crispi and his friends had borrowed or received from Tanlongo's bank. Giolitti's presentation of these documents to parliament reflected almost as much against himself as against Crispi, for they did not amount to a great deal, and yet they raised the awkward question of why they had not been shown to Mordini's parliamentary inquiry. Too many people had an interest in stopping any further disclosures, and powerful interests thus protested against statesmen continuing to blacken each others' reputations while social unrest and a war in Ethiopia were threatening the country.

Crispi sensed and exploited this feeling. He first told the deputies that he would answer these grave charges, but the very same evening they were astonished to find that a royal decree had closed parliament after by far the shortest session on record. One pretext Crispi gave was that the House should not continue discussion while tempers were so heated. Another was that a few mischief-makers were just trying to make trouble. His real reason was that parliament still had a Giolittian majority, and he intended to change the prefects and organize a new general election. Di Rudinì gathered some of the conservative deputies together to register a protest against his action. Further over to the Left, Cavallotti for the radicals and Zanardelli for the liberals drew the obvious conclusion that Crispi was artificially prolonging the state of emergency so as to distract attention from his own dishonest behavior. This belief was further borne out by the suspension of parliamentary government for the next six months, during which even some taxation had to be authorized by royal decree. All this time Crispi continued in office, though he lay under the gravest suspicions, and the revelations of the *plico* could thus not be discussed until parliament was recalled in June 1895. His prorogation of parliament showed the grossest contempt for representative government, and it also implicated the king himself who had signed the decree in full cognizance of the facts.

"At my age," said Crispi, "after fifty-three years of service to my country, I have the right to believe myself invulnerable and above all these libelous accusations." This was an astonishing claim. But some people took it seriously just because Crispi claimed to stand as a defense against socialism and anarchism, and because parliament had been discredited by the dishonesty and corruption of deputies on both Right and Left. Crispi privately told Farini in December 1894 that he was coming to believe that parliamentary government was not possible in Italy. But in the elections of May 1895 he managed to win about 350 *ministeriali,* including people from the Left, the Center, and even from the extreme Right. Coercion on an unprecedented scale was required to give such a result, and two years later a parliamentary inquest into the finances of the ministry of the interior suggested that money voted for the relief of a great earthquake disaster in Calabria might have gone to his election fund. And yet one must assume that, had Crispi not suffered a heavy reverse in Ethiopia, he would almost certainly have managed to consolidate his partial dictatorship. The young journalist, Guglielmo Ferrero, commented that Italians admired Crispi's political courage and strength of will just because they lacked these qualities themselves; and concluded that, since so many of the ruling elite liked his violent methods of government, Italians therefore were still not ready for liberty.

Crispi's methods were indeed becoming increasingly imperious, and his private conversation suggests that his character and even his mind were weakening. In October 1895 he celebrated his seventy-seventh birthday. His advancing senility, his lack of tact, together with the personal animus which separated him from Giolitti and Di Rudinì, and then the defeat of Adowa, all these finally combined to cause his collapse. Grave and detailed moral accusations had been leveled at him publicly, to which he made no adequate answer. Although he had Catholics in his ministry, the clericals were frightened when his irascible nature led him into another contest with the Church over the grant of exequatur to bishops. The conservative liberals did not forget that he had been the enemy of Cavour. The Left feared his authoritarianism and his aristocratic pretenses—the daughter of this ex-redshirt married a prince in 1895, and he contemptuously attacked those deputies who neglected to wear the traditional frock coat. The elections may have heavily reduced the personal followers of Di Rudinì, Giolitti, and Zanardelli, but the five socialists of 1892 were increased to fifteen in 1895. All Crispi's personal enemies were back in parliament—Cavallotti, Colajanni, De Felice, Costa, and Imbriani—and there had been many previous examples of a large government majority dissolving almost overnight.

Above all there was the fact that Italy was already overspending her income by a large margin, and yet Crispi wanted to incur even more expense on a campaign in Africa. A coalition was therefore forming against him of those who wanted a sane financial system, together with those who thought that money should be spent on colonizing Italy rather than Africa, those who wanted to fight for the Trentino rather than for Abyssinia, and those Milanese who opposed the "southernization" of public life. Some ordinary citizens might appreciate Crispi as a protection against social disorder, but they were to turn against him when he asked for sacrifices to make Italy a big colonial power, and they mercilessly overthrew him when he led them to military defeat.

24 The Ethiopian War and the Eclipse of Crispi

After setbacks over Tunisia and Egypt in 1881–82, the prospects for Italian colonization in the Mediterranean were poor. Libya was still "unoccupied," but it looked like an unpromising desert, and the opportunity of securing international recognition of Italian interests there had been missed. In 1882 a first colony was therefore established instead on the Red Sea where there was less chance of clashing with other European interests. Considerations of prestige were thought to demand expansion somewhere, and, unprofitable though this particular venture might seem, it was possible to find reasons which if sophistical and contradictory were felicitous on the tongue. It was said that Italy must escape from her "imprisonment in the Mediterranean," or alternatively that the "key to the Mediterranean was in the Red Sea." Geography was thus obscured by rhetoric.

This Red Sea settlement originally dated from the time when the Rubattino company set up a small commercial station at Assab. When the British became alarmed for their interests at Aden, Cairoli had to state that there was no intention of establishing a military post, but Gladstone came to power in 1880 and was more sympathetic. Trouble in the Sudan made it desirable for Britain that Assab should be held by a friendly power which could control the traffic in slavery and arms smuggling. In June 1882 it was proposed to the Chamber that Italian sovereignty be declared over Assab. Some of the more independent deputies objected that the Red Sea was both remote and profitless; but now that national pride was involved, few parliamentary leaders were rash enough to damage their political future by committing themselves to a policy of dignified withdrawal while it was still possible.

The acquisition of this port was soon said to demand the occupation of the interior in order to ensure its safety. The Triple Alliance worked in the same direction by encouraging Italy to look away from the Austrian frontier and seek compensation elsewhere. When the Khedive of Egypt decided in 1885 that he could no longer keep a garrison at Massawa (another port further up the Red Sea), Italy sent an expedition thither, trusting that the British would welcome Italy's presence as a background support of their campaign against the Mahdi. Mancini reassured the Chamber with his novel phrase about the Red Sea being the key to the Mediterranean, but Mancini was a lawyer not a politician, and he never explained the meaning of this extravagant hyperbole.

Quite apart from the improbability of reaching the Mediterranean by this route, Mancini's geography was otherwise at fault, for he ordered a sortie from Massawa to Khartoum as though it was but a few miles' journey through friendly country. The defeat of the British general Gordon left Italians alone in a hostile country. Commercial stations were soon in need of military support, and this involved Italy with the tribes of Ethiopia as well as the dervishes in the Sudan. The colonial venture which had begun with the Mediterranean in mind was thus compelled to change direction and look south.

In 1887 a rash decision was taken to move the troops away from the sandy and feverish coastal area to more healthy quarters in the interior highlands. At once Negus John of Ethiopia became alarmed. Already in Massawa and Assab he had lost two natural outlets for the northern provinces of his empire, and he was justifiably sensitive lest this new move should conceal a design on his country's independence. Twenty years earlier the British had sent a successful expedition against Negus

Theodore, but they had never intended to stay, because they calculated that Ethiopia would involve much expense for little return. Italy, on the other hand, did not count the cost until too late, and underestimated the strength and intentions of her opponent as she also overestimated the possible gains in commerce and prestige.

Inevitably, the usual "incidents" took place in the indeterminate frontier region. Di Robilant spoke in a classic phrase of sending a punitive expedition against "two or three robbers," and he made no allowance for the fact that the same kind of nationalistic pride which drove Italy to conquest might also be inspiring other people to defend themselves. The result was that in 1887 a column of five hundred men was surprisingly destroyed by Ras Alula at Dogali.

This dealt a wounding blow to Italian morale, especially as France had to be asked for help in transporting reinforcements. Worse still, Italy was thereby drawn even further into a war of conquest. Amid unruly scenes, the Chamber approved an aggressive policy by 332 votes against 40. Approval was given to increased military appropriations, and the minister of war, General Bertolé-Viale, provocatively spoke of a long-term goal of several million men under arms. As Crispi told Bismarck, "duty" would compel him to revenge. "It will be a war of little importance," he wrote in his diary, "and it is a war we cannot avoid." He had no idea of permanent occupation, "yet we cannot stay inactive when the name of Italy is besmirched." Bismarck's comment was that Italy had a large appetite but poor teeth.

At least one minister chose to resign rather than accept Crispi's argument, but Crispi, undeterred, threw himself further into Ethiopian domestic politics. He first suborned the most important tribal chieftain, Menelik, King of Shoa. The poet Rimbaud was for a while engaged in gunrunning for Menelik, and saw more clearly than the Italians that here was an excellent businessman who knew exactly how to profit from any conflict between Italy and the Negus. For a while, however, fortune seemed to be with Italy, since Negus John was killed by the dervishes in 1889, and Menelik, who was John's son-in-law and claimed descent from Solomon and the Queen of Sheba, succeeded to the imperial throne with Italian support.

Six weeks later Menelik signed the Treaty of Uccialli, which was interpreted by Rome as giving Italy a virtual protectorate over his empire. Menelik had merely wished to secure formal Italian support against possible pretenders, but misinterpreted by Crispi this treaty gave Italians a false sense of well-being. Italian arms were sent to the new emperor, and Crispi ordered the further occupation of Asmara in the interior. He followed this in January 1890 by the official proclamation of a new colony on the Red Sea with the name of Eritrea. This forceful move was soon combined with patent evidence of Italian weakness, and the rebel ras therefore joined Menelik against their common enemy, Italian imperialism. It was finally discovered that the Amharic text of the treaty made no mention of an Italian protectorate, for the copies in each language had simply not been checked against each other. Yet this unjustified claim to protectorship ironically became a point from which Italy could not back down without loss of face.

Crispi had gone characteristically from one extreme to the other. As a righteously indignant member of the Pentarchy he had once objected to the Red Sea venture and had spoken against the annexation of Assab and Massawa, and yet he now outdid all others in his imperialistic zeal. In a dangerously false analogy he recalled how easily Garibaldi had conquered Naples with very slender means. A colonial war, he believed, would be good for the prestige of Italy and of Crispi, and by providing a counterattraction to irredentism would also reinforce the Triple Alliance. He therefore informed the *Almanach de Gotha* that the name of Ethiopia would soon disappear from the map, and a new silver coinage was struck in anticipation with Umberto wearing the imperial crown.

Parliament was still deliberately left in the dark. Little account was given to it of money spent, and when new grants were requested these were carefully said to be for defense of existing commitments only. The deputies continued to think in terms of a peaceful commercial colony, whereas in fact it was a prestige venture under a military governor and with aggressive intentions.

§❧

It would be hard to discover any campaign undertaken with obscurer aims and methods than that which led to the defeat at Adowa. Opinion was divided, official policy inconsistent. Crispi wanted a protectorate over all Ethiopia. General Baldissera, the military commander at Massawa, wanted no more than the Tigre. Baldissera distrusted Menelik, and on his own initiative, backed by the minister of war, made contact with neighboring and rival princes. Crispi himself, on the other hand, relied and acted on advice from Count Antonelli which directly contradicted that which reached the War Office.

Finali, who was a minister and a friend of Crispi, says that the cabinet was never once allowed a full-dress discussion on the colonies while he was in office between 1889 and 1891. Apparently, the cabinet did manage to overrule Crispi when he wanted to occupy Asmara, urging the financial, political, and military reasons against it, and adding that the Italian people were absolutely against making sacrifices for what they saw as neither glorious nor useful. But the ministers were as surprised as anyone to find in August 1889 that, despite their decision, the occupation had taken place. Such were the devious workings of the Italian constitution under a strong prime minister.

Among other politicians, Giolitti and the finance minister Sonnino opposed any increased expenditure on Eritrea, while Blanc the foreign minister wanted a purely defensive war, and Saracco the minister of public works advocated abandoning even Massawa. Opposition came naturally from the patriotic irredentists who disliked colonial wars, and also from merchants and industrialists of Milan who (apart from those few engaged in armaments) saw no profitable market or investments in Ethiopia. Above all there were imperative financial arguments, for the government was regularly spending each year a hundred million lire more than Italy could afford, and no statesman dared associate himself with any project for increased taxation. The veteran statesman Jacini, who had been a minister with Cavour, spoke up for common sense. It was vain, he said, for Italian newspapers to magnify the promising future of East Africa, and the only arguments they could find were mere phrases and generalities. Some other people highly placed in politics and the services were even beginning to say that a minor reverse in Africa would not be unwelcome if it would act as a salutary check on this overmighty premier.

The Italian political system militated against the formation of a large party in opposition which could focus these dissentient voices. The conservative leader, Di Rudinì, may have been sorry that Italy was engaged at all in East Africa, and he was determined that the military budget be reduced by at least thirty million a year, but yet he felt that the nation could not back out altogether without losing face. When he succeeded as prime minister in 1891 he sent a parliamentary commission to Africa, but unfortunately they would not assume any positive responsibility and merely recommended no surrender of positions already held. On Baldissera's advice, Di Rudinì chose to support the Tigre faction against Negus Menelik, but then his successor Giolitti returned to the old alliance and so gave Menelik every reason to distrust the changeableness of Italian policy. While both these successive prime ministers were agreed on preventing any further penetration, neither was bold enough to draw back, even though military men on the spot now advised that the inland plateau should be evacuated if no further advance was in view.

One explanation of Crispi's return to office in 1893 was that so many people objected to Di Rudinì's project for economies on the army. The generals, the armament manufacturers, the Court, the enthusiasts for the Triple Alliance, all were agreed on this point. Farini, who as president of the Senate was one of the most important and influential politicians in the country, believed that the army must be strengthened rather than decreased, for it might be needed against lower-class unrest, and "the army is the only existing cement which holds the country together." A strong military state had to be created as "a *sine qua non* of Italy's continued existence," said Farini. General Cosenz went one better and told the king that the army would become demoralized if it was not given a war to fight soon.

Crispi thus realized that a warlike policy in Africa offered him a last chance of political success. An expansionist policy was therefore resumed and the Tigre occupied. Subsequent recriminations make it difficult to trace responsibility for the development of this campaign. Coordination between Rome and Massawa was so bad that Crispi could accuse Baldissera's successor of first occupying Adowa against orders, and then of retiring once the home government had become convinced of the need to stay. General Baratieri occupied Kassala in the Sudan, though Crispi confessed that the government's financial situation made this inadvisable, and the critics blamed the occupation on the general's personal pique after some subordinate had won a minor victory in his absence.

Crispi for his part went on refusing demands from his generals for money and supplies, while still inciting them to strong action. He explained to them that public opinion insisted on colonies paying for themselves, and reminded Baratieri how Napoleon used to pay for his wars with money extracted from the people he had conquered. This was not wise. The fact was that Crispi did not want to face parliament until he could pose as a triumphant conqueror, for he knew that heavy taxes and a financial deficit were handing weapons to his opponents. Yet the same financial anxiety prevented him from properly reinforcing his generals, and so he made this sought-for triumph impossible. Giolitti was later able to criticize the inadequate provision of food, clothing, medicine, and arms. He pointed out how "Crispi's second ministry completely changed our colonial policy, occupying both Kassala and Tigre, forcing the ras of Tigre into alliance with the Negus, and inviting the joint opposition of a united Abyssinia and the dervishes. This policy was wrong and its execution even worse. One part of the ministry wanted war, the other just allowed the drift into war while refusing the means necessary to win it. On top of all this there was incredible incompetence in the organization and military direction of the enterprise."

The critical moment came when, at the end of 1895, Menelik with his Italian-made arms won a small victory at Amba Alagi against heavily outnumbered advanced units of the main Italian forces, and Crispi, who had chosen to disregard military advice over the question of reinforcements, now let political arguments again take precedence over military, even to the point of taunting his commanders with incapacity and cowardice. Politicians in Rome still seem to have been more preoccupied with what terms they would impose when victorious than with planning for victory. Crispi had taken on a big personal responsibility by his constant provocation of the Ethiopians. He continued to call them rebels who somehow owed allegiance to Italy, and he went on thinking that it was a simple colonial war in which the Italians could not be beaten and which therefore did not need serious preparation. He also continued to deceive parliament into permitting further military appropriations by saying that these troop movements were purely defensive, and by insisting that the Ethiopian war would turn out to be a profitable investment.

But he should have chosen another man to taunt with cowardly inactivity than General Baratieri, a man who had been in Garibaldi's Thousand, who was both rash and incompetent and apparently quite capable of carrying out a blind advance without proper calculation. Hearing that Baldissera had been sent to supersede him, Baratieri tried for a quick success and marched in four badly integrated columns to Adowa. Far from his base at Massawa, with no accurate maps, with thoroughly ineffective intelligence, he led six thousand men to their deaths in a heroic but hopeless engagement. In one single day, as many Italians lost their lives as in all the wars of the *risorgimento* put together.

§✿

This defeat concluded Italy's first attempt to conquer Ethiopia. Troops were withdrawn, an indemnity paid, and the silver coins bearing Umberto's head were melted down. The Ethiopian currency was still to be that bearing the face of Maria Theresa. In 1897 Kassala was ceded by Italy to Britain. The colony of Eritrea was retained, but the Red Sea was evidently not a key to anywhere. A successful colonial enterprise would have needed more thought, more men, more money, and more time than Italy had expected or could afford. As Di Rudinì told his constituents in March 1897, they had lost eight thousand soldiers and spent nearly five hundred million lire in exchange for bitterness and disillusion. Eritrea was unsuitable as a colony of settlement because of its climate, and instead of paying for itself it would devour money through the costs of administration. Despite all the absurd nationalist propaganda, colonialism was materially a dead loss. It had already helped to ruin Italy's finances and diminish her military authority in Europe. She had wanted an empire, and had acquired at great expense a desert.

The moral setback was the most important of all, for old wounds were reopened by the humiliation of Adowa. General Baratieri, in a coded telegram to the minister of war, hinted at cowardice on the part of his men, hoping thereby to excuse his folly in allowing them to be so hopelessly outmaneuvered and outnumbered, and unfortunately this telegram was published in Rome. The general also blamed the government for not giving him enough supplies at the same time as they jeered at him for his reluctance to fight. Baratieri himself was brought to trial, like General Ramorino and Admiral Persano before him, and though he was acquitted, it was in terms that branded him with incapacity and reflected poorly on the government which had chosen him. Crispi did his best to calumniate this incompetent but unfortunate general, yet the official Green Book, despite the "loss" of certain important telegrams from the files, showed up the primary responsibility of the prime minister himself and his minister of war. It was a political rather than a military defeat, and the responsibility was Crispi's for thinking that such a war could be won, that it was worth winning, and that it could be won cheaply.

For the Italian people, this public washing of dirty linen was particularly painful. In a more just perspective they might have looked on Adowa as the British looked on defeats at Khartoum or Isandhlwana, but they were in no mood to balance passion with realism, and the battle was magnified by Crispi's political enemies in order to get rid of him. The country had ill-advisedly been persuaded to accept war as a test of nationhood, and defeat therefore inflicted on her a psychological wound for which the whole of Europe was one day to suffer.

The news of Adowa reached an Italy which was already tense with panic over social revolution and political jobbery. The country had turned desperately for deliverance to a strong man, but he had produced only disaster. Jacini called Crispi a megalomaniac, and it was inevitable that many others should now combine to blame their leader's futile exaggeration of prestige and national dignity, his lack of foresight or restraint, and his dangerous approximation to military dictatorship. But one cannot help feeling that these criticisms were directed less against Crispi's authoritarianism than against the fact that he had failed to succeed. Crispi had been the one great hope even of people who knew his weaknesses, and in the land of the blind the one-eyed man had deliberately been made king. Some men, Carducci among them, still hoped in 1896 that Umberto would confirm Crispi in office again, so that Italian honor could be satisfied in yet another and more extravagant campaign, and Crispi himself remained insanely confident that he alone could cope with the situation. Queen Margherita would have stood by him, for she believed passionately in both his "Africanism" and his doctrine of martial law at home. It was noted that the queen and Crispi both refused to contribute to the religious mission which collected money for the Italian prisoners with Menelik, cruelly alleging that a virile race should liberate its own kin by force or not at all.

Mercifully, these fine sentiments were too rarefied for ordinary people. Fortunato roundly called Adowa a well-merited and salutary defeat for a second-class power which had become puffed up with vain and grandiose ambitions, and Italy's simultaneous pursuit of prosperity and *grandezza* seemed to him a ridiculous piece of confusion. Popular feeling had been shown by railroad track being torn up to prevent the further embarkation of troops. Cries had been heard of "long live Menelik," and the mayor of Milan had publicly asked the government to retreat from an enterprise which so much damaged Italy's good name and commerce. Evidently Crispi, to make himself more powerful, had imposed on the country a war which the great majority had not really wanted.

Fortunately, King Umberto, who in general approved of the authoritarianism, the imperialism, and the pro-German bent of Crispi, was not so close a friend and sympathizer as to let the prime minister continue unhindered in his despotism. To Crispi's disgust, the king accepted his resignation. This was done even before parliament had time to give its views, and the expedition for revenge in Ethiopia was not allowed to take place. The same deputies who had applauded Crispi's aggressiveness now witnessed his collapse with little pity, and there was even a call for his impeachment. Finally, in 1898, they officially censured him for his peculation with the banks—the first example of such an outright parliamentary condemnation in Italian history.

Boldness, patriotism, and energy could not make up for Crispi's many weaknesses of mind and temperament. He had taken so much power on himself and tried to run so many departments that details were bound to get lost and subordinates to be ill-chosen. Social unrest had become exacerbated, parliamentary government less efficient, and socialism stronger, all unintended results of his premiership, and nationalism had been purposely and dangerously activated. At the age of nearly eighty he left politics, unwillingly enough, and had to watch the reversal of all he had stood for. Socialism and Catholicism were now to become still more active in public life, government more tolerant, foreign policy less anti-French, and colonial policy less ruled by considerations of dignity.

In his time Crispi had contributed much to the making of Italy and to the rallying of left-wing radicals to the Crown, and some people felt guilty that he was allowed to die in poverty and disgrace. To some liberal historians such as Croce his period of office was disastrous, a break in the normal liberal development of the country. But other liberals and all fascist historians were to call him a hero, and correctly demonstrated that, far from being a hiatus in Italian history, these few years of aggrandizement and megalomania were by no means wholly unconnected with the traditions of the *risorgimento* before and with the febrile nationalism which was to come after.

25 Parliamentary Government Endangered, 1896-1900

The obvious successor to Crispi would have been Giolitti, a restrained colonialist, unopinionated, undemonstrative in domestic policy, and anxious to curb the military and germanophile proclivities of the Court. But Giolitti's attitudes toward tax reform and social unrest were too liberal for the parliament elected in 1895. It was a time of emergency, and the king ran true to form in turning to another military leader. General Ricotti was asked to form a nonpolitical cabinet, and chose to take junior office himself under the Marquis di Rudinì, who became premier for the second time.

This brought a welcome sense of relief. A decree of amnesty was published for De Felice and Bosco, two champions of the *fasci* who had since been re-elected to parliament. Many others implicated in the Sicilian rising were also released, and a special commissioner was appointed to carry out emergency reforms in the island. Ricotti resigned quite shortly, because as minister of war he wanted the army reduced from twelve corps to eight, and this the king vetoed. The left-wing liberal, Zanardelli, was brought into the cabinet later in 1897 in order to broaden the ministerial majority. Giolitti tried to prevent this, but Zanardelli like everyone else had come to accept the process of transformism. In so far as these labels now meant anything, the cabinet included five men of the Right and six of the Left, so it could hardly agree on any constructive or forceful policy.

The problem of social disorder was the most urgent of all, as it was also the most difficult for a cabinet of such varied composition. Contemporary newspapers in 1896–97 tell of the cabmen at Rome and Naples going out on strike aganist the new streetcars, of a monetary crisis which forced a reversion to paying wages in kind, of people in Sardinia eating grass and dying of hunger, and of fifty arrests at Ancona for pillaging the municipal granaries. So manifold and various were these symptoms of unrest that quite clearly there existed a deep-seated malaise. In the past twenty years many great fortunes had been made by fair means or foul, and the contrast between riches and poverty was becoming more and more conspicuous and unhealthy. Protests were made in parliament against the large numbers of Italian children being exported to work in French factories. We hear again of town halls and local customs houses being burned, of peasants moving to occupy the land on the large grazing estates of the Chigi, Colonna, and Barberini in the Agro Romano, and of anarchists making attempts on the life of the king. On one occasion the minister of education, Gianturco, was mobbed by the students at Bologna, and could escape only when soldiers arrived to take over the university; and at Rome university too the army had to garrison the lecture rooms before the professors could lecture undisturbed.

In the face of this turbulence, and especially after the reinforcement of the extreme Left in the elections of 1897, Di Rudinì had no plausible social policy. Few politicians since 1861 had ever had time to wonder how far a regime of liberty was possible while some people were on the point of starvation, though in fact the whole future of parliamentary government depended upon this emergent proletariat being somehow made less revolutionary and more contented. The best answer to these bread riots would have been to suspend the local excise on grain and flour which was so cruel an imposition in a time of rising prices, but any coalition cabinet risked a split if it proposed such a measure. When at last Di Rudinì dared to stand up to the vested interests behind this excise, it was too late.

ॐ

Peasant unrest and an increase in the parliamentary *estrema* went along with the development of Marxist socialism among some of the city workers. Socialism was the product of a new civic society which advanced *pari passu* with Italian industry under the protection of tariffs. After several centuries of relative stability, the leading towns in Italy were once more expanding, as the surplus rural population was gradually persuaded to come and serve the new factories. The population of

Milan was under 200,000 in 1871; within a few years it overtook that of Turin and Rome, and by 1921 was over 700,000. Turin doubled its size to 500,000 in the same fifty years, and Rome expanded from 220,000 to almost 700,000. Urban expansion at some moments was quite hectic, and any depression would provide material for socialist propaganda among this new proletariat.

But the tardiness of Italy's industrial revolution meant that socialism at first appeared to be more an intellectual than a proletarian movement. At Milan in 1891, Turati, Bissolati, and other socialists who frequented the salon of Anna Kulishov, founded the review *Critica Sociale,* which was to have considerable importance in educating the next generation. Simultaneously, Antonio Labriola's lectures at Rome university dramatically and cogently introduced Marxist materialism to the educated world, and on a less serious level the sentimental humanitarianism associated with Garibaldi influenced some of Italy's foremost writers. The poet Pascoli had gone to prison in 1879 for his propagation of socialist doctrines. De Amicis, who was the most widely read Italian novelist, the writer Ada Negri, and the composer Leoncavallo were all sympathizers. The brilliant lawyer, Professor Ferri, was converted in the early nineties. Lombroso the criminologist, Ferrero the historian and sociologist, and for a while Pantaleoni the economist and Benedetto Croce the philosopher, all were tinged with socialist ideas.

For these men socialism came to replace a sense of disillusion and emptiness, and to inject real distinctions and controversies into political life. The conservative Villari wrote in the *Nuova Antologia:* "socialism has faith in itself; it has order and discipline; and what is more, it fights with a program of its own, while other parties lack such a program and are all more or less personal. . . . Socialism is not only held as a belief by the most cultured and civilized part of the country, but everything is contributing to favor its progress." Likewise Croce later wrote about this same period that "socialism conquered all, or almost all, the flower of the younger generation. . . . To remain uninfluenced by it, or to assume, as some did, an attitude of unreasoning hostility toward it, was a sure sign of inferiority." Marxism acted as a tonic on the decadent liberalism of the 1890's, and as a purgative which eventually destroyed the outmoded radicalism and republicanism of the Left.

Some of the old-guard radicals remained in their backwater. Cavallotti, for instance, the natural leader of the *estrema,* wrote pungent articles which helped to make *Il Secolo* for a time perhaps the most powerful journal in the country. Cavallotti was the idol of the people, a man who had fought under Garibaldi in Sicily, honest and combative, poet and playwright as well as politician. He was essentially a radical, and yet he was far from socialism and far from even recognizing the importance of economic problems. In 1898, fighting his thirty-second duel, he was killed by the editor of a rival conservative newspaper who was fighting his fifteenth—the continuation of this primitive and grotesque method of controversy was a sure indication of retarded political education among the deputies. The next time that Cavallotti's opponent arrived in parliament, the whole of the Left silently filed out of the Chamber, but the disappearance of this romantic and generous figure symbolized the passing of leadership on the Left from the radicals to the socialists.

In 1892 the new Italian Socialist Party, or PSI, met for its first conference at Genoa. Its deliberations were a little unreal and pedantic, and already there existed a tendency toward debilitating divisions over hairsplitting points of dogma. The chief decision made was to break finally from the anarchists, and a composite program was then formulated, Marxist by inspiration but moderate in tone, to which both extremists and moderates might adhere.

A second congress at Reggio Emilia in 1893 tried with less success to define a socialist attitude toward the radicals. Ferri led one wing of the party which was ready to work with the radicals for social reform; the other wing followed Turati who at this point was intransigent and for strict independence. Enrico Ferri was a political mountebank: handsome, eloquent, and vain, he was to change his mind many times before he ultimately flirted with fascism. Filippo Turati was more of a realist, as he was also to become a great patriot, a believer in gradualism, and above everything he put socialist party unity. After much debate the congress agreed to compromise over whether to collaborate with other parties and try to make parliamentary government work. It was arranged that socialist deputies might sit in parliament, but not vote for any bourgeois government.

Social reform found another champion from an unexpected quarter in Pope Leo XIII, during whose pontificate a group of Catholics appeared with the name of La Democrazia Cristiana. Leo in 1878 had condemned socialism as a deadly peril for the Church, as his predecessor had condemned liberalism, but in 1891 the encyclical Rerum novarum laid down that property should be more equitably divided and that workers' unions were not necessarily bad. The Church thus recognized more quickly than many liberals how important it was not to leave all the good tunes to the devil. Catholic laymen were still not permitted to vote, but they were encouraged to intervene more in public affairs.

§●

Although social reform thus became almost respectable, the generation of Di Rudinì lacked the imagination to apply it. The price of bread
continued to rise, especially during the Spanish-American War, and a
general economic crisis was the inevitable result of Crispi's expensive
enterprise in Africa. Violence smoldered throughout 1897. Riots in
January 1898 led to Rome being put for several days in a state of siege
with troops posted at every street corner. In Parma the mob ran loose
cutting telegraph wires and smashing the new electric lights. At Florence
they broke into the Palazzo Strozzi where the Queen of the Netherlands
was staying, and for one day virtually took over the whole town. A government circular of May 1898 complained that everywhere the local
authorities were invoking the aid of the army, and sooner or later this
was bound to mean heavy casualties. An extra class of conscripts was
even drafted. Colajanni spoke of tens of thousands in prison, and socialist deputies were camping in the parliament buildings so as to avoid
arrest. Worst of all, in May 1898 a violent clash took place at Milan.
After two policemen had been killed in the rioting, General Bava-
Beccaris turned cannon and grapeshot against the unarmed mob, mis-
taking a concourse of beggars around a convent for a revolutionary
army. At least eighty people were killed, and minor street fighting lasted
for four days.

This tragic episode was, on very slender evidence, attributed to socialist machination, and hence a repressive policy was adopted. The unfortunate general, who had probably just lost his head, was misguidedly
rewarded by the king with the Grand Cross of the Military Order of
Savoy to signalize his courage and foresight. The *estrema* leaders at
Milan, including the radical Romussi and the republican De Andreis,
were arrested, together with Costa, Bissolati, and Anna Kulishov, and
Turati was sentenced to twelve years in prison, although convicted of no
more than spreading socialist propaganda. Railroadmen and civil servants were put on a military footing so that disobedience could be punished under military law. The universities of Rome, Naples, Padua, and
Bologna were closed; chambers of labor, village banks, and philan-
thropic associations were dissolved, together with some three thousand
Catholic groups and organizations. The Milanese *Osservatore Cattolico*
was suppressed and its editor brought before a military tribunal, and
among a hundred other newspapers suspended was the radical *Secolo,*
though it had not supported the riots. Such procedure was legally irregular and politically inept, and suggested that the government had
little understanding of all this turmoil. It compared most unfavorably

with the failure of the courts and the government to act against blatant examples of political and financial corruption.

Responsibility lay with Di Rudinì for this abrogation of constitutional rights. Not only was he prepared to use the army to enforce his domestic policy, but he even threatened to make financial appropriations by royal decree. Once again, however, the king proved too timid, and perhaps in the last resort too sensible, to give his ministers more authority as the queen and many of his advisers wished. When parliament met in June 1898, he refused to permit a dissolution. Di Rudinì therefore resigned without waiting for a parliamentary vote. He had played the *gran signore* too much to be popular at Court. He was also distrusted for his incongruous *connubio* with Cavallotti and Zanardelli and his attempt to mix Left with Right. The conservative Visconti-Venosta had had to resign because of Zanardelli's anticlericalism, whereas Zanardelli had resigned as a liberal protest against martial law. Transformism at a certain point could mean incoherence and lack of an agreed policy; and as soon as such a government was forced by circumstances to act decisively, the coalition was almost bound to be shattered.

Once again in a time of crisis the king turned to a general for his next premier, and four other ministries were also placed under serving officers. Parliamentary opinion was not consulted in advance, for by a strict reading of the constitution it was now being regularly asserted that the government was responsible not to parliament but to the king. General Pelloux seemed an uncontroversial choice. Earlier in the year, when sent with full powers to restore order in Apulia, Pelloux had refused to proclaim a state of siege, for he appreciated that disorder did not arise from political rebelliousness but was a manifestation of extreme economic need. He was a conservative with liberal leanings, and he included in his coalition Fortis and Nasi from the Left Center. For seven months, indeed, he governed as a liberal and refused to enforce Di Rudinì's repressive edicts.

Before long, however, Pelloux's training as a soldier and his parliamentary inexperience made him an instrument for those who advocated strengthening the executive against the legislature. As an army officer he was also subject to a direct order from the king in a way which other prime ministers were not. Instead of granting the expected amnesty of political prisoners, in February 1899 he introduced legislation to control public meetings and the press and to send political offenders to the penal settlements. When the more liberal members of his cabinet objected, he replaced them by Salandra and Di San Giuliano. Some of his opponents argued that Article 28 of the constitution explicitly permitted freedom of expression in the press, and indeed that the very creation of Italy had depended on this freedom as a means of educating people in patriotism. The Left urged that the extraordinary powers which he claimed should not be allowed save when specifically requested by the judges, but the committee appointed to examine the bill in parliament was mainly one of conservatives, and instead modified its provisions the other way to allow the executive even greater discretionary power. Still unsatisfied, Pelloux in June 1899 announced his intention of ruling by royal decrees which would give his projects the automatic force of law without the need of facing parliamentary criticism. Never before had anything like this been heard.

The promulgation of this decree law forced the liberals into extra-constitutional action themselves. Deprived by the censorship of more normal modes of criticism, without party organization, without redress in the ordinary courts whose harsh sentences were undermining popular confidence in the judiciary, they fell back on the method of obstruction in the Chamber, and so forged for themselves a powerful but dangerous weapon. Zanardelli and Giolitti stood aloof at first from this obstructive policy, but the socialists Bissolati, Prampolini, and especially Ferri began to talk continuously through entire sittings, and when Sonnino in response proposed to introduce the same guillotine procedure which had been used to quell the Irish at Westminster, they merely turned their filibustering on to this procedural point. In a memorable session of June 1899, the Speaker, claiming to save the dignity of the House, suddenly declared that the debate was closed and the motion could be put. This arbitrary action provoked Bissolati and De Felice to overturn the voting urns. Pelloux thereupon arrested them and closed parliament for three months, and Costa when he protested this closure was promptly arrested himself. The socialist town council at Milan was also dissolved and replaced by a nominated royal commission.

The scene of conflict then shifted from parliament to the higher courts. The *Corte dei Conti,* which had the right to register all government edicts, had already made certain reservations about the decree law, and in February 1900 the high court of appeal, on the straightforward request of a single citizen, declared it an unwarranted act of the executive and with no more authority henceforward than as the text of a bill before parliament. This was a notable decision, and Pelloux had to accept it if he did not want to carry out a *coup d'état.*

For another month he fell back on trying to alter the parliamentary regulations and restrict freedom of debate, and at the end of March 1900 he once more attempted to cut short the interminable discussion and vote his proposed restrictions so that he might then be able to win parliamentary sanction for his decree law. But rather than be party to such a violation of usage, the extreme Left walked out of the Chamber in protest. Paradoxically, it had been the "anticonstitutional" groups of the *estrema* which had defended the constitution in these two years since martial law had been declared at Milan. This time, however, in April 1900, Zanardelli rose to say that he and the Left Center would also withdraw from parliament rather than countenance such despotic governmental action.

This strike of the parliamentary opposition resembles that secession of the "Aventine" liberals which twenty years later was to present Mussolini with a clear path toward absolute power, and no doubt it was Zanardelli's success in 1900 which led Amendola to try to copy him in 1924. Had Pelloux been so minded, he might have arbitrarily altered the standing orders and then used his large majority to pass any measures he fancied, but in fact he had sufficient belief in liberal and parliamentary methods to put his case to the electorate. No doubt he was confident that a general election would confirm his policy and so give him a mandate for more forceful behavior.

The broad alliance against Pelloux was an important development in Italian politics. Until now, even radicals and republicans in the old *estrema* had been reluctant to band together in parliament, but repression gave them a common experience and persuaded even socialists of Turati's school not to be wholly intransigent. Thus, the socialist congress of 1895 agreed to support the more progressive liberals even to the point of voting for them on the second ballot at elections. This alliance became an established fact only after Di Rudinì in 1898 forced all the more democratic groups together in face of persecution. The sixty-seven deputies of the *estrema,* when they perceived that Sonnino and other conservatives intended to modify the constitution, welcomed the aid of the more enlightened liberal newspapers. The important liberal-conservative daily, the *Corriere della Sera* of Milan, moved into opposition against Pelloux as it had also opposed Crispi in Africa—this was another big difference between 1899 and twenty years later. Some of the conservatives objected to Pelloux's extravagant attempt to start a colony in China, just as others objected to the fact that this attempt was such a failure. A useful weathercock was the young poet D'Annunzio, who, elected deputy for the extreme Right, with theatrical exhibitionism now ostentatiously crossed the floor of the House. "On one side of parliament," he exclaimed, "there are many people who are half dead, and on the other a few who are alive, so as a man of intellect I shall move toward life."

This strengthening of the opposition was far from being a straight-forward union of progressives against conservatives, but it saved Italy from reverting to a pre-1860 type of government, just as a similar alliance might have saved her from Mussolini in 1922. Despite all that Pelloux could do to "make" the elections of June 1900, the representation of the *estrema* increased from sixty-seven to ninety-five seats, so that all the opposition groups together formed a loose-knit bloc numbering 212 out of 508. This election was noteworthy for the appearance of an organized and nationwide electoral campaign on the part of both the *estrema* and Zanardelli's "constitutional opposition." At Turin a socialist lost by only six votes against the ministerial candidate, but the ballot box was then found to contain ten more voting cards than the number of registered voters. D'Annunzio, now a candidate for radical socialism, failed to be returned as such (a lesson he took to heart), since most people could not follow his highly charged language, but at Milan a socialist beat the same conservative Speaker of the House who had tried to invoke the parliamentary guillotine against the filibusters. Pelloux still had a majority, but feared to push matters to extremes, and when the new Chamber gave him a majority of only twenty-eight in electing the new Speaker, he chose to resign in June 1900 to give the king a chance to find a stronger coalition.

Moderate at heart though he may have been, Pelloux had mismanaged the situation, and stirred up an enormous amount of ill-feeling without being prepared to introduce that emendation of the constitution which some of his friends advocated. Sonnino and others were discussing the merits of a Bismarckian type of chancellorship, or of returning to the pre-Cavour tradition of strongly monarchical government. But here the conservatives were being dangerously radical, and these suggestions had the effect only of shaking people's confidence in parliamentary government of any kind.

§❧

Unfortunately, this episode had involved the monarch in political controversy, and cries of "down with the king" were heard even from deputies in the Chamber. Pelloux's resignation revealed the fact that King Umberto had kept up no relations with Giolitti or other possible premiers; he even refused to answer Giolitti's letters. Being unfettered constitutionally in his choice of a successor, the king departed from precedent and chose a member of the Upper House, the characterless octogenarian from Piedmont, Senator Saracco. A few days later Umberto was assassinated by a former emigrant, Bresci, who had been chosen by a group of anarchists in the United States to return and avenge the deaths of those shot by the army in Milan.

In a sense King Umberto had been the victim of the ultras who sought a more authoritarian mode of government. He himself had taken no public initiative in this movement, though it was true that he had become far too intrusive in politics and Queen Margherita was notoriously a bigoted conservative who could not abide even the moderate liberalism of a Zanardelli. In choosing Pelloux and Saracco the king had shown small regard for the recognized leaders in parliament. Admittedly, the royal right of veto on parliamentary resolutions had never been used except when the king was once begged by his ministers to correct an error they had made, but the issuing of regulations by royal decree had again become general practice in the nineties. Finally, the king, who was theoretically a "sacred" person above the clash in the arena, had allowed himself to be involved personally (and not merely through his ministers) on one side of a struggle which divided the nation.

Umberto was recognized to have a special prerogative in foreign and military policy, and the Triple Alliance was thought to be largely his handiwork. This made him unpopular not only in those conservative circles which wanted to cut the military budget, but also among the irredentists who opposed Austria, and it compelled him to interfere still more in domestic politics. For example, Zanardelli's project to form a government in 1892 had failed because the king refused to have the irredentist General Baratieri as foreign minister, and the fact that this refusal was known to be in response to a specific request from Austria made it doubly unacceptable. After Adowa, Umberto had further insisted that Di Rudinì should not yield too much to the demands of the victorious Menelik, because "neither I nor the army will stand for it." Di Rudinì's minister of war had also been overruled by the king when he asked for a reduction in the army.

All this together was hardly a plot against the constitution, for existing constitutional law gave the king considerable latitude, and Umberto lacked the strength of mind and perhaps also the interest to go further. Moreover, what he had lost to the monarchy in prestige and popularity was in part to be recovered during the more peaceful and prosperous years which lay immediately ahead.

26 Defects in the Constitution

The assassination of Umberto ended a decade of violence, and even the republicans in parliament joined in a testimony of homage to the dead sovereign. A more tranquil and prosperous age was coming. The rapid building of factories in the North was evidence of this, and so was the habit of seaside vacations for the well to do at Viareggio, Venice, and Posillipo. The great tide of emigration was partially relieving country districts of the surplus manpower which had depressed standards and caused unemployment. The age of electricity had begun, the first automobiles were on the roads (Queen Margherita became a great enthusiast), and the first reinforced-concrete buildings were being planned. *Giolittismo* was something new in politics, as *d'annunzianesimo* in literature. The age of Verdi was giving way to the age of Puccini—Verdi died in 1901, and it was a sign of the changing times that the young Mussolini made a speech to commemorate the event.

§●

In politics the most notable feature at the turn of the century was a sad derangement in parliamentary behavior. Now that forty years of history could be reviewed in perspective, it was clear that parliament had never been robust. Italy had not yet been able to assimilate or supersede the experience of France, England, and America, and develop stable conventions of her own. Parliament had not succeeded in preventing corruption. In 1896, more bank directors at Turin and Naples were arrested for fraud, and it was found that Palermo had not published its municipal accounts for five years—a million lire could not be accounted for by the city treasurer, who was another of Crispi's shady acquaintances.

Ever since 1860 the centralization of government had proceeded apace, without a parallel development in representative institutions to ensure the essential freedoms and enough public criticism. Cavour had long since realized the dangers to liberalism inherent in the advance of mass democracy, yet had himself been forced to use plebiscites with manhood suffrage. He had foretold how the idea of equality, once assimilated into social habits and codes of law, might end in the centralization of all power until any dissentient minority was buried beneath the weight of numbers. Rattazzi, Nicotera, and Crispi were examples of this leaning of radical democracy toward authoritarianism—even Garibaldi had chosen to be a dictator and a *duce* during his only period of political rule.

There were similar tendencies latent on the Right. Di Rudinì and Sonnino inherited from Spaventa and Ricasoli the paradoxical notion that liberty could be imposed from above, which led to the idea that governments might have the right and duty to increase their powers and eradicate criticism. The menace of socialism in the eighties and afterward only served to increase the intolerance and authoritarianism of those who felt threatened by class war, and to reinforce the pervasive sense of disquietude about parliamentary institutions.

The executive—the king and his ministers—had always possessed a preponderance of power under the 1848 *statuto,* and not even Cavour had been interested in setting up checks and balances once he himself had risen to power. The judiciary was hardly distinct from the executive, and through the minister of justice the government had wide powers of nomination to and promotion on the bench. There were few if any political forums outside parliament, no wide circle of newspaper readers, no well-developed party organizations linking up rural areas with the capital. The Senate rarely showed independence, and subserviently came to heel at the mere threat of nominating an *infornata* or "ovenful" of new senators. In the Lower House a skillful premier could usually build a majority by the patronage emanating from the ministries of the interior and public works.

Crispi when out of office in 1886 described this exercise of influence: "In parliament a kind of bilateral contract is often made: the minister gives the local population into the hands of a deputy on condition that the latter promises the ministry his vote: the prefect and the chief of police are nominated in the interests of the deputy in order to keep local interest in his favor. . . . There is pandemonium in parliament when an important vote comes along, as government agents run through rooms and down corridors collecting votes and promising subsidies, decorations, canals, and bridges." Much power was concealed in the ability to promise tariffs, government contracts, and titles. Railways, roads, barracks, drains, and aqueducts would be built wherever deputies most required them for the assertion of their own influence, and local interests thus placated would vote for the government candidates. The authorities would bargain with the camorra, the mafia, the local landowners, or the banks which owned the mortgages on so much property, and thus they managed by persuasion or coercion to control many southern electoral districts. A friend of the government who owned large estates might easily be elected without visiting his constituents—as Lacaita for instance had been.

On the relatively few occasions when a serious contest seemed probable, the government would simply instruct the prefect which candidate to favor. A corollary of this was that new prefects would commonly be appointed by each successive administration, and in the years 1886–96 Salerno had ten different prefects (this was Nicotera's constituency) and Girgenti twelve. Opposition voters in the South were sometimes arrested on trumped-up charges the day before the elections; criminals could be released from prison to use their influence on behalf of the official candidate (Crispi in private once threatened to release all the prisoners in Sicily); and names of opponents might be erased from the lists on the spurious plea of illiteracy. Government servants—under which category came schoolmasters, university teachers, magistrates, and railroadmen—might be threatened with loss of employment, or removal to some inhospitable post on the islands. On an average there were only some 4,500 voters in each constituency around the year 1900, and so it was not hard for the prefect to find a majority.

If Depretis, Crispi, and Giolitti were in turn able to build up a kind of parliamentary dictatorship, it was largely due to this electoral manipulation. Very seldom indeed did any election lead at once to a change of government, for it was the government which made the election, not the election the government. The very regularity of this practice suggests that it evolved naturally out of the constitution, or at least that Italians were glad to sacrifice electoral freedom for some of the order, discipline, and deeper "sense of the state" which they felt themselves to lack. The instinctive anarchism of so many Italians thus produced an equal and opposite trend toward authoritarianism as a corrective. History had shown them that necessary reforms, in education for instance, might have to wait until an emergency when they could be effected under plenary powers: whereas, under ordinary conditions of parliamentary life, such reforms ran the risk of perishing stillborn for want of either the habit of give-and-take or the force of authority.

This nostalgia for authority was always present, even if submerged. Some of those who dared not inform against brigandage must have secretly hoped that one day they could support law and order without being thought dishonorable or having to fear the penalties of private vengeance. In like manner, many of those very taxpayers who defrauded the government of millions may possibly have hoped that a more just and efficient fiscal system would one day make it possible to reduce the level of taxation even at the price of making subterfuge impossible. In an even greater degree the poor knew that true liberty for themselves might come only from a strong central authority which curbed the over-mighty landlords. As things were, trial by jury in the South, far from safeguarding the liberty of the subject, was—when it operated—a nor-

mal means of perverting justice on behalf of the local magnate or cama-
rilla whose interest the jurors dared not gainsay. By a paradox, the
curtailment of "constitutional rights" thus appeared to some people the
only guarantee of freedom. The deputies themselves connived at this
process, and would accord a government full powers so that reforms
might be made; or alternatively the government would rule by decree
and then be acquitted retrospectively by statute.

The reputation of parliament naturally suffered when the process of
government could be thought of as a succession of administrative edicts,
and the function of deputies as mainly to talk and hinder. Parliamentary
prestige also suffered when the bank scandals revealed how much the
deputies, who received no payment (and life at Rome was expensive),
had been connected with the Banca Romana and so were possibly
the mouthpieces of corrupt financial interests. Over a hundred deputies
had finally been implicated in the reports on this bank, and Crispi and
Giolitti, together with a number of ex-ministers or future ministers such
as Nicotera and Di San Giuliano, had been censured publicly for irregularities or peculation.

It was particularly disturbing that deputies seemed to represent the
wrong people. In 1895, to check the influence of vested interests, all
government contractors and representatives of companies subsidized by
the state were made ineligible for the Chamber, and no more than ten
professors and ten magistrates were allowed in the House, any excess
being removed by lot. Probably half the whole number of deputies were
lawyers. So far removed were these so-called representatives from the
productive life of the nation that in 1900 only eight of them called themselves agriculturists and a dozen declared themselves engaged in industry. Hence the reputation of the House as a parasite community.

The practice of filibustering naturally lowered the dignity of parliamentary proceedings and the reputation of parliament. Unseemly behavior by deputies during debate was much too common, and life in the
Palazzo Montecitorio became increasingly wild, especially once the
socialists entered politics after 1882. The Speaker might on occasion be
showered with paper missiles or worse, and forced to suspend the session
by putting on his hat, while it was not extraordinary when the minister
of marine was assaulted by an admiral whom he had retired on half pay.
More than once there was a fight on the very floor of the House, and the
temperature of politics could probably be charted by the charges for
broken desks and chairs. The newspapers naturally fastened on these
scenes and on tales of parliamentary corruption as being more newsworthy than normal parliamentary business, and this too helped to lower
deputies in popular estimation.

Toward the end of the century the standard of speeches declined, perhaps because a widening electorate demanded a more rhetorical and demagogic delivery. Speeches were too often declaimed toward the press gallery, and the parliamentary correspondents thus became a power in the land. A deputy rash enough to go on speaking after 7 P.M. might find that for a time, depending on the magnitude of his offence, his pronouncements would receive no notice in the press, and his dearest object would thus be frustrated.

§●

The chief limitation on the power of a man such as Crispi was the lack of cohesion among the groups in his majority and the consequent succession of ministerial crises. Groups were customarily composed of clients acknowledging the same patron, of deputies forming a common regional interest, rather than of men accepting the same political principles and program. As Petruccelli remarked, "a gust of wind, and these leaves which call themselves deputies will be blown about and mixed up anew." A chance insult was enough to permit one of the group leaders to work up an artificial excitement and stampede the Chamber, so that the prime minister might have to reshuffle his entire cabinet. This helps to explain how, in the seventy-four years between the granting of the constitution and Mussolini's accession, seventy different ministries held office.

One interesting constitutional custom was that a prime minister would not normally wait for defeat in either House before resigning. In 1892 Crispi estimated that during the last thirty-two years there had been twenty-eight ministerial crises, of which only six had been strictly parliamentary, and of these six, he added, not one had been resolved by giving power to the man most representative of the parliamentary majority. In the decade 1891–1900, ministries invariably resigned without waiting for a parliamentary vote against them. Crispi claimed to be quite justified in this, and had the audacity to say that he feared to compromise the great interests of the state by a vote in the Chamber.

The king was thereby at least left more freedom in choosing a successor, "unhampered" by a parliamentary decision. The outgoing minister knew that, having once paid this price, there was no reason why he should not be re-employed in some new combination, or at any rate have a say in placing his friends in the vacant jobs. His justification in thus sidetracking parliament would be that the Chamber, possessing no solid basis of party, seldom knew its own mind and seldom in fact objected to the royal choice. Crispi's constitutional doctrine insisted that "the king is not responsible before parliament but before the country," and he once explained that "when the king turns against a ministry, he conspires in parliament with the deputies whom he thinks most influential, and organizes a hostile movement." The king certainly conspired against Cavour and Ricasoli in this way, and no doubt often again where documentation is not yet possible: Crispi had good reason to know this procedure at first hand.

Because of the absence of well-knit parties, a man was powerless in opposition except by some temporary combination of groups. Crispi and Giolitti when out of office rarely played an active part in political life—one may be reminded of Cavour's unhappy example in 1852 and 1859—and they made little attempt to build up an organized party. It suited their interests to remain uncommitted so that they would have more scope when their turn to build a coalition came again. Crispi, for twenty years the leader of a so-called democratic element in politics, seldom precisely defined a policy or effectively disciplined his followers. Perhaps this was because he stood for no simple policy and knew the absurdity of trying to impose political discipline in Italy, or perhaps he preferred to be free to profit from the continually shifting balance of parliamentary power.

Every government was a coalition, for no group was ever powerful enough on its own. This usually meant that when any real division or clash of principle emerged, it was driven underground in order to prevent the majority breaking up. For example, the condition of the poor scarcely seemed a subject for profitable debate in a cabinet that included both Di Rudinì and Nicotera or Zanardelli. The Roman question was likewise too delicate for the usual composite ministry. We know that individual ministers were often sharply divided from each other on the vital question of colonies, and also on the size of military expenditure, yet resignation on such issues was infrequent. More striking still was to be the way in which half a dozen successive cabinets after 1919 avoided the whole issue of fascism while there was still time to avert a *coup d'état,* and Italian parliamentarism thus dug its own grave.

The tacit agreement to submerge these conflicts of principle hinders the historian in labeling political groups and pinpointing the significance of parliamentary debate. Many politicians refused to question military expenditure or the Triple Alliance, for they knew that they could hardly reach office against active royal disfavor, and it was important to avoid the hostility of the local prefect at the next election. Had the Catholics in general not held back from parliamentary life, they might have acted as a healthy challenge backed by political courage and a principle of cohesion, and this would have forced the anticlericals, from Turati to Zanardelli and Crispi himself, into a common alliance over a point of real substance. But without such a challenge, as Villari remarked in 1902, no feature of Italian political life was in fact more remarkable than the small amount of real change effected by the succession of one government to another. The real political life of the country was thus sometimes quite unreflected in parliamentary proceedings, and the petty consideration of match taxes and pensions made politics seem even more desultory and unsubstantial. Although some parliamentary criticism was extremely vocal, and sometimes physical too, the critics came from a nonconformist fringe outside the game of transformism—there were lonely eccentrics such as Bertani on the Left, Villari and Mosca on the Right, or Garibaldi and the socialists who disapproved of parliamentary institutions as a point of principle.

The lack of great political issues was associated with a lack of the kind of party which could have manufactured a real or artificial conflict of ideas. America and Britain had in common a two or three party system, and this ensured—however artificially—that each problem was threshed out in the open and presented before the public as susceptible of alternative solutions. Among Italy's more important political theorists, Cattaneo and Mazzini had similarly believed in the formation of parties with a good organization, possessing members, membership subscriptions, and newspapers, and De Sanctis and Minghetti on the other side (and also Crispi and Giolitti when not in office) spoke in general approval of a two-party system. But Cavour and most of the liberals, despite their imitation of England, tended to believe that parties were factions which put sectional before national interests. Cavour set the fashion of believing that the art of politics was to find a coalition based on a highest common factor of agreement, obscuring where possible— or else absorbing—what was controversial. That this caught on was probably due to the existence of extreme views, ultraconservative or republican, communist or fascist, which wanted to alter the whole basis of politics, and against which the groups of the Center had to try to combine. Cavour at least knew how to use this method of group combination for the purposes of efficient government, and was brilliantly successful at preserving his majority while not shirking the controversies of the day. His successors copied his methods indifferently and with less political courage. Their practice was to open an umbrella at the first rumble of political storm, and wait until the clouds had passed.

Political theorists were not lacking who justified this concept of "government by the indeterminate middle." They easily proved how even Mazzini and Cattaneo, for all their teaching, in practice lacked the first requisite of good party men, the readiness to yield on doctrine and tactics in order to keep party cohesion. Italian politicians, it was argued, were too individualistic, too used to a clientelistic tradition, to form parties of any size or durability. Even when, as in 1898–1900, issues of great moment could no longer be buried, there were no simple parties which emerged to voice them, but two broad alliances containing a wide range of view. And between these broad alliances there was a dangerous lack of mutual respect and tolerance. A healthy parliament could hardly exist where one side attempted to alter the rules and suppress criticism, while the defeated side walked out of the Chamber after upsetting the voting boxes.

It was the socialist party which made the first serious attempt to cut loose from transformism and the group system. The socialists theoretically believed in discipline, dogma, and organized opposition, and they therefore brought new life into political controversy. Before long, however, their own lack of internal cohesion revealed them as yet another example of the atomic individualism of Italian politics. It remained for the fascists to show how a party could discipline its members to achieve certain selected ends, and unfortunately fascism like socialism was pledged to overthrow the constitution. Parties and parliament evidently did not go together in Italy. One may note that the same old means of transformism and coalition were also to be used by fascism in order to conquer its disorganized opponents, and Mussolini himself veered from extreme Left to extreme Right and then back again.

§

It is difficult to know how far the defective working of parliamentary government was due to the system itself, and how far to the defective quality and political education of the men who operated that system. A number of changes in the constitution were in fact suggested, for instance strengthening the authority of the prime minister and widening the suffrage. Experiments were in fact made with proportional representation, with single-member constituencies and *scrutin de liste*. The English system of three readings to a bill was considered as a replacement for the French system of committees and interpellations, and regulations for parliamentary procedure were changed successively in 1863, 1876, and 1888. But such experiments still left political behavior much as before; one unfortunate but inevitable result was that they also helped to prevent the growth of an indigenous political tradition and to deprive Italy of a useful check on revolutionary change.

Experience convinced many people that they had to blame not only procedural and institutional deficiencies, but also what a famous editor of the *Corriere della Sera* called the "political immaturity of the country." Cavour had told parliament in July 1850: "Yes, gentlemen, I tell you frankly that, until our liberal institutions are animated by real political life in the smallest villages as well as in the largest cities, we shall never have a genuinely liberal system, but be driven to and fro from anarchy to despotism like the French." Centuries of rule by tyrannical governments had covered up what native traditions there were of local self-government. There was no middle way: either provincial and communal government was centered on prefects nominated by the minister of the interior, or else, when elected councils were given more authority, local cliques and camarillas merely reinforced their personal power, and the prefect in this case took care to let well enough alone.

The result suggested, once again, that only strong central government would check the countertendency toward anarchism, and that Cavour's hopes had in fact been utopian. Since there was corruption in the progressive city government of Milan as well as in the backward communes of the South, evidently democratic methods did not grow naturally in this milieu. A year or so after the Left had upset the voting urns in parliament, Mussolini's socialist father was arrested at Predappio when one of the customary election battles in the village had ended with broken ballot boxes. Given little incentive to take their share in politics, people abstained: the Rome elections in 1871 were an extreme case, when only a few hundred people took the trouble to vote.

Local self-government was not a program with much popular appeal. The chief aims of the general public were less for self-government than for security and prosperity. One result of this was that active politics became more professionalized. Instead of portfolios going to traveled men of culture like D'Azeglio and Cavour or to philosophers like Gioberti and Balbo, office was regularly conferred on accomplished bureaucrats such as Depretis and Giolitti, or on lawyers who coveted the deputy's title of *onorevole* to help widen their legal practice. When Giolitti once quoted Dante in parliament, there was an audible gasp of astonishment at such unexpected breadth of culture—but then someone pointed out that he had probably lifted his quotation from some other speech which he had found in the parliamentary records.

§♠

Complaints against the working of parliament had been heard ever since 1860. Cattaneo registered his protest by repeatedly refusing to take his seat. Mazzini was elected more than once, and his election arbitrarily vetoed by parliament itself, but he regarded the whole system as a corrupt and bogus method of falsifying the general will of the people. Garibaldi ostentatiously resigned three times from the Chamber, and notoriously believed in the quicker methods of dictatorship. Cavour alone of these great names was a great parliamentarian, but he died without establishing sufficiently solid traditions of liberal government, and after him most notable political thinkers lacked his enthusiasm and optimism about parliamentary institutions. The 1848 *statuto* could be stretched to cover monarchical paternalism, enlightened liberalism, parliamentary dictatorship, mass democracy, even fascism, but most of the suggestions heard in the eighties and nineties were for reform in an authoritarian direction such as Cavour would hardly have countenanced.

In 1882 Pasquale Turiello published his first reasoned criticism of Italian politics. His argument was that government would continue to be paralyzed until the Crown could act more independently of an elected majority and the chance decision of the electorate. Turiello used to apply the Darwinian terminology to politics, and spoke crudely of the "struggle for life" between nations and between elements inside a nation. He not only believed, but was apparently proud, that Italy was "the most violent and bloody nation in Europe," and he hoped that, with a strong hand to quell their natural factiousness, Italians could be piloted into a war which would stiffen their moral fiber. Turiello was an early representative of a new right-wing school of nationalism, and his views are important for a true understanding of Crispi's Italy.

From a different standpoint there was the criticism of parliament made by Ruggero Bonghi, a disciple of Cavour and an intellectual who had translated Plato's dialogues and was much admired as a journalist and pamphleteer. Bonghi maintained that the sentimental wish to apply English governmental methods was anachronistic and unwise, since Italy still lacked the essential prerequisites, namely a widespread political education, a sense of social responsibility, and a strong middle class. Like Croce and many other Italian thinkers, Bonghi took his views to the point where liberalism became not only distinct from, but fundamentally opposed to, democracy. He recognized that parliamentary government in Italy had worked well only when Cavour had made himself almost a dictator. He agreed with Turiello that the gradual abandonment of the king's discretionary power had left the cabinet without one very essential limitation to its authority, and pointed out that, while in England parliament had become an effective countercheck on the executive, in Italy this had not happened. His solution was that the king should be given a consultative privy council of well-known people chosen for their ability to put national before group loyalty, and whose age, status, and reputation would enable them to strengthen royal authority and prestige.

Bonghi had once adhered to *trasformismo,* but only with the hope, shared by Minghetti, that new parties would emerge once the unreal distinctions of the old Left and Right had disappeared. Regretfully he had to acknowledge that these hopes had been excessive, that parties were still to seek and that petty egotism and ambition for office continued to take the place of principle. The alignment of parliamentary groups bore little relation to political forces outside, but was the product of corridor intrigue; and the various leaders conspired to parcel out offices by private and sometimes squalid backstairs compromises among themselves, instead of putting issues honestly to the electorate for its criticism and sanction.

Largely in agreement with this diagnosis was another liberal thinker, Gaetano Mosca, who lived to raise his voice against Mussolini, and who at the end of the nineteenth century was firmly opposed to the extension of democracy. Mosca not only criticized the practical workings of parliament, but even posed theoretical objections against it as a method of government. He concluded that, if the problem of politics was to find the best governors, this was quite obviously not being solved by the present representative system. The will of the people never expressed itself freely and honestly in electoral contests, for elections would always be won either by the ministry or by the local bosses. Mosca propounded the doctrine, which subsequently became a political cliché, that in every society there was a political class or elite in control. Formulas such as "the rights of man," "liberty and equality," or "votes for the people," were merely used by that class as a device to conceal the basis of its power. With the spread of democratic methods, there was still an elite, but it was one of demagogues and wirepullers instead of detached and liberal statesmen.

Vilfredo Pareto, the economist and sociologist, developed still further this idea of the ruling class. He suggested that the decadence of parliamentarism in Italy, especially after 1876, had simply sacrificed the mass of the people to the interests of a small class of rulers, and that this class, by incorporating any potential leader into the system as he appeared, had been able to keep a monopoly of politics. Such a doctrine of the transformation of ruling elites was to become of considerable importance in the study of politics. If its chief exponents were Italians, this may have been due in part to the fact that the ruling class in Italy was narrow and more or less clearly defined. As this class was also receptive to new blood and new ideas, young revolutionaries such as Carducci and Nicotera, Crispi and Mussolini, were eventually drawn into it and made monarchist and conservative.

These various critics agreed that parliament in Italy was defective if

not altogether unsuitable. Fortunato went one step further and regretfully concluded that Italians were authoritarian by nature and temperament. In practice, the Chamber of Deputies had had virtually no say in
the accession of Di Rudinì, Giolitti, Crispi, Pelloux, and Saracco. The
conservative leader Sonnino asserted anonymously in an article published in 1897 that this fact should be regularized by a formal return to
the original purpose and spirit of the constitution of 1848, so that cabinets might in practice be made responsible not to a majority in the
House but to the king by whom they were chosen. He agreed with
Bonghi that the dominance of the Lower House was an idea of foreign
importation without warrant in the *statuto* and without correspondence
to Italiar. traditions and experience. As he saw it, "parliamentarism will
kill liberty if we cannot oppose to the concept of collectivist tyranny
the ideal of the liberal state."

Sonnino here concurred with those who wanted the Cavourian revolution undone and a different system of checks and balances set up; and
since parliamentary dictatorship had grown through the atrophy of the
royal prerogatives, it might best be checked by their restoration. Some
of those who believed this took their opposition to democracy so far
that they impugned the very principles of liberalism itself, but others
sincerely admired parliamentary government in theory and were merely
perplexed at its failure in an Italian context. Their plan to return from a
parliamentary regime to what they termed a constitutional regime was,
however, a futile attempt to put the clock back. Umberto and Vittorio
Emanuele III were not of the caliber to restore personal rule.

Parallel with this antiparliamentarism on the conservative Right,
there was a similar trend on the extreme Left. The anarchists were a
small body, but their importance was considerable. Exiled and kept in
prison, sometimes without trial, they declared war on society and refused
to collaborate in parliament. They were especially strong in the Romagna, as were also the residual republicans who shared their attitude
of nonco-operation. The more extreme socialists and syndicalists also
had theoretical objections to parliamentary government, and among the
Left generally there was a tendency to think of parliament as a class institution from which no good would come. The great criminologist Cesare Lombroso saw, as early as 1897, that universal suffrage was likely
to undermine freedom rather than increase it. In his study on political
crimes he concluded that "parliamentary government, which has with
justice been stigmatized as the greatest superstition of modern times,
offers greater and ever greater obstacles to the introduction of good
government, and some of the elected representatives obtain a freedom
from responsibility which tends to the advantage of crime."

Zanardelli of the Left Center was not nearly so pessimistic as those on the extreme Left, nor did he follow those conservatives who proposed schemes of institutional reform, for he mistrusted the monarchy and attributed the constitutional malaise rather to excessive royal power than to too little. He also recognized that representative institutions alone offered an adequate opportunity for new men and new forces in society to penetrate the ruling elite. It was the sanity of men like Zanardelli which tided over this difficult period in Italian history, and after him Giolitti, another moderate, worked out a new system of liberal parliamentary dictatorship which accepted the aims and methods of democracy.

The many criticisms of parliament nevertheless gave the dangerous impression that the constitution of 1848 could and should be altered. The belief gained currency that liberal democracy could not be so fine, and might one day have to be replaced by open despotism. The more prosperous conditions after 1900 postponed the further undermining of confidence only for a decade, after which the fascists were able to look back on Turiello, even on Pareto and Sonnino, as precursors.

27 Liberal Government Resumed, 1900-1904

Vittorio Emanuele III had been born in 1869 in the presence of ministers, generals, and the mayor of Naples; he became king in July 1900, hymned by Pascoli and D'Annunzio; he survived the rise and fall of Mussolini, and died an exile in Egypt. He was not a great king. Physically he was delicate and deformed, and he possessed an obvious sense of inferiority. His father and grandfather had both married their first cousins, and a fear that the dynasty might have become dangerously inbred had occupied people's minds when in 1896 the young prince was married to the daughter of a Montenegrin chieftain. Up to the age of twenty Vittorio had lived under the severe military rule of his tutor, Colonel Osio, and only twice a week had he been allowed to take meals with his parents. It was a soldier's education, and it effectively suppressed any liveliness he might have possessed.

The new king's tastes were soberer than his father's. The royal stables were quickly dispersed, as were the royal mistresses. Queen Elena herself, so it was said, liked to prepare the family meals. Only on state occasions did they live in the Quirinal palace, for the king preferred a private residence where his children could break windows and he himself could drive a nail into the wall without bothering about its cost to the national exchequer. His one great passion was for numismatics, and he personally supervised a voluminous catalogue of Italian coins. As Bolton King noted, already on his accession "he had the tastes of an old man or a bookworm."

This was no way to popularity, and Vittorio's prosaic, disillusioned, retiring nature cut him off from the common man. He was served with great loyalty, but was not liked or admired. When in 1904 his heir, the future Umberto II, was born, the town council of Milan refused to fly the national flag from the cathedral. Nor was he even a good Catholic, despite all the prayers of his pious mother and the instruction of his English governess, Elizabeth Lee. Indeed, he was the most anticlerical and unreligious of a generally anticlerical dynasty. He was appreciated neither by the "black" papal aristocracy, nor by the Left, nor by the *mondain* society which went on crowding the salon of the queen mother.

If personally he was not a great success, yet his common sense and modesty temporarily gave the throne a solid support, at least until his love of a quiet life allowed him to surrender Italy to the fascists. His father, in the years 1893–1900, had seemed to be trying to halt the liberal development of the constitution, and in successive ministerial crises had never received the liberal leader Giolitti or even answered his letters. The new king, too, was never friendly with Giolitti or indeed with any of his ministers, and Osio's papers show that Vittorio had always been more or less contemptuous of parliament. But he did try not to seem committed to one side or the other and to avoid being tainted like his father with partial responsibility for an unpopular government policy. He even abandoned some of the constitutionally recognized methods of influencing his ministers, and was never to refuse, for instance, when Giolitti requested a dissolution.

§♠

The conservatives had been slightly weakened by the elections of 1900. The eighty-year-old Saracco with his invariable top hat and redingote was hardly the man to keep a majority intact, and so the king broke with his father's example in February 1901 and turned to the Left Center liberals under Zanardelli. There was no obvious parliamentary mandate for this, but since the old ministerial majority had been broken, it was for the king to find a new combination which could settle the country after the violence of recent years. The experiment in authoritarianism had not quelled disorder but had increased it. Though the conservative Saracco had to some extent restored confidence and tranquillity, he had still relied too much on censorship and the police, and his hostile attitude toward labor organizations had provoked several paralyzing strikes. That the conservatives were by now on the defensive was shown by an article Sonnino wrote for the *Nuova Antologia* of September 1900, in which he moved away from his proposal to modify parliamentary government and instead advocated the union of "all national parties" to defend the constitution against the "so-called popular party."

Giuseppe Zanardelli, by this time an old man, who had served successfully with Depretis, Cairoli, Crispi, and Di Rudinì, took the premiership without any departmental portfolio, thus allowing considerable scope to his minister of the interior, Giolitti. He did not hesitate to include conservatives in his cabinet, for instance Prinetti the foreign minister, but he was himself a staunch liberal, an anticlerical, and something of an irredentist. His weakness was that he had not learned, as Giolitti was to learn, that a prime minister without a firm party basis could only afford the luxury of strong opinions if they were such as would bring his ministry solid support in parliament or in the country at large.

Zanardelli's achievement was to restore the full practice of parliamentary government and the proper discussion of state expenditure. He also reduced some of the more oppressive food taxes, and refused to follow Saracco in sending the army to break agricultural strikes. When the landowners complained in parliament that they would then have to do the ploughing themselves, they were astonished to be told that this was not a bad thing for it would teach them to pay their men better, and that the really important point was to convince the peasants that the government and the troops were not always their enemy.

Although in this way Zanardelli succeeded in making the socialists break their rule and vote on at least two occasions for a bourgeois government, he still misunderstood socialism and underestimated its importance. He flouted the extreme Left by increasing military appropriations, and he kept as minister of war San Martino who had served continuously in that post under the conservatives Pelloux and Saracco. The socialists shook his government by exposing how naval contracts were placed at absurd prices to keep up the profits of the Terni steelworks; and when their paper *Avanti* described how these profits had soared every time Admiral Bettolo was minister of marine, it was not only socialists who were impressed with the coincidence.

Zanardelli was a theoretical liberal, not a trimmer of Giolitti's quality, and so could never forge many various interests into a sufficiently malleable coalition. Giolitti observed the tactical defects of his policy, and after twenty-eight months in the government he chose to resign as soon as the scandal over armament production had weakened the government majority. Zanardelli's proposal to introduce legislation about divorce also broke one of the tacit compacts on which coalition government depended. Giolitti, therefore, wanted to free himself for being called in as Zanardelli's successor. Although he did not vote at once against the government, he took care not to involve himself in its growing unpopularity.

§♠

In November 1903, Giovanni Giolitti became prime minister for the second time. He had begun his career as a civil servant under the expert tuition of Sella at the ministry of finance. After a late entry into parliament, Crispi made him finance minister in 1889, and by 1892 he was prime minister. He was then just under the age of fifty, whereas Crispi reached the premiership at sixty-eight, Zanardelli at seventy-four, and Saracco at over eighty. He was to be prime minister five times, and on one further occasion to hold the pivotal ministry of the interior, so that the period 1901–14 can justly be called the age of Giolitti.

In administrative realism and knowledge of men, as in financial experience, Giolitti was equal if not superior to Depretis. No doubt his administrative training and his phlegmatic Piedmontese background helped him to eschew the rhetoric and bombast of Crispi, and his speeches have a logical clarity and economy reminiscent of Cavour, another northerner. This low temperature was thought to be un-Italian by many of his countrymen, who therefore considered him a man who did not believe in "Italy's mission in the world." Hence they gave him their respect rather than their affection. None could deny, however, that he was a crafty and masterful parliamentarian, and he was particularly adept at manipulating any controversial issue to make it a simple matter of administration on which most people could agree.

Giolitti learned much from the liberal precepts and practice of Zanardelli. Together they had opposed Crispi and Pelloux, and withstood the "exceptional laws." They had maintained against Sonnino "that the parliamentary regime is the method of government best able to reconcile stability with liberty and progress"—so Giolitti had told his constituents in March 1897. In their opinion the conservatives had endangered existing institutions quite as much as the socialists had done, and were therefore as dangerous and insidious.

Giolitti declared that social questions were now more important than political questions, and would henceforth differentiate one political group from another. In a speech of September 1900 he made his position quite clear: "Sonnino is right in saying that the country is sick politically and morally, but the principal cause of its sickness is that the classes in power have been spending enormous sums on themselves and their own interests, and have obtained the money almost entirely from the poorer sections of society. We have a large number of taxes paid predominantly by the poor, on salt, on gambling, the *dazio* on grain and so forth, but we have not a single tax which is exclusively on wealth as such. When in the financial emergency of 1893 I had to call on the rich to make a small sacrifice, they began a rebellion against the government even more effective than the contemporary revolt of the poor Sicilian peasantry, and Sonnino who took over from me had to find the money by increasing still further the price of salt and the excise on cereals. I deplore as much as anyone the struggle between classes, but at least let us be fair and ask who started it."

Once back in the government, Giolitti insisted that justice and expediency alike demanded "a policy which is frankly democratic," and that not only the tax system but local government and even the law code itself should be changed to suit this new trend. In February 1901 he told parliament that "the administration of justice can certainly not be said to win general confidence, and everyone knows what the state of our public security is, and how communal administration in many places is in the hands of a real camorra"—a political assassination in Sicily had lately shown how illicit interference with police and judges was perverting the course of justice. It was useless to preach the virtues of parliamentary government to people who were hungry: "If you wish to defend our present institutions, you will have to persuade these new classes that they have more to gain from those institutions than from utopian dreams of violent change. . . . It depends on us whether they will turn out to be a conservative force, a new element in the greatness and prosperity of the country, or a revolutionary force for its ruin." Giolitti thought it impossible to prevent the lower classes from eventually seizing some share of economic and political influence, and anyhow it would be a political, moral, and economic error to drive what was in fact a majority of Italians into irreconcilable rebelliousness.

Finding that since Jacini's inquest of the 1870's no official statistics had been collected about agricultural wages, Giolitti made inquiries through the prefects. In Lombardy he discovered agricultural laborers earning one lira a day or less, which meant that, in the intervening thirty years, wage levels had declined from a standard which had even before been insufficient. Agrarian unemployment proved to be much more serious than he had imagined, and the facts convinced him that in no other country were taxes on ordinary articles of food so high, or the gap between rich and poor so wide.

§•❦

While Giolitti was thus coming halfway to meet socialist demands, a distinct current of socialism moved in his direction and proclaimed that gradual and evolutionary methods were the surest path toward social justice. From 1896 the party paper *Avanti* appeared with the moderate Bissolati as its editor, and during the struggle over the decree law it was persuaded to make a tactical alliance with radicals and democratic liberals and to champion liberty and the constitution. Under this compulsion the socialist party produced a "minimum" program which, while retaining long-term ideas of social revolution, in the short run allowed socialists to collaborate for tactical reasons inside parliament. This program included the right to combine and strike, universal suffrage, the payment of deputies, compulsory insurance, a progressive income tax, reduction of interest on the national debt, administrative decentralization, and government neutrality in disputes between labor and capital. Most of these aims Giolitti would have found unexceptionable.

At the socialist party congress in Rome of 1900, two programs, a minimum and a maximum, were proposed, to approve either of which might have split the party, and so Turati, believing in socialist unity, secured the approval of both, the one being held as a means to the other. This compromise papered over an internal division which remained fundamental. It was much the same cleavage as in other countries, where the revisionism of Bernstein and the reformism of Millerand condemned the policy of violent revolution and showed a willingness to collaborate with middle-class governments. Giolitti welcomed this cleavage, and adopted much of the minimum program in order to win over its supporters and so strengthen his own majority. He was not far from Turati, who in the *Critica Sociale* was urging that social reform should be achieved through slow and gradual changes in society without upsetting present institutions.

But Giolitti failed to capture the practical support of the working masses, and many leaders of Italian socialism were more interested in a utopia of their own devising than in the wage concessions which he offered. Indeed, for those who adhered to the maximum program, ordinary social reforms might even seem harmful, since they would make the workers more contented and less revolutionary. The maximalists were made strong and uncompromising by the belief that history was on their side, and that the process of dialectic would bring them success without their having to contaminate themselves by fraternization with the liberals.

At the Rome Congress of the PSI in 1900, a more extreme group of syndicalists had gathered around the Neapolitan professor, Arturo Labriola. These syndicalists believed dogmatically in violence and the general strike: their aim was to win control of the socialist party in some annual congress, and so to secure the management of *Avanti* and of the party funds on behalf of their revolutionary policy. They failed in this, and so became another example of that tendency toward schism which was to be a main characteristic of Italian socialism. The anarchists had seceded in 1892, and syndicalists, reformists, and communists were to follow suit in 1908, 1912, and 1921, and numerous other small groups thereafter.

These successive breaks eventually left the maximalists in sole command of a diminutive remnant, but for the moment, in 1900 and again in the 1902 congress at Imola, Bissolati, Bonomi, and the reformists carried the day. The revolutionary leaders, Ferri and Labriola, had to contain themselves awhile. This was the opportunity for Giolitti's sweet reasonableness to break up the socialists and strengthen his Center coalition.

§⬧

Giolitti's approach to socialism was most perceptive. He recognized that, with its concentration on class and social problems, socialism was rapidly outpacing republicanism and radicalism as a political force. It had positively thrived on the repressive measures of Crispi, Di Rudinì, and Pelloux. Giolitti read it as a sign of the times when Milan, the largest and wealthiest Italian city, elected a socialist mayor. He was himself a friend of Turati and had studied *Das Kapital* with application and profit. Instead of attributing the Sicilian revolt of 1893 to political propaganda, he recognized it as an understandable explosion of discontent which would have been met better by reform than by repression.

Giolitti assumed that persecution was the one thing which would heal the cleavages inside socialism and make it a force to be feared. He also advanced the novel doctrine that labor unions were welcome as a safety valve against unrest, for organized forces were less dangerous than those which were disorganized. He observed in February 1901 that "the badly nourished industrial worker is always weak in body and mind, whereas the countries which have high wages are at the head of industrial progress. A period of social justice inaugurated by the government would recall the common people back to their affection for our institutions. I am not asking privileges for either workers or capitalists: the government ought to stand above these disputes between capital and labor except where the law is actually broken." Impartiality suited Giolitti's temperament. In the damping down of controversial issues he saw most hope of maintaining his majority, and he wisely aimed to avoid a situation where groups might be maneuvered against him before he had time to prepare the elections. He also believed that wages, like profits, were best fixed by the free working of economic laws, for example by permitting strikes, instead of by Crispi's alternative method of putting the prefects and the *carabinieri* at the disposal of employers. In this way he hoped to edge Marx off the political stage, just as Bernstein and Croce were simultaneously attacking Marxism in philosophy and history.

Giolitti was soon put to the test by an outcrop of strikes. On the municipal street railways, in the sulphur mines, the docks, the iron and steel factories of Liguria and Leghorn, everywhere there were strikes, as the proletariat began to envisage a fairer balance between the classes. In 1901 there were 629 reported strikes in agriculture and 1,042 in industry, and in the space of three years there were at least eleven armed conflicts with the authorities, and 242 recorded casualties. Nevertheless, Giolitti persisted in thinking that employers would be more ready to compromise where both sides had to conduct the dispute on more or less equal terms. He refused to let soldiers take over the work of agricultural strikers, for the knowledge that such help was at hand had simply increased the landowners' intransigence. The peasants therefore bettered their wages, and the state won more of their confidence.

Yet toleration was combined with firmness. On the grounds that the government should always put down disorder, the anarchist Malatesta, who had been Bakunin's favorite pupil, was arrested. Giolitti also claimed that freedom to work was as important as freedom to strike, and if strikers prevented other people from working this "would set up artificial conditions which in turn would make a new conflict inevitable." A strike by railroad workers, he maintained, was in a different category since it might cause unemployment if not actual starvation, so he threatened to call up those railroadmen on strike who were liable for military service. He argued that all public officials must be subject to some extra discipline, especially as they had secure contracts and guaranteed pensions to differentiate them from ordinary workers.

When Turati accused Giolitti of opportunism in all this, the latter took it as a compliment. As a true empiric he claimed to be both conservative and radical, and wanted above all to secure existing institutions by wise reforms. His enemies put it differently, saying that he tackled no fundamental problem but wanted just enough reform to keep people quiet—and himself in office. Whatever the reason, opportunism quickly brought him to appreciate the transformist technique, and in 1903, renouncing any belief he may once have had in party government, he was ready to choose his cabinet from many different sections of the Chamber.

Once he had offered the socialists their minimum program, he drove the wedge further by asking the reformists to be logical and join his government. The age of barricades was indeed over when the very men Crispi had outlawed in 1894 were invited to take office. Some of the

Fabians who believed in the inevitability of gradualism were inclined to accept this invitation, but Turati knew that acceptance would split the party, and Bissolati had to inform the premier that his offer was premature. The explanation was offered that acceptance would be misunderstood by the politically immature rank and file, and would merely discredit the reformists: that is to say, for some socialists refusal of office was now a matter not of principle but of expediency. This marked an interesting stage in political development. Some people have plausibly suggested that acceptance of Giolitti's offer might well have prevented the rise of fascism. Turati in private deplored that the socialists could not join Giolitti, the one real radical and practical statesman whom Italy possessed, but in public he had to side with the maximalists in refusing the advantage of any tactical interpretation of dogma.

When both socialists and radicals refused his alliance, Giolitti as easily turned toward the Right, and appointed Luzzatti to the Treasury and Tittoni to the Foreign Office. The rest of the cabinet were liberals of the Center. Apart from Luzzatti, all of them were in office for the first time, since it was Giolitti's avowed intention to bring new blood into the governing class and prepare himself a new basis of political power. He and Zanardelli had already created fifty new senators. Meanwhile, his policy of social reform was not pushed so far as to antagonize the majority in the Lower House, which was still that elected under Pelloux in 1900. By a vote of 284 to 117 they gave him their confidence.

In the meantime the reformists were losing control of the socialist party. In 1903 Ferri captured the editorship of *Avanti* from Bissolati, and in the 1904 congress at Bologna he became virtually the leader of the party. Many socialists distrusted Ferri, knowing him to be a late convert who was as unversed in Marxism as he was inexperienced in working-class affairs and a notorious opportunist who never adhered to one policy for very long. He was, however, a clever and dangerous man, and his growing extremism was alarming.

Still more alarming was the development of syndicalism inside the party. The Italian edition of Sorel's book on syndicalism obtained wide circulation after 1903, and the *Reflections on Violence* by the same author was published in translation by Laterza in 1907. Popularized in Italy by Croce, Sorel was to instruct many in the cult of violence and antidemocracy. Probably he had more influence in Italy than anywhere else. Against the milder socialists who were beginning to yield to the allure of power and compromise, he taught that workers' syndicates, instead of relying on parliamentary action and the betterment of conditions, should be a weapon of violent class war against the bourgeois state. After triumphing at the regional conference at Brescia in 1904, Arturo Labriola and Leone strongly advocated this view to the national congress of Bologna.

In September 1904 the Milan revolutionary socialists tried out for the first time Sorel's idea of a political general strike as a protest against bloody collisions between police and workers in Sardinia and Sicily. For four days life over large areas of the country came to a standstill: newspapers did not appear, public services were shut down, even the gondolas suspended activity, and Venice was virtually isolated. Such success surprised no one more than the strikers, who had enjoyed the holiday and the spectacle but had little idea what to do next.

Giolitti alone was certain what to do—which was, nothing. He thus avoided bloodshed, confronted the strikers with the futility of such a purely negative action, and also encouraged the reformists to recapture their former leadership in the party. The *Corriere della Sera* blamed him for what appeared to be cowardice, but wiser men appreciated that his restraint had shown the harmlessness of this new syndicalist weapon. Giolitti was sensible enough to allow wages as well as prices to find their own level, and even let the magistrates form a union to increase their salaries. Instead of using force, as Crispi or Di Rudinì might have done, he simply dissolved parliament in October and held general elections the following month, intending to punish the labor leaders for preferring violence to negotiation. His object was partially gained, for the *estrema* was reduced from 107 to 94, a total made up of thirty-nine radicals, thirty-one socialists, and twenty-four republicans. Another significant point was that six Catholic deputies were elected to strengthen the conservatives. Catholic intervention was before long to upset the whole shape of Italian politics.

§❧

In this, the second of Giolitti's five general elections, electoral chicanery was said to be more prominent than ever before, but some allowance must be made for the exaggerations of defeated candidates, and in any case these sharp practices were by now a well-established custom. In the elections of 1895 Crispi had easily been able to strike many opposition voters from the electoral lists, and had drawn heavily on the Banca Romana for his electoral expenses. In 1891, the year before Giolitti's first election, Pareto described how a special language had already grown up: "It is called the *blocco* when the whole contents of the voting urns are changed, or the *pastetta* when one changes only a part of them. There is still no word for when absent people and even the dead are made to vote, though one will soon appear when this usage becomes

general. . . . Such practices have always been endemic in southern
Italy, but for some little time now they have begun to infect the whole
country."

These methods were brought to a fine art by Giolitti's election managers: blotting paper was issued to voters which had to be returned showing the name of the favored candidate upon it; banknotes were torn in
two and given half before and half after voting; secret service funds
were appropriated to the election campaign; electoral lists included
fictitious names, sometimes gathered from tombstones in the town ceme-
tery. Mussolini's father once described in the local paper how fifty
cows were registered by name for the elections in Predappio. Giolitti
knew what was going on. He once described how a mayor had apolo-
gized to him for two negative votes being cast against the government
candidate: "We have found out who cast those two votes," reported
the mayor, "and the men have had such a time of it that they have emigrated to France." "I replied," so Giolitti recounts somewhat naïvely,
"that this was really too much."

His own policy was to allow the more advanced parts of Italy to vote
in relative freedom, and to confine his intimidation and corruption
mainly to backward areas, where they worked better, and where, if he
did not use them, someone else would. "There are places in Italy where
the law does not operate at all," he informed parliament, and he more
than once referred to a large Sicilian municipality which avoided taxes
by persuading the police to register it as "missing and untraceable"—his
implication being that this kind of fact had to be either endured or exploited. A later prime minister, Bonomi, estimated that three-quarters
of the electoral districts in Italy were feudal enclaves or private perquisites where there was never a serious contest, and he concluded that
the moral significance of an election would emerge just from the hundred
or so seats where there was a genuine fight. Giolitti could afford to allow
a more or less free vote in these hundred cases, but elsewhere found it
easier and more profitable to use the local machines than to destroy them.

28 Clerical and Radical Co-operation, 1904-1906

Papal hostility had been such that it was rare after 1870 for any leading minister of the Crown to be a devout Catholic: Crispi had called himself a deist, and the Freemasons claimed such names as Depretis, De Sanctis, Spaventa, Di Rudinì, Crispi, Cavallotti, Carducci, and even the king himself. The policy of such men had reflected an instinctive prejudice against a Church which was a state within the state. The Church claimed jurisdiction in mixed matters, arbitral authority over all moral issues, and the supremacy of its own law over that of the nation. For sixty years it refused to recognize the very existence of an Italian state, let alone the occupation of Rome.

The Martinucci case of 1882 had decided that, the Pope apart, every inhabitant of the Vatican might be held subject to the Italian courts. Though the crucifix still hung in lecture rooms, an anticlerical minister in 1881 appointed the heretical ex-canon of Mantua, Ardigò, to a professorial chair at Padua, and religious seminaries were threatened with closure if they refused to permit government inspection; in the universities, theological faculties had already been suppressed before the accession to power of the Left. A decree of 1888 put the onus on parents to ask religious education for their children, instead of having to request exemption from it. Then Zanardelli's penal code of 1889 increased the penalties on clergy who condemned from the pulpit existing institutions or acts of the government.

After much opposition, the compulsory payment of tithe was abolished, and most of the remaining church charities were taken over by the state in 1890. This last was a great blow to the clergy, who had obtained much influence from the distribution of alms and doles. Crispi asserted on this occasion that there were 9,464 pious fraternities with a total revenue of nine million lire a year, a sum of which only one-tenth had been devoted to the main function of public assistance, the rest being spent on masses, candles, and fireworks on gala occasions. Finally, and most wounding of all, in 1895 Crispi made an annual public holiday of

September 20, the day on which the royal army in 1870 had turned its cannon against the walls of Rome.

§❧

Such measures were anticlerical rather than anti-Catholic; they were, indeed, supported by many sincere Catholics who recognized that Cavour's ideal of "a free Church in a free state" had been repudiated by Rome and was now effectively replaced in liberal dogma by Luzzatti's more realistic formula, "a free Church in a sovereign state." By 1900 the controversy between Church and state was looking more and more unreal. Liberalism might be condemned and its products placed on the *Index,* and Catholic protests were heard even against King Umberto's burial in the Pantheon, but the lay state was now untroubled by such censure. In May 1904 Giolitti laid down that "Church and state are two parallel lines which ought never to meet."

Even Popes had to recognize that they had been less disturbed by outside pressure since the loss of temporal power, and the eighty-six encyclicals of Leo XIII have been called collectively the most important contribution to Catholic doctrine since the Middle Ages. The verbal *non possumus* having saved honor, good sense was always at hand to make a compromise in practice. The Pope had been forced to allow bishops to ask for the royal exequatur, just as he had to endure the statue of Garibaldi looking down provocatively from the Janiculum onto the few remaining acres of papal territory. On the other hand, monasteries had been re-endowed since the dissolution, and the census figures of 1881 and 1901 show that, in defiance of formal law, monks and friars increased in number from 7,191 to 7,792, and nuns from 28,172 to 40,251. Sella in the 1870's had been able to say that "the black International is far more dangerous to our liberties than the red," but by 1900 this fear seemed ridiculous. Both sides were developing a mutual tolerance, and the danger of red revolution was giving them a point in common.

There continued to be extremely conservative Popes, especially those of humble origin like Pius X and Pius XI, but there were also the more aristocratic Leo XIII and Benedict XV who intimated that the alliance of the Church with political absolutism was not in itself absolute and irrevocable. Both these men had been trained in diplomacy, and like good statesmen were ready to meet an opponent halfway or nearly halfway. It was Leo who opened the Vatican archives in 1881, and who advised French Catholics to rally in support of the Third Republic. His encyclical of 1888, *De libertate humana,* seemed almost to argue away the antiliberal syllabus of Pius IX a quarter of a century before.

Catholic socialism appeared late in Italy, for the condemnations of both Pius IX and Leo were too recent and uncompromising. Theologians had feared that the Christian virtues of patience and charity might be prejudiced if people stressed the rights of the poor and the duties of the rich. But Leo recognized that, as the poor were the great majority, it was bad policy to leave the materialists a monopoly of the claim to speak on their behalf. Perhaps the encyclical *Rerum novarum* of 1891 contained no very definite doctrine, but a new spirit was abroad when a Pope could give his blessing to the Knights of Labor and affirm the desirability of trade unions. Professor Toniolo and Monsignor Bonomelli, two leading churchmen, were meanwhile providing a requisite theoretical justification by distinguishing the natural and absolute right to property from the limited uses to which it might be put, and by insisting that ownership carried duties as well as rights.

In the turmoil of 1898, Christian-democrat groups were formed which —to the concern of the Vatican—did not scorn alliance with the *estrema*. Other Catholics were busy organizing agricultural unions, cooperative dairies, and village banks. Padre Curci, founder of the Jesuit paper *Civiltà Cattolica,* was preaching that the Church should come to terms with democracy, though after writing a work called *Christian Socialism* he was dismissed from his order. The monks of Monte Cassino, under their famous Abbot Tosti, had already in 1870 shown that they put national unity before the temporal power of the Pope. The heirs of these men were Toniolo and Meda who in the late 1890's developed the propaganda organization of Christian democracy. When this was suspended by Pius X in 1904, Romolo Murri, although a priest, founded the "National Democratic League" and entered parliament, but was defrocked and excommunicated.

Parallel with this political movement, there were certain kindred heresies which Curci and Murri did not share and which collectively earned from their orthodox ecclesiastical opponents the generic label of "modernism." The modernists suggested that dogma was not to be formulated once and for all, but could be expected to grow organically and change to suit the times. This suggestion, with all its complex of associated ideas, was condemned outright by a new papal syllabus in 1907, though the accused denied many of the beliefs attributed to them. The chief enemy of modernism was Pius X, who reigned from 1903 to 1914 and who was the first Pope of modern times to be canonized—it is interesting that he was elected Pope only after Austria had vetoed the election of the pro-French cardinal Rampolla. Pius felt obliged to protest against the growing materialism and positivism of the age and against the false logic which might lead through modernism to Protestant heresy. Even Fogazzaro, the most popular novelist of the day and a Catholic, had his study in religious psychology, *Il Santo,* placed on the index of prohibited books.

Fifty years earlier the state might have risen to the rescue of a minority within the Church, but Croce and the liberal anticlericals were by now indifferent, and admitted that the Church should regulate itself as it wished. Furthermore, while the Vatican was careful to distinguish what it thought incorrigibly erroneous, it was gradually becoming reconciled to the prevalent trends in modern society. Once the heat of controversy had passed, the Church throughout its history has managed to come to terms with all manner of diverse philosophical and political beliefs, wisely acting to moderate the more extreme views, and warning against irresponsible flirtation with the latest fashionable craze. Its gradual and partial reconciliation with the ideals of liberal democracy was to help Giolitti bring Catholics more actively into political life.

Many churchmen were beginning to conclude that their policy of non-co-operation since 1870 had been quite ineffective. The Vatican had made a brave effort to challenge the secular state and prevent it from taking permanent shape, but with every year that passed success became less likely. Church abstention from politics had hurt no one but the conservatives, and co-operation might be by now, if not a positive good, at least a lesser evil. There was a need for Catholics to appear in parliament and present the church's views on marriage and education, especially when the year 1904 saw the shocking fact of a world congress of freethinkers in the Holy City itself. The new king was accused of atheism—it was said that the only church he built was the Jewish synagogue at Rome—and in February 1902 the speech from the throne had announced another of Zanardelli's projects for permitting divorce. This called for urgent political action in reply. Moreover, the black nobility could not be expected to refuse Court invitations forever, and from contemporary fiction one can see that they and other Catholics were inevitably coming around to take their share in national life. Far from being the enemies of the new state, many Catholics were beginning to think of themselves as its defenders, alike against socialism on the Left and the parallel anticlericalism of Sonnino and Di Rudinì on the Right.

Giolitti, though personally favorable to the idea of divorce, was too realistic to antagonize Catholicism directly, and when his plans for socialist support fell through he gladly welcomed as an alternative this other nonconformist faction at the opposite extreme. The election campaign of November 1904 was first opened on a liberal platform, but when the results of the first ballot proved disappointing, Giolitti made positive overtures to the Catholics. It was a novel sight to find the

Roman aristocracy haranguing the crowds. *Avanti* calculated afterward that the clerical vote caused the defeat of socialist candidates in twenty-six districts. Then, in June 1905, the encyclical *Il fermo proposito* allowed each bishop to decide whether the Catholics of his diocese might participate in political life, for the recent rupture between the Vatican and France made reconciliation with Italy the more desirable.

§⁂

Giolitti's object was to find the highest common factor of agreement for a majority, and hence the apparent contradiction of his offer to the socialists in 1903 and to the Catholics in 1904. His change of front left him in an equivocal position, especially as the various groups of the *estrema* together constituted a powerful enemy. The socialists were close to capturing that nerve center of the country, Milan, and the grand master of Italian Freemasonry, the English-born Nathan, became mayor of Rome itself. The republicans still existed as a party, if without much following—Scarfoglio, the most prominent contemporary journalist, asked what purpose would be served by working for a republic when no one so much as noticed that a monarchy existed. The radicals still exerted considerable influence, especially through their newspaper, *Il Secolo,* and they did not forget that Giolitti had passed them over when he invited the more extreme socialists into office.

Accordingly, Giolitti made yet another transformist gesture. He appointed the radical Marcora as Speaker of the House, arguing publicly that due balance must be maintained between the various groups, and hoping secretly that the radicals might thus be weaned from the rest of the *estrema*. Enemies of the government read this as new evidence of Giolitti's lack of principle, but in any case the uncertain basis of his parliamentary support still left him insecure.

The government was further shaken when one of its subordinate ministers, Rosano, on the very day of his appointment committed suicide because he had been accused in the press of corruption. The cabinet was lashed from the Left by the bad-tempered oratory of Ferri, while the Right complained of the government's inability to deal with a "go slow" campaign of the railroad workers. Giolitti was therefore glad to take the opportunity of resignation afforded by a bout of influenza, his designation of the insignificant Fortis to be his successor suggesting that this was merely a temporary tactical retreat in favor of one of his lieutenants. Probably, he felt himself unable in the present state of parliament to put through his nationalization of the railroads, or at least he hoped to divert to his stopgap successor any unpopularity that this measure might bring.

The great railroad boom of the late nineteenth century had left behind it much inefficient and uneconomic construction, and the network was notoriously unable to cope with the growth in foreign trade. Many bankruptcies had been registered in the course of railroad building, and the profits were significantly less than in France and England. A government commission nevertheless recommended that no change be made in the system of private ownership. Giolitti disagreed; the restlessness of the railroad employees was seriously interfering with trade, and exporters wanted the aid of subsidized transport rates which private companies could not afford. The railroad strikes of 1904–5 brought this problem to a head and forced the state to intervene.

An act nationalizing the principal lines was eventually put through by Fortis, though without a full study of its implications. The first director of state railways, Riccardo Bianchi, did much to improve services, but his accounts soon showed a deficit. Critics claimed that the loss was inherent in state ownership; others replied that the private companies, whether in fear or hope of state intervention, had latterly been exploiting the lines to their limit without making any provision at all for repairs and replacement. The new administration certainly gave better service, and differential freight charges were introduced to subsidize long-distance freight traffic. But such an increase in state involvement provided scope for corrupt patronage and added to an already unwieldly bureaucracy, while to many conservatives it seemed an unwise concession to the pressure of organized labor. Giolitti was very prudent to have left to Fortis the responsibility for so contested a measure.

᠑᠅

The cabinet formed by Fortis was, like Giolitti's, predominantly of the Left Center, and met with the same opposition from both extremes. One of its chief problems was to reconcile the economic interests of North and South. The northern deputies forced through a commercial treaty with Spain to assist the outflow of northern manufactures, but southerners were threatened with grave loss by its compensatory grant of preferential treatment to Spanish wine. Giolitti had supported Fortis here, so he was not himself able to succeed as prime minister when this brought the government down. There was still technically a large "Giolittian" majority in parliament, but the Chamber was divided far more over personalities than over principles and never could be entirely relied upon. In February 1906 the inheritance fell to Baron Sonnino of the Right Center.

Sidney Sonnino was a solitary man, rigid, austere, and taciturn. He was the child of a Welsh mother and a rich Tuscan Jew, and had the reputation of combining strict honesty with a somewhat narrow conservatism. It stood to his credit that he had written a commentary on the sixth canto of Dante's *Paradiso,* and he had given up a foreign-office career to do research on Tuscan and Sicilian agriculture, but he had come back into active politics as a minister under Crispi and had then advocated a reduction in the powers of parliament. Sonnino himself headed a group of only about thirty people, and in order to find himself a majority he had to leave out the Center and approach the *estrema* in what was hailed as the most audacious political experiment since Cavour's *connubio.* He formed his first ministry with Luzzatti, Salandra, and Boselli from the Right, all of them future premiers, and the radicals Pantano and Sacchi from the extreme Left. This added one more to the long list of extremist factions made respectable by the offer of power. Although Salandra and Pantano had been at opposite poles in almost everything, Italian political tradition contained no prescription about collective cabinet responsibility, and governments had seldom needed to possess a collective policy.

Even more surprising than this association of ministers was the support which came from Ferri. Although at the socialist congress of Bologna in 1904 he had agreed with the revolutionary syndicalists in repudiating parliamentary collaboration, he now switched around. Since Bissolati's reformists and Turati's "integralists" were on the fringe of Giolitti's group system, Ferri chose to go one better and join the conservative Sonnino. This opportunist stroke was suggested in part by the failure of the general strike which had discredited the syndicalists. Then at the socialist congress of Rome in 1906 the split inside socialism was temporarily healed, and although Bissolati and Turati were dumbfounded at the inconsistencies of the vain and unprincipled Ferri, they all united under the banner of what was called integralism to put him and the syndicalists in an unimportant minority.

Obviously, the PSI was too academic and doctrinaire a party. Marxism was proving more successful with lawyers and students than with the working classes of the Po Valley and had a negligible influence among the peasants in southern Italy and the islands. As a result, the socialists tended to value doctrine above tactics, a fact which was to have serious consequences in the not so distant future.

Sonnino's policy was one of conservative reform. He condemned the use of secret service funds for bribing the press, and he promised to try to relieve the burden of taxation in the South, especially the tax on land. He also promised to give more state aid to local village schools, and to limit the power of prefects in confiscating newspapers and dissolving the elected councils in communes and provinces. Pantano, as minister of agriculture, even sketched a project for breaking up and colonizing the large estates, a scheme which cannot have had much appeal for some of his colleagues. But after three months the government resigned when a conflict at Turin between workers and police led to another general strike. Ferri had been overruled by his party who still considered that the class struggle was incompatible with supporting a middle-class government, and Ferri's defection gave Giolitti the cue for his next entry upon the political stage. With such a composite government, Sonnino was almost bound to fall when a fundamental controversy arose to divide his followers. Perhaps he had been unwise to abandon the secret service fund, and indeed its immediate resumption by Giolitti was to have a noticeably favorable effect on the press.

The same parliament which had just given a majority of 150 to Sonnino now applauded Giolitti as his successor. The new government was to last for three years, longer than any for a generation. Almost all its ministers except Tittoni were from the Left Center, but this time Giolitti determined to ask no favors from an extreme Left which had compromised itself with Sonnino. His aim was to outdo his predecessor in reforms, to attract the working-class vote by a policy of moderation, and if possible to restore the cohesion of the Center liberals. Not only did he take back the secret service funds, but he vetoed a bill which Sonnino had introduced limiting the right of the central government to overrule local government authorities. Indeed, in September 1906 Giolitti dissolved the civic administration of Naples for the fourteenth time since 1861 and appointed to govern the city a royal commissioner who could resist local graft and perhaps make Naples more *giolittiano* in time for the next elections.

One signal accomplishment in June 1906 was to carry through the scheme prepared by Sonnino's minister, Luzzatti, for conversion of the interest on government bonds from 5 to 3.75 per cent. The success of this conversion reflected a growing confidence in the stability of the state, for very few people at home or abroad chose the alternative of cashing their bonds at par. It enormously lessened the annual load of interest payments on the eight billions of national debt and allowed the government to borrow money more cheaply and so to lighten the food taxes. This sign of greater financial independence was also reflected in the larger gold reserves and in the greater amounts deposited in savings banks. Cheaper money for the government also meant cheaper money for industry and agriculture.

But Giolitti still believed that the dominant problem was how to improve the life of the working classes. Legislation was accordingly passed to control conditions of employment and contracts of service. Tenders for public works were accepted from workers' co-operatives, to the great disgust of other contractors, and parliamentary commissions were set up to examine alleged irregularities in the administration of the army and navy. Above all, an effort was made to study the intricate and distressing question of southern Italy.

29 The "Southern Problem" and Emigration

For some time after 1860 most of those who protested their ardent patriotism most keenly were completely ignorant of the South and its people, for few of them ever went there if they could help it. Minghetti called the South the most fertile part of Europe, and even Cavour, who refused an urgent invitation to go and see for himself, believed that Naples could become the richest province in Italy. Probably this illusion provided one of the reasons why some northerners accepted the national movement, and the subsequent disillusion partially weakened national feeling. After closer acquaintance the inhabitants of the South were soon being referred to by one responsible cabinet minister as "an army of barbarians encamped among us." D'Azeglio even suggested that the South should once again be separated from Italy, since other provinces were incapable of supporting such a burden, and "even the best cook will never make a good dish out of stinking meat."

Very gradually the double legend was thus fostered of a naturally rich area impoverished by the inefficient rule of the Bourbons and by the sloth and corruption of its inhabitants. Having made these false assumptions, deputies assumed that the enlightened government of United Italy would automatically improve matters, and hence that there was no need for scientific study and legislation on the "southern problem." They forgot that the island of Sardinia was in worse shape even than Sicily, despite one hundred and fifty years of rule from Turin. They disbelieved what the less doctrinaire economists told them of the real condition of this imagined garden of the Hesperides, and Fortunato was even reproached with having "invented" malaria as a polemical fiction. Piedmontese statesmen such as Cavour and Depretis never considered traveling to the South to see things for themselves, and Giolitti went only once, during the emergency which followed the terrible earthquake in the Strait of Messina. These three statesmen all lived in the far north-west, and to them Rome was as far south as was pleasant to go.

The southern question was not studied seriously until the two Tuscans, Franchetti and Sonnino, jointly tackled it in the seventies, and not until after 1901 did politicians in general become aware that the South was still not righting itself automatically under enlightened northern rule. Luzzatti warned parliament in that year that, if nothing were done, the North would inevitably sink to the economic level of the South, and that the future of the nation therefore depended on solving this awk-ward problem. The fabled wealth of the South had evidently been a myth; it was the North which had capital, established industries, better education and communications, contact with the rest of Europe, a more enlightened ruling class, a better climate, and more raw materials, and complicated irrigation works built up through many centuries. Corbino computed that the average Piedmontese in the nineties was almost exactly twice as rich as the average Sicilian.

Under the Italian system of government there tended to be a con-spiracy of silence among politicians about inconvenient issues which threatened to displace the balance of groups in parliament. The condition of the poor had long been such an issue, and hence there had not been much to choose between the social policy of Cavour and Rattazzi, Minghetti and Depretis. Only after 1900 did the growing importance of the proletariat force both sides to compete for popular sympathy. The conservative reforms of Sonnino were thus met by the liberal reforms of Giolitti, and each faction now vied with the other in discovering the facts about the South upon which policy should be based.

The South was bound to gain in the end from national unity, by en-joying honest and efficient administration and the benefits of political education under a freer regime, but there had inevitably been severe economic dislocations in such a violent change. Before 1860 the South was a country of low taxes and negligible national debt, with the col-lective capital asset of large domanial lands, and having a paternal gov-ernment which above all tried to keep food cheap. After 1861 its auton-omy was gone, taxes leaped upward, and by 1865 the loss of industrial protection had forced the closure of many factories at Naples, Messina, and elsewhere. The British consul at Naples reported that trade declined by 16 per cent as a result of the increase in municipal octrois between 1861 and 1866.

In 1864 Garibaldi informed the king that the semimilitary government of Turin was hated more in Naples than that of the Bourbons had been, and ten years later a newspaper campaign was opened there with the slogan "we are Neapolitans before we are Italians." There had been progress, but apparently less than in the decade of French rule at the beginning of the century. Resentment was reciprocal. The South was sometimes reproached for having made so few sacrifices in the struggle for unity, and, in Franchetti's cruel phrase, it was thought of not as a region to be wisely governed, but simply as a group of deputies to be conciliated and bribed.

Then in the eighties the agricultural depression caused another setback in the South just when the industrialized North was beginning its rapid advance under the protection of government tariffs. The price of wheat fell first to 22 lire a quintal in 1888, and then to 13.5 in 1894, and Sonnino as minister of the treasury chose this moment to increase the *dazio* on grain and to raise the price of salt from 35 to 40 centesimi a kilo. This hit both landowners and peasants in the predominantly rural South, for the payment which Sicily made on the *dazio* was now as much as that paid by the infinitely wealthier region of Lombardy, and three times that of Venetia. Meanwhile, the decline in agricultural prices made it increasingly difficult for southerners to pay the interest on debts incurred by their enormous increase in vineyard acreage, and hence each year many thousands of smallholders forfeited their holdings. The South had to pay with its depreciated products for manufactured goods which protection now made dearer, and thus yet more capital was drained from the South in a deliberate policy of accumulating resources in the North where it was thought that they could be better employed.

§◈

It has often been said that two stages of civilization coexisted in Italy, for in the South there were far more murders, more illiterates, superstition, corruption, and poverty than in the North and Center. Alexandre Dumas *père* described what he found at Naples in 1862: "While the *signore* feeds his dogs on white bread, the people live on roots and grass, eked out with an insufficient quantity of coarse bread. The *signore* puts his horses in stables shut in from the winds and the rain and properly paved. His peasants live in damp, unhealthy hovels, open to all the winds, without windows, without a roof. The whole family will sleep on the same bed of straw, in the same room with their donkey, their pig, and their chickens." For this accommodation they paid the equivalent of seventy days' wages. Fifty years later these people could still be found earning only half a dollar a working day, and working days meant probably only half of the year. Malaria determined the way they lived, their methods of land tenure, the type of crops, and the relative density of population. Extensive agriculture and large estates continued to accompany malaria. Where families had to live huddled together in hill villages raised above the malarial plains, crops were needed which could be looked after by people living some distance away, which could be left without close attention in the most dangerous months, and which did not require the additional help of female labor in the fields.

Fortunato fought a great battle against chemical manufacturers and drug stores to obtain state provision of quinine. He described how in his native Basilicata you could travel ten or twenty miles without sighting a village, and could live for months and years without ever seeing an open or joyful face. The number of expropriations for tax default in this province alone was twice that for the whole of northern Italy. In the Abruzzi, Franchetti related how the *contadini* were in every way slaves: they worked on their lord's farm for a stipulated number of days, they kissed his hand, suffered the gratuitous exactions which indeterminate clauses in contracts of service allowed him, and showed a groveling deference to anyone who was dressed at all respectably. Early in the new century he wrote: "Peasant risings, which usually lead to bloodshed, are characteristic and normal events of public life in the South. . . . Without any middle class, even without workers who are above the poverty level and possess a rudimentary education, the practice of representative government in fact works directly against the objects it might hope to achieve."

The Neapolitan, Villari, said the same, that the peasants still thought their lord almighty and all-knowing, but that, when anything happened to destroy this belief, a long suppressed hatred would flare up with all its accompaniment of vindictiveness and savagery. Only a small rise in the price of bread might set off rebellions like that of Sicily in 1893, and every year there were minor clashes. Travelers from the North thought southerners were idle, said Villari, when in fact they merely lacked employment. He described how two-thirds of the population of Naples, still in 1881 the largest city of Italy, had no certainty of daily work and daily bread. Not until after the terrible cholera outbreak of 1884 did Naples obtain a reasonably pure water supply along the Serino aqueduct.

In Sicily it was not so much a class but the whole province that was poor. A parliamentary commission in 1876 cheerfully reported that the Sicilian peasants were not so badly off as the Lombard rice growers or the shepherds of the Roman Campagna. Franchetti and Sonnino, however, criticized this parliamentary inquiry for seeking evidence only from the local gentry and only from the main provincial centers. They themselves concluded that the idea of liberty was quite meaningless in such conditions as they found all over the island and that violence would remain an important local industry unless and until the whole social and economic situation could be changed. No wonder that Verga left his fashionable writing and went back to his native Sicily to find a proper setting for *Cavalleria rusticana,* those sketches which he published in 1880 to describe the violent passions of a downtrodden peasantry. His novel *Mastro Don Gesualdo,* published in 1888 and later translated into English by D. H. Lawrence, likewise told of the misery and anger of Sicilian peasants in revolt against their environment.

Four-fifths of the island population were still illiterate in 1900, and nine-tenths of Sicilian conscripts continued to be medically unfit. Drains, pure water, and even cemeteries were often entirely lacking well into the twentieth century. Once the granary of old Rome, Sicily now no longer fed itself, and a primitive system of agriculture was progressively exhausting the soil. It was a country like Ireland, of great estates, absentee landlords, secret societies, rebellion, and emigration. Sicily was not so much oppressed as neglected by Italy. Considerable support was sometimes found for separation from the continent, and Franchetti echoed D'Azeglio in saying that the island should be given back its independence if the existing government from Rome continued to be so ineffective.

The southern problem was basically a problem of poverty. Except for a few fertile areas, like the Campania around Naples and the Conca d'Oro around Palermo, the soil seemed burned up by the sun, frequently a barren wilderness of clay and rock. Even the generating of electricity was more difficult in the South where rivers dried up for half the year. Statistics for wheat production in the decade 1909–20 show that, compared with nineteen quintals per hectare in the northern district of Ferrara, Reggio Calabria could produce only 4.9 and Syracuse 5.5. The twelve provinces with the lowest production were all from the South, whereas no more than two provinces from the South came into the top half of the list at all. The same figures show a striking annual variability of output as equally characteristic of the South.

Landslides and earthquakes were also a specialty of the lower Apennines and the islands. Some indication of this constant menace may be gathered from the fact that Croce lost his parents and Salvemini his wife and children in such awful natural calamities. In the space of a few

years an eruption of Vesuvius in 1906 and another of Etna in 1910 engulfed whole villages. Hundreds were killed by earthquakes in Calabria
in 1905, and in 1908 a terrible convulsion and tidal wave in the straits
of Scylla and Charybdis destroyed three hundred townships, burying
fifty thousand people at Messina and twelve thousand in Reggio.

Capital to repair such disasters was short in the South, and when it
was available there was little spirit of enterprise and no proper institutions for its protection and investment. Peasants might conceal their
savings at home, or more often their whole "surplus" income went in
discharging usurious interest rates which might be well over 100 per
cent. Usury was profitable enough to take capital away from industry
or agricultural improvement, and landowners had to lend money to
their men against bad harvests instead of using it to increase production.
The vast sums spent in purchasing ecclesiastical and domanial lands
between 1865 and 1890 had also absorbed much of the free funds available, and prevented the transition to a more intensive form of agriculture.

Any remaining money tended to go into state securities. Centuries
of misfortune had made security appear the primary requisite, and
speculative ventures or even investment in public amenities were generally distrusted. Loans were refused by many southern municipalities
when offered by the government on easy terms for use in road building
and the like, although such offers were readily snatched up by enterprising northerners who sought long-term rewards for present absti-
nence. A false economy led the Neapolitan town council, thinking more
of the municipal rates than of public health, to turn down successive
projects for drainage and water supply, while the lavishly ornate municipal theater was given every priority.

§♥

It was perhaps natural that southerners should try to shift the blame
from their own deficiencies on to the wicked devices of statesmen at
Rome. Giolitti was always being attacked by them for favoring the
North. No doubt he had good reason to be more afraid of social revolution among the northern industrial proletariat than among the southern
peasants, but to reward the rich North and penalize the poor South
seemed an unfair conclusion for him to draw from such a fear. It was
even suggested that brigandage was deliberately publicized in the national press just to keep tourists away from the South. After the Messina
earthquake, when the government prohibited the return of fugitives for
fear of indiscriminate looting, it was bitterly complained that this had

prevented the rescue of many people, and even that northern insurance firms bought up individual claims to government compensation so as to gain the best street sites.

More justifiably it was argued that, while Sicily alone among Italian provinces enjoyed a demonstrable export surplus (sulphur, marsala, and fruit were all export trades), the rest of Italy swallowed up its profits. The Sicilian waste land was the last to be reclaimed, and it was in Lombardy and Emilia that the new state built its canals and roads and carried out its biggest schemes of land reclamation. Government contributions to elementary education were assessed on the basis of existing schools rather than on the need for new schools, and this naturally favored the North. Such public works as were carried out in the South were frequently entrusted to northern contractors, and northerners alone possessed sufficient capital and enterprise to take over the farming of the tobacco monopoly and the construction and running of the railroads.

The economist Pantaleoni computed in 1910 that northern Italy, with 48 per cent of the national wealth, paid 40 per cent of the nation's taxes; the Center, with 25 per cent, paid 28 per cent; and the South, with 27 per cent of the national wealth, paid 32 per cent. This was an unfair proportion. Fortunato in 1904 asserted that the immense wealth being built up in Lombardy almost entirely escaped the existing net of taxation. Another minor but perhaps typical form of unintentional discrimination was the taxation of farm buildings. Rural property was less heavily taxed than urban, but primitive peasant huts clustered in large southern hill villages were considered urban dwellings, while the equivalent farm buildings in the North were more obviously rural and so exempt. Again, while the old Kingdom of the Two Sicilies had had barely any national debt, after 1860 the vast increase in debt payments by the state at once impinged on the hitherto sheltered southern taxpayer. Rich men in the North, instead of investing in backward areas, bought national securities which bore attractive rates of interest, and the heavier taxes after 1860 therefore appeared to divert money from the South to pay the interest of northern bond holders.

ဒ❧

Cavour had once written to an English lady that "the reason why Naples has fallen so low is that laws are held not to apply to a *gran signore* or a friend of the king, or to their friends and confessors. Naples can rise again only by a severe but just application of the law." Unfortunately, Cavour's successors had failed to practice this precept. The land-tax qualification in the administrative franchise confirmed the landlords in possession of local government, through which they could influence the national elections and even the administration of justice itself. The Marquis di Rudinì virtually inherited the mayoralty of Palermo in his middle twenties, as did the Marquis di San Giuliano that of Catania.

Some mayors treated their office as a perquisite which, by its control of electoral lists, could be used to perpetuate family graft and the exploitation of communal property. We hear of another Sicilian marquis who diverted a river for the benefit of his own watermills, and in return said a mass for the people on feast days in his private chapel. A survey of Calabria in 1910 found in one commune eighty-three usurpations of the common land, two of them by brothers of the mayor, seventeen by his first cousins, two by his nephews, and a dozen more by communal councilors and their friends. After the great Calabrian earthquake, some of the relief money disappeared altogether, and accusations were made that far too much of it was diverted to rebuilding the houses of the rich. Poor-law boards sometimes worked so that relatively little of the revenue from local charities reached the real poor, and commissioners of the *monts de piété* lent themselves money under assumed names. The condemnation of the Sicilian ex-minister Nasi for embezzlement added to the belief that the island was thoroughly corrupt, and Ferri once said in open parliament that there existed only a few "oases" of honesty in the whole South.

Franchetti recounts how he found one prefect who was removed for trying to clear up such corruption; and another mentioned the arrival of orders that he was to wink at it. One man said that "our mayor is the king of the village and can arrest whom he wants." Franchetti here discerned the emergence of a new and different feudalism: instead of *corvées* and *banalités* there were the communal taxes which could be suitably rigged, and though the peasants were not tied to the soil in law they were still so in fact. Prefects who came from the North regarded their tenure of office as a penance, while prudent silence would be repaid by a transfer northward. If they were by origin southerners, the educational system ensured that they were of the landowning class, whose interests they normally pursued.

Among the principal instruments of oppression were the mafia of Sicily and the camorra of Naples. The mafia was a collection of gangs which protected pockets of graft from the law and organized smuggling and kidnapping. They exacted hush money and protection money. Their sanctions ranged from murder to the burning of ricks and killing of cattle, or to preferring trumped-up charges against opponents by suborning false witnesses. The mafia was a way of life, part of the social habits of a whole people, infecting and comprising members of every class and profession. That man who administered his own justice with his own hands was praiseworthy: this was the code of *omertà*. In 1875 the vice-prefect of Palermo confessed to Sonnino that he was a *mafioso,* and many of the town officials and lawyers took a profitable share in the racket. Landlords used it to keep their peasants in subjection, or an ambitious man would purchase its support at election time by promising to represent the interests of the *mala vita* at Rome. Its objects were not always bad, and clearly it had given invaluable support to the revolutionaries in 1848 and to Garibaldi's volunteers in 1860. But it could almost always be relied on to oppose the government, whether the Bourbons or the House of Savoy, unless officialdom connived at its illegalities. Sometimes the government made halfhearted efforts to investigate the whole system, but the mafia always continued as before.

The name *camorrista* was bestowed at Naples on anyone who used cleverness or strength to exploit the weak. Here, too, a perverted sense of honor supported a criminal conspiracy to live by intimidation and blackmail. The camorra became a sort of unofficial police force and was sometimes engaged as such by the government. More frequently it supplied the place of the magistrate, for its justice was commonly cheaper and sometimes more just than that of the regular courts. Like the mafia, it sold its electoral support, and blacklisted candidates who did not subscribe to its funds. It had considerable influence inside the Naples town council, and it could even send its own deputies to parliament.

The camorra was never very highly organized, but it seems to have developed something of a hierarchy, with peculiar laws, initiation ceremonies, and conventional language. In the city of Naples it was said to take a tenth of the winnings in gambling houses, and to impose a specified tariff on porters, cabdrivers, and prostitutes. A camorrista lurked at every city gate, at railroad stations, and in the market and imposed levies at every stage on the cartage, unloading, distribution, and sale of food. Peasants bringing their wares to town would gladly pay their tithe for its protection, and so would the merchant who wished for the safe unloading of his ship. The society had its own methods of influencing customs and excise officials, and its agents even when in prison were paid a regular monthly tribute to which all other prisoners would contribute. It was the pawnshop of the poor. It might also put a tax on a priest when he said mass. If a more than ordinarily scrupulous prefect tried to crush it, the organization might temporarily disappear, but the way of life remained, and the prefect himself usually disappeared more permanently. No wonder if, from Minghetti to Garibaldi and Lombroso, leading Italians voiced their shame over the criminal statistics in a country where such things were normal and apparently incorrigible.

§✿

Not until the end of the century did the government begin to take active responsibility for reform in the South. Acts were passed in 1897 for the betterment of agricultural conditions in Sardinia, in 1904 for the Basilicata, and in 1906 for Calabria. The state now recognized that certain regions had special needs which demanded special treatment, and northern industrialists gradually realized that a more prosperous South would provide an expanding market. But action continued to be slow, and expenditure far too small. In 1905, after forty years of talk, a contract was signed for an aqueduct to pierce the Apennines and carry water for two million people down from the river Sele into remote Apulia; the work dragged on and was not finished until 1927. If by then the southern question was less acute, this was due not so much to government schemes of development, as to the spontaneous action of southerners themselves in emigration.

§✿

The great exodus or *Völkerwanderung* of the Italians is one of the most striking features of their recent history. Many districts had long been acquainted with a migrant life. In the Alps and Apennines, for example, there was little work to be done in the winter. Men moved freely over the frontiers, and shepherds would take their flocks for seasonal grazing far away to the plains below. There had always been an annual migration for temporary work between Umbria and the Marches on the one hand and the Agro Romano and the Tuscan Maremma on the other, and the harvesting and polishing of rice in Lombardy has always attracted additional seasonal labor. About 1900 it was estimated that a million workers spent up to two months in the year working away from their families in other provinces of the country.

For permanent migration abroad there are no exact figures until 1932. The *Annuario Statistico* of 1861 gave 220,000 Italians as resident abroad—77,000 were in France, 47,000 in the United States, and 18,000 in Brazil and Argentina. By 1876 a hundred thousand people were leaving Italy a year, by 1901 half a million, and in the single year of 1913, 872,000 people left the country, that is to say one person in every forty. By 1914 there were thus five to six million Italians living abroad as compared with thirty-five million inside Italy.

The early emigrants were casual wanderers or political refugees. Mazzini, Foscolo, and Rossetti had gone to England, Pareto's father to France, Da Ponte, the librettist of Mozart, and Garibaldi himself to

America. In the middle of the nineteenth century the chief trend was from northern Italy to other European countries, the emigrants being mostly urban workers who intended to return. The image-hawkers from Lucca were celebrated the world over, and some remote Italian villages exist to this day where a substantial number of the menfolk have learned English on their regular travels in search of work. In the next phase the casual laborers, the agricultural *braccianti* who had no property to bind them to the soil, left Liguria, the Veneto, and the coastal areas of the South. The adult males would go first, and only later might summon their wives or write home to their families to choose a wife and send her out to them. Usually, they would return to Italy once they had made their fortune. Only at the end of the century, particularly after 1887, did whole families in the inland districts tend to go abroad together and for good.

The poor peasant in Italy, if he did not rebel, had no choice but resignation to his lot or else emigration. His motive in going was not always simply land hunger; on the contrary, it sometimes looked rather like flight from the ungrateful soil. Deforestation, soil erosion, and enclosures had upset his rural economy, destroying his fuel supplies and grazing rights and encouraging the spread of malaria. Heavy local and national taxation skimmed off that small margin of cash which could have made these backward areas more fruitful, all the more so now that Italy had pretensions to being a great power; and as a result, an Alpine valley in Italy might be poor while the next valley in Switzerland was prosperous. This constituted an immediate reason for moving to a place where conditions were easier.

The national population rose to forty-two million by the census of 1936, having doubled since 1861. Though the birth rate began to decline during this period, the fall was much slower than elsewhere, and in 1906 there was still an annual surplus of eleven per thousand in births over deaths. Agricultural families were particularly large, and, especially in the more barren and mountainous regions, fathers would send some of their children abroad to avoid too much division of the family inheritance. The depression in agriculture after 1887 made unemployment acute, for fewer hands might be needed if grain land were converted into pasture to serve some local cheese industry, or if a *latifondista* simply wanted to reduce his wage bill.

For this "surplus population" there were counterattractions in the mines of Lorraine and Luxemburg, in the building of railroads, bridges, and harbors from Scotland to Siberia, in planting coffee in Brazil or vines in North Africa, in pedaling ice cream or shining shoes in New York. Navigation companies made so much profit on the traffic in emigrants that they gave good publicity to the existence of labor shortages abroad, while those who returned also brought back with them higher standards of living, which made their friends at home discontented and ambitious to better their own fate.

In 1876 north Italy had provided 85 per cent of the annual emigration. The Piedmontese went to France, the Venetians often spoke German and had a long tradition of movement to and from Austria. Only after the agricultural slump did emigration begin to be predominantly from the South. By that time the industrial development of Lombardy and Umbria offered alternative employment for agricultural workers in the North and Center, while in the South the depression helped to break down that attachment to the land which had hitherto deterred people from moving abroad.

The proportion of emigrants who actually went overseas rose from 18 per cent in 1876 to 50 per cent by the end of the century. At first the exodus was directed to South America—mainly Brazil and the Argentine—whence, after the harvest months, a man would often return in time for the spring sowing in Italy. Later, the swelling stream poured instead into the United States, as the available free land in South America declined and the requirements of capital increased. Garibaldi and Cavour had both on occasion looked to the United States as the country destined to lead the world in a new age of liberty and human progress. Cavour had once threatened to emigrate there himself, and Garibaldi lived there long enough to call himself an American citizen. Above all there was the attraction of relatively high wages and a seemingly inexhaustible capacity for assimilation. In 1898, of all immigrants coming into the United States, there were for the first time more from Italy than from any other country, and more than twice as many Italians as British. In remote villages of the Abruzzi, American politics were followed closely even by people who had never been there and who could neither read nor write. By 1927 the Italian government computed that over nine million Italians were living abroad, including three and a half million in the United States, and one and a half million each in Brazil and the Argentine. Over half a million were in New York city alone, a hundred thousand in Philadelphia, and as many in Buenos Aires.

The economies of Tunisia, Argentina, and the south of France had already been substantially altered by the work of Italians, and on Italy itself the effect of such a mass exodus was incalculable. It was a safety valve and took away many anarchists and other undesirables—Mussolini himself, when out of work in 1909–10, had plans for emigrating to the United States. Perhaps in early years it helped to postpone the development of an organized labor movement in the country. It resulted in raising domestic wages, but also in inducing landowners to save labor by abandoning rice for cattle. A particular benefit was that about 500 million lire—a sum larger than that produced by tourism—returned in annual remittances to the families of emigrants in the years just before 1914, and this not only helped to restore the balance of foreign trade, but by bringing capital into the countryside dealt a blow to the local usurer and made the land more profitable. The *Americani* who returned, easily recognizable from the gold and silver prominently displayed in their teeth, brought with them new habits, new needs, new skills, a higher level of education, a greater sense of independence, and a consciousness of their rights against the *padrone* and the government. Among other things they were convincing proof that literacy paid. The prospective emigrant feared that he might be turned back at the port of entry if he were illiterate. He needed to be able to write letters to his family, and his family needed to be able to read them. This was a far greater educative force upon such a family-conscious nation than edicts from Rome about compulsory schooling.

Apart from wanting to keep men at home until they were no longer liable for military service, the government cared little about emigration. Only in 1901 was an office set up to try to control the speculators and transportation agencies who were running a virtual slave trade in human flesh. When Zanardelli traveled specially to see conditions in the South (apparently the first prime minister who thought this half of Italy to be worth a visit), he was surprised and shocked when the mayor of Moliterno greeted him "on behalf of the eight thousand people in this commune, three thousand of whom are in America and the other five thousand preparing to follow them." But the government's policy was normally one of laissez faire, and only under fascism was every emigrant considered a potential source of manpower lost to the country.

Mussolini substituted for the word emigrant a more patriotic title of "Italian abroad," and developed the new doctrine that these *émigrés* did not reflect the poverty of his country but rather the superabundant energy of a young people with a mission to civilize the world. But by then, immigration laws in other countries were refusing illiterates and discriminating against poorer and more backward nations. This spelled disaster for Italy.

30 Economic and Cultural Revival

Although Italy was an essentially agricultural country, few deputies were much concerned about rural society. Said Professor Villari: "If I try to interest a deputy in the working conditions of the poor, he is only bored, but if I talk to him about the latest shuffling of parties, his face lights up and he regards me as a sensible man of the world." The government seemed little interested in statistics, and the census which should have been taken in 1891 was put off for ten years from misguided motives of economy. It was left to individual students like Franchetti and Pareto to try to fill the gap.

Villari's interest in the conditions of life of the poor was particularly close just because they made up such a large majority of Italian citizens. Workmen's unions designed to increase wages had usually been considered illegal, though employers could legally combine to stop overproduction or to bring pressure on the government. This discrepancy was too unfair to last. Despite persecution, friendly societies and co-operatives began to appear in agriculture toward the end of the century: we have an early example in the landless *braccianti* of Ravenna who in 1883 formed a co-operative to obtain contracts for land drainage. By 1889 chambers of labor were being formed, and in 1892 there was in existence a Federation of Agrarian Co-operatives. There were co-operative dairies and wine factories, as well as co-operative rural banks, and for perishable truck-garden produce a joint sales organization was most necessary. Agricultural experts were employed by a society and sent around to give demonstrations on market days, to teach pruning and wine production and the use of vegetables in the rotation of crops.

Self-help and mutual help were important, but the government alone had resources large enough to tackle the problem of land reclamation, especially as marsh and mountain formed such a high proportion of the total land surface. Rome itself had been partially surrounded by uninhabitable land ever since Belisarius and Witige cut the aqueducts in the early Middle Ages, and the three hundred thousand acres of the Pontine marshes stretched from the Alban hills to the coast, almost as a shallow gulf of the Tyrrhenian sea. The marshland of the Maremma ran northward along the coast between Civitavecchia and Leghorn, and near Ferrara there was another almost uninhabited swamp, twenty by thirty kilometers in size. In the still water of such marshes bred the mosquitos which propagated the parasites of malaria.

Another problem calling for state action was the rapidly dwindling forests, especially in the Apennines, which had been cut down to provide timber for the shipping and building industries, or deliberately burned to provide a soil which for a few years would be highly fertile before being washed away. In Sardinia the bark of oak trees had been indiscriminately stripped off for the cork trade or the tanneries, and much of what remained of the forests was cut down in the seventies and eighties to feed a flourishing trade in charcoal. In all, by 1890, between four and five million acres of woodland were computed to have been destroyed in living memory. Great numbers of peasant families had thereby lost an important source of livelihood, and severe problems of soil erosion had been laid up for the future. In the single province of Cosenza, the forest inspectors reported 156 landslides during 1903, covering some five thousand acres. The River Basento in the Basilicata, a raging flood in winter, almost dry in summer, was estimated to carry 430,000 cubic meters of mud into the sea each year, washing the soil away from under the feet of the inhabitants and blocking the river mouth. Deforestation in this way destroyed capital as well as income, and was a prime cause of the barren rocks, sterile pastures, floods, avalanches, marshes, and malaria of Italy. Men out for quick profits had not stopped to think that woodland might in some areas be the most profitable type of cultivation.

In time, when the damage could no longer be overlooked, a third of the total area of the country was to come under one scheme or another of land reclamation. Something had been done by private hands: successive Popes had built canals along the old Appian way to drain part of the Pontine marshes; Prince Torlonia in 1876 brought to a conclusion the draining of Lake Fucino, later to be the scene of Silone's novel *Fontamara*—this one project involved the construction of 800 bridges and 250 kilometers of roads, and a living for thousands of families was provided on the land reclaimed. The government made a forlorn effort in 1865 to build a network of dikes for flood control, and in 1873 the mention at least was made of expropriating nonco-operative landowners. A law of 1877 encouraged reforestation, and the Baccarini act of 1882 recognized that the cost of draining large areas would have to be borne almost entirely by the state.

Successive edicts of 1883, 1903, and 1910 then tried to force the landowners in the Agro Romano to drain their land and settle people on it, under pain of forfeiture. In the province of Ferrara, two hundred thousand acres were said to have been reclaimed for productive agriculture in the thirty years before 1907. The great plain of the Tavoliere, stretching from the sub-Apennines to the gulf of Manfredonia and down to Apulia, had its medieval pasturage customs curtailed by statute to make it an area of more intensive cultivation. Bounties were given to families that settled in these newly reclaimed areas, and new villages were given certain tax exemptions. Altogether in the forty years before 1900 it was claimed that one and a half million acres were reclaimed; even the fertile lava on the slopes of Mt. Etna was broken up for profitable cultivation.

But the figures are suspect, and sometimes seem to refer rather to projects than to completed work. The bureaucracy was slow; reclaimed land fell back only too easily into primitive wildness; and landowners usually were more than satisfied with the income from these extensive, unreclaimed pasture lands where so little labor was required, while their lethargy and in many cases their poverty made it difficult to enforce the law. The complexity of internal politics made stringent measures impossible, and as there were no effective sanctions so there was little expropriation. On the contrary, the landlords could all too often arrange that their own estates were the chief beneficiaries from public expenditure, especially as these laws put the onus of action on local authorities. The provincial governments were in general poor and lazy, and preferred to spend their money on theaters and festive occasions. Giolitti declared that state action had not secured the planting of a single tree in provinces which were hostile or indifferent.

It was long before the magnitude of the task was fully grasped. Apart from the difficulty of making laws effective, a project might be useless if it did not fit into a composite regional plan. Road building might thus be a prerequisite of expenditure on river beds and embankments, and schemes of drainage would be insufficient if they failed simultaneously to arrange methods of land tenure and cultivation and find settlers for the land. Since poor Alpine areas could not be expected to pay for work in the mountains which chiefly benefited the plains, only the central government could provide the necessary finance and co-ordination of effort, and maintain the results once achieved.

§❧

The return of prosperity after 1897 was, of course, due only in small part to government action. The end of the tariff war with France, the growth of the co-operative movement and emigration, the increased use of electricity, all had their share. Fairer negotiation in labor disputes was now possible, and the outburst of strikes after 1901 was a symptom of improved conditions. From one lira a day, wages rose to three and even five lire in the countryside. Another indication is the comparison of mortality figures for 1901–5 with those for 1909–13, when the number of deaths in the two worst provinces diminished from twenty-seven to twenty-two per thousand inhabitants.

In the years 1899–1910 the annual Treasury budgets show a favorable balance of income over expenditure for the only continuous stretch in modern Italian history. The habit of travel, of taking vacations at the seaside or in the mountains, was a further indication of growing prosperity. Genoa easily held its place as the third port of the Mediterranean for traffic, and it was hoped that completion of the long Simplon tunnel in 1906 might enrich her still more by creating a new route from Central Europe. Foreign trade, which had diminished in the decade 1880–90, grew again between 1890 and 1900 from two to three billion lire in value, and then to six billion lire by 1910. Even after corrections have been made for advancing prices after 1906 and for the increase in population, imports rose by 61 per cent in value between 1901 and 1913, and exports by 47 per cent.

One significant qualification is that the discrepancy between imports and exports was larger than anywhere else in Europe, and from a yearly average of about 175 million lire in the period 1896–1900, the gap had increased to 1,300 million by 1912. Another qualification, though less important, is that in 1913 two-thirds of Italy's maritime trade was still being carried in foreign ships and that the Italian merchant marine was, despite heavy protection, very largely foreign-built. Income per head in Italy in 1911–13 was considerably less than half that in France, less than a third that in Britain, and little more than a quarter that in the United States.

Nineteenth-century Italy had produced many distinguished scientists and mathematicians, but names like Betti and Cremona were eclipsed in popular renown by the work of those who, from Volta to Marconi, made important discoveries in the field of electricity. In 1883 the Italian Edison company set up a generating plant on the River Adda, using some of the dynamos of the defunct Holborn Viaduct station in London, and Milan became one of the first European towns to use electricity for streetcars, street lighting, and industrial power. By 1886 there was an automatic telephone system in the Vatican library. Streetcars were running from Florence to Fiesole in 1890, and two years later from Tivoli to Rome—the famous falls of Tivoli being used to supply Rome with her light and power. Marconi's great work on wireless telegraphy took place between 1896, when he took out his first patent at the age of twenty-two, and 1909 when he became a Nobel prizewinner.

After this early start, it was surprising that a country so lacking in coal and with such great hydraulic resources did not develop hydro-electric energy much faster. Generating stations were rather considered by the state as a new source of taxation revenue, and it was fortunate that the enormous profits attracted private capital despite all the bureaucratic difficulties encountered. As an indication of the government attitude, foreign bids for big schemes of railroad electrification were turned down in 1897 because the minister was unwilling to allow foreign companies too great a control over Italian resources. Not until just before World War I was Nitti's scheme adopted for large generating plants on the River Sila in Calabria and the River Tirso in Sardinia, and only the pressure of war itself forced Italy to develop her latent potentialities. Even so, Mussolini after 1919 was naïve enough to blame Nitti for allowing so much American capital to come in and build up this vital industry. The topsy-turvy economics of the new age assumed that it was better to do without than to accept foreign help.

Electricity was at last to provide a cheap and abundant form of power, and this supplemented the meager deposits of lignite in Italy and the importation of foreign coal which by 1914 amounted to one million tons a month. All these various sources of power gave a great impetus to Italy's industrial revolution. Hitherto, land and government bonds had been the favored form of investment, and silk alone of Italian industries had been of great international importance. Now a wide range of other manufactures began to offer the same combination of profit and security.

The replacement of wood fuel by coal had originally been a severe threat to the subalpine ironworks of the Val d'Aosta and the Val d'Ossola, far away from supplies of coal. After 1878, however, government protection began to be lavishly granted, and in proportion to the political weight of industries as well as to their economic need. In many direct and indirect ways the state was thus to bear the cost and risk of expansion in the heavy industries, and government protection was followed by the forming of cartels. A metal trust had been formed at Florence in 1896 to stop internal competition and raise prices, and in 1905 two rival companies, which had competed for mining concessions in the island of Elba, joined to form the Ilva group, linked with the Terni steelworks and the Orlando shipyards at Leghorn. A second composite group was that of Ansaldo, using the mines of Cogne in the Val d'Aosta, shipyards at Sestri Ponente, and mechanical and electrical shops at Sampierdarena. Combination, though perhaps unavoidable, was bound to result in keeping superfluous and inefficient workshops in existence, and did not suffice to prevent chaotic overproduction after 1907. In 1911 a convention had to be made between the Ilva and other smelting concerns to reduce stocks and prevent further capital being sunk in the industry.

Armament production was always closely involved with politics. The Terni factories in Umbria had a monopoly in the supply of some armaments, and a parliamentary inquiry in 1906 showed that they were misusing the heavy state subsidies in order to pay dividends of 20 per cent, as well as possessing unhealthily close contacts with Krupp and Vickers. Yet the Italian steel cartel was able to use the evidence of German infiltration to extort still further subsidies. Some of the resultant profits, guaranteed as they were by the government, were undoubtedly spent in bribes to obtain even more favorable tariffs and bounties. The cartel was backed in particular by the Banca d'Italia, and in time came to be run more by financiers than industrialists, the industrial companies sometimes appearing to be pawns in an enormous game of speculation.

The new industries were never really healthy and vigorous. They did not prove remarkably efficient during World War I, and they collapsed with disastrous results in the slump after 1919. Without heavy protection they could not have survived so long, since the high charges for coal and other imported raw materials told against them. The heavy duties placed on imported steel and pig iron had meanwhile harmed the mechanical industries by increasing costs all around. And again with shipping, bounties based on tonnage did not encourage efficiency and economy in the shipyards. Protection brought together politicians and speculators, and with the growth of *affairisme* it is not surprising if taxpayers' money was sometimes misspent.

After 1900 the concentration of industry in the North became more pronounced. Even when laws required that one-eighth of the material used for the railroads should come from Naples, the absence of skilled labor there made this quota impossible to meet. Milan continued to increase its commercial and industrial predominance and was becoming a highly efficient but soulless city which the other Italy of Puccini and Verdi was often tempted to dislike for its wealth and materialism. Between Milan, Turin, and Genoa lay most of the nation's industry and wealth, and this disproportion became greater and greater with the passage of time.

Italians had been experimenting with internal combustion engines ever since the 1830's. The first Italian automobile was made at Turin in 1895, and in 1899 a group of industrialists under Agnelli created the Fabbrica Italiana Automobili Torino, or Fiat for short. By 1903 there was an output of thirteen hundred cars a year from four factories, and, shortly after the grant of protection in 1905, as many as seventy different concerns were engaged in the automobile industry. But this new group of factories came into activity just when a contraction of sales set in. Overhasty expansion brought with it severe financial and technical difficulties, and in 1907–8 Fiat had to write off seven of its nine millions of capital. After the industry had rationalized itself, production of cars increased to 18,000 a year in 1914. World War I turned Fiat into the largest group of factories in Italy, responsible for over 70 per cent of the automobiles produced. In addition, Alfa Romeo at Milan specialized in racing cars; Isotta Fraschini, also at Milan, was to be one of the first firms interested in aircraft motors; Bianchi and Prinetti made bicycles; and the factories of Lancia at Turin and Maserati at Bologna also became world famous.

৯✿

Fifty years after unification, northern and central Italy were becoming prosperous under the benevolent rule of Giolitti. Not even the experience of the 1890's had undermined his confidence in parliamentary government, and his tolerant attitude produced a more natural balance of social forces. Both clericals and reformist socialists were now being drawn into the orbit of the constitution. This was the most buoyant period in modern Italian history, and affluence brought with it optimism and a sense of greater political maturity. Giolitti did not greatly exaggerate when in 1911 he claimed that no other people had in so short a period of time gone through such a profound transformation politically, morally, and economically.

If the nation now felt itself internally less divided, this came partly from a developing social conscience and the realization that conservatism might best be served by a policy of enlightened reform. Giolitti insisted that one of society's main tasks was to improve the condition of the poor. He had already more than once proposed the introduction of death duties and a progressive tax on incomes. In 1902 parliament passed a factory act to regulate the work of women and children— though only three inspectors were appointed and one of these was soon dismissed. Giolitti's proposal for a compulsory Sunday holiday was defeated in 1904, but two years later night work was forbidden for women and children in the cotton industry. Agricultural workers were less vociferous and less easily organized, but they also benefited. The right to strike was confirmed. Giolitti laid down a special code for unhealthy activities like rice cultivation, and tried to insist on the provision of healthy sleeping quarters, medical attention, good food, and drinking water. He also reduced food taxes, after being shocked to discover that salt paid fifty-five times its price in tax, while alcohol and tobacco paid only four times. Acts were passed to enforce public holidays, to provide free quinine against malaria, and to prescribe rules for accident prevention. The socialists commented that no fundamental reforms were being tackled and only enough was conceded to avoid revolution; nevertheless it was noteworthy that some of these socialists were becoming far less unco-operative as prosperity spread.

In matters of culture, Italy had tended to lag behind France. Marinetti, Pareto, and D'Annunzio chose to write some of their works in French, as did Papini, Soffici, and Ungaretti; and the most celebrated Italian painter, Modigliani, was French in almost all but name and origin. There had been little of great note in art or architecture during the Humbertine period, and the flamboyant style of the early twentieth century was epitomized by the tasteless Palace of Justice. This had been planned to cost eight million lire, but in fact cost thirty-nine, and four deputies had to resign after a parliamentary committee had reported in several volumes on this interesting discrepancy. Far worse aesthetically was the hideous Vittorio Emanuele monument which desecrated the skyline of Rome. Covered with warlike emblems, built arrogantly and aggressively on the Capitoline hill, a typical and far too expensive product of top-heavy state enterprise, Sacconi's edifice was a monument to what was worst in the age.

In opera Italy had been supreme, and popular demand was here insatiable. Donizetti was dead by 1860, and Rossini's work was over, but Giuseppe Verdi was then beginning to set the fashion of a new dramatic and lyrical style which protected Italian music from too slavish an admiration of Wagner and Debussy. Verdi's enormous output was crowned in 1871 by *Aida,* to celebrate the opening of the Suez Canal, by the *Requiem* in 1874 to commemorate Manzoni, by *Otello* which was first performed at La Scala in 1887, and finally, when the composer was over eighty years of age, by *Falstaff* in 1893. During the next ten years his successor in popular esteem, Puccini, wrote *La Bohème, Tosca,* and *Madama Butterfly.* Mascagni's *Cavalleria rusticana* appeared in 1890, and Leoncavallo's *Pagliacci* in 1892.

De Sanctis had proclaimed as long ago as 1861 that the national *risorgimento* needed to be and would in fact be intellectual and artistic as well as political. Mazzini, too, had confirmed that Italy was bent on an intellectual movement "more stirring, more *initiating* than all French and German *systems* had been or ever will be." But in practice, far from being stimulated by the political revolution, artistic and intellectual life continued at a low ebb after 1860. French novels had a better sale than Italian, not only with people like Cavour himself, but also with later generations of his countrymen.

In a famous essay, Bonghi showed why Italian literature was not and could not be popular, for the language of 1860 was too refined for simple prose and was difficult to write naturally without seeming either precious or vulgar. There was too wide a variety of local idiom, and, in treating the life of ordinary people, realism demanded too much dialect for complete intelligibility. Characters in Fogazzaro's novels sometimes spoke Venetian, those in Fucini, Tuscan. In Naples, Rome, and Lombardy, furthermore, there continued to exist an entirely dialect literature, and even D'Annunzio had to leave his native Abruzzi to learn a purer diction at school in Tuscany. But although many years of city life and popular journalism were needed to fix the language more firmly, by the beginning of the new century a literate public was coming into existence. This was not only for journals and reviews. Carducci died in 1907, De Amicis in 1908, and Fogazzaro in 1911, and their books reached quite a large audience. Carducci's achievement was signalized when in the year before his death he received the Nobel prize for literature.

In philosophy there was an even more significant and successful effort to break free from the mixture of narrow provincialism and characterless cosmopolitanism which had previously distinguished Italian culture. Unification had found the country with no indigenous tradition which could survive the invasion of Parisian art, English liberalism, and German philosophy and historiography. There was nothing to justify Gioberti's boast that "because Italy is the center of Catholicism, it follows that she is the natural leader of our modern civilization, and Rome the real metropolis of the world." Perhaps the very strength of clericalism in Italy had deprived her of the stimulus which in France was to create a flourishing school of lay Catholic philosophers. Instead, the return of her exiles after 1860, Bertrando Spaventa, De Sanctis, and others, had brought from northern Europe an invigorating injection of Hegelianism, non-Catholic and often anti-Catholic. When Garibaldi in 1860 made De Sanctis minister of education at Naples, thirty of the old timeserving professors were removed from the university and at least three notable Hegelians figured among their successors. Naples thus became the center of philosophical studies in Italy, as it had been before in the time of Bruno, Campanella, and Vico.

The rival school of scientific positivism was to meet special difficulties in a country where education was fundamentally classical and literary, and where the Church stood firmly against the new heresies of Darwin, Comte, and Spencer. An article by the Neapolitan Villari in 1886 marks the first appearance of philosophical positivism in Italy, but although it was to be taught in some universities by Ardigò and his disciples, its chief importance was in practical application, for example through the psychological and sociological criminology of Ferri and Lombroso.

Against the somewhat arid achievements of the positivists, speculative thought was revived in philosophical idealism, especially in the writings of the Neapolitan, Benedetto Croce. Books on aesthetics and logic by Croce began to appear soon after 1900, and continued through the next half century, sometimes more than one volume a year. Eschewing all remote metaphysics, his attack on current fashions of thought from D'Annunzio to Marxism brought new life into Italian thinking. Croce never held an academic post, yet his academic influence was enormous. His fine style and universal grasp made him read or read about by all intelligent people, and he became a sort of secular anti-Pope, an uncrowned philosopher king. His Sicilian friend, Giovanni Gentile, was more of a pure philosopher, and perhaps had a larger following in the schools and universities. Until fascism divided these two men, their common respect for spiritual values seeped down through the whole educational curriculum to color the outlook of ordinary individuals on a host of subjects.

ᔐ

A morbid phenomenon which not even Croce's literary and philosophical criticism could exorcise was the fascinating prose and poetry of Gabriele d'Annunzio. This man spent his time in sensuous and extravagant living, almost always in debt, doing nothing that was not exaggerated or at least spectacular. Perpetually lonely and unsatisfied, he took everything to excess, seeking always for new experiences and indulgences, for greater speed, greater passion, a more shocking private life, a more violent assault on convention than anyone else. His cult of beauty was in itself an excess. Reveling in the decadence of the aesthetic movement, he preached that everything should be forgiven the artist, who was a superman above ordinary morals, just as he should also be above the payment of debts. Poets were for him the acknowledged legislators of mankind. D'Annunzio affected colored cravats, a monocle, and perfumes so pungent that some people could not stay in the same room. It was a fair warning when on the doorway of his luxurious villa he put "beware of the dog" on the left-hand pillar and "beware of the master" on the right.

As a writer, D'Annunzio claimed to be the successor of Carducci.

Against the orthodox, romantic tradition of Manzoni, then represented by Fogazzaro, and against the unmitigated realism of Verga, he set a new fashion of sonorous rhetoric that was captivating even when it was not meaningful. His characters were not sympathetic or amiable, all of them lacked nobility, nearly all were unbalanced, and they have been called case histories of degeneracy. The very titles of his books were significant: *Pleasure* (1889), *The Triumph of Death* (1894), *Songs of Death and Glory* (1911).

D'Annunzio gradually moved away from aestheticism toward politics, with the result that his writing grew increasingly empty, and he himself came to seem what Nitti called "a literary Barnum." He entered parliament in 1897 in order to experience a new sensation, and to experience another he crossed over from extreme Right to extreme Left at a moment well-chosen for dramatic effect. Moving quickly through socialism, he had become by 1909 a burning nationalist, summoning his countrymen both to revenge their colonial defeats and to conquer their unredeemed provinces from Austria.

In a famous speech, one of the characters in his play *La nave* called on Italians to "man the prow and sail toward the world," a dubious exclamation which had an enormous *réclame* and somehow helped to make nationalism the fashion. In a poem of 1911 he reached the point of saying that "Africa is only the whetstone on which we Italians shall sharpen our sword for a supreme conquest in the unknown future." Beneath his crepuscular, delphic terminology lay half-concealed visions of unmentionable splendor and excitement, and though exposed again and again by Croce and the critics, his rhetoric and his nationalism fitted so exactly the mood of his time that he molded as well as reflected Italian taste. It was to be expected that D'Annunzio would be well to the foreground in the two dramatic moments when Italy entered World War I and then raised Mussolini to power.

31 The Last Years
of Liberal Reform, 1909-1911

The elections of 1909 increased the representation of radicals, republicans, and socialists, and this extreme Left rose to 108 in the Lower House, the socialists holding nearly half of these seats. The militant Catholics also were up to about 20. Whether or not this advance of the two extremes convinced Giolitti that it was time for another of his temporary retirements, or whether he was simply planning to strengthen himself with the Left, he now brought up again his provocative plan to raise income-tax and death duties. A parliamentary tumult ensued, during which a duke was moved to throw an inkpot at the prime minister, and, when the *estrema* still refused him their support, Giolitti ended his third and longest ministry in December. Without waiting to sound parliament by a vote of confidence which might have prejudiced his later return to power, he advised the king to revert to Sonnino and the right-wing liberals.

Sonnino's second administration, like his first, lacked the support of a carefully prepared majority. While Giolitti always kept some personal friends among his political enemies, Sonnino had few friends anywhere, and possessed none of Giolitti's suppleness in debate. His Jewish antecedents and "Anglican" faith were against him in some quarters—good Catholics were advised not to read his newspaper, *Il Giornale d'Italia*. This time Sonnino avoided the radicals and included just the Right plus a few stray Giolittians. He also packed the Senate with thirty new nominees, among them Benedetto Croce himself. Croce had already been put up for this honor to the previous government, but Giolitti said he had never heard of the man. After three months, however, Sonnino had still made no headway, and when Admiral Bettolo ran into severe opposition over his proposal to increase the subsidies of shipping firms, the cabinet did not wait to be defeated in parliament but gave way to another under one of the other ministers, Luigi Luzzatti. Both of Sonnino's ministries had lasted less than a hundred days.

These successive cabinets are not easily differentiated. No parliamentary leader had any very distinct party support outside parliament, and inside they all claimed the title of liberal—not only Giolitti and Zanardelli, but Sonnino and Salandra, Crispi and Di Rudinì. As Giolitti told Salandra, they were all liberals of a sort, but the word now covered so many different shades of opinion that it ought to be dropped. Most of these liberals were eventually to draw closer together when socialism became more an object of fear, but usually Right Center and Left Center competed against each other with competitive projects of reform, and the radicals could without dishonesty take office under Sonnino, Luzzatti, and Giolitti in turn.

Luzzatti was, like his predecessor, a Jew. He was a famous and erudite economist, and already had been five times minister of the treasury. Luzzatti himself inclined to the Right, but his cabinet included two radicals, Sacchi and Credaro, and several Giolittians including Facta. Laudable measures were announced to put down usury, to control food adulteration, to abolish the truck system of wages in the mines, and for schemes of compulsory insurance and cheap housing.

Early in 1911, however, when Luzzatti proposed a moderate electoral reform, Giolitti sensed a drift of opinion which gave him a new opening. Dramatically, and despite his former scruples, Giolitti overcalled the government and demanded universal suffrage, for the democratic trend of society was evidently irreversible, and he wanted to gain for himself the prestige of such a concession, and to win power in time to prepare the ground for the next elections. The radicals thereupon broke away and helped to defeat the ministry, indicating how cleverly Giolitti had chosen the issue on which to regroup a new coalition and resume office. The same Chamber that had welcomed Luzzatti by 393 votes against 17 hailed his successor by 340 votes to 87. How unreal was the change appeared from Giolitti's retention of seven out of ten of Luzzatti's ministers, even including those radicals whom he had fought in the elections of 1904 and 1909.

§♠

Once again, however, the socialist party refused Giolitti's offer of collaboration. The indecisiveness of Italian socialism, its internal divisions, and its continued threats of violence and revolution, all these were to make a tiresomely complicated story but were to be of the greatest importance in the next few years. The Rome party congress of 1906 had recorded a victory for "integralism," and the syndicalists had been heavily outnumbered, yet revolutionary socialism continued to spread, especially in Milan and in the agricultural centers of Parma, Reggio, and Ferrara. The two extreme wings of the official party manifestly disagreed strongly over ends as well as means, yet even the right wing feared to split socialism still further by explicit collaboration with the government.

The syndicalist program was to boycott parliament, to make the trade unions a kind of antistate, and to assume control of the means of production by using general strikes. The agricultural strikes of 1908 in Parma and Ferrara were the real test of this program, and their failure discredited the theoretical ideas of De Ambris and Bianchi. This premature and futile attempt at socialist revolution merely drove the landowners into defensive leagues and counterrevolution. It was a foretaste of the future when, in 1908, the landowners of Emilia collected a defense fund and formed a motorized volunteer force equipped with arms. This force assisted the troops in street-fighting at Parma and marched through a barrage of missiles and boiling water to surround and occupy the working-class quarter of the city. Similar scenes were to occur more frequently in the not so distant future.

Some of the syndicalists, Arturo Labriola among them, saw that their best hope of revolution was by accepting a far more fervent nationalism. Olivetti demonstrated how easily these extremists of the Left could accept an imperialism in which war and conquest became ends in themselves, and he even advocated voting for reactionary representatives so as to bring the parliamentary system into contempt and collapse. The movement's proletarian wing under Corridoni was soon left an impotent remnant.

The ordinary working man was far less extreme than these firebrand leaders, and the reformists were therefore voted into control of the trade unions when a General Confederation of Labor was formed in 1908. Reformists also proved successful when they joined with radicals and left-wing liberals to win many town administrations including Rome for a popular bloc. The positive and immediate success of this collaborative method secured a decisive victory for reformism in the 1908 socialist congress at Florence. It was there declared that the general strike and any strike of state employees were dangerous weapons not to be lightly used. As a result the revolutionary syndicalists were expelled and the extremists around Ferri who remained were placed in a clear minority.

From 1908 to 1910, the moderates Bissolati and Treves used the pages of *Avanti* to try to educate the workers in a policy of gradual reform, and to wean them from unqualified faith in the international solidarity of the working classes. These two "reformists" held that the practice of democracy and a wider suffrage could be regarded as steps toward socialism, while Turati, once again the party leader, was not far from them in his views. Eventually, but much more slowly than Bissolati, Turati was to agree that socialists might consider taking office.

In the party congress of 1910 at Milan, the revolutionary remnant of the party was led by Lazzari and the young Mussolini. The voting at the congress showed that these revolutionaries were still in a minority of about one to four, and Giolitti concluded that sweet reasonableness must have worked and that "Marx had been relegated to the attic." The revolutionaries answered him by producing a journal called *The Attic,* and his confidence was made to look premature before many months had passed.

Giolitti's fourth ministry had some support from the moderate socialists. Although Bissolati reiterated their refusal to enter the cabinet, it was at last true that a socialist had entered the Quirinal—albeit in a soft hat and lounge suit which scandalized the Court—to advise the king over a ministerial crisis. In a private letter to Giolitti, Bissolati confessed that only a temperamental predilection for being "against the government" had motivated his refusal to become a minister, not any difference of principle. Nevertheless, he resigned from *Avanti* in favor of Treves, realizing that the majority of socialists preferred a more uncompromising attitude.

The moderates had gone too far and too fast for their party. At the congress of Modena in 1911, Bissolati and Bonomi therefore found themselves against a coalition of intransigents and "integralists," with whom were temporarily associated the other school of reformism under Turati, Treves, and Modigliani. Bissolati claimed in defense that he was right as a socialist to be pleased that the head of the state had recognized the political power now held by the Italian proletariat. More significant, perhaps, was the point of view put forward by Rigola, secretary-general of the Confederation of Labor, that the time was past when Marx could say that the workers had nothing to lose but their chains; on the contrary they now had something to defend and were not anxious to risk it in revolutionary action. But while this may have been true of the industrial workers, most party leaders had been nurtured in the dogmas of class war and revolution, and it was the extremists who in 1912 were to capture the party organization and funds.

Meanwhile an act of 1911–12 greatly extended the franchise concessions of 1882. Having effectively pre-empted Luzzatti's platform, Giolitti surprised everyone by the so-called concession of universal suffrage and raised the electorate from three to eight million. It was arguable that the partial project which Luzzatti had proposed would mainly have enfranchised the town artisans and so have aided socialism, whereas manhood suffrage included the illiterate southern peasantry whose vote would offset the radically minded workers in the North. A wider suffrage would give a firmer basis to the social structure, since excluding the

masses from political and administrative life had left them open to subversive ideas. Giolitti viewed the question realistically. On the one hand
he wanted to appear as a progressive liberal in order to offset his imperialistic policy in Libya; on the other hand he admitted that a social
revolution had taken place in the thirty years since the last electoral concessions and that this had so advanced the well-being and intellectual
status of the masses that they had obtained a right to participation in
political life.

The new law gave the vote to all males who were over thirty or who
had served in the forces. This meant illiterates too, so henceforward
symbols were to be included on voting cards in order to differentiate
the various parties. Votes were not granted to women, though this had
been desired both by the socialists and also by the conservatives around
Sonnino. In the 1860's women had participated in the administrative
elections of Lombardy, Venice, and Tuscany, but the liberals had withdrawn this privilege fearing that it would add to the clerical vote, and in
1911 Giolitti put forward this very same argument against it. Sonnino
made a bid for proportional representation, but Giolitti opposed this too,
saying that it would benefit the smaller parties and so make a working
majority even harder to build. His prophecies were to be fulfilled when
these two reforms were conceded some years later. The payment of
deputies was agreed to in 1911, and Giolitti also promised to check the
use of fraud and violence in elections—disingenuously, as his own conduct in 1913 was to show.

One or two dissentient voices were heard. The political philosopher
Mosca foretold that this wider suffrage would add to the problems which
it was intended to solve, and he considered it merely a dodge by which
some people hoped to attain or keep power. His opposition to it was that
of a liberal who discerned in this reform the beginning of the end of
liberalism. Manhood suffrage, he said, would decrease that proportion
of the electorate which had "political capacity," and increase the proportion which was moved by local or class interests. The *Corriere della
Sera* also shied at this latest step on the dreaded path to democracy and
regretfully watched rival liberal groups competing for the favor of the
mob. When a minor peasant revolt broke out late in the summer of 1911
against the "spreaders of cholera dust," it shocked and frightened many
people who realized belatedly how ignorant and superstitious was the
new electorate to whom they had surrendered some of their power.

Salandra, Sonnino, and Luzzatti, however, had all approved of the
law, and these conservatives even hoped that its provisions might be extended to make voting compulsory. This was not only because they

wanted to avoid the label of reactionary; they also deluded themselves that the southern peasant would overthrow the local cliques which had been used to guarantee Giolitti's majority. Manhood suffrage would, they believed, shatter the socialists' claim to speak for the people, and "contradict the argument that parliament was just a shareholders' meeting to promote bourgeois interests." Among the Catholics likewise there were many who thought that they could rely on the peasant vote, at least until free elementary education began to produce its corrosive effects. Hence Catholics and conservatives virtually agreed with radicals and socialists, each of them hoping to exploit popular sovereignty for their own ends.

Giolitti had apparently triumphed. Having stolen his opponents' program, he found support for it from both Right and Left. And yet he had unwittingly done himself harm, for instead of the popular vote helping him grind his own private axe, it was shortly to generate new mass parties which spelled ruin to the existing balance of politics. A larger proportion of people had been given the vote than was usual in other European states, but these newly enfranchised masses did not as yet possess a vested interest in the preservation of social order, and hence might have more reason to overthrow existing society than to defend it.

Democratic in appearance, Giolitti's reform in effect simply changed the composition of the ruling elite, and favored those adept at manipulating elections and utilizing the democratic myth. It produced more demagogy and rhetoric and promised power cheaply to those who offered most bread and circuses—which in the end meant fascism. Giolitti himself perhaps looked upon democracy as something which should grow naturally out of liberalism, though he did not possess the skill or the imagination to control the difficult process of transition. Croce and Mosca, on the other hand, were satisfied that liberalism and democracy were irreconcilable and indeed antithetical, both in theory and in practice. As the liberals in general were therefore too happy and self-assured in their monopoly of power to yield willingly, democracy was going to develop less by evolution and gradual concessions from within liberalism than as something revolutionary grafted on the state from outside. Since the liberals were too proud and insensitive to court popularity, and the socialists too doctrinaire to collaborate in government, it was the fascists who won in the end. Universal suffrage was thus to assist in destroying the liberal party: the old liberal ruling classes were soon so afraid of the new popular parties, whether socialist or Catholic, that to combat them they signed their own death warrant by supporting Mussolini.

Together with his franchise act, Giolitti obtained approval in April 1912 for the government to take over a monopoly of life insurance. State monopolies had already yielded a good revenue from salt and tobacco, and Giolitti showed that the profits of private life insurance were sometimes above 100 per cent a year, even though its risks were more or less accurately calculable. He also argued that too much capital was thereby concentrated in a few hands, and those for the most part foreign hands, so that too much money was leaving the country. Opposition to his proposal was encountered from the leading economists of the day, Pantaleoni, Einaudi, and De Viti de Marco; also from the conservatives, Sonnino and Salandra; and from the insurance companies and other financial interests who feared more nationalization to come. The editor of the radical *Secolo* was won over by the probability that this profitable government monopoly would make heavy borrowing from the banks (often paid for by doubtful political concessions) unnecessary. The chief spokesman in parliament for the bill was the Neapolitan radical, Professor Nitti, whom Giolitti had made minister of agriculture. After a stormy session, parliament agreed to it, but such were the vested interests involved that its repeal was one of Mussolini's first measures after 1922.

Another reform which Giolitti took over from Luzzatti was an education act to supplement the Casati law of 1859 and the Coppino act of 1877. Individual teachers in Italy had been men of great distinction, but the educational system itself had been widely criticized. One complaint was that it concentrated too much on literature and the classics, another that religious instruction was neglected (or some people said overstressed). Education was generally held to be overcentralized, since the king appointed the rector of each university and the heads of faculties, and the minister determined the curriculum of gymnasiums and lyceums.

The chief criticism was that the establishment of "compulsory" elementary education in 1877 had in many areas remained a dead letter. There had been little if any sanction of force behind it, and far too few school inspectors had been appointed to supervise its application. Parents preferred their children to earn money. They associated education with taxes, and hence protests against taxation sometimes took the form of assaults on school buildings. Local authorities were always tempted to economize at the expense of popular education; government loans for school building were thus refused or diverted elsewhere; and teachers, whose salaries should have increased by one-tenth every six years, were often dismissed and reappointed at the old salary. The poverty of schoolmasters was to be an important contributory reason for the spread of socialism, and the Church had this among other things in mind when it opposed or retarded the development of secular state education. But in any case, so easy was it to disobey regulations in Italy that for one reason or another millions of children managed to escape schooling, and almost half the population was still illiterate according to the census of 1911.

The chief problem in the universities was the reverse of that in the schools: education was too cheap. Italy had not only more illiterates but also more university students than many other European countries, and an intellectual proletariat was thus growing up which was more dangerous and multiplying faster than the real proletariat. A university education was a useful qualification even for minor government posts, and such was the social prestige of government service and the professions that parents successfully combated any attempt to increase the fees or raise standards.

Professors complained that they were still paid the same as fifty years previously despite the fall by a half in the value of money, and the need to find other part-time work gave them little contact with their pupils except at examination times. We hear of students breaking up a course of lectures (since by law this would exempt them from examination), and there might be riots against professors who insisted on attendance at lectures or who dared to fail their examinees. Examples are on record of corruption or intimidation by the family of a student whose career was at stake. In Sicily there were cases of lecturers and even schoolmasters having to be given a police escort after the examination results were announced, and of prizes not being awarded because the master did not dare choose between students. Moreover, the subjects favored for degrees suggested that professionalism had all too often overcome the desire for either general education or disinterested speculation and research. Technological education was backward, and it was something quite new when in 1902 the famous Bocconi university, specializing in economics, was founded at Milan. Since by far the greater number of students read law or medicine, these two professions in particular suffered from chronic overcrowding. Fortunato noted it as a morbid sign that even in 1900 there was one lawyer for every 1,300 people in Italy, and in Sardinia there was one lawsuit pending for every three inhabitants.

The radical minister of education, Credaro, had been inherited by Giolitti from the previous cabinet, together with his draft of reform. Both of these men realized clearly that the electorate would need better schooling if the new suffrage act were to work and that a primary need was to raise the salaries and social esteem of the teaching profession. Most teachers were being worked too hard to carry out their job effectively, though elsewhere Giolitti noted that professorial chairs were being created even where there were no pupils, just to provide employment for a largely parasitic class of people. He also commented unfavorably on the ease with which one could obtain a diploma: it would be the easiest thing in the world, he thought, to find an institute to award a degree that would allow him to teach Chinese.

Credaro's chief contribution was to make a larger grant-in-aid by the state, and to give the control of elementary education to the provinces instead of to the small communes which had not been able to afford the expenses involved. Unfortunately, a comprehensive plan had small chance of being drafted and applied when thirty-five ministers of education followed each other in the thirty-eight years after Crispi's first accession to power. The new regulations of 1911 had barely time to be effected before World War I upset everything, and it remained for Professor Gentile in 1923 to attempt a more fundamental reform of education.

32 The German Alliance, 1896-1911

The Triple Alliance with Germany and Austria was renewed in 1891 and 1902, but the old objections continued that this did little for Italy's maritime interests and actively thwarted her ambitions in the Adriatic and the Balkans. Italians, therefore, sought to make a supplementary agreement with Great Britain, the strongest Mediterranean power. Britain had sometimes been thought to covet Sicily for her empire, but most Italians feared British hostility far less than British indifference. French and German influence were so pervasive that Britain was a welcome counterpoise. There was no common frontier to cause trouble as there was with France, and Protestant Britain was always a reliable check upon the Pope. By 1900 an understanding had therefore been reached with Britain about Mediterranean affairs; the King of Italy was called upon in 1902 and 1905 to arbitrate between Britain and Brazil and Portugal over colonial disputes; and it was even hoped that the Triple might shortly become a Quadruple Alliance.

In the early nineties Franco-Italian relations were severely strained. Crispi's trade war had serious psychological as well as economic results, and the latent ill-feeling burst out after some riots against immigrant Italian workmen at Aigues Mortes in 1893. But some people were beginning to question this one-track foreign policy, for Crispi's breach with France had lost Italy the scope for maneuver which she had enjoyed as undistributed middle between France and Germany. While the initial commitment to Germany in the *Triplice* had helped to restore Italian morale after the French annexation of Tunis, it now served no such useful purpose. The defeat at Adowa, moreover, proved that Crispi, deluded by his own fine gestures and flagwaving, had overestimated the country's strength and so had misjudged its true interests in picking a quarrel with France.

The Marquis Visconti-Venosta then became foreign minister. He had already held this position in 1863–64, 1866–67, and 1869–76; and in two further periods of office between 1896 and 1901 this experienced and professional diplomat had renounced the heavy-handed policy of Crispi for the more subtle and opportunist expedients of his old friend Cavour. Visconti-Venosta had been alarmed at Crispi's submission to Bismarck, and rightly feared an Austrian advance into the Balkans, so the pendulum now swung back in the direction of France. In 1896 Italy at last recognized the French position in Tunis, and two years later Luzzatti was sent to Paris to terminate the ten-year-old tariff war. From the other side, Barrère, who was French ambassador at Rome for the next twenty-five years, worked cleverly to weaken Italy's attachment to the *Triplice.* Early in 1900 the Italian fleet visited Toulon. Then, in December, an exchange of notes clarified the frontier positions in Somalia and recognized the paramount French interest in Morocco and the Italian interest in Libya.

In addition, Vittorio Emanuele III was much less Germanophile than his father, while Queen Elena came from Montenegro, a country hostile to Austria, and she had been brought up in Russia and was bound to Russia by family ties. In one of many *faux pas,* the German emperor visited Italy with a retinue of giant Pomeranian grenadiers, which delighted the cartoonists but infuriated the diminutive king. Instead of overawing people with German strength, this was taken as bad manners and bad psychology. On another naval visit some cruelly disparaging words by the emperor were unfortunately overheard and reported by a German-speaking Italian. As a gesture of independence, Vittorio Emanuele pointedly traveled to Paris, London, and St. Petersburg.

More seriously, Zanardelli's foreign minister was the Milanese industrialist, Prinetti, who even went so far as to encourage irredentism against Austria. In November 1902, Prinetti assured Barrère that Italian obligations under the Triple Alliance were limited: "If France is directly or indirectly attacked, Italy will maintain a strict neutrality, and it will be the same if France, as a result of direct provocation, is compelled to declare war in defence of her honor and security." This secondary entente with France was a partial return to the traditional foreign policy of make-weight between rival power groups. Von Bülow accused Italy of flagrant adultery, but later admitted that a husband might occasionally dance with someone else's partner, especially as Austria and Germany themselves made subsidiary agreements with Russia and Turkey outside the alliance. The Triple Alliance for reasons of expediency continued in force until 1915, but some subtlety has been needed by Italian historians to explain the import and morality of its protracted existence. An Italian foreign minister had told Barzilai as far back as 1892 that the alliance with Germany was a piece of bluff and there was no intention of ever acting on it. The dubious conduct of the Italian foreign office in 1914–15 seems to support Admiral Brin's private but memorable remark.

Though Giolitti as prime minister in 1903 welcomed the commercial accord with France, it was not necessary to take this to the point of throwing over the *Triplice*. After the French president Loubet visited Rome in 1904, Giolitti pacified the German chancellor by journeying to Hamburg, and the Triple Alliance was formally renewed again in 1907 and 1912. The foreign minister Tittoni ingenuously repudiated any intention of securing a balance of power, "for that would be unworthy of a great nation"; but in practice he and his successor continued to flirt with both sides. Giolitti's personal disregard for foreign affairs was proverbial, and he was criticized for spending too little money on supplying the armed services and bribing the foreign press. If he renewed the Triple Alliance this was largely out of inertia, because it was a useful and inexpensive piece of reinsurance, and it was not his nature to want to copy the far more complicated and exacting foreign policy of Bismarck or Cavour.

§◆

The outward continuance of the German connection incidentally reflected cultural and financial links forged in twenty years of alliance. Parallel with the political and economic breach with France, people had noted a retreat from French rationalism and a marked preference for German erudition and scientific method in philosophy, religion, technology, and law. French influence had continued to prevail in some fields: in painting through the impressionists, in literature through D'Annunzio and Soffici. In their several directions, Sorel, Maurras, Barrès, and Loisy each had a sizable following in Italy. Croce and Gentile, on the contrary, oriented Italian intellectual life around Hegel and German philosophy. The study of German became more common, and students went to Germany to complete their education, while textbooks were modeled on, or translated from, the German. Writers of Prezzolini's generation, nurtured in French culture, began to wonder whether post-Bismarckian Germany was not politically more admirable than the France of Panama and Dreyfus. Even the Italian socialists abandoned Bakunin for Marx and named their paper *Avanti* after the German *Vorwärts*. This German penetration into Italian intellectual life was a pattern repeated after 1933. It was stimulating—but also carried with it the danger of suffocation.

When Crispi's tariff war led to the withdrawal of French investment capital, Germany became the chief alternative source, for British money went in preference to British colonies. Early in the 1890's the Deutsche Bank sent Siemens to make a financial agreement with Giolitti in Rome, and the renewal of the *Triplice* in the following year was accompanied by the grant of commercial facilities to Italy, of which the corollary was the opening of the country to German investment. Many Italian firms were owned by Germans, others were dependent on German patents or on the German chemical and electrical industries. Eighty per cent of the cotton machinery used in Italian factories was said to be made in Germany. German finance was heavily engaged in the construction of railroads to develop Trieste. The Banca Commerciale Italiana, for which most of the capital was Austrian and German, controlled several important shipping lines, half the electric companies, and much of the steel industry, and this also implied a concealed influence over the press and in politics. Simultaneously, the habit of vacations and Alpinism was bringing German settlers and travelers along the Brenner railroad and down the Adige Valley.

German cultural and financial influence would hardly have been very dangerous but for its political implications. It was the fear of exclusive dependence upon Germany which, at the conference of Algeciras early in 1906, caused Visconti-Venosta to lean toward France. Unofficially, this trend was given impetus by a vigorous renewal of irredentism. At the same time, general currency was given to the name Alto Adige to describe what Austrians preferred to call the Südtirol. Special journals and learned societies were founded wherein individual Italian savants, with a deliberately political end, proved the affinities of the local dialects with Italian, and postulated that the water system of the Trentino, like the geological formation of the Carso, made these regions essentially part of Italy. Minority rights were demanded at Trent and Bozen, and when these were refused there was talk of rebellion. Cesare Battisti and his irredentist companions took it upon themselves to spy on the movement of war material in this Austrian province and send details to Rome. Italian-speaking professors at Innsbruck tried to make the university bilingual, and lectured in Italian, so provoking student riots which triggered off violent outbursts all over Italy and Germany. Two foreign ministers, Tittoni and Di San Giuliano, felt obliged to state in public that irredentism was dead, but an instinct of self-preservation kept Italian language and culture alive in these border provinces. The Speaker of the Chamber, the radical Marcora, embarrassed the orthodox by publicly referring to "our Trent," and Giolitti later had the effrontery to confess that he himself used government money to assist the victory of the Italian element in the municipal elections at Trieste. The alliance with Austria was clearly wearing thin.

In 1908 Aerenthal announced the formal annexation of Bosnia and Herzegovina, thus drawing attention to the altered balance of power in the Balkans. This stirred up the peoples of that unstable area to seek revenge, and other neighboring countries to claim compensation. Italians in particular were resentful. It was no accident that the following year the Czar visited the King of Italy at Racconigi. Hitherto, the Left had resisted any friendly gesture being made toward autocratic Russia, so much so that on this occasion Giolitti apprehensively threatened the prefects with dismissal if the Czar's visit provoked any hostile demonstration, but the event proved that even some of the *estrema* were prepared to back Russia against the Austrians. At Racconigi an agreement was made to keep Austria from further disturbing the *status quo* in the Balkans and to look benevolently on each other's designs in the Dardanelles and Tripoli. Thus yet another blow was struck at the spirit of the *Triplice,* and we now know that the Austrian general staff began to meditate open hostilities against so uncertain an ally.

Italy meanwhile was being swept by the same jingoism which pervaded the Kaiser's Germany, Theodore Roosevelt's America, and the England of Joseph Chamberlain and Kipling. To some extent this Italian nationalism was a healthy reaction against people such as Lombroso and Ferrero who had tended to praise the superiority of Anglo-Saxons to Latins; but it was soon taken to excess. We find protests against French menus and fashions in dress, against foreign words creeping into the language, against too many works of art going to America, against foreign contributions for the terrible earthquake disasters in the South, and even against foreign generosity when in 1902 the campanile of St. Mark's in Venice unexpectedly collapsed.

From something natural and not unhealthy, jingoism thus became a disease, and it was a disease which found an easy prey in a people whose two most deadly enemies (according to Count Sforza) were nationalistic vanity and literary overemphasis. One can discover both these qualities in Mazzini, who had proclaimed that Italians were "the Messiah people" called to redeem mankind. The irredentism which looked toward Trent, Trieste, even sometimes to Nice, Corsica, and Malta, was in one sense a projection of *risorgimento* patriotism. But where Cavour spoke of the country's good, Crispi spoke rather of its greatness and its predominant position in the Mediterranean. In 1894 Farini, the president of the Senate, talked of the army alone keeping Italy united, and he had ominously remarked that Italy must become a strong militarist state or cease to exist.

The wish for a strong army and navy was thus not merely the sovereign's personal whim, but was shared by ordinary liberals and Catholics at many different levels of society. In 1907, Baron Casana was appointed the first civilian minister of war in Italian history specially so that he might persuade parliament to increase military expenditure. When he still insisted on saying that Italy must proportion her forces to her means, this unexceptionable statement provoked considerable disapproval, and he had to resign in favor of General Spingardi who then continued in this office through four successive cabinets. In 1908, as a result of the war scare over Bosnia, four more ironclads were laid down.

The military men thought this armament policy too modest, the radicals called it too grandiose, but the real objection should have been to its inefficiency. In July 1906 a parliamentary commission reported—in five volumes—on scandalous incompetence in provision for the navy. Not only did ships apparently take six years to build, but the report also exposed the administrative disorder, the use of defective steel, and corruption in the placing of contracts. As high protective duties had now freed domestic industry from its worst fears of foreign rivalry, there was no great incentive for cheapness or modernization, and the armed forces were thus made dependent on inferior and expensive goods. The Terni company once again received particular blame, heavily financed as it was by the state for the profit of influential shareholders. This report led to an angry debate, but the government forced through an innocuous motion which blamed no one and merely hymned the glories of the Italian navy. A violent tumult then ensued, during which the Speaker's chair was overturned and the Chamber had to be forcibly cleared.

In the Florentine magazine *Il Regno* from 1904 to 1906, Corradini and a new group of extreme nationalists, alongside more moderate men such as Prezzolini and Papini (later author of a celebrated *Life of Christ*), began to prepare for another great age of Italian expansion. A new paper at Venice was significantly entitled *Mare Nostrum,* another in Milan *La Grande Italia.* At the Milan exhibition of 1906 a special section was devoted to the work of Italians abroad, and in 1908 and 1911 national congresses were held in the United States by Italian emigrants. Religious orders and missions from Italy spread in Syria as in North

America, and in 1907 the Pope was persuaded to substitute Italy for France as the protecting power for Catholics in Turkey. Most decisive sign of all, in 1910 the first congress was held in the Palazzo Vecchio at Florence of a new Nationalist Party, claiming the inheritance of Crispi's imperialist tradition and going far beyond the patriotism of the *risorgimento*. In the following year, on the anniversary of Adowa, Corradini and Federzoni launched its journal, *L'Idea Nazionale*.

This party was not without a certain admirable idealism, but its less worthy elements were soon in charge, inebriated with the vulgar imperialism of violence and conquest. Count Sforza says that its publicity was heavily subsidized by the big Ansaldo combine, whose huge steelworks and machine shops relied on armaments for their continued prosperity. If the Nationalist Party was irredentist, this was only incidental, and until after the outbreak of war in 1914 it was not sure whether to stand with or against Germany so long as blood could be shed and great victories won. Its adherents believed with D'Annunzio that paradise lay in the shadow of the sword, with Papini that war was a quick and heroic means to power and wealth, and with Corradini that the sacredness of human life was an outmoded piece of sentimental idealism. Corradini, who was one of the more moderate and balanced, said that with a hundred men ready to die he could give Italy new life. For him nationalism was the antithesis of democracy, and without an authoritarian state there could be no true freedom. The ideals of liberty and equality were to be replaced by discipline and obedience; instead of life being sacred, he insisted that it should be lived aggressively, dangerously, and with hardship. Clearly, this was one of the particular scrapheaps where Mussolini was to scavenge in order to clothe his ideological nakedness.

Mingled with these novel ideas, nationalism took other notions on the political use of violence from Sorel and the syndicalists. From Darwin and Spencer were derived such terms as the fight for existence between nations, natural selection, and the survival of the fittest. Hegelians supplied the concept of an ethical state which was far greater than the sum of individuals who composed it. Alfredo Oriani represented yet another current of authoritarian thought, discontented with liberalism and believing in the right of an elite to seize power and rule. Oriani campaigned to take the statue of Julius Caesar out of the Capitoline museum and raise it high in some public square as a reminder of the Roman conquest of Europe. This Oriani was the man later hailed as a prophet of fascism, to whose tomb Mussolini was one day to lead a "pilgrimage." His remarkable and most readable books are full of talk about "Roman eagles," "imperial destinies," and the *"virtù* of our race," but they are bitter in their recollection of the recent past, vainglorious and aggressive in their hopes for the future. Whatever the direct influence of such writing, it revealed a climate of opinion at once morbid and dangerous.

To take another example, in art and literature the "futurists" thought of war as "the only purifier of the world," and Marinetti's Futurist Manifesto of 1909 repudiated the criterion of justice and extolled conquest and power: "We sing the love of danger. Courage, rashness, and rebellion are the elements of our poetry. Hitherto literature has tended to exalt thoughtful immobility, ecstasy, and sleep, whereas we are for aggressive movement, febrile insomnia, mortal leaps, and blows with the fist. We proclaim that the world is the richer for a new beauty of speed, and our praise is for the man at the wheel. There is no beauty now save in struggle, no masterpiece can be anything but aggressive, and hence we glorify war, militarism, and patriotism."

In fulfillment of this general theme, Carrà in 1910 produced a manifesto of futurist painting and Boccioni in 1912 one for futurist sculpture. Thirsting after novel sensations, Silvio Mix wrote a futurist ballet called *Cocktail,* Russolo in 1912 began to write "noise music" for an orchestra of thirty different noises, and Folgore wrote odes to coal and electricity. Contemptuous of intellectualism, or even intelligibility, these hermetic poets tried "to free words from the tyranny of syntax and meaning," and made their poems a phonetic and illogical concatenation of symbols. Papini in his futurist period described the essence of futurism as all that was fantastic, rebellious, destructive, and agitated. It was the breaking of all rules, for Italian culture had too long been simply copying other nations or its own past. Papini wanted to burn all libraries and museums, to end the vacuous adulation of Dante and Giotto, and to throw away the traditions of university academicism represented by Carducci and Pascoli. The best concerto was the noise of a busy city, so he said, and the most profound philosophy was that of a peasant ploughing or of a carpenter whose mind was a complete blank. Marinetti went one better and started a campaign against spaghetti as too middle-class and respectable a food.

These were the petulant and rebellious manifestations of would-be artists who felt a need to create something new and yet discovered that short of this nonsense they had nothing very novel or noteworthy to say. It is interesting that, despite their *avant-garde* attitude toward art, in politics the futurists earned the title of reactionary, for this at the moment was the "progressive" thing to be. They believed in force at home and abroad, and together with the nationalists they reacted strongly against Italian passivity in North Africa and the Balkans, where other nations advanced and their own stood still. They discovered that the younger generation in the universities had an unsatisfied longing for greatness, and Marinetti and Corradini fed this contemporary malaise by leading dissatisfied youth via nationalism to a spiritual home among the fascists. Educated on the stirring exploits of Garibaldi (and of that man whom they regarded as an honorary Italian, Napoleon Bonaparte), these surplus graduates were humiliated to find themselves keeping accounts or writing for cheap magazines. Such men were an easy prey to emotional propaganda.

The combination of these various groups gave Italy at last the beginnings of a self-confessed and active party of the extreme Right. Many industrialists provided money for its organization and its newspapers, approving both its foreign policy of expansion and its domestic policy of authoritarianism and the disciplining of labor. The socialists naturally opposed it; so did Croce on intellectual grounds, and Nitti and Salvemini from their various radical standpoints. But some of the liberals were converted. Maffeo Pantaleoni the economist, for instance, impelled like many others by his compound dislike of socialism, nationalization, parliamentary degeneration and labor unrest, moved over toward a party which took pride in being anti-liberal, anti-democratic, even anti-parliament.

Giolitti saw what was happening, and as his policy was always to bring inside his majority as many as possible of the live forces of the nation, he now proceeded to satisfy these new currents of opinion on the extreme Right, just as he had already made some gestures toward the clericals and the moderate socialists. At the first nationalist party congress in 1910 Federzoni, the future fascist minister, called for the invasion of Libya, and a year later Giolitti launched Italy on another colonial war of conquest.

33 The Libyan War, 1911-1912

Although the disaster of Adowa had halted active colonial expansion, Eritrea was retained (though Luzzatti had a project for exchanging it for Cyprus), and a protectorate was established over much of Somaliland. Colonies were still much in people's mind. During the South African war, Ricciotti Garibaldi had offered to fight for the British, and though most Italians were for the Boers, some newspapers suggested aiding Britain in return for the gift of Malta, Gibraltar, and Egypt. More practically, trade concessions were won from the sultan of Zanzibar, and Crispi made a not very successful attempt to rival France in Morocco, building warships for the sultan at Leghorn and securing a contract to set up an arms factory and a mint. Morocco had subsequently to be written off along with Tunisia and Egypt as barred from Italian exploitation. But in Libya the Italian consul, Grande, was used by Crispi to intrigue with dissident Arab groups as a possible preliminary to occupation. Naval bases had been constructed in southern Italy at Taranto, Brindisi, and Augusta, and warships were being built at Taranto from 1898 onward. This southward shift away from the old ports of Spezia and Venice was a move toward Africa.

Considerations of prestige sent Italy yet further afield, to China. Pelloux never published the documents on the military expedition to China 1899–1900, and Giolitti's biographer, Natale, says that Giolitti privately persuaded the opposition in the national interest not to press for information on a fiasco which was almost as expensive as it was unnecessary and unsuccessful.

The China expedition was generally recognized as absurd, and Nitti was not alone in thinking it wasteful to go chasing after sandy deserts in Africa. Radical humanitarians remembered the embarrassing remark of Giuseppe Garibaldi that, as the world had been on the side of Italy's fight for freedom, if Italy then set about conquering other people he himself would regretfully but firmly side against his own fellow countrymen. Southern Italy in any case desperately needed the money that was being squandered on these prestige ventures abroad, and it was ironic to see railroads being built in Africa when some Italian districts had been awaiting them for fifty years. Trade figures by no means justified these colonies, and despite the constructive work being done by such an enlightened governor as Ferdinando Martini, they remained an economic liability—all the more so if one remembers the enormous cost of the colonial wars of 1896 and 1911–12. The arguments about colonies absorbing surplus population were beside the point, for only 1 per cent of Italian emigrants would go to Italian colonies in Africa, as against 40 per cent to America. If they had known the poor as well as Fortunato did, the propagandists would have understood that peasants would never voluntarily go to Libya where soil and climate were even worse than in Sicily and the Basilicata. A commission under a British geologist, Professor Gregory, reporting in 1909 on the possibility of Jewish settlement in Libya, advised against the colonization of such arid desert, and was unable to find the great mineral deposits which had been so trumpeted.

Yet all these bogus arguments went on being used in Italy, for hard economic facts were buried under considerations of emotion and prestige. Turiello, for example, considered the nineteenth century as above all that of the expansion of the white races, and in the struggle for life each nation had therefore to seek out colonies to make itself powerful and respected. "Destiny" had imposed an obligation on Italians; there was an "umbilical cord" between them and Africa, apparently vital for their national existence. Oriani about 1900 was writing that conquests in Africa and the Balkans were a duty, part of Italy's historic mission which she could not abdicate, a necessary seal on the *risorgimento*. The worth of peoples, he said, was to be measured by the extent and celebrity of their expansion—and he therefore offered to go on a polar expedition as its official poet and historian.

In the pages of *Il Regno* this frenetic mood was taken up by people who glorified war for its own sake and the Italians as a naturally warlike race. Dogali and Adowa, said Martini, had so depressed national morale that Italians were losing heart and confidence in themselves. Hence successful war was essential to restore self-confidence, and the fiftieth anniversary of unification must be celebrated by the conquest of Libya to prove that Italians were worthy of nationhood. Such was the spirit with which Giolitti had to reckon in 1911. When Ricciotti Garibaldi assembled some hundreds of red-shirted volunteers in that year to reconquer an Italian empire on the Albanian coast (one of them was a youngster of fourteen named Italo Balbo), it was possible for the government to decide that this nationalism could be more safely and profitably canalized into an official invasion of North Africa.

§❧

By 1911, Libya had become in popular imagination a veritable Eldorado, and a book about it with the title of *Our Promised Land* appeared that same year. History and geography were invoked to establish a proprietary right over this former dependency of ancient Rome. Sicilians as diverse as Crispi, the socialist De Felice, and the conservative foreign minister Di San Giuliano, all agreed on the strange doctrine that similarities of cultivation and climate made North Africa a natural outlet for surplus Italian population. Sicilians in particular became emotionally involved in Libya, for they knew the economic argument at its most urgent, and there was as yet insufficient evidence to show them that this was the wrong remedy.

The first plan had been one for simple economic penetration without the risk and expense of military conquest. Hitherto most imports into Libya had come from England, while Libyan ivory and esparto grass went principally to England, and her ostrich feathers to France. But after 1905 the Banco di Roma secured mining concessions, and launched an exaggerated propaganda campaign about the plentiful raw materials to be found there. The bank was soon the largest landowner, and controlled grain mills and part of the sponge industry. Then in 1908–9 this advance was threatened when the Young Turk revolution took place at Constantinople, for the Turkish nationalists naturally feared any one European state becoming too deeply involved in their empire, and guessed that Italian contractors were politically subsidized. Inside the Turkish empire, therefore, Krupp went ahead of Ansaldo, Siemens of Marconi, and the Deutsche Bank of the Banco di Roma, and when an Italian firm submitted the lowest bid for the harbor works at Tripoli, the Turks preferred to drop the whole project.

Italians therefore began to become alarmed, especially when Britain and France took greater interest in North African shipping lines and in "archaeological research." It was said that the Egyptian frontier had advanced in the last thirty years almost to Solum. When French troops entered Morocco in 1911, and when Germany after the Agadir crisis was thought to be picking her way toward other vacant stretches of North Africa, Italians were driven to consider military conquest if they did not want to give up what they took to be a generally recognized right of pre-emption over Libya. They did not like the prospect of another humiliation such as over Tunis in 1881, nor that of Germany turning Benghazi into another Agadir. The Banco di Roma, furthermore, deliberately circulated a rumor about selling to Austrian and German banks its considerable interests in Libya.

Giolitti himself now became worried. He had opposed earlier efforts at colonization, and at the Treasury under Crispi's administration had even refused to allow his chief some of the supplementary estimates demanded. But he had been genuinely annoyed that the Turks, instead of yielding gracefully to economic penetration, chose instead to offer alternative concessions in Mesopotamia. Giolitti, like Cavour, never allowed himself to fall far behind public opinion, and he sensed that national prestige now required a more assertive foreign policy.

In the summer of 1911 he therefore decided to move. If he were forestalled in Libya, this might ruin his delicately poised political machine, whereas forceful action might win over the nationalists and the new mass electorate which he was in the process of enfranchising. Hastily he prepared an offensive while the ambassadors were still away on summer vacations and while the weather still permitted. Because of the need for secrecy and haste he could not make entirely sure that the army was ready for war, let alone for a desert campaign. He could not stop to verify his assumption that the local Arabs would be hostile to Turkey, nor could he prepare public opinion at home or governments abroad for war. These omissions were to prove costly.

ﾟ‍

Left-wing opinion in Italy clearly disliked the prospect of war, and the ordinary citizens who were expected to do the fighting sometimes mutinied or tore up railroad tracks to stop the movement of troops. Anticlericals in general resented that the Catholic Banco di Roma, the bank of the Holy See, should benefit from state expenditure and be saved from the consequences of its very ill-judged investment policy. Salvemini, in his paper *Unità,* showed that he knew far more about the unpromising conditions of Tripoli than did those who considered it potentially a great economic asset, and Ferrero saw in Italian imperialism the mark of typically German power politics. According to these radical intellectuals, Italy should renounce her idea of being this kind of great power, for clearly she could never afford it, and all that Libya promised to be was not an Eldorado but the grave of Italian settlers.

The socialist party congress at Modena therefore declared against the war, as did the official socialist paper, *Avanti,* and the reformist Treves and the *Critica Sociale.* Turati wrote that the war was one of pure aggressive violence, which would do nothing except arouse brutal mob instincts and prepare the return to power of the reactionaries. As for the revolutionary socialists, they were even more violently pacific: Mussolini and Nenni tried to raise the workers in a general strike against war, and both were sent to prison for a treasonous anti-imperialism which the Duce later tried to excise from the record. Leone and De Ambris among the syndicalists were also against the war, stressing the bankruptcy of Italian colonialism in Eritrea and Somaliland.

But on such a major issue the socialists were always hopelessly divided, especially now that nationalism was beginning to cut across class interests, and on this occasion their reformist and revolutionary wings were each split internally. Among the moderates some were becoming very close to Giolitti, and the veteran Costa before he died in 1910 had even been elected deputy speaker of the Chamber. Although Turati and Treves feared to give up the myths of their creed too suddenly, Bissolati and Bonomi were coming to agree that "vital interests" and expansion were proper considerations for a young state. Another current of socialist thought welcomed colonial wars as a logical development of capitalism which might hasten the ultimate victory of the proletariat. Ferri approved of the war, and De Felice embarrassed the high command by asking to be the first to disembark in North Africa. Among the syndicalists, Arturo Labriola and Angelo Olivetti were behind the government. Olivetti explained that war was a school of virility and courage, and the conquest of Libya would be a wonderful example of syndicalist methods, for it would mean breaking treaties and throwing aside international law. These various socialist attitudes explain why, while Mussolini and Nenni were reading Sorel together in prison to study the technique of violent action, their antimiltarist campaign found little response outside, and Mussolini's *volte-face* in the subsequent war of 1914 was a tacit admission that Olivetti's analysis in 1911 might have been the more correct.

Support for the Libyan war came from the columns of Giolitti's *Stampa,* and from the *Corriere della Sera* which represented the more conservative liberals. The *Corriere* admitted frankly that little material gain could be expected from colonies, but was equally sure that, with France now in Morocco, it would be demoralizing if Italy did not find compensation somewhere. Support also came from Catholics who looked forward to a crusade of Cross against Crescent. Chiesa and Barzilai stood apart from the other republicans in favoring the war, and Alessio divided the radicals by supporting it. Nonpolitical humanitarians such as the poet Pascoli were convinced that Italy needed colonies to settle her surplus population, and even the wise and moderate liberal, Giustino Fortunato, while realizing that Italy might be ruined by this "fruitless and wasteful" effort, yet genuinely rejoiced at what he took to be the first real proof that Italy was at last a united state. D'Annunzio, with his usual bravura and full of the joy of conquest, burst into streams of historically allusive patriotic poetry which did much to obfuscate or etherealize the rational arguments on either side, and his chief theme in *La nave* is imperialism and the white man's burden. He was echoed by other hysterical poetasters such as Marinetti. Mystical nationalists like

Corradini rashly promised that Libya would fall without firing a shot and that a few honest Italian laborers would then suffice to make the desert blossom like a rose. The nationalists were in their element and began to beat up their enemies in the street—sometimes without Giolitti's police interfering.

§⁕

War was declared at the end of September 1911. Giolitti first went through all the usual deceit of saying that the Turks had stirred up trouble against Italy and had provocatively resisted Italian economic penetration. He was also bold enough to talk of the civilizing mission of Italy and to protest that the Turks had not reciprocated the invariably frank and honest conduct of Italy toward them. All this was capped by a twenty-four-hour ultimatum. With unusual promptitude the Turks declared themselves ready to make concessions and asked what guarantees Italy might think necessary. But Giolitti was not to be balked of his war; any delay might give time for his allies, Germany and Austria, to intervene and mediate.

Early in October, Tripoli was bombarded, and within one month most of the coastal towns as far east as Tobruk had fallen. A compromise settlement was proposed by Germany which would let Italy occupy the area while Turkey remained nominally sovereign, but Giolitti foiled this plot by deliberately burning his boats, and in November a simple royal decree proclaimed the formal annexation of all Libya. In thirty years of occupation in Egypt, Britain had never been so rash as to cut off all room for maneuver in this way. But Giolitti no doubt wanted to engage Italian honor so that there should be no possible chance of any compromise solution; a conspicuous military victory was indispensable for his own and Italy's prestige. The unexpected result was that a war intended to last a few weeks at a negligible cost dragged out in fact for over a year and seriously depleted Italian strength.

The general unpreparedness and overconfidence was quickly apparent. Although Tripoli had been an objective of policy for decades, neither the nature of its tribal society nor even its geographical features had been adequately studied. The diplomats had been in such a hurry with their ultimatum that they had given little warning to the armed services. Ships had to sail with provisions for a single day, and it was over a week after hostilities began before an army corps was ready to embark. General Caneva had little idea how to fight a mobile war against guerrillas, and had been appointed commander simply on the results of the summer maneuvers in the Po Valley. His chief of staff,

General Pollio, had mistakenly assumed that Turkey, unable to send reinforcements, would surrender after a token protest. He also made the expensive miscalculation that the local Arabs would oppose their Turkish masters and coreligionists or would at least remain neutral, and that twenty thousand soldiers would therefore be sufficient.

Caneva's first proclamation to his troops spoke proudly of the conquests of ancient Rome. Nevertheless, the early resistance he met was a painful reminder of Adowa and perhaps made him overanxious to avoid defeat. He therefore hugged the coastal strip that was under range of his naval guns. In the end he found that not twenty thousand but a hundred thousand men were needed, even though fighting against only some ten thousand Turks under a colonel and about twenty-five thousand Arabs. For the whole terrain and type of warfare were unexpectedly difficult. The Italians had been accustomed to pitched battles in Ethiopia, and it was not easy to adjust their technique of warfare to an enemy who knew the countryside and could quickly vanish into the desert. Heavy artillery was not much use here. Bombing airplanes and dirigibles were employed for the first time in history, but the Arabs had few permanent works to destroy, and most of the bombs buried themselves harmlessly in the sand.

Contrary to all expectation, the Arabs proved far more difficult to conquer than the Turkish troops. For when irresponsible Christian bishops talked of a crusade, the Arabs replied with a jihad and "treacherously" defended themselves against the invader by attacking the Italian lines from the rear. This provoked Caneva into terrible reprisals, since ununiformed Arabs were by definition spies and not soldiers, as Italians were by definition their protectors against Turkish oppression. Some grisly and authenticated tales emerged which dismayed the rest of Europe, and Marinetti and Boccioni traveled all the way to Surrey to challenge an Irish newspaperman to a duel for having evaded the censorship with some highly colored and most un-Italian stories. Marinetti himself claimed that the whole war was a typical manifestation of futurism and wrote a book about it which positively reveled in the slaughter. Corradini spoke of the Arabs as savage beasts who should be whipped and not shot but hanged.

Although Giolitti had assumed that other countries would accept a *fait accompli,* the fact was accomplished too slowly to be well received abroad. We have Nitti's word that the government expended money lavishly on French newspapers, yet France had much capital invested in Turkey, and Italians were clumsily disturbing the Mediterranean equilibrium. The attempt at blockade was disliked and so was the spreading of war toward the Dodecanese Islands and Asia Minor. In particular there was a celebrated incident in January 1912 when two French steamers were hauled into Cagliari under suspicion of carrying contraband. Great Britain also had reasons for regretting the decline of Turkey, fearing that all Europe might be sucked into the vortex and Russia move into the Straits. Worst of all, the other powers of the Triple Alliance intended to teach Italy a lesson for acting on her own initiative. Austria instructed her nominal ally that the war must not come near the Balkans, and Germany, smarting from Italian "desertion" at Algeciras, was more than friendly to Turkey and openly claimed to be the protector of Islam.

There was no decisive victory in Africa, but Rhodes was taken in May 1912, and secret negotiations then dragged on throughout the summer. Giolitti adroitly instructed his delegate, a crafty financier from the Banca Commerciale called Volpi, to put forward extreme claims so that subsequent Italian concessions would enable the Turks to yield without too much loss of face. The agreement reached at Ouchy, and shortly confirmed at Lausanne, recognized Italy as *de facto* ruler of Libya and the Dodecanese. In return, Italy paid a large sum to the Turkish national debt (some Italians objected that this looked too much like an indemnity), and a dangerous concession was allowed by which Constantinople kept its religious authority in North Africa and hence also some kind of say in judicial and political affairs.

§

Italian morale was greatly uplifted by this colonial success, and its importance was signalized by the establishment of a ministry of colonies in 1912. Although the war brought little access of material power, it nevertheless could be called proof of national vigor. Croce and Mosca insisted that, though Italy had gone to Libya mainly for sentimental reasons, such sentiment was beneficent and beneficial, and even a purely "moral victory" was well worth all the expense and loss of life. Evidently, the dangers concealed behind these sentimental considerations of honor and prestige were not yet apparent even to some highly intelligent and sensible people.

The glamor of empire, however, could not permanently conceal that there were also disadvantages. The new provinces produced much the same crops as southern Italy, so that domestic prices were depressed and raw material imports not greatly increased. Over half a million Italians left Italy in the first six months of 1913, but they still preferred French Morocco to Italian Libya, and far more were going to America than ever before. Colonies without colonizers proved an expensive concession to sentiment. Tripoli needed capital, but Italy had not enough even for herself, and few notable public works could be set on foot, though if an equivalent sum had been spent on reforesting the Apennines, this might have provided living space for thousands who otherwise had to starve or emigrate. Fifty thousand resident Italians were expelled from Turkey in retaliation, with a great loss of business and of contacts built up over centuries. A Moslem boycott of Italian goods, reinforced by unwise Italian protectionism, made Rhodes under Italian rule lose importance as a trade emporium, and for the textile centers of Biella and Schio the first result of colonial expansion was a decline in overseas orders. Commercial disadvantages were also accompanied by financial. Not only was the Banco di Roma badly hit and forced to reduce its capital by half, but the war had begun an inflationary price revolution. As Luzzatti admitted, no one had ever imagined that hostilities would last so long and cost so much. Giolitti announced this cost as 512 million lire, but he had deliberately falsified the balance sheet, and the true cost was twice as much. He also falsified *communiqués* to make people think that the army had fought well. After ten years of budgetary equilibrium, a huge deficit of 1,305 million appeared, and was now to grow steadily worse with each year.

Italy, wanting colonies to exploit, was herself exploited by them. The Treaty of Lausanne applied only to the Turks, and a recalcitrant war whose cost is still unknown continued on and off for years against the native population. By the beginning of 1916 the "rebel" Senussi were successful enough to have reduced effective Italian occupation to a few coastal garrisons again, and, by the Treaty of Acroma in 1917, Italy was obliged formally to admit their independence. Italian prestige never quite recovered from this setback in the eyes of the North African population. The Turks had garrisoned the vilayet peacefully with a few thousand soldiers, but Italy found it difficult with many times this number.

Moreover, the administration of Libya was poor: the men chosen, the frequent change of policy and of governors, the remote control from Rome by inexperienced bureaucrats who negotiated directly with local chiefs and bypassed their agents on the spot, all marked an inauspicious beginning in colonial government. Not until 1922 could enthusiasm be generated for an extension of Italian dominion into the Libyan interior, and even as late as 1928 there were apparently only 2,800 Italians resident in the 680,000 square miles of this most expensively earned colony. The argument that Libya could take up any surplus population from Italy had been used with cynical irresponsibility by the nationalists who in fact wanted colonies just for purposes of prestige.

Most important of all the results of the Libyan war was the dangerous fanning of nationalism and the cult of violence. Italian newspapers of the time give ample evidence of this. In Europe, by weakening Turkey, it led on to the Balkan wars and so was among the causes of World War I. In Italy itself the liberals were rapidly losing their comfortable monopoly of politics to new groups which demanded a more imperialistic policy. These new parties were to prove more intractable than the other social forces which Giolitti had hitherto managed to control or corrupt, and were shortly to overthrow the whole Giolittian system of government. The prime minister had learned his lesson that war gained too little and cost more than Italy could afford, but he dared not tell the nation the facts which had given him this conviction. Partly as a result of this reticence, in 1915 other people were to fight another war at a time when his own private experience correctly foretold disaster.

The spokesmen of tolerance and moderation had been given little chance to make themselves heard in 1911–12, especially as hostilities had been deliberately commenced at the beginning of a seven-and-a-half-month parliamentary recess. Parliament was neither called to sanction the war, nor to debate the royal decree which proclaimed annexation. When the deputies met at last in February 1912, Turati was shouted down, and the foreign minister announced that they ought not to be allowed to debate political or military matters. In the flush of victory a retrospective vote was secured for the taxes already raised by decree, and there was hardly a voice so bold as to object. These were ominous signs.

34 Giolitti's System Collapses, 1912-1914

The victory of Mussolini and his friends at the socialist congress at Reggio in July 1912 reflected working-class impatience with the middle-class leadership of Bissolati and Turati. Doctrinaire concepts and Fabian tactics had less and less appeal as the party became a mass party. The war of 1911 gave a fillip to those socialists who believed in violence and weakened those who accepted the methods of parliamentary government. Bissolati shocked the other socialists at the Reggio congress by his reformist heresies, and especially by the hope that "our country, which today is the equal of England and I think even surpasses her in matters of liberty and political institutions, tomorrow may become the forge of a great democratic movement." Because of this bourgeois belief he was forthwith expelled, together with others of the *libici* who had voted in favor of the war against Turkey. Also expelled was Bonomi, who was one day to be the first socialist prime minister, and Podrecca, who among other offences was overfond of attending the opera in evening dress.

Against Bissolati's democratic reformism, Cicotti proclaimed at Reggio that the socialist party was an eminently antidemocratic party and that democracy was a bourgeois expedient. Extremists of this type were henceforward to control the party until its dissolution a dozen years later. They were ambitious men, more dangerous to the liberal creed than syndicalism, but assimilating some of syndicalist ideology and technique. The young Benito Mussolini, who scored a great oratorical success in this congress, publicly called the class war not a question of economics, but essentially a matter of revolution and the pursuit of power. At the age of twenty-nine he became, with Lazzari, the most prominent party leader, and as editor of *Avanti* in the next two years he tripled the sales of the official socialist paper. Under his guidance socialism utterly renounced the policy of tacit co-operation with the liberals.

From the parent brood of the original workers' party there had successively split off anarchists, syndicalists, and now the right-wing reformists under Bissolati and Bonomi, but none of these were formidable on their own. Bissolati's group was doctrinally not unlike the British Labour Party, but it was cut off from any broad popular base, and so was already moribund long before its leader died in 1920. The left-wing reformists, Turati and Treves, remained behind as a right wing of the official party, though heavily outnumbered. A natural split along the grain might have divided reformism from revolutionism and left Turati and Bissolati both on the same side, but Turati believed that these internal divisions could only make socialism powerless, and he would not sever himself completely from his proletarian origins. At the same time he refused the seats on the party executive which were now offered to his group, arguing that the revolutionaries should be solely responsible for the failure which he hoped would attend their policy. In retrospect this seems a muddled and irresponsible attitude.

§❧

Giolitti, when the socialists again proved recalcitrant, turned more to the parliamentary Right. Perhaps he was beginning to be alarmed at the results of his policy of social laissez faire. Perhaps he also calculated that the enfranchisement of the illiterate peasantry might after all mean a more conservative or even a Catholic vote in rural areas. Salandra described how, paradoxically, the Italian peasants were socialists only out of a desire for land, which was the same as to say only so that they might cease to be socialists. More reliable as a sign of a conservative trend in public opinion was the expansion of the *Corriere della Sera,* whose circulation shortly touched 750,000, far larger than that of any other daily. Its weekly supplement, the *Domenica del Corriere,* reached almost two million. In the municipal administration of Rome, Nathan's radical-democratic bloc was defeated by a combination of Catholics, liberals, and nationalists. In the country at large the nationalists were obtaining the active assistance of heavy industry, and they had the sympathy of the foreign minister Di San Giuliano and of the Court. The Catholics, now more prominent in public life, also were a more than normally conservative influence during the pontificate of Pius X.

With elections imminent, Giolitti needed to trim his sails to the prevailing wind. Instead of continuing to try to absorb the popular parties, he therefore adopted Sonnino's policy of forming a national bloc against them, and his group momentarily joined with Sonnino's for this purpose. In the summer of 1913 he briefed the assembled prefects at Rome and then dissolved parliament. The subsequent elections were manipulated even more than those he had already organized in 1892, 1904, and 1909, and this time the new instruments of the motion-picture projector and phonograph were also employed. About half the electorate voted, and the constitutional liberals were returned with about 318 seats instead of 370. Alongside them the first three nationalists were elected, and the militant Catholic deputies increased from 20 to 29. On the Left Center the republicans were reduced from 24 to 17, but the radicals rose from 45 to over 70, even though they lacked a distinct party consciousness and for the most part continued to support Giolitti. Four different socialist groups together obtained almost one vote in four, and although their number of deputies increased only from 41 to 78, 52 of these were pledged to the subversion of parliament as an "institution devised by the *bourgeoisie* for their own interests." With proportional representation, these 52 would have been 89. The cause of liberal constitutionalism was indisputably on the wane.

Giolitti still possessed a comfortable majority for the immediate future. He had renounced his anticlericalism sufficiently to make an electoral compact with Count Gentiloni, president of the Catholic Union, whereby those liberals who were against socialism and who signed a declaration to oppose divorce and to favor the religious orders and private schools would receive Catholic votes. This did not prevent the clericals from pushing their own candidates wherever they hoped to succeed on their own, nor Giolitti's machine sometimes helping radicals, Freemasons, and even the independent socialists. Yet Gentiloni claimed the adhesion of 228 ministerialist candidates to his pact, and those people may well have been correct who estimated that without this support Giolitti's following in the new House might have numbered less than two hundred.

§⬦

For the duration of this one parliament the liberals were more or less to hold their own. But Giolitti's endless compromises were wearing thin. Salandra and the *Corriere* criticized the Catholic alliance, and when Giolitti subsequently made civil precede religious marriage, this only antagonized the Catholics without others taking it as repentance. The consequent defection of the radicals was to deprive Giolitti of office at a critical moment, so that the outbreak of war in 1914 found him unexpectedly on the opposition benches. He had upset a delicate balance of forces and had leaned too far in one direction to preserve his amorphous majority. This was a small premonitory sign that the whole tradition of parliamentary government was breaking down, the transformist compromise becoming ever less easy to work.

As the socialist Raimondo protested to parliament, under a democratic banner Italy had imperceptibly been led into what he roundly termed a dictatorial regime. People had said this of Cavour, Depretis, and Crispi in turn, and were now saying it of Giolitti. Four times he had "made" the elections, as often as Cavour himself, and by now he had nominated most of the senators, prefects, police officers, and other administrative officers of the state. But the worm was beginning to turn, and in 1913 some of the deputies demanded his impeachment before the high court for violating the freedom of the vote. Salvemini vehemently attacked what he called *"il ministro della mala vita"* and this electoral gerrymandering: "The police enrolled the scum of the constituencies and the underworld of the neighboring districts. In the last weeks before the polls, the opponents were threatened, bludgeoned, besieged in their homes. Their leaders were debarred from addressing meetings, or even thrown into prison until election day was over. Voters . . . favoring governmental candidates were given not only their own polling cards, but also those of opponents, emigrants, and deceased voters, and were allowed to vote three, five, ten, twenty times. The Government candidates were always the winners. Any deputy who dared Giolitti, had to confront a bad time at his next election. In Italy people used to say that Giolitti sold prefects in order to buy deputies. . . . When, in 1913, he was confronted not with a mere two or three thousand voters, but with ten thousand or more voters in a constituency to be "managed," he was forced to increase the dose of violence to ensure success. He won another of his overwhelming electoral victories. But the scandals of that campaign provoked bitter indignation everywhere. On the eve of the war of 1914–18, Giolitti was the most powerful man in parliament, but the most unpopular man in the country."

In February 1914 the radicals decided to withdraw their support from the government coalition. Radicalism was now an indiscriminate mixture ranging from liberals to quasi-socialists, from free traders to protectionists, from irredentists to pacifists, and had no roots in any solid sectional interest, but on paper its seventy-eight deputies represented a third force of considerable power inside Giolitti's political system. In 1913 a group of Masonic radicals attacked the Gentiloni pact, contending that the Vatican as an international and religious body should be excluded from temporal and national affairs. The radical ministers, Sacchi and Credaro, were then forced by the radical congress of 1914 to resign, and Giolitti, although he still had his majority, took this as a cue for what he intended to be another temporary exit. The Libyan war in any case had entailed serious financial difficulties, and there were visible shoals ahead in the shape of a railroad strike and agrarian disorders in Emilia. Another period of retrenchment out of office might be beneficial to his reputation and career. He had successfully used the extension of suffrage and the African war to divide the opposition groups, but had also unwittingly begun to cut the ground from under his own feet. Socialists, Catholics, and nationalists were all increasing their representation, and these three groups were before long to upset the whole applecart of upper-class liberalism.

§♠

Giolitti's active career was virtually at an end. He had been accused of dictatorship, but the accusation cannot easily be reconciled with the simultaneous charge that he fatally let things slide, and this second charge contained some truth. No doubt Giolitti's Italy had something of the police state about it: the memoirs of Armando Borghi, for instance, give examples of imprisonment without warrant or even without any accusation at all, and of being beaten up by the police. But this was not remarkable in contemporary Europe. Giolitti made no attempt to subvert institutions, but only exploited what already existed, and if he left politics in a not altogether healthy state, it was existing traditions and institutions rather than himself which were primarily responsible.

No one will deny that much was wrong with politics during this period of *giolittismo*. Several commissions of inquiry had to be appointed, on electoral corruption, on misappropriation of money for the armed services and on the building of government offices. The Saredo commission had shown up shocking abuses in the administration of Naples. Memories of the bank crisis were evoked when in 1908 the Sicilian professor Nasi, a former minister of education, was convicted by the Senate of embezzling the funds of his department. It did not restore confidence when the culprit was given but a short term of imprisonment which he was allowed to serve in his own home, nor was it reassuring that there was an uprising in Sicily to protest his prosecution. Some of his adherents at Trapani even raised the French flag and proclaimed a republic, and afterward they regularly went on electing him to parliament. No one seemed to mind very much at discovering that ministers and prefects had considerable perquisites attached to their office, and the assumption was that Nasi had been unlucky to be caught abusing them. Far from trying to reform such scandals, Giolitti, in the general opinion, made use of them for his own political purposes.

Fundamentally these abuses were the product of an unhealthy political system and an ineradicable anarchism among ordinary citizens. This anarchism had shown itself in the political assassination of King Umberto and in numerous other crimes of blood. Brigandage was still endemic in many provinces, and when a law was passed to restrict the length of knives, manufacturers evaded it by making hilts that would enter a wound along with the blade. Politicians set a bad example of illegality by corruptly feathering their own nests, and from Cavour onward they had fought duels among themselves at the same time as they were trying to punish crimes of violence among their inferiors. We find another aspect of this contempt of the law in the boycott of politics by the clericals, and not only by them but by such radicals as Cattaneo. We also find it in the thin attendance of deputies at parliament, and in their inability to cohere as organized parties with a collective policy. The theoretical anarchism of Bakunin and Malatesta was thus supported by a widespread empirical anarchism which took a multitude of forms. It is seen in Garibaldi's succession of private armies, in the Sicilian *fasci* of 1893, in the agrarian leagues for self-help which grew up after 1906, in the frequent student riots against university discipline. The Sicilian mafia was the perfect expression of such a society, and Mosca assures us that the mafia itself was an anarchic confederation of gangs, each *cosca* working on its own or even against its neighbor. This general lawlessness was made worse by the fact that the magistracy was badly paid and was therefore undistinguished either by intelligence or status. Both Giolitti and Mussolini were, in their different ways, natural products of such an environment. History was to show that this exaggerated individualism, which had been the great glory of Italy, was also her greatest peril. The police state was accepted as an attempt to remedy it, but so rooted was the disease that this remedy only made it worse.

〽

The most common accusation against Giolitti by historians has not been that he was authoritarian or corrupt, but that he was prosaic and pedestrian. To an even greater extent than that of Sonnino and Zanardelli, his policy looked as though it had no special characteristics except for a somewhat vague democratization of political life, and while his policy was not very positive, his tactics were opportunistic and shifty. He was always feeling for his majority, grouping and selecting different tendencies and trying to synthesize them. Like Depretis, he tended to equate politics with administration, and to this extent he brilliantly made the most of a political system which favored coalitions and decried clear commitments. Sonnino made the criticism that Giolitti's policy was to patch up each leak in turn, to placate the most noisy of his opponents, but only taking care of day-to-day problems as they arose. He was not concerned to prevent an individual remedy from creating an even worse problem tomorrow, and perhaps making impossible a more complete and radical reform in the long run.

The enemies of Giolitti continued to say that his cynicism robbed Italian politics of even such idealism as remained. Interpreting everyone's wishes in terms of self-interest, he played on people's defects rather than on their virtues. As the king later recalled to Count Ciano, Giolitti kept a dossier on each deputy's private weaknesses so that he knew how to manage each one. No wonder he sometimes seemed contemptuous of parliament when deputies and electors could be so easily influenced, and, indeed, when he was not in power he spent years without attending the House. In November 1916 he told Senise that there was no point in him attending parliament, for it was no longer asked even to vote taxes or give advice, and had in fact become a mere legal fiction. If this was true, it was in part his fault. Deprived of both leadership and a healthy conflict of ideas, parliament was losing its vigor and even its usefulness.

There was, however, a good deal to be said in favor of a realist who was in his way a sincere if disillusioned liberal, an enemy of magniloquence and overemphasis. Prezzolini adjudged that this unemotional, industrious, and practical administrator was the right person for a people who were so prone to enthusiasm and rhetorical exaggeration. As Giolitti was never eager to superimpose any theory on his practice, his variegated liberalism often deceived contemporaries, but later generations construed him as one of the foremost statesmen of United Italy. One thinks of him along with Cavour and De Gasperi, alike in technique and temperament, scornful of doctrinaire ideologues, resourceful in parliamentary maneuver, all three of them fighting a vanguard or rearguard defense of a workaday down-to-earth liberalism. For nearly thirteen years Giolitti governed Italy. During this time, even when out of office, he was the most important politician in the country. Fortis, Sonnino, Luzzatti, Salandra, and also Bonomi all became premier on his recommendation, and after the war he even returned to office himself for a year. Although Giolitti did not receive a good press at the time, Croce was later able to conclude that Italy had reached a pinnacle of success in 1914 under his skillful and benevolent rule.

Croce was here going to the other extreme of exaggeration. The liberals who, like him, served under Giolitti, mistook their own well-being and that of their friends for constitutional balance and social stability in the community at large. Italy was prosperous in 1914— Mosca noted as one sign of change that more peasants now wore shoes and carried handkerchiefs. A few of the liberals realized nevertheless that the country was on the brink of political disaster and social revolution. Mosca analyzed the dangers of universal suffrage, Pantaleoni those of nationalized insurance, Croce those of *d'annunzianesimo,* and here they spoke as experts; but in many other respects they were too close to the system to judge it correctly. From the relative detachment of Switzerland, Pareto noted the gradual defection of people toward socialism and Catholicism and explained it by the corruption and lack of leadership of the Italian ruling class and their growing divorce from the rest of the nation. He thought that Italy could have chosen either military power or economic wealth, and success either way would have reconciled ordinary citizens to this system of government; but she had tried for both and so had fallen disastrously between one and the other. On the politicians who encouraged this, and even on those politicians who allowed it to happen, he concluded that a grave responsibility must lie.

35 Italy Remains Neutral, 1914

Austria and Italy were still allies in name, but hardly so in fact. Austria remembered her loss of Venice in 1866 and the danger to which this exposed her only port at Trieste. Especially after 1906, under the hereditary prince, Franz Ferdinand, and General Conrad von Hötzendorff, the anti-Italian party grew in power, and strategic positions were occupied in the uncertain mountain regions along Austria's southern frontier. The foreign minister, Aerenthal, for a time successfully moderated Conrad's aggressive schemes. But Italian counterirredentism toward Trent and Trieste was then fanned by the Austrian annexation of Bosnia in 1908, and by the chilly unfriendliness of Austria and Germany during the Libyan war of 1911–12.

The Triple Alliance had to be either denounced or renewed one year before its expiration in the summer of 1913. The Italian foreign ministry was occupied through the years 1910–14 (under three successive premiers) by Di San Giuliano who passed for a confirmed triplicist. On the other hand, the irredentists were dismayed at the prospect of renewing the treaty, especially as, with general war becoming more likely, Italy's hands might thereby be tied too tightly for diplomatic finesse. But denouncing the alliance after all these thirty years would have been too active and positive a foreign policy for Giolitti, and would have looked too much like an overt act of hostility against Austria. Rather than have to think out any alternative line of action, in December 1912 he confirmed the existing treaty for the fourth time in thirty years.

Nevertheless, this treaty relationship with Germany and Austria was by now of very limited potentiality, for Italo-Austrian recriminations continued, and Italy had also reached an understanding with the rival Triple Entente of France, Russia, and Britain. In August 1913, Trieste was ordered by Prince Hohenlohe to dismiss Italian-speaking civic employees not of Austrian nationality. Formerly, the Italians in Trieste had looked toward Vienna for protection against the advancing Slovenes, but a novel Austrian solicitude for the Slavs now threatened Italian livelihood as well as Italian culture and language there. The Triple Alliance, which had never meant very much, now obviously meant less than ever.

Giolitti's resignation early in 1914, though at the time it seemed to be just another of what Salandra cynically called his calculated political vacations, was in fact to prove decisive in Italian politics. Giolitti was not the man who would have let Italian animus against Austria build up into open hostility in World War I. He had gone unenthusiastically into Libya and was disinclined toward heroics and wild hopes of glory. He was aware as early as July 1913 of Austria's aggressive intentions toward Serbia, though he concealed this knowledge for more than a year so as not to alarm the public. Despite this fact he continually resisted the financial appropriations for which the army pressed, and he was convinced that Italy's best policy was to remain neutral in any European conflagration.

Successive ministers of war had tried to reorganize the armed services within the limits imposed by the Treasury and their own competence. That General Spingardi could remain minister of war successively under Giolitti, Sonnino, and Luzzatti allowed some continuity of policy under royal supervision. Lacking adequate parliamentary criticism and enough financial support, however, the best that such a man could do was not good enough, and the unpreparedness of the armed forces was to be the greatest argument for Italian neutrality when the European war broke out.

On Giolitti's resignation, and on Giolitti's advice, the king in March 1914 appointed as premier Professor Salandra, who had been in Sonnino's cabinets of 1906 and 1909. Antonio Salandra was a conservative, aloof and distant, and less ready than Sonnino to accept Giolitti's democratic reforms. Yet he made the usual pastiche administration. His appointment of one of Giolitti's enemies, Ferdinando Martini, as minister of colonies brought him some initial support from the radicals. The Court insisted on his retention of Di San Giuliano as foreign minister, and this ensured the simultaneous adhesion of the nationalists and the clericals. Misreading the situation, Giolitti even helped Salandra to form his ministry; indeed, the government could scarcely have existed without such assistance, for Giolitti's habit of resigning while he still had a majority in parliament was meant to keep his successor from taking any initiative. This was one of Giolitti's great miscalculations. He saw Salandra as a mere stopgap who would take the responsibility of government during a difficult period, but who had neither the political courage nor the parliamentary following to take any decisive step. Instead, Salandra proved to be an ambitious gambler, who was ready to break free from Giolitti's system and throw Italy into a crippling war.

ᶎ

In the month of June 1914 the new ministry had to cope with a near revolution almost like that of May 1898. In parliament the voting boxes were again overturned, and Chiesa, the deputy responsible, was severely manhandled by his colleagues. In Emilia and the Romagna there was another peasant *jacquerie*. The landless *braccianti* in this inflammable area had developed co-operatives in order to obtain from the *mezzadri* more employment and better terms. Socialist trade unions here and there were winning a virtual monopoly of agricultural labor, and municipal employees might even be paid in credits at the co-operative shop. To this the landowners and *mezzadri* replied by forming mobile squads of strikebreakers to exert a counterpressure. Here were all the elements of a conflict. While in the South the local tyrant was a landowner, in parts of the North the local party boss was king. One such boss was Mussolini, who at the congress of Ancona in 1914 expelled the Freemasons from the socialist party for not being sufficiently revolutionary or class-conscious. Another kindred spirit was Nenni, also from the Romagna. Pietro Nenni had once been a republican for whom the works of Mazzini were a sacred text, but by now he was a militant leader of the socialist *braccianti* against the republican *contadini* as well as against the conservative estate owners.

These two firebrands were both involved in the "red week" of June 1914, and so was the chief anarch, Malatesta. At Ancona an antidraft demonstration had provoked firing by the police and consequent reprisals. A general strike was declared, though it was only partly effective because so many of the moderate socialists were of two minds. Shops were sacked, railroad tracks again pulled up, telegraph poles knocked down, and the royal insignia removed. Soon the red flag was flying above the town hall of Bologna, and Ancona and other towns declared themselves to be independent communes. When a republic was declared in the Romagna, most of the authorities went into hiding. The future Marshal Balbo, of ill-fame, was observed to leave Ferrara with a posse of bicyclists to make such trouble as he could, clad once again in a Garibaldian red shirt. Here and there an army commander took orders from a socialist dictator, and General Agliardi of the regular army had to surrender his sword to the rebels near Ravenna. None of this was the work of Mussolini, but he justified it in the columns of *Avanti* even though in later life he pretended otherwise. Over a hundred thousand men had to be called up before law and order were restored, and the expense of this was considerable, while the drain on magazines and uniform stores left Italy unprepared when the war of 1914–18 began.

§❧

In this electrically charged atmosphere, Salandra was confronted with the Austrian ultimatum to Serbia. Many years later, by the time Italy began to publish her prewar documents, the main facts were fairly well established. Giolitti had already made it clear to Austria that Italy would not join her ally in any attack on Serbia. Salandra did not know that Austria had been warned in 1913 not to count on Italian support, for Giolitti kept the relevant papers after he left office, and did not give his successor this vital information. But Salandra had several other cards at his disposal to play against the Austrians, for the Triple Alliance required first the imparting of prior information to an ally and second the offer of compensation for any disturbance such as they were apparently contemplating in the Balkans. Austria defaulted under both heads when in July 1914 she sent her ultimatum to Serbia, and Italy knew nothing of this ultimatum until after it was sent.

Nine months later Italy was fighting on the side of France and Britain, but in July 1914 there was a distinct possibility that she would have to fight alongside Germany and Austria. The obligations of the Triple Alliance suggested, without requiring, such a course, and the general staff had naturally based its strategy on joining the Central Powers with whom Italy had been formally allied since 1882. At the foreign office, Di San Giuliano believed that young and energetic Germany was in the ascendant, while corrupt France and self-satisfied Britain were declining. Sonnino thought that Italy should at once declare war on Germany's side. Missiroli of the *Resto del Carlino* and Scarfoglio's *Mattino* were also for favoring the Central Powers with a policy of benevolent neutrality at least, and Croce, like the germanophile Banca Commerciale Italiana, put his weight into the same scales.

Those who wanted war were, however, in a very small minority indeed, for to fight on the same side as Austria—the possessor of Trent and Trieste—would be to betray Italian nationalism and the inviolable *risorgimento* itself. Austria's aggressive policy in the Balkans had technically freed Italy from her obligations under what was an essentially defensive pact. One provision of the treaty excluded any war in which England was involved, and the 1902 accord with France equally indicated Italian nonbelligerence. Clearly, Italian governments had again contrived by skill as well as luck to secure a position where they could jump either way or neither.

There was furthermore a possibility of internal trouble if Italy decided to fight for her Central European allies. Radicals like De Viti de Marco, the reformist socialists around Bissolati, and the republicans Chiesa and De Andreis had no sympathy for Austria, and powerful francophile and anglophile newspapers existed, including Salvemini's *Unità* and the *Secolo*. Verdi's collaborator, Boito, represented a generalized nonpartisan patriotism which already wanted war against Germany, and two of Garibaldi's grandsons were killed as volunteers with French troops in the Argonne. But for most people the immediately urgent thing was not so much to fight against Germany as to stop Salandra from fighting against France and Britain. France had been courting Italian sympathy of late and had established cultural institutes at Florence and Milan. Of Italy's coal, 90 per cent came from Britain. Active participation in war would thus dislocate trade, and the minister of the treasury, Rubini, threatened to resign if Italian finances were required to withstand another war so soon after the Libyan venture. On the other hand a neutral Italy would be very well placed economically.

Giolitti, now out of office, stressed the political advantages of neutrality, for he knew that Italy's interest was in maintaining the balance of European power, and for this she needed to keep all her forces intact and uncommitted. Libya had taught him that the army and the machinery of state were too weak for hostilities, and it was tragic that the needs of propaganda forced him to keep this conviction a secret—to the great loss of his country. When the outbreak of war caught Giolitti in London, he came over to Paris and there sent a telegram to warn his inexperienced successors that there was no obligation to fight. By simple negotiation Italy could gain a good deal, he believed, and perhaps the war might break up the Austro-Hungarian empire and set free its subject populations to Italy's advantage. Italy therefore ought at least to wait and see who was likely to win before committing herself, and his own vote was for remaining quite free.

The decision for neutrality was taken by the cabinet at the end of July. Parliament was not called to ratify it, but was allowed to sleep on on through a five-month recess despite Turati's urgent request that the deputies be summoned. Full powers were just arbitrarily assumed, and policy was entirely determined by the cabinet and the Court. At such a moment Albertini's *Corriere della Sera* was more of a political force than the Chamber of Deputies, so irrelevant had representative institutions become. Unaided and uncriticized by parliament, Di San Giuliano, timid and pro-German, the one politician whom the king really appreciated, was able to promise what was in effect a benevolent neutrality to Austria. Far from trying hard to hold Austria back, and far from making it quite explicit that the ultimatum to Serbia freed Italy from any treaty obligations, he refused to denounce the Triple Alliance, but hoped for war so that he might then claim the compensations which by treaty were payable by Austria if she annexed territory in the Balkans. He did not defend neutralism on grounds of principle, but used the negative arguments that war alongside Austria might involve Italy in a republican revolution and a bombardment of her seaports by the British navy.

Salandra was later deceptive on this point, for in retrospect he wanted to give his foreign policy a more consistently patriotic look. He said that as early as July 27 or 28 he had clearly suggested to Austria that she should cede her Italian provinces; and he added that he had even threatened otherwise to break the Triple Alliance. The German and Austrian documents record this somewhat differently, and the Austrian chancellor announced with the authorization of the Italian ambassador at Vienna that Italy had promised "to assume a friendly attitude in conformity with our alliance." It was on August 4 that Di San Giuliano seems to have put the stress on compensation, that is to say when the Entente powers had declared their attitude and so given Italy a more arbitral position. Even then he mentioned the Trentino alone, and this was to be the price not for impartial neutralism as he later implied, but for nonbelligerent complicity alongside Austria.

§⬦

In October Di San Giuliano died. His successor as foreign minister, Sonnino, was another triplicist whose electoral program of February 1909 had specifically deplored Visconti-Venosta's policy of weakening the Triple Alliance and of retaining the ability to negotiate with both sides. In August 1914, Sonnino was one of the few politicians who had protested against neutrality and favored joining Austria. But once the battle of the Marne had destroyed the legend of German invincibility, he changed his ground and preferred to exploit a position in which each side was competing to promise Italy any advantage that would not cost them too much.

In this mood an Italian "sanitary commission" landed unopposed at Valona on the Albanian coast, and in December, as no voice of protest had been heard, the city was occupied by troops. This was a pledge to be held against the victory of either side, and it constituted another stage in that expansionist policy which had already engulfed Libya and the Dodecanese. Italians had lately built ports and railroads in Dalmatia, and an Italian company had secured the tobacco monopoly of Montenegro. But economic penetration had inevitably encountered increasing resistance from local nationalism—by 1913 there was in existence a new Albanian state—and the developing conflict between Italians and Slavs had also aided German infiltration in Trieste. The Austro-Serbian war in 1914 therefore offered an excellent excuse to improve a deteriorating position and stake out a claim on this defenseless part of the Adriatic coast.

On December 9, once Valona was securely in pledge, Sonnino officially asked Austria to discuss the compensations Italy might claim under Article 7 of their treaty of alliance. In other words he was still very much out to secure the enforcement of the Triple Alliance rather than ready to throw it over. Salandra later claimed that he was only playing for time, having already agreed in private to go to war in the following spring on the side of the Entente. But, if this Machiavellian explanation was really true, more war preparations would without doubt have been made in the next few months than Salandra in fact permitted. Italy still seems to have been much closer to Germany than to France, and it is fairly certain that Sonnino still hoped to gain Trent and Trieste by gift of Austria without actually entering the war himself.

Meanwhile, the Central Powers rose to the bait of Italian benevolent neutrality—at a price. The German generals particularly wanted to gain several months for the development of their Carpathian offensive, and the diplomats were therefore directed to play out time in talk but not to make any premature concessions to their ally. The former German chancellor, von Bülow, with his Italian wife, was sent to Rome, there to use, as occasion demanded, blandishments or threats. Dark hints were dropped about possible concessions over the *terre irredente,* yet also about restoring the temporal power of the Pope if Italy proved recalcitrant. The considerable commercial and financial hold which Germany had obtained in Italy provided another useful weapon for him to use.

As the war dragged on, Austria moved to meet Italian claims, but very slowly and partially. Franz Joseph had declared war as a last resort to prevent his great multinational empire from breaking up, and he would not therefore lightly yield Trent to Italy lest this should touch off a dozen other claims from the other insurgent nationalities. He could also argue with some force that Italy already possessed in Valona all the compensation she could expect. But the fortunes of war gradually strengthened Italy's demand for nothing less than her *terre irredente,* and by March 9, 1915, von Bülow had persuaded Austria to agree in principle to make some concession. Perhaps the Germans felt hopeful that they had thus assured Italian neutrality.

36 Intervention Against Austria, 1915

As the war gathered momentum, some Italians began to think that neutrality was undignified for a nation of their status, whereas intervention
would mark them indisputably as a great power. In support of this it was
also sophistically argued that the victory of either side would upset the
balance of forces upon which they relied for the proper assertion of
their influence, so that as neutrals they were bound to lose. Behind both
of these dubious arguments was the hard fact that Italy still thought of
herself as an unsatisfied nation. Her "natural frontiers" were still to be
reached, and civilians and military alike were avid to wipe out the
memories of Custoza, Lissa, and Adowa in some great victory that
would prove their mettle.

Once intervention was decided upon, Italy could have chosen either
to fight against her allies for the Brenner and the Adriatic, or with them
for Nice, Corsica, Malta, and Tunis. Opinion gradually hardened in
favor of the first course, mainly because the Entente powers had more
to offer and were better placed than Austria to do so without damage to
themselves. Victory on the side of France and Britain had the advantage
that it would not only liberate Italian-speaking people, but it would
at last achieve a proper Alpine frontier, and gain control of the Adriatic
and a share in the Turkish empire.

The interventionists were a nondescript collection acting with very
little common purpose. Among them there was the king, who had been
brought up as a soldier and wanted to break free from Giolitti's influence
as his grandfather had tried to break away from Cavour's. D'Annunzio
by January 1915 already had private information that war might be
declared against Germany before the summer. Most of the Freemasons
and most politically active university students seem also to have been
among the *interventisti,* and the irredentists were of course with them
to a man. The nationalists, as soon as the chances of war against France
began to vanish, grouped together against Germany, considering any
war better than none. Likewise, the futurists were absolute for war, and
as early as September 1914 they had interrupted an opera of Puccini's
at Rome in order to burn an Austrian flag on the stage. Marinetti declared that futurists had always considered war to be the only inspiration

of art, the only moral purifier. In his view, war would rejuvenate Italy, would enrich it with men of action, and force it to live no longer on its past but on its own strength. Strange bedfellows with this *avant garde* were the old conservatives perpetuating the francophile tradition of Visconti-Venosta and Bonghi. Stranger still, there were Salvemini and the reformist socialists who wanted a war of generous idealism waged in the name of freedom and democracy and against the invader of Belgium.

The revolutionary socialists under Mussolini had been momentarily surprised to find themselves in the same neutralist camp as their three chief enemies, Giolitti, Turati, and the Pope, but official dogma was fairly clear on the point, and so in September 1914 Mussolini condemned the war outright as the ultimate form taken by class collaboration. By October, however, he had modified his standpoint to one of "conditional neutrality," and by November to the other extreme of uncompromising belligerency. This strident *volte-face* may have been partly due to French money, but it must also have come from a realization that war might prepare revolution and accustom the common people to violence and arms. At all events, De Ambris, Corridoni, and other remnants of revolutionary syndicalism gathered around him; so did Farinacci, and Caldara the socialist mayor of Milan, and Nenni who called neutrality a sign of impotence and humiliation. In November Mussolini launched a new paper, *Il Popolo d'Italia,* to support the cause of war against Germany; it is certain that he was subsidized for this by the French and by Italian industrialists.

The socialist party itself, scandalized by Mussolini's irresponsible desertion of the true Marxist position, reacted by summarily bundling their late leader out of the fold, as they had recently ejected his opponent Bissolati. The remaining socialists were left divided between the moderate Turati and Treves, and the revolutionary faction of Lazzari and Bombacci, all of them advocating neutrality. Deprived of its two interventionist wings, yet still divided internally, the party was now more ineffective than ever.

§❧

Support for intervention was thus found in many different directions of the political compass. All told, the interventionists were far from numerous, and more than one member of the cabinet has put it on record that the government's war policy was quite deliberately in the teeth of the great majority both in parliament and the country. What was more, the motives of different groups for intervention were quite irreconcilable in logic. Nevertheless their momentary agreement in practice urged Salandra to a bold stroke of duplicity. On February 16, 1915, despite concurrent negotiations with Austria, a courier was dispatched in great secrecy to London with the suggestion that Italy was simultaneously open to a good offer from the Entente. At the same time the screw was given a twist at Vienna, for it was hoped that both sides would now need Italian support enough to compete for it. The final choice between them was aided by the arrival of news in March of Russian victories in the Carpathians. Salandra began to think that victory for the Entente was in sight, and he was so anxious not to arrive too late for a share in the profits that he instructed his envoy in London to drop some of the Italian demands and reach agreement quickly.

The memorandum which had been originally given to Grey showed that earlier irredentist demands no longer satisfied. Not only Trent and Trieste, but all cisalpine Tyrol, much of Dalmatia with its islands, and a share of the Ottoman empire, all these were demanded, together with a monetary subsidy, the exclusion of the Pope from any peace conference, and equitable treatment in any distribution of colonies. On March 27, however, Grey's compromise counterproposals were accepted for fear that the war might soon be over, and because Russia as protector of the Slavs insisted on halving Italy's claims in Dalmatia. Even so, the final provisions of the Treaty of London would have taken Italy's eastern frontier down as far as Cape Planka and included most of the Adriatic islands, so that she would have dominated that sea. In return, Sonnino gladly allowed the Serbo-Croats an outlet at Fiume, for as yet this town did not feature among Italy's ambitions—it was time enough in 1919 to see the error of bartering away Italian Fiume in exchange for Slav Dalmatia.

The secret Treaty of London was concluded on April 26, binding Italy to fight within one month from that date. The Entente powers had assumed that Italian armed assistance was not worth more than a certain price, especially when they surmised from Salandra's proposals that the von Bülow mission had failed. Nevertheless, it cost them little to be generous, as Italian demands hardly ran against their vital interests. Thus, for one week Italy managed to be in alliance with both sets of combatants simultaneously. Not until May 4 did Salandra denounce the Triple Alliance in a private note to its signatories, arrogantly and inaccurately calling this Italy's first spontaneous political action since the *risorgimento*. And never, despite a formal promise, did he consult Giolitti.

Salandra and Sonnino also deceived their own cabinet, and none of the ministers and military leaders of Italy knew that these secret negotiations were proceeding at London: nor, of course, was there any suggestion of consulting parliament. The text of the treaty was brought to parliamentary notice only some years later when it was published from Russian sources by a newspaper in Stockholm. Salandra had thus committed the nation to war on his own responsibility and against a large known majority in parliament and the country. He was quite within his legal rights, but Italy was to suffer terribly for this constitutional anomaly. He had not even consulted General Cadorna and the General Staff.

Quite apart from the question of constitutional propriety, some people felt guilty about denouncing the *Triplice* in this roundabout manner just when its termination could do most harm to their former allies. Nitti, for instance, in his acid reminiscences, concluded that these simultaneous negotiations with each side let Italy into the war in the most dishonorable way, and he called the Treaty of London a monumental piece of folly. Nevertheless, however clumsy the manner of this diplomatic revolution, Salandra could claim that there were good arguments for trying to sway the balance between rival power-groups, and hence a turncoat policy might be a necessary condition of survival. What was more controversial than breaking from Germany was his decision to enter the war, for even if Italy emerged on the winning side, the balance would have been upset and her own influence would thereby be reduced. Either as victor or vanquished she stood to lose.

Giolitti, the leader of the neutralists, was living far away from Rome on his Piedmontese estates. His long absence from the political scene—and it was by no means something unusual when out of office—was another reflection on constitutional practice. His farsighted view had been that what looked superficially like an easy and attractive war of national aggrandizement might turn out to be the first step in a domestic revolution. It was also the view of this most experienced of Italian statesmen that skillful diplomacy could in any case satisfy national aspirations without war. As Salandra said, Giolitti had been disillusioned by the Libyan war over the fighting qualities of the army and the morale of the civilian population, for his calculating mind was impressed less by sentiment than by hard facts and material interests, and he knew all too well the niggardliness of his own expenditure on the army, the lack of military tradition, and the inadequacy of the generals. Unfortunately his reasonable arguments were discounted because they were thought merely to conceal an ambition to return to power. Giolitti had a majority in parliament and had been waiting for a suitable moment to displace Salandra, but now he suddenly found himself completely hamstrung. He feared to press his case for neutralism too publicly, for that would have weakened Italy's hand in negotiating with Austria, and he would not then have been able to become premier without Austria reducing the price she was ready to pay for Italian nonbelligerency.

§❧

Salandra could nevertheless expect considerable opposition when the time came to make public the engagement he had undertaken in the name of Italy. He frankly admitted that in May 1915 the very great majority of Italians were against intervention, and everyone else agreed with this estimate. Mussolini himself even thought it a matter for pride that the people were dragged into this war by a minority, and his fateful conclusion was that a dynamic minority would always prevail against the static masses.

This was a striking lesson for the future Duce to learn at so little cost to himself, and not for nothing have historians spoken of May 1915 as a dress rehearsal for the *coup d'état* of October 1922. What D'Annunzio in 1915 helped to do by his inflammatory speeches at Genoa and Rome, De Ambris and Corridoni did by their agitation in the nerve center of opinion at Milan. Secret-service money could be used on propaganda for this purpose, and the police had long since been instructed by Giolitti in the art of contriving "spontaneous popular manifestations." Above all, Salandra noted, these manifestations were headed by young university students, the same *déraciné* intellectuals who also prevailed in such other revolutionary years as 1860 and 1922. Cavour in 1860 had acknowledged that "shouts in the piazza cannot be taken as manifestations of public opinion," but it was sometimes convenient to forget this truth, and the riots of May 1915 were an artificially stimulated appeal to have Salandra's policy confirmed against the known will of parliament.

Gabriele d'Annunzio was asked to return for this purpose from his hideout in the south of France whither he had fled from his creditors some years previously. According to his own testimony, the government privately informed him about the Treaty of London before he left France, long before the parliamentary leaders knew the first thing about it, and the obvious conclusions may be drawn from the fact that his financial embarrassments now ceased for awhile. Once back in Italy he delivered a declamatory harangue at a meeting to celebrate the anniversary of Garibaldi's expedition of the Thousand, and this was only one day after Salandra's repudiation of the Triple Alliance. Great scenes of enthusiasm ensued, and nothing was left to the imagination in his exuberant apostrophe to "an Italy which shall be greater by conquest, purchasing territory not in shame but at the price of blood and glory. . . . After long years of national humiliation, God has been pleased to grant us proof of our privileged blood. . . . Blessed are they that

have, for they have more to give and can burn with a hotter flame. . . .
Blessed are those young men who hunger and thirst for glory, for they
shall be filled."

From Genoa the poet made a triumphal progress to Rome, where he
declaimed war poetry in the Roman theaters and on May 12 and 13
staged other speeches on the Capitoline hill: "No, we are not and do
not want to be just a museum, a hotel, a vacation resort, a Prussian-blue
horizon where foreigners come for their honeymoons, a gay market
where things are bought and sold. Our genius demands that we should
put our stamp on the molten metal of the new world. . . . Comrades,
it is no longer time for speeches, but for action, and for action after
the high Roman fashion. If it is a crime to incite people to violence, I
boast of now committing that crime. . . . This war, though it may seem
destructive, will be the most fruitful means of creating beauty and virtue
that has appeared on the earth."

While war fever was beginning to mount, Austria made her last attempts to keep the peace. Late in March she had offered to cede Trent
as a bribe to stop the defection of her wayward ally. Then on April 17
she agreed to part of the Italian counterdemands for regions further
north in the Adige Valley. On May 7, two weeks after Italy's secret commitment to the Entente, Sonnino notified the Italian cabinet of still further Austrian offers which included Valona and the Italian Tyrol, with
Trieste becoming a free city. The Germans carefully ensured that these
final concessions were generally known, hoping that Italian public opinion would then force Salandra to back down from his rash policy of war.

᛫᛫

Giolitti did not arrive in Rome until May 9, though von Bülow warned
him on the 4th what the government was doing. This was a disastrous
wait, and perhaps he had been hoping that the king would approach
him directly. Salandra's cabinet had at last agreed to inform the chief
parliamentary leaders how things stood, and Carcano, a friend of
Giolitti, therefore went to see him on his arrival and astonished him
with the news about ending the Triple Alliance. Giolitti visited both
the king and Salandra, and urged upon them that parliament would be
against fighting, that the Italian generals were not up to it, that a German victory was likely, and that war might last longer than they thought
and bring invasion and even revolution in its train. He suggested that,
without any loss of honor for Italy, a vote in parliament could be used
to upset any unratified arrangement with the Entente, and then another
or the same ministry could resume negotiations with Austria on the
basis of offers already made. By this suggestion Giolitti hoped to make

his political opponents compromise themselves. According to his own account—in the autobiographical memoirs which Malagodi wrote in his name—he had still not been informed about the Treaty of London. Salandra's contradictory version is more likely to be true, that if Giolitti had not been shown the actual treaty (for it was secret), he had at least been roughly apprised of its contents. Even so, for a few vital days Giolitti allowed himself to be deceived about how deeply Italy was committed to begin fighting at the latest by May 26.

This difference of opinion soon became generally known, and since parliament itself was closed, within a few hours of his arrival at Rome over three hundred deputies personally left cards at Giolitti's apartment to demonstrate their opposition to fighting. The parliamentary majority had been elected on a Giolittian ticket, and they must have felt him to be the safer man to have in charge of affairs. They also had to think of their newly enfranchised constituents, most of whom were believed to want peace. Bissolati, himself an interventionist, computed that no more than sixty deputies sincerely wanted war, whereas on the other side these three hundred were an absolute majority of the Chamber, and undoubtedly their number would have grown had parliament been in session and more deputies present in Rome. Salandra admits that he was fighting against the majority and that his opponents were growing more numerous every day.

Salandra's position was highly delicate and irregular. It made things worse that (again this is from his not wholly reliable memoirs) the king asked him to try to win over Giolitti so that the war would be begun without a division inside the so-called constitutional parties. For the fear of impeachment by this hostile majority made Salandra most unwilling to meet Giolitti publicly in parliament, and he confessed that he himself ruled out any possibility of letting parliament decide. The decision had already been taken, and the king had given his full approval to a policy of war. The cabinet therefore agreed to resign and so lay responsibility upon the king for reconciling Giolitti. Salandra also postponed the opening of parliament from May 12 to 20 so as to gain more time. He had been particularly alarmed to find that the general staff, when informed of the complete switch in alliances, declared that they would need time for their preparations.

The king himself was so far committed that Salandra felt quite safe in offering resignation. Owing to Giolitti's absence, Vittorio Emanuele had been inveigled into a war policy, and now insisted that, despite the fact that they had resigned, the ministers should continue to prepare for war. When Giolitti heard that the king thought his honor was pledged, he agreed to make things easy by withdrawing his political challenge, and then cravenly recommended a premier who would support a war policy which he knew might be fatal. Others gave similar advice when the king approached them. Giolitti had something in his nature which made him reluctant to take office when things became difficult, and to return to politics now would have been too much of a challenge. Once he knew the scope of the treaty, he understood that its repudiation might not only impugn Italian good faith, but could result in the abdication of the king who had signed it. Salandra was therefore reinstated, and another radical weakness was exposed in the constitution of 1848.

The decision between peace and war had already been irretrievably taken, and the need to cover the king had resulted in the government mobilizing for war before parliament had even been consulted over this complete reversal of policy. Deputies known to be neutralists were being manhandled in the street, and Salandra cynically connived at this. Students rowdily invaded the very Houses of Parliament, and Sonnino's *Giornale d'Italia* was not alone in abusively insinuating that Giolitti's friends were in the pay of Germany. D'Annunzio's language about Giolitti became obscene and unquotable, and this former premier had to be given a guard through the streets. Mussolini preferred the method of fighting duels as his contribution to showing that the promised age of violence had dawned. No weapon was illegitimate, for the honor of Italy and the king's reputation were at stake, and the wishes of parliament and public opinion were therefore irrelevant. This was the result of the fact that Giolitti had not bothered to organize a parliamentary opposition, and had sulked at his country house hoping to remain uncommitted until the time arrived for a comeback. Being uncommitted he was also impotent just when a challenge to the government was most needed.

So loud were D'Annunzio's shouts in the piazza that the king could recall Salandra on May 16 without the wishes of parliament mattering in the least. Nitti later looked back on this as the day when the constitution was abolished and liberty destroyed. As again in 1922, the king, placed between parliament and the demagogues, chose the latter, and there was no constitutional means of restraining him. Giolitti for his part, by not being ready to form a ministry, had acknowledged defeat, and on the seventeenth, even before parliament met, he scuttled away again to far-off Piedmont whence to watch the verification of his gloomy forebodings in years of solitude. In private letters he explained that he did not dare raise his fundamental opposition in parliament, for in the first place it would have done no good, and in the second place such opposition must not be allowed in time of war. These were melancholy and damaging admissions.

Giolitti's followers drew their own conclusions from his flight, and by

May 20, when parliament met for the first time during the crisis, they had astonishingly changed sides. Under severe intimidation, forsaken by their leader, and knowing now the extent of the king's involvement, the deputies gave the government full powers "in case of war" by 407 votes to 74. This decision was greeted by salvos of applause from all benches save those occupied by the fifty official socialists, and a patriotic hymn of the *risorgimento* was begun in the public galleries and taken up in the body of the House. Some of the deputies cried out "long live the war," and were to have their wish granted more literally than they may have intended. In the Senate the decision was unanimous, for the band wagon was now palpably moving and he who did not jump on might be left behind. War was declared on May 23, and on May 24 the army marched.

୨୶

It redounds to Giolitti's credit that his first major defeat in fifteen years was at the hands of extraparliamentary forces, the piazza mob and the royal prerogative. All his reasoned arguments and all the dangerous implications of fighting in a European war were now overwhelmed by the excitement of the moment and by the infectious enthusiasms which swept through the land. No doubt a historian must not lightly accept his view that Italy should on no account have fought, but one may agree with him that the prevalent motives were usually irrational and bad, as the consequences of fighting were also to be disastrous. Parliamentary deputies, when all is said, are more intelligent than mobs and (in this case) than poets or kings, even though all of them finally succumbed to a wave of nationalistic hysteria. Mussolini's followers joyfully concluded from this course of events that parliament had been superseded and would disappear at the end of the war. They were right, for parliament was thoroughly discredited, and the war was going to create the conditions out of which Mussolini emerged a dictator.

So charged with emotion was this moment of May 1915 that men of many different political opinions were to look back on it as one of regeneration, the moment when Italy chose to fight for righteousness and to win the war for democracy. Salandra, however, in his justification to parliament at the time, stressed egoistic rather than idealistic motives for intervention, just as in August 1914 he had stressed the egoistic motives for neutrality. According to Giolitti, indeed, Salandra's main motive in fighting was to strengthen the conservative interest in Italian domestic politics. Salandra and Sonnino were not notoriously anti-German or antimilitarist, nor were they much in love with democracy, and the liberation of subject peoples could not deeply interest a government whose chief war aim was Italian dominion over the Adriatic and the southern Slavs.

As if to prove the point, Salandra declared war not against Germany, the violator of Belgium, but only against Austria upon whom Italy had selfish territorial claims. Apart from this being a breach of the Treaty of London, it gave to subsequent operations more the appearance of a private grudge war than of a war of liberation and righteousness. Hence the mistrust of Italy which her new allies began to show, for her simultaneous negotiations with all the major belligerents had hardly inspired much confidence, and the prime minister's memoirs show that he continued to treat France with coldness and hostility. About Salandra's unfortunate public reference in October to *sacro egoismo,* Nitti concluded that it damaged Italy as much as a military defeat. The realist Salandra quite properly derided the specious ideology of the Allies, but a still shrewder realist would have seen that, with some more ideal motive, Italians might have fought better and might have deserved a better press abroad and a better peace settlement.

37 The Conduct of War, 1915-1918

So complete was Italy's unpreparedness that her entering the war looked lightheaded and irresponsible in retrospect, but Salandra at the time imagined the fighting to be nearly over, and indeed this was the only reason he had risked his own career and the future of his country. In negotiating the Treaty of London he had requested financial help from his new allies only for several months. He had omitted to ask for any assistance with oil and raw materials, and he defended his forgetfulness by the remarkable assertion that he did not want to dishonor Italy by bargaining over peace and war—as if this was not what he had been doing for months. He bravely called Nitti a pessimist for thinking that the war might continue past the winter of 1915. Here was irresponsibility on a colossal scale.

Salandra admitted later that the military operations were unsatisfactory. This was partly his own fault, because he thought he could make Italy a great power cheaply, and indeed General Porro in 1914 had refused to become minister of war specifically because of Salandra's parsimony over the army estimates. Such was the premier's secretiveness about negotiating with both sides at once that the general staff was finally told about the reversal of alliances only on the evening of May 5, and the generals were thus given less than three weeks to prepare for war against Austria after having based their plans on the Austrian alliance. The development of hostilities then showed up their obsolete military theory and their failure to think in terms of a war of attack. Cadorna confirmed that, when he took up the supreme command in July 1914, he found the existing campaign studies to be exclusively defensive, and the in-

grained habit of invasion-mindedness continued to be an important restraining factor. The Austrians were the first to be surprised at it. There
was also the fact that the Libyan war had used up reserves of munitions
and finance and had left military morale slightly impaired. The chief of
staff reported later that the Italian army had begun the war in a state of
real disintegration.

It hardly helped matters that the king, in conformity with what he
took to be the traditions of his house, left immediately for the front and
stayed there almost uninterruptedly until the end of the war. Cadorna
himself had never held active command before, and his chief qualifica-
tions were that his father had liberated Rome in 1870 and that his own
manual of army training had become a standard work. He was a good
organizer, but he and his chief colleagues were unresourceful, unimaginative, and inflexible, and inspired little confidence or affection in their
men. He could not abide interference by politicians, and replaced the
existing minister of war by his own nominee, General Zupelli. Nor would
he brook much advice from the Allied military leaders, with the result
that the principle of a unified Allied command was not extended to Italy.
Cadorna was thus fatally remote from any adequate check.

Salandra's ministry was more conservative than the Chamber or
Senate. Though he brought in the radical Carcano and the liberal Orlando in October 1914, and the ex-republican irredentist Barzilai in the
summer of 1915, it was nearer one-party government than had been
customary. Neither Salandra nor the king even set eyes on Giolitti for
some years after May 1915, for this "leader of the opposition," though
a salaried deputy, did not turn up in parliament until November 1917.
Parliament was in fact of no importance whatsoever during the war,
and government by decree was more extensively adopted than in other
belligerent countries.

§�

Italy had hoped to find Austria on her last legs, and was disagreeably
surprised when Russia's withdrawal from Galicia after her defeat at
Gorlice in May 1915 let Austria switch more troops to the south. Ironically enough, this German advance against Russia had begun the day
before Italy denounced the Triple Alliance, and hundreds of thousands
of Russians were taken prisoner in the next three weeks before Italy
declared war. Salandra admits that, had this been known in time, Italy
might not have intervened at all.

The main Italian activity was along the River Isonzo, and here the
mountains and a lack of munitions made Cadorna's task particularly
difficult. Though his army was superior by three or four to one, the war

settled down into a dozen successive battles for position which left him about where he had begun. On the Carso tableland beyond the Isonzo there were numerous caves and other natural defenses which hindered the conversion of any tactical success into a big strategic victory. Cadorna had also based his strategy on active Serb co-operation against Austria, but Sonnino had never intended this when he arranged the Treaty of London. The Serbs had in the interim discovered Sonnino's intention to annex Dalmatia, and as they therefore feared their Italian ally even more than they feared Austria, they understandably concentrated against the "brigands" in Albania near the Italian beachhead at Valona. Sonnino's Dalmatian ambitions had clearly been misconceived: they had been opposed by Cadorna, for he guessed that they would be a military liability, and now they were also proving a political disaster.

The first major movement on the Italian front was in May 1916, an Austrian offensive in the Trentino down the Brenta and Adige valleys. Cadorna claimed to have known about it well in advance, but evidently he had believed that the mountains and the single-track railroad would prevent any great concentration against him. The Austrians on this occasion penetrated within six miles of the Venetian plain, and to crown their victory they captured and executed the irredentists Chiesa and Battisti for being Austrian-born subjects fighting for Italy.

As a result of this reverse Salandra fell, though three months earlier he had received an overwhelming vote of confidence. On his own confession, after twelve months of war the Italian defenses were still most defective. The faith of the country was shaken, and some of the deputies had not forgiven the way he had stampeded them into war. The prime minister was not a man who easily made himself liked, but he treated parliament with quite unnecessary disdain, and quarreled seriously with Cadorna. His unforgivable error was to have gambled on the war being over by early in 1916, and Italians were now beginning to find that Giolitti's warnings had been amply justified.

Salandra's successor was Boselli, an undistinguished trimmer of the Right Center, than whom no one could have been less suitable as a war leader. This time, Giolitti's advice was not even asked by the king. Seventy-eight years old, perhaps the oldest deputy in parliament, Boselli was a nonentity and a stopgap. Bonomi—who was in a position to know —seriously but ingenuously recorded that a younger man was avoided lest he might impose a strong will on the cabinet. Boselli's lack of personality nevertheless permitted a coalition which extended from Meda of the Catholics, through Sonnino and Orlando, to the radicals Sacchi and Carcano, and to Bonomi and Bissolati of the reformist socialists. On paper this looked like a broad expression of national feeling, however useless for the taking of the quick and decisive action that is necessary in war. Only the independent socialists failed to join in the general satisfaction over his appointment.

The Austrian offensive was contained by desperate fighting, and then in June the coincidence of Brussilov's offensive in the East with a British offensive on the Somme brought some relief. In August a forward movement under General Capello and Colonel Badoglio then proved that, with careful preparation and readiness to take losses, positions which had defied assault for fifteen months could be won in a few hours. The capture of Gorizia was one of the signal Allied successes of the year. But then the war settled down once again into the situation typified by D'Annunzio's isolated and irresponsible raids by land, sea, and air. The propaganda value of D'Annunzio had demanded that he be given what was virtually a quite independent command in all three services at once. He was ecstatically happy in this freelance life with all the limelight, though he lamented that no more than three medals were allowed for gallantry, since he thought he deserved at least six.

This counteroffensive on the Carso was reassuring not only to Italian morale, but also to the Allies. Lack of mutual confidence had here been deepened through political differences. For example, the Allies wanted Greece as a belligerent to offset Bulgaria's entry into the war, but Sonnino feared Greek aspirations in southern Albania, and antagonized the Greeks by suddenly proclaiming Albania an Italian protectorate in June 1917. Another difference arose over the fact that Italy was at war only with Austria-Hungary; and France and Britain therefore arranged between themselves the eventual partition of the Turkish empire in the Sykes-Picot agreement of April–May 1916. To regularize this anomalous position, Boselli did what Salandra had always refused to do, and declared war on Germany in August 1916. A settlement then reached at St. Jean de Maurienne in April 1917 recognized Italian claims against Turkey, but it was never fully ratified, and so a fruitful source of disagreement was left over until after the war.

§❧

Toward the end of 1917 Italy suffered a disastrous military reverse which some ascribed to poor morale. There had been much defeatism among both civilians and soldiers enervated by a static war that was already much longer than anyone had intended. Italians fought well enough, but great numbers of them had entered the war reluctantly and without feeling involved. The prefects as well as the deputies were largely Giolitti's nominees, and this helped to make local co-operation unenthusiastic. There were bread riots at Turin in the summer of 1917, with forty-one deaths recorded. Shortages and restrictions caused a lowering of civilian morale, which inevitably affected the soldiers, and unsavory legends were current at the front about the *pescecani* or sharks who made fortunes out of war profiteering.

Clerical pacifism was so strong that Pope Benedict XV called for a "white peace" without annexations, and his unequivocal reference to "useless carnage" received wide publicity and was much deplored in Allied circles. The Pope was here strangely at one with the official socialists, but the socialists' slogan, "Oppose the war, but do not sabotage it," palpably reflected their internal differences of opinion. Turati, in his gradual rise to respectability, moved toward the view that the proletariat had more to lose from defeat than from fighting. A pacifist deputation was nevertheless sent to the international socialist congresses of Zimmerwald in 1915 and Kienthal in 1916, and the maximalist majority in the socialist party helped to disaffect those important cities like Milan and Bologna which had socialist administrations. Later, it was found necessary to imprison Lazzari and Bombacci, the secretary and vice-secretary of the party.

The defeat at Caporetto was not altogether unconnected with this crumbling of morale. Cadorna wrote of the cowardice of the Second Army in a shameful communiqué, though his solicitude for military honor demanded that defeat be attributed primarily to "red" and "black" propaganda. General Caneva's later inquiry into the catastrophe attributed the shattered confidence of the troops quite as much to what Sforza called Cadorna's "mystical sadism," for the commander was even accused of having soldiers shot in decimations for crimes committed when some of the victims were absent. He had never believed in catering to the comfort of his men. Furthermore, senior officers were rendered nervous and irritable by the fact that scores of generals had been suddenly and without explanation relieved of their commands. Basically, however, the defeat was due to poor generalship by Cadorna himself. In October 1917 certain regiments under Badoglio's command gave way; when other units retired to cover the breach thus made, a rumor suddenly spread that all was lost, and the general rout began.

Considered dispassionately, this was a straightforward military defeat. Cadorna had been too isolated to sense what was afoot, and Boselli was too invertebrate to criticize the conduct of operations adequately. Lloyd George and Foch both agreed that poor organization and staff work were chiefly responsible. Cadorna had disagreed seriously with his corps commander, General Capello, and the wiseacres tried to point some deep moral from the fact that the former was a clerical and the latter a Freemason. Both of them later wrote books to try to justify themselves against each other, and both were later dismissed by the government for their alleged mistakes. Caneva's report showed that the Second Army had been too much a law unto itself, since despite the collapse of the Eastern front after the Russian revolution it had persisted in offensive plans. Too little attention had been paid to the formation of reserves and the technique of defense in depth, and units had repeatedly been incited to gain territory even if this left them in an untenable position.

The situation had further been changed by the surprise arrival of German troops on the Austrian front, and one young German officer who particularly distinguished himself was Erwin Rommel. Their attack was directed first against Caporetto, a small Alpine market town where the angle made by Italian defenses was too sharp. This point was chosen because a good road and railway led back to Cividale, and once there an advancing column could quickly turn the flank of the whole Isonzo line. The movement began in the early hours of October 24, achieving tactical surprise against slightly demoralized troops, and by midday the Italians were in full retreat. It was a tremendous collapse when seven hundred thousand men had to fall back so suddenly for a hundred miles, and on the River Tagliamento there were not enough bridges to carry them. Only by a herculean effort was this penetration into the plain of Lombardy halted at Monte Grappa beyond the River Piave.

The psychological impact of this retreat was enormous. The king even mentioned the word abdication. But among politicians, when confronted with an actual invasion even Turati and Treves spoke of resistance to the last, and for the first time in history the Italian people stood together almost as one. Giolitti, too, gave up his backstage pacifism. The futile Professor Boselli gave way in October 1917 to the Sicilian Professor Orlando—again Giolitti was not consulted—and Nitti from the radical Left was included as finance minister in a reshuffled cabinet. Cadorna was succeeded by Diaz, a Neapolitan of Spanish ancestry, who took some thought for the welfare of his men and set up propaganda offices to tell the soldiers about the conduct and purpose of the war. Diaz also tried hard through people like Sforza and Wickham Steed to make Sonnino waive his political objections to co-operation with the Slavs, because such co-operation was still thought necessary by the general staff. The winter was then spent in consolidation, and in June 1918, to everyone's relief, the army successfully held a new push on the Piave.

As the war drew to a triumphant close on the various European fronts, the government overrode the advice of reluctant generals and pointedly ordered Diaz to advance. Orlando's view was that circumstances could not be better for taking such a risk, and everything should be staked on wiping out the memory of defeat. He pointed out how the

Allies now had the initiative, how Bulgaria had collapsed and a revolution was taking place in Austria, how even the Germans wanted an armistice. Exactly a year after Caporetto, on October 24, Caviglia's army therefore crossed the River Piave with Allied contingents in support. By the thirtieth they had reached the village of Vittorio Veneto from which the victory would derive its name, and a huge number of prisoners had been taken. On November 3 Trent was captured, and the navy landed in Trieste. Austria-Hungary was in complete dissolution and had to concede an armistice.

§

The war was over, and the belligerents could begin to count as much of the cost as was countable. By the end of 1918 Italy claimed to have put five million men under arms, fifty thousand of whom had fought on the French front, and she had made an immense industrial effort. The number of combatants killed is sometimes given as nearly seven hundred thousand, but General Caneva's commission put it as a good deal less. Financially, the drain had been enormous. The yearly imports, which in 1914 had been valued at three billion lire, were running three years later at fourteen billion, and this total was covered only to one-third or less by exports. Meanwhile, the current figures for state expenditure had multiplied in an alarming ratio:

	million lire
1913–14	2,287
1914–15	5,224
1915–16	10,550
1918–19	30,857

The Treasury announced in 1930 that the final figure for the cost of the whole war had been 148 billion lire, that is to say twice the sum of all government expenditure between 1861 and 1913.

This total is a symbol for an enormous consumption of energy and natural resources, in return for which Italy obtained little joy and much grief. A great deal of idealism had gone into the war on Italy's part, and much elevated patriotism, but one need not look many years beyond 1918 to see that it had been one of the great disasters of her history. A plot hatched by Salandra, which also involved the king, had irresponsibly exploited the patriotism of Italians. He and his friends had been forced to keep their plot secret, and so had neglected to notice certain quite elementary miscalculations which criticism could have brought out. A secondary result of the constitutional weakness which allowed this to happen was that Italy suffered twenty-five years of revolution and tyranny.

38 The Peace Settlement, 1918-1920

United as never before, Italy had made a notable contribution in the last stages of Allied victory, but internal squabbles reopened at once, and this weakened her position at the peace conference. The sharp division of 1915 between interventionists and neutralists had continued under the surface of politics, and superimposed on it by 1918 was an equally fundamental division between those who claimed Dalmatia as Italian and those who renounced it.

Sonnino, who remained foreign minister continuously from 1914 to 1919, had no use for the "renouncers." In his eyes, liberating the submerged Slav nationalities would be to replace defeated Austria by a new enemy, since the names of Croat and Slovene recalled the hated units of the Austrian army which had played a cruel part during the *risorgimento.* Against much military and political advice, Sonnino therefore failed to meet with the Slavs and support their parallel claims against Austria. For him the Adriatic was *Il Golfo,* as in the days of Venetian hegemony. It was embarrassing as it was surprising to him that the Greeks and Yugoslavs had ended as his allies, for the Yugoslavs wanted Trieste and Dalmatia, while Greece rivaled Italy in her claims to Anatolia and the Dodecanese.

On the other hand, at least one minister, Leonida Bissolati, had openly advocated the breakup of Austria-Hungary into its national constituent elements. As a good Mazzinian, Bissolati could not deny to others in the Dodecanese and Albania the self-determination which Italy claimed in Trent. When in June 1917 Sonnino declared his protectorate over Albania, Bissolati had resigned, especially as this declaration had not first been put even to the cabinet, but he subsequently withdrew his resignation lest a ministerial crisis should weaken Italy's position with her allies. As a result, this important difference of opinion was suppressed just at the moment when its discussion was most needed. Bissolati as a minister without portfolio was impotent, and decisions reached his ears only after the executive departments had already settled them. The cabinet had deliberately not been consulted when the Treaty of London promised Dalmatia to Italy, nor over this occupation of Albania, and hence a highly dangerous and controversial decision had been taken irresponsibly and without proper debate. Worse still, prime minister and foreign minister disagreed on many fundamental points; yet Orlando could not dismiss Sonnino without dissolving his coalition and allowing Giolitti back into power.

The defeat of Caporetto, however, had made Slav military help suddenly desirable, and in April 1918 Sonnino permitted a Congress of Oppressed Nationalities under Senator Ruffini to be convoked at Rome. From it emerged a "Pact of Rome," wherein was declared that the unity and independence of Yugoslavia was a vital interest of Italy. This declaration must have been of considerable help in the downfall of Austria, and although not promulgated officially by the Italian government, it was welcomed by Orlando the prime minister, and was regarded as at least semiofficial. The Italian delegation to the congress had been widely representative, and included such people as Albertini, Amendola, Barzilai, Federzoni, Mussolini, Prezzolini, and Salvemini.

Even though Bissolati's slavophile policy continued to meet strong opposition, some of the realists thus recognized that Italy would need the new Yugoslavia as a friend, and hence idealism and enlightened self-interest combined to recommend renouncing some Italian ambitions in the Adriatic. The *renunciatari* included men of such diverse sentiments as Giolitti and Turati, Nitti and Salvemini, and newspapers ranging from the *Corriere* to the *Secolo* and *Avanti*. On the other side, with Sonnino, were such groups as those attached to Mussolini, Barzilai, and D'Annunzio, who wanted their pound or more of flesh from the Treaty of London. Mussolini, as a signatory of the Pact of Rome, wished to have it both ways, and was already trying to be all things to all men.

§❧

The peace treaty with Austria was signed in September 1919 at St. Germain, and that with Hungary in June 1920 at the Trianon. Italy's main demands were based on the 1915 Treaty of London, but the situation had changed in the interim. For one thing the unexpected breakup of Austria-Hungary made Italy's domination of the Adriatic less essential for her security than it was in 1915, and it was in fact both unnecessary and unwise to press her old claims against the new successor states with whom Italy should have been on terms of friendship, not enmity. Furthermore, the United States had become a belligerent, and the State Department, not being bound by the Treaty of London any more than were the Serbs, stood squarely by President Wilson's fourteen points. Of these points, the ninth was quite repugnant to that treaty, as it stated that "a readjustment of the frontiers of Italy should be effected along clearly recognized lines of nationality." Sonnino was not formally committed by the fourteen points in his armistice with Austria, but Italy had exploited the victory value of Wilson's idealistic war aims, and the President's tumultuous reception in Rome suggested that ordinary Italians might prefer self-determination to the mere right of conquest and strategic advantage. Orlando himself, at the time of the Pact of Rome, was on record as having said that the Treaty of London was made against an enemy, Austria, and could not be invoked against a friend, Yugoslavia. But, the war once over, Sonnino increased rather than reduced his claims to the Dalmatian coast, perhaps in order to have something which could be surrendered in a compromise. Prime minister and foreign minister thus seemed to be in disagreement.

The American territorial experts opposed Italian claims upon the Dalmatian coast and its islands, as well as on the Dodecanese and much of Venezia Giulia. They even urged that the Upper Adige above Trent, although south of the Alps, should continue Austrian, since its inhabitants spoke German. Against this expert advice, and despite his cherished principles, Wilson decided entirely in Italy's favor regarding her northern frontier. He realistically acknowledged that here if anywhere a strategic boundary cut across the confines of nationality and language. Italy thus obtained the Brenner for her frontier, and annexed the Italian-speaking Trentino and German-speaking Alto Adige. In some sectors of her northeastern frontier, indeed, she obtained more than her due under the Treaty of London—for instance by the inclusion of Tarvis.

The eastern frontier was yet more confused, geographically, linguistically, and by historical tradition. The only safe generalization was that many of the cities had been predominantly Italian, the countryside Slav. Trieste itself was given to Italy without much debate. As the terminus of the *Südbahn,* and a great mercantile emporium for Central Europe, this annexation was a rich prize. It was not such an unqualified advantage for Trieste itself, since a political frontier now severed the Triestini from their German and Slav hinterland, leaving the city a head without a body and its inhabitants often without occupation.

On the other side of the Istrian peninsula, Fiume was more difficult. It had not featured among the usual Italian irredentist claims, not even in the Treaty of London where so much of the Dalmatian coast had been assigned to Italy. But in 1919 some of the nationalists for once joined with the *renunciatari* in renouncing their treaty claims on Slav-speaking Dalmatia if in exchange they could obtain Italian-speaking Fiume. The Italian peace delegation was divided on this point. Sonnino would have liked Dalmatia without Fiume; Orlando preferred Fiume to Dalmatia. In the end they demanded both, although the arguments for one might have seemed logically to exclude the other. This excess of appetite did Italy no service at the conference, and it played into the hands of those among the Serbs, Croats, and Slovenes who wished to sink their differences and form a state united against Italian imperialism. Orlando professed that he could not abandon Fiume lest a violent outburst in Italy should endanger peace. This irresponsible threat covered his real motive, which was partly one of pure prestige, and partly that if Fiume lay outside Italy it would destroy Trieste by becoming the main outlet for Central Europe and the Danubian lands.

There was obviously no boundary in Istria and Venezia Giulia which would satisfy both Italy and Yugoslavia, and Wilson was right to insist on compromise. But the so-called Wilson Line was propounded so tactlessly that Orlando played his reserve card and withdrew the Italian delegation from Paris. Wilson's recommendation offered considerable strategic and ethnic advantages to Italy, even exceeding her demands in some places. Thereunder she would have obtained most of the Istrian peninsula with Trieste and Pola, and all the railroads which connected Gorizia and Trieste to each other and to Italy. The fact that a quarter of a million Slavs would have come under Italian sovereignty proved once more that Wilson could be a realist who recognized that self-determination was no absolute shibboleth.

Italy's objection to this boundary was the omission of Italian-speaking Fiume and of the independent railroad which made that city more accessible than Trieste to the commerce of Vienna and Budapest. Wilson replied by saying that if self-determination applied to the city of Fiume apart from its Slav surroundings, then it might also apply to regions of New York City where there were many Italians, or even to Alto Adige where there were many Germans; in other words, that Italy could not have it both ways. Britain and France stood with him on this point, and intimated that, if Orlando persisted over Fiume, this would impair the rest of his case under the Treaty of London. Italian intransigence thus shook other Italian claims which might have gone unchallenged, and the result was that Fiume became a free state, and Wilson, from being the most revered of all men by the Italians, suddenly became the most detested.

Italian pretensions to the rest of the Dalmatian littoral were so sharply urged by Sonnino that in December 1918 Bissolati once more resigned from the cabinet. Whereas Sonnino said that he could not distinguish Yugoslavs from Austrians, Bissolati in a speech at La Scala in Milan drew attention to the simple fact that Yugoslavia existed and nothing Italy could do would alter the fact. This speech was made almost inaudible by nationalist agitators, since it betrayed the cause of "our Adriatic." In their eyes, Slav friendliness might have been welcome in the dark days of 1917, but now victory enabled the true national interests to be reasserted. These vocal nationalists may have been a negligible fraction of the population numerically (and their party won only ten seats in the 1921 election), but their influence was strong at the Court and in army and industrial circles. D'Annunzio had loudly proclaimed that the Slavs ought to be "slaves": "Dalmatia belongs to Italy by divine right as well as human law, by the grace of God who has designed the earth in such a way that every race can recognize its destiny therein carved out. . . . It was ours and shall be ours again. No German from the Alps, no Croat either caring nothing for history or else falsifying it, not even the Turk disguised as an Albanian, no one shall ever hold up the rhythm of fate, the Roman rhythm. . . . What can avail the brute force of the barbarians against the law of Rome!" Only a temporary access of sweet reasonableness enabled Italy to yield this point and sign the Treaty of Rapallo with Yugoslavia in 1920, momentarily renouncing her Dalmatian ambitions.

Italy also had designs on Asia Minor. Despite the rival claims of Greece, Sonnino fought to the last for Smyrna, and mutual differences on this point caused the resignation of several Italian representatives at Paris. Finally, Italian troops were landed at several places in Turkey on the plea of keeping order, and plans were even made for an expedition to the Caucasus. But Turkish resistance soon made it clear that there was to be no partition of Asia Minor after all, and the troops had to be withdrawn. By the Treaty of Lausanne with Turkey, in July 1923, Italy had no more than her sovereignty confirmed over the Dodecanese Islands where she had ruled *de facto* since 1912.

The colonial settlement was affected by Article 13 of the Treaty of London whereby Italy should have *compensations équitables* if her allies extended their colonies. Italian statesmen were chiefly concerned about frontier adjustments with Tunisia and Egypt; they also would have liked Kassala in the Sudan which Italy had ceded to Britain in 1897; and if only Eritrea could be linked with Somaliland, there were chances of dominating Abyssinia as well. Nevertheless, the fact that during the war Italy had undertaken no colonial campaign whatever, and had even been forced to withdraw from most of Libya, made it seem improbable that she had sufficient interest or sufficient resources for much extension of colonial territory. Another handicap was that her delegates at the peace conference were of several minds about colonial expansion.

The Allies, not with much good grace, admitted the justice of compensations, and when Balfour announced the appointment of a committee to consider them, Orlando expressed himself content. Again, when the German colonies were finally distributed as mandates to other countries, Orlando entered no demurrer. Personally, he was not much interested. He wanted instead to yield on the matter of colonies so as to establish his right to compensation nearer home, for his own over-mastering concern was still the Adriatic, and he was also persuaded that the reconquest of Libya would be expensive enough without inviting more colonial responsibilities. In the end he therefore signed the German and Austrian treaties before obtaining satisfaction on the colonial question. Italy received only Jarabub and Jubaland from Britain, and some minor French concessions on the frontiers of Libya and Eritrea ten years later. With these results fascist Italy was altogether unsatisfied.

In sum, as a result of these treaties, the Italian mainland was extended by about nine thousand square miles, winning most of the 1915 program but by no means all. Her hitherto most vulnerable frontier now was extended to run from the Brenner to Monte Nevoso, which was more than self-determination would have allowed, and rocks and glaciers contributed to form a new natural barrier for several hundred kilometers. Mussolini's newspaper—which was to veer abruptly when the wind changed—rejoiced at this consummation, delighted that all the roads by which the German barbarians had invaded Italy down the centuries were now firmly barred. Even more than this, whereas France was still confronted by an undivided Germany, Italy's hereditary enemy was now but a cipher. Instead of Austria-Hungary with fifty-one million subjects, there was Austria with six million and Yugoslavia with twelve. One of the more perceptive Italian foreign ministers, Count Sforza, expressing a view which other Italians would have done well to ponder, concluded that Italy was the nation to win most from the war.

This was not the same as being satisfied, because Italian war aims, unlike those of her allies, were mainly territorial, and if judged by territorial results the outcome of modern wars must seem quite incommensurate with the sacrifices demanded. Inestimable potential benefits were gained, but these were obscured by mismanagement of the bitter controversy over Fiume and the Adriatic. As Salandra at least recognized, absolute national security was impossible without complete domination in that area, and this was inconceivable. On the contrary, once the intoxicating illusion of Vittorio Veneto had passed, Italy to her surprise found herself playing a minor role at the peace conference. The brutal fact was not that her allies deserted her, not that she had "lost the peace"—these were artificial and unscrupulous nationalistic legends—but that the collapse of the Central Powers in 1918 prevented her acting as the makeweight in the balance of Europe. It was the war rather than the peace which defeated her. The war revealed what in normal times skillful diplomacy could conceal, that Italy was a great power by moral and not by physical authority.

The Italians were scarcely treated with complete fairness at the peace settlement, but later propaganda exaggerated their disappointment in order to exploit it. A peace conference is hardly the time for perfect justice, and most of the other belligerents had lost incomparably more than justice would have allowed. One must add that the Italian representatives were unbending and feckless in negotiation. It was no doubt unfair and tactless when, in April 1919, Wilson appealed to Italian public opinion over the head of Orlando, seeming to imply that the latter was not representative of his country. But Orlando did not improve matters by stumping huffily out of the conference, and waiting two weeks at Rome in the hope of being given an apology and asked to state his conditions. Fearing that Italy might be left to sign a separate treaty, he and Sonnino had to pocket their pride and return, just in time to witness the presentation of the peace proposals to Germany, and without the opportunity of putting the Italian case on controversial points.

Orlando and Sonnino had hoped that their importunity would force the conference to yield, and they therefore did not trouble to explain tactfully the historical, economic, and strategic grounds upon which their demands were based. By comparison, the Yugoslav memoranda were more subtle and calculated to please the American president. Italy lacked first-rate leaders, not for the first time since the death of Cavour, and her ruling coalition always included many divergent points of view —her traditional system of government made this almost inevitable. The Italian case was therefore clumsily presented. No doubt, too, the people of Italy were confused about their genuine national interests and misled by sentimental considerations. Certainly they were no more selfish than the other belligerents. But had they renounced generously in 1919 what they were forced to yield to Yugoslavia in 1920, these concessions might have enabled them to bargain for less illusory economic advantages.

As Sonnino talked so much of territorial acquistion, the Allies were given no help in understanding that the most vital needs of Italy were economic, and neither did Sonnino begin to realize this himself. In 1915 Italy's fixation on frontiers had obscured her need for adequate financial and economic help, and again in 1919, for precisely the same reason, questions of raw materials and of wider Italian economic interests in the Mediterranean were completely neglected. In this strange world of exaggerated sentimental nationalism, Sonnino thought it undignified to ask for a loan, but apparently not at all undignified to ask for a piece of someone else's territory which had not even been conquered. He had not apparently appreciated how far Italy had been dependent on her allies for munitions, nor how much the feeding of Italy through the war had been helped by the Allied Wheat Executive, nor did he realize how only the unlimited credit given to Italy by her allies had kept Italian currency stable during the war. This made the rude awakening in 1919 all the more of a shock. There are indeed many instructive lessons to be learned from the contrast between Italy's economic collapse after victory in 1918 and her recovery after defeat in 1943.

39 New Political Currents 1919

The end of the war brings us to the question of why Italy, so proud of her liberties, should have been the first important European country to succumb beneath the tidal wave of fascism. Postwar problems were everywhere difficult, but in Italy the ruling classes were so bewildered that they lost both control over events and confidence in themselves. The programs of each party and politician show little evidence of the imagination and honesty that the situation required, but successive governments connived at illegal and revolutionary actions for dark purposes of their own and played up popular discontent merely for tactical reasons of domestic or foreign policy. Liberals and antiliberals alike, and particularly those people who had been guilty of dragging an unwilling Italy into the war, devised the myth of an Italy cheated of her due in 1919 by other nations. The gain achieved by the destruction of Austria-Hungary was deliberately minimized, and popular dissatisfaction with the treaty deliberately aggravated, with the intention of influencing Europe still further in their favor.

Italy had been psychologically damaged by the defeat of Caporetto, emotionally overexcited by the sudden triumph of Vittorio Veneto, and then depressed again when the peace did not bring the utopia which irresponsible leaders had promised. Inflation was meanwhile undermining middle-class security, and this helped to break the tacit agreement between classes which Giolitti had created in the prosperous and expanding prewar world. The astonishing number of one hundred and fifty thousand deserters from the forces were in hiding, and were once more raising the serious problem of brigandage in the provinces. Demobilization caused yet another unbalancing anticlimax and created widespread unemployment just when the old remedy of emigration was becoming impossible, and a dangerously large number of generals who did not adjust themselves easily to the pedestrian and ill-rewarded tranquillity of civilian life had to be retired on half pay. Allied economic help dried up almost immediately, leaving Italy billions of dollars in debt. Wheat subsidies for farmers, steel subsidies to the heavily overcapitalized war industries, bread subsidies for consumers, all helped to increase inflation and the budgetary deficit, and yet were insufficient to relieve distress.

Only a government possessed of courage, vision, and popular approval could have met such a situation. But once again there was the inevitable parliamentary paralysis in which no government had a reliable working majority, and politicians inevitably resorted to tactical maneuvering from one side to the other for their parliamentary support. By ill chance there was one Italian who had the correct combination of ability, fascination, and unscrupulousness to exploit this situation to the utmost.

Benito Mussolini was born in 1883, the son of a socialist blacksmith, and of peasant rather than bourgeois origin. He was named after Benito Juárez, the Mexican revolutionary who had executed the Emperor Maximilian in 1867, as his brother Arnaldo was named after Arnold of Brescia who had once led a revolution at Rome against the Church. During his youth he was too insignificant for many reliable facts to have survived. But like Crispi, that other anticlerical, Mussolini was brought up in a Catholic seminary, from which he had at last to be expelled by the Salesian fathers after he had stabbed a fellow pupil. Again like Crispi, his upbringing made him a displaced intellectual and revolutionary. In 1901 he graduated as an elementary schoolmaster, and henceforth he passed among his socialist friends for a "professor" who tried to play the violin and who wrote jejune essays on German literature. There is some evidence that he could not control the boys in his class.

Mussolini in those days opposed military service, and so emigrated to Switzerland in 1902 to avoid the draft. There he held a quick succession of jobs, among others that of errand boy for a wine merchant. He was arrested in July 1902 for begging in the streets of Lausanne, and was expelled from one canton after another for holding a forged passport. His belief in illegal action, learned from the anarchists and republicans of his native Romagna, was now refined and formalized by reading Sorel and Nietzsche. Among other occupations he probably attended a course of lectures by Pareto in Lausanne and discovered Pareto's theory of the new elite rising to supplant the decadent humanitarians of parliamentary democracy.

Angelica Balabanoff knew Mussolini well in Switzerland, and she has left a graphic picture of a dirty, unkempt vagrant, who slept under bridges and cheated his fellows, but who thought of himself as a privileged intellectual and who would rather do no work than manual work. She had small regard for him as a socialist and saw that he was moved rather by the desire for recognition and for revenge against society. She had met his type before, a man as violent in word as he was insincere in belief and a coward in deed. Even disparaging words made him happy provided he was noticed in some fashion. He was afraid of walking home alone by night. He told her that he meant one day to write something more frightful and hair-raising than Poe, and the book would be called "Perversion." He was of the crude, loudmouthed, soapbox-orator kind, with obvious signs of instability and hysteria. The picture is no doubt overdrawn, but recognizable.

Mussolini returned to Italy in 1904 and modified his principles (not for the last time) so far as to undergo military service. He then took up what always remained his primary interest, journalism, and worked hard as a local organizer for the socialist party. At Trent he was secretary of the Chamber of Labor and in those days actively fought against Battisti and the nationalists. In view of his later pose as a patriot, one may note that in 1911 he was jailed for condemning Italian imperialism in Libya, when he called the national tricolor "a rag to be planted on a dunghill." He was in prison more than once for agitation. Between 1910 and 1912 he edited a pseudo-Marxist magazine called *The Class Struggle,* and he produced an anticlerical book on *John Huss, the Man of Truth.* All these activities in later years he tried to conceal.

As a result of party divisions in 1912, Mussolini, as editor of *Avanti,* became with Lazzari the most outstanding personality in Italian socialism. Yet, in retrospect he seems less like a socialist than like that typical product of the most anarchic and revolutionary province of Italy, the Romagnol tyrant, a petty Renaissance despot in modern dress. Among socialists he inclined to the belief of Babeuf and Blanqui in violent insurrection by a minority in order to establish authoritarian rule. His articles reveal a retreat from belief in class solidarity, and a growing attachment to revolution for revolution's sake, power for the sake of power. In this he was gradually to be joined by many miscellaneous malcontents of Right and Left.

A few weeks after the outbreak of war in 1914 he veered around abruptly and completely from ardent neutralism to ardent intervention, instinctively sensing that war would be a highroad to revolution. In return for this change, Ansaldo and the sugar and electrical industries helped him to publish a paper of his own, *Il Popolo d'Italia,* with a quotation from Blanqui on its front page. Most of the war years he spent as a journalist. For a while he was in uniform, attaining like Hitler the rank of corporal, and the self-dramatization of his heroism was to be a feature of official biographies. With a gusty humorlessness, not unworthy of Baron Munchausen, he described to Emil Ludwig how he was " 'so badly wounded that it was impossible for me to be moved! One of the newspapers had mentioned where I was laid up. Thereupon the Austrians shelled the hospital.' 'Is it true that when they performed a necessary operation you refused to take chloroform?' He nodded affirmatively." This dramatic posturing, another characteristic shared with Crispi, was typical of Mussolini's megalomania. He may have been a moderately good soldier, but the more likely story is that he was wounded after grenade practice and did not take part in any serious military engagement.

Fascism began as a Milanese and not a national movement, when late in March 1919 two hundred discontented zealots met at Milan in the Piazza San Sepolcro. They were still socialists of a sort, and their program is interesting in the light of later fascist developments—it included death duties, a heavy capital levy, an 80 per cent tax on war profits, workers sharing in industrial management, and confiscation of unused houses and ecclesiastical property. Mussolini had been envious of the bolsheviks, and for a while fancied himself as the Lenin of Italy. He still talked the language of expropriating exploiters and seizing the factories as a first step in social revolution. But in the general elections of November he discovered that this line had little appeal and no future. Not a single fascist was successful (Mussolini himself had also been unsuccessful in 1913), and they polled less than 5,000 votes against 170,000 for the socialists at Milan. Several assistant editors of *Il Popolo d'Italia* protested against Mussolini's appropriation of funds which the paper had collected from America for D'Annunzio's conquest of Fiume. Most fascists now resigned, and Mussolini's career seemed at an end.

This catastrophic electoral failure was partly due to fascism being such a medley of different ideas and tendencies. Balbo was a republican, Bianchi a syndicalist, but De Vecchi and De Bono were monarchists and conservatives. Marinetti wanted to expel the Pope from Italy, but Grandi and De Vecchi were to finish up with honorific titles from the Vatican. Nenni was another adherent in these early days before he became the leader of Italian socialism. Toscanini was a fascist candidate in 1919, though he later rebelled when they tried to make him introduce the fascist song *Giovinezza* into his concerts, and Puccini too in his last years welcomed the new movement. Idealism and gangsterism were thus in familiar harness.

Only when these elections showed the folly of competing with the official socialists for working-class support did Mussolini reveal his true colors as those of pure opportunism and change to the conservative side. His only consistency was in the use of violent means for the pursuit of power, and the agrarian disorders of Emilia and the Po Valley soon gave him the chance to launch a civil war against the socialists who in 1914 had thrown him out of their party and defeated him in the elections of 1919. Gangsterism came out on top once electoral failure had turned him not only against socialism but against the parliamentary system itself.

§♠

Far more successful than fascism in 1919 were the two mass parties, the socialists and the *popolari* or Christian democrats. The leader of the *popolari* was Don Sturzo, a Sicilian priest, whose sincerity, moderation, and administrative capacity at last welded many Catholics into a political party of their own. Another young enthusiast alongside him was Alcide de Gasperi. This revival of Christian democracy—different only in degree from that which Pius X had condemned early in the century— seemed to augur well. Unlike Murri, Sturzo had not rebelled against condemnation, but had quietly submitted until the time was ripe for a Catholic movement which also tried to be democratic.

The new party which launched its manifesto in January 1919 had been formed in no wise on papal initiative. Benedict XV, one of the wisest among modern Popes, avoided ecclesiastical intrusion, but gave incidental assistance by finally lifting the *non expedit* and so letting Catholics vote more freely. Technically, there was no official connection with the Church, but Sturzo, though not a conservative himself, was strictly orthodox and obedient, and his party was thus the more open to influence from the conservatives who, especially after the death of Benedict in 1922, predominated in ecclesiastical circles. Pius XI did not speak ex cathedra on politics, yet on "mixed questions" he was always the judge, and here he could often touch politics by implication. Moreover, disobedience to his private and fallible communications would rank, if not as mortal sin, at least as very close to the sin of pride. Hence Don Sturzo's position was often rendered ambiguous and ineffective.

The *popolari* were a mass party inclined if anything to the Left. Their official program included theoretical plans for condemning imperialism, introducing proportional representation and votes for women, and for dividing up big estates among the peasants; an extreme wing around Miglioli was almost Marxist. Their leaders knew that only a sympathetic attitude toward agrarian strikes would win the allegiance of the agricultural laborers on whom they depended. By 1920 trade unions associated with the *popolari* had one million people inscribed, and though the rival socialist unions boasted over two million, it was the Christian association which included most agricultural workers. In the fight against socialism the *popolari* would have been far more effective than Mussolini, but Pius XI was to choose wrongly and let in seven devils worse than the first.

The elections of 1919 gave this Catholic party the remarkable number of one hundred deputies in parliament, yet their weakness was that they spoke with no single voice. Along with genuine social reformers, they comprehended some conservatives and reactionaries, and therefore each party congress fought shy of any practical policy which might cause a split. Miglioli's proposal to collaborate with the socialists was rejected, and although Sturzo resisted those at the other extreme like Padre Gemelli who wanted his movement to become strictly confessional, political tactics dictated an attempt to try to include the moderate Right as well as the moderate Left. Any suspicion of affinity between *popolari* and socialists was embarrassing to Pius XI in 1922. So perhaps was their emblem, a shield carrying the word *Libertas,* for this sounded too much like what the syllabus of 1864 had condemned as a cardinal error.

In sum, although strong enough to hamper other parties, the *popolari* were not themselves sufficiently united to have the influence on politics which their number and quality deserved. The one thing common to all of them was opposition to the anticlerical liberals who had almost monopolized Italian government since the time of Cavour. They might allow a tactical alliance with liberalism, but they were particularly conscious of their new power and were determined to use it to see that this oligarchic minority of liberals should now take more note of the Catholic populace over whom they had uncomprehendingly ruled for so long. The *popolari* thus too often played an unfortunately negative and disintegrating role in parliament and so were easily dissolved by Mussolini after a brief life. It was a great tragedy (as it was also a reflection on both parties) that both they and the Giolittians preferred to ally with fascism against each other rather than with each other against fascism.

§

In 1919 the real rival to the *popolari* was not fascism but socialism. Socialism flourished mainly in the big industrial centers, Milan, Turin, and Genoa, where the war had concentrated many workers in factories, and also in the Romagna where there were Mazzinian and anarchist traditions of rebellion and unrest. By 1919 large groups in industry had an eight-hour day. The membership of the socialist party had risen from 50,000 before the war to 200,000 in 1919, readers of *Avanti* to 300,000, and trade-union membership in the Confederation of Labor from half a million to two million. In the November elections the official socialists raised their representation in parliament from 50 to 156, and after the local elections of 1920 the party and the Chambers of Labor controlled some two thousand municipalities as well as twenty-six provinces out of sixty-nine. It was easily the largest party in Italy and, at least more than any other, was organized and disciplined. Here was something quite new in Italian history, and many people took fright at it.

Italy's misfortune was that socialism lacked responsible leadership, and from the benches on the Left hardly a single constructive step was proposed which went beyond the vaguest generalization. The only constant factor among the socialists was their association of violent language with a timid uncertainty in deed, and this was bad tactics as well as self-deception. They positively refused to collaborate against fascism with the governments of Nitti, Giolitti, and Bonomi in turn, and so doing they made a right-wing victory almost inevitable. Yet they had little idea of effecting a communist revolution on their own. They simply sat back under the cosy illusion that time was on their side and that universal suffrage inevitably signified the approaching end of liberalism and the dictatorship of the proletariat. There was no hurry to carry out reforms, no need to compromise or win allies, no obligation even to make their policy attractive or practicable. Even a moderate such as Turati shared these views. He did not like the idea of cooperating with the old ruling classes, but argued that those who had involved Italy in the war should be left alone to take responsibility for its results.

The language of socialism nevertheless continued full of sound and fury signifying very little, and a fierce proclamation by the party executive in December 1918 announced that they aimed at a socialist republic and the dictatorship of the proletariat. The original Genoa program of 1892 had allowed the party to work inside the existing institutions of government, but this was modified first by Mussolini in 1912 and again more uncompromisingly when the "maximalists" triumphed in the sixteenth party congress at Bologna in October 1919. The so-called reformist section led by Turati and Treves was there outvoted by four to one, and the congress decided that "the proletariat must have recourse to the use of violence for the conquest of power over the bourgeoisie. . . . The existing institutions of local and national government cannot in any way be transformed into organs which will help to liberate the people.

Instead we must use new and proletarian organizations such as workers' soviets, and we must adhere to the Third International." Turati prophetically warned the congress that if their provocative propaganda for expropriation ever forced the dominant class to counterattack, "then goodbye to parliamentary action and goodbye to the socialist party," for such a challenge would gratuitously arouse the self-protective instincts of many otherwise well-intentioned people. Unfortunately, the point was not well received.

Most of those who spoke airily of a dictatorship by the proletariat did not know what they meant, or at least did not mean what they said; such alarmist statements merely gave them a pleasant illusion of power. The submerged half of Italy was seething with excitement in 1919 as they discovered at long last that they could stand up to the bosses and terrify them. Minor communist risings took place, the "red days of Mantua" for instance, but were isolated and unco-ordinated. All bark and no bite, they needlessly provoked counterrevolutionary reprisals. The socialists may have taken pleasure in feeling themselves to be feared, but they soon had to pay for their pleasure when Mussolini discovered that his gangs could break up the printing presses of *Avanti* without the police or the other liberal newspapers acting as though he had done wrong.

Lenin and Trotsky, like Sorel, were mystified by this folly and incompetence. Despite their great number, despite the sporadic general strikes and local peasant revolts, the Italian socialists were just waiting for the bourgeois state to fall into their lap instead of themselves trying to coerce events. Some of them admitted later that the conditions had existed for a Russian type of revolution. But with the expulsion of the syndicalists and of Mussolini they had lost much of their revolutionary zeal. During the war they had been pacifists and defeatists, and this had evidently damaged party morale. They went on mouthing the orthodox formulas of their religion, but many of them remained pacifists at heart and had developed a sneaking sympathy for liberal-democratic methods. The socialists in parliament were more moderate than the maximalists who had captured the party itself, and above all the powerful Confederation of Labor voted in February 1920 against hastening the day of proletarian dictatorship.

One must conclude that socialism did not believe wholeheartedly in either revolution or collaboration, and hence it was merely going to provoke fascism and antagonize all straightforward patriots, without taking the only sort of action which could defend Italy against the inevitable counterattack from the Right.

40 Nitti and
the Rape of Fiume, 1919-1920

The war ministry of Orlando lasted until June 1919, when its mismanagement of the peace negotiations was the pretext for a parliamentary
defeat by 262 votes to 78. Nitti, the southern radical, then became prime
minister for a year at the head of three successive cabinets. Francesco
Nitti was a professor of political economy who had written profusely on
economic problems. He was certainly honest and well-meaning, and he
was sensible enough to veto Orlando's extraordinary plan to send an
expedition to the Black Sea for the conquest of Soviet Georgia. But he
was too academic, too much the journalist, and had become facile and
rhetorical in his political views. Often hasty and unsound in judgment,
he was also prone to acid sarcasm, and this made many enemies among
the miscellaneous radicals and liberals who might have given him a
majority.

In an attempt to bargain with the socialists, Nitti gave way more than
most liberals liked. He did not see sufficiently that Italy was in a fervor
of nationalism and militant class consciousness which would make
the former kind of coalition government particularly hard. The old system of intricate coalitions had worked best with many small groups, and
was far less practicable now that a wide suffrage had created mass
parties of Catholics, nationalists, and socialists. Unlike the prewar varieties of Left and Right, these new mass parties believed more in doctrine
than in personalities, so that transformism was less easy, and yet none of
them was large enough for any alternative possibility of party government to emerge. The old ruling class, too, was now radically divided.

Parliamentary institutions were therefore in danger of no longer working at all, and only the military rule of the war years had concealed the
fact. During this military interregnum, parliament had seldom met and
even taxes had sometimes been raised by simple decree. As a result,
traditions of parliamentary behavior had been lost. Giolitti had formerly
known how to bind the selfish interests of almost every denomination to
his chariot: his complex electoral system had extended everywhere, and
his use of patronage yoked pressure groups, municipal cliques, trade
unionists, the landed families, even sometimes the parish priest, in common harness. This machine had now broken down. Parliament was filling
with new men of whose private weaknesses there was no account in the

government dossiers. Moreover, Nitti personally was antipathetic to Giolitti and many other liberals, while his accession to power was hailed by the communist Gramsci as the counterpart of Kerensky's in Russia, denoting the incipient collapse of the Italian bourgeois state.

§●

Nitti's plan to form another Left Center ministry made it necessary to hold a long-overdue election, for which, under Catholic and socialist pressure, he introduced the new method of proportional representation. By instituting large constituencies and large party lists, Nitti's electoral law aimed to sever the often reprehensible attachment between deputies and local pressure cliques, and no doubt the new method also produced a more exact representation of the people. Among other things it increased the power of party leaders who now could choose to accept a name or omit it from their list. This reform was approved by a majority of 277 against 38, though many of the older parliamentary leaders, for instance Salandra, Boselli, and Luzzatti, abstained from the vote.

Sonnino opposed proportional representation; so did Giolitti, though he did not trouble to come to Rome and vote against it. The new constituencies would be far too large for the immediate sympathies or comprehension of the people. Lists of candidates were now to be pre-selected by a party caucus, and deputies were to be elected en bloc without their individual character or intelligence being appreciated by voters. The number of small parties was not thereby reduced. Although the liberals were weakened, the mass parties were strengthened, and the general effect was once again to make either transformism or single-party government more difficult. Significantly enough, the *Popolo d'Italia* welcomed this reform, though Mussolini tried later to conceal the fact; and indeed, according to Giolitti, proportional representation was indirectly going to be one of the chief causes of ultimate fascist victory.

The elections of November 1919 were run with quite unusual fairness by Nitti, but their results showed how very important formerly in securing a working majority had been the unscrupulous use of government influence. The real victors turned out to be the official socialists and the *popolari*—one reason undoubtedly being that they had both tended to oppose the war. Together these new parties made up just over half the Chamber, and, as the socialists were always in opposition, this left the Catholics as arbiters of the parliamentary scene. Fifty years after 1870 the wheel had come full circle. The old liberals had been hopelessly riven between neutralists and interventionists, renouncers and imperialists; and instead of closing the ranks, Salandra in 1919 was still blaming Giolitti for Italian military weakness five years before. One can read from these results that there was strong opposition to Salandra and the men who had involved Italy in war.

Out of over five hundred seats, the right-wing liberals obtained only about twenty, Giolitti in the Center about ninety. The *popolari* emerged with a hundred instead of fifty as Nitti expected. He was ready for sixty socialists, but in fact there were 156, of which it is interesting to note that only ten came from the South, and none from the islands of Sicily and Sardinia. The fascists won no seats at all and only four thousand votes in the one area they contested. The radicals were down; the republicans were reduced to nine deputies; the independent socialists around Bonomi were negligible. The tragic failure of these elections was that no possibility of a liberal-democratic bloc emerged from them against the avowedly unconstitutional programs of socialism and fascism, and with a parliament like this it was going to be almost impossible to reach agreement on anything. Little more than half of the electors had voted, and it is likely that many of the younger generation were already being taught by their parents and schoolteachers to have small regard for parliamentary institutions: in 1915 parliament had easily and unprotestingly been overruled by the king and the piazza, and so it was equally contemptible in the eyes of both interventionists and noninterventionists.

An ominous sign in December was that the socialists interrupted the speech from the throne by cries of "long live the socialist republic," and then marched out of the chamber singing the *Red Flag*. The king was humiliated and frightened. Yet these were the true representatives of the people, for this was the freest election so far in Italy (as it was the last relatively free election until 1946), and the socialists were the largest party in the House. Universal suffrage and proportional representation were thus building a bridge into fascist tyranny. The many-headed multitude which was now coming to power was less intelligent than its more oligarchic predecessors, perhaps less disinterested, and certainly less practiced in government. If the old governing classes of Italy had been deficient in political education, how much more so were these new voters who often lacked education of any sort?

Most of the deputies were new to parliament and inexperienced. Few admitted that to make effective government possible some sacrifice of interest and program was indispensable, and few showed the honesty and disinterested high principles which had governed Sella and Ricasoli fifty years before. Thus, in March 1920 the Chamber unanimously decided to continue the bread subsidies simply because no one dared antagonize the voters, even though they knew that this would ruin the country's

balance sheet—wheat was apparently being fed to cattle because its artificially subsidized price was only a quarter of that on the free market in
Europe. Each parliamentary group in turn, finding the reality of power
out of reach, made sure that no other group would succeed where they
had failed. As one example of the consequences, five different ministers
of education succeeded each other in the three years 1919–22, each
leaving behind him a scheme of reforms which he had had no time to
enact.

§◆

The end of the war brought not only political decomposition but
economic collapse. Nitti could say in an open letter to his electors that
"present state expenditure exceeds receipts by more than three times;
all state concerns are in debt, and billions every year are being lost by
the artificial fixing of the price of bread; the national debt is increasing
at the rate of one billion a month; and each month our expenditure on
the army is greater than it was each year before the war." The value of
money was greatly changed, especially after New York and London
ended their exchange controls in March 1919, and the dollar, which
had stood at 6.34 lire in the second half of 1918, rose to 18.47 in the
first half of 1920. Prices followed the same index, and only wages lagged
behind. In July 1919 there were widespread riots against the cost of
living, and the inevitable slump in heavy war industries led at once to
widespread defaulting on wage agreements.

Another threatening trend was the growing disparity in wealth between social classes, for some people had done well out of the war,
others not, and hence new hatreds were generated. For instance, government contractors had often made fortunes, and so had many farmers,
because the old rents were by now ludicrously small and agriculture
had been freed by inflation from much of its burden of mortgage payments. It was noticeable that among the first to join fascism were many
of the wealthier peasants, as well as the landowners and war profiteers
who feared the advance of socialism. Many landless laborers had meanwhile returned from the relative comfort of service life to primitive conditions, depressed wages, and unemployment, and had a burning grievance against those who had stayed at home and made their fortunes.
The difference was that the workers had now acquired novel standards
of comparison, and many of them could write and add, so that they
could check the *mezzadria* accounts with the *padrone*. The war had
like all big wars brought a revolution in habits and social relationships,
and this was something the king and Salandra in 1915 had not foreseen.

Even a professor of political economy might quail before such a prospect, and in fact the impossible task of assembling a majority frightened Nitti away from proposing drastic measures to stop inflation and pay for the war. An impost on capital was decreed during 1919–20, but it was to be spread lightly over twenty years. War profits, too, were declared taxable, but this did not affect the agriculturalists who were already threatening "a strike of taxpayers." As was noted by an observer at the British embassy in Rome, the outcome of such experiments in taxation "depends on the will of the people to contribute and on the ability of the government to collect the taxes," and both these were lacking. The bread subsidies threatened national bankruptcy, yet Nitti's final move toward trying to abolish them by decree only made the Left decide to hound him from office. On the other hand, Giolitti's subsequent tinkering with income-tax and war profits pushed many of the rich into the camp of *squadrismo* and civil disobedience. Left and Right were each too much preoccupied with their own private selfishness to be able to join in promoting the commonweal.

§❧

In September 1919, a calamity at Fiume should have made clear whither such progressive disobedience was leading. D'Annunzio's invasion of this somewhat unimportant town was the first instance of international violence in postwar Europe. It prepared the way for fascism inside Italy, and outside it helped to destroy the mutual confidence between states for peaceful negotiation over their differences.

The principle of self-determination, conveniently ignored by Italy in South Tyrol, had been very usefully invoked during the victorious advance of October 1918 when Fiume was said to have proclaimed its union with Italy. The Italian claim did not greatly impress the Allied statesmen at Paris, and local elections were later to show that the Italian nationalists had no mandate from the civic population, but D'Annunzio determined to improve the Italian case by resort to arms. An Allied commission under an Italian general had eventually decided that, to avoid local clashes which were threatening, Italian soldiers in Fiume should be replaced by British police, and in September 1919, when this change was to take place, D'Annunzio made his coup as the first step toward annexing the whole east coast of the Adriatic.

The end of the war had left this poet laureate starved for amatory and military excitement. He was now bald, one-eyed, nearer sixty than fifty, and no longer a hero in the headlines, nor had he any more government funds to preserve him from bankruptcy and keep his muse and his mistresses indulged. General Caviglia, the minister of war, tells how D'Annunzio asked him to lead the army in a mutiny to overthrow parliament. This failing, the poet petitioned Nitti for three million lire of government money with which to visit the East and there find new inspiration for his art. Finally, he succumbed to the prospect of glory and pelf which the nationalists were working up over Fiume. As usual, he let himself be guided by aesthetic motives, by his flair for the *beau geste,* and for what he had once called the "move toward life." A buccaneering expedition, which Badoglio and other generals were to call the finest since Garibaldi's invasion of Sicily, seemed in every respect suitable. Already at the end of May 1919 the nationalists in Fiume were writing to him as the "one and only *Duce* of the Italian people."

Support for this escapade was easily obtained from many patriots who had no intention of honoring Orlando's signature at Versailles, and D'Annunzio spoke for such people when in November he stated that "the Yugoslavs are excited by a savage spirit of domination and we cannot avoid perpetual quarrel with them." In addition, there were hundreds of supernumerary generals and fifty thousand other officers whom Nitti had already managed to ax. Many of these had been under arms since 1911 and knew that it would be hard to find other employment or retain their standard of living on a pension. One general even publicly threatened to become a shoeshiner in his uniform and decorations. The blackshirted *arditi,* or shock troops, were especially dangerous when demobilized, and in such circles there had been talk of a military *coup d'état* long before D'Annunzio arrived on the scene. The war had accustomed such people to brutality and the use of force. A continuation of the war under the respectable cloak of patriotism would be a godsend to them, and Fiume was the obvious place.

Mutineers as well as demobilized soldiers were actively involved, and when reminded that desertion was high treason, they recalled how Cavour had secretly connived at regular troops joining Garibaldi. Perhaps this precedent was in the mind of Admiral Millo, commanding in Dalmatia, when he visited D'Annuzio, publicly and presumptuously swearing to uphold Italian claims. The cause of disinterested patriotism was becoming sadly and dangerously confused when, not only did Nitti refuse to dismiss Millo, but the king had to write a personal letter to prevent this high officer from deserting to D'Annunzio.

Worse still, public opinion had been encouraged by the government to solidify in favor of annexing Fiume, and the possible international repercussions of this were completely disregarded. Powerful interests at Venice and Trieste were out to destroy their rival's commerce. Even patriotic socialists of such diverse stripe as Nenni and Bissolati called for annexation. So did the liberal Albertini of the *Corriere della Sera,* however much he disliked D'Annunzio's method of conquest, and Sonnino's *Giornale d'Italia* devoted pages of lyrical excitement to both the method and its results. Giolitti's position, too, was at least equivocal, for he could not help applauding in secret even while he deplored the undermining of military discipline. Certain members of the royal family were more open and paid public visits to D'Annunzio in Fiume. The seamen's union was evidently behind him and so were some among the heads of the moribund Banca di Sconto and the Ansaldo munitions cartel.

A particular responsibility must rest on Nitti, the prime minister. Subsequently he explained that, while appalled by these events, he did not turn D'Annunzio out because this would have risked revolution and weakened Italy's bargaining position with the Allies; hence D'Annunzio was emboldened to defy the world, knowing that no violence would be used against him. Nitti hoped that the Allies would restore the government's prestige in parliament by conceding Fiume, and he staked his reputation on succeeding in this. While forced by European protests to deny the nationalists in public, in private he thus abetted them so as to convince Europe that there was no alternative to Italian annexation. A Yugoslavian expedition could have chased D'Annunzio out, but Nitti himself prevented this by a direct military threat. When, after a hand-to-hand fight in parliament, the deputies affirmed that Fiume should be Italian, Nitti was not the man to court unpopularity by trying to calm them. Instead, he actually boasted of giving government money to D'Annunzio in order to keep this artificial revolt alive, and when the next prime minister showed how this Ruritanian state would collapse at the first sign of force, Nitti's reaction was to blame him for throwing away such a useful diplomatic counter. Apparently it meant nothing to him or to the king that military indiscipline was unpunished and even praised and rewarded.

❧

D'Annunzio's "Regency of Carnaro" lasted for over a year. Although it was a petty and ridiculous affair in itself, its example was an inspiration (and another dress rehearsal) for fascism, however much Mussolini's jealousy made the early fascists doubtful about it at the time. The *comandante* let few days go by without a speech, usually from a balcony, and with stage effects which later became familiar, as the crowd answered his cry, "Whose is Fiume?" "Ours"; "To whom the future?" "To us." The black shirts of the *arditi* were to be seen in Fiume as people shouted the future fascist warcry, *"A noi . . . eja, eja, alalà."* Here, too, was seen the first sketch of the "corporative state." All this was later to be copied, without acknowledgment, by Mussolini. Here at Fiume was the same amalgam Mussolini was to use, an alliance of nationalists, army veterans, dissident socialists, idealists, and adventurers who turned up at the first smell of blood, men who fought duels with hand grenades in D'Annunzio's presence. The Regency proved an irresistible attraction to undesirables, as fascism did later. Schoolboys ran away there as they had run away to join Garibaldi, for this was a generation which had learned D'Annunzio's poems at school. For their food his army relied in part on piracy in the best old style, and D'Annunzio's marriage legislation incidentally drew a profitable revenue from those who could not afford or otherwise procure a "divorce" in Italy. His effrontery and panache in all this were superb. In a typical gesture he dropped a manifesto on Paris from the air giving the "foreign policy" of his state. He also worked out an elaborate constitutional document, and proclaimed to the world that he would make Fiume the center of a world revolution. On one occasion, according to his biographer, Antongini, he flew over Rome and dropped on the parliament buildings a chamber pot full of carrots. The same futility and bad taste would have been typical of Mussolini, though Mussolini never possessed D'Annunzio's imagination, and fascist theatricality was to be distinctly less subtle and individual.

The end came in the last few days of 1920, aided perhaps by an epidemic of Spanish influenza. The new premier, Giolitti, for six months had continued to provide government money and food for Fiume. Soleri's memoirs confirm this, and the minister of war, Bonomi, thought it a matter for boasting that he had helped finance D'Annunzio on the budget of his ministry. But when an armed clash led to the death of a dozen soldiers, Giolitti was emboldened to reverse his policy. First he bargained for the support of the fascists and the army leaders. Then he acted. At Caviglia's first shot, D'Annunzio, after having gratuitously declared war on Italy, withdrew hurriedly into honored retirement, a wealthy man again, and held up to the next generation of schoolchildren as a national hero. Mindful of his oaths for "Fiume or death," he continued to bewail that death had not taken from him the shame of being an Italian, but then he concluded that Italy was not worthy of such a loss. As Nitti remarked, he had treated Fiume just as he treated his mistresses and had left it exploited and exhausted. The cause had meant little to him, his own self-indulgence everything.

Meanwhile the good conscience of Italy had temporarily triumphed. D'Annunzio lamented that if only half the Italians had been of the same stamp as the inhabitants of Fiume, Italy could conquer the world. To this the *Corriere della Sera* responded: "Italy has no wish to conquer the world, but does need to gain mastery of herself. . . . D'Annunzio should be warned not to provoke civil war and unmake the very nation whose territory he is trying to complete." Albertini, the editor of the *Corriere,* and in private life D'Annunzio's good friend, echoed Cavour's admonition that the capture of Fiume would be barren if it implacably alienated the Slavs, and added that the use of violence would not go unpunished. But unfortunately this generally sensible and moderate editor still had to learn the same lesson himself when it came to domestic politics and the violence of the fascist *squadre.*

41 Giolitti and the Suicide of Liberalism, 1920-1921

Nitti's government was eventually submerged under an accumulation of discontents. The army deplored his amnesty for deserters, capitalists his schemes to nationalize sugar, coffee, coal, and oil, while the nationalists resented his unwillingness to set up a protectorate in Georgia or Armenia. Some of the more conservative liberals were suspicious of his proposal for an eight-hour day, his laws in favor of compulsory unemployment insurance, workmen's compensation, and old-age pensions. Salandra eventually characterized Nitti's government as the worst he had known in all his long parliamentary career. The fascists and socialists feared his specially created security force of twenty-five thousand "Royal Guards," for this threatened all those who had an interest in disorder. Nitti's personal nucleus of radicals was small, and Giolitti disliked him as he disliked all professors on principle, while the establishment of proportional representation had alienated other groups in the Center. When even the *popolari* turned hostile, Nitti first tried to rule without them from March to June 1920, and then discreetly retired.

His immediate successor was the elderly revenant, Giolitti, who had first become prime minister thirty years before. Giolitti's diagnosis of the situation was interesting, if inadequate. He complained to the press that parliamentary prestige had fallen because the deputies had abdicated their power to the executive and to government by royal decree. Parliament should recover its legislative action, said Giolitti. The king should be deprived of his ability to prorogue the legislature and should no longer be allowed to carry on his own distinct policy. Article 5 of the constitution should be repealed under which the king in 1915 had secretly reversed the system of alliances and decided upon war without resort to parliament. This last proposal, coming from the man who had first become premier in 1892 as representing the Court party, was something which the king never forgave. Giolitti also spoke in favor of more local administrative autonomy, of the workers' right to share in the management of industry, of revising wartime contracts and imposing a capital levy. At this price he hoped to obtain left-wing support for abolishing the bread subsidies and so arresting the deficit. But this attempt to please both Right and Left in fact antagonized everyone. Radicals, socialists, *popolari,* and even Benedetto Croce backed his government, but the results were to show that in postwar Italy there was no longer enough in common to bind a composite Giolittian coalition of the Center. This calm, impassive, laborious *faux bonhomme* was no longer the man of the moment.

One thing Giolitti inherited was agrarian strikes, made possible by a labor shortage on the land brought on by war casualties and epidemics. During the darkest days of the war the conservative Salandra had optimistically promised plots of land to the soldiers on their return to civilian life, but no serious action was prepared or perhaps even intended, and in 1919–20 the peasants illegally scrambled among themselves for what they could get. In a time of inflation, ownership of land spelled security, and hunger drove people to excesses in their search for it. The state appeared helpless before strikes and civil disobedience. By the Visocchi decree of September 1919, and the Falcioni decree of April 1920, Nitti had to give retrospective sanction to many peasant occupations. Not only were the landowners highly indignant at this, but social reformers objected that wealthier peasants in this way obtained more than the destitute and that the surrender to violence discriminated against the law-abiding. Above all, it was dangerous to show people that armed illegality would pay.

On the industrial front a similar problem arose over the so-called occupation of the factories in September 1920. A breakdown of wage negotiations in the metallurgical industry had led to a lockout by the factory owners, and this aroused the workers to seize some of the large factories in the North. For some eight weeks the red flag flew over these buildings in what was wrongly regarded as part of a systematic attack on private property and the first step in a political revolution. Far from planning this operation, the socialists themselves were surprised and baffled, however ready they may have been to try to profit from it. They had little idea how to apply their revolutionary theories in practice, and this sudden challenge to their bluff was spontaneous and unexpected. Neither the party nor the Confederation of Labor could agree as to the onus of responsibility or the action to take.

There is evidence that some industrialists welcomed or even provoked this incident in order to compel Giolitti to use compulsion against the workers, but in any case the prime minister refused to be drawn in, and he continued his vacation. He even suspected that the industrialists were behind it, and his personal belief was that force would only unite the various socialist factions and convert industrial into political revolt. He knew that only the skilled workers were participating in this occupation, and that without clerical and managerial staff they would find the factories impossible to run. Giolitti therefore chose his moment to suggest a peaceful compromise, and the occupation petered out in an anticlimax. It was all going to be much magnified by parties interested in exaggerating the danger of socialism, whereas in reality the occupation demonstrated that Italian socialism was inept and harmless. Governmental nonintervention, however, though it admirably exposed the ineffectiveness of these strikes, gave another example of unpunished lawlessness. Insubordination spread to the railroad workers, who held up trains used for transporting troops and police. Hence property owners everywhere became afraid for their livelihood, and, when the protection of the law seemed to fail, they engaged private armies of hooligans. The technique which Giolitti had used so successfully with socialist strikers in 1904 and 1920 did not work when he tried the same passive inaction with these fascist bravos in 1921.

Giolitti's public excuse had been that he possessed insufficient police to reoccupy the factories. Yet we know that a few thousand resolute men with cudgels and castor oil were shortly to succeed in taming agrarian and industrial disorder, while in many areas the local police were siding openly with the fascists, and they sometimes even led the peasants in marching to occupy the land. Giolitti's real reason was not lack of men; he had deliberately abstained from intervention in the belief that this was the best policy, and he guessed that such hectic symptoms would tend to disappear with the revival of tourism and foreign trade and investment. At the same time he lacked the imagination to recognize that these disorders were not just the same process of lower-class emancipation he had experienced with the Sicilian *fasci* of 1893. His old remedy had been to let any new social forces either work themselves out or find their own level, but whereas this neutral attitude had formerly aided the common people, it was now going to benefit their employers who had the means and the resolution to act on their own in a contrary sense.

§◆

Giolitti's affectation of neutrality at the end of 1920 gave free rein to the general economic turbulence of the times, and this was to play into other hands than his own. Strikes occurred even among government officials and schoolteachers, while labor unrest at Turin resulted in five fatal casualties, and an incident in a football game at Viareggio caused splutters of insurrection all over Tuscany. Mussolini himself was to be the chief gainer. Although he later used both this lawlessness and the government inactivity as excuses to justify his own coup, at the time he supported both one and the other, just as at first he had openly encouraged the occupation of the factories. Fascism profited most from these strikes, for they dispersed the energies of the Left while rallying all who wanted efficiency and economic recovery.

Mussolini had been left high and dry since his defeat in the 1919 elections. Without a policy, without friends and backing, without the ardor or the theory of the official socialists behind him any more, he was in serious danger of ending up as just a confused and egocentric demagogue with a talent for histrionics. But the Fiume episode had now given him a chance to feel the prevailing nationalist mood of Italy. It was time for him to emulate D'Annunzio and "move toward life," and before Italy became too prosperous again he needed to encourage anarchy and civil strife so that he could pose as the nation's deliverer.

These strikes of 1920–21 were later built up into a justification of Mussolini's rise to power, so it is important to stress that labor unrest was found in other countries including England without such fatal effects. Despite what was said, the strikes had no master plan behind them and were usually unrelated. The railroad workers, who had not taken part in the so-called general strike of 1919, walked out only after the post-office employees had returned to work. Individualism and spontaneity was the keynote, and this makes it fairly clear that bolshevism was not the threat in Italy that it was in Germany and Hungary, fascist propaganda notwithstanding. In any case, such dangers as it did present were virtually past by 1921. Giolitti's refusal to intervene had been a principal factor in this return to more normal conditions in 1921, though it is interesting to see that the fascists could not afford to let him take the credit, and they soon began to blame him for the remedy as well as for the disease.

It was the bogey of socialism which, with however little justification, made newspapers like the *Corriere della Sera* connive at fascist injustice. What they saw was a pattern made up of proletarian lawlessness, of Giolitti's plan to increase income-tax and death duties, an attack on wartime profits, an eight-hour day in industry, socialist administrations in several thousand towns, and Nitti's idea about state ownership of fuel and power. Landowners in some areas were at the mercy of the Red Leagues, and sometimes of their own employees who were in charge of local government. Labor might even be doled out to them at the fiat of union leaders, and squatters were often settling on their land. Moreover, not only the socialists, but also the *popolari* were quite serious about intending to split up the big estates.

Property owners were not alone in forming pressure groups to draw private advantage out of the common pool. Without being less selfish than other people, they were usually more individualistic and less easily organized, and by owning real estate they had survived inflation far better than most. By 1920, however, they were alarmed and took the offensive. A General Confederation of Industry was formed, and armed bands of retainers were enrolled from the unemployed and demobilized. These bands later became the nucleus of the fascist *squadre,* and from this period dates Mussolini's *connubio* with the agrarians of the Po Valley. Under the pretense of saving the country from bolshevism, the fascists were thus able to attack governmental authority and create anarchic conditions which would make people long for authoritarian government.

Contemporary plays and novels reflect the impact of this proletarian challenge upon the hitherto unquestioned supremacy of the old ruling classes in public life and industry. In politics Giolitti found that he could be outbid in electoral appeal by both socialists and *popolari,* and he was alarmed when neither would fit into his system. The liberal heirs of Cavour were at last proving unable to absorb the new forces in Italian politics, and many of them acted on the false assumption that the fascists would prove more easily digestible than either the Catholics or the socialists, both of whom were by definition enemies of liberal government. Croce and Mosca had been elaborating their theories about the antithesis between liberalism and democracy, and some of Giolitti's liberals were so confused that they allied against democracy with men who ostentatiously despised the liberal state.

The postwar generation was slow to perceive how profoundly antiliberal fascism was, and people preferred for a while to believe dogmatically that revolution could come only from the Left. Croce, who was a member of Giolitti's cabinet, explained that fascism was safe because it had no program, as though this were not precisely the fact which should have put him on his guard. Social disorder and parliamentary breakdown sent even moderate men looking for a strong man to deliver them, and Mussolini's well-timed renunciation of republican socialism labeled him superficially in their eyes as a comfortable transformist of the old school. As many of these liberals analyzed the situation, the primary need was for a stronger state, and for this purpose Mussolini would serve, while they themselves would meanwhile stand apart and retain their reputations uncontaminated against the day when they could return in safer conditions and replace their puppet. Any alternative remedy to this might require probing under the surface to discover the more fundamental maladies of the body politic and might thus expose their own social and constitutional position to the knife of criticism.

This was a failure of perception and of leadership. The experience and intelligence of Croce and Giolitti would have been invaluable if only a profounder analysis and greater moral courage had equipped them to do effective battle for liberal principles. Giolitti, now nearly eighty years old, was all for a quiet life—under no circumstances was the prime minister to be disturbed at night. When D'Annunzio collapsed so readily, this fostered in his mind the fatal delusion that fascism could be safely invoked to crush socialism, and then brushed away with equal ease to leave the liberals in control. Hence, astoundingly, Giolitti included the fascists on his own list for the elections of May 1921, telling Sforza that this would make them respectable and would enable him to assimilate fascists as he had assimilated radicals and others in the past. It was this electoral alliance which guaranteed Mussolini representation in the new House, whereas in the elections of 1913 and 1919 he had completely failed. Liberalism to Giolitti was thus shown to be a matter less of principle than of means which could be modified when necessary. Despite all his progressiveness and his contribution to the advance of his country, he had, like Hindenburg later, based his calculations on a formidable error in psychology, and conjured up a monster which he could not subdue.

§

Giolitti had achieved one notable triumph when he withdrew Italian troops from Albania. Sforza, his foreign minister, combining liberal views with astuteness, understood how sentimental considerations had made Sonnino try to annex too much of the Dalmatian shore. Ever since 1914, for instance, a virtual Italian protectorate had existed in Albania, which had cost much money and yielded nothing to Italy except local "rebellion." In 1920 a war continued there in which each day a hundred Italian soldiers were dying from malaria alone, and so unpopular was this that the railroadmen again refused to transport reinforcements. In June 1920 mutiny broke out in one of the best Italian regiments which was about to embark for Albania. Here was yet another sign of the prevailing spirit of insubordination and government paralysis, but at least it persuaded Giolitti to withdraw completely from this unprofitable venture.

Naturally, such a withdrawal outraged D'Annunzio and the nationalists. They were still more infuriated when in November Giolitti signed with Yugoslavia the Treaty of Rapallo, finally renouncing Dalmatia and recognizing an independent state of Fiume. The nationalists noisily persisted in regarding Yugoslavia as an artificial creation invented by the rest of Europe to cheat Italy of her due, and General Caviglia had even threatened to resign his command if Dalmatia were not annexed. Giolitti paid no attention to this nationalist bluster, and thought that, if anything, his new treaty included too many Slovenes inside Italy and thus was likely to cause trouble in the future. When Salandra criticized him for abandoning Fiume, Sforza answered with a pertinent reminder about Salandra's complete failure to mention Fiume in the Treaty of London. Sforza was able to boast that by unscrupulous mendacity at Rapallo he had at least kept Zara for Italy, though he disingenuously tried to conceal his promise to cede Port Baross to Yugoslavia in exchange. The agreement confirmed Italy in possession of Istria, Gorizia, Trieste, and several more important islands, but the main point was that all this was settled by negotiation and not force. It is interesting to note that Mussolini was as yet more jealous of than identified with the nationalist party, and his approval of the Treaty of Rapallo was another fact which he later forgot and tried to make others forget.

§⦿

A still better omen for Giolitti was the defection of the communists from the socialist party. Ever since the Russian Revolution, the communists of Turin had been trying to capture the party from the maximalists entrenched at Milan. The word had come from Russia that the European socialist parties had failed in their attitude toward the world war and that the socialist utopia required a violent revolution to overthrow capitalism. To this Turati replied with the heretical statement that conditions in Italy were not the same as in Russia and that he still hoped to achieve socialism without passing through the horrors of civil war. He was supported here by the trade unionists, and the Confederation of Labor in a meeting at Verona decisively turned down a communist motion for a general strike.

Disturbed by such a turn of events, the Third International chose this critical moment in Italian history to split the largest party in the Italian Chamber, for the socialists were now requested from Moscow to expel the last remnants of reformism and integralism along with all who believed in the efficacy of a bourgeois parliament. They were also required to sever relations with the co-operative movement and the Confederation of Labor. This astonishing directive was still more astonishingly endorsed in the party executive in September 1920 by seven votes to five, but at Leghorn the following January the party congress decisively repudiated their executive by a democratic vote. The left wing of the socialists then trooped from the hall chanting the *Internationale,* and seceded to form a separate communist party, thereby depriving the main socialist body of its most courageous, single-minded, and unscrupulous leaders. Because of this folly and confusion, a hundred thousand socialists gave up their party membership altogether. The way was further opened for a "counterrevolution" from the Right.

This communist secession still left the nonco-operative and illiberal elements around Lazzari and Nenni in charge of what remained of the socialist party. At the Leghorn congress some 58,000 votes went to the communists, against 98,000 for the majority decision, while only 14,500 voted for the democratic reformists represented by Turati, Treves, Modigliani, and Matteotti. Yet the maximalist majority possessed little obvious *raison d'être* on their own. Mere logic would seem to have demanded one of two clear alternatives, either reformism with its faith in compromise and co-operation, or else Gramsci's uncompromising determination upon class-conscious revolt. But the executive clung to the one policy which averted the need for positive action, and reaffirmed the illogical compromise of the Bologna program of 1919. Nor did Turati's reformists leave the party to join Bonomi's.

Events were moving toward the final destruction of Giolitti's precarious political equipoise. The failure of the 1920 harvest had been disastrous, and over two-thirds of wheat requirements had to be bought abroad at a price far above what Italian consumers would pay. This aggravated the existing deficit, and yet any move to increase taxation was bound to alienate Left or Right and so undermine Giolitti's coalition. He had begun with the support of every large group save the official socialists, but he foundered when these financial difficulties at last forced him to challenge the tacit connivance in tax immunities for the wealthy.

On Giolitti's estimate, securities of some seventy billion lire in value were escaping income-tax and death duties through being held as unregistered bonds made out to the unnamed bearer. In September 1920, therefore, the Chamber eventually agreed to his law making these shares compulsorily registered and taxed. This law was one of elementary fairness, but it threatened the income of the rich and also affected those ecclesiastical bodies which used these bearer bonds to evade the law against the Church holding property. The Vatican now pressed the *popolari* to take the decisive step of breaking from Giolitti and so protect the assets of religious corporations. As a result, the Catholics did break away, and their subsequent refusal to join any new coalition with Giolitti was to be of the greatest help to fascism in 1921–22. Such was the immediate collapse of the Stock Exchange, that Bonomi in August 1921 had to suspend application of the law on bearer bonds as one of the first acts of his premiership, and Mussolini shrewdly abrogated it altogether. This form of investment was thus allowed to keep its partial tax immunity, though the national income was wildly out of balance, and although the poor were made to give up their bread subsidies in February 1921. By thus increasing the price of bread, moreover, Giolitti offended the Left as much as his former proposal had offended the Right.

Uncertain about his majority, Giolitti held elections in May 1921, a decision which Sforza and others never quite forgave him. He had won four elections, and did not guess that a fifth was beyond him. By a gross tactical error he organized a national bloc including the nationalists and fascists and using the fasces as one of his electoral symbols. This was his protest against Nitti's new scheme of proportional representation. Wanting fascist help against socialists and Catholics, he even thought of offering Mussolini a cabinet post. In his memoirs he lamely justified this alliance with Mussolini as of real benefit to the country, arguing that fascism was now a live political force which ought to be represented in parliament. Mussolini thus won thirty-five seats, for he had the powerful aid of Giolitti's prefects and government toleration of terrorism. Whereas until this moment fascism had only a marginal importance, Giolitti's rash invitation now gave it an accolade of presumed respectability. Fascists with clubs were responsible for dozens of deaths on polling day alone, and they had rendered socialist propaganda completely impossible over large areas. Giolitti must bear full responsibility for this shocking fact, and there can be little doubt that the police had orders to wink at anything which weakened socialism. Yet it must always be remembered that, in the last pretense at free elections for twenty-five years, fascism obtained only 35 deputies out of 535.

Grandi described how the fascists looked upon this electoral struggle only as one more episode in their civil war against socialism. But that war was not won yet. Twice in succession, and despite this fascist violence, the rump of the socialist party had emerged as the largest group in parliament, and the Right thus learned the dreadful lesson that socialism could not be eliminated without altering the whole system of parliament and elections. Grandi in 1921 began to criticize Mussolini for not overthrowing parliament and the whole structure of the liberal state, and Mussolini himself recognized increasingly that this course of action might at last be possible.

The numerical strength of parties in the new House was variously estimated. There were about 123 socialist deputies, apart from 29 independent reformists and 15 communists who ran on separate slates. The *popolari* actually increased their representation to 107. There were also 68 radicals under their new name of liberal democrats. The national bloc itself won little more than a hundred seats, and this meant that Giolitti had failed to obtain a majority, however much he had triumphed over Nitti. What he called the "constitutional parties" had captured about half a million votes which had formerly gone to the "subversive parties," but inside his bloc he had lost more than this to the extreme Right, who were shortly to prove far more subversive in their own way and quite as contemptuous of the constitution.

Mussolini, elected at Milan, was now determined to exploit and canalize the counterrevolutionary enthusiasm which he had observed behind D'Annunzio. He himself, as a good republican, boycotted the opening of parliament, though some disobedient monarchic fascists turned up to sing *"Giovinezza"* on this inauspicious occasion. When Mussolini first addressed the Chamber he explained to an unheeding or uncomprehending audience that his speech would be reactionary because he was against parliament and against democracy. Though elected with the government bloc, he at once ranged himself with the opposition, and Giolitti's coalition was thereby stillborn. Mussolini still chose to think of himself as a republican, but he sat on the extreme Right where normally no deputy liked to be seen for fear of being thought an impossible extremist. In fact he seldom came to parliament, for he preferred the more powerful and less competitive rostrum of his editor's office in Milan.

One by one the various groups were turning against Giolitti. Salandra and the nationalists belabored his "renouncing" policy over Albania and his support of the League of Nations. An important class was antagonized by his proposals for surtaxes, a capital levy, expropriation of war profits, and war on tax evasion. The *popolari* and the Left could never forgive his electoral compact with the reactionaries. Nitti and Salandra he disliked on personal grounds, not least because of his rooted objection to university academics. Orlando and De Nicola refused to collaborate. So Giolitti in the end had to conclude that the traditional practice of coalition government was completely unworkable in this kind of parliament. In a final effort he asked for full powers to cut down the enormous number of state employees and so put some sense into the national budget. But parliament refused to sign away its prerogatives, and Giolitti resigned. The full powers which they refused to him, this same parliament was uncritically to give Mussolini in the following year.

42 Bonomi and Facta, 1921-1922

It is astonishing that so many liberals took fascism at its own valuation, not as a positive element of disorder but as the incarnation of legality. When the fascist Giunta once drew his revolver in parliament, one of Giolitti's ministers was bold enough to protest, but it was Giolitti himself who forcibly pulled that same minister back into his seat and told him not to take sides in the developing civil war between Left and Right. Mussolini himself came from the Romagna where there was a tradition of armed banditry which went back to time immemorial. Here and in Tuscany the practice of *squadrismo* developed wherever the agrarian leagues were pitted against socialist co-operatives, and it spread rapidly when its leaders found that they went unpunished and that socialist opposition was crumbling. Balbo's diary shows him as typical of many ex-*arditi* who smuggled bombs and machine guns back into private life, and he strutted about Ferrara making passers-by take off their hats when the black flag of fascism went by. Dumini was another, and every Sunday fascist shock troops followed him and his fellow murderers in punitive expeditions through the Tuscan villages, with a death's head embroidered on each black shirt.

Sometimes these sorties were pointedly political, sometimes just anarchical, sometimes they seemed to be an urban revolt of the small middle class against peasant uppishness and price-fixing in the countryside. Alternatively, it was the age-old struggle for control of town administration. At Bologna, for instance, fascism had a minor triumph in November 1920 and caused many casualties, since the socialists had to be punished for winning in the local elections, but only the socialists found any voice to protest. In January 1921 Matteotti thus expostulated in the Chamber: "The government and local authorities are assisting unmoved at the overthrow of law and order. Private justice is in operation, substituting public justice. . . . So the workers are saying that the democratic state is just a joke, and has renounced its duty of guaranteeing the same law for everyone." But as Giolitti did nothing to stop this, neither did parliament do anything to make him stop it, for the socialists were deliberately trying to sabotage parliament and so were thought a fair target. In the two years before October 1922 the antifascists computed that altogether three hundred fascists and three thousand of their opponents were killed in riots. There are no completely reliable figures, but the newspapers show a growing number of political assaults, and by autumn these were happening at the rate of at least a dozen a day.

That the fascists went unpunished must be read as damning evidence of government complicity, for a few hundred gangsters could have been controlled with the greatest ease. According to Matteotti, in December 1921 there were 240,000 men in the services, plus 65,000 *carabinieri* and 40,000 *guardie regie,* all at the government's disposal in addition to the ordinary police, but they were not used, not even when the fascists gave ample notice of their nefarious intentions. The police and the magistracy seemed to be in collusion against law and order, and one clue to this may possibly be found in a dark threat by the fascist-party secretary that he might "put his cards on the table and so embarrass certain politicians." Collusion went fairly deep during the 1921 elections. Often the squads were organized by army officers, and obtained arms and trucks which must have come from the military authorities. Possibly this assistance was more by negligence than design, for after a war there are always many firearms in private circulation, yet it was not easy to explain away an official circular of advice to local military commanders in September 1920 that fascism should be supported. Bonomi, the war minister, was able to claim that there had been some mistake and that the government was not officially involved, but this ex-socialist Bonomi was to fight the next election on the same slate as the fascists, and it would not be surprising if some elements in his department used government influence to help their political friends, especially during the occupation of the factories.

Socialist counterviolence in the countryside was equally horrible and inexcusable, only it was not so systematic, nor was it official policy as with the fascists. Whoever started the reign of terror, the fascists certainly were better organized, better armed, and had more money; their raids were more numerous, more widely felt, and infinitely more successful. A legend later created around the fascist martyrs done to death in the "massacre of Sarzana" and the "butchery of Modena" was designed to give an excuse before history for the fascist "counterattack." But the official socialist party, irresolute and defeatist, was at the time advocating instead nonresistance or passive resistance for its members, in order to give the government no further justification for its mock neutrality.

There remained to the socialists only their strong parliamentary representation, but this they refused to use. Freedom might yet have been defended if the parliamentary Left and Center had stood together as in 1898–99, and the communists fairly taunted their socialist ex-colleagues with the folly of nonresistance if they were never going to take the further logical step of accepting power or joining a government coalition. Such a step would, however, have been against the doctrine hallowed by the sacred books of socialist law and sanctified by decades of party congresses. At the congress of Milan in October 1921, Modigliani, brother of the painter, again put the case for collaboration in a social-democratic alliance, but again Lazzari's maximalist counter-proposal carried the day.

Since the liberals refused to govern, and the socialist party was still a slave to dogma, fascism had to cope only with the local trade unions and co-operatives. Without leadership and organization, these were helpless, and the Left was thus expelled forcibly and piecemeal from its control of hundreds of municipal councils and chambers of labor. Fascism first captured the country districts, and then played on the old animosity of country against town to invest the larger urban centers. So successfully did it break the spirit of the opposition, that as the blackshirt lorries were seen approaching, the Red Guards and union officials used to fly into the fields, and retaliation was gradually renounced after it had been regularly met with redoubled cruelty. No doubt many people in and near the government were secretly pleased to see the unions broken without having to take any activity or unpopularity upon themselves. No doubt they also intended that fascism should wear itself out in the process and disband spontaneously once its purgative mission was complete, but if so they were egregiously optimistic and simple-minded.

§❧

Giolitti's successor as prime minister was Bonomi, who held office from July 1921 to February 1922. Ivanoe Bonomi was the same who had been expelled from the socialist party for supporting the Libyan war in 1911–12. In character he was honest and good-natured, and he had some reputation as a historian, but in politics he was colorless, imperceptive, and irresolute. Salvemini said he lacked any authority whatsoever and was thus unable to do either good or evil. The other socialists always regarded him as a renegade, and among his supporters the *popolari* and the democratic liberals did not see eye to eye. For Bonomi's cabinet was another broad coalition, though tending more to the Left than its predecessor. His finance minister has recorded that, when the *popolari* objected to a plan for the expensive military reoccupation of Libya by Volpi, Bonomi decided to authorize this expediture on his own authority and did not even tell the cabinet for fear of a split. This was the compulsive logic of coalition government, but it was also a fact that Bonomi was oddly naïve and credulous as a politician. He still thought that he could remain impartial between fascists and socialists, and he therefore made an attempt to reconcile them to each other, hoping to find himself a new government majority in this unpromising quarter.

That a coalition was conceivable between fascism and socialism is witness to Mussolini's opportunism and tactical skill. The man who in May 1921 gave a republican statement to the *Giornale d'Italia* was shortly to take over from the nationalists their cult of monarchy. At one moment he threatened that any police measures against fascism would make him join with communism to overthrow the state; at another moment he mobilized his handful of deputies to beat up the communist deputy Misiano inside the parliament building itself—with impunity of course. In his autobiography he warmed at the memory of this latter gesture of strength and recalled how it had cleared the air and made it easier to breathe in the stuffy atmosphere of parliament.

All these oscillations and diverse policies were typical of the split mentality of fascism. Many of its provincial organizations retained an individual character. In Trieste they were anti-Slav, in Sicily they were particularly against land occupation by the peasants, in Apulia they were linked with the *mazzieri* who were organized by a notorious clique of political bosses. Fascist leaders could vary in being republican or monarchist, socialist or conservative, Catholic or Masonic, anarchical or *étatiste*. This was often a diversity of practice rather than of rational belief, for apart from the futurists, and perhaps the *salon* of Margherita Sarfatti at Milan, there was a notable lack of intellectuals (as distinct from students) in the party, and the movement was professedly and arrogantly irrational.

Mussolini was shrewd enough to embody in himself many diverse elements, and this was one reason why he remained head of the party. For tactical considerations he would stress one rather than another. In

June 1921 he thus made a strategic speech in parliament declaring himself to be on the side of both Catholics and liberals. He favored administrative decentralization and the limitation of government activity to little more than foreign policy and the police. Secondary education, too, should be in private hands. Italy should abolish the collectivist state which had been a legacy of the war, and should return to the Manchesterian state. In the same month, June 1921, he also gave in when his colleagues overruled his extreme statement of republicanism. Mussolini here showed signs that he was becoming more respectable as part of a deliberate attempt to move into a new level of society. He now shaved every day, partly abated his excessively sordid language, and wore a stiff butterfly collar and spats when he thought his fascist uniform too aggressive for the occasion—the later and more disrespectable Mussolini did not like to be reminded of this middle phase and its bourgeois accouterments. When the people who appreciated this social respectability also wanted a nationalist foreign policy, again he adjusted his views to suit them.

Simultaneously with this more seemly trend on the part of the leader, there continued inside fascism a rowdy element represented by the *ras,* local leaders who took their suggestive name from the tribal chieftains whom Italy had met in Ethiopia. There was Grandi's variety of fascism at Bologna, Balbo's at Ferrara, and that of Farinacci the labor boss of Cremona. It was a symptom of the changing times when Farinacci, who as a socialist had seen nothing of World War I, now began to talk emotionally of national grandeur. The *ras* tended to be against too much centralization of power in the hands of Mussolini. They were also against too much respectability. *Squadrismo* had won them a powerful and profitable enclave of local graft in their several regions.

Mussolini could be vulgar and disorderly when he wanted to, none more so, yet he could also be charming and correct, and Bonomi and Giolitti pinned their political faith on this fact. Moreover, Nenni, then a correspondent of *Avanti,* records that even Gramsci and Turati believed until early 1922 that fascism would soon be decently absorbed in the constitutional bloc and lose its more boisterous elements. As prosperity returned and the Left became manifestly impotent, it was thought that the trimmers in fascism were likely to adapt themselves to the more moderate tenor of public opinion. Mussolini was the first of the trimmers, and resenting the independence of Grandi and Balbo with their technique of uncontrolled gang warfare, he adopted Bonomi's idea and suddenly signed a pact of pacification with the socialists in August 1921. "It is ridiculous to talk as though the Italian working class were heading for bolshevism," he argued in this transient and uncharacteristic phase. "I shall defend this pact with all my strength," he asserted, "and if fascism does not follow me in collaboration with the socialists, at least no one can force me to follow fascism."

Socialism and fascism still had much in common, and a coalition of these two "anticonstitutional" parties had its own logic as a possible path to power. But Mussolini proved to be not strong enough to swing his followers. The *ras* rebelled against making a pact with the very people they had lately been hired to massacre, and they would not be done out of their punitive weekend expeditions into the countryside. What was more important, their rebellion against the leader was apparently backed by the landowners and businessmen who held the purse strings and so could call some of the tunes. Mussolini momentarily had to resign from the executive of his fascist movement, and some regional meetings passed resolutions to renounce his leadership altogether.

He was, however, too skillful a tactician not to be able to eat his words almost at once, and at the fascist congress in Rome during November 1921 he capitulated and buried this stillborn pact with socialism. Subsequently, he fabricated the legend that there had been some attempts at fascist secession and schism which he had removed with a wave of his wand, but the history of fascism to which Farinacci gave his name interpreted these events rather as an abortive attempt by Mussolini to break free from the agrarians and industrialists. He failed and skillfully altered course back again, for it was power and not program that mattered to him. "We are relativists par excellence," was how he put it himself in this congress. Unfortunately, the other political groups in parliament did not yet see him as simply a professional adventurer, and so did not exploit this momentary split. Although fascism was still not very strong except in a few provinces, and had made little impression at all on Rome and southern Italy, the poison was spreading day by day, still abetted by one liberal government after another.

§

Early in 1922 the socialists decided to overthrow Bonomi, presumably in the deliberate hope of upsetting the whole parliamentary system, for there was hardly any other conceivable parliamentary combination which they can have preferred to him. The king was at a complete loss and sent Bonomi back to force a vote which might indicate a possible successor, but parliament failed dismally to give any such indication. All party leaders, including Mussolini, were summoned to the palace for their advice, but each was waiting anxiously for the groups to rearrange themselves and for a "formula" to suggest itself. Until this happened, no one dared to hazard a program, for with such an irresponsible parliament, divided into about thirteen diverse groups, each leader feared to compromise his reputation and political future by any positive statement or initiative which might weaken their hand in negotiation. So this twenty-sixth legislature in the history of Italy signed the death warrant of liberal government, and, after nearly four weeks without a government, admitted to power another of those pitiful weaklings traditionally reserved for this familiar condition of impasse.

Luigi Facta was designated as another stand-in for Giolitti. He had little experience of heavy responsibility, being a timid, ignorant provincial lawyer who had risen in politics by seniority alone. His appointment at first was taken almost as a joke, but it was a wry sort of humor. He brought into his cabinet some ministers of the Right, in power for the first time since 1916. But after an ineffective career, Facta's stopgap ministry fell in July 1922 before a hostile vote of 288 to 103. No formula had appeared, the groups in parliament showed no sign of agreeing on any policy, and fascist violence had meanwhile continued with astonishing impunity. In five months, remonstrated Turati, daily outrages against life and property had taken place without a single one of them being punished. The *popolari* for once therefore joined the socialists in this vote against Facta; and Mussolini, too, anxious not to be left in a minority, turned against the administration.

For several weeks the country again lay helpless without any government, while sporadic gang warfare continued all over northern Italy. Orlando, De Nicola, Bonomi, Meda, and Giolitti each declined the poisoned chalice, none of them having the courage and practical common sense to join together, though any one of them might possibly have called on the patriotism and right-mindedness of individual deputies and summoned them to unite in self-defense while there was yet time. The Catholic Meda declared that he would join a ministry but not lead one; Nitti, the doctrinaire, was flirting with both D'Annunzio and Mussolini, and said he would not take office again until there was a parliament likely to approve his paper reforms; Salandra preferred to sketch out a plan to link his conservative-liberal remnant with the fascists and nationalists on the extreme Right. Turati the socialist at long last crossed the threshold of the Quirinal to give advice with the other party leaders. Had this move come earlier it might possibly have saved Italy and socialism, but he had gone on too long trying to save party unity. *Avanti* now blacklisted him as a traitor to his class.

Mussolini, too, was consulted by the king, and apparently recommended another Giolitti administration. He knew that the more chaotic the situation the more call for an autocrat, and he was content to bide his time. An article he published in February had ostentatiously advocated a military dictatorship, and his speech against Facta in July threatened that his few fascists might shortly abandon parliament forever. Mussolini also told parliament quite openly that he would initiate a full-scale revolt if any prime minister were chosen who stood for "antifascist reaction." But not even this did Giolitti and the rest take seriously. Giolitti himself was at Vichy, determined not even to give advice in such a situation. He felt tolerably certain of becoming premier again, but wanted his hands free to make a coalition with Mussolini, and so supinely waited to be summoned back into power—only to be foiled when the gratuitous folly of the socialists returned Facta to office on August 1.

§♠

At this moment of all moments a general strike was declared, a last fatal example of the strike myth which had deluded Italian socialism for twenty years. It was said to be intended to help the government against the growing unruliness, but this was ridiculous, and it was pathetic to see a negative and pacifist strike used as an answer to active fascist terrorism. In this case the public was merely exasperated, and the last vestige of socialist authority was thus nonsensically thrown away. No one even knew whose decision the strike had been, and the editor of *Avanti* was on the point of denouncing it out of hand as a plot of the reformists. In fact it originated from an irresponsible secret committee of action set up by a group of unions in the *Alleanza del Lavoro*, so secret indeed that no one knew whom to obey. The final absurdity of the situation was that the news had leaked out early in a Genoese paper, and hence the fascists were fully prepared to take counteraction.

Mussolini had hitherto been uncertain in his movements, witness his successive tactical alliances with everyone from Giolitti to the socialists. Now, with an intuitive grasp of the revolutionary moment, he realized that the socialists had unwittingly played into his hands, and he launched an ultimatum that the fascists themselves would break the strike if the government did not immediately intervene to stop it. This would enable his gangs to pose as defenders of law and order, and at the same time would afford an excellent chance to seize some of the important towns not yet captured for fascism. On August 2 at Ancona his squads therefore moved in from the countryside and razed all buildings occupied by the socialists. The same thing happened at Leghorn and Genoa and elsewhere. This was a planned movement, and the choice of these arterial cities was well made.

The biggest prize of all was Milan, the brain center of Italian socialism. Here, on August 3 and 4, after three hours of street fighting, the fascists advanced to break up the printing presses of *Avanti* and burn its buildings. To the satisfaction of the *Corriere* and many Milan industrialists, Farinacci then ejected the socialist civic administration, and from the balcony of the town hall no less a man than D'Annunzio spoke to exhort the multitude. The commercial classes of Milan especially detested any transportation strike and were therefore duly appreciative when the fascists took over trains and stations and operated a reduced service for the public. Their gratitude undoubtedly took a tangible monetary form. Among such people the excuse was being manufactured that Italy was on the edge of economic collapse and needed a savior, whereas in fact, when compared to 1921, the year 1922 was witnessing a notable decline in the number of strikes, an improved balance of trade, and an important revival of tourism. Once again myth took the place of reality. It was these economic improvements, indeed, which no doubt made Mussolini in a hurry to create greater political confusion, for they threatened to take away much of the justification for his revolution if he let recovery go too far.

Once again, government passivity in face of this criminal rowdyism by the fascists is the important thing to explain. Irresolution, cowardice, and criminal conspiracy have all been advanced as explanations, and all of them plausibly. The very ease of Mussolini's success against this strike, coupled with the fact of public indifference to or even approval of his action, is a condemnation of Giolitti and the others who feared the unpopularity of trying to enforce the law. As it was, the strike enabled the fascists to put themselves on the same side as the police and public opinion. Though Forlì held out against a similar invasion, and though Balbo was repulsed by clever tactics at Parma, this could not conceal that the socialists were at this moment leaderless or at least thoroughly misled. To crown all, Turati was induced by Facta to promise the strikers that no action would be taken against them if they returned to work at once; then Mussolini vetoed this pardon, and Facta had to wriggle out of his promise—possibly it had been designed only to split Turati still further from his fellow socialists.

43 Italy on the Eve, Summer 1922

Facta presented his new cabinet to parliament early in August, and the mixture was much as before. One American visitor noticed more revolvers brandished in the Chamber, for the sirocco was blowing from Africa and the tremendous heat made politics particularly tense and difficult. Perhaps this was one reason why Facta was now confirmed in office by 247 votes to 122 though two weeks earlier these same deputies had rejected him by 288 to 103.

Even among his cabinet there were some who later regretted their folly in accepting his leadership a second time. It was not an administration to inspire confidence, and the ministers had been selected rather to give a due quota of representation to the eight or so groups whose support was necessary to avoid defeat. Taddei had the reputation of a strong man, and he, together with the radical liberals, Amendola and Alessio, was the main hope of the constitutionalists. On the other hand, Riccio at the department of public works seems to have always vetoed any action against fascism, and apparently kept Grandi informed about cabinet discussions. There were thus several quite irreconcilable factions inside the same cabinet, and yet the radicals dared not expose this fatal flaw by resignation. The absence of collective cabinet responsibility was on this occasion to prove expensive. Alessio once said that if Riccio would not resign, neither would he. This was bad doctrine and bad tactics.

All depended on Taddei at the vital ministry of the interior. This man recounted how one of his first actions was to advise the prefects on August 4 to use arms against disorder if necessary, but the prefect of

Milan, Lusignoli, sent a defeatist rejoinder in acknowledgment. Senator Lusignoli had been a follower of Giolitti, but, as the government representative at Milan, he was now veering toward the city's fascist captors by whose sufferance he maintained his prefecture. He was in fact playing a triple game between Facta, Giolitti, and Mussolini in his attempt to keep a finger in every pie.

Lusignoli sent a telegram on August 6 to Facta after long talks with the fascist leaders. He described how Milan had become the center of a widespread revolutionary movement and how the fascists intended to invite the king to constitute a directorate with dictatorial powers until parliament could be re-elected by other methods. Here was an example of the state authorities already treating with the fascists as with an independent sovereign power. Taddei himself saw another fascist leader two or three times in this week to plead that the fascists reduce their violence and bloodshed, and apparently the minister regarded such a petition as nothing very extraordinary. He merely noted that, since Bianchi was a real fanatic who believed what he said, such a man was not so amenable to negotiation as was Mussolini. To this nadir had liberal Italy descended on the eve of its eclipse.

§❧

It is important to note the king's attitude toward the developing situation, for this was one of the rare moments when the royal actions were to be conclusive for the life of the state. If he and his government had acted in concert against fascism, all might yet have been retrieved, for the king retained the loyalty of the army and the Senate, as the cabinet did that of the police. But Vittorio Emanuele was aggrieved: he seemed to possess less authority than before the war, his own wishes were consulted less, and parliament contained far more republicans and socialists. Following the habit of his dynasty, he had not kept in touch with the opposition groups which one day he might have to invite into office—for many years he never once met Sonnino. So much had his political conscience been attenuated in two decades of transformist practice that he could not understand why Turati and Mussolini should not solve the crisis by joining the same cabinet, preferably under the premiership of Giolitti. The minister of the royal house, Pasqualini, seems to have been an opponent of fascism, but on the other side there militated the influence of Margherita, the queen mother, who was an overt fascist enthusiast. Above all the king was seriously worried by the threat that, if he opposed the fascists, they would depose him and give the crown to the far more spectacular and personally attractive branch of the family led by his cousin the Duke of Aosta. The duke had already in 1920 put forward a scheme to make himself prime minister and dissolve parties as Horthy was doing in Hungary. The king had not permitted this, and now Aosta was reputed hand in glove with Mussolini, a fact which is confirmed from personal knowledge by Jacini of the *popolari*.

The king's misjudgment eventually precipitated the revolution, and for the constitutional impropriety of his final act he must bear full responsibility, especially as he was acting against ministerial advice. There nevertheless seems to be considerable truth in his defense that, when he finally invited Mussolini into power, this action appealed to a growing number of people in every class of society. Everyone must have known of the barbarities which from the second half of 1920 had devastated Emilia, Tuscany, and the Po Valley, and yet there had been no outburst of indignant public feeling which would have compelled the government to send the police into action. On the contrary, many moderate men had psychological and economic reasons for welcoming a movement of revolt and adventure which was directed against anarchic socialism. Students, and many ex-soldiers who after the war found it hard to return to office life, discovered in *squadrismo* the same outlet that their grandfathers had found with Garibaldi. Fascism for them meant that desirable thing, a uniform, as it also often spelled a job in either the well-stocked party hierarchy or the squads. Many of the white-collar unemployed therefore joined with the nationalists, the futurists, the violence-loving syndicalists, and those malcontents with a grudge to settle. Many peasants and small farmers had a permanent grudge against the liberals who in sixty years of power had done so little for their welfare. There were landowners too who wanted strikes broken and their tenants and laborers kept in order, and there were shopkeepers who would have liked to end the competition from socialist co-operatives.

Along with the blatant plebeians like Starace and Farinacci, fascism was to have a large following among men of property, and among its leaders there was, for example, the shrewd and enormously rich banker, Count Volpi, who became a party member in January 1922. Industrialists in general wanted a strong government to force through a new strike law, to keep wages low, and to raise tariffs for protection against the postwar slump, while others had private information that the existing government monopolies in railroads, telephones, and insurance would be released by fascism to private enterprise. Mussolini's first speech in parliament in June 1921 tried to wheedle these people by saying that "the history of capitalism is only just beginning"—this from the man whose newspaper had only recently dropped its front-page subtitle of "a socialist daily," the same man who was going to become the archpriest of state collectivism once he had found enough innocents to put him in power.

Support also came from the poorer middle classes whose fixed incomes were depreciating in the economic inflation and who thus became a revolutionary force. There were patriots who had been humiliated by socialist opposition to the war and liberal "renunciation" of the peace. Many Catholics looked upon Mussolini as a defense against red atheism; while he courted Vatican support, ecclesiastical influence was now used to divide the *popolari* and win them to alliance with fascism. Other groups were moved by their irritation at an incompetent and corrupt parliament where politicians jockeyed for place and let things slide. To such people fascism represented an efficient administration which would act more and talk less and make the trains run on time.

§

No one is ever likely to know for certain how far these various motives had gone by 1922 in winning general support for Mussolini, but their existence showed the real weaknesses of liberalism in Italy. The liberals evidently put riches and comfort before liberty, and the philosopher Gentile teased his liberal friends with conniving at fascist cruelty wherever it served their purpose. Not only the conservative *Giornale d'Italia,* but the big liberal and radical dailies, the *Corriere della Sera,* the *Secolo, La Stampa,* and *Il Messagero,* all on occasion showed distinct sympathy for the squads against the Reds. When *La Stampa* began to suggest that, since socialism was now palpably beaten, the liberals in self-defense might veer back again toward the social democrats, the *Corriere* stood firm: "Much better remain alone around a beacon light than venture into the darkness in bad company."

Albertini, the editor of the *Corriere,* boasted that he was an intransigent liberal, but he was unable to see that his liberalism was blunted, and in fact his paper did not seriously oppose fascism in these early, decisive years. After (or even because of) yet more dreadful acts of fascist prepotency, he even advocated in August 1922 that Mussolini with his three dozen deputies be asked to form a government, for he thought this the only way to avoid a *coup d'état* and preserve legal forms. Like the London *Times* on which it was modeled, Albertini's paper was a powerful influence with the governing classes. It had taken a not unworthy share in liberalizing the conscience of its three-quarters of a million readers, and Albertini, like Croce and many of his other chief contributors, later regretted that he had supported Mussolini at a time when his anathema might have carried great weight. But psychologically this type of liberal was unprepared for the possibility of revolution from the Right. Perhaps after the failure of the general strike he thought that all real danger of revolution was past.

The fascist gangs must have cost a good deal, and so must *Il Popolo d'Italia*. Some contributions came from Ansaldo and the shipowners of Genoa; also from Milan, the town of bustle and reinforced concrete, where many big concerns were pledged to the fight against strikes, bolshevism, and nationalization. The saying went that both fascism and socialism obtained their money and brains from Milan, their thugs from Tuscany, and their orators and agitators from the Romagna. Fascism had been supported so far by the agrarians, who were now doubly terrified since the Chamber in June 1922 had passed a law to break up the large estates. Now finance and industry also began to see that their own vital interests were involved. Although national prosperity was returning, in a period of demobilization the heavy industries were crippled: Terni and Fiat just managed to weather the postwar economic crisis, but the big industrial cartels of Ilva and Ansaldo were forced into liquidation in 1921, and this caused a succession of bank failures. The General Confederation of Industry therefore seems to have placed itself in close contact with Mussolini, since a party which promised to maintain the honor of Italy abroad had obvious attractions for the war industries with their excess capacity. Mussolini himself, who had gone to prison as a pacifist in the Libyan war, now trimmed his sails deftly to the nationalist breeze. In the middle of August he is said to have borrowed heavily from the Roman banks. For these banks were not only big owners of land, but closely involved with the financing of heavy industry, and on both counts, after some initial perplexity, their directors seem to have backed fascism to win, and purchased a useful financial interest in its success. The industrialist, Pirelli, later recollected how a committee of the *Confindustria* called on Mussolini at the office of the *Popolo d'Italia* on October 26, 1922.

The socialists were now a parody of their former selves, and it is difficult to see why they inspired so much fear. The official party no longer had any resources to protect itself against fascism. Yet Serrati reasoned that to join a bourgeois government would morally be the end of the party; socialism might be overpowered by violence and yet recover, but in his view there would be no recovery if they meekly surrendered. Their one weapon was the general strike, yet this had now failed dismally. Unable to face their enemies, they turned petulantly on their friends, and at this critical moment the congress of Rome in October by a bare majority expelled Turati, who thereupon formed a separate Labor Party with Treves, Modigliani, and Matteotti. Turati had at long last come out for collaboration with the Catholics and Giolitti, and his expulsion was therefore correct in dogma even if pointless in practice. The residuum of the official socialists was now led by Bombacci, who later became a fascist and ended in 1945 strung up alongside Mussolini in the Piazza Loreto, and Bombacci was vainly attempting in October 1922 to rejoin the communists. Many socialist as well as communist leaders were away in Moscow.

This fatal month thus found the socialists completely ineffective and unimportant. The largest group in parliament was divided into squabbling factions around Bonomi, Turati, Bombacci, Labriola, Bordiga and Gramsci; and Ferri was already trying to persuade some socialists to support fascism. Socialism as well as liberalism had proved to be a hollow sham, and fascism was therefore to conquer less by its own strength than by its enemies' weakness.

§◆

Meanwhile, the fascists empirically acquired a plan of campaign. Ferrara, Cremona, Parma, Ravenna, Leghorn, as well as Milan, all had their town councils forcibly taken over, for these towns were strategic points in the coming insurrection. When a fascist was killed at Fiume, his fellows even seized a destroyer and captured the city from the antinationalist party which had won the civic elections of April 1921. Bologna was besieged and its prefect forced to flee the city under cover of night. Yet, almost unbelievably, the government took no action and the liberal ministers did not resign. The fascists thus were given a free rehearsal in mobilizing their legions and cohorts and received welcome proof of the paltry temper of Facta's cabinet.

On a much larger scale, an invasion was planned of the Alto Adige where Senators Credaro and Salata, the acting high commissioners, had been sensibly trying to win the affection and loyalty of the recently annexed German-speaking population. Farinacci and De Stefani simply took over the government of this region themselves in protest against such a soft and un-Italian policy. The occasion and the particular area were admirably chosen to secure nationalist approval for fascist depredation, and thus the moral position of both government and governed was gradually weakened, as they first connived at lawlessness in little and then suddenly found themselves to be accomplices in large.

Mussolini later recalled how every day brought him the growing conviction that he alone was in charge of events. Such success was due in part to luck, and in part to the fact that neither Giolitti, Bonomi, nor Facta had the sense and fortitude to say that this daily slaughter was illegal, but in part it was also due without doubt to Mussolini's own personality. Like the mass-oriented journalist he was, he held that a smattering on any subject was real knowledge, and that he could easily solve problems which baffled everyone else. This type of superficial self-confidence was further reinforced by an opportunism which was ready to accept any policy or any kind of alliance. His hand was sometimes forced—for example by the ex-syndicalist Bianchi, who was party secretary and the real drive behind the "march on Rome" when Mussolini himself was too timid and uncertain to force the pace. It was, however, Mussolini's own deliberate inactivity which cleverly or by accident and from fear left open to the very last moment the choice between collaboration and insurrection, and this kept everyone guessing and allowed him to pose as everyone's friend.

One by one he neutralized each party by threat or bribe, and left most of them hoping to join a coalition with him. Mussolini was in touch with Facta and Giolitti through the prefect of Milan, with Salandra and the Right through Federzoni and the nationalists, with the radical Nitti through General Capello, and also in contact with D'Annunzio, with the Court and the queen mother, with the Duke of Aosta through General De Bono, with the Church, and with both branches of Italian Freemasonry. It was a grand new transformist effort to darken the waters of politics, and he had not watched Giolitti's tactics in vain. He was even ready to make another move toward the socialists until this was vetoed by Federzoni, and he played up to the conservatives by at last making a formal acknowledgement of the monarchy in a speech of September 20. In typical fascist verbiage he justified this latter *volteface,* saying that the reason why he had hitherto been republican was that in a sense the monarchy had not been sufficiently monarchical.

Many fascists no doubt genuinely believed that they and they alone could save the country, though most of their leaders were adventurers of the worst sort, either ignorant bullies or mercenaries in search of booty and rapine. D'Annunzio, the archadventurer, had no hand in the final blow, but only because he had been incapacitated in August by a mysterious fall from a window after an assignation with a lady. He declaimed to a congress of his Fiume legionaries that parliament and the parliamentary system were the cause of national ruin and were a great mephitic sewer which had to be destroyed. These were the views of the man whom Nitti, in a presumably aberrant moment, hoped would join a coalition with himself and Mussolini. Jealousy, if nothing else, made such a coalition most unlikely. Although only a febrile imagination like D'Annunzio's could have conceived the choreographic *mise en scène* of a march on Rome (as Mussolini once admitted in 1944), the poet could hardly have led such a march himself; he had no tactical sense of how to arrive and was worried that he might not know what to do on arrival. The fascists neither knew nor cared, and this fortunate inability to care was shown in their typically vulgar motto, *me ne frego*. The fact was now their strength, as later on it was to be their ruin and the ruin of Italy.

By early October, Mussolini and his handful of deputies were virtually masters of the situation even though the other parties were slow to recognize as much. The government writ scarcely ran, and though pockets of state authority still survived around the police and the prefects, people were even being referred to Mussolini for safe-conduct passes. Taddei emptily threatened once more that he would resign unless the cabinet approved stronger measures; but when they still could not agree, he withdrew his resignation, arguing with unconscious irony that for him to leave now might have provoked a crisis.

If Taddei's behavior was futile and cowardly, his colleagues' refusal to act as he advised was criminal negligence. That a strong policy to punish illegalism might possibly have failed is no excuse for not having tried it; and moreover, from what we know today, it is extremely unlikely that repression could have failed. Fascism was still a small minority, and the state authorities had not even been allowed to go into action against them. What the government lacked was not the strength but the will, and perhaps it was not fascism but its backers of whom they were really afraid. Another explanation can be found in a comment by Facta's secretary, who noted that several ministers were now expecting the cabinet to fall and were determined to see that themselves fell on their feet. In the expectation of a new government, everyone intended to play their cards so as to have a good chance of inclusion, and offending Mussolini or any other of the group leaders was something they would try to avoid.

44 The March on Rome, October 26-30, 1922

The machinery of government was fast running down when Facta, who had hitherto implored other ministers not to precipitate a cabinet crisis by resigning, on October 26 proposed a collective cabinet resignation himself. Alessio and Taddei were horrified, for at this very moment the fascist congress at Naples was proclaiming revolution. Resignation before now might have worked against fascism, but coming at this particular moment it could not have been better timed to suit Mussolini, for the prefects could only interpret it as a sign of surrender. All Italy knew what was being said at Naples. One fascist delegate at the congress delightedly observed that there was no government any longer, only a few prefects who would follow the prevailing current. Another declared openly that the fascists, even though they were in a minority, had the right to govern, because they had saved the country. And yet, according to Soleri, who was minister of war, Facta on October 26 decided to shuffle his cabinet and bring in the fascists, and to this a majority of ministers presumably agreed.

Late on the twenty-sixth, the prefect of Pisa reported the beginning of fascist mobilization and added that some of the telephone lines had been cut and men were leaving in small groups for Rome. Their strategic headquarters was at Perugia, where Bianchi, De Vecchi, Balbo, and General De Bono were a quadrumvirate directing operations. Mussolini was a notable absentee. Had he been sure of success he would no doubt have fought where the glory was greatest, but instead he beat a hasty retreat out of harm's way, and until all was over stayed close to the Swiss border. Balbo used to say in private that the other leaders forced Mussolini into action only by the threat that otherwise they would proceed without him. Michele Bianchi eventually persuaded him to drop his negotiations with Giolitti and Salandra, and to insist on supreme power. For the moment, however, Mussolini kept his options open and relied on bluff, because bluff was needed to conceal the fact that the fascist militia was often without arms or food and had been ordered not to fire on the troops even if they themselves were fired on. Mussolini's chief fear was that the army might shoot, and this was one reason why he was so eager to enroll retired generals in uniform.

Facta nevertheless insisted upon resignation and was delayed only by the extraordinary fact that at this turbulent moment the king was away on vacation near Pisa. While awaiting his return, Facta and

Taddei consulted the military authorities at Rome, and General Pugliese guaranteed that, so long as the government gave precise written orders, absolute trust could be placed on the troops to suppress fascism. Facta, it must be assumed, was still hoping for a coalition with Mussolini, and he simply assured Pugliese verbally that such orders would be issued when needed. This was a betrayal of weakness, and the army leaders, whether or not against their own feelings, must have taken it as a caution against overzealousness.

At about 8 P.M. on October 27, Facta met the king on his arrival at the Rome station. Then again at 9 P.M., after Lusignoli at Milan had telephoned to say that no mere cabinet reshuffle would be acceptable to Mussolini, Facta took to Villa Savoia the prepared resignation of his ministry. During the evening, prefects had reported some trains and telegraph offices illegally requisitioned, and even in some cases fraternization between the rebels and the army. The ministers therefore agreed that, until a new cabinet was in office, they should continue responsible for law and order to the best of their ability. Facta told Senator Bergamini that the king had consented to this and had also authorized him to declare martial law if necessary. So, astonishingly, he went to bed. There was no general alarm so far, and the telephone service at the ministry of the interior was not operated through the night.

§❦

We still do not know with complete certainty the motives and actions of the chief actors in this tragedy. It is generally assumed that Facta had been secretly working for the return of Giolitti, and we also know that Facta was in touch with the fascists. Giolitti himself, the man who had the best hope of saving the country, was celebrating his eightieth birthday hundreds of miles away and never came near the scene of action. He later regretted that he had not returned to Rome, and gave it as his belief that Facta, whom he had once thought to be a personal disciple, was playing false after he had been won over to the fascists by the hope of some place in a new coalition. Actually, Facta seems to have sent a telegram on the twenty-seventh to Giolitti saying that the king wanted to see him. It is likely that the king intended to ask Giolitti to form a government, and the chances are that he could have formed one and so altered the course of history. But this venerable statesman was not a man for a crisis. He would not leave home without first having an express command to form his own ministry. There had indubitably been negotiations between Giolitti and the fascists through the medium of both Camillo Corradini and Senator Lusignoli, though this had only been to keep the old man quiet. At the very same time that Mussolini dropped these deceptive hints of a coalition, he had also told the fascists at Naples that he did not mean to come into power "by the servants' door." As Mussolini knew, Giolitti had once ordered the army to fire on D'Annunzio and was presumably capable of doing the same against fascism if ever the Giolittians were back in the government.

Of all the other party leaders, Salandra was perhaps the most likely candidate for the premiership. Salandra led a conservative group in parliament some thirty strong, and they sat with thirty-five fascists and ten nationalists on the extreme Right. His bitter rivalry with Giolitti was now fatal for Italy. Hoping to form his own ministry with Mussolini's collaboration, he had worked to overthrow Facta. He was supported by Senator Albertini of the *Corriere,* by Senator Bergamini of the *Giornale d'Italia,* and also it seems by Senator Frassati who owned *La Stampa* of Turin. He was also backed by his friend Federzoni of the nationalist party, and, it was supposed, by powerful elements in the army. Mussolini himself visited Salandra's house on October 23 when passing through Rome to Naples, and Grandi and De Vecchi came to see this former prime minister often on the twenty-seventh.

The loyalty of the army leaders to the king and the general nonintervention of the army in politics had been features of Italian history since the time of Garibaldi. But the generals were far from being irremovably wedded to a parliamentary regime, and a succession of ten war ministers in five years was too many to make the system specially attractive to them. Demobilization had created a dangerous class of needy men who were accustomed to battle and military discipline. Generals De Bono, Fara, Ceccherini, and Gandolfo helped to organize and lead the "march on Rome," and numerous others, for instance the more important Giardino, were marginal sympathizers. Salvemini adds that Diaz, the wartime commander, sympathetically addressed the fascists of Florence on October 27. At a critical moment in the night of October 27–28, the king is said to have consulted General Diaz and General Pecori Giraldi as to the loyalty of the troops in the event of civil war, and Diaz is supposed to have answered that the army would do its duty, but had better not be put to the test.

There is, however, no conclusive evidence to suggest that the army would have disobeyed the king, and twenty years later Vittorio Emanuele said that this particular story about Diaz was fictitious. At Fiume the army and navy had fired on other Italians when ordered to do so, and D'Annunzio's rebellion had thereby been dissolved in an instant. In October 1922, General Badoglio, who had succeeded Diaz as chief of staff, said in an interview at Rome that at the first shot the whole of fascism would crumble. Badoglio asked to be given full powers, and a determined government might have granted his request at once. His opinion was confirmed by General Pugliese, the military commandant of Rome, who told Facta at the time and has subsequently repeated that he could have put down any attempt at revolt. Road blocks and *chevaux de frise* were ready on the roads, and even some of the blue-shirted nationalists had apparently asked to help defend the capital against the blackshirts. The deficiency was in political sense and in morale, not in physical strength.

About midnight on October 27–28, Taddei telephoned Pugliese that he should assume military powers over Rome at once, for the ministry had decided this unanimously after Facta had received the king's agreement. But Pugliese, fearing to be disowned like other Italian generals in the past, had again insisted on written instructions, and no such instructions were sent. Shortly after this, Bianchi telephoned from Perugia, pretending to be the prefect, and informed the government that bloodshed could be avoided only by surrender. This at last caused Facta to suspect that Mussolini had deceived him, and he was heard to remark that revolt must be resisted. A cabinet meeting was urgently summoned for 6 A.M.—one minister was untraceable in a hotel on some *affaire de cœur*—when everyone, even Riccio, agreed that violent revolution must be repressed, and written orders were finally sent for the army to stop the fascists by every means at their disposal. The form of decree used for martial law at Milan in 1898 was hurriedly looked up—it is interesting that this had been neglected until so late—and soon it was in the newspapers and on the walls of Rome. At once, says Pugliese, the fascist bands began to dissolve. The order even went out for the arrest of the fascist *quadrumvirs,* but the telegraph office at Perugia had been captured and the order was received by De Bono himself.

৯৯

Then came the real shock: for when, soon after 9 A.M., Facta went to obtain the promised royal ratification, the king refused to sign. One must remember that Vittorio Emanuele knew that the rebels were moving on Rome. We also know that his official military and civilian advisers had told him that order could be restored if he signed. His refusal was therefore not only an infraction of constitutional procedure, it also clinched the success of the revolt. It is inconceivable that the king had misunderstood Facta the night before. Alternatively, according to Soleri's first and enduring impression, Facta himself when alone with the king may have dissuaded the latter from signing, since Bianchi had assured him of a place in Mussolini's cabinet. Taddei later told Sforza that he agreed with Soleri's version. Facta cannot have pressed the king very hard to carry out his constitutional duty, but the prime minister would not have published the decree overnight had the king not approved it the previous evening. There is even evidence that the latter had threatened to abdicate if it were not published.

There is no doubt that the king must have changed his mind during the night. Vittorio Emanuele's glamorous cousin the Duke of Aosta, perhaps seriously aspiring to the throne, had conspicuously stationed himself near Perugia and was said to have reviewed fascist militiamen lately near Merano. The king therefore had to go warily. Very early that morning, on his own responsibility, he had been talking to the wrong people. He had not consulted Badoglio who was known to be ready to fight, but he had spoken with at least one fascist, and with Federzoni who left his presence to put a call through to Mussolini at Milan. Judging from Federzoni's tone of conversation immediately afterward, the nationalist leader probably mentioned to Mussolini over the telephone that the king was afraid of civil war and hoped to prevent it by allowing a peaceful fascist arrival in Rome.

This was apparently the first time in twenty-two years that the king had acted against his ministers' advice. The fact that some reputable parliamentarians defended his action is perhaps a commentary on the dubieties of the Italian constitution which had led directly to this state of affairs. But most people have argued subsequently that the ministers were still in office and the king should have accepted their policy until a new cabinet had been sworn in. It was not a valid excuse to say that proclaiming an emergency by decree would have been unconstitutional, for emergencies might happen in a parliamentary recess, and Umberto had acted by decree in 1898. A better, but not publishable, excuse was that in 1898 the villains had been the Left, whereas in 1922 they were the Right, and by definition the Right represented law and order, property and the establishment, Church and state.

The King of Italy had learned a dangerous lesson in 1915, namely that he was entitled and able in emergencies to short-circuit parliament and appeal directly to the man in the street. He saw that fascism claimed the more or less open allegiance of many leading liberal newspapers and deputies of Center and Right. Local elections in October were undeniably turning in favor of fascism—aided by the powerful argument of castor oil and the *manganello*. As the king may have known, people such as Croce, the liberal high priest, advocated Mussolini's assumption of power as better than the existing anarchy, and believed that fascism might be gently directed into good constitutional usage. In the turmoil of the moment it might have seemed possible for the House of Savoy to absorb and convert Mussolini, as it had already absorbed Garibaldians and Mazzinians, Catholics and reformist socialists. There was nothing new in the king calling into power a minority group, and there was plenty of precedent for omitting the prior authorization of a parliamentary vote. On the other hand, a less impressionable sovereign might have seen that the use of bludgeons and hand grenades indicated that fascism was still a minority opinion, and no doubt the appointment of self-confessed murderers was as immoral as it was also to prove inexpedient.

The king himself on October 28–29 still did not perceive that the stable door was open, and asked Salandra to form a ministry. Salandra, too, still hoped for a coalition with fascism, and entirely supported the king in refusing to sign the martial law decree. But he was being duped like the others. Mussolini used Federzoni and the pivotal prefect of Milan to notify Rome that, if he were not called upon to form a fascist government, things would soon become ugly. A number of prefects had in any case delayed promulgating the martial law decree, and this apparent nonco-operation of a few local authorities was magnified into a feeling of general helplessness, which also played into Mussolini's hands. Once the king's revocation of the decree indicated that the government was powerless, nonco-operation spread rapidly, since no prefect who hoped for promotion would publicly oppose fascism until he could see which way the cat would jump.

This was the real disaster about the king's refusal. In the first place, the public authorities were convinced thereby that the government would do nothing to stop fascism, and hence adjusted their loyalties accordingly. In the second place, Mussolini now knew that the king, having once yielded to a threat, would always do so again, for he had now been made an accomplice and his only alternative was abdication. Mussolini was always uncertain in later years whether to implicate the throne by publicly insisting on its collusion at this moment or to ascribe the whole success to his own courage and intuition; with typical inconsistency he usually tried to have it both ways.

§❧

The most effective means of undermining public confidence during this fatal weekend was through the newspapers. The *Corriere* was therefore asked by the fascists to drop all talk of a Salandra coalition, and on proving obstinate it received a direct threat. For one vital day the paper ceased publication, and the next morning it surrendered. Albertini had feared for his wonderful new typesetting machinery, and in face of Mussolini's veto he thought it more dignified to say nothing at all than to voice his objections to this ungentlemanly behavior. Events were thus showing how right Mussolini had been to concentrate his intimidation and bribery on Milan, the "moral capital" of the kingdom. One of his great discoveries was that intimidation was more than half the battle, and he studiously cultivated an outward mien of inflexible determination in order to conceal the indecisiveness which his best friends knew lay underneath. Albertini was frightened enough to ask the prefect and the army for protection, but the answer came that this was impossible and he would have to let his offices be occupied by the blackshirts.

A different technique was used with *La Nazione* of Florence. There was an urgent need to control Florence, as it held the largest garrison on the highroad to Rome. So Malaparte, the journalist, led a fascist deputation to "encourage" the editor of this newspaper to print the false story that the king had invited Mussolini to form a cabinet, and two hours after this interview, fascist trucks were distributing the news in a special edition all over Tuscany. The tale was believed, perhaps because many people wanted to believe it, and, by thus implicating the king, the army was neutralized. The local military commander, Prince Gonzaga, thought that he could quiet his conscience and excuse himself by a personal visit to fascist headquarters in order to hear the rumor confirmed.

Meanwhile, Salandra, when charged to form a government, pleaded with Mussolini to come to Rome for consultations. In reply, De Vecchi and Grandi were sent from Perugia to Rome, and spent the evening of October 28 with Ciano senior and Federzoni discussing a possible coalition of the Right. By midday on the twenty-ninth they were able to advise Mussolini not to hold out any longer. Mussolini, however, thought otherwise, and once again his instinct was right. In the security of Milan he did not appreciate that the few fascist squads encamped around Rome had been sitting in the rain, hungry and on the point of going back home to work on Monday morning. Mussolini required complete assurance of victory before he moved. He also wanted to show that he was responsible to no one for office and could therefore be absolute in his exercise of power. A well-staged coup would better satisfy the hooligan element than simply joining someone else's coalition, and it would give far more publicity, for it would be good theater as well as a good self-indulgence.

Whether from timidity or calculation, Mussolini therefore would not budge from the safety of Milan unless invited to form a cabinet himself, and without him a coalition of the Right proved to be impossible. So Salandra, disgruntled at finding himself a pawn in someone else's game, renounced his attempt. At the king's request, De Vecchi then telephoned from the palace and invited Mussolini to Rome, but Mussolini still insisted on a positive invitation by telegram to form a ministry, and even the offer of a special train to Rome did not move him. A discreet hint was, however, dropped by the fascists to Bergamini of the *Giornale d'Italia,* and that evening all Italy knew through a special edition of the virtual ultimatum which they had sent to the king. This was clever journalism, and it helped build up the illusion that Mussolini was a necessary man.

The required telegram was finally sent, and during the night of October 29–30 Mussolini crossed the Rubicon in a sleeping car, arriving the next morning at Rome station. Meanwhile, a group of what was probably about twenty-five thousand fascists—the king claimed that there were a hundred thousand—had been mobilized into "columns" within forty miles of Rome, many of them unarmed and quite out of touch with headquarters at Perugia. The troops at Rome could easily have dominated such a motley collection. But the Duce arrived at Rome before his men, and, surrounded by a few blackshirts dirty with mud and rain, singing and brandishing their sticks, he made his way to the palace. The "march on Rome" was thus a comfortable train ride, followed by a petty demonstration, and all in response to an express invitation from the monarch.

Subsequently, however, Mussolini managed to twist appearances more in favor of a violent conquest of power. When the squads refused his express order to disband, he persuaded the king to allow his desperadoes to come in ten special trains from their encampments, ostensibly to make a demonstration before the palace in homage before being packed off home, but photographers were there on the thirty-first to give this some semblance of a dictator's private army overpowering the constituted authorities of the state. There were priests among this crowd, and the Duke of Aosta later told Mussolini's wife that he too was with them. Many other senior officers were also observed among the fascists, including the war hero General Capello who wore a half-army, half-fascist uniform that looked quite South American. Indeed, there was something South American about the whole business, and the *caudillo* Garibaldi with his red shirt and poncho would surely have seen the humor of it.

45 Dictatorship Emerges, 1922-1924

At the age of thirty-nine, Mussolini was the youngest prime minister in Italian history. In November 1922 he still had only his three dozen fascist deputies in the House, less than 7 per cent of the whole, and the important thing was to go easily and placate everyone until he was strong enough to do away with parliament altogether. Hence, while keeping in his own hands the foreign office and ministry of the interior, he carefully included ten nonfascists and only four fascists in his cabinet. At least three of these ten called themselves liberals, two were *popolari* (the future national president, Gronchi, was an undersecretary), and two social democrats. The king said that Mussolini's first suggested list also included the name of Einaudi and that the royal permission was also asked and received for including a socialist. The armed forces were rewarded and cajoled by choosing the popular Admiral Thaon di Revel and General Diaz for the service ministries. Diaz had hoped, unsuccessfully, to obtain from Nitti some public recognition or grant to signalize his war services, and was delighted now to find himself more appreciated.

When parliament met in November, Salandra noted that the benches on the extreme Right were unexpectedly filling up and becoming almost crowded, as deputies of the Center experienced a timely conversion. Mussolini's first speech in parliament, along with certain equally timely invocations of God's help, threatened in Cromwellian tones to "make an armed camp of this House." He boasted that his government had been formed without reference to parliament and was therefore hardly accountable to it. His numbed audience, far from challenging such a statement, took it without protest. Giolitti, when questioned by his followers, said that he thoroughly approved of this speech and that parliament at last had got the government it deserved; as the deputies had not known how to find a workable administration, the country had found one for itself. De Gasperi and the *popolari* also approved, and even radicals such as Salvemini still preferred Mussolini to Giolitti, whom they considered the arch-corrupter of political life.

No doubt many of these deputies were only too relieved to find that someone at last knew his own mind and was prepared to act. One moderate socialist, Matteotti, who was soon to pay for such audacity with his life, was bold enough to cry "long live parliament." But the communists led a shout of "down with parliament" in reply, and their prayer was to be answered sooner than perhaps they wished. The Marxists had been misled by their dogma into completely misreading the situation. Their diagnosis that fascism was the last counterattack of the conservative classes was only a half-truth.

In the Senate, too, the liberals were quite disoriented when Mussolini asked rhetorically: "Who could have stopped me from proclaiming an open dictatorship? Who could have resisted a movement that represented not just 300,000 party ticket holders but 300,000 rifles?" The liberal Albertini gave a favorable vote and tried hard to prove that there had merely been a normal constitutional accession to power, "since the spirit of the country is evidently in favor of fascism and its leader." He wistfully cautioned Mussolini not to abuse his victory, but to disband his armed squads and revert to liberal methods. "Mussolini has given to the government freshness, youth and vigor, and has won favor at home and abroad. . . . He has saved Italy from the socialist danger which had been poisoning our life for twenty years." Coming from a true liberal of the old school, these words give a reliable clue to how the great party of Cavour had sunk to supping short-spooned with this impostor.

The Senate voted confidence in Mussolini by a larger majority than any liberal ministry had received in a long time. In the Lower House, Giolitti, Salandra, Bonomi, De Nicola, as well as the *popolari,* ranged with two successive government majorities of 215 against 80 and 306 against 116, and by no means all the 160 miscellaneous socialist deputies voted negatively. Pareto had written to reassure Mussolini that, parliament being divided into so many groups, fascism would find an easy majority, and he was right, though Mussolini's feckless predecessors had somehow failed to discover the key to this riddle. Both Houses in fact accorded Mussolini what they had refused Giolitti, the exercise of extraordinary powers for twelve months, despite (or because of) his threat to use force if they refused. The committee appointed to consider this concession included Bonomi, Salandra, and five other liberal ex-ministers, all of whom approved Mussolini's request.

The elected representatives of the people were by now inured to government by decree and had also become fully convinced of their own incapacity to rule. By condoning and virtually confirming the monarch's refusal to promulgate a state of emergency the deputies took on themselves a responsibility for future events. Albertini rightly ascribed the fascist victory to a love of *quieto vivere* by the liberal parliamentarians. What adds up to the most serious criticism of liberal Italy is that he and they opposed fascism only after active opposition had become impossible. Even Nitti in April 1923, while he refused to support Mussolini, also refused to criticize him and stated that the fascist experiment should be allowed to continue undisturbed.

For two years some people were able to go on hoping that parliament and the King were still free at any time to undo what they had done and that Mussolini was a new Giolitti who stood for national union against the subversive parties. Friends and critics alike had their different reasons for trying to make out that there had been no revolution. Fortunato, that aged relic of liberalism, coined the epigram that fascism was not a revolution but a revelation—a revelation of servile, boastful, bigoted Italy which properly derived from the Counter Reformation and the Spanish occupation and in whose history liberalism was a mere parenthesis. From another point of view Mussolini convinced others as well as himself that he was not the destroyer but the defender of the constitution, whereas Facta, on the other hand, could be said to have violated constitutional convention, first by urging the king to an illegal act and then by proclaiming martial law without the royal signature.

Cautiously, Mussolini lulled people into a sense of false security, and this gave time for the opposition groups to be singled out for piecemeal and surreptitious destruction. His immediate aims were to stress continuity and tradition and to develop the myth that he spoke for the "general will" and knew men's interests better than they did themselves. He was quite within tradition in governing by decree, and there was nothing illegal or novel in depriving Rome of its elected municipal council on the pretended grounds of bad administration. Gradually, during 1923, however, prefectures, police offices, and the state administration were restaffed with fascists. A batch of new senators was created in March, including De Bono, Pareto, Pantaleoni, Corradini, Martini, Casati, and Agnelli the director of Fiat. The structure of a new state was thus being built up unobtrusively, and as far as possible without recourse to revolutionary methods.

§�

For a time Mussolini tried to remain uncommitted to any positive policy. He had, in any case, few very constructive ideas himself, but he also wanted to hold together the diverse elements in his party and give himself time for a series of *ballons d'essai* to test popular reactions. At least until the 1924 elections he had to go carefully. There was the big problem of how to balance Left against Right, the extreme fascists against his liberal sympathizers, monarchists with socialists, clericals with anticlericals, idealists with rogues and *affaristi*. Volpe, the enthusiastic historian of the movement, trod delicately over this muddle. Fascism was not a party but an anti-party, he said. It was an organ not for propaganda but for combat, a synthesis of every negation and every affirmation, and he admitted that the precise objectives for which it was fighting were none too clear even to those who fought.

Mussolini in time found that people expected a policy from him, indeed that policy was a prerequisite of useful action, but his own hodge-podge of pseudo culture was so barren and inconsistent that he preferred to let any general political ideas emerge empirically from *ad hoc* responses to the problems of administration as they arose. Circumstances thus forced him to create a party militia, which made a legal institution of *squadrismo* and transferred to the government payroll the hoodlums he did not dare dismiss. This done, he then claimed that the militia made redundant the Royal Guards which Nitti had instituted as an extra force of police. These Royal Guards he condemned as a "blind instrument of national hatred," and the angry tone reveals his vindictiveness against one of the few public bodies which had been available to maintain public order in the civil war of 1920–22.

The dissolution of the *guardie regie* provoked armed resistance and fatal casualties in some places, as did also the dissolution of the nationalist blueshirts, but no one was ready to exploit the fact, and the socialists disliked these bodies for precisely the same reason the fascists did. Mussolini's enemies were thus allowing themselves to be picked off one by one. There was minor friction even inside the fascist party itself during 1923, and armed conflict occurred between various factions for the possession of headquarters and funds in Rome, Venice, Bari, and elsewhere. But the hierarchic element soon overcame the democratic inside fascism, as the state became ever more closely identified with the party.

Fascist policy was built up by a wholesale borrowing of ideas, the intention being to make the regime look progressive and yet sound. Measures and ideas did not need to be consistent, so long as they were popular, showy, easy to administer, preferably noncommittal, and pre-digested enough to need no extra thought or definition. Mussolini thus picked Gentile's brains for the education act of 1923, which became "the most fascist of all reforms," until it was replaced in turn by other educational reforms which were each said to be more fascist than their predecessors. In foreign policy the same man who had offended many of the patriots by his socialistic anti-imperialism now appropriated from the nationalists their flagwaving and drumbeating. A pact of fusion was made with the nationalist party in March 1923, and so a potential rival was won over, together with more support from high finance, heavy industry, and the nationalist intellectuals behind Federzoni and Corradini. This also brought him ten more deputies, to make forty-five.

Mussolini was politic enough to take from the Catholics such ready-made ideas as fitted his own brand of anticommunism. The Catholics formed the vast bulk of the Italian electorate, and without at least benevolent neutrality from them and the Vatican he could not hope for easy success. So he jilted Marinetti, renounced his own silly theme of "Go back to Avignon," and overrode Farinacci by declaring that both factions of Italian Freemasonry were incompatible with fascism. Red atheism was decreed the common enemy. Influential prelates readily took the hint that a few well-directed political sermons would help forward the new Catholic university at Milan and the introduction of compulsory religious instruction in schools. Salvemini also found evidence that in January 1923 Mussolini secretly saw Cardinal Gasparri, the papal Secretary of State, and discussed an alliance with the Church and possible help for the Catholic Banca di Roma. Certainly Pope Pius XI turned against Don Sturzo's Catholic party in 1922, and so helped to confound one of Mussolini's few potential rivals.

With an eclectic, empirical policy it was hoped to keep all classes happy and convinced that fascism had a real rationale of its own. While on the one hand some of the syndicalists were attracted by a mock version of guild socialism, on the other Mussolini pandered to the monied interests, taking care to create the impression that he was the exploited and they the exploiters. A few days after October 28, the General Confederation of Industry put out a manifesto welcoming the new government, as well they might. One of Mussolini's first acts was to decree the abrogation of Giolitti's law on registering bonds in the owner's name, a decision which sent the stock market soaring, and his suspension of the law on land reform was welcomed with acclamation by the agrarians however much it weakened the popular basis of fascism in the South. A few months later another decree reduced death duties by half, and the commission of inquiry on wartime profits was dissolved, in both cases reversing what had been fascist policy in 1920.

Mussolini's former socialistic speeches were now withdrawn from the official canon, and De Stefani, an economics professor close to the old-fashioned liberal school, was brought into the cabinet with a policy of denationalization, to free industry and trade and to repeal quasi-socialist land legislation. It was De Stefani's policy to withdraw government subsidies from co-operatives, to abolish the government life insurance monopoly, and to hand the telephone system over to private enterprise. Einaudi and his liberal friends heartily approved, and so did the big businessmen of the *Confindustria*. The railroads still remained under state control, perhaps as a sop to the ex-railroad worker Farinacci and the other "national socialist" elements in fascism, but also because they were too unprofitable. Nevertheless, a policy of decontrol and economy continued until De Stefani's dismissal in 1925, and this helped to win the initial support of industry and finance.

One transient phase thus succeeded another. Up to 1919 Mussolini had been a socialist. In April 1920 he had so far changed that his newspaper claimed to believe only in the "religion of anarchy." "I am for the individual and against the state," he was saying at this stage in his career: "Down with the state in all its forms and permutations." Subsequently, he posed as a free-trade liberal. Then, after 1925 he reversed this trend and proceeded through an exaggerated phase of monopoly capitalism to end up after 1938 reverting back to his original views as a class-conscious, revolutionary socialist. Here is an example of the violent oscillations and fundamental unseriousness which characterized fascist policy in every field.

§❧

Mussolini's chief object in 1922–24 was to entrench his party in power but without acting so fast that his enemies were frightened into stopping him. It was therefore important that the most revolutionary step should have been not by decree but by parliamentary vote, the passing of the Acerbo electoral law at the end of 1923. This law declared that the party or coalition obtaining the largest number of votes, provided this was at least 25 per cent of the votes cast, should automatically have an absolute majority with two-thirds of the seats in the Chamber. When this utterly decisive matter came up for discussion there was still only those forty-five fascist deputies in parliament, but Mussolini also received the support of Salandra, De Nicola, Orlando, Giolitti, and their respective groups, for these liberals had all come to the conclusion that transformism was unworkable and must somehow be replaced by party government, even if that party should be the fascists.

The *popolari* decided that they disapproved of this electoral reform, as also did Bonomi's reformist socialists and Amendola's democratic liberals, yet as they still retained general confidence in the government these groups decided to abstain from the vote. Thirty-nine of the *popolari* deputies opposed this decision to abstain, and some of those who voted, either for or against, had to leave the party. Some senators, too, who were intimately connected with the Vatican, resigned their party membership, and this was interpreted to mean that the Church had decided against the continuance of a popular Catholic party which was beginning to break free from its earlier collaboration with fascism. The disintegration of such a large group was just what Mussolini desired, and it was well worth some concessions to the Church in his ecclesiastical policy.

His vote of confidence on this occasion was carried by 303 to 140, and the second vote on the disastrous Acerbo law still gave him 235 against 139. The Senate majority was 165 to 41. While the representatives were voting, black-shirted troopers in the galleries of the Palazzo Montecitorio ostentatiously toyed with pistols and pared their nails with daggers, while the *onorevoli* down below pretended that this childishness meant nothing. A minority was thus presented with dictatorial powers and the assurance of at least 356 seats out of 535, because, with control of the ministry of the interior, fascism could hardly fail to obtain the necessary 25 per cent poll. There was no hope of a parliament elected under these conditions giving an adverse vote, let alone any chance of a change of ministry. The parliamentary system had simply been voted out of existence by Giolitti, Orlando, and their friends. Speaking on the first anniversary of the "march," Mussolini said that his government would last five years, but then corrected himself and said "or rather twelve times five."

The subsequent elections showed that, political tradition being what it was, the Acerbo law had hardly been necessary. The elections were fought on a national not a constituency basis, and the fascists contrived to form a splendidly transformist electoral coalition containing the names of Salandra, De Nicola, Orlando and other liberals, together with the first batch of trimmers and *arrivistes* from socialism and the *popolari*. Against this single government bloc, the communists suggested organizing a broad opposition alliance to try to win the necessary 25 per cent of the vote, but the other parties would not hear of it, and six individual opposition slates were formed, none with any possibility of success. There was also a seventh independent slate—that of Giolitti and his liberals—which flanked fascism and was not in opposition. Mussolini told his men not to take these "election sports" too seriously, for good fascists should regard such things as a mere survival of the old outworn order. Nevertheless, in the elections of April 1924 the party militia was on duty inside the polling booths, and the familiar tale of casualties and killings was repeated. The principal opposition newspapers had been systematically intimidated all through the campaign, and armed raids and arson inflicted heavy financial losses on them.

Perhaps, after all, it was remarkable that 2,500,000 votes were cast for nonfascist parties. But Mussolini's coalition obtained four and a half million, or 65 per cent of the vote, and was easily assured of its majority. The *popolari* obtained 640,000 votes; the reformist labor party which had broken off in 1922, 420,000; the maximalists who controlled the socialist rump, 360,000; the communists, 268,000; and the liberals, 233,000. The twenty-seventh legislature in Italian history had 403 ministerial deputies, apart from qualified supporters in the 15 independent liberals, 10 social democrats, and 4 deputies of the so-called peasant party. The opposition included 39 *popolari,* 24 reformist socialists, 22 maximalists, 19 communists, 2 deputies of the Sardinian party of action, and 1 dissident fascist. Even opponents of Mussolini such as Salvatorelli admit that this was a genuine majority, and that in a sense it gave retrospective sanction to Mussolini's conquest of power. Fascism already had behind it the clear authority of the king and the two Houses of Parliament; from now onward it also could claim to represent the will of the electorate.

46 The Defeat of Parliament and Press, 1924-1925

Now that he was backed by the largest clear majority since the time of Cavour, Mussolini had less need for caution. In June 1924 many assaults occurred on opposition deputies, and we now know of a personal telegram from Mussolini to the prefect of Turin ordering him to "make life difficult for Gobetti." Worst of all was the cruel assassination of Giacomo Matteotti. This man was a moderate socialist deputy who had been brave enough to point out how Mussolini had once fought for many things which fascism now opposed on principle. Furthermore, he dared to accuse Mussolini in parliament of being determined to use force if the elections turned against him, at which remark a triumphant cry of "Yes!" went up from the fascist deputies and Mussolini nodded his head. Why, asked Matteotti, did fascism make it a matter of pride that Italians alone in the world should be incapable of running their own affairs and must be ruled by force? His question went unanswered, and a few days later Dumini's band murdered him for his outspokenness. Only a few months had gone by since the Italian representative at the League of Nations had poured public scorn on Greece as a primitive nation where assassination was still an instrument of politics.

So great was the outcry at this crime that Mussolini had to stand in sackcloth and suspend De Bono from his command of the police. He later explained it, and perhaps correctly, as an act of extremists who wanted to arrest the current trend of fascism toward respectable parliamentarianism. Whatever the motive, some of the leading fascists were in fact sufficiently scandalized to turn king's evidence, and certain opponents of the regime, for example Sforza and now even Albertini, contemplated a *coup de main* when they saw the incriminating memorandum compiled by undersecretary Finzi. At long last, liberals and socialists drew together. But unfortunately Amendola, who had succeeded Giolitti as head of the truly independent liberals, decided that the monarch could be relied on to take any action that might be necessary, and only a few days after this murder the Senate passed a vote of confidence by 235 to 21.

The king apparently did consult Giolitti, Salandra, and Orlando and then determined to do nothing. Not only were his own fortunes now bound up with the revolution he had abetted, but he could hardly act against a solid fascist majority in the Lower House. Moreover, the only alternative to fascism would involve the socialists whom he disliked far more. Giolitti stated in so many words that only a government under Mussolini could restore social peace; in the eyes of the ruling classes in Italy, social peace was an overriding consideration. Both Giolitti and Salandra, so the king told Bergamini in 1945, advised him at this moment to retain Mussolini, though Orlando was no longer so sympathetic. Senator Campello presented Vittorio Emanuele with Finzi's implication of Mussolini in Matteotti's murder, but the king covered his face and said that he was deaf and blind and that the Chamber and the Senate were his ears and eyes. A few months later the sovereign returned unread to Bonomi certain other inculpating evidence presented by dissident fascists. Too late he now affected to play the constitutional monarch who could do nothing without his ministers' advice. When a deputation of veterans came to protest at fascist crimes, he changed the subject at once: "My daughter shot two quails today" was his only rejoinder to their complaint.

Faced with a solid majority of blackshirts, in June 1924 most of the opposition deputies decided as a protest against Matteotti's murder to abandon the Chamber altogether. This was called the Aventine secession, after the plebs in ancient Rome who once withdrew from the city to the Aventine hill. It was led by Amendola, one of the finer minds and more attractive characters in recent Italian parliamentary history. Amendola had already been assaulted in Rome during 1923 and was to receive fatal wounds from a second manhandling in July 1925. A final speech from him in parliament listed the sins of fascism: using state funds for the party militia, overriding local authorities, intimidating the opposition by physical force, and truculently claiming to rely on violence and not on parliament. Mussolini interrupted twenty-seven times during this forty-minute speech, using his worst vein of uncouth, ungrammatical, and quite unparliamentary language.

Amendola hoped that the Aventine secession would give the king an excuse to intervene by making clear to him that parliamentary government in the old sense was at an end. Nevertheless, it was of little use for these seceders to wait in the wilderness for public opinion to develop; public opinion needed leadership. The Aventine episode thus proved to be yet another example of the ineffectiveness of constitutional opposition in Italy. It could only have worked had there been a fairly general abstention, but Giolitti refused to join. Giolitti told Amendola that elected and salaried deputies had no right to absent themselves from parliament, perhaps forgetting the lamentable precedent which he himself had set in 1894 and 1915. At this particular moment when fascism was confused, hesitant, and even on the retreat, all the independent forces remaining in the state were passing the buck in turn, and so were severally and effortlessly to be defeated by a man who had the nerve to wait for his luck to turn.

Even though the parliamentary opposition thus ran away from the scene of battle, fascist uniforms and badges began to disappear, party membership cards were returned, Mussolini's *anticamera* was deserted, and criticism became quite outspoken. Worse than a crime, the murder of Matteotti was proving to have been a blunder. Even Balbo had to resign his position. Yet some of the liberals remaining in parliament continued to insist that they still hoped for Mussolini's success, or at most that their protest was only moral, and they had no wish to unseat the one man who could guarantee effective rule and social order. When on June 25 the Senate overwhelmingly supported Mussolini, however, some well-known and respected names figured among the opposing minority—Albertini, Bergamini, Ruffini, and Sforza. Even so, only three senators spoke against fascism on this occasion, and Albertini's speech contained many words of cautious praise. Facta was in September made a senator for his help, and Salandra's opinion was still that fascism had not yet completed its function in history, but was the best available representative of the liberal tradition.

It was this attitude of the so-called liberals which betrayed the hollowness of parliamentary Italy. The liberal party congress had lately given its blessing to fascist rule, and Casati and another liberal were somehow persuaded to join the cabinet in July 1924, unmoved either by Matteotti's murder and its repercussions or by the decree of July 1924 which introduced heavy restrictions on the press. The fear of socialism among these men was evidently greater than their love of liberty, and they still regarded Mussolini as a negative antisocialist instead of someone with a positive ambition for power on his own absolutely illiberal terms.

Don Sturzo commented most unfavorably on the inaction of Giolitti, Orlando, and Salandra. According to him there were many timeservers in Mussolini's party who would have been glad to desert the government coalition if only some of these parliamentary leaders had set an example. The electoral coalition with fascism in fact shows that what the liberals really feared was not so much Mussolini as the mass parties which were threatening to oust them in popular favor, and by this they meant the *popolari* as well as the socialists. Christian democrats, said Croce, were doubly to be feared in that they were both democratic and papal, and this monstrous blend of irreconcilables showed that they also must be illogical and insincere. Giolitti, too, had harsh words for both Sturzo and Salandra, but was never openly heard to make any disparaging remark about Mussolini. Croce had publicly, if reluctantly, sanctioned the violence used in the 1924 elections, for it had been the only way to obtain a fascist majority. In January this philosopher had made an explicit and public statement: "The heart of fascism is love of Italy, the safety of the state, and the true conviction that the state without authority is no state at all. . . . Fascism is overcoming the traditional indifference of Italians to politics . . . and I value so highly the cure which Italy is undergoing from it that I rather hope the patient will not get up too soon from his bed and risk some grave relapse."

The prestige of a liberal like Croce would have been of great effect if used to condemn what early in 1925 he was to revile as an "onagrocracy," or government by wild asses, but in the confusion of the postwar world the liberals like all other parties had in fact lost their bearings. Giolitti and his friends originally believed that the political rules laid down in the past by their own kind were inviolable and beyond controversy. They had tried to use the fascists to give the Left a few salutary rebuffs in punishment for its nonco-operation and its attempt to demolish class privilege. Even when their former servant began to call the tune, they either failed to understand the menace or at least were ashamed to confess that they had been wrong. The *Giornale d'Italia* was beginning to move toward opposition, but still the *Corriere* decided not to print hostile comment against fascism if it imperiled the newspaper's existence. People did not appreciate that so long as liberals refused to stand with socialism in opposition, neither the general public nor foreign observers could properly judge what was happening. Giolitti went on attending parliament with unwonted regularity, to show his solidarity with the government; he listened deferentially to Mussolini's speeches and was seen to applaud them. The king noted all this and assumed that all must be well. Meanwhile Gobetti asserted the need to make liberalism more radical, as Gramsci saw the need for socialists to discard the old myths of socialism, but they were heretics and a small minority, and their protest came too late.

The fate of fascism was still uncertain in October 1924, and it was noted that the war veterans association refused to take part in the anniversary celebrations of the "march on Rome." But as soon as it appeared that the opposition did not mean business, the job hunters and timeservers re-emerged with their fascist insignia. Men of every party sincerely or insincerely began anew to bow to the rising sun: Romolo Murri who had once been a leader of Christian democracy, the philosopher Gentile, the former liberal prime minister Boselli, senators of renown and scholarship like Marconi, Scialoia, Tittoni, and Pantaleoni, all confirmed their allegiance to the regime. This was a testing time during which many consciences were racked and many friendships broken.

In November Giolitti set a belated example of independence as he at last realized how he had been deceived. In particular he rebelled against the fact that freedom of the press had been abolished by a simple decree, for this was violating an express provision of the constitution. Orlando followed Giolitti a few days later. Provoked by these signs of disaffection, Mussolini then boldly launched a challenge in the Senate to see if they were prepared to back words with deeds. If His Majesty were to call him today and say he must resign, he would come to attention, salute, and obey, but his allegiance was to King Vittorio Emanuele, not to "his majesty the *Corriere della Sera*." In the absence of the Aventine seceders, however, there was barely a handful of liberals and communists left in parliament to take up this challenge. During a noisy session, in which Mussolini himself was several times called to order, Albertini claimed that all the leading politicians had gone over to the opposition; but Federzoni, minister of the interior, pertinently shouted, "except the majority of parliament." By 208 to 54 the Senate again supported the government. Mosca and Croce could not suddenly restore confidence in the parliamentary democracy whose theoretical justifications they had spent so long helping to undermine.

At the end of December 1924, another memorandum implicating Mussolini in assault and murder was publicized by Amendola in his paper, *Il Mondo*. The author, Cesare Rossi, had been very close to Mussolini as director of the fascist press bureau. There was an awed hush for a few days, and Salandra and Riccio joined the opposition. Amendola assured his friends once more that they need only keep quiet and do nothing, since Mussolini was bound to resign. But on January 3, 1925, the Duce dealt characteristically with this pitiful parliamentary remnant, and at last gave up his earlier explanations and claimed personal responsibility for Matteotti's murder: "I declare before all Italy that I assume full responsibility for what has happened. . . . If fascism has turned out to be only castor oil and rubber truncheons instead of being a superb passion inspiring the best youth of Italy, I am responsible. . . . Italy wants peace and quiet, and to get on with its work. I shall give it all these, if possible in love, but if necessary by force. In the forty-eight hours after my speech the whole situation will be changed." He proceeded to taunt his hearers by reminding them that Article 47 of the constitution allowed the Chamber to impeach ministers before the High Court. Of course no one dared to take up his defiance; on the contrary, the speech was accepted with acclamation, and only thirty-three votes in the Chamber were cast against him. The two liberal ministers, Casati and Sarrocchi, at last resigned, the second not very willingly it seems. Sforza told a friend that a new ministry would have to be formed with Giolitti, Orlando, and Salandra, as it was unthinkable that a self-confessed murderer should continue to govern the country. But the king knew that his own action in October 1922 tied him firmly to the existing government. The moment passed, and organized opposition henceforward was impossible.

Forty-eight hours after this speech of January 1925, Mussolini's government had ceased to be merely a ministry and had become a regime. He had isolated his opponents and beaten them individually so that he could now drop all pretense and come out in his true colors. Salandra withdrew from politics in bitter disillusionment, even though fascism still retained the enthusiastic allegiance of most of his conservative-liberal friends who represented the landowners and northern industrialists. The liberal party of Giolitti and Croce, without which Mussolini would never have achieved power, was outlawed along with all other independent parties. The 123 deputies of the Aventine, when they lamely tried to return to parliament, found the stable door shut; they were in 1926 declared to have made "an anticonstitutional and clearly revolutionary secession" and so to have forfeited their seats. As was henceforth the rule, this decision was carried unanimously. In the words of Morandi the opposition now left the Aventine for the catacombs, among them the liberal Amendola and the *popolari* leaders De Gasperi and Gronchi. The communist deputies had not seceded from parliament with the rest and were mostly imprisoned. Some of these antifascists fled abroad. Most were left unmolested so long as they abjured politics.

৯৯

After January 3, 1925, it was no longer possible to deceive oneself into believing that Mussolini was intent on becoming respectable, because he had publicly acknowledged his responsibility for the local ras and their squads. He was evidently more interested in power than good government, and any criticism of him in parliament or the newspapers was now declared intolerable. In a last outburst on January 4, Amendola's *Il Mondo* said: "This man Mussolini constitutes a pathological case not foreseen in the constitution. . . . Everything is subordinated to his mad ambition. . . . Apart from his personal coarseness, he is altogether alien to what the English call 'fair play.' " This illumination came too late, and independent journalism was thenceforward forcibly silenced.

Nenni, editor of the socialist *Avanti,* had already been arrested for "defamation of the fascist government." His paper proclaimed to the last that ultimate victory was assured "if only we remain quite intransigent. . . . This is not the first time that our party has been dissolved, but persecution has never held up the march of socialism." Such a philosophy may have consoled, but did not heal, and *Avanti* paid the full penalty for its intransigence. The radical *Secolo* also fell into fascist hands. The *Corriere della Sera* had whole issues confiscated in an attempt to ruin its sales. The liberals who remained on the municipal council of Milan had already been frightened into disavowing their paper, and in November 1925 the owners of the *Corriere,* the Crespi family who were cotton manufacturers in Milan, were persuaded by Farinacci to dismiss the Albertini brothers from its editorship. Liberal writers like Einaudi, Parri, and Croce were banned from its columns, and a less recalcitrant editor, Ojetti, was appointed on the Duce's special designation. So passed one of the great papers of Europe. Likewise,

Frassati had to hand over *La Stampa* to a fascist group, and its editorship was later given for a time to Curzio Malaparte.

A new ruling class of journalists was appearing to replace Salvemini, Gobetti, Salvatorelli, and other notable figures who had striven to keep liberal thought and criticism alive. Hitherto, says Perticone, the opposition journals had been selling ten times as well as the official press. Henceforward, if a quasi-socialist paper managed to exist in Genoa for a number of years, this was probably due only to fascist inefficiency and impercipience. Journalism was standardized from now on, and Farinacci and Balbo found it highly profitable to launch new papers at Cremona and Ferrara which obtained a sure sale as the mouthpiece of government policy.

Mussolini himself, who always remained a journalist at heart, was to spend much more time and thought on publicity than on policy. Daily instructions came to the press from the dictator's personal office in order to mold opinion and ensure that a uniform and ideologically correct impression was created. It would be ordained for example that no mention should be made of his birthday, of his being a grandfather, of him dancing, for the authoritative impression was to be one of youth and serious-mindedness. Photographs of himself smiling were not to be printed. "Say that the *Duce* was called out on to the balcony ten times." "Put out a special edition with his speech under an eight-column headline." "You may comment on his speech, and we shall shortly circulate the requisite comment for inclusion."

This ridiculous behavior was, of course, contraproductive as well as productive, and though there is no means of testing sales resistance, one may guess that the individualism and humor of Italians made them less susceptible to this kind of treatment than Mussolini can have wished. Even his own paper, *Il Popolo d'Italia,* never reached at its peak a circulation of 500,000, a figure which the liberal *Corriere della Sera* had far surpassed in the old days.

47 The Machinery and Personnel of Fascism

Having overcome the independent organs of public opinion by 1925, Mussolini could spend the next few years a law unto himself, gradually transforming the nature of the state and making it more authoritarian and personal. All over Italy the nominated *podestà* was to supplant the elected mayor in each town and village. A committee of "eighteen Solons" including Gentile, Volpe, and Angelo Olivetti the ex-syndicalist was appointed in January 1925 to reform the constitution. In December a law gave the prime minister a new legal existence as head of the state, no longer the first among equals but singly responsible to the king. Whereas under the 1848 constitution the king nominated and dismissed ministers, he now could do this only on Mussolini's proposal, and every motion for debate had first to be approved by the Duce. Mosca was a lone voice in opposition to this. A law of January 1926 then gave Mussolini power to issue decrees having the full force of law—there were to be more than one hundred thousand decree laws issued under fascism, making administration and justice impossibly complicated. Mussolini's person was declared inviolable, and after the attempts on his life by Major Zaniboni in 1925 and the Irish Miss Gibson in 1926, capital punishment was prescribed for those who so much as contemplated his death.

By a law of December 1928 Mussolini was to enter the plentitude of power, for the king then lost his right even to select the prime minister. The Grand Council of fascism was empowered to list the names from among whom Mussolini's successor should be chosen, and the king not only agreed to this but apparently he was once given such a list. This promotion of the *Gran Consiglio* of the fascist party into an organ of state was a constitutional innovation of which Mussolini was particularly proud. Its secretary continued to be secretary of the fascist party. Mussolini alone could convene it and determine who should attend; he was its president by right, could decide its agenda, and use it as a check on the cabinet. He even gave it a right to intervene in the succession to the throne itself, since the heir Umberto was reputedly lukewarm in supporting the regime. Behind all these theoretical attributes, however, there is no evidence that the Grand Council had any importance in practice until in July 1943 it turned on its creator and toppled him.

A new electoral law of May 1928 also changed the representative system once again, receiving only fifteen hostile votes in the Chamber. Parliamentary candidates in future were to be selected from a list drawn up by unions of workers and employers, and from the names on this list the *Gran Consiglio* would choose the candidates who were then put to the electorate for approval or rejection en bloc. Only in the impossible event of their rejection were second elections to be held between competing parties.

Mussolini told the Senate when presenting this bill that universal suffrage was merely a conventional fiction and that the constitution was dead and buried, not because it had been abolished, but simply because Italy was now profoundly different from what it had been in 1848. The senators who sat quietly through this kind of talk were still very largely the liberals appointed by Giolitti and Orlando, but a counterresolution made by Ruffini on this occasion received only forty-six signatures. Albertini made the point that the victors in World War I had been the free peoples, "while those ruled by more or less despotic forms of government were either defeated or else fell out of the struggle before its end. . . . I am a survivor of a liberalism that even though defeated cannot accept dishonor, and mindful of the oath taken in this very hall of the Senate, I feel it my duty in this hour to reaffirm my unshakable faith in those principles which the bill before us denies." Hundreds of new senators soon swamped these antediluvian survivors, and because it became *de rigueur* for the whole body sometimes to wear black shirts and shout ritual slogans, the liberals preferred to stay away.

In 1929 when elections were held, 136,000 votes were officially declared to have been cast against the national list of candidates, but this number may have been pure guesswork. The next elections in March 1934 showed only fifteen thousand votes for the opposition, though 95 per cent of the electorate was said to have voted. These were absurd figures in view of the number of policemen and political prisoners who testified to the strength of popular resistance. Plebiscites of this sort were a bogus test of public opinion and merely indicate how easily such elections can be manipulated to give a required result.

But this is not to say that Mussolini was unrepresentative of his country. Opposition there may have been, but it could not be very vocal, and where most people wanted security and prosperity above everything, Mussolini could easily persuade them that he had these gifts at his disposal. The plebiscitary dictatorship was in its own way a manifestation of democracy. Other politicians in history had already discovered that liberty and equality could be exclusive as well as complementary, and that by careful handling the mob could be used to make a dictator more autocratic. The argument for Leviathan grew ever more attractive to the generality of people as international relations became more perilous and as the problems of government escaped further from their knowledge and experience. Internal liberties might seem to be too expensive when they meant delay, division, and inefficiency. And so Mussolini was able to establish what he called an "authoritarian, centralized democracy," in which he could talk contemptuously of the "putrefying corpse of liberty" to the applause of a uniform nation.

๛

The central organ of the revolution was the fascist party itself, and parallel with each existing institution of state there grew up a new one which was dependent on the party: the fascist militia alongside the army, the Roman salute with the military salute, the special tribunal cutting across the ordinary law courts, and the federal secretary at the side of each provincial prefect. There was also the Palazzo Venezia which after 1929, when Mussolini made it his private office, overtook the Quirinal palace as a fount of patronage and power, and there was the party song *"Giovinezza"* which, to the king's disgust, began to oust the *"Marcia Reale."* At the apex, the Duce of fascism was simultaneously the Head of the Government, and these two offices were soon considered identical. Gradually, the party was thus absorbing the state. Fascist law became the only effective law, and the nationalization of the fascist militia transferred an onerous burden from the shoulders of the rich party backers onto the taxpayer. Emblazoned on the state coat of arms was the party emblem of the lictor's fasces. The party secretary in the end assumed ministerial rank and attended cabinet meetings; he came to be a *de jure* member of the defense council and the board of education and was given precedence in ceremonial processions and court functions.

Another tendency was for the party itself to become increasingly centralized, and throughout 1923 there was a purge of its provincial directorates, as local fascist units were subordinated to the center at Rome. Several times before 1922 the local *ras* had rebelled and over-ruled the leader, but never again for the next twenty-one years. After 1926, instead of the *Gran Consiglio* being elected at the annual party congress, nomination was introduced from the top—"supermen elect themselves," declared Mussolini. The *Gran Consiglio* then chose the party secretary, and the latter appointed the provincial secretaries who together made up the national council. These provincial secretaries then appointed the lesser officials of the local *fasci*.

Membership of the party fluctuated considerably in number, for there was an oscillation between considering the party as a mass and treating it as an elite. At one moment the *tessera fascista* was a document requisite for many types of employment. At another, large expulsions were decreed when the party was suddenly thought to be unwieldy or ridden with factions. Its hard core was the "fascists of the first hour," the *sansepolcristi* who had inaugurated the movement in 1919 and who continued to set the tone. These obtained special privileges, as did all real or self-styled "pre-march" fascists, and for this reason the hooligan element remained on top.

§❧

Few of the party leaders were more than mediocre men, and few were even efficient. Most of them were unintelligent, grasping, jealous, and incompetent, and jockeyed for place by telling tales against their rivals, or else boosted each other's morale by organizing "spontaneous" crowd demonstrations for one another. With the possible exception of D'Annunzio, there seems to have been no living Italian for whom Mussolini felt any admiration. When he later claimed that the party leaders had let him down, the answer must be that he had the subordinates which he deserved and whom he had himself advanced. No doubt he deliberately promoted their rivalries and conflicting policies. Frequently, he replaced nearly all the ministers and party leaders in a sweeping "change of the guard," and he publicly boasted in 1929 that he used to announce these wholesale changes without even consulting first with the people he intended to appoint or dismiss. This was a revealing manifestation of *ducismo*.

Each party secretary was quickly superseded by another, so as to prevent anyone winning too much influence or building up a private empire within the state. In 1923 Bianchi was displaced as general secretary by Sansanelli, he in 1924 by Giunta. In 1925–26 the post was held by Farinacci, one of the more illiterate and brutish of the hierarchy, anticlerical and anti-Semitic. The term of his successor, Augusto Turati, ended when he was charged with immorality, suspected of lunacy, and confined at Rhodes. He was succeeded in turn by Giuriati, Starace, Muti, and Serena; of these only Starace reigned long enough to have much influence, his consulship extending from 1931 to 1939. Then, with Vidussoni in 1941 was appointed a party secretary still in his early twenties, of whom no one knew anything at all except that he had failed his examinations and had a medal for valor. After him came Scorza.

Mussolini's sons were but shadows of their father. Bruno was involved in running an airline to South America, and Vittorio tried to assume direction of the film industry. Edda, their sister, had a more forceful character. Mussolini's younger brother Arnaldo was the most worthy of the family, a man of some conscience and religion, and one of the few men to keep Mussolini's affection and confidence. His job was the running of *Il Popolo d'Italia*.

Of the other leaders the Duce was always a little suspicious, sometimes with reason. Emilio De Bono was fifty-six years old in 1922, a white-bearded, somewhat puny army general who helped organize the militia and whom Mussolini was to execute in 1944. Italo Balbo in 1922 was only twenty-six, thirteen years younger than Mussolini. The most genuine and gallant of the fascists, he was always a *frondeur,* with his own private aims and ambitions which often differed from Mussolini's, and he was suspected of courting Prince Umberto in the hope of some time succeeding to supreme power. Mussolini was a little afraid of Balbo it seems, as well as envious of his youth. Eventually, this potential rival was to be shot down by Italian antiaircraft guns in 1940, probably by accident. A more senior and more absurd figure was Cesare De Vecchi, created count of Val Cismon, poetaster and pseudo academic, who was the general butt of his colleagues and eventually helped to remove Mussolini in 1943. Dino Grandi was another young "first hour" fascist, and a callous squad leader in his youth. He also had some ambition to succeed or replace Mussolini. His chief official task was to fill up the ministry of foreign affairs with party hacks; later he took over the London embassy during the thirties. Grandi was a competent diplomat, but fawning and obsequious toward Mussolini until he too deserted the sinking ship in July 1943.

The younger generation was represented by Galeazzo Ciano, whose father, Costanzo, was an admiral who had done very well financially out of running the ministry of transport. The younger Ciano rose rapidly to become foreign minister in 1936 at the age of thirty-four. He compared moderately well with his associates, being generally good-natured, and having something of wit and even intelligence to make up for lack of education, but he was corrupt and self-indulgent, superficial to a degree, idle, frivolous, and quite without weight of character. Ciano was an exhibitionist who lived for the camera, and sometimes used to play irresponsibly with the destiny of nations just out of vanity or pique. He is said to have been liberal in giving away vital public secrets to friends in high Roman society, who found in him almost alone of the fascist leaders a man of conversation and polish, and he defended their interests against the quasi-socialist elements which occasionally threatened to dominate the party. The old-guard fascists of the first hour resented him as an upstart and were more than enraged when in 1930 he was chosen by the Duce as a son-in-law. For years Ciano remained the dictator's favorite, until in 1944 his father-in-law had him shot in the back for treason in order to placate the Germans.

On the left of the party was Rossoni, leader of the fascist labor unions and an erstwhile revolutionary agitator in the United States. Bianchi and 'Professor' Bottai also inclined toward this left wing, together with other ex-socialists like Farinacci and Bombacci on the extreme fringe. The relative importance of this group is hard to gauge, but union leaders in general gained in power and prestige from the new centralized organization of trades and professions. More and more individuals in search of a job after 1922 had to abandon the socialist and Catholic unions and join the fascist syndicates. Under government pressure, in October 1925 the Confederation of Industry and the Confederation of Fascist Trade Unions signed the Vidoni pact, when their spokesmen, Gino Olivetti and Rossoni, each recognized the other as representative of his whole class. Olivetti, however, was far more genuinely representative than Rossoni, and Mussolini thus obtained industrial peace at his own price, although workers were placed in a clearly inferior position by the abolition of strikes and penalizing labor unrest. Clearly, the left wing of the fascist party was not very strong in itself until Mussolini reverted to his earlier socialism toward the end of his life.

§●

It will not be very helpful to list many of the numerous laws decreed by fascism, because in any case they rarely corresponded with achieved results. But one reform obtained particularly wide publicity, and it must therefore be noted how the socialistic and bureaucratic tendencies in fascism together resulted in creating the so-called Corporative System. Mussolini was eager to demonstrate that his movement, despite appearances, was not simply conservative, but was simultaneously full of new and seminal ideas. The party intellectuals were therefore enlisted to expound and apply his oracular assertion that "the Corporative System is destined to become the civilization of the twentieth century."

This was one of a number of ideas borrowed from the nationalists and Catholics. Its author, the nationalist Rocco, became justice minister in January 1925; a new ministry of corporations was created in 1926, and in 1930 a National Council of Corporations was called into theoretical existence as a deliberative assembly. To it were attached all the workers in the state through their respective trade organizations. When at last the system took more positive shape in 1936, there were said to be twenty-two separate categories for various trades and industries —for instance, the fifth for the sugar and beet industries, the ninth for metallurgy, the twenty-second for the professional classes and artists. All workers were fitted into an appropriate category, and each category was given political as well as economic functions. The union officials were of course appointed from above, because this was good fascist theory and because jobs had to be found for party members. The workers themselves had but to pay their subscriptions and do what they were told, for instead of being citizens with rights and independence, they were now cogs with a function. Having abolished political liberalism by 1925, Mussolini thus buried economic liberalism soon afterward.

The idea of corporativism seemed so attractive and typically fascist that Mussolini's claims for it far outdistanced actuality. In November 1933 he promised the National Council of Corporations that they might one day replace the Chamber of Deputies: "The Chamber has never been to my taste; it has now become anachronistic even in name; as an institution it is foreign to our fascist cast of thought, and presupposes a plurality of parties which no longer exists." Two years later he shamelessly assured them that they were "perhaps the most imposing assembly in the whole history of Italy." Finally, in 1939 the Chamber of Fasces and Corporations was created, and the old parliamentary system disappeared in name as well as in fact.

Imposing though the name of this new body may have sounded, the corporations were more an aspiration than an actuality, and Salvemini rightly called them an elaborate piece of imposing humbug. In practice the new system was simply an attempt to keep a tight hold on the workers in straitly centralized unions. The machinery of corporativism was tremendously expensive, and this invited much jobbery and corruption, while a vast organization had to be built up to do things which voluntary unions did more willingly and more efficiently elsewhere. Whether they performed any genuine function which had not been done before is still a mystery.

Mussolini in March 1936 told the Council of Corporations that he "did not wish to bureaucratize the entire economy of the nation," but in practice the extension of governmental activities everywhere brought with it a top-heavy organization, slow and unresponsive, and quite out of close touch with ordinary people. Party members and officials constituted a huge new vested interest, since the party, the militia, and the corporations provided what was admitted to be as many as a hundred thousand jobs for secretaries and organizers. Fascism in this way helped to satisfy that deep-rooted desire among Italians to find a respectable post in government service, poorly paid but easy work and a sure pension. The census returns of 1931 and 1936 reveal strikingly how the greatest increase in occupation statistics was made by administrative and professional categories. The bureaucratic capital, Rome, now regained the lead in size (lost about 1875) over the industrial capital, Milan. A writer in the London *Economist* thus described the position in 1935: "The new corporative state only amounts to the establishment of a new and costly bureaucracy, from which those industrialists who can spend the necessary amount can obtain almost anything they want, and put into practice the worst kind of monopolistic practices at the expense of the little fellow who is squeezed out in the process."

With all this increase in government expenditure and patronage, corruption became the besetting sin of the regime, even though the Duce personally did not seem to profit from the graft which riddled every department of state. While he was in prison on the island of Ponza in 1943, the local policeman explained to him why the tap in his room did not run: although money had been lavished on an aqueduct, most of it had been channeled into the pockets of good party men and their friends. In every locality the party hierarchs or *gerarchi* were petty tyrants with an unlimited call on public money and the assurance of being acquitted of any crime. As they were almost invariably bad men to begin with, this conscious immunity was especially damaging.

Authenticated and unauthenticated stories of malversation were legion. Mussolini's friends, unfortunately, included people interested in the marble trade from Carrara, and the monstrous public buildings erected in the best *stile fascista* all over Italy and its colonies are probably not unconnected with this fact. Fictitious "industrial zones" were declared to exist so that state subsidies would be forthcoming, and mock factories were built for this same purpose, though they were never apparently intended to produce anything. There was a lively trade in titles. In another field, Farinacci the railroad clerk easily picked up an honorary doctorate of law, and the incontrovertible nature of his forensic arguments secured him the rewards of a good legal practice. Ciano was also said to have used his inside knowledge to buy up ships prior to the Ethiopian war. And thus the ungodly flourished.

In most cases this corruption was no doubt petty and unimportant. For example, even an unfriendly American press agency could usually buy up a monopoly of pictures from a party official on any newsworthy event, and a reporter with ready cash could jump an important story even when a simultaneous release had been promised. But sometimes matters were not so trivial. High civilian and military officials are known to have diverted funds away from aircraft development, and as there were always enough people who would keep silent for a consideration, Italy lost World War II before hostilities had begun. Salvatorelli, who is the safest historian of this period, concludes that this corruption became really scandalous only from the moment when Mussolini began his liaison with Clara Petacci in the middle thirties; thenceforward, it was not only something normal and unconcealed, but even regulated and taxed.

§❧

That this rickety machine kept running so long was due largely to the personality of its leader. Mussolini lacked all nobility of character, but he knew the Italians and knew how to make them serve him. He was always able to inspire confidence and make people think him sincere, whatever his beliefs or lack of them. Skill consciously employed was here allied with a fascination he exerted almost unconsciously.

In 1932 Mussolini dropped some revealing remarks to Emil Ludwig: "Today people have not so much time to think as they used to have. The capacity of the modern man for faith is illimitable. When the masses are like wax in my hands, when I stir their faith, or when I mingle with them and am almost crushed by them, I feel myself to be a part of them. All the same there persists in me a certain feeling of aversion, like that which the modeller feels for the clay he is moulding. Does not the sculptor sometimes smash his block of marble into fragments because he cannot shape it to represent the vision he has conceived? Now and then this crude matter rebels against the creator." His interlocutor asked whether a dictator could be loved. "Yes," answered Mussolini with renewed decisiveness, "Provided that the masses fear him at the same time. The crowd loves strong men. The crowd is like a woman."

Mussolini was a play actor who knew how to produce himself in public. With his bulbous and unsmiling face he created a legend of the strong man who was victorious and always right, the wise man who knew the inmost thoughts of people, the industrious servant of the public frequently photographed when toiling in the harvest field stripped to the waist. Foreign diplomats were impressed and frightened when they had to move past a double column of his unpaid corps of pugnacious-looking black-uniformed musketeers with daggers held out at arm's length, and any reception in Mussolini's gigantic marble study was always carefully staged to humble the visitor. His most important quality was thus that of being a stupendous poseur. His mixture of showmanship and vulgarity appealed to the common people, who liked to hear of his adulterous relationships and illegitimate children because he then became more human and virile. They were not allowed to know about his ill-health or his use of eyeglasses, and foreign journalists would be expelled if they mentioned his ulcer, let alone if they hinted at syphilis.

Only in retrospect do we notice Mussolini's deep inferiority complex and his extraordinary timidity and reluctance to decide between alternative lines of conduct. What was stressed at the time was the carefully contrived swagger and braggadocio of a Benvenuto Cellini. On top of this was superimposed the quite different legend of a temperate man who did not smoke, who seldom drank wine, and ate little but fruit, milk, and vegetables. A light would burn in his study far into the night to persuade people that he was at work, when in reality he was asleep, or dallying in the dark with Signora Petacci. Stories circulated of his skill on the violin, and his abiding affection for Dante, without which no Italian politician can pass muster for long—it was even claimed that he knew whole cantos of the *Divine Comedy* by heart. His fencing and horsemanship were legendary, for he had to excel in everything, and a public fall from his horse would be stringently concealed from the newspapers. Since there was no possibility of contradiction, he even convinced himself of his ability as a brave soldier, a daring aircraft pilot, and (most dangerous of all) a great strategist and war leader. In his "autobiography" he was childishly vain about driving cars so fast that experienced drivers were astonished.

Some of this deceived nobody except himself, and even the witless party leaders had their private laugh when requested to record some flatulent *mot* for posterity. But propaganda makes people gullible and uncritical, and fascism inevitably bred a low average of sense and discrimination. After one visit Mussolini paid to Genoa, a journalist was not ashamed to write: "To die without lament, and with a vision of light in one's eyes, and an infinite sweetness in the heart, that is what we should be glad to do after the experience of today, while our hands still keep some of the warmth of his masculine hand which we kissed, our hearts in tumult and full of a sense of liberation." When people began to turn against fascism, it was not so much for its tyranny and bellicosity as for this sort of embarrassing bad taste which permeated the whole of public life.

There was perhaps some slight excuse for foreigners to approve of Mussolini from a distance when Italians found so much to idolize on the spot—and in this connection one may note that Italians living abroad were wheedled at great cost to the exchequer into becoming his most blatantly enthusiastic fans and propagandists. Croce later tried to exculpate himself for supporting Mussolini in 1922–24 by describing fascism as a disease which came to Italy from abroad and largely because of foreign help (as also he insisted that it was brought to the South from northern Italy and by northern Italians). Croce even took this piece of patriotic consolation to the point of asserting that fascism was wholly alien to Italian traditions and temperament. The evident sophistry of this thesis must not make us ignore its tiny germ of truth. Among the British, Bernard Shaw whimsically defended the Ethiopian invasion. Winston Churchill in 1927, after an hour with Mussolini, spoke of his charm and gentleness and praised those Italians who backed fascism against the Reds. Churchill and Lloyd George both referred to the Corporative System in Italy as a highly promising development. One British foreign minister was accused of giving the fascist salute at a press conference in Rome, and the wife of another on a celebrated occasion was seen to be wearing the party badge. From the United States many useful loans were advanced to fascist Italy until the Debt Default Act was passed, and one version of Mussolini's "autobiography" was apparently written for him by an ex-ambassador of the United States at whose house he used to stay.

There was a fair amount of uninformed foreign approval for fascism, though no one has been able to prove that this had much effect in practice. Those Italians who say that Britain and America ought to have condemned Mussolini should pause to think whether foreign interference in domestic affairs does not usually have the reverse effect of strengthening a regime, as indeed happened later over sanctions. All that foreigners could see was the applause which the Italian press and parliament (and the electorate) gave to fascism in 1922–24, and by 1925 the damage was done irretrievably, short of war. One may add that the shopwindow aspect of fascism was deliberately dressed with an eye to foreign inspection. When Axel Munthe asked him to make Capri into a bird sanctuary, Mussolini saw the advertisement value of the idea to impress sentimental foreigners—though his forgetfulness or his discourtesy was such that he is said to have given Munthe skylark pie for lunch when the latter arrived to thank him for his benevolence.

§♠

Mussolini's flair for publicity is undoubted, but it masked a profound lack of skill in policy and administration, and so in one sense was to prove his undoing. His journalistic bent is revealed in the periodic anonymous articles he continued to write for the press, and it was on the profits of journalism, authorship, and newspaper ownership that he lived, for it was claimed somewhat dubiously that he never took his ministerial salary. Press clippings from abroad were dilligently studied and became lamentably influential on policy, while Mussolini's own mental processes never ceased to be governed by slogans and eight-column headlines. This was to prove disastrous. Mussolini was a facile assimilator of superficialities and possessed an ephemeral but sometimes surprising secondhand culture—"forgive my learned references" was a phrase which once amused his entourage. He preferred to argue and speechify rather than to penetrate behind words to reality, and so never properly dissected a problem, but thought he could solve anything after a cursory survey. Fascism, which affected to despise speeches and talk, was itself essentially rhetoric and blather. Mussolini was a moderately good talker, and some good listeners said they found his conversation delightful, but he was a bad administrator, and his policy was too often empty, contradictory, and misapplied.

The motto "Mussolini is always right" was nevertheless stenciled on wayside houses all over Italy, winning credence by repetition—it was even embossed by *devots* on their notepaper. And yet his opinions were inconsistent as well as shallow. On and off he preached and then abandoned socialism, anticlericalism, republicanism, anti-imperialism, and pacifism, and one should remember his campaign in April 1919 against dictatorships of every kind. At one moment he claimed to be the categoric antithesis of democracy, at another its most perfect manifestation. His one constant belief was that action was for the sake of action and consistency mattered not a whit, so that ideas and opinions were of minor importance, simply tactical means to win the alliance of the Church or the conservatives or the trade unionists. Patriotism meant little to him, and, to judge from his abuse of them, he despised Italians even more than he did humanity in general. He glorified Italy only in so far as this redounded to his own glory, and he as readily handed her over to German occupation and civil war when she threatened to fall short of that purpose.

Mussolini was easily influenced, and his lieutenants quickly discovered his vexatious habit of always agreeing with the last person he had spoken to. But perhaps no one held any continuous influence over him until the Petacci family cornered him in his premature dotage. He was no respector of persons and had little sense of loyalty to former friends and collaborators. Indeed he despised friendship. He boasted to Senise that he had never possessed a friend in his life, and very few people were ever asked home to the Villa Torlonia. The truth was that, apart from an impressive interview technique, he did not shine in dealing with individuals, whereas he loved crowds and felt enlarged when addressing them. He was as self-consciously unsure of himself in private as he was self-consciously aggressive in public.

Mussolini was careful to take upon himself all the credit for any success, because this not only fed his vanity, but it also prevented his lieutenants from gathering any popular support and becoming anything but abjectly subservient to his person. For the same reason he discouraged them from taking any bold political initiative. In return they were allowed to strut in fine uniforms and amass private fortunes, the chief losers being the Italian people who consequently were exploited and misgoverned by the dregs of the nation. Yet though Mussolini tried to monopolize the credit for success, he always found someone else to blame for failure, and perhaps he reached that last fatal pitch of delusion where he genuinely thought that he could do no wrong. This divorce of power from responsibility was ruinous, and it was, for example, to allow Mussolini to declare war without full appreciation of Italy's inordinate unpreparedness. Such was the deliberate concentration of power in himself that there was only himself to blame for the result. In 1926 Mussolini personally held the offices of prime minister, president of the council, foreign minister, minister of the interior, minister for the Corporations, minister for all three of the service departments, and commander in chief of the militia. At other times he was also minister for colonies and for public works. Mindful of the Code Napoléon, he also had to put his own amateurish stamp on the new codes of law which were introduced during his period of government.

This was quite absurd, for no one could attend to so many jobs, and power thus became confusedly dispersed through a jungle of under-secretaries, *gerarchi,* and *ras,* who were frequently changed, and who were seldom given either the time to carry out any reform or the authority to consider policy over a broad enough field. The dictator's personal permission was needed before the police could change into their summer uniforms, but high policy went disregarded, and as minister of war he confessed to Bottai in 1939 that he had had no idea that the artillery then in use dated from World War I. Again and again he buried his head in the sand, either from ignorance and carelessness, or from a genuine fear of having to take the responsibility for policy decisions, and unfortunately he could never abide the existence of a vice-Duce to supply his deficiencies.

48 Economic and Social Policy

Fascism began with no particular economic policy; its doctrines of planned economy were one day to be called typically fascist, but in fact they came as an afterthought. The first minister of finance, De Stefani, started rather by reducing government expenditure. He partly rationalized the tax system, and in the years 1924–26 the budget once again was balanced. Italy was meanwhile sharing in the general prosperity of contemporary Europe, and liberal economists could approve of government policy. Financiers and industrialists, however, did not like the minister's "moralization of the Stock Exchange," nor his reduction of the sugar tariff.

In July 1925 De Stefani was therefore succeeded for three years by the financier and industrialist Count Volpi, and certain vested interests at once began to profit from protection and central planning. First, import duties were heavily increased on grain, sugar, silk, and other commodities. Then the currency was heavily overvalued, for reasons of prestige and in order to put the lira on a par with the franc. Note circulation was heavily reduced, and credit was so restricted by the banks that the value of the dollar fell from 32 to 18 lire in the single year 1926–27. This raised export prices and severely damaged trade, though it benefited the bureaucrats and some of the middle classes whose salaries had depreciated during the postwar inflation. Meanwhile, by the Vidoni pact of 1925, trade unions were forbidden to strike, and thirty rather vapid aphorisms were officially coined in 1927 and issued with the grandiose title of a Charter of Labor. Mussolini in 1926 then opened up his national "battle for grain," followed by a "battle for population." The new trend of the times can be seen in decrees issued for reducing the size of newspapers to save wood pulp, for diluting gasoline with alcohol made from wine or grain, and for allowing a nine-hour working day again. Gradually, a planned economy was introduced, at least on paper. Self-sufficiency had become the principal aim by the early 1930's, and the Leader had declared that "laissez faire is out of date." No one could obtain employment without a special worker's pass, and on this pass were included details of a man's political as well as his industrial experience.

The immediate postwar economic recovery began before fascism came into power, and so reflected no very positive credit on the government. But the slump in Italy started earlier than the collapse of the bull market on Wall Street and must be ascribed in great part to Mussolini's policy of revaluation and autarky. Tourism and the trade in luxury commodities fell off. The rich began to complain that the lira was valued too highly and that the multiplying bureaucracy ate up too much of the community's taxable wealth. Accordingly, the salaries of government employees were cut by 12 per cent. Those affected by this cut and by parallel wage reductions found it cold comfort when Mussolini told the Senate in December 1930 that "fortunately the Italian people were not accustomed to eat much and therefore feel the privation less acutely than others." When recovery commenced after 1933, he contrived to attribute it to fascism, but he then started preparing for war and so began the progressive ruin of the whole economy.

Fascism found it hard to alter Italy's dependence on foreign imports —in 1925 this dependence included 99 per cent of her cotton and mineral oil, 95 per cent of her coal, and over half of her metals. Industry did make considerable progress, but mainly in the field of military supply. Production of electricity was subsidized and increased about fivefold between 1917 and 1942. The automobile industry produced 38,675 cars in 1938, though only 30,032 in 1939. In an attempt to modernize shipping, bounties were given for the scrapping of old vessels, though unsound investments were made in big prestige liners such as the "Rex" and the "Conte di Savoia" which might win the "blue ribbon" for a brief year but could not compete economically in transatlantic traffic. Moreover, shipping construction seems to have declined in the 1930's, owing to the high cost of steel plate which resulted from exorbitant protection and the system of trusts. Schemes were devised to build oil refining installations at Bari and Leghorn, and perhaps Mussolini believed his own statement that he would make Italy self-sufficient in oil and gasoline by 1938. But achievements fell ludicrously short of this aim, and had he taken the trouble to discover the real precariousness of Italian industry, he might have been less bellicose in foreign politics.

౸

Mussolini was no mere instrument of business and agrarian interests, yet his ignorance about economics and human nature left him an easy target for sharks who wanted protective duties or who extracted money from the state for quite impossible schemes of industrialization. Fascism seems to have had a close reciprocal understanding with the big trusts from which both sides gained, and several presidents of the *Confindustria* became ministers. When Count Volpi of the Banca Commerciale Italiana took over the ministry of finance, this began another involvement of banking with politics which aroused as much talk of scandals as the Tanlongo affair in the 1890's, only this time the talk was suppressed. In 1928 the heavy taxes on company amalgamation deeds were reduced. The industries of the Ansaldo group, which had collapsed in 1921, clearly banked heavily on a government which would stimulate armament production and "nationalize" their losses. A new steel cartel arose in the early thirties which helped to keep inefficient firms alive, its express intention being to maintain high prices and restrict production, and consumers thus compulsorily subsidized inefficiency in order to prevent a large uneconomic investment from losing its value. With such help, the Edison electricity company, Montecatini chemicals, Snia Viscosa artificial silk, and Pirelli rubber lost none of their dominant position. The Agnelli family, which controlled Fiat, became responsible for four-fifths of Italian automobile manufacture, as well as for numerous other operations which ranged from mining and smelting to making vermouth, cement, and newspapers. These were private concerns. Italian economy under fascism was not typified by direct state ownership, but in 1933 the *Istituto per la Ricostruzione Industriale* was founded by the government to subsidize industry and to save those banks which had been too liberal in giving long-term credit. By the time the war came, the I.R.I. controlled many of Italy's leading firms in the heavy and mechanical industries and had interests stretching over a wide field of banking and manufacture.

Nevertheless, as employers found it increasingly necessary to go to Rome for credit, permits, and protection, they were bound to be irked by the delays and restrictions involved in this growing dependence upon the government. Milanese businessmen had welcomed fascism's nationalization of labor unions, but in the thirties they felt the brunt of capital levies, compulsory loans, and the high taxes which imperialism demanded. The war industries doubtless continued to thrive, but even here it is evident from Italy's weakness in 1940 that billions of lire must have been misappropriated. By a paradox, the obverse of dictatorship was inefficiency, and such a fact cannot have helped to ingratiate this type of government with the generality of businessmen.

An overvalued currency led to devaluation of industrial wages, and as early as 1926 the hard-earned eight-hour day was surrendered. The official index of wages told such a tale that its publication was suspended in 1927, the year in which a general wage reduction was decreed. Figures given by the International Labor Office in 1930 suggested that real wages in Italy were lower than anywhere in western Europe, including Spain. Even the *Corriere della Sera* admitted that they had been reduced by almost half in the four years before 1932, and Professor Chabod, after trying to reconcile many conflicting statistics from various ministries, now concludes that between 1926 and 1934 farm laborers lost 50 to 70 per cent of their wages. Unemployment figures still showed a million out of work in 1932–35.

By a typical *volte-face* Mussolini abandoned his boast about increasing prosperity, and in May 1936 bragged instead that he was enforcing a more vigorous way of life: "We must rid our minds of the idea that what we have called the days of prosperity may return. We are probably moving toward a period when humanity will exist on a lower standard of living." Mussolini had by this time engaged on a policy of war and was taking money away from welfare in order to invest it in imperialism. People have estimated on official figures that three or four hundred thousand Italians at this time were still living in hovels made of earth and sticks, and many others in caves or crowded ten to a room. To these classes of the abjectly poor a showy apparatus of social services was offered, which was much more than the liberals had ever considered, but in great part this was just another piece of window dressing, and expenditure on social services probably absorbed less of the national income than in nearly all other European countries. Foreign visitors would not notice the increase in child labor, but punctual mainline trains and strict police action against beggars would impress them, and depreciation in other far more important regards might thus pass unobserved.

§❧

These twenty years witnessed a big exodus from the land. The census of 1921 gave three-fifths of the working population as still employed in agriculture, but that of 1931 gave less than half. Mussolini strongly disliked this drift to the cities, in particular because industrial labor was factious and socialistic, and a law was therefore passed in 1930 to stop workers moving except by permission of the prefects. The landowners were grateful for this, because it kept their peasants tied to the soil and wages low. But industry suffered badly and rural overpopulation thereby became worse, so much so that proprietors were sometimes obliged to employ a fixed proportion of workers per unit area of land. Nobody liked this increasing degree of coercion all around, and one is not surprised to find it only in part effective.

Mussolini maintained that Italy was the classic land of the small-holder, but on the one hand some seven thousand small properties a year continued to lapse to the exchequer for failure to pay land tax, and on the other hand nothing was done to divide up the large estates. A bill had already passed through the Lower House in 1922 by which part of these large estates should be given out to the peasants, and indeed this was a policy which *Il Popolo d'Italia* had itself specifically proclaimed in January 1921, but after 1922 Mussolini was too much in thrall to the agrarians, and the bill was quietly dropped. Some fifteen noble families such as the Borghese, Caracciolo, Chigi, Colonna, and Torlonia continued to hold between them well over a million acres of land, which in a small and crowded country was a sizable proportion of the total agricultural area. It was estimated that in 1930 there were some 3,500 *latifondi* each over 1,200 acres in size, together comprising a fifth of the land under cultivation, while 15,000 people held other estates of 250 acres or more; all these together covered half the cultivable area of Italy. No doubt many of these large farms could not be split into small holdings without loss in productivity. Nevertheless, satisfaction of land hunger was probably the only way to reconcile the peasantry and prevent that flight from the countryside which Mussolini so deplored.

Some idea of the principal imports and exports of Italy at this time may be gained from the following tables for 1933:

Imports   (*in million lire*)

Raw cotton	737
Coal and coke	685
Wheat	504
Machinery	365
Wool	361

Exports   (*in million lire*)

Fruit and garden produce	1,091
Raw and artificial silk	820
Cotton fabrics and yarn	676
Cheese	241

It will be noted how much Italy was still an agricultural nation and yet how dependent she was upon imports of grain.

Perhaps the most striking alteration in her economy under fascism was in domestic production of wheat. Ever since 1870 the annual production had been little more than forty million quintals, but by 1930 Mussolini had raised this to sixty million, and by 1939 to eighty million quintals. This *battaglia del grano* was highly successful. Medals for the most successful farmers were distributed each April 21—this date being now set up to rival the socialist May Day—and progress was such that wheat imports were cut by 75 per cent in the ten years after 1925. The price paid was, however, dangerously high. Cereals were a type of agricultural product which long experience had shown to be the least economical for Italy, and the result was to lower the total output of agriculture and with it the national income. Mussolini's obsession about self-sufficiency drove him to produce the maximum quantity of wheat at any price, instead of as much as could be produced economically. Marginal land was therefore changed over from cattle pasture, fruit, and olives, thus quite distorting the economy, and the cost of Italian wheat was 50 per cent higher than of American.

While the large-scale cereal growers grew fat on government subsidies, consumers were not in the best position to make their voices heard. As wheat cost more, some Italians simply had to eat less of it, and the switch in land usage also meant that there was less livestock and olive oil. Political motives thus played havoc with Italian agriculture, and autarky added to Italian economic problems instead of solving them as Mussolini had assumed. The relative index of variations in consumption per head given in the *Enciclopedia italiana* shows the effect of a rising cost of living:

	1922–29	1930–38
Wine	123	101
Wheat	100	91
Tobacco	99	81

With this decline in consumption of basic foodstuffs, it is small wonder that the infant mortality figures remained twice or thrice those in Scandinavia.

§

Another fascist "battle" was that for land reclamation, under the generalship of undersecretary Serpieri. Mussolini soon discovered the advantages of *bonifiche* as an ostentatious testament to his own skill and enterprise, and in 1928 large government funds were appropriated to schemes of water regulation and mountain conservation which were beyond the scope of individual proprietors. Positive achievements were the Emilia canal, and the partial colonization of the Volturno Valley and the Pontine marshes. The Agro Pontino was near Rome, and hence its reclamation was a particularly useful advertisement with foreign visitors. Several hundred thousand acres were reclaimed, and hundreds of peasant families were settled in a more ambitious and successful scheme than any previous ruler of Italy had attempted. Here again, however, the work was marred by its primarily political motivation, and it was said that proprietors who had the ear of some *gerarca* diverted the money to land of their own which was in good shape already. When Mussolini turned away to pursue his grandiose schemes of imperialism after 1934, payments on land reclamation dried up. Many of his improvements were then lost in World War II, for as soon as dikes were left unrepaired, water crept back over the old marshland. Farm buildings scattered irrationally over the Sicilian *latifondi* also had to be abandoned when insufficient investment was forthcoming to change the prevailing type of extensive agriculture.

Progress was maintained in the development of communications. The mainline tourist trains did run punctually, and by 1939 some five thousand kilometers of track had been electrified. Fast traffic roads called *autostrade* were built to connect the principal towns and tourist centers in northern Italy, Turin to Milan, Milan to the Lakes, Florence and Rome to the sea. The aircraft industry never developed quite as successfully as Italian skill in automobile manufacture might have predicted, but Italian planes won the Schneider trophy in 1920, 1921, and 1926, and Major de Bernardi set new world speed records in 1927 and 1928 with a Macchi seaplane powered by a Fiat motor. It is interesting to note these dates, for the gradual encroachment of fascism over the whole of Italian life was reflected in a diminution and not an increase in this kind of success, and only 11,000 planes seem to have been produced in World War II. Prizes and subsidies were liberally offered, and by 1939 Italy's civil airlines covered a considerable mileage, but the war found her deficient in types of warplane and industrial capacity. Mussolini boasted that he could blot out the sunlight with his air force, but he had no idea of the inefficiency and corruption attending his sort of totalitarianism.

The eighth national census in 1936 showed that Italian cities had absorbed two million more people during the previous fifteen years as the industrial fever took hold. Between 1871 and 1943 Rome grew to seven times its former size, and Milan to six. In the period 1921 to 1931, Rome increased its population from 690,000 to over a million. The coastal towns, Taranto, Bari, Genoa, and Spezia also expanded considerably. The drying-up of overseas emigration contributed powerfully to this movement, and after 1922 urbanization continued despite attempts by the government to stop it.

The damming of the stream of emigration was one of the biggest changes of all in postwar Italy. In 1920 the current still ran strongly, and about 350,000 Italians entered the United States alone. Then came the American immigration law of 1921 which laid down an annual quota for every nation, namely 3 per cent of its share in the U.S. foreign-born population as of 1910. The Italian quota was thus reduced to about forty thousand, and another law of 1924 cut this figure to about four thousand a year. After other countries had followed suit, there were often more old emigrants returning to Italy each year than new ones leaving, especially as Mussolini was shortsighted enough to encourage this trend. This lowered the standard of living in emigration areas, and reduced the remittances sent home by emigrants. By 1939, as links with the homeland became severed, the sum of these remittances had dropped from about five billion lire to about five hundred million a year, a not inconsiderable loss in the balance of payments.

૭১

This drastic fall in emigration might have been compensated in part by a fall in the birth rate. But Mussolini for some reason thought that national honor demanded a high rate of fertility, and so launched a "battle for births" with the fantastic target of increasing the population by one-third to sixty million before 1960. When the incredulous asked how such a number could live in Italy, the reply came in typical fascist language that they would live because they could not die, adding that such questions were pernicious and insidious and revealed a weary or anemic mentality. A large population meant more cannon fodder, and would perhaps impress foreigners with Italy's need for colonies; it would also keep wages conveniently low. Faced with Italy's most chronic and intractable problem, it is interesting to see that Mussolini aimed to make it worse and not better, for he harked back to a pre-Malthusian age when the birth rate might have been considered an index of a nation's virility.

Mussolini therefore subsidized matrimony. Fathers with conspicuously large families received higher wages, and the most prolific mother in each region was made an honorary member of the fascist party and might even be ceremonially received by the Duce. Loans were advanced to newlyweds, to be repaid only if there were no children or not enough, and specially favorable insurance policies were distributed by the officiating priest along with a copy of Pius XI's encyclical *Casti connubii*. Being unmarried was a serious impediment in most careers, and in February 1939 it was declared an absolute bar to promotion in government service. A progressive bachelors tax was introduced in 1926, and exemption allowed only to clergy and disabled veterans. This interference in family life was taken to the point where parents were forbidden to give their children names which might sound like an offence to fascism. Women were also encouraged to stay at home so as to have more time for children and to reduce unemployment. There was the feeling that women as schoolteachers might be too religious and too pacific for the planned indoctrination of Italian youth, and in the end they were dismissed altogether from jobs in government service. The potential labor force of the country had thus been heavily reduced just at the moment when war preparations were beginning, and there was no corresponding gain elsewhere to make up for it.

Results were once again incommensurate with intentions. Excluding the war period, 1932 was the first year since 1876 in which there had been fewer than one million live births—a fact which perplexed and infuriated the Duce.

49 Fascist Doctrine

Fascism at first boasted of being a movement and not a doctrine. Action, said Mussolini, was of primary importance, even when it was a blunder, and the theory or purpose behind action was largely irrelevant. The battle was what mattered, no matter for what cause. "Believe, obey, and fight" was his motto for Italians, inscribed in Article 4 of the fascist party constitution, even though the belief to which he was referring was not in a creed but in a person.

The success of fascism in 1919–22 was due less to any interior logic or merit of its own than to the vacuum left by the failure of other parties. Hence no doctrine was required, and indeed victory was even helped by this negative philosophy, for fewer people were antagonized. Mussolini's life had been a succession of negations, against the state, the socialists, and the Libyan war; against law and order, and then against disorder; against parliament and liberalism, Versailles and the League, bolshevism and democracy. When asked to replace these negations with something positive, he became evasive and contradictory, for he had no serious beliefs of his own, and any positive statement was likely to offend some possible ally. In this way, astoundingly enough, Mussolini came into power before people had more than a vague idea of what he stood for, and the fact that such a person as Croce could think fascism empty of doctrine and therefore innocuous was a powerful motive in neutralizing potential opposition.

The only truly original contribution of fascism to politics was probably the technique of castor oil. Nevertheless, from this unpromising start, Mussolini skillfully maneuvered after a few years into a position where he was actually claiming that for the first time in modern history the Italians had given the world a doctrine, a philosophy, a new style of living. This he did by making a patchwork of bits and pieces collected from friend and foe. He had learned the theory and practice of revolution from the socialists; his foreign policy, after a few false starts, was taken bodily from the nationalists; the liberals around Gentile contributed a pseudophilosophical terminology; and from certain authoritarian parties abroad he discovered how Catholicism could be used to underpin a strong state built on order and obedience.

This strange amalgam was never given quite enough time to set, and Mussolini went on mouthing negative or meaningless slogans of doubletalk long after he had decided that fascism was after all a doctrine as well as a movement. Indeed, this doubletalk was thoroughly typical of him. Sometimes he instructed fascists to live with a high seriousness and passionate conviction; sometimes they were prescribed the "could not care less" attitude summed up in their uncivilized motto *me ne frego*. Relying on people's forgetfulness, he said that he was a friend of England and yet her irreconcilable enemy. He was the only disinterested champion of the League, and yet also its destroyer—both these incompatible facts being treated as matter for boasting. He meant to bring both peace and a sword:

We represent a new principle in the world, the clear, final and categoric antithesis of democracy, plutocracy, Freemasonry, and the immortal principles of 1789.

The ideals of democracy are exploded, beginning with that of "progress." Ours is an aristocratic century; the state of all will end by becoming the state of a few.

Fascism is the purest kind of democracy, so long as people are counted qualitatively and not quantitatively.

§●

This last remark is taken from the famous article on fascism in the *Enciclopedia italiana,* an article which was written about 1931, signed by Mussolini but obviously composed by a number of hands including that of Gentile. Here at last it was boldly asserted that fascism had a doctrine, that of the Ethical State which manufactured its own system of morality and owed no allegiance to anything outside itself, that of the Nation in Arms which had to fight in order to justify its own existence:

The fascist conception of the state is all-embracing, and outside of the state no human or spiritual values can exist, let alone be desirable.

Perpetual peace would be impossible and useless. War alone brings all human energies to their highest state of tension, and stamps with the seal of nobility the nations which dare to face it.

Mussolini's article became the last word in philosophic speculation, just as his speeches had already become a bible for the faithful from which texts could be dug out to suit all occasions. Every few hundred yards along the roadside the traveler would see emblazoned in large letters on the whitewashed walls of a house the terse and pregnant quotations which every schoolboy had to know by heart: "He who has steel has bread"; "Better to live one day as a lion than a hundred years as a sheep"; "Nothing against the state, nothing outside the state"; "Nothing is ever won in history without bloodshed." In order to immortalize these great principles of 1922 a fascist faculty of political science was established at Perugia in 1927, followed by the creation of a "School of Fascist Mysticism" at Milan to debate what these principles meant. The true fascist, said a decree on the militia, must have his mind "pervaded by a profound mysticism." Groups of professors were given lectures by visiting party bureaucrats on not trying to put their own reasoning capacity on a level with the Duce's for between them and the leader was "a simply astronomical gap."

One of Mussolini's chief mentors in establishing the intellectual content of fascism was the Sicilian philosopher, Giovanni Gentile, who had split away from Croce and his fellow liberals. Early in 1925 Gentile drew up a fascist manifesto to send to foreign intellectuals, signed by Pirandello, Ungaretti, Soffici, Pizzetti, and Panzini among others. Croce wrote a countermanifesto signed by Einaudi, Ferrero, Fortunato, Mosca, Salvemini, Salvatorelli, Jemolo, Ruffini, Calamandrei and others who formed a far more distinguished list. Gentile became minister of education, member of the *Gran Consiglio,* president of the *Istituto Fascista di Cultura,* and general editor of the *Enciclopedia.* He was a person of intelligence and it seemed also of integrity, but his vanity was tickled when fascism adopted the philosophical jargon of Actual Idealism. Croce, who had formerly been his friend, had also once preached the necessity of a strong state, yet drew back as soon as he realized what was happening. Gentile on the contrary turned somersaults to prove that all true liberals must be fascists, and he had insufficient self-respect to rebel when Mussolini contemptuously declared that "one *squadrista* was worth two philosophers."

Gentile's official task was to justify fascism theoretically, to rationalize its boasted anti-intellectual bias, to demonstrate how its proclaimed lack of a philosophy might be itself a philosophy, and how its frequent changes of policy could be theorized and comprehended into a program of higher opportunism:

Often the Duce, with his profound intuition of fascist psychology, has told us the truth, that we all participate in a sort of mystic sentiment. In such a mystic state of mind we do not form clear and distinct ideas, nor can we put into precise words the things we believe in, but it is in those mystic moments when our soul is enveloped in the penumbra of a new world being born that creative faith germinates in our hearts. . . . The fascist spirit is will, not intellect. . . . Intellectual fascists must not be *intellectuals.*

Again, with another paradox, he adapted Croce's Hegelianism to attract right-wing Italian liberals into the fascist party:

The *Duce* once discussed whether action should be by force or consent, and concluded that the authority of the state and the liberty of the subject are counterparts and inseparable. . . . Fascism does not oppose authority to liberty, but sets a system of real and concrete freedom against an abstract and false parody. . . . Even in the nineteenth century people were beginning to think that a strong state was necessary in the interests of liberty itself. . . . One can even say that the new Corporative State, by stressing the identification of liberty with authority, and through a system of representation which corresponds better with reality, is actually more liberal than the old.

There was apparently sufficient speciousness in all this to appeal to many of those steeped in the fashionable idealist philosophy. It was easy to make fun of the skeptical prewar liberalism

. . . which dared do nothing because it believed in nothing and saw no point in sacrifice; which used to measure the national fortunes by the standard of individual well-being, but never liked to compromise itself or to get heated about anything, preferring to put on one side any question that might imperil *quieto vivere;* which threw the cold water of prose upon the enthusiasm of poetry, and recommended moderation at all costs.

Nevertheless, Gentile leaned over backward to the other extreme, justifying the cruelties of *squadrismo* and writing pages of nonsense about the economy and austerity of the *stile fascista*. He was bold enough to say that in the corporative system the Italian genius was once again leading the world, for the first time since the age of the Renaissance.

Many of Gentile's ideas were later repudiated to his great chagrin. Fascists did not like people who were clever, and Gentile's use of an umbrella indicated that the professor was out of touch with the true fascist style. One of his *gaffes* was the attempt to set up a special fascist university at Bologna, as if any other sort of university might still be extant. He also made an unguarded remark about fascism being a minority movement, and had to be publicly disavowed. Then after 1929 came Mussolini's reconciliation with the Church, which was most upsetting to those who had first been attracted to fascism by its anticlerical leanings. Gentile's own educational reform of 1923 had been inspired by the belief that the dogmas of the Church were no more than a useful halfway house to the truth, and suitable for primary schools alone. When fascism sensed the need of full alliance with the Church, Gentile fell from grace. He remained on and off an officeholder, and was eventually assassinated by the antifascists in 1944.

༖

Mussolini's inspirational method of extempore speechmaking sometimes led him to pose as a philistine and say that he cared not the least bit for the past, but in his contrary pose as an intellectual he set great store by rooting his movement in Italian historical traditions. Research was vigorously organized for this purpose under De Vecchi, who set up a control of historical publications, and under whose aegis facts and documents were sometimes treated with scant regard for the truth. One deliberate intention was that fascism should be differentiated from everything in Italian history that was unwarlike, parliamentary, or bourgeois, and in this sense, said De Vecchi, history knew no more profound revolution than that of fascism. On the other hand the regime had to be linked with Mazzini, Foscolo, Dante, and the great names of the past. Both in history and politics it had to be simultaneously ultraconservative and ultrarevolutionary.

Imperial Rome was a favorite hunting ground for moral lessons and heroic exemplars. Mussolini thus announced that Caesar was the greatest man who had ever lived, and he innocently and comically called Shakespeare's *Julius Caesar* the finest school for statesmen. The fascist symbol had itself been derived from the lictors of ancient Rome, and such words as consul, cohort, and centurion were now halfheartedly and self-consciously resuscitated. Archaeology therefore came into its own. "Fascism," said the egregious De Vecchi, "has solved the most formidable problems of archaeology and of art through the mind and will power of the *Duce*." An ambitious excavation of the Forums at Rome was started in 1924, and in ten years had completely altered this region of the city, bringing to light what was Roman at the expense of what was Christian and medieval. A monumental Via dell'Impero was built as an ugly scar through the city, and there was even vandalistic talk of opening up another imperial route between the Pantheon and the monument to Marcus Aurelius in Piazza Colonna. Meanwhile, large outdoor maps in marble relief showed the extent of the Roman Empire, with the implication that what Rome had done once she could do again. In the new penumbral jargon, life had to be lived *romanamente*. Mussolini set the example in his revival of pagan rites, and in October 1928 instituted a ceremony in which patriotic citizens presented their national savings certificates as a burnt offering on an ancient altar of Minerva specially brought out of its museum for the purpose.

The great names of other periods were likewise taken as forerunners and examples. The Middle Ages were deliberately played down as a period of weakness, though Dante was transmuted into a premature nationalist. The Duce said he studied Plato's *Republic*. He used to recall listening to his father read Machiavelli's *Prince* aloud by the family fireside, and he himself frequently quoted it and chose the theme of this book when he wrote a slight disquisition for his honorary doctoral degree at Bologna. The Renaissance itself was not, however, uncritically accepted in the new canon, as it was said to have diverted Italians into a ruinous individualism, and works of art were generally anathema to Mussolini. Renaissance rulers had spent money on beauty instead of on making a strong and victorious state.

The nineteenth-century *risorgimento* showed more of the authentic fascist ebullience and gave Mussolini the comfortable feeling that he was the fulfillment of a logical process of history. Garibaldi had been a Duce with a colored shirt and was marked as a precursor by his acts of piracy, his balcony speeches, and his militarized youth corps. Newspaper correspondents with Garibaldi had commented on the electrifying communion of mind between him and the masses, and on the religion of Garibaldianism for which people were ready to die. Benevolent and liberal-minded though he was, Garibaldi had chosen the title of dictator when he ruled over half the peninsula, for in his own words, "I had become more and more convinced that the only way to get Italians to see eye to eye and agree with each other is by using armed force, nothing less."

The official professors similarly had an easy time with Mazzini, who had spent much of his life crusading against parliament and socialism, and against what he called the excessive individualism of the Americans. Mazzini, as a collectivist, had come near to suggesting that the individual had only duties, while the state alone as a moral entity had rights. His ideal state looked like a totalitarian theocracy, in which there was no distinction between Church and state and no conflict between classes. Mazzini and Garibaldi would certainly have opposed much of fascism, but with much of it they might also have sympathized, and together they represent an authoritarian tradition on the radical Left to which some of the fascist leaders belonged.

On the Right, a parallel tradition could be traced back to the time of Cavour, and especially to those of Cavour's colleagues like Spaventa who followed Hegel in theorizing about the state. Some of these right-wing liberals had from the start advocated an extension of governmental controls, and it was the Right not the Left which had first advocated nationalization of the railroads. Bonghi, although a good liberal, had concluded that Italian parliamentary government worked well only when a man of genius like Cavour had coerced it into operation. The young Orlando, likewise disillusioned with parliament, had written in 1884: "Our only hope is in the appearance of a *deus ex machina,* that is to say a man of such demonstrably superior qualities, and such determined intention, that he would seize the rudder of the state and pervade every aspect of peoples' lives with a sense of positive government action." The arrogant Crispi had been vain enough to imagine himself just such a superman, and had had good reason to think that Italians would welcome a disciplined authoritarian state. The pessimists pointed out that, except for a brief and imperfect interval since 1860, absolutism had been the sole political experience of most Italians. Furthermore, while other countries had inherited a disbelief and an individualism from the Reformation, Italians had nearly all been brought up in a church which demanded perfect obedience.

These historical facts no doubt help in part to explain why parliamentary government had broken down in 1922. Fascist historians were able to find precursors everywhere and to suggest that arbitrary rule came naturally to the national temperament. From Rienzi to Masaniello and D'Annunzio there had been many notable demagogues before Mussolini, and Gregorovius in the nineteenth century said that he found three types constantly recurring in Italian history—Machiavelli, Cesare Borgia, and the *condottieri.* Enlightened despots, Jacobins, Bonapartism, national unification by conquest and plebiscite, irredentism and imperialism, all of these were wrought into an arid and melancholy pattern by obedient official historians. The intent was to confer an aspect of inevitability on the events of 1922 and to make Italians feel that by nature and history they were destined for this high fate. All roads led to Rome, to the Third Rome in which Mussolini aimed to outdo all the Caesars and Popes.

50 The Standardization of Culture

Artists and intellectuals can be as unreliable as anyone when dealing with politics. Pirandello signed the manifesto of fascist intellectuals and put on the gaudy fascist uniform of Mussolini's new academy. Shortly before his death, Puccini gave his blessing to fascism and was made a senator for his trouble. The *doyen* of Italian economists, Pantaleoni, was also made a senator and so was the sociologist Pareto. Marconi, too, had his pride caressed when he was created a marquis and his advice was asked on politics. Mussolini later wrote of this period as "the time of the carrot and the stick," and his own experience taught that these two weapons were effective with most people in attaching them to the regime. A decree of 1933 prescribed, on paper at least, that party membership was necessary for any administrative post, and Croce and the Church both agreed that this was a formality which could be accepted even by nonfascists if it were needed for office or promotion. Few people in fact could afford to hold out.

Croce himself, though his writings might be removed from schools and libraries, possessed an integrity and an economic independence which allowed him to remain adamantly distinct from fascism after 1925. D'Annunzio, on the other hand, easily capitulated to the grant of a pension, and a palatial villa was bestowed on him as a national monument in which he could indulge his unamiable eccentricities. Since he was never able to throw off the memory of the absolute power he had enjoyed as Regent of Fiume, he was also presented with the forecastle of a naval ironclad which he erected in his garden by Lake Garda;

sentries stood on duty there, and the poet used to welcome visitors by a salute of guns corresponding to their merit or title, just as though he were still a sovereign power. D'Annunzio was also created Prince of Monte Nevoso, one of the few examples of princely rank conferred in modern Italian history. The old aristocracy resented the way in which fascism cheapened titles and granted them in batches. Mussolini invented several completely new titles for himself, and he made De Pinedo a marquis for flying around the world in 120 days.

The intellectuals were drilled into corporations like everyone else, because fascism liked to have everyone and everything organized and wanted to prevent any untidy leftovers or people who claimed some vestigial independence of thought. After 1933 compulsory uniforms were introduced even for professors and civil servants as a symbol of their new uniformity of mind, and medals were distributed annually for "fascist" achievements in art, culture, and sport. A National Council of Research was created, over which Marconi and Marshal Badoglio presided with considerable powers of patronage. There was also a Fascist Institute of National Culture under the presidency of Gentile, which published periodicals and set up libraries for the study of fascism.

Between 1926 and 1929 the Fascist Academy was conceived, to coordinate all work in the arts and sciences, to "preserve for our intellectual life its national character according to the genius and the tradition of our race, and also to favor its expansion abroad." There were to be sixty academicians, all chosen by Mussolini, paid a salary, addressed as "Your Excellency," receiving free first-class travel, and given a mock-antique uniform complete with plumed hat and gilt sword. Pirandello, Marinetti, and Panzini were obvious choices as inaugural members, and its secretary was Volpe, the best of the fascist historians. Tittoni, Marconi, D'Annunzio, and Ferderzoni, successively its presidents, wore ostrich feathers and had perquisites on an even more luxurious scale.

In return, the duties of academicians were negligible. They awarded titles and decorations, banned words of foreign derivation, and decided that every good fascist ought to address his neighbor only in the stilted language of the second person plural. Inevitably, they were a dull body, chosen generally for their artistic and political orthodoxy and suffocated by worldly success. Most of them became as much at home in fascist parades as in the arts and sciences, and the photographs of them goose-stepping at the Roman salute have a macabre fascination. Papini and the composer Mascagni look oddly placed in this *galère*. But the honor and perquisites did without doubt cause many a crisis of conscience among an important class of people. Some of the signatories of Croce's antifascist manifesto in 1925 had become apologists and even propagandists for the regime ten years later, because Mussolini used the carrot to good effect.

A mild rap with the stick was also used to conscript the intelligentsia when professors in 1931 were required to swear an oath of loyalty not only to the king but to fascism. This oath, too, was generally considered a mere formality, and the Church again held that it was a legitimate claim by the government for obedience. The world-famous mathematician Levi-Civita added a private reservation, and the government showed that it was quite ready to accept the substance without the form. About twelve hundred professors did as they were bid. Orlando and De Viti de Marco preferred to resign before the oath was put to them. Eleven others made their names celebrated by refusing to swear, and so forfeited their posts. They included De Sanctis the ancient historian, Lionello Venturi the art historian, Ruffini the canon lawyer, and Buonaiuti the modernist theologian who had come under ecclesiastical ban. The students were incited to mob those teachers who refused to burn their pinch of incense, but sometimes had the sense to respect such signal courage and integrity. Nevertheless, the oath was a big success for the regime, and if only there had been several hundred refusals instead of eleven it would have been a sharp challenge which would have carried weight with public opinion and abroad.

When the racial laws were introduced in 1938, some ninety scholars were dismissed. Of the two leading Italian mathematicians, Volterra had refused the oath, and now Levi-Civita also went. Others who had Jewish friends and relatives followed these into voluntary or involuntary retirement and exile. The physicist Fermi had already refused to return home after receiving his Nobel prize in Oslo, and as two of his leading followers in Rome also left, the loss to Italy in the field of nuclear physics was incalculable. Together with the bureaucratization of universities and the selection of professors for political reasons, this persecution helps to explain the backwardness of Italian science in assisting the war effort after 1939.

In literature and history some of the party bosses put their names to —and perhaps even wrote—articles and books purporting to be serious contributions to scholarship. In Croce's magazine, *La Critica,* a true scholar like Omodeo was able to expose some extraordinary examples of plagiarism in their work, but he had to pay for his courage and irony, and not many people were thus ready to risk their careers. The vagaries of the censorship were notorious. Fisher's *History of Europe* was confiscated from bookstores in 1939 by order of a new dignitary called the Minister of Popular Culture. An index of prohibited books was also drawn up for libraries, in which, along with Robert Graves and Axel Munthe, Machiavelli and Boccaccio were in 1939 declared "unsuitable to the fascist spirit." By this time the lunatic elements of fascism were clearly in full control. It may seem surprising that good work could ever be done in such an atmosphere, and yet the pervasive inefficiency, plus a certain amount of good-natured tolerance, allowed much more freedom of expression than was ever possible in contemporary Germany.

ᔓ

It is too early to estimate what posterity will find durable in the artistic and cultural achievements of this quarter of a century. The arrival of fascism seemed to coincide roughly with the end of a period. Pascoli and Fogazzaro had disappeared before the war; Modigliani the painter died in 1920, Pareto in 1923, Puccini and the Duse in 1924. The leaders of the next generation were of smaller stature, and the central controls of fascism were inevitably a brake and a hindrance upon them. Political motives also helped to weaken the literary and aesthetic links with France and so to cut off Italy from the most vital source of challenge and renewal. German influence was more encouraged, especially as Mussolini himself had acquired a fair superficial acquaintanceship with German culture and went on taking German lessons to the end of his life. Beethoven and Wagner he much preferred to Puccini, or so he said, but Vittorio Mussolini often saw his father asleep during Wagner's operas.

Mussolini intended fascism to be strikingly creative and sought hard to discover for it a cultural identity. Successive experts thus restlessly pursued one novelty after another, though there was an absence of strong traditions to build on, and the results usually lacked individuality and character. The ubiquitous but hazy "fascist style" was eventually dragged into art as well as into manners and even religion. Dragged is the only word, for Mussolini himself in his poverty of spirit had no love of art, and had once praised Marinetti's fantastic suggestion to dispose of the national galleries in exchange for good foreign currency. What he would have liked, he told Ciano, was fewer pictures and statues and more enemy flags captured in battle. He boasted that he had never set foot in a museum or art gallery until Hitler took him on a minute examination of the Pitti and Uffizi, and the boredom and physical exhaustion of this occasion was to remain a painful memory.

Marinetti the futurist had been the earliest literary influence in fascism, but futurism had been more talk than achievement, and in any case was passé long before the fascists had caught on to its usefulness. The religious conversion of Papini about 1918 was symptomatic of an already existing return from these futuristic excesses back to order, discipline, and traditional language, and Papini too became a keen fascist. Bacchelli, Baldini, and Ungaretti were turning to more classical models of prose and poetry after the crude paroxysms of yesterday's *avant garde,* but these people were too intellectual for Mussolini. In an attempt to show what the fascist style meant in literature, the Duce himself set up as a playwright, and so did the barely literate Farinacci, with unimpressive results.

Pirandello's best work was already written by the end of 1921, in which year he had composed *Enrico IV* and *Six Characters in Search of an Author.* In 1934 he won a Nobel prize for literature. But he was never outstandingly popular in Italy, and after the first performance of *Sei personaggi* he had been hissed into the street. In his lugubrious characters it is possible to glimpse something of the spiritual emptiness of postwar Italy; they believed that life was a bad joke, vain and useless, and that private illusions alone afforded any protection—an apt enough commentary on fascism, even though not Mussolini's idea of the *stile fascista.* Among the younger generation, Moravia's brilliant novel of 1928, *Gli indifferenti,* held another mirror up to fascist Italy, and described a cynical, existentialist world, peopled with sensual, repugnant characters and devoid of belief and purpose.

In sculpture and painting, fascism lacked both attractiveness and character, an understandable state of affairs in an organized and artificial culture where the prizes went to those who depicted fascist successes and martyrology. Since the death of Canova a hundred years before, the academic school of sculpture had been coasting on its past momentum, and the *risorgimento* had brought only a horrid outcrop of heroic groups and rhetorical statues in most *piazze* up and down the kingdom. Then at the turn of the century, the embellishments on the Vittorio Emanuele monument in Rome demonstrated official art at its biggest and unhappiest. Fascism inherited no ready-made school or tradition except this, together with an indigestible ferment of fashionable novelties, and not much success was registered in creating a new style which reflected the inner nature of Mussolini's revolution. Futurist artists such as Carrà, metaphysical painters such as De Chirico and Morandi, the sculptors Marini and the younger Manzù, with neocubists, neorealists, tonalists, hermetic poets, and the rest, managed to exist alongside the safe academic art which flourished on official patronage.

In architecture the fascist period showed more character. It has been said that architects flourish under a dictatorship as much as lawyers in a democracy. Buildings can become good publicity, and countless post offices and town halls proved to be effective vehicles for the grandiose and magniloquent impressions which fascism hoped to convey. A veritable building fever overtook the regime. Compared with the baroque Rome of Bernini, the much larger "Humbertine" Rome palpably lacked a consistent style and is remembered mostly for its gigantic official follies. The new fascist style was unashamedly modernist. It transplanted, or rather translated and traduced, Gropius and Le Corbusier, using harsh geometrical lines and large white plain surfaces to replace the pilasters, loggias, and elaborate façades which had for so long been used to soften the glaring sunlight of Italy. At its most successful there was Michelucci's railroad station at Florence, and a younger school of engineers led by Nervi and Ponti was to show an artistry in reinforced-concrete hangars and office buildings which won worldwide admiration after 1945. At its worst, Mussolini's taste showed a reversion to the classical and "Roman," almost always spectacular and violent, and usually vulgar. At international exhibitions, the Italian pavilion had if possible to be higher and showier than others, and the unfinished tower of Babel outside Rome was to be a melancholy reminder of shoddiness and vainglory.

The history of these twenty years was not, of course, synonymous with that of fascism. There were Toscanini and the other exiles abroad, and even in Italy there was always some nonconformity to interrupt the monologue which issued from Palazzo Venezia. It is tempting to say that the only interesting creative work came from the nonco-operators. There were fine works of historical scholarship by Omodeo, De Sanctis, De Ruggiero, Chabod, Salvatorelli, Spellanzon, and many more. The better novelists of Bacchelli's generation showed no purely official qualities in their novels, and much of Treccani's huge and impressive *Enciclopedia italiana* is free of political slant. Einaudi and Gramsci were major figures. Above all there was Croce, who as a writer, thinker, and critic of art and literature had an immeasurable influence on all intelligent people. In a hundred ways Croce exposed the bad taste and shoddy thinking which were in danger of typifying a whole generation of Italians, and luckily he was himself too big a figure with too great a world reputation to be suppressed.

Fascism was too casual, and perhaps too self-consciously on the defensive, to be as insidious and deep-rooted an evil as nazism. Nevertheless, despite the few creative artists who had the courage, integrity, and means of livelihood to hold aloof from official direction, the damage done was incalculable. Many writers, artists, and thinkers had to depend on official money, and this made it the more disastrous that a policy of artistic autarky ran parallel with that of political and economic autarky. The music and drama of "sanctionist" states was thus forbidden during the Abyssinian war, and jazz was always deprecated as something alien to the race. Such a doctrine of cultural self-sufficiency betrayed a lack of confidence and an unwillingness to compete which was both a symptom and a cause of artistic decay.

§❧

The education of the young was vitally important for a government which boasted of upsetting all the conventional standards of morality, justice, and civilization. Official policy laid down that Italians must be brought up to be more warlike and tough, less artistic and less "nice," and to be always "desperately serious." Above all they had to become less individualistic and more amenable to discipline.

The education act of 1923 sponsored by Gentile was passed before Mussolini knew what he wanted. It had allowed considerable freedom to private schools and greater autonomy to universities. It stressed the value of humanist education and promoted the teaching of philosophy at every level. It also laid down the sensible doctrine that examinations were to test not facts learned by rote, but understanding and expression. Gentile's philosophical method became vacuous and rhetorical in the hands of lesser men, and it could be argued that Italy's chief need was not for more philosophy but for that very scientific and technological education which Croce and Gentile thought to be of minor importance. Nevertheless, Gentile's reform contained few of the usual fascist banalities, and it helped to preserve some independence of mind in education during the dark days to come.

It was again typical of fascism that one reform should cancel out another. Instead of the stability which Mussolini had promised to bring, he soon had to invert his thesis and proclaim that fascism was not a revolution once and for all but a perpetual revolution. His own ministers changed almost as rapidly as their predecessors. Eight ministers of education, eight ministers of public works, and nine ministers for the colonies followed each other in the fourteen years after 1922; the syllabus and curriculum for schools were repeatedly changed; textbooks were rewritten when Fedele wanted more religion, or when Ercole wanted more economics, and yet more radically when De Vecchi ordained that every detail of education must be infused with the highest fascist principles. Bottai then put an end to mixed schools, since male supremacy was a fascist principle. But the basic problems of education remained unsolved, and the seventh national census in 1931 still gave 20 per cent of illiterates (48 per cent in Calabria), while the eighth in 1936 pointedly omitted to give any figures at all.

"Fascist culture" and "corporative law" were introduced into the schools, though teachers must have been puzzled what these topics really meant. Professorships of political economy were renamed professorships of corporative political economy. The subject of history was disciplined and twisted in order to illustrate the primacy of Italians. Out of 317 history textbooks, 101 were forbidden by a special commission in 1926, and ten years later a single standardized text was in compulsory use. The polarization of history around the year 1922—*anno primo*—was indicated by a new calendar superseding the outmoded reckoning of dates from the birth of our Lord, and no one was allowed to point out that this was just aping the French Revolution. Balbo's description of his flight across the Atlantic in 1933 became Italian literature and a set text for secondary schools. Foreign literature was represented among other books by translations of Benjamin Franklin and Samuel Smiles. The Italian language was enriched with new words coined by Mussolini which Panzini had to include in his dictionary, and books were written to analyze the subtlety and vigor of the leader's literary style—though his more scatological expressions were if possible concealed from the public eye. The words chosen for spelling lessons were connected with fighting, and children were taught how Italy had saved Britain and America in World War I and how Mussolini had now made Italy again "the first nation in the world."

Selected phrases from the compulsory reader issued for eight-year-olds in 1936 give some indication of the kind of education which fascism now intended to impart.

The eyes of the Duce are on every one of you. No one can say what is the meaning of that look on his face. It is an eagle opening its wings and rising into space. It is a flame that searches out your heart to light there a vermilion fire. Who can resist that burning eye, darting out its arrows? But do not be afraid; for you those arrows will change into rays of joy.

A child, who, even while not refusing to obey, asks "Why?," is like a bayonet made of milk. . . . "You must obey because you must," said Mussolini, when explaining the reasons for obedience.

How can we ever forget that fascist boy who, when near to death, asked that he might put on his uniform and that his savings should go to the party?

To the victor who has conquered the Abyssinians we owe eternal gratitude and obedience for winning the greatest colonial war that history has recorded. . . . The Empire has been created by the rooted conviction in us that "Mussolini is always right."

An essential part of fascist education was the conscription of youth into quasi-military units. At the age of four a child became a "son of the she-wolf" and put on his first black shirt; at the age of eight he joined the *Balilla,* at fourteen the *Avanguardisti*—Balilla was the nickname of an unknown Genoese boy who was said to have thrown the first stone against the Austrians in a civic rebellion of 1746. These children were trained to military discipline, and special toy machine guns were made for their entertainment. They were also instructed in *cultura fascista,* which they were then expected to retail among their families. Official chaplains were attached to the *Balilla,* and this partially appeased the Church for the fact that a monopoly on youth clubs had been obtained by organizations which were pagan in fact and militaristic in both fact and theory. Millions of Italian boys and girls passed through this poisonous process of indoctrination, though no doubt it was often applied or absorbed in a casual and slipshod manner.

৯৯

Other methods of propaganda were limited, since most Italians had not yet acquired the habit of radio or even of newspapers. Even the provincial Catholic press had to fill three of its four pages with fascist nonsense in order to purchase the use of one page for the bishop's letter and events of the ecclesiastical calendar. Mussolini made his first broadcast speech over Marconi's new system in 1924, but a technical hitch made his words unintelligible and for fear of ridicule he was cut off. Radio was of course monopolized by the government, and a law of 1927 set up a special organization which later became *Radio Italiana.* A policy was eventually laid down for radio programs to be governed by "a rigorously autarkic cultural spirit," and when the minister of culture announced this to the fascist Chamber he was greeted with loud applause. Mussolini himself only two or three times in his life gave talks specially for the radio, because he quickly discovered that impersonal fireside chats were not much in his line.

The Italian film industry was not organized until relatively late. Historical films were always a favorite in Italy, as they could give full scope to the feeling for pageantry and national greatness. Lucrezia Borgia, the battle of Lepanto, the last days of Pompeii, Nero, Julius Caesar, even Dante, all were filmed at least once. On the introduction of talkies about 1926, another speciality was opera and dramatizations of the lives of composers such as Verdi and Bellini. After 1929, films with a fascist bent became more common, but people found them dull, and American importations were more diverting as well as technically superior. Mussolini had films specially shown for him most evenings. He himself preferred comedies to tragedies. He tried at first to forbid films with foreign dialogue, and then allowed foreign products a quota of only one to ten instead of ten to one. This caused American companies in 1939 to withdraw from Italy, and the consequent decline in foreign competition gave Italian producers a guaranteed market however poor their efforts. For this reason, and because of the demands of propaganda, good films such as the *Siege of Alcazar* were exceptional. Yet subsequent development of the new realist school with De Sica and Visconti revealed a fund of latent talent, and with the removal of central direction and ideological prejudice, Italy was ready to take a front place in the world of cinema.

৯

A totalitarian regime had of necessity to stake out moral dominion over every sphere of individual life, and this included recreation and sport. Here national prestige could be asserted ostentatiously, and the nation's physique could be improved against a day of bloodier battle. The vogue of sport, like the word itself, had been introduced from Great Britain late in the nineteenth century. In 1857, Englishmen formed the first Alpine society, and the first ascent of the Matterhorn was in 1865. In 1870 the first cycling club was founded in Milan, and after 1909 the *giro d'Italia* became one of the big events of the year. The second favorite sport was football, for which a club was started as early as 1890 in Genoa. From 1908 when the first Italian championship was held, football spread rapidly, until there were ten thousand recognized clubs. Fox-hunting also was brought in from England, and there was a golf society in Rome by 1903.

Mussolini did his best to organize these miscellaneous importations, and one party secretary even tried to instill the fascist style into sport through a new and short-lived game called *volata*. The organization of leisure was a paramount aim of the new ideology, so *"il weekend"* was abolished and in 1935 became by law *"il sabato fascista."* Sport eventually became a fascist monopoly: for example, the Olympic Games committee had to be affiliated with the party, and the party appointed the president of the Italian chess association. The physical education of the young benefited incidentally from this official encouragement, and the *Dopolavoro* institution provided excellent cheap vacations and recreation for workers. Many international victories were also won in bicycle and motor racing, and in 1933 the carpenter Primo Carnera beat Sharkey at New York to become world heavyweight boxing champion, the newspapers being carefully instructed never to show pictures of him knocked down in the ring. Boxing, said Mussolini, "was an essentially fascist method of self-expression." In February 1939 the Italian lawn tennis association decreed that all players in international matches should wear fascist uniform and should respond with the fascist salute when their opponents offered to shake hands.

Once again, thinking to aim at the sublime, the movement had fallen by an internal and inevitable logic into the ridiculous.

The football industry was purged as early as 1926, and reorganized on lines "more consonant with the new life of the nation." The game was said to be not a foreign importation, but a development of the old Tuscan *calcio,* which had long ago been forbidden because of the casualties it caused and then had been taken to England. Its control now passed from local clubs to a central body with a honeycomb of divisional, zonal, and federal directions. By 1937 there were 52,000 players licensed by their membership cards to play, and 2,700 authorized referees under the chief referee at Rome with his gold whistle. As a "typically Italian creation," there was a new official, the *commissario di campo,* who was sent by the federal director to "invigilate" both the behavior of the public and any fouling on the field which might escape the referee. No one knew who he was, but he drew up a private report on the game and sent it to the zonal Directorate of Football, where it was then compared with that of the referee. Sport, as in other countries, was thus encouraged to pass from dilettanti to professionals, and also from the countryside to the large metropolitan towns, for only big stadiums could pay for the grand spectacles which were part of the choreography of fascism.

51 Persecution and Its Effects

The tale of misery caused by fascism will never be fully told, for most of the victims are dead. The natural humaneness of Italians prevented anything remotely resembling the wholesale murder practiced in Germany, and there was a soft and sentimental side to Mussolini which had unexpected if unimportant manifestations. Yet fascism deliberately exalted brutality into an officially imposed creed, and the police did not interfere when the squads were on a weekend spree. Harmless citizens, if they escaped the *manganello* (the word, significantly, comes from the Romagna dialect), might have their heads shaved and painted with the national colors, or they might have to perform some revolting act such as consuming a live toad in public. More commonly they would be forced to drink a pint or two of castor oil, in the fascist "baptism" designed to purge people from the sin of opposition and intended to impose the maximum public indignity on its victims.

This purgative action was so capricious and unsystematic that in one province a man might be in danger of his life and yet be a minor public figure in another. In general the liberals and *popolari* were left in peace so long as they abstained from open political action, but occasional severities were designed to generate fear and make a public example of any lukewarmness. People who had joined the Aventine in 1924 or who had signed Croce's "antifascist manifesto" in 1925 suffered in their profession unless they groveled in penitence, and any former Freemason or socialist might find himself at the mercy of some private enemy who wished to pay off a grudge without cost to himself.

In November 1926 a special police body was created to prosecute antifascism. A special tribunal was also set up, an organ of the fascist party rather than of the state, from which there was no appeal and which could hear cases *in camera*. While the *carabinieri* were a semi-military police force who kept some loyalty to the king and finally carried out Mussolini's own arrest, the OVRA, or secret police, was essentially an arm of the party. Luckily, Bocchini, the head of the police, was a not disagreeable cynic who saw through Mussolini, and he seems to have kept a residual sense of legality and decency which was sometimes used to modify the letter of the law. Luckily, too, the characteristic carelessness of fascism created what the head of the OVRA says were as many as twenty separate and rival police forces, often unknown to and working against each other. OVRA itself was a meaningless name which Mussolini invented about 1930 just to frighten people. Over one billion lire per annum were soon being spent on police services, a figure which reflects Mussolini's sense of insecurity as it is said to be ten times the prewar equivalent—though certainly it also concealed a good deal of secret expenditure on bribery and corruption. Bocchini and Senise were seldom mentioned in the press, for Mussolini was careful not to build up potential rivals. Their political prisoners were confined on the islands, while lesser suspects such as the painter-novelist Carlo Levi were sent under surveillance to some remote and primitive village.

§

Between 1924 and 1926, many people had to decide whether to take the path of exile. Among the first political expatriates were Nitti, Sforza,

Don Sturzo, Amendola, Gobetti, Salvemini, and De Ambris. Then followed Turati, Treves, Nenni, Saragat, and Modigliani. Of the communist leaders, Gramsci returned from Russia to live the rest of his life a captive, but in his stead Togliatti left to represent the party on the Comintern at Moscow. One or two exiles came back later: Labriola, for instance, arrived from New York to support the Abyssinian war. In a different category was the gifted young writer Lauro de Bosis, who first went to scrape a living in Paris as a concierge and then returned to meet a heroic and mysterious end in 1931, after dropping antifascist leaflets over Rome from the plane he had barely learned to fly.

The story of these exiles is tragic, not least in its exemplification of all the doctrinaire extremism, political fecklessness, and intolerance toward each other which had been chief among the original reasons for fascist success. The bitterness and the idleness of exile were enough to break the spirit of all whose quality was not of the finest, and there was a continuous succession of quarrels and splits between the various parties and inside each party. Nevertheless, those who survived were to bring back a priceless tradition and experience of freedom after 1943.

Of those who died, the most famous antifascist martyr was Carlo Rosselli. He had been driven to politics by his horror at the murder of Matteotti. In association with Salvemini and several of the younger liberals like Bauer and Ernesto Rossi, he first ran a clandestine paper called *Non mollare* (*Don't Weaken*), which had to be printed in one house after another so as to avoid discovery. In 1926, Rosselli and Parri (who survived to become prime minister in 1945) smuggled the aged Turati by motorboat to Corsica and then chose to return to imprisonment themselves. In 1929 a famous escape was organized from the Lipari Islands by Rosselli, and thereafter he lived a precarious existence in Paris editing that most famous of antifascist papers, *Justice and Liberty*.

This provoked the undying hatred of Mussolini. Close watch was kept on these exiles in Paris, and a grandson of Garibaldi was employed as an *agent provocateur* to try to secure their expatriation. When Mussolini intervened in Spain on the side of Franco, Rosselli went to Spain with Nenni and the communist Longo to fight for the republic, as did five thousand other Italian antifascists, and many future Italian partisans of 1944–45 received their training in the Spanish Civil War. But in 1936, as again in 1944, political differences seriously diminished their military effectiveness. Rosselli returned to France disillusioned with this particular fight for freedom, and he and his brother Nello were shortly afterward assassinated near Paris by Mussolini's hirelings.

§❧

Fascist persecution was also directed against the two hundred thousand southern Germans whom the Treaty of Versailles had given to Italy in the Alto Adige, and even more against the half million Slavs who had been annexed in the five provinces of Gorizia, Pola, Trieste, Fiume, and Zara, which made up the region of Venezia Giulia. Fascism proclaimed that there could be no minorities in Italy, only Italians. As early as 1923, German place names were changed, use of the German language was greatly restricted, and Italians were imported to dilute the German character of the Trentino-Alto Adige and its "ethnographical relics." Lawyers now had to plead in Italian, and schoolboys to take their examinations in Italian, despite the severe hardship that this involved. Local government was controlled by nominated Italian prefects. When monasteries were forcibly handed over to Italian abbots, the Prince Bishop of Trent, Endrici, did more than connive at this, and in 1926 his order went out that religious instruction was to be given only in Italian. The local priesthood appealed to the Pope, and 227 priests announced their intention to disobey this order when the Vatican would not or could not reply. Luckily, the Gentile education act in the early and more anticlerical days of fascism had allowed the children of dissenters to opt out of religious instruction altogether, and even the most devout Catholic German parents now preferred to invoke this provision rather than submit. Later on, when Austria asked for more lenient treatment of these unfortunates, the Italian minister was indignantly recalled from Vienna; but after Hitler's *Anschluss,* Mussolini was forced to offer people the choice of emigration to Germany if they wished, and some seventy thousand seem to have departed.

Bishop Fogar of Trieste, unlike Endrici, showed himself a courageous champion of minority rights, but the Vatican in the end found that obedience to Mussolini was a lesser evil, and in 1936 replaced this bishop by another who was more amenable. Slav inscriptions in the churches and on tombstones were then forcibly removed, and it was even prohibited to call children Cyril, the name of their patron saint. Whereas Hitler could speak for the German minority, the Slavs had no powerful champion, and their cry went unheard. Italy had once been full of moral indignation against the treatment given to the Italian-speaking minority in the Austro-Hungarian Empire and had even justified her own *risorgimento* by the immorality of this persecution. But her own treatment of minorities was proving to be far more cruel, and Italian nationalism was thus being brought into contempt. By 1938 even the French-speaking parts of the Val d'Aosta were being forcibly

Italianized, and in 1942 the party secretary was cheerfully talking of exterminating a million Slovenes. Italy was to suffer for this after 1945 when the Slavs and the French were in a position to fight back.

§●

The reaction of Italian public opinion to such fascist behavior cannot be easily gauged. Without the continued collaboration of most Italians, however, fascism could not have been so successful. Economically and politically it may have been in the long run their ruin, but at the time it gave them reassurance and self-importance. There was no need to be an enthusiast, for so many inconsistencies and half-truths existed in the official claptrap that people could choose any one interpretation of fascism, and some of its aspects appeared harmless enough.

Some people were thus convinced simply by success. Some clung to the illusion that autocratic government would moderate itself once the emergency was over. One way or another, so long as fascism offered an ordered regimen, an end of class war, and the fruits of victory without war itself, ordinary citizens seem to have been content. Individual liberty they sacrificed as the price of purchasing collective power and renown, and they rejoiced at last in the delicious sense of being feared abroad. There were parades and speeches, bunting and national self-admiration, and great hopes were constantly fostered and sometimes partly realized. Some people, indeed, will possibly look back with nostalgia on these twenty years as a golden age, for so much of what is unpleasant may be forgotten and refined in retrospect.

Up to 1936, so far as one can see, support for Mussolini grew rather than diminished. In the early days a few more people as bold as Matteotti might have sufficed to overturn the hollow colossus which bestrode Italy, and we are told, for instance, that when in May 1925 the news spread at Reggio Calabria that fascism had fallen, the town was momentarily convulsed with joy. But forcible suppression of press and parties after 1925 proved to be unanswerable. Consciences were gradually dulled, as people were driven from one small connivance to another. From the king downward they found that, once the first mistake had been made, there was no point of retreat, no unviolated principle worth a battle, until the means of opposition no longer existed. Antifascist outbursts therefore diminished through the twenties as they became more obviously useless, and fascist violence and cruelty dwindled proportionately. A circular from the Duce to prefects in January 1927 said that *squadrismo* was now "anachronistic," and that "the period of reprisals, devastation. and violence is over." By this time, according to

Nitti, sentiment, necessity, and calculation had combined to make almost all Italians content and loyal. It was enough that Mussolini could fool most of the people most of the time. They were Mussolinians if not fascists by conviction, and antifascism had been reduced to negligible proportions.

The liberals of the old school were the most easily deceived, and many of them merely tried to escape from their own responsibility by looking on what had happened as inevitable, something which just needed analysis and justification. "It may be," said Albertini to the Senate, "that the Italian people were not sufficiently penetrated with the sanctity of liberal principles, and needed a reactionary experiment in order to learn to appreciate them." Opposition would therefore be culturally and politically sterile and would mean effectively a complete severance from the active life of the country.

Indeed, it could in fact be maintained that the task of intellectuals should not be to oppose, but rather to try to influence fascism for good, to develop the healthy conservatism in it, and to relate this new movement to the rest of Italian history and culture. Thus, their own surrender could be made out to have been justified, and fascism would appear as necessary and logical. Given the reluctance of these older liberals to stoop to conspiracy, this was a not unworthy attempt to salvage something from the wreck of the past and make fascism more safe and respectable. Placing the cause of Italy above that of its rulers, they hoped to serve fascism with their fingers crossed.

§♠

Giolitti and his liberals had admitted the need for dictatorship, and such opposition as they now allowed themselves was intellectual rather than political. By 1928, the year when Giolitti died, their party had been proscribed, and Croce, Ruffini, Casati, Bergamini, and Albertini had been compelled to reconsider the fundamentals of their political philosophy. The few people who gathered for Ruffini's funeral in 1934 had some of them given indispensable support to the government in its earlier and more difficult years, but they now seemed the last survivors of a defeated age. Croce found that his philosophical ideas were beginning to lose ground to the neoscholasticism of the Catholics and the heresies of the renegade Gentile. While on the whole he had welcomed the authoritarianism of the regime, Croce could not abide its bad taste and materialism, its brute ignorance and muddleheadedness, its worship of callow youth. People who had received his kind of liberal education could not be expected to approve a creed of irrational mysticism, nor the fact that Mussolini encouraged culture only as an article for export and prestige.

The younger liberals, Gobetti, Parri, and Bauer, were prepared to go one stage further, to revise their creed to meet these new conditions, and then fight and suffer for it. Gobetti was a remarkable youth who endured assault and arrest from the fascists and died in Paris in 1926 at the age of twenty-five. A pupil of the great liberal economist, Einaudi, at Turin, he then worked on Gramsci's communist paper *Ordine Nuovo,* and in 1922 himself edited the weekly magazine *Rivoluzione Liberale,* a successor to Salvemini's *Unità,* which became for several years perhaps the liveliest opposition journal in Italy. Gobetti remained in close touch with the communists, but found them too rigid, and spent the few active years of his life in trying to socialize liberalism and strengthen it with new forces and ideas from below. His was an inspiration which fired many leaders in the future war of liberation.

After 1926 there was hardly an antifascist movement, only antifascist tendencies. Outside Italy these ranged from the communism of Togliatti, through the liberal socialism of Rosselli and Salvemini, to the radicalism of Nitti, the Christian democracy of Don Sturzo, and the republicanism of Sforza. A broad Anti-Fascist Concentration was formed at Paris, but the republicans later broke away from it, and the reuniting of Nenni's maximalists with those reformists adhering to Saragat proved only a temporary access of worldly wisdom.

Inside Italy a skeleton communist organization continued in secret existence, perhaps the only existing party apart from fascism itself. Besides this there were ex-premiers like Bonomi and Orlando who as titled "cousins of the king" had a right of access to the throne which they were able to use with effect in 1943. There were liberal aristocrats like Duke Gallarati Scotti and Prince Doria, aghast at the vulgarity and irresponsibility of the fascist leaders, and scholars such as Luigi Einaudi, whose intellectual honesty was beyond all doubt and whose international position kept them in touch with world opinion. Croce's magazine *La Critica,* and books from the publishing houses of Laterza and Giulio Einaudi gave currency to a shadowy and allusive antifascism and surreptitiously helped to preserve some independence of mind and teaching. It was impossible to suppress altogether the occasional pasquinade, and some illegal manifestos were even printed in the offices of *Il Popolo d'Italia.*

§❧

Further down, the great mass of educated public opinion had no possibility of manifest opposition until Mussolini overreached himself and success failed him. But his government was not much more immune to privately felt criticism than were liberal governments. What people particularly resented was the increasing interference of fascism in private life, for this came home to them far more than the cruelties of the *squadre* and the penal settlements. Mussolini thus forbade people to shake hands, despite the fact that this used to be one of his own favorite poses in front of the camera and he continued to practice it sometimes in private. What was worse, he introduced instead the ostentatious arm-length Roman salute which made them feel ridiculous—it was more hygienic than a handshake, he apologetically told Ludwig. Addressing a group of doctors in 1932, he said he meant to change popular habits of eating and even of sleeping. Italians were encouraged to date their correspondence from *anno primo,* and had always to use *Voi* instead of *Lei* in private address. As well as their vocabulary, their clothes and the style of their bathing suits were subject to political control. Such intrusion into private behavior was naturally hated and despised.

The absurdity of the system was further exposed in the mania of party members for uniforms, civilian state employees being obliged to wear uniforms by a law of 1938. It was also seen in the importation from Germany of the goose step under its inadequately disguised name of the *passo romano.* The height of ridiculousness was reached when public gymnastic exercises were prescribed for elderly party leaders who were made to scramble up walls and jump through flaming hoops in the Mussolini Forum. With a strange humorlessness, films of this activity were publicly shown in cinemas as propaganda for physical fitness. It was indeed hard to take some of the fascist leaders seriously. And their malpractices were notorious. Although the gold lace and the *carnavalesque* had once been appreciated, the point was reached where these became childish. Wealthy men, who had approved of fascism so long as it confined itself to strikebreaking, became maddened by its extravagance and bureaucracy, and the government which they had originally welcomed for its efficiency no longer had the same appeal when it proved to be corrupt and inefficient.

Such intellectual and moral opposition may have been widespread, but it could never have had any political effect until the king, or a general insurrection, or foreign armies could first undermine the edifice of fascism. Absolutism was tempered only by inefficiency and popular disobedience. Nevertheless, the elephantine bureaucracy which grew out of the corporations and the government departments did put a certain restraint on action by its very unwieldiness and gave scope to the natural disobedience of Italians. The unruliness and insubordination which had been major forces behind the *risorgimento,* and also behind the success of fascism, were in the end to be Mussolini's undoing, and much of the money he spent on organization and propaganda must have been corruptly diverted on the way—to the king's private satisfaction. In June 1942 Ciano made a revealing entry in his diary, which said that the cabinet was for the first time considering the possibility of penal sanctions for tax evasion. In the end the proposal had to be withdrawn, because whereas they recognized that it might work in more advanced countries, they knew that in Italy everyone would go on swearing to their false statements. This would just make fascism look ridiculous, and the extra revenue would largely have to go on building prisons for the disobedient. As Mussolini later lamented, fascism in a sense failed because it was not totalitarian enough. "I am the most disobeyed man in history," was the pathetic cry of this absolute dictator.

Even more than among the wealthy taxpayers, many of the poor peasants must have regarded fascism as just another invasion from the towns, bringing more taxes and more wars which the peasants would have to fight. Indifferentism and passive conformism or nonconformism were instinctive remedies for this. Sicilians thus merely transferred to Mussolini's government their ancient insular resentment against the mainland. The prefect Mori was sent to crush the Sicilian mafia by ruthless measures, only to find in it something more lasting than fascism, the habit ingrained in all classes of falling back on self-protection and self-help. Such was Mussolini's resentment against Sicily that in 1941 he took the absurd and impossible decision to transfer all its officials to the mainland. The more backward a province, the more flourishing was this conspiracy of nonco-operation against rationing and monopolies, against requisitions and the compulsory dispatch of crops to government storage centers. The shrewd Sardinian peasant guessed that government pools and fixed prices were primarily a means to enrich the local party hierarch, and fascism pitted itself in vain against uncooperative rustics who hid their wheat and even fired on government officers sent to collect it.

This example of rebelliousness may stand as symbolic of the shrugging shoulders, the caustic *bon mots* and *barzellette,* the amused skepticism at fascist claims, and an unchronicled passive resistance at all levels of society. Unfortunately, these were all compatible with great enthusiasm for other more dangerous aspects of fascism. Unfortunately, too, the general indifference, the habit of dissimulation and passive disobedience were going to prove one of the most evil and ineradicable legacies of the regime.

52 Surviving Institutions

Mussolini's ideal was to have everything organized under the state. As he told the magistrates in 1939, "in Italy we have no longer a division of powers, only a division of functions." Despite all he could do, however, some more or less independent institutions still survived. In particular there was the monarchy and the Church, and also the armed forces were never completely identified with the party.

The army had played a surprisingly small part in Mussolini's revolution; it remained broadly loyal to the throne, sometimes aloof from fascism and occasionally hostile to it, though open mutiny was inconceivable. Diaz, Caviglia, and Badoglio were each placated by the offer of a marshal's baton, but General Capello was dispatched to the penal settlements, and even Badoglio—to judge by his own special pleading—always retained some independence. When Balbo in 1926 tried to head a republican pressure group inside fascism, Badoglio apparently was strong enough to force its dissolution.

The fascist militia had been created with the deliberate intention of offsetting the regular army, and an important rivalry developed from this fact. The regulars disliked going short of weapons so that the militia could be armed. The militia soon duplicated the army's duties in the field, and blackshirt divisions played an active part in Ethiopia and Spain. Their officers were also given rank equal in status to officers in the army, and this caused acute jealousy among those who had attended the crack military school at Turin.

The increased use of civilian uniforms and the growth of civilian militarization in any case undermined the distinctiveness and caste consciousness enjoyed by the services. When General Gazzera, the minister of war, seemed to be resisting this process of depreciation, Mussolini in 1933 permanently took over this department himself—he had also held it until 1929. His undersecretary, General Baistrocchi, was a fascist who obeyed orders. Many entrenched susceptibilities were now offended when old regimental distinctions were abolished, when the goose step and the fascist salute were introduced, and undignified songs and war cries given to the troops. The best recipe for advancement in the military profession now was to have a large family of children, to join the party, and to applaud the Duce's hyperbolical speeches about breasts of steel and forests of bayonets.

This effort to *fascistizzare* the army introduced favoritism and corruption, while it allowed the wrong type of officer to come to the top. At the same time the weakening of the army's *esprit de corps* undermined morale, and the results appeared after 1940 in a lack of self-reliance and competence among the generals. The air force was yet more demoralized, having been born under fascism, and its first loyalty having always been to the regime. Here was proof that the very touch of fascism spelled death to honesty and initiative. But the navy remained an efficient fighting force, and many of the admirals retained enough independence of mind to disobey Mussolini in 1943.

§◈

If the king had been a more vital personality the loyalty of the armed services might have been used to save Italy before the final defeat. Vittorio Emanuele III was an unsympathetic man with none of the character and spirit of his forebears nor any of their popular vices. His consort, Queen Elena, kept her Slav accent and preferred to speak French. She was a woman of simple tastes and never content unless in the mountains far from Rome and the Court—"my cousin the shepherdess," so the Duchess of Aosta was said to call her. Such unsophistication made them the happiest royal family in modern Italian history, but did little to win popularity or ensure good government.

The king was pedantic and pettily scrupulous over the details of dispatches, but relatively uninterested in policy or politicians. To his ministers he appeared cynical and cold, without enthusiasm, and without any capacity at all for friendship. Despite his obstinacy, he was easily frightened, as he was also very sensitive about his diminutive height—people noted that when seated at audiences his feet used to dangle in the air. Whereas his grandfather had ordered the army to fire on the national hero Garibaldi, Vittorio Emanuele was awed by Mussolini and shrank from unwelcome realities or any difficult decisions which might compromise his dynasty. He would always swim with the tide, whether of liberalism in 1900, nationalism in 1915, reaction in 1922, or panic in 1943. He was not, in fact, a man from whom any courageous determination could be expected, and it seems that he never seriously contemplated rebelling against the man whom he sometimes must have regretted lifting into power.

There was no love lost between Mussolini and the king. The minister was seldom invited to the royal house, and the king stayed once only with the Duce. Etiquette was usually observed, and a Mussolini in civilian clothes would call officially at the palace on Monday and Thursday mornings at 10:30. In private, however, we hear of many petulant threats to abolish the monarchy once and for all. It was resented that when Hitler visited Italy he reviewed parades beside the king, while Mussolini had to stand behind. It was also resented that the king, so rumor said, had placed some of his large private fortune in safe custody with Hambro's bank in London. Prince Umberto, too, even though conforming outwardly did not belong to the party and was not seen in a black shirt. The press therefore was instructed not to use his title of "Hereditary Prince," and broad hints were given that the Grand Council was going to alter the succession. It was regarded as a notable occurrence when Maria José, Umberto's wife and daughter of the King of the Belgians, wore the party badge with her Red Cross uniform in 1940.

Right-wing antifascists clung to the monarchy as an anchor, when it was in fact the frailest of reeds. If the king ever protested against the lamentable trend of the times, it was not in defense of the constitution which he had sworn to uphold, but against some trivial invasion of his royal prerogative or some uncouth and disrespectful treatment of his majesty. His independence was limited to raising objections when the Collar of the Annunciation was presented to Ribbentrop and Goering, or when Starace entered the presence in his black shirt-sleeves, or when parliament without any notice suddenly gave Mussolini the altogether new title of First Marshal of the Empire—on this occasion he threatened to abdicate, for the king was commander in chief by constitutional right. The Duce made jokes about a diarchy, but in fact all effective power lay with the Mayor of the Palace, and both of them knew it. The fasces were added to the royal cross of Savoy, and Mussolini's portrait displaced that of the queen in schools and barracks, at the same height and in the same-sized frame as the king's. The Duce pardoned criminals on his own initiative, and laws were said to have been "approved" before receiving the royal signature.

As Mussolini became increasingly unhinged toward 1939, he reverted more and more to his earlier republican sympathies and even prepared a secret dossier on the private lives of the royal family in which Umberto at least was accused of the most horrible vices. But this ammunition was never used, because the approach of war made the co-operation of army and monarchy indispensable to him. The king, moreover, was troublesome rather than dangerous. He had severed all contact with the opposition after the murder of Matteotti, and it was almost impossible for a man of his aloofness and indecision to renew it. In his isolation he could hardly make alliance with the Church when he himself was so little inclined toward religion, and he had too long relied on the advice of politicians like Giolitti to be able to act decisively now that he lacked it. Only in Piedmont and Naples did he have any broad popular support, while the Roman aristocracy seem to have thought him, correctly, a bore and a boor.

The monarchy, unlike that of Great Britain, had failed since 1861 in its attempt to win both power and the appearance of powerlessness. On the contrary, it had merely succeeded in being saddled with responsibility for events without being able to control them, and as an instrument of government it had therefore become discredited in the eyes of fascists and antifascists alike. Abdication certainly would have focused world attention on Mussolini's iniquities and divided Italy (and perhaps even fascism) against itself. But though his great-grandfather had abdicated in another dark hour to save the country, Vittorio Emanuele III does not appear to have felt the duties of his office and the liberties of his country in the same way. Cut off from good advice, his actions therefore led him step by step to the collapse and disappearance of the dynasty in 1946. One of his daughters perished tragically in a German concentration camp; he himself died an expatriate in Egypt; and his son too was to be condemned to exile as soon as a free popular vote could decide that the oldest ruling house in Europe should cease to reign.

§◆

Parliament was a far less independent institution than the king or the army. Mussolini as late as June 1939 republished the *statuto* of 1848 as the fundamental constitution of the realm. Without being abolished it simply atrophied as his party absorbed the state. Both Senate and Chamber learned to break into fascist songs and war cries, and the whole body stood up when the Duce entered or left. Voting was generally by acclamation, even at the passage of the racial laws or, ironically enough, when the Chamber of Deputies abolished itself altogether in January 1939. A sample extract from the proceedings of the new Chamber of Fasces and Corporations on April 27, 1940, will show the quality of Italian politics at a time when the rest of the civilized world was overwhelmed with dismay and apprehension: "The Chamber and public galleries broke out into an intense and enthusiastic ovation. The cry of 'Duce, Duce' resounded through the hall again and again. The Duce responded with the Roman salute. The Assembly then sang *'Giovinezza.'* Again vibrant acclamation. The president ordered that the Duce should be saluted, and the Chamber answered with a powerful *'A noi.'* When the Duce left his seat, the National Councilors crowded around him with enthusiastic and continual acclamation."

After January 1939, members sat simply by virtue of holding some office in the corporations or the party. The new body had no importance except as window dressing for a regime that was personal and strictly unconstitutional. Laws were passed about the exact status and competence of the various institutions of government, but they were empty words. The Duce of fascism was declared not only *ipso facto* head of the government, but for a time the press even spelled DUCE in capital letters. By this time constitutional niceties had ceased to matter.

§

The Church was another institution which managed to remain autonomous. Very few leaders of fascism were practicing Catholics. Mussolini himself repeatedly boasted of being an unbeliever and of ruling an irreligious nation, and his personal servant, Navarra, never knew him to attend mass. One of his early works had been a eulogy of the heretic Huss, and he named his son after another heretic, Giordano Bruno. A scurrilous novel by him appeared in an American translation in 1928 entitled *The Cardinal's Mistress*. Yet he was prudent enough to realize how indispensable was ecclesiastical support. His first program in 1919 had called for the confiscation of Church property, but the prospect of power made him change direction, and by 1922 his party seems to have come to some tacit arrangement with certain high dignitaries of the Church.

Before the election of 1924 Mussolini cleverly played for clerical support. The crucifix came back into schoolrooms, chaplains were appointed to the party militia, Freemasonry was abolished, and a substantial sum was granted toward repair of the war-damaged churches. Wide exemption was also given from military service to clergy and seminarists, and a timely increase was made in the state subsidy for clerical stipends. This was something quite new in Italian history since 1861. The Laodiceans were confounded and the prestige of the parish priest augmented when religious ceremonies were at last officially attended by the local political leaders, and when religious blessing was given at party functions. The anticlerical Gentile was shortly replaced as minister of education by a Catholic, Professor Fedele, who inaugurated a more sympathetic educational policy in the years 1925–28, and at the Pope's request deprived the excommunicate modernist Buonaiuti of his teaching post in a state university. Mussolini himself also began to have his children baptized, and in 1928 he yielded sufficiently to go through a religious form of marriage with Donna Rachele.

This friendly policy toward the Church helps to explain the powerful support which Mussolini received during the twenties when he needed Catholic help in establishing his power. Church encouragement was withdrawn from the Christian democrats in 1922, and Sturzo was urged to resign his secretaryship of the party lest as a priest he should compromise the Vatican in the developing civil war. When the *popolari* collaborated with the socialists in the Aventine secession, the *Osservatore Romano* condemned this impious association. On the other hand Mussolini was apparently less impious; he could at least be relied on to oppose the Reds, and it could not yet be guessed that fascism would prove no barrier but rather a great encouragement to the spread of atheistic communism in Italy. After all its secular experience of tyrants of all kinds and creeds, the Church refused to say that fascism with its ruthless bludgeoning, its glorification of the state and of war, was incompatible with Christianity. The Vatican had in 1861 and 1864 protested uncompromisingly against liberalism, and before long it determined that no communist should be allowed to remain in the Church, but most rank-and-file fascists were Catholic in name at least, and some high prelate was always at hand to give a public blessing to all the important actions of fascism.

For fifty years the Pope had refused to leave his "prison" or even to recognize the existence of Italy. So when reconciliation was at last announced in 1929, it was rightly hailed as a great victory for Mussolini, and doubtless brought him a great accession of support in the country and the world at large—though the British foreign secretary, a Methodist and a socialist, refused to send his congratulations. In almost the first subsequent papal pronouncement, Pius XI paid a tribute to "the man sent to us by Providence," the man who fortunately lacked the "preconceptions of liberalism." These casual phrases were to be quoted too much by the anti-Catholics, but in a sense they did mark the culminating point of Mussolini's career, and they help to explain how one month after this reconciliation he was able to hold a plebiscite which showed overwhelming support for the regime.

This reconciliation in 1929 comprised a treaty and a concordat, by which the Church at last recognized the existence of Italy and the Italian occupation of Rome and retained for itself only the sovereign territory of the Vatican. The Vatican City, with a population of a few hundred, was to have its own army and police force, its own courts, railroad station, radio, newspaper, and prison. The Church also obtained confirmation from the state of its own establishment as the state religion, with a call upon government protection. The compact was finally sealed with a huge sum of money which made the Church perhaps the largest holder of Italian state bonds, and thus gave it a much-criticized financial interest in the stability of Mussolini's regime.

Other concessions were also obtained. There was to be no further distribution of Protestant Bibles in Italy, and the holding of evangelical meetings in private houses was forbidden. The state promised to take its marriage laws from the Church. Ecclesiastical schools received preferential treatment, and religious teaching was extended from elementary to secondary education. Ecclesiastical corporations were exempted from taxes, and legal personality was again allowed to religious orders. A national holiday was also affixed for February 11 to commemorate this conciliation, replacing the provocative September 20 which had commemorated the conquest of Rome in 1870.

Amid the general applause, Croce alone spoke in the Senate against the concordat. While he welcomed the treaty and the reconciliation, he strongly disliked the manner and the details of this "surrender" by the lay state. "Against those who think Paris is worth a mass, there are still some who must protest on grounds of conscience." These must have been the last words of serious criticism in parliament that Mussolini ever heard.

The Church soon realized the barrenness of its victory, for Mussolini would not have signed the concordat had he not intended to profit substantially himself. On his first ceremonial visit to the Vatican after the reconciliation, he refused to kneel and kiss the Pope's hand and forbade the photographers to picture him as the humble servant of the Church or the mild man of religion. He explained to parliament that in practice he had conceded nothing of note. In the field of education, he added, he would show himself quite intractable. Mussolini the realist had given up his claim to out-of-date jurisdictional rights and was quite ready to modify the fascist attitude on women's sports so as to meet objections from the Vatican; he would even bring his wife down from Milan and pose as a model family man; but the corollary of establishment was that the state should keep a tight grasp on the Church and a voice even in ecclesiastical nominations. This was no longer Cavour's "free Church in a free state," for ecclesiastics now knew that the government could block their promotion or even secure their dismissal if they did not keep in with fascism. Mussolini could not afford much latitude to any institution which tried to stand apart from his machine. Almost immediately he launched a violent attack on Catholic Action, and the Pope was forced to yield and to diminish the activity of Catholic organizations in the training of youth.

This conflict over Catholic Action produced some signs of renewal of the old conflict between Church and state which historically had been one of the great forces working for liberty. In particular it prompted the outspoken encyclical *Non abbiamo bisogno* in 1931, in which the independence of the Church was asserted against totalitarianism, though it was explained that the fascist party was not specifically in question. The authoritarian state was welcomed by the Church, but with reservations: as Pius stated, "We cannot allow freedom of discussion, for that might imperil the faith of less enlightened hearers and damage the established religion." But authoritarianism on a Mussolinian scale was by 1931 cutting too close to the bone. The racial laws and the fascist attempt to monopolize youth education, though approved of by Father Gemelli, were bound to be anathema to most Catholics.

This encyclical was the most categorical public challenge that Mussolini had received inside Italy since Croce's manifesto in 1925, but for politic reasons this criticism had to be partial and indirect. As a rule, Mussolini knew that he could rely on Church support. In the plebiscitary elections of 1929, the president of Catholic Action instructed all members of his organization to support fascism, and the Jesuit organ, *Civiltà Cattolica,* which had been so relentless in its criticism of liberal governments, looked with far greater benevolence on this military dictator. The secretary of the fascist party was in 1930 received by the Pope in solemn audience, a favor never previously conceded to any other political party. In sum, while the Pope boldly protested at Mussolini's more strident heresies, no government in modern Italian history had received anything like so much ecclesiastical approbation. Thousands of sermons exhorted the faithful to be loyal to their great leader, and a cardinal inaugurated the school of "fascist mysticism" in Milan, while in the world at large Mussolini became for a time, until the arrival of General Franco, the ideal pattern of a Catholic statesman.

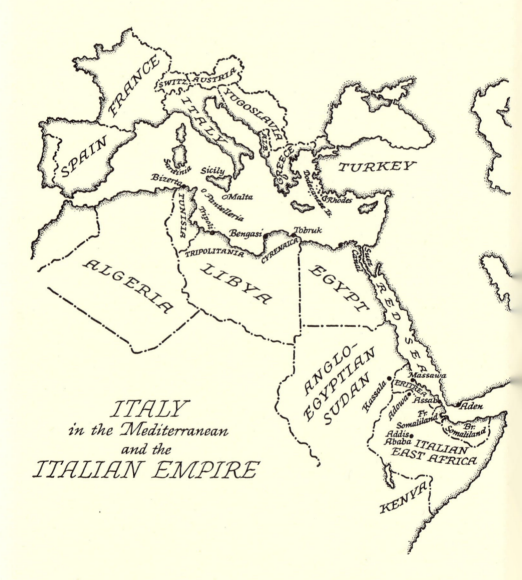

SWITZ. AUSTRIA
FRANCE
SPAIN
ITALY
YUGOSLAVIA
Sardinia
Sicily
Bizerta
GREECE
Dodecanese Is.
TURKEY
TUNISIA
O Pantelleria
O Malta
Rhodes
Tripoli
Bengasi
Tobruk
TRIPOLITANIA
CYRENAICA
ALGERIA
LIBYA
EGYPT
RED SEA
Suez Canal
ANGLO-
EGYPTIAN
SUDAN
Massawa
Kassala
ERITREA
Adowa
Assab
Aden
Fr.
Somaliland
Br.
Somaliland
Addis
Ababa
ITALIAN
EAST AFRICA
KENYA

ITALY
in the Mediterranean
and the
ITALIAN EMPIRE

53 Foreign Policy, 1922-1936

Mussolini gave an early foretaste of what the fascist style meant in foreign policy when he bombarded Corfu in 1923. An Italian, General Tellini, had been assassinated on the borders of Albania and Greece while with an Allied mission. Without stopping to examine the facts, Mussolini sent a truculent ultimatum to Greece and immediately ordered his warships to shell the island when his conditions were not accepted unreservedly. He wanted to eclipse D'Annunzio in the Adriatic and to earn the reputation of a man of action who knew how to make Italy feared throughout the Balkans.

Despite a warning note from Britain and acceptance by Greece of a settlement arranged not at Rome but in Paris, the episode was to rank as a moderate success in Italian eyes. It set an ominous example of unpunished violence, at the same time as it defied the League of Nations, and Mussolini tried to make out that the rest of Europe was admiring and jealous. It was not in his nature to see that there might be disadvantages for Italy if he earned the reputation of a bully and a trickster so quickly.

Until he was able to assert himself more emphatically than this, Mussolini tried to reassure the world that fascism was not an article for export and that ideology and foreign policy would be kept distinct. His sympathies and antipathies were well known, so he said in a phrase which became famous, but he did not base his policy on them. In his less restrained moments, however, he completely spoiled the effect, publicly demanding an essentially anti-English attitude to bring about the downfall of the British Empire, to turn the Mediterranean into an

Italian lake and drive out its parasites. The antithesis here was palpable, but foreigners were easily deceived. They were not to know that the export of fascism was something very close to his heart and that he was secretly going to subsidize the rexists, the cagoulards, the Italian party in Malta, and other fascist organizations all over the world.

Little by little Mussolini moved toward a policy of treaty revision. In 1923 he backed France against Germany over the occupation of the Ruhr. He signed the Pact of Rome with Yugoslavia in January 1924, by which Italy took Fiume and recognized Susak and Port Baross as Yugoslavian—all without reference to the League, of which Italy was officially a member. He did what he could to penetrate into Balkan politics and prevent any close alliance of states there. He also signed commercial treaties with Germany and Soviet Russia, on whose support any revision of the Versailles settlement seemed ultimately to depend.

Mussolini himself held the office of foreign minister until June 1936 (except for the years 1929–32), but his first departmental secretary, Contarini, was a career diplomat for whom national interests came before fascism. Contarini tried to continue Sforza's foreign policy, to restrain the intrusion of ideology and whimsy, and to prevent the giving of gratuitous offence to other nations. In this spirit of accommodation the Treaty of Locarno was signed in 1925. Contarini resigned in 1926, for by then the party machine was beginning to permeate the foreign service with men who lacked either intelligence, honesty, or even the most elementary knowledge of the outside world. In their blindness to genuine national interests, and their ignorance of how lines of retreat could be kept open from every diplomatic position, these party placemen were to do grave harm to the prestige of Italy and to begin an unhappy chapter for her in foreign politics.

Miscalculations and confusion in foreign policy were to be Mussolini's eventual undoing. From the very beginning he was dangerously muddled between on the one hand thinking that he could convince foreign admirers that Italy was a safe and stabilizing force in Europe, and on the other hand incessantly proclaiming that the settlement of 1919 must be smashed in order to allow further Italian expansion. The urge for expansion always won in the end, however, and by 1927 his statements should have left Europe with little room for doubt. On their testimony, between 1935 and 1940 Italy would arrive at a crucial point in European history and see her rights at long last prevail. By that time Italian aircraft would blot out the light of the sun. Italy was thus made out to be an unsatisfied power, and one with a grievance which would justify the most barefaced acts of imperialism.

Once firmly seated in the saddle, Mussolini could not resist the temptation to cut a figure, and it was merely a blind when in 1928 he adhered to the Kellogg pact to renounce war. By 1930 fascism was being declared of universal application, and hence very much for export. "Though words are beautiful things, rifles, machine guns, planes, and cannon are still more beautiful." Two years later Mussolini told an audience at Milan that the twentieth century would be the century of fascism, during which Italy would return for the third time to be the directing force in human civilization. In ten years' time, he insisted, all Europe would be fascist. In 1934 Mussolini further announced that Italians had to be a bellicose as well as a militarized nation, and the Council of Ministers decreed that all citizens between the ages of six and fifty-five should be thought of as soldiers.

Fascist foreign policy typically cut free from tradition and veered unstably from ideological arguments to momentary whims and intuitive fancies, but all this was compounded with a modicum of shrewd realism and a real virtuosity in propaganda and showmanship. Though he had come to power on the pretext of opposing bolshevism, Mussolini was realistic enough to be almost the first to recognize the revolutionary government in Russia. "Both we and the Russians are opposed to liberals, democrats, and parliaments," he said, and not until Russia joined the League and seemed to abandon revisionism did Mussolini turn to prefer German help. Evidently, the central core of fascism was not antibolshevism (Mussolini was himself more like a bolshevik than were most Italian socialists), but rather the deliberate intention to blow sky-high the peace of Europe; antibolshevism had just been a pretext for tricking the *ingénus* at home and abroad into becoming his accomplices.

Italy and Germany were almost certain to become allies if once they could agree about Austria. In her weakened state Austria was a natural cushion on Italy's most sensitive frontier, and the fascists therefore furnished arms and money to help Dollfuss maintain Austrian independence against Germany. When in July 1934 Dollfuss was murdered, an infuriated Mussolini mobilized troops at the Brenner to check any threatened German advance, and momentarily crossed back from revisionism into the camp of the League. This was a fateful moment in the period between the wars. Britain and France came to meet Italy at the Stresa conference in May 1935, and Mussolini hoped that, in return for his support against a rearming Germany, the democracies might be won over to guarantee Austria and support his conquest of Abyssinia. The crucial issue was Abyssinia, and here a chapter of accidents intervened which broke the Stresa front and lined up Mussolini in a fatal marriage with the nazis.

§❧

General De Bono has put on record that Mussolini had been preparing to invade Abyssinia since 1932, though the invasion was subsequently sold to the world as an answer to "unprovoked aggression" by the Abyssinians in 1934. The fascists were ambitious to make a splash, no matter what or where so long as it was large and provocative. Italian history since 1922 seemed to belie their early promises. Apart from the Lateran Treaty there had been no great achievements, and only idle rhetoric and paper devices so far exemplified the much trumpeted creativeness of fascism. Furthermore, the economic depression made it desirable to divert people's gaze from home discontents and to unite the nation around its common patriotism. "We have a right to empire," said Mussolini, "as a fertile nation which has the pride and will to propagate its race over the face of the earth, a virile people in the strict sense of the word." Colonial expenditure was already up from 107 million lire in 1921 to 530 million in 1930, but this had mostly been dissipated on the profitless desert of Libya. Hence arose this project for a more glamorous colonial war against the last unoccupied region of Africa, the same country whose inexplicable defeat of Italy in 1896 still rankled. So often had Mussolini extolled war and conquest that now he was finally obliged to find an easily beaten opponent in order to practice what he had preached. He needed to justify fascism by success and prove in battle the boasted virility of his regime and people.

While the new undersecretary Suvich providently stressed the overriding need to defend Austria against the Germans, the amateur politician Mussolini ill-advisedly thought he had time to indulge in acquiring a waste and sandy empire, imagining that he would still be able to regroup his forces on the northern frontier before Germany was ready to annex Austria and risk hostilities. For a long time he had directed his thoughts to Africa. He had looked with some benevolence on the nationalist movement in Egypt, for this was against Britain, but in the Italian colonies of Tripoli and Cyrenaica he naturally did the very reverse, and these provinces were gradually reconquered from the Berbers and Senussi by the heavy hand of Volpi and the even heavier hand of Graziani. The "revolt" of these newly conquered peoples after 1915 took fifteen years to suppress before the Senussi chief could be captured and publicly hanged before the eyes of his followers. Only then could Mussolini seriously push that settlement of Italian peasant families by which he designed to establish in North Africa a stronghold of *italianità*. Despite a considerable expenditure, only about two thousand

Italians had settled in the enormous area of Libya by 1930, though big schemes for irrigation and road building were under way.

Meanwhile Italy reasserted her benevolent patronage over Abyssinia, introduced this independent country into the League, and in 1928 signed a pact of friendship with the Negus. But the latter, justifiably fearing that economic pressure was only a prelude, began to take advisers from other countries as well, and was said to be hindering the development of roads and trade connections with Italian territory. This opposition turned Italian patronage into a veiled hostility. Mussolini repeated until the last moment that there was absolutely no question at all of wanting territorial conquest, and he continuously expostulated that he was no collector of deserts. Both these statements were in fact untrue, but many people believed him, and this capacity to inspire belief was proving to be an important asset until its long-term results could be seen.

A preliminary step toward the conquest of Abyssinia was to obtain from Laval in January 1935 a general statement of French approval. Later in the year, as an attempt to avert war, Eden offered to compensate Abyssinia with a corridor to the sea through British territory if only she would placate Italy with part of Ogaden, but Italy vetoed this arrangement, objecting to Abyssinia keeping an independent outlet to the sea which would free her from Italian economic pressure. Sforza vouches that Mussolini said he would not take Ethiopia except by war, not even if it was offered him as a gift. The Hoare-Laval plan, which proposed to give Italy a large part of Abyssinia while still preserving it as a separate state, was for the same reason unacceptable as a permanent answer. In any case the unexpected outcry against the plan by British public opinion in December 1935 effectively split the Stresa front and drove Mussolini to seek the friendship of Hitler. Germany was thus able to reoccupy the Rhineland unopposed and then to engulf Austria without a protest from Italy. From this moment the Italian dictator was doomed to play a subordinate and finally a servile role in Europe. The Ethiopian venture was going to prove more expensive than he had bargained for.

§✿

The incident regarded as the actual provocation of war had taken place a year earlier at Wal-Wal, an oasis which was marked even on Italian maps as Abyssinian territory, but where the Italians claimed a right of usage. Mussolini eventually began military operations in October 1935. He knew from an intercepted message that the threat of British naval action against him was all bluff, and Grandi at London claimed to have private information from members of the British cabinet who opposed Eden and favored the Duce. It was all too simple, for Italy thus stood to gain a maximum of effect with a calculated minimum of risk.

Condemnation by the League inevitably followed the outbreak of hostilities, and in November came the imposition of economic sanctions, but this suited Mussolini very well. It seemed to prove that Italy was persecuted and encircled, that it was the nation and not the regime which was in danger, and that the austerity campaign for self-sufficiency had been no mere caprice but a vital national interest. Sanctions in any case did not hold up his war effort. Ridiculously enough, coal and oil were exempted, although without fuel he would on his own confession have been brought to a halt. Soviet Russia provided a considerable part of Italy's requirements for this imperialistic war, and Germany also refused to join the other nations in their embargo, while of course the United States merchant marine was not legally bound by a League decision. The Germans tried to inflame the situation still further. They were delighted at this diversion of Italian energies so far away from Austria, especially as in the process it split Italy from France and destroyed the self-confidence and mutual trust of the League powers.

The Italian people seemingly betrayed considerable enthusiasm over this call on their patriotism, and the war strengthened rather than weakened Mussolini's internal position. Wedding rings were gladly sacrificed to provide currency, and Prince Doria's Scottish wife was assaulted when she refused this tribute. Some former political exiles rallied to the regime, while Orlando, Albertini, and Croce apparently welcomed this continuation of the liberal policy of African expansion, and the dramatist Sem Benelli volunteered to fight in person. Imperialistic poetry poured from Soffici, and prose from D'Annunzio and Ojetti. Even the Papacy, which had angrily condemned World War I as a useless carnage, on this occasion said nothing to give the slightest offence to fascist imperialism, and most of the bishops bestowed their public blessing on this self-styled Protector of Islam in his war against the Christian Abyssinians.

Military operations began under General De Bono, who as a first-hour fascist had the honor of capturing for the party any laurels there were to be gained. Mussolini flooded him with telegrams of instruction, sometimes a hundred of them a day, all top priority even when they dealt with the tiny details over which the Duce was anxious to show his masterly sense of control. After a few weeks of fighting, however, De Bono had to be promoted marshal and replaced by a commander from the regular army, Badoglio. Thenceforward, the war progressed smoothly, about half a million men being needed before it was over. Badoglio, relying on speed and penetration, struck at the main centers without worrying very much about his lines of communication, and in six months Addis Ababa fell. This was a workmanlike job of strategy, and the engineers and roadbuilders in particular proved remarkably efficient, although sizable military operations had to continue against "rebels" and "brigands" for many months longer.

Admittedly, the enemy was in no position to put up more than a token resistance, and hence the victory was achieved almost too easily and gave Mussolini a dangerous feeling of overconfidence. Later, he lamented that only 1,537 Italians had been killed and that the war had been won at too small a cost and without hardening the national character as much as fascist doctrine prescribed. Italian credit incidentally suffered because of the supererogatory use of poison gas, and young Vittorio Mussolini published a much admired and widely circulated account of the fun of bombing native horsemen, which ecstatically described how they looked like a budding rose as the bombs exploded. While justifying the war by talking at Geneva about the barbarity of the Abyssinians, fascism thus attracted this label of barbarism to itself.

The efficiency of Badoglio was in time superseded again by the pettiness and corruption of the party bosses, who appeared in droves in order to earn their campaign medals and fill their pockets. In February 1937 stories circulated of a pitiless massacre of thousands of Abyssinians, for the Duce had expressly ordered Graziani to shoot all captured "rebels," to use gas against them, and to enforce the law of "ten eyes for an eye." There were further demoralizing stories of fortunes being made by companies formed for building roads and factories, and exaggerated reports were sent home about the natural resources of Abyssinia in order to obtain the necessary state subsidies. Political jobbery led inevitably to jerrybuilding, since there was little competition for public contracts, and the Duke of Aosta was later to report that half his colonial civil servants were incompetent and half the rest corrupt. Effective supervision was lacking to remedy this deficiency, and when a ministry of Italian Africa was created in 1937, the Duce simply added it to his existing profusion of conflicting responsibilities.

Much fine work continued to be done by individual Italians in Africa, but it was overshadowed by the damage left behind by fascism. If Italy gained little from what she invested in her colonies, this was not only because the empire was mostly unprofitable desert, but also because mismanagement was the invariable companion of fascist exploitation, and great sums were squandered each year on "fascist" objectives which were concerned mainly with prestige and propaganda. Despite Mussolini's economic arguments for expansion, in 1939 Italy's trade with her colonies was only 2 per cent of her total trade. She was spending on them ten times their economic value to her, and the Italian population of New York City was still ten times that of the entire Italian colonial empire.

Some of those who had welcomed Mussolini's domestic policy apparently began to fear the inebriation of cheap success after 1936, and with reason. Financial exhaustion, moral disrepute, and diplomatic isolation were all threatening. And yet for most Italians his victory in Africa seemed a glorious success at the time. It had mortally wounded the League, it had defied a vote by fifty-two nations at once and had rocked the prestige of Great Britain. It had also provided few casualties and many medals. Since 1860, many an attempt by Italy to cut a more heroic figure in the world had crumbled to dust and ashes. Now at last there was something substantial to show, and Mussolini could prove that it was a fascist and not a liberal achievement: indeed he was succeeding in 1935 precisely where parliamentary government had failed in 1896.

This parody of an empire nevertheless gave many Italians a wholly false impression of their country's potential strength and their leader's abilities. After the reconciliation with Rome in 1929, the proclamation of the empire in 1936 was the second deceptive peak in this rake's progress. Instead of seeing that the campaign had seriously depleted war reserves, the illusion spread that victory over half-armed tribesmen could be repeated as easily against France. Instead of recognizing the palpable fact that the war had been won on credit, bad habits of lavish expenditure had been acquired, and retrenchment was becoming psychologically ever more difficult.

The tragedy of Italy in the next ten years was the working out of these misconceptions to their bitter end. Mussolini shared both the illusion and the subsequent disillusion, though few if any people had been better placed than he for knowing the real truth. Flattery went to his head. He was extolled by the king for winning the greatest colonial war in all history, and so increasing the prestige and power of the fascist fatherland. Many years later he recalled in Ciano's hearing how everything had gone well until 1937 and how he wished that his stomach ulcer had killed him at that moment of success.

In truth, however, Italy seems to have been already well on the road to destruction by 1937. The Ethiopian war had created an exaggerated *ducismo* which in the end proved fatal. It forced the extortion of compulsory loans and a capital levy and caused a resumption of irremediable budgetary deficits. It also isolated Italy and thus compelled her to make the German alliance that proved her ruin. By teaching her to underestimate Britain it broke the Anglo-Italian entente which had been for so long the basis of her foreign policy. And thus the results of a policy of prestige were already becoming evident. They could already be seen in the fate of Trieste and Fiume under fascist rule, because, cut off from their natural trade routes, the one city was declining despite heavy protection, while the other was almost destroyed, grass growing on its railroad track and its port installations in decay.

Fifteen years of fascism had left most Italians too confused for honest self-criticism, and the many internal contradictions in the system had now become quite bewildering. For example, Mussolini persuaded them that the Ethiopian war was defensive, fought against a savage and brutal aggressor, though at the same time he had gone on arguing that war should be welcomed and provoked as a good in itself. The Ethiopians were to be condemned for their cruelty and their failure to conform with the Geneva convention, wheras he was to be praised for his realistic recognition that humanitarianism was mere cowardice and international law a fictitious device used by decadent powers. At one moment he was the champion of tradition, at another the herald of a new age.

> Stiff in opinions, always in the wrong;
> Was everything by starts, and nothing long:
> But, in the course of one revolving moon,
> Was chemist, fiddler, statesman and buffoon.

At once revolutionary and conservative, Catholic and antireligious, socialistic and bourgeois, the champion of law and then the negation of all law, Mussolini brought out the cynicism and opportunism in his fellow countrymen. The great majority ceased to possess much capacity for firm belief, and trusted only that the Duce, with all his apparent contradictions, was really infallible and was merely using these stratagems to delude the enemies of Italy. The delusion was rather his, and theirs.

54 Lack of Restraint, 1936-1938

Two such dissatisfied countries as Germany and Italy were natural allies, and the two regimes were in many ways nearly identical. Hitler seems to have admired Mussolini almost alone among mankind, and in the end these two dictators surrounded themselves with so many sycophants that each imperatively needed the other as an alleviation for his own cosmic loneliness.

Hitler had been using the Roman salute by the middle twenties, and the word *Führer* copied that of *Duce*. The unknown Hitler is said to have been refused when he requested a signed photograph from his successful prototype, but Salvemini has collected evidence to show that nazism was being subsidized from Italy at least by 1932. Goering spent a year of exile in Italy, and another future nazi, the Prince of Hesse, became Vittorio Emanuele's son-in-law in 1925.

Mussolini was so convinced of his own intellectual superiority that he genuinely believed for a time that he would be the senior partner in any alliance with Hitler, just as he continued up to the 1940's to tell his friends that he was the more intelligent and skillful of the two. He had been overjoyed to find someone in Europe who took him seriously and aped his dogmas and institutions. Nazism flattered his vanity by confirming his negation of liberalism and democracy and by accepting much the same combination of state socialism and state capitalism. Nazism employed the same methods of cruelty and conquest and echoed his sadistic and mystical belief that "only blood can turn the bloodstained wheels of history." Hitler took from Italy the military organization of youth, as indeed he took some of the posturing and the hysterical crowd scenes. As a result, according to Ambassador Guariglia, Mussolini was already by 1930 allowing nazi formations to train on Italian soil where the other treaty makers of 1919 could not observe or check them.

As time went on, Hitler proved immeasurably more successful and fertile in ideas, while Mussolini degenerated both physically and intellectually. On paper the two ideologies may have looked alike, but in practice fascism lacked organizing genius and either the intention or the ability to take theory to its logical extreme. It became the turn of the fascists to admire the efficiency, the "know-how," the national discipline, and the supposedly shattering thoroughness of the nazis. Mercifully, the very individualism of Italians, which at first had prepared the way for Mussolini, always constituted an invaluable differentiation from the totalitarian methods of Hitler. Mussolini could casually order the cold-blooded murder of prisoners taken in Spain, but there was little system in his cruelty, and his fierceness was far more in word than deed. Croce's conclusion was true in part: "There was a deep and important distinction between nazism and fascism, because the first was a terrible crisis which had been brooding through centuries of German history, and the second was a superfetation quite alien to the history of Italy. . . . The first had a tragic and diabolical aspect, but the second kept an incorrigibly clownlike appearance even in the crimes it committed, and anybody could see as much at a glance by contrasting the appearance of the two chiefs." At least the second of these statements was true.

In comparison, Mussolini was a lightweight, a crude novice in the art of government. There was an abysmal pettiness about the man who ordered Italian journalists in the gallery of Geneva to hiss Haile Selassie when he came to defend Ethiopia before the League. Mussolini's violent changes of policy were sometimes accepted on his own valuation as brilliant strokes of Machiavellian deceit, part of a superplan which the fullness of time would reveal, but Ciano's diary now confirms that they were rather a pathological symptom. At one moment he vetoed the *Anschluss* and began to fortify the Brenner; at the next he struck an attitude and announced to the world that he was standing beside Germany in shining armor. At one moment he was ranting against Hitler and hoping that the Russians would beat Germany; then in a matter of days he suddenly changed when a recollection of Chamberlain reminded him how contemptible were the pluto-democracies.

Sometimes, when the issue of peace or war appeared to lie in his hands, and when the world stood breathless to know his will, Mussolini had no policy at all and no idea even what was happening, but sought his information from the press like everyone else. National and international politics were merely being directed to subserve a personal vanity, and on a level of irresponsibility which sometimes passes belief. Again and again when trying to explain the collapse of his regime one comes back to the vanity and irresponsibility of this one man. Hitler was great enough to endure some powerful subordinates and to deserve their fear and loyalty, but apart from Balbo there was not a single top-level fascist leader with a strong will and personality of his own. Indeed, one could argue that almost none of Mussolini's chosen apostles had any admirable qualities even of a purely technical order.

§❧

Evidently, the western democracies had nothing to offer Italy comparable with what she thought she might obtain from alliance with Germany, and this was the decisive fact. Italian territorial claims against the German peoples had been largely satisfied in 1919, and any ambitions which remained were directed primarily against France, Britain, and French client states in the Balkans. Mussolini failed to appreciate that revisionism, if it implied a German alliance, would probably upset the balance of Europe to Italian disadvantage. He preferred to reason superficially that, since Germany had refused to impose sanctions, she must therefore have Italian interests at heart.

In the summer of 1936, despite or perhaps in part because of German rearmament and the reoccupation of the Rhineland, there came a *rapprochement* between Italy and Germany. Mussolini christened it when he remarked that the Berlin-Rome vertical was not a diaphragm but an *axis* around which all other peace-loving states in Europe could group themselves. Once the Austrian question had been "solved," once Germany could forget Italian "treachery" in 1915, and as soon as fascist doctrine could be modified to include Italians within the Aryan race, all was ready for the Pact of Steel. It was under this German influence that the goose step was imported into Italy, though Mussolini went on protesting that he never imitated anyone. When people grumbled that the goose step was Prussian, he became indignant and humorlessly replied that the goose was a Roman animal for it had once saved the Capitol from the Gauls. But he also promised them that he would never stop his campaign to "prussianize" Italy. His feelings toward Germany were a mixture of admiration, envy, fear, and dislike; and admiration predominated at this critical moment.

The traditional foreign policy of noncommittal was therefore thrown overboard. Mussolini even burned his boats and gratuitously insulted the western powers. A cleverer man would have retained sufficient independence to play the *tertius gaudens,* and so incidentally would have extorted more respect and consideration from his new ally. Instead of this, Italy became a camp follower in the march of German expansion, and whether victorious or defeated she thus stood to lose all. Even when fate restored her to the position of mediator between two power groups in September 1939, Mussolini obtusely threw away this undeserved good fortune, and since he had crushed all opposition there was no effective voice which could show him his error. Bottai murmured against the Axis, as Balbo against the Roman salute, but these murmurs were drowned in the rhythmic cries (artificially amplified where necessary) of "Duce," and Mussolini was reinforced in the view that his own instinct must be infallible.

꿎

One can follow this lack of restraint developing rapidly after June 1936. Just after the Ethiopian war there was another "change of the guard," and without the least preliminary discussion with anyone Mussolini suddenly handed over the foreign ministry to the thirty-four-year-old Ciano. Up to this moment the Duce's many other preoccupations had allowed foreign affairs to be in part directed by his undersecretary Suvich, but, as in other departments, the restraints put on by the old civil servants were by now fairly ineffective; Suvich was dismissed and Ciano now put the seal on what Grandi had already begun. The existence of an Italian empire was proclaimed in 1936, and Italy was somewhat prematurely pronounced to be a satisfied power. In yet another contradiction, however, satisfaction was also declared to be a bourgeois and unfascist sentiment, and Ciano in particular still needed to attach his name to some new conquest.

This was the moment when Franco initiated his revolt against the Spanish republic, confidently relying upon Italian intervention. The Spanish republicans had sinned in Mussolini's eyes by restoring free speech and more democratic government at a time when fascism was supposed to be winning everywhere. Intervention in Spain, disguised before the world as a campaign against communism, would punish them, as well as possibly winning the Balearic Islands for Italy. The ruinous search for prestige and reputation had to be continued in this backstairs way, for Italians had been told to expect success after success, and any failure to repeat the prescription might expose the whole sham upon which fascism was built.

In return for all the money and effort expended on intervention in Spain, Mussolini received nothing for his pains. When the Italians suffered a minor defeat on the Guadalajara, the foreign press began to suspect that fascism was more bark than bite, and this irritated him excessively, because not being taken seriously was his greatest fear, as it was also the greatest danger to his government. He therefore soon made Roatta's expeditionary force less "voluntary," and replaced the blackshirted militiamen with more regular soldiers. Seventy thousand Italians were engaged in Spain during 1937, and the initial promise of arms had led by degrees to an inextricable involvement. While victory would bring little reward, defeat would mean a loss of face which he dared not contemplate. Here was a political mistake which was as elementary as it was now irreparable.

Completely misinformed by the incompetent new fascist diplomats, Mussolini continued to belief that this Spanish war might end at any moment, whereas in fact it dragged on for nearly three years until the fall of Madrid in March 1939. Apparently, he did not even use the fighting to learn any helpful lessons on weapons or tactics. The Germans, on the other hand, seized a greater political and economic hold on Spain in return for a much smaller effort. Germany was not averse to seeing Italian troops tied down there, for again, as in the Ethiopian war, this gave Hitler a freer hand in Austria and made the breach between Italy and France so wide that Germany could depend upon the Italian alliance without the need of further concessions. Mussolini's own remoteness from this kind of political reality can be seen in a strange speech to the Senate in March 1938 in which he claimed that the Abyssinian and Spanish wars had in the first place increased and not weakened Italian strength, and in the second place had led him to the conclusion that modern armies should not be too heavily motorized. Perhaps he realized that he lacked the resources to emulate what he had seen in Germany, or perhaps on the contrary he had no conception of the nature of modern war or of the difficulties of equipping his army to fight under such conditions.

ॐ

For some while yet, Britain gambled in the hope that appeasement would prevent a European war, guessing from experience that Italians would probably try to keep a foot in each armed camp. But the so-called Gentleman's Agreement of January 1937 was a mere blind to cover the fact that fascist Italy was geared to upsetting the Mediterranean *status quo,* necessarily at British expense. Fortifications were built in Pantelleria, Tobruk, and the Dodecanese. Italian newspaper correspondents were withdrawn from London, and no Italian representative attended the coronation of George VI because the deposed Negus of Ethiopia was also invited. In March 1937 Mussolini made a provocative speech at Tripoli in which he again claimed to be the defender of Islam—by implication her defender against Britain and not presumably against Christianity. All this may have been pasteboard and window dressing, but it was intended to impress and alarm, and it certainly was alarming, even though almost all British statesmen of the Chamberlain era lacked the political and psychological awareness to read the signs of the times.

In September 1937, wearing a new and specially designed uniform, Mussolini set out for Germany and was there given a tremendous reception. The display organized for his benefit, especially at the Essen factories and the army maneuvers in Mecklenburg, finally convinced him, as was intended, that Germany would win the inevitable war. The 800,000 Germans listening to his speech on the Maifeld were something impressive beyond anything he had seen before, and Hitler's personal and unfeigned admiration was intoxicating. To his last moments Mussolini clung to this myth of German invincibility, and his reception in 1937 was a fateful and fatal event in his life.

In November he therefore joined the anti-Comintern pact, and an Italian ship carrying armored cars to the Chinese was even ordered to wreck itself off the Chinese coast so as not to offend his new ally, Japan. In December, after an absurd two-minute meeting of the Grand Council, he announced Italy's withdrawal from the League. Quite apart from the cardinal sin of being dominated by the Western powers, the League was obnoxious by being democratic in procedure and because of its outmoded intention of securing peace, friendliness, and the maintenance of international law.

In this same mood Austria was finally sacrificed as the price of German friendship, and in March 1938 Hitler was allowed to swallow the rump state which had once looked to Italy for protection. This caused the immediate collapse of the friendly Danubian bloc which Italy had tried to build up. It also lost Italy her chief advantage under the 1919 settlement, since a strong European state was now back again at the head of the Alpine valleys. Here was the most unanswerable condemnation of Mussolini's foreign policy, and this was an important moment in the progressive enslavement of Italy to the Germans. What annoyed Italians quite as much at the time was the promise to give Germany the famous Discobolus of Myron; they could not know that this was the beginning of a big artistic emigration, but the Duce said he wanted fewer statues and more trophies captured from the enemy.

୨ଈ

As dictatorship became more firmly established, there was less need for showing consideration to the monarchy, or to the Church, or big business, and the dictator was increasingly ruled by his whimsical intuition. Criticism, destructive or constructive, became rarer, and even his old cronies found him unapproachable and impervious to reason. The chief weakness threatening a personal dictatorship was this absence of a sufficient internal conflict of wills and institutions. Some people trace the beginning of Mussolini's decay to his appointment of Starace as party secretary in 1931, and of the cynical Buffarini as his own undersecretary at the ministry of the interior in 1933. Some time between these two dates he had met Clara Petacci. But only in 1937–38 was decline obvious, aided by the fatal illusion of cheap success in Ethiopia.

As his tactical alliance with the men of wealth became less necessary, Mussolini reverted to type, to his plebeian associates and his former socialism. In the autumn of 1938 he began to inveigh particularly against the Italian bourgeoisie for preferring private gain to national victory, and in his last six years of life this notion became a positive fetish. He thus gratuitously provoked the enmity of a most powerful class which had hitherto been an important source of strength. The first-hour fascists had always been nostalgic for the radical party program of 1919, and among these radicals was Achille Starace who was principally responsible for this new antibourgeois campaign. Starace was typical of all that well-to-do northerners detested in the proletarian South. In payment for their contempt he attacked the "bourgeois mentality" and tried to make it a scapegoat for fascism's failure to permeate the whole of national life. This mentality he defined as something which was pacifist, pro-League, pro-England, and antisport; it was a preference for conserving gains already made rather than risking in order to gain more; it was the habit of mind which always counted the cost and which for example considered mass propaganda flights in formation across the Atlantic only as a waste of aviation spirit.

Mussolini himself became virulent on this point. Looking back to his socialist youth, he wondered what he would have done if he had really understood the Italian middle classes in those days instead of just knowing them through the medium of Karl Marx, and he concluded that he would have outdone Lenin himself in the cruelty of his class war. He now turned with inverted snobbery against the top hat, butterfly collar, and spats which he had once affected. Party hierarchs were told to avoid wearing them, also to avoid night clubs, to stop drinking coffee (he himself loved coffee but his indigestion forbade it), not to dress for dinner, nor to use starch in the collars of their black shirts, for all these things were bourgeois. Mussolini also in the end tried to abolish sleepers, dining cars, and first-class compartments on the railroads, and talked once more of closing the stock exchange. A later party secretary, the juvenile Vidussoni, even tried to prohibit golf, to the great vexation of the social climbers, Ciano and Grandi, who ultimately managed to get his decision overruled.

One intention in all this was to toughen up the Italian people and be revenged on their soft middle-class mentality. Mussolini told Ciano that in reforesting the Apennines his idea had been to make the climate more severe, for this would kill off the weaklings and make the race more robust. Toughening the race was also one reason given in all seriousness for his entry into World War II, and again he expressed the astonishing wish that more Italians might be killed, so as to bring home to them the glory and the sacrifice of war. Too many automobiles would make them soft. Italians, he used to say, must be made less *simpatico,* more hard and ruthless; he would even like to see them become hateful and disliked.

The Italian middle classes, however, did not appreciate these efforts on their behalf. Nor did they like the higher death duties imposed in 1939, nor the attempt once again to compel the registration of bearer bonds in order to close up a major tax loophole. Nor would they have approved if they had known that Mussolini was meditating what he obscurely referred to as a complete alteration in the system of private property. The growing unbalance in the national accounts was already alarming enough to taxpayers without these new threats to middle-class prosperity.

Vastly increased government expenditure at home and imperialism abroad had by this time created huge debts which not even prestidigitation with the budget and "deferred payments" could altogether conceal. In only fifteen of the years since 1861 had revenue apparently balanced expenditure, but not until after 1934–35 was the unbalance catastrophic. The following table of published state expenditure reflects the loss of control in fascist foreign policy (the excess of expenditure over revenue is given in parentheses):

(in million lire)

1934–35	20,926	(2,119)
1935–36	33,057	(12,687)
1936–37	40,932	(16,230)
1937–38	38,642	(11,174)
1939–40	60,389	(28,039)

Thereafter, the deficit doubled itself in each succeeding year. Evidently, the totalitarian powers enjoyed by fascism had not resulted in more accurate tax payments, and the increasing complexity of so many decree laws may even have made evasion easier. The minister of finance, Guarneri, who was a former director of the *Confindustria,* repeatedly told the Duce that imperialism was ruining the country, but the latter in time became too accustomed to these jeremiads to listen, and the job hunters politicly tried to conceal facts which he evidently preferred not to know. A new ministry of the press and propaganda, created in 1935, reflected the fact that fascism was coming to depend not on efficient action, but rather on pretense and on persuading people that the government was efficient.

Gradually, however, the existence of this deficit lost Mussolini the confidence of the financiers who had once found him a good investment. Volpi went on making public pronouncements thanking the Duce on behalf of Italian industry for his policy of imperialism and national self-sufficiency, but not all of the big industrial barons can have been so naïve, and one would not be surprised to find that Pirelli, Cini, and Agnelli were becoming increasingly restive. As for ordinary citizens, what struck them was the heavy devaluation of the lira in 1936 which led to an admitted increase of over 20 per cent in the cost of living by May 1937.

Another symptom of Mussolini's decline was his imitation of the German racial laws. According to the 1931 figures, there were only fifty thousand Jews in Italy, though others came later as refugees from Hitler's persecution. Mussolini could therefore boast that there was no racial problem in Italy. The article on "race" in the *Enciclopedia* had denied that there was any Italian race, and the article on anti-Semitism had even been written by a Jew. Some fascist *gerarchi* were Jews. Mussolini in the early 1930's talked disparagingly of Hitler's anti-Semitism, for it was a sore point that the German racial doctrines also excluded Italians from the *Herrenvolk*. Then came the conquest of empire, and this at once led to the development of a new race consciousness. No doubt Mussolini's journey to Germany in 1937 accentuated this trend. On Hitler's return visit in May 1938, the two countries agreed to harmonize their internal as well as external policy. In July the newspapers had to print an impertinent declaration signed by a number of well-known university professors who had the audacity to state that Italians were Nordic Aryans of unmixed stock since the Lombard invasions and should be alive to the "peril" from this less than one-tenth of 1 per cent of the population. Mussolini in private expressed the hope that the resultant persecution would make Italians more hated abroad.

Many world-famous scholars thus had to leave their posts. Admirals and generals were dismissed, and Mussolini himself had to change his dentist. The law said that Jews could not become journalists, teachers, or notaries; recent immigrants were to be expelled; Jews could not join the fascist party or attend state schools; they could not go to university or possess listed telephone numbers, and some of their property was declared forfeit. The "Italian race" had to be kept pure from corruption by "inferior elements," and hence contaminating marriages with people of other "races" were no longer valid without special permission from the government—it was perhaps forgotten that one of Marconi's parents had been English and one of Cavour's Swiss. Marriage or concubinage with "natives" in Africa was punishable by five years in prison.

As with all fascist legislation, these laws were carelessly and ineffectively enforced, especially as many people, fascists such as Balbo included, were shocked by such unscientific, shameless imitation of the barbarian Germans. The fact that a dictator could suddenly change his mind and decree that this much-conquered peninsula was inhabited by a pure Italian race must have given the more intelligent fascists something to ponder. But perhaps by this time there were not many intelligent fascists left.

55 The Drift Toward War, 1938-1940

Great Britain was still credulously hoping that Mussolini was too sensible or too timid to join Hitler, and the Anglo-Italian pact of March 1938 marked another stage in what turned out to be a futile policy of appeasement. Mussolini had already decided the other way. A few days before signing this pact he bravely told the Germans that he would fight England singlehanded if necessary. Once Italy had become united, he explained, she was obliged to continue further and become an empire, and so was forced by an internal logic to try to dominate other countries; fascist imperialism was the culmination and not in any sense the antithesis of the *risorgimento*.

Neighborly concessions by Britain merely encouraged this impressionable dictator to think that the British must have been corrupted by wealth and comfort and hence that their empire was moribund. This view was confirmed by the Munich conference, where Mussolini had his biggest moment in foreign policy and where he was able to pose dramatically as the savior of peace and the virtual arbiter of Europe. The decadence of Britain was also borne out by Chamberlain's secret negotiations with Grandi behind Eden's back, and when Chamberlain and Halifax came as supplicants to Rome in January 1939. The liberal *Manchester Guardian,* astonishingly, wrote in this same month that Mussolini was the most formidable statesman in Europe, for Hitler was "a smaller man in charge of a heavier nation."

Such successes were as intoxicating as they were false and deceptive, but only the intoxication mattered at the moment. Ciano's reference in parliament to Italy's "natural aspirations" was a prearranged cue for the well-drilled deputies to rise to their feet and shout "Nice, Corsica, Tunis" in unison, as the French ambassador watched ruefully from the gallery. Since Germany had won control of Austria and Czechoslovakia, fascist Italy felt obliged to do something comparably ruthless, and France was the chosen victim. When more evidence was received of the falling French birth rate, and when Chamberlain even asked Mussolini's opinion on the text of a speech which he intended to make at Westminster, the Duce was finally convinced of the decline of the West. Appeasement thus had a completely contraproductive effect, for it gave an inherently weak country the ridiculous conviction that she had nothing to lose by pulling down the pillars of European society. Annoyance was added to Mussolini's disdain when another diplomatic intercept informed him that certain uncharitable remarks had been made at his expense by the new French ambassador. Instead of being useful, these secret pieces of information always made Mussolini too angry to act sensibly, and when the Belgian ambassador sent home reports on pacifist feeling in Italy, the embassy received an anonymous letter of protest drafted personally at the Palazzo Venezia. Early in 1939, without so much as warning the Germans, a tremendous press campaign was therefore opened against France, though the only people to suffer were the hundreds of thousands of Italian seasonal emigrants who earned their living across the frontier.

The ambassador to Berlin, Attolico, was one of the few surviving Italian diplomats who put the interests of his country above those of the regime, and he did what little he could to keep Italy from complete subjection to the Germans. He repeatedly sent warnings that Hitler was being deceitful and would drag Italy into the wrong kind of war, but Mussolini's increasing capriciousness and unpredictability made these warnings vain. On a sudden impulse in May 1939, enraged by an American press report that Ribbentrop had encountered hostility from a Milanese crowd, Mussolini telephoned Ciano to conclude an immediate formal alliance with Germany. Ciano was astonished, for no detailed plans had been prepared for this, and it seemed to be merely a decision on instinct by someone who placed dignity and prestige before national interest.

So unready was Ciano that the text proposed by Germany for an offensive alliance had to be accepted with only several short amendments, and Italy suddenly found herself pledged to support Germany even in an aggressive war. Ribbentrop reassured Ciano at the time that Germany looked forward to at least three years of peace, but no steps were taken by the Italians to include any precautionary clause about this in the pact itself, and unknown to Italy the German general staff was in fact already under orders to prepare war against Poland. This was irresponsibility on a colossal scale. Thus easily could a self-styled realist be fooled. It has even been suggested that Mussolini, anxious about his own timid and volatile nature, was trying on purpose to commit himself so far that he could not back down. At least his action should be contrasted with that of General Franco, who, in a very similar situation, managed to retain some independence of Germany and so saved his country from the horrors of another war.

Ciano admitted that the Pact of Steel was unpopular in Italy, though an attempt was made to conceal the fact by numerous missions pouring into Germany to exchange decorations and compliments. He also privately revealed his own doubts about its desirability. The foreign minister's personal diary here shows how trivial and irresponsible were the architects of policy. Essential decisions were not made at all, or else were based on gossip and personal animosities. Ciano refused to read any memorandum if it were over a page long, and his "diplomacy" was usually carried out on his almost daily visits to the golf course and at gay society functions. Neither he nor the king seemed to be truly aware of impending tragedy, and up to June 1939 he was still talking in private as well as in public of London's aggressive intentions against Italy. The Italian ambassador in Moscow could go for more than three years without being consulted or instructed on policy; and yet almost every day Mussolini insisted on reviewing the press photographs and documentary films of himself and drew up detailed orders about their publication. The Duce had discovered that he could do at a pinch without political success, but never without propaganda, and increasingly he sought refuge in a make-believe land where he was insulated from the truth by mass meetings and eight-column headlines.

꿎

The invasion of Albania on Good Friday in April 1939 bore the perfect hallmark of fascist Machiavellism and carelessness. Fearful that Germany might become a satisfied power before he had satisfied himself, and piqued at not being informed about Germany's invasion of Czechoslovakia in March, Mussolini determined to fend for himself. It could have been objected that Albania was hardly worth conquering, for it was already a vassal state and useful as such for asserting Italian influence over the Little Entente. Subsidies and connivance at the financial irregularities of the puppet king Zog had so far proved much cheaper and perhaps more effective than actual occupation of the country, and already the small Albanian army was partly commanded by Italian officers. But the logic of fascism was inexorable in its demand for blood.

General plans for an invasion had been prepared a long time back, but the actual decision was made at the eleventh hour. This seemed to betoken an absence of calculated political planning, just as hitches over disembarkation came as an unwelcome sign of inefficiency in the army. The Italian press, too, was unsure whether the agreed story was to be that Italian strength had overcome fearful odds, or that the Albanians were welcoming with open arms their delivery from the tyrant Zog. It was a typically fascist confusion.

The conquest of Albania apparently met some opposition from the king. It was widely resented in Europe, and it destroyed what was left of the confidence which Italy hitherto had tried to inspire in the Balkans. When the simple feudal patriarchs came to greet Starace, they were given a good dressing down because they offered to shake hands instead of using the Roman salute. This was all most obtuse and heavy-handed, and its effects were probably the very reverse of what Starace had in mind.

The Albanian affair reinforced Mussolini in the view that he would need three years at least to prepare for general war, and in May he told Hitler as much in the "Cavallero memorandum." Apart from his armament requirements, he needed time to pacify Albania and Ethiopia and to repatriate the million Italians whom he claimed were resident in France. He was already running out of foreign exchange, and he knew that a major war would dry up the proceeds of tourism which kept the national accounts from an impossible deficit. He was also planning to obtain foreign currency from a big exhibition for the twentieth anniversary of fascism in 1942. A quite absurd reliance was placed on this exhibition. But the chief argument for delay was military and industrial unpreparedness. Between 1860 and 1939, a good third of total state expenditure had been used for military purposes, and yet this was now seen to be either too much or insufficient, or else it had been most corruptly applied. In his saner moments, Mussolini appreciated how completely unprepared Italy was for a general war and how vulnerable was her position, but his capacity for self-deceit was unlimited, and it was unquestionable fascist dogma that one must never count the cost.

The measure of Mussolini's competence was that he continued to proclaim the inevitability of war and yet had no idea how to prepare for one. His own forte was publicity, and he was unsuited to a situation where deeds were required as well as words. The Italian nation had not become military-minded, despite drilling children with the goose step and miniature machine guns, and despite the weekly half-holiday which workers were meant to spend on the parade ground. Mussolini confessed to Admiral Maugeri in 1943 that Italy had been much better equipped for war in 1915 than in 1939, so that the seventeen years of fascism had apparently been to no purpose. The regrettable fact was that the long and painful struggle for autarky, far from increasing Italian strength as had been promised, had done the very reverse. Fascism, indeed, was being defeated by its own dogma.

As Mussolini had personally directed all three service ministries from 1925–29 and again after 1933, his later claims to have been misinformed merely reflect on himself. So long as things went well he was determined to keep all the credit for himself and hence simply ignored his chief of staff; and when Badoglio protested at being left in the dark, the answer came that military men could not appreciate the complex political issues involved. Hitler used to bring Keitel to his meetings with Mussolini, but Mussolini occasionally arrived alone in case Italians should think that he needed advice on strategy. In 1938 correspondents were told that military matters took up most of the Duce's time, as they were also told that his working day was twelve to fourteen hours long. The reality was, however, utterly different. More time was probably spent on his passion for cheap novels. In any case, trying to run half a dozen departments at once, he left all the work and the decisions to other people and just kept the publicity and credit for himself. It is even on record that he inadvertently made incompatible decisions in different ministries at the same time, for he always had to rely on subordinates, and some of them were incompetent and untrustworthy. His undersecretary of the navy from 1933 to 1940, Admiral Cavagnari, had told him the true state of affairs, but was not believed. His undersecretary of the army, General Pariani, and of the air force, General Valle, had both deceived him and were relied on to the extent that Mussolini seriously thought that "by a single order and in a few hours I can mobilize eight million bayonets." This delusion was a symptom of *folie de grandeur,* and was a fatal result of such a centralized regime.

The war was in fact to show up all the weaknesses of fascism, its carelessness and corruption, its insincerity and lack of proper criticism. With the army, for instance, training had not been built sufficiently around the hypothesis of a possible enemy, and the target date for military preparations had been far away in 1942. Graziani grumbled about the plethora of generals and about the party placemen who held high military command without sufficient training. He himself was made army chief of staff, but with little power or responsibility, and he was even given a simultaneous operational command in Africa. There was a notable deficiency in munitions. Italian artillery in 1940 was still mostly of 1918 vintage, and included guns captured from Austria in that year. The rifle issued was that of 1891. There was a serious shortage of anti-aircraft ammunition, and people grumbled that this was due to the firm of Breda having acquired a lucrative monopoly of its manufacture. Colonel Canevari in October 1939 sent a memorandum to Mussolini which described the motorization of the army as derisory and tried to convince him that, despite what other people were saying, armored divisions just did not exist. Parades of old-time cavalry were put on even during wartime, but these did not impress the Germans. When more serious parades were required, Senise describes how the police had to lend their trucks to the army and have them painted khaki for the occasion. Never in fifty years, said General Favagrossa, had Italy been so weak, and she was not even ready to fight a colonial war.

The air force, according to Graziani, was antiquated and ridiculous, though some interservice rivalry may lie behind this criticism. A project for making air torpedoes and torpedo bombers had been turned down by the chiefs of staff in 1938, and Italy had no aircraft carriers because Mussolini had persuaded himself by one of his slogans that the country was itself one big aircraft carrier and needed no more. There were only two searchlights. There was no naval air arm, and no co-operation between navy and air force; hence no plans were ready for an attack on Malta, and no adequate techniques worked out for night fighting or for the use of light craft to cut communications in the Mediterranean. Captain Bragadin of the naval staff has confirmed the incredible fact that no study was made of the defenses of Malta, and clearly the navy cannot have considered very seriously the likelihood of war against England. This unpreparedness, however, was not only apparent in all three services, but was also industrial, psychological, and administrative. When Italian experts prepared for Hitler a list of essential requirements, Mussolini personally doubled some of their estimates before forwarding the figures to Germany, and so revealed to his ally the ineffectiveness of a system which could not even estimate the consumption of raw materials on a rational basis. He could hardly grumble when the Germans in future sometimes cut Italian requirements by half.

No doubt the Duce had too often let himself be gulled by subordinates who wished to delude him that they had spent the service grants honestly and efficiently. The Albanian mobilization surprised him by revealing that many divisions were only about a regiment strong, and after the summer maneuvers in the Po Valley he had to admit that the fully effective front-line troops numbered only ten divisions of all his boasted seventy. Ciano's diary for April 29, 1939, speaks of the extraordinary piece of bluffing which the service departments had carried out. Valle reported that he possessed 3,006 effective aircraft, whereas the naval authorities had positive information that the number was only 982. This time Ciano was worried enough to tell the Duce. A census was taken, and planes were apparently flown from one station to another to give the illusion of strength. But Mussolini, who would easily lose his temper if the *passo romano* were done badly or at a feeble display of drill in front of German generals, apparently paid little attention to these military deficiencies, and Ciano's comment was that he was afraid to face the truth. No doubt he also feared to expose the hollowness of his regime. Hence the calculation of peace or war was going to be based on evidence which the calculators knew to be false.

୬๑

Technically, the Pact of Steel obliged the Italians to fight alongside Germany if war broke out, and Hitler thus had in his possession an unconditional warrant which he could present at any time. Attolico's reports from Berlin about German double-dealing had been unheeded. Since Mussolini had not the courage to confess to Hitler that his own warlike posturing had been bluff, the Italian ambassador was not instructed to speak with sufficient firmness, but was expected merely to confuse the issue and so gain time. Mussolini's psychology was thus to play an important part in the failure to avert one of the most gigantic catastrophes in world history. He was acutely sensitive lest the world's newspapers might suggest that he was afraid to fight or that he was betraying his ally, and his own belief and hope was that there would be another Munich, since the democracies were too decadent to take up arms and he would thus simply win more cheap kudos as an intermediary. At the end of August he therefore began partial mobilization so that it would later look as though England had given in to his threats, whereas in fact this merely removed British confidence in his mediation and so eliminated one of the last chances of averting war.

Mussolini was to discover soon enough that he had lost any control over the situation. His associates suddenly found him old and touchy and ill, fearing that the Italians would laugh at him, and grumbling that Hitler treated him with scant respect and merely sent him another message as Germany conquered each country in turn. One such message arrived on August 21 saying that Hitler was signing an agreement with

Russia, despite the anti-Comintern pact, despite the crusade in Spain to save civilization from bolshevism. This caused the Italian minister of culture some difficult moments before the newspapers could be swung into line. A second casual note announced the invasion of Poland just when Mussolini had cast himself again as the brilliant mediator who was to attain eternal glory by dramatically saving the world from war.

It was a surprise for Ciano to learn that Hitler, bent on hostilities, cared not a rap for Italian opinion. Ciano probably was a convinced neutralist, but he lacked the moral courage or the integrity to assert his views, and in fact held his post only because of his constant submission to, and his frank admiration of, Mussolini. He now confessed that he was disgusted with Germany. Hitler had lied to the Italians and was now dragging them into an adventure which they had not wanted and which might ruin fascism and Italy itself. Personally, he did not know whether to hope for German victory or defeat. The Duce's reactions were first to say that Ciano was right, then to declare that honor obliged him to march with Germany, and he added that he wanted his share of the booty in Croatia and Dalmatia. Already in August, Ciano said that he had no further doubts; it would be Hungary's turn tomorrow, and then Italy's; they would have to act quickly while there was yet time. Besides Ciano, there was the king, the general staff, Balbo, De Bono, Bocchini, Federzoni, and Bottai, all of whom probably desired to stay neutral. Salvatorelli avows that, so low was morale in September 1939, a resolute move by the king would easily have crumbled the whole edifice of fascism. Perhaps, on the contrary, people were so inert after years of dictatorship, so numbed and uncritical, that war and defeat came as an inevitable fifth act to conclude the tragedy.

Mussolini was never at his best when he had to decide between two conflicting pieces of advice, and in September 1939, while De Bono insisted that army morale was terrible, Alfieri and Starace reported on the contrary that the Italians were rejoicing at the prospect of war. For the moment, however, Mussolini supported the peace party, because Britain and France had unexpectedly sided with Poland, and he grudgingly recognized that discretion should come before valor until the dust had time to settle and show who was winning. Starace was therefore replaced as party secretary by Muti, the immediate pretext being that Signora Mussolini had seen Starace's dogs being taken for a walk by a uniformed official. Pariani, Valle, and Alfieri were also supplanted, and the neutralists thus remained temporarily in command.

It was too much to hope that the dictator would not change his mind at least once more, for after all his talk of war and national virility this discrepancy between word and action was a grave confession of weakness. On September 24, smarting at the memory of Salandra's double policy in 1914–15, he explained that Italy would have to intervene or lose her good name; this time Ciano did not dare to contradict him, because contradiction now made him still more frenetic. Not being able to stand the word "neutral," Mussolini brought in the more manly phrase "nonbelligerent" to describe himself. On October 3, however, the pendulum had swung again to the other extreme, and he told Ciano that he was jealous of the glory which Hitler was winning and would be pleased if Germany should meet with some salutary setback. A few months later he took this to the ridiculous point of warning Holland and Belgium when the Germans confidentially gave him advance notice of their invasion, for he hoped that this might help to administer such a check.

Mussolini had learned from his brother dictator that bold intuitive decisions were a hallmark of the *Führerprinzip,* and he therefore convinced himself that his own sudden changes of opinion were a true sign of Napoleonic genius. Bocchini, the chief of police, gave this inconstancy a different interpretation, and believed that Mussolini was becoming deranged and should take another syphilis cure. Clearly, the Duce was not himself. Bottai once saw him quite convulsed with pain, and so did his son Vittorio. Clara Petacci had now left her husband, who had been for safety exiled to Japan, leaving her as mistress of a secret apartment inside the Palazzo Venezia. People noted this as another small sign of her paramour's increasingly eccentric and impossible behavior.

Mussolini's more sensible counselors were convinced that, as in 1914–15, neutrality was far the more profitable attitude, with both belligerents competing for Italian interest and support. Trade statistics were rocketing, and the stock exchange showed how high Italian credit stood. Nevertheless, this artificial prosperity, like the tactical relaxation of the British blockade in his favor, merely increased Mussolini's illusion of strength, and he was eager to punish his countrymen for being so unfascist as to prefer peace and affluence to war and conquest. His whole regime depended on a journalistic mastery of propaganda, and he dared not now disillusion the people whom he had taught to believe in his infallible intuition. He had lately spoken to his biographer De Begnac of his need always to keep up a spectacle and always to satisfy the public. Failure in either respect would mean ruin. Hence he could endure neutrality only until he again suspected that people might be sneering at him as a coward, or until he thought that they needed a new conjuring trick to keep up the illusion. Finally, in June 1940, after waiting through the winter to pick the winner, he was to choose the wrong side.

§ॐ

Some people have argued that this was the point where, after many years of skillful and beneficent government, Mussolini accidentally miscalculated and took the wrong road. Against such a view, however, one must consider whether this was not another typically fascist decision and whether war was not the logical conclusion of totalitarianism and of the propaganda which taught Italians that they and the Germans constituted a mighty master race which should inherit the earth. Early in 1939 Mussolini had publicly threatened "to make *tabula rasa*" of all civilized life, and by hurling Italy into battle he was just making good a long series of such promises. Here he was a pathetic but inevitable victim of his own rhetoric. Mussolini quoted Bernard Shaw to prove that dictatorship was the central theme of the age, that never in history had conservatism triumphed over revolution, and hence the democracies were bound to crumble at a touch. Juggling with words thus took the place of informed argument. It was part of the same logic when, instead of "eight million bayonets," one and a half millions alone could be mobilized in June 1940, and this only at tremendous cost to the economy and by accepting very low standards of equipment. The chickens were coming home to roost at last.

Misinformed as to his own strength, Mussolini had been misled, too, about foreign opinion, about the capacity and readiness for war of the Spanish republicans in 1936, and of the British in 1940, not to mention the Greeks. For his diplomats feared to give their true opinion and advice on foreign countries. It has even been said that fascist diplomacy was tested more in the relations of these ambassadors with the home government than in their relations with foreign governments. Once again one must conclude that war was declared just because fascism could not free itself from its own intricate network of deceit.

Not only the foreign service but also the intelligence service was untrustworthy. The *Servizio Informazione Militare,* apparently, had a passable information service inside Germany, but Ciano asserted three months after the outbreak of war there was still not a single agent in Great Britain. According to the head of this military intelligence, each of the services had distinct counterespionage organizations, which sometimes planted false documents on each other and arrested each other's agents. The complexity of such deceitfulness soon becomes bewildering. For instance, the army chief of staff in February 1938 had stated that munitions production would be completely ready for war by the spring of 1939, yet the director-general of munitions found himself in June 1940 with only one month's supply. Mussolini may or may not have been taken in by this kind of irresponsible remark, or by the federal secretaries of the party who told him how the people of Italy were agog for war. But these deceptions were in fact to cost Italy dear, and they were a characteristic product of the *stile fascista.*

56 Military and Political Defeat, 1940-1943

Cut off from reliable advice, even cut off from reliable information, Mussolini gambled blindly with his country's fate as he changed his mind from one extreme view to another and then back again. In January 1940 he wrote sensibly to Hitler that they would now gain most from peace, though less sensibly he also added that there might possibly be some point in fighting Russia. Hitler did not reply for two months, and by this time Mussolini's intuitive sense had divined once again that the time for intervention was near at hand if he did not want to be "left behind by history." The thought of leading a victory parade through an enemy capital was irresistible. It was humiliating to stand around with one's arms folded while others were writing history. To make a people great, he said, they must be forced into combat, even if necessary pitchforked into it by a kick in the backside. He felt that he was becoming the laughingstock of Europe, but he warned Ciano that he would make the English sorry for their continued resistance, and Italy's intervention would be the signal for their defeat. A month later he repeated that he would fight only when there was, as he put it, an almost mathematical certainty of winning. Yet his preparations were still niggardly: air-raid shelters were given barely a thought, no plans were prepared for the evacuation of civilians, no industrial mobilization was decreed (there was no ministry of production until 1943). Mussolini even continued to export essential armaments in 1940. He sent some of his scanty supply of airplanes to help Finland, and Favagrossa confirms that munitions were even being exported to England as late as May 1940.

The king apparently realized for a brief moment that many Italians would look to him as their last chance of preventing this final folly, and the chief of police thought that he could have arrested Mussolini at this point. Vittorio Emanuele was timidly supported by Badoglio and the general staff, who pointed out in May that there were still almost no armored cars and little more than a thousand planes available. But military men are trained to obey orders, and Badoglio hardly pushed his objections very far. The tremendous sweep of the German army through Norway and France seemed to offer glory with a minimum of effort and risk, and unfortunately it also gave a fatal example of how the intuitive genius of Hitler had successfully overriden technical objections made by the military experts.

At the end of May, Mussolini therefore took over the high command himself, despite the constitutional claims of the king and the military claims of Badoglio to this position. Ciano had seldom seen him so happy, for at last he had his dearest wish, to be a military leader in time of war. No advice was sought from the *Gran Consiglio*, which in fact did not meet until 1943. Nor did Mussolini consult the council of ministers, for he wanted all the credit of victory for himself, as much as he later wanted to saddle the generals with all the responsibility for failure. Badoglio, the chief of staff, tells us that the army was given only two weeks' notice of war, because the surrender of Belgium and the Dunkirk retreat meant that there was no time to lose if Italy intended to join in before peace was declared. "It is suicide," he told Mussolini, and received the extraordinary reply that the army need prepare only for a defensive war. The fighting would be all over by September, said this presumptuous dictator; he only needed a few thousand dead so as to be able to attend the peace conference as a belligerent. It had not entered his calculations that Britain might fight on. He himself was joining in the war to obtain the profits of victory and not to fight.

ॐ

On June 10, war was announced from the balcony of the Palazzo Venezia. It was the anniversary of Matteotti's murder. The exiled socialist, Pietro Nenni, wrote in his diary: "This is a war without any reason, for no real Italian interest is at stake; it is without excuse, because a German victory would mean for Italy and the rest of Europe just the brutal and intolerable hegemony of Hitler; and it is without honor, because Mussolini is attacking a France which already languishes on the point of defeat." Italian intervention did the Germans no good, but only closed a useful aperture in the blockade system, and committed Germany to the eccentric schemes of an incompetent megalomaniac. Hitler admitted that it was a major disaster for the cause, and it was also a disaster for the Italians. As in 1914–15, they had delayed as long as they dared, and then, on a mistaken hypothesis about the war's duration, they suddenly threw themselves into a conflict from which Italy had little to gain and much to lose. History was repeating itself, only this time the fascists made the mistake of choosing the wrong side.

A full-dress war was a fair test of whether behind all the rhetoric of fascism there lay anything substantial. After all these months of threatening talk there were still no adequate plans ready for the invasion of France, and Prince Umberto and his troops were by Mussolini's express order still in defensive positions when he suddenly instructed them to attack. The army said that this would need twenty days to prepare, but the Duce would allow them only three, for France had already asked for an armistice and he had at all costs to appear on the stage before the curtain rang down. Without adequate clothing, and with "cardboard" boots that became legendary, many soldiers were frozen to death in this sudden Alpine campaign. Mussolini was determined to use his single much-vaunted motorized division even in unsuitable mountain fighting. General Armellini, of the chiefs of staff committee, has called it a completely farcical situation, since the army was just praying that the French would not attack. Armellini called Mussolini's decision in so many words the desperate bluff of a poker player, and the Duce was described as ordering war just as he would ask for a cup of coffee, with no idea of even making the right munitions first. He was jealous of the army leaders and determined that he and not they should have the credit, so he gave detailed orders to their subordinates before they heard a word and then blamed them for the complete disorganization which ensued.

Luckily, the Germans had already beaten the French before the Italian advance began, though Mussolini himself hardly appreciated his good fortune. Only a slight penetration into Savoy had been made when, as Ciano said, fortunately for Italy the armistice was signed. But Mussolini himself was much upset; this unforeseen outbreak of peace quite disconcerted his plans. A tenth of Italy's submarines had been lost in these two weeks, a third of her mercantile marine, and 217 soldiers had been killed. But Italy received for her reward neither Nice, Savoy, Corsica, nor the French Tunisian ports which would have been so useful later in the war, because Hitler and not Mussolini had won this battle, and the alliance of a defeated France was apparently of more use to the Germans than was that of their Italian ally.

Mussolini was certain that the war would not drag on into the winter, and, without even consulting his Chiefs of Staff, decided to begin demobilizing. Three hundred thousand men were said to have been sent back to civilian life, and in the meantime work continued unconcernedly on the thousand-acre site designed to carry the immense marble weight of the "Third Rome" which was being built for the twentieth anniversary of fascism in 1942. When Mussolini repeatedly asked for the honor of assisting in the bombardment and invasion of England, the German reply was a tardy, grudging acceptance. Fiat bombers were in fact attacking Britain by the end of October, but a counteroffer by the Germans to help Italy bomb Suez showed Hitler's more realistic sense of priorities. Mussolini even betrayed pleasure over the German defeat in the Battle of Britain. He was still not taking the war seriously, but made decisions with an eye on showmanship and propaganda. His three hundred thousand men in East Africa were equipped with only 160 airplanes.

In particular, lack of plans made it impossible to profit from Britain's critical position and invade Egypt; and this must have had an important effect on the course of the war. Precious time and supplies were wasted on the occupation of British Somaliland in August, with the intention of embracing the largest possible expanse of territory before Britain followed France and sued for peace, and indeed this was the first British colony to be conquered for a hundred years. But the army made every excuse for not moving toward Suez. In September, Mussolini finally drove a reluctant Graziani into an offensive with ill-equipped troops, and some early successes seemed to promise at last the glory which he said Italy had been seeking in vain for three centuries. Nevertheless fascist dignity again led to the fatal mistake of turning down the offer of help from German armored divisions, and the only result of this miscalculated and halfhearted offensive was to leave Graziani's army in an untenable salient.

According to General Amè of the military intelligence, interception of American messages betrayed detailed figures to the Italians about British armor in North Africa and about the Malta convoys. But this could not prevent Graziani with ten divisions being beaten in January 1941 by two divisions perilously but efficiently supplied from distant England, and he was then chased out of Egypt in a five-hundred-mile retreat, with the loss of over a hundred thousand prisoners. Eritrea fell in February, Somalia in March, and Addis Ababa in April, so that Italian East Africa had also collapsed, and the Duke of Aosta had surrendered with nearly a quarter of a million men. Courage and patriotism could not possibly compensate for gigantic political errors, nor for military unpreparedness, nor for the fact that fascism had filled up so many posts with party placemen and had crushed individual initiative and taught people to rely blindly on an organization which was bureaucratic, corrupt, and inefficient. A court of inquiry censured Graziani's conduct, and Badoglio reported that this rival general had proved thoroughly incompetent, having spent most of his time in a bombproof shelter. The man who had lost one reputation through his cruelties in Ethiopia, now lost another through sheer military incapacity. But the incompetence was quite as much that of Badoglio himself, who for fifteen years had been in charge of both staff planning and industrial research into munitions production and had so little to show for it. Graziani now went into disgruntled retirement, and Badoglio was shortly to follow him.

ᔕ᠗

Once again, however, the chief villain was not the generals but fascism and its political folly. This is exemplified in Ciano's scheme to invade Greece. Once more a principal motive was irritation against Germany, this time against her sudden occupation of Rumania, and again one must note that Italy's unheralded initiative was in flat contradiction to Hitler's wishes. Mussolini complained bitterly that Hitler always confronted him with a *fait accompli,* but this time he meant to pay the Germans in their own coin and make them learn from the newspapers that Italy had taken Greece. In this way the balance would be restored. Mussolini added that he would resign from being an Italian if anyone found any technical difficulties about fighting the Greeks. It had never occurred to him that German secretiveness might be fully justified by the scandalous and even deliberate leakages of information at Rome. He likewise never dreamed that Greece had any chance of successful resistance, but instead he halved the estimate of Greek strength given him by Amè and the intelligence services.

The chiefs of staff protested vehemently against such a purely political decision to invade the Balkans, but were nonchalantly overridden and allowed only three weeks to switch all their plans to this difficult campaign. Mussolini changed his mind almost hourly about its timing, says General Armellini, and once five times in fifteen minutes. The date he eventually chose for the attack was October 28, the anniversary of the "march on Rome," though it was madness to begin mountain warfare so late in the rainy season. Armellini adds that staff headquarters learned about the final ultimatum only by listening to the London radio. As an ultimate folly, on October 5 another order had been issued for demobilization, and thus planning continued quite out of phase between one department and the next.

This Greek adventure soon proved to be the greatest national disaster for Italy in modern times, because after a few days' fighting the Italian army was in full retreat toward the coast. Hitler was furious that Mussolini had provided the British once again with continental bases, and bombing of the Italian fleet and the oil wells of Rumania could now be expected. In November half the Italian battle fleet was thus put out of action at Taranto, since the lack of reconnaissance planes allowed enemy carriers to come within a few miles unobserved. Almost as bad, Franco had lately intimated the possibility of Spain entering the war, and it was the Italian failure in Greece which chiefly restrained him. Mussolini and Ciano were personally to blame for these miscalculations. They were also to blame for the military defeat, though they pretended that the general staff had purposely sabotaged the affair. Ciano lamely assured Mussolini that he had bribed the Greek forces to give way, but this was excessively naïve, and no doubt the money had become stuck in fascist pockets en route. Even the replacement of Marshal Badoglio by General Cavallero could not save the Duce's reputation, especially as Cavallero had been a director of the Ansaldo munitions trust and therefore had a bad reputation in army circles.

Hitler now had the pleasure of pointing out the folly of acting without German advice and assistance, and he confessed to his friends that there was a complete lack of leadership in Italy. German troops had to be brought in to rescue Mussolini, or otherwise his troops might well have been driven out of both Africa and the Balkans. The arrival of German divebombers in Sicily after January 1941 completely altered the pattern of war in the Mediterranean, and, after paying the piper, Germany henceforward called the tune in both strategy and politics. From these early defeats in the winter of 1940–41 Italy never recovered, and the regime suffered accordingly in popular esteem. Fascist propaganda could not altogether ignore the fact that the British navy was able to bombard Genoa unmolested.

§❧

The closer their relations with Germany became, the more Italians admired German skill, and the deeper became Italian fear and dislike of Germans personally. It was natural for the ruling power in Austria to be regarded as a potential enemy, and the *Anschluss* therefore inevitably carried the threat of growing friction. Italians were staggered by German cruelty, and even Mussolini was surprised that his allies could surpass him in brutality and yet feel no compunction. Moreover, he had staked everything on Hitler's assurance of a quick German victory and never quite forgave the *Führer* for letting him down. Owing to their very totalitarianism, it was never possible for these two Axis powers to develop such a joint military command as the democracies constituted naturally among themselves, and this must have been a factor in the final result. Hundreds of thousands of Italian workers were drafted into labor service in Germany to replace Germans sent to the front and were often treated there like prisoners of war or another subject race. Italy herself soon became almost a colony of the Reich, and inevitably this built up a huge fund of anger and resentment.

Mussolini sorrowfully described himself as only "the taillight" of the Axis, and was not pleased when the king told him his nickname of "the Gauleiter for Italy." Had not the alliance been the last prop to his personal dictatorship, no doubt he would have tried to extricate himself. In June 1941 his entourage heard him say that he had just about had enough of that man Hitler and of being simply summoned like a waiter by a bell. At their joint conferences, Mussolini had to stand for five hours or more listening to futile and boring monologues. The Duce therefore decided to go on with plans for fortifying the ridge of the Alps. One day those fortifications might be useful. Mussolini now began to find the *Führer* less heroic and more lachrymose and hysterical. He was justifiably piqued when Hitler's personal messages were timed with obvious deliberation to arrive so that he would have to be wakened at night to receive them. So vain was Mussolini that in his meetings with Hitler he sometimes refused an interpreter lest this should bring into question his own highly imperfect knowledge of German; hence the Germans had it all their own way, and the Italian staff sometimes barely discovered what was happening. In July Mussolini told one of his ministers that he foresaw an inevitable crisis in relations with Germany. He even seriously wondered whether it would not be better for the English to win the war. He was very glad that they were bombing Germany by day and night, because one day Italy would herself be fighting Germany and so must not build up any legend of her invincibility. He also said he would keep fifteen divisions on the northern frontier ready for the day of reckoning against his nominal ally.

This was the talk of a madman. In fact, the worse the situation became, the more his personal security depended on the presence of the Germans in Italy. The Gestapo was in Rome; Rommel virtually took over the Libyan campaign early in 1941, though nominally always remaining under Italian command; and Kesselring set up his headquarters at Frascati in December. German help offered the last hope of winning the war, yet in Germany Mussolini was up against a force obviously stronger than himself, and it was incorrigibly his nature to resent the fact. The Germans had duped him into signing a blank check in the Pact of Steel. They had then duped him into a war several years before he was ready and into staking the whole future of his people on the German determination to win a lightning victory. Finally, they were now taking over the Italian war effort because fascism had proved itself so incapable. The pill was a bitter one, especially as it was administered so publicly.

§❧

Italians, whether fascist or antifascist, fought hard and loyally in their country's defense. Yet many of them felt from the outset that their cause was wrong, and as visions of a quick and easy victory receded the war grew increasingly unpopular. Mussolini was forced to admit to his foreign minister that events in Greece and Libya had shaken people and that he had little faith in the Italian race. At the first bombardment that destroyed a famous picture they would be overcome by a crisis of artistic sentimentalism and throw up the sponge. He even said that the Italians of 1914 were better than those of 1940, despite the fact that this was a poor commentary on the achievements of fascism. Italians he now described as a race of sheep. Eighteen years had not sufficed to change them; it would need eighteen centuries or more. His attempt to mobilize the civilian population and pervade them with a new fascist style of living had evidently failed.

By July 1941 the undersecretary for the interior, the rascally Buffarini Guidi, described in private how antifascism was rooted everywhere, threatening and implacable, even though on a small scale and unostentatious. Newspapers had been ordered not to mention queues and shortages. The mass of the people was becoming torpid and cynical as the theory of fascism was so obviously belied by the facts, and the soldiery were openly sarcastic against a government which had led them into such a war so irresponsibly and so ill-prepared. What Italy stood to gain from the war was not clear. Everyone was listening to the London radio, even the generals and the fascist leaders who wanted to know what was really happening.

By the spring of 1942 there was news of strikes once again, of clandestine newspapers, and of *carabinieri* firing into the air over crowds of hungry women. A sudden fascist decision to reduce prices by 20 per cent simply led to the disappearance of foodstuffs from the stores, and a black market grew up in every commodity as a necessary counterpart to official disorganization. The price of land soared as people defied regulations and scrambled to invest in something solid, and this inflation of prices was progressively undermining the loyalty of the fixed-income groups.

Further signs of disaffection appeared in a second struggle with Catholic Action in 1941, and from May 1942 onward in successive and drastic purges inside the fascist party. Ciano, Bottai, Grandi, Farinacci, Starace, and others were on one occasion suddenly ordered to leave their comfortable sinecures and go on active service in the front line: some of them appreciated the chance to earn more decorations, but others were not so keen, especially when the number of medals had to be limited because of evident abuse. A young man called Vidussoni was then appointed to run the fascist party, whose sole qualification was hero worship of the Duce, and under whom organization and discipline became quite out of hand. It seems that only the army and the Germans held the country together. Discontent must have been widespread, particularly after military failure and the growing subordination to Germany, and yet this discontent was never such that the least glimmer of revolution shone through.

§♠

The fortunes of war had meanwhile gone to and fro. Rommel's offensive in North Africa was launched in March 1941 and caught Wavell unguardedly trying to stretch his limited forces in support of Greece. Bypassing Tobruk, the Afrika Korps reached the Egyptian frontier after barely a fortnight. In April an offensive against Yugoslavia was started, provoking a fierce nationalistic uprising against Italy which in the end was to obliterate all the gains won by prefascist diplomats at Rapallo. Two weeks sufficed for the Germans to conquer Greece, after the Italians had failed to make any headway in six months.

In June 1941 began the German invasion of Russia. Mussolini had been given only the vaguest intimations of this fatal move and was caught in the middle of negotiations with Russia for a commercial treaty. Once again, however, he was completely taken in by Hitler's confident assurances of easy victory, and in a gross miscalculation he insisted on sending 200,000 Italians to the Russian front, again contrary to Hitler's wishes and without consulting even his own generals. In support of this purely political decision he even used the incredible argument that his divisions were superior to the German divisions in equipment and men. These Italians in Russia found themselves faced with an impossible task, and they only learned to hate the haughtiness and brutality of their German allies. If used in Libya, so many men might possibly have tipped the scales the other way.

In December 1941, Japan wantonly brought America into the war, and so sealed her own fate and that of the Axis too. Mussolini appeared to be delighted at this new turn of events, and at once declared war on the United States himself, apparently thinking that this would make the task of victory more simple. The more grandiose the war, the more he felt himself to be the destined man of history. He declaimed against

Roosevelt as someone who had all the time been planning the war with diabolic skill, and his continuing underestimation of the Americans was a clear sign of an infirm mind that had become accustomed to work by intuition and not intelligence. Pride was relentlessly preparing the fall, and the sins of violence and self-worship were bringing their inevitable nemesis.

For a brief moment, however, victory seemed within sight. After a second offensive by the British through the western desert in November 1941, by May 1942 the British front in Cyrenaica had again crumbled. Tobruk fell with thirty thousand men, and in June the Germans reached El Alamein. Mussolini really thought that his hour had come and flew to Africa, intending a triumphal entry on a white horse into the Egyptian capital, but his premature arrival only aroused the mocking ridicule of the Germans, and after waiting three weeks he had to return home with all his entourage.

In reality the battle of supply was already lost. Before the war, 80 per cent of Italian imports had come through Gibraltar or Suez, and both these routes had now been closed for over two years. Hitler's altered directives and Mussolini's lack of strength and forethought had left Malta impregnable, though it was only twenty minutes' flying distance from Sicily, and a few battered British reinforcements continued to reach the island. On the other hand, Italian convoys in the short passage to North Africa sometimes lost every ship through the Allies' radar and intelligence, and the German naval records indicate that nearly three-quarters of the supplies for the Afrika Korps were being sunk. Rommel was thus checked for lack of fuel at El Alamein, whither all his supplies had to be brought for hundreds of miles under enemy fire. Montgomery's victory in October 1942, coming together with the Allied landing in French North Africa and the battle of Stalingrad, must have convinced most Italians that the war could not be won.

Mussolini had lately suffered what was probably the recurrence of an old stomach ulcer (though an autopsy suggested that it may have been psychosomatic), and his mental weaknesses were simultaneously becoming more marked. Bottai noted this combination of intellectual and physical decline and reported that the Duce no longer possessed his former fascination, but was soft and dependent on flattery and deceit. Basically, he was turning out to be a weak-minded and superstitious man, afraid of the evil eye, afraid of being ridiculed. Even his flair for publicity was gone, and his war bulletins were less and less happy in their content and effect. He compared himself more frequently to Napoleon and even to Jesus, as delusions of grandeur grew to compensate for his weakness. He grumbled to Ciano that it was the material to work on which he lacked, since even Michelangelo had needed true marble to make his statues. He was glad to see so many German casualties in Russia and positively vexed that so few Italians were killed in North Africa. He rejoiced at a heavy snowfall or a reduction in the rations, because it would kill off the weaklings and so strengthen the fiber of what he termed this mediocre Italian race. He expressed a ghoulish delight that Naples was being heavily bombed: the race would thus become harder and more Nordic. This, it must be remembered, was the man who was not only prime minister, but head of all three service ministries and acting commander in chief. Megalomania could go no further, and this by itself spelled defeat. Another measure of his declining ability was the scandalous power which his mistress's family came to exercise in the government. They evidently secured a decisive influence in many appointments which ranged from ambassadors to professors at Milan university, and built up a fortune which was dispatched to safekeeping in Spain by way of the diplomatic bag.

By the beginning of 1943, half Mussolini's armies in Russia were lost; the navy, which had almost all the time been immobilized for lack of fuel, was now working on only 24,000 tons of oil a month; and in May, Marshal Messe surrendered with the remaining Italian forces in North Africa. By early July the Allies were in Sicily, just after the fascists had "celebrated" the third anniversary of their entry into the war. There were only 500 effective aircraft left. Nevertheless Mussolini retained the loyalty of many. Perhaps he had given false encouragement with his sinister references to a secret weapon which he forbore to particularize, or by his delusions about an imminent and decisive revolt of India against the British and of the Negroes in the United States. In May he had assured Hitler that Sicily was impregnable, and in June he made a fantastic speech to tell Italians that "the enemy has no further card to play." Yet there was still no revolution inside Italy, and the evidence hardly suggests that his government can have been all this time imposing itself on a country burning to be free.

᎒᎒

Under all these crushing blows, cracks were beginning to appear inside the fascist ruling class, even though imperceptible to outside observers. The party leaders did not like being put through assault courses and sent to the front. The least dishonest among them must have been amazed at the revelations of industrial and military weakness, just as they were dismayed at the symptoms of their leader's decline. Bottai mentions that the Duce, when he informed the cabinet of the loss of North Africa, could only try to defend himself with the argument that the Germans had yielded first, and that events would certainly turn in Italian favor by August. Bottai, De Bono, De Vecchi, Grandi, even Ciano were therefore becoming increasingly afraid that the war might be quite out of control. In February 1943 Mussolini dismissed the *frondeurs* and those remaining ministers who still preserved some independence of mind. They were replaced by insignificant, unknown men, at least one of whom was under treatment for mental disorder, and the new party secretary was Carlo Scorza, a first-hour fascist who had been implicated in the mortal attack on Amendola in 1925.

Some of the dissident fascists now began to edge toward the king and to wonder whether the Allies might possibly accept them as a new government if they managed to defenestrate Mussolini. As early as November 1942, Vittorio Emanuele had privately urged Ciano to discover some link with the enemy, but this had remained without effect, and even after the North African defeat the king was still not prepared to take any positive initiative which might compromise or endanger his own person. He was waiting for a move by some subordinate who could be repudiated in the event of failure.

Working along parallel lines with these dissident fascists were the old-school liberals, some of whom still kept in remote touch with the Court, and all of whom remembered with nostalgia the prefascist era of political liberty. Hitler thought in May 1943 that certain Italians would be glad to become a British colony if this were the only way to free themselves. Almost everyone at least wanted freedom from German colonialism, especially these former disciples of Giolitti who had been disarmed and virtually deposed by fascism. In 1942 Bonomi had received a vague hint from Prince Umberto to expect an important message about possible political action, but then heard no more. Early in June 1943 Bonomi called on the king, so did Soleri; Orlando and Casati were also consulted. But Vittorio Emanuele had shut himself so far away as to be quite out of touch with liberal opinion or with public opinion generally and was embarrassed and hesitant when dealing with the prefascist politicians whom he had once betrayed.

It was a long-standing tradition of the dynasty to turn in an emergency to the army leaders. General Ambrosio, who in February 1943 succeeded Cavallero as chief of staff, saw the king every week, and is known to have pressed Mussolini to make peace. Marshal Badoglio, too, had a national reputation and a known loyalty to the throne. But these officers had been schooled always to await orders and to insist on being covered by the responsibility of higher persons. Revenants like Admiral Thaon di Revel and General Zupelli also went to see the king, but no one was ready to risk the initial step without a positive command or at least without a fairly distinct understanding that they would be supported.

The final impulse came rather from the malcontent party leaders, especially those who had been dismissed earlier in 1943. At the center of this plot was the Duke d'Acquarone, the minister of the royal household, who had recovered a political importance for this particular office similar to that won by Gualterio in the 1860's and Rattazzi in the 1890's. Through him the king learned that some of the chief lieutenants of fascism were considering ways of saving themselves by the removal of Mussolini, and hints were dropped in return that the king might act if a public appeal were made to him.

So strongly entrenched was Mussolini in power that not until the invasion of Sicily was anyone ready to rebel. This invasion came as a staggering blow. The bombing of Rome in July was another fact which startled a great many civilians into rebelliousness, for hundreds of thousands had swarmed to the Holy City as a place immune from attack. At this point Mussolini arranged a meeting with Hitler on July 19, their thirteenth encounter. At the last moment he did not dare carry out the suggestion that he might break loose from Germany. Hitler was able to make some acid references to the feckless conduct of Italian troops in Sicily and was unwilling to send extra help against the Allied invasion because he was doubtful whether such help would be properly used. If Mussolini, despite all his boasting, was not able to defend Italy and not even able to maintain confidence between Italians and their German allies, this was his supreme moment of weakness, and Acquarone therefore intimated to Badoglio and Ambrosio that a change of government was now at last possible.

§❧

In the night of July 24–25 came the meeting of the *Gran Consiglio* in which Grandi suggested a motion of no confidence in Mussolini and invoked the king's prerogative to restore the national fortunes. A number of different accounts have been given of this dramatic occasion, for no stenographer was allowed to attend. Grandi brought a live grenade in case of emergencies, and gave another to De Vecchi, but unnecessarily. Mussolini seems to have been ill and tired, and again he had little better argument to put up than an obscure reference to a secret weapon which he had in store to resolve the situation. After ten hours of discussion, Grandi's motion was carried by 19 votes to 7. De Bono, De Vecchi, Federzoni, Ciano, Alfieri, Bottai, De Stefani, and Rossoni were among the majority nineteen, five of whom were executed a year later for this "betrayal" of their leader.

Mussolini now tried to defend himself by claiming that opinions of the *Gran Consiglio* were advisory and no more, but the king quickly seized his chance. By 6:00 A.M. on the twenty-fifth Vittorio Emanuele knew of the fascist revolt, and before midday he had signed the appointment of Badoglio as premier. General Cerica, commandant of the *carabinieri,* was ordered to arrest Mussolini when he was leaving the king's private residence. This was done without fuss or difficulty, and a proclamation announced that the king "intends to resume effective command of all forces according to Article 5 of the constitution, and the supreme initiative of decision which our institutions allow him."

The Great Dictator had collapsed, and the emptiness of his whole system was suddenly exposed. He had been ousted with astonishing ease, not by popular revolution nor by the antifascists, but by a royal edict coming on top of action by the fascist leaders themselves. Mussolini told a friend a few months later that the Italian people hated him in defeat as much as they had loved him in victory, and this was a truer statement than many he had made before. One fascist committed suicide at the news of his removal, but in general it caused little stir except in the sense of relief, and not one voice was raised publicly in his defense. The historian Salvatorelli concludes that perhaps not a single regime in all history had fallen under such unanimous condemnation.

This may be true, but it leaves us wondering why in that case this fall had been so long delayed. By waiting so long, people had allowed fascism to lose Italy her colonial empire, ruin her homeland, and temporarily throw away her good name. Mussolini had perverted the national character, coarsened the language, and generally undermined national self-confidence. For twenty years he had educated people in subservience and corrupt practices, and now he was to crown all by dividing the nation in a futile and shocking civil war. It needed far more than the joyful shouting and illumination of that fatal Sunday in July 1943 before this incalculable damage could be repaired.

57 Liberation, 1943-1947

For his new prime minister, the king did not choose an antifascist, nor Marshal Caviglia who Grandi urged on him, but Badoglio, who had held office fairly continuously under Mussolini. Fascism was thus replaced not by the old liberals, nor by Grandi and Federzoni, but by a monarchical autocracy founded on the army, the police and the ex-fascist civil service. Ordinary citizens had to rest content with the promise of free elections once hostilities were over.

Meanwhile, however, the fighting continued, since the king was afraid to break from the Germans, and indeed he gave Hitler his word that he had no intention of deserting the Axis alliance. The fascist party was declared illegal, but the political censorship continued, most fascist appointees remained unpurged, and Badoglio did not dare to disband the fascist militia. Such an ambiguous policy had one grave failing, for it forced both the Germans and the Allies to treat Badoglio as a potential enemy. If he privately intended to change sides, at least he took his time over it, and probably his hope was to wriggle free from both sides without risking either throne or army. An immediate armistice would have found the Germans heavily outnumbered in Italy, but these few weeks of paralyzed indecision gave them time to treble their strength and be ready for anything; the Italians, on the other hand, were so afraid of giving the game away to Hitler that they still made almost no military preparations of any kind.

On September 3, when the Allies were poised to attack the Italian mainland, Badoglio finally agreed to capitulate, trusting that the Anglo-Americans could quickly overcome the inevitable German resistance. Two landings were made, in Calabria and south of Naples, but the king and Badoglio failed to make a stand at Rome. They fled precipitately to the South, leaving the Italian army without orders, without even a commander, and with no positive instructions how (or even whether) the Germans were to be opposed; they then fabricated a fictitious story in an attempt to throw all the blame on the Allies for the resultant catastrophe. Although the bulk of the navy escaped from German hands and sailed for Malta, most of the generals allowed their forces to be disarmed without a shot, for a totalitarian education under fascism had encouraged neither personal initiative nor individual responsibility. In the space of a few hours the Germans occupied Rome and then the whole peninsula down as far as Naples, meeting little resistance. Only in Naples did a popular insurrection help the Allied forces check this advance—and in retaliation for that brave effort the Germans destroyed much of the priceless Neapolitan archives, permanently obliterating many chapters of Italian history.

§◆

Mussolini spent his sixtieth birthday a captive. He passed the time translating Carducci into German, skimming through twenty-four volumes of Nietzsche sent by the Führer, and trying to discover how the blame for defeat could be pinned on the German army or the Italian people. Then a brilliant operation by German glider troops set him free, while Badoglio's Italian police guard in his mountain prison, despite orders to shoot him in such an emergency, stood to attention and saluted his captors. Nothing much remained now of Mussolini's earlier character, none of the political flair, none of the skill in propaganda, nothing of the swagger and braggadocio. Physically, he looked a beaten man, hollow-cheeked, and often in pain. Though he had eighteen months still to live, the personal magnetism had disappeared. There remained only the colossal conceit which claimed his recapture to be one of the most dramatic moments in the course of human history.

§◆

When the king reformed his government at Brindisi, one hopeful sign was that Italian politicians had learnt in bitter years of persecution to underplay the factious dissensions which had helped Mussolini into power. In June 1944 Badoglio's "nonpolitical" administration thus gave way to a broad coalition under Bonomi in which six reconstituted parties, from liberal to communist, were all represented. A number of familiar names from pre-fascist Italy now reappeared. Among the conservative liberals, Einaudi, Orlando, De Nicola, and Casati had survived to contribute a sense of continuity to a younger generation with no experience of self-government. Among other survivors were Sforza, Croce, Nitti, and Don Sturzo. At the head of the Christian democrats was not the elderly Sturzo but Alcide de Gasperi, who had spent most of the fascist period as a papal librarian in the Vatican City.

Unlike the Christian democrats, Italian communism had retained some clandestine organization under fascism; and, equally important, the cohesion and combativeness of the communists enabled them to form excellent partisan units, so that they emerged from the final stages of the war with a special degree of prestige. Palmiro Togliatti was an able politician, and his deputy, Luigi Longo, was one of the two or three most active leaders of the Resistance. On his return from Russia in 1944, Togliatti showed unexpected tactical mobility by joining Bonomi's government, as well as by promising to respect religion and not to collectivize small properties. This was communism with a difference, a far more positive political force than in 1921–22, and the party remained inside the government coalition for three years. Very close to this extreme Left were the socialists, whose leader, Pietro Nenni, proved more intransigent and less agile a tactician than Togliatti; he usually ranged his supporters alongside the communists in a united popular front, though he refused to stay with them in the government when Bonomi formed a new administration in December 1944.

Another group with a radical program was a new Party of Action, which tried for a brief while to act as a "third force" between this popular front and the conservatives. These *actionists* were second only to the communists in their contribution to the Resistance, and so held considerable authority in the years 1943–45. Their leaders were high-principled men, greatly respected for their courage and integrity— among them were Ferruccio Parri, Carlo Sforza, Ugo La Malfa, and Ernesto Rossi. Most of them had been disciples or companions of Salvemini, Gobetti, and Rosselli. Their hostility to the monarchy, to the Church, and to Bonomi's government was far more doctrinaire and uncompromising than that of Togliatti. They included a high proportion of writers and intellectuals, men such as Omodeo, De Ruggiero, and Salvatorelli, and, as was inevitable with a party of intellectuals, they liked to make fine distinctions which eventually undermined their political solidarity. Until elections could be held, however, the degree of popular support behind their or any other party was anyone's guess.

§❧

Meanwhile, the war dragged on. The Allies made a further landing at Anzio in January 1944. In May the Gustav Line collapsed and

Cassino fell. Rome was entered in June, Florence in August, but the Germans then managed to dig in for the winter along the so-called "Gothic Line" which stretched from Spezia to Rimini. This halt to the Allied advance, with all its tragic results in prolonging what was now a civil war, resulted from a policy decision to make the Italian front subsidiary to an invasion of France.

Mussolini was thus given time to establish his new fascist administration—as its various departments were mostly scattered around Lake Garda, it became known as the Republic of Salò. The trimmers and the practical men had already abandoned fascism in or before 1943, and there were left only the rogues and the dreamers, such as Gentile, Farinacci, Buffarini Guidi, and General Graziani the embittered rival of Badoglio. The German army allowed little scope to this fascist rump, for Hitler had no interest in Italy except as a battleground on which to fight the Allies and partisans.

Though Mussolini went on grumbling against the Germans, he nourished a desperate faith in ultimate German victory, and one Italian scientist persuaded him to believe in a "death ray" which would turn the scales. He was convinced that the western Allies would soon break with Russia. He was quite prepared to abandon Germany in order to make a separate peace with either West or East, though he thought he would rather be a Russian satellite than an American colony. He was comfortably sure anyway, win or lose, that fascism had by now destroyed the British Empire: his defiant assertion was that above all he had been against Britain, and he fancifully recalled how British and French ill will had foiled his self-sacrificing efforts in the 1930's to bring peace to Europe.

Defeat only accentuated Mussolini's bitterness against his fellow Italians, for they were the people who had shattered his imperial dreams. He lamented their factiousness which he had failed to correct, though he was glad to think that this same factiousness, which made them confuse democracy with individualism, would ruin all their attempts at liberal government. He now conceived the idea that he had not created fascism but merely exploited the fascist tendencies existing subconsciously in all Italians. It comforted him to believe that, even if he should be beaten, they would one day return to his methods.

Two traits noted by Mussolini's new German doctor in 1944 were an extreme credulousness and an absolute inability to say no to anyone when face to face: these characteristics help to explain why his encounters with Hitler had been so one-sided and why his preparations for war had been so hopeless. The prospect of possible defeat revealed a stupendous incapacity for self-criticism. He was seldom seen, but played solitaire by the lake, and found it hard to secure obedience from the many discrepant factions in this Republic of Salò. Buffarini Guidi was even tapping his telephone. Dozens of new uniforms casually appeared, and many authorized and unauthorized police forces came into existence. The chief internal enemy he identified as no longer communism but capitalism, and he therefore proclaimed sweeping measures of nationalization to "liquidate" the bourgeois classes whose inertia and defeatism had been too strong for him. Once more, however, these were dreams not deeds. We hear that he was applying himself again to the study of Plato's *Republic,* and he made searching inquiries of a French visitor about the astrological predictions of Nostradamus.

This fascist republic is of little importance in Italian history, and the Duce's office was later found to contain mostly photographs and newspaper clippings about himself. Some Italians, remarkably enough, were still willing to launch their country into further civil strife on his behalf. Some of the last-ditch adherents, the philosopher Gentile among them, were assassinated in a growing fever of reprisal and counterreprisal. Other fascists came to a different sort of violent end, for Mussolini had De Bono and his own son-in-law, Ciano, shot in the back as traitors, because of their hostile vote in that final meeting of the Gran Consiglio. Grandi escaped to Lisbon, where he was said to have lived by giving Latin lessons; De Vecchi took refuge in a monastery; and a few other *gerarchi* quietly followed Mussolini's surviving son to South America. As for the *Duce* himself, in April 1945 the partisans caught him near Lake Como, disguised in a German greatcoat, clutching packages of mysterious documents which he theatrically asserted could be used to win Italy the peace. Of all his companions, only the faithful Clara Petacci stood with him. Both were summarily shot, and their bodies strung upside down with the corpses of Starace and Farinacci in the Piazzale Loreto at Milan.

With this gruesome scene the curtain fell on the period of fascism. Italy, which had endured and assimilated so many barbarians, had been forced to support yet another cruel tyrant and a twenty-year sack as bad as any in her history. The fascist regime had in some respects penetrated deeply into Italian life, but mostly had been just empty pomp and vacuous speech. Benedetto Croce somehow satisfied himself, despite all his own theories of historical continuity, that fascism had been essentially extraneous to Italy and was tied by no more than a casual connection to earlier Italian history. This was a dangerously simple view; and yet totalitarianism in Germany had been infinitely more thorough and hateful. In his last years Mussolini fondly manufactured a legend with which disciples might be able to justify his life and prepare a second more nationalistic *risorgimento*. He could not be expected to see that aggressive fascist nationalism had held Italy back from greatness, nor that his countrymen were poised to break free of this incubus and achieve a great national rebirth.

§❧

In April 1945 the Anglo-Americans overran northern Italy, and a popular patriotic movement helped to bring about the German capitulation in May. Although there had been no sign of a resistance organization during the occupation of Rome, antifascist cadres of fighters had subsequently been formed all over the North: working sometimes on their own, sometimes with the Allies, these partisan groups tied down a number of German divisions and started many successful insurrections. Parri, one of their commanders, claimed that in August 1944 there were 80,000 fighters on this clandestine front, and perhaps as many as 200,000 by April 1945. Possibly the partisans suffered greater casualties than the regular armies in this campaign; certainly their achievements were a big factor in restoring Italian morale and self-confidence. Some of the very best elements in the country were prominent in the Resistance, and it provided a fine training in social consciousness as well as a new kind of idealistic patriotism. No one who lived through such an experience could forget it; never before had so many citizens participated so actively in national life. From many sources—not least the poetry of Salvatore Quasimodo, as in stories by Pavese, Vittorini, and Pratolini—the impression emerges that this liberating war against Mussolini and Hitler penetrated far more deeply into peoples' consciences than the nineteenth-century *risorgimento* had ever done.

Although men of different political beliefs fought alongside each other in the Resistance movement, most partisans were well to the Left, so that the Left captured considerable influence in local government and hence in what would soon become the electoral machine. This posed a strong political challenge to the ideals and leaders of old-style liberalism; and one result was that, during the five-months premiership of Parri who followed Bonomi in June 1945, Italy came closer to a radical process of social and political change than at any time since 1861. That the country stopped short of drastic social changes was due to the conservative instinct of so many of her people and the entrenched strength of vested interests.

The aftermath of war was a very difficult period, not least because the partisans put a keener edge on the class struggle and gave many people a new political awareness; but gradually the country returned to something like normal. The problem of political purging was less divisive than in France, since in Italy nearly everyone had been involved in fascism and therefore the apportionment of guilt seemed not very relevant. Cobelligerency alongside the Allies had partly atoned for belligerency against them, as it also helped to mitigate the terms of peace which Italy was obliged to accept in 1947. Because of Mussolini's earlier misdeeds, the peace settlement awarded Istria and Fiume to Yugoslavia, but at least Trieste was saved for Italy, and so were the German-speaking areas of the South Tyrol. In the northeast, De Gaulle tried to occupy the Val d'Aosta for France, but the other Allies stood firm, and French annexations were ultimately confined to several small Alpine villages. The colonial empire in Africa, which had cost so much in men, money, and emotional commitment, had to be surrendered, as had the Dodecanese Islands. All this aroused bitter feelings, and Croce tried to argue that, since in his view fascism had been external to Italy and imposed on her by outside forces, it was highly unfair to penalize Italians for fascist mistakes. Good patriots did not readily accept that other countries in Europe and Africa, having suffered at Mussolini's hands, would not accept this metaphysical argument, but might want reassurance and perhaps compensation.

On top of the mortification of defeat and the agony of civil war there had been tremendous damage to the physical endowment of Italy, to buildings, shipping, and internal communications. This would take years to repair. Nearly half of state expenditure remained uncovered by revenue, and successive governments were at first afraid to enforce severe measures of austerity. By 1947 the wholesale price index had risen to 55 times its prewar level. There were millions of unemployed, and for very many people conditions of life were desperate.

On the credit side, well-organized partisan action enabled the port installations of Genoa and the factories of Milan and Turin to suffer relatively little damage in the final German evacuation; this was a big element in the return of prosperity. Even more important, the Allied occupation, though distressing, was effective in lessening the internal divisions which had made the previous postwar period after 1918 so unhappy. Defeat in 1943, paradoxically but mercifully, proved less disturbing than victory in 1918. This time there was less social unrest and far less political anarchy. Another bonus was that the United States and Britain forwent their claim to reparations, and American generosity was to make reconstruction much easier than after World War I. Not only was much-needed food supplied, but two billion dollars in foreign aid helped the country on to its feet, and a defeated Italy ended the war with considerable credits owed her by victorious Britain. One incidental gain was the gift of new insecticides which brought the centuries-old scourge of malaria under control—in terms of human happiness this must rank among the most important events in all modern Italian history.

§●

Had Vittorio Emanuele III abdicated in 1943 as did Carlo Alberto at another moment of defeat in 1849, the monarchy might have survived. Instead, he self-righteously repudiated the indictment of unconstitutional collusion under Mussolini, arguing that a parliamentary sovereign was not responsible for his ministers' actions. His son, Prince Umberto, placed the blame for the events of 1922 firmly on the Italian people, and imprudently stated in public that their enthusiastic approval for fascism had forced the king to accept Mussolini's appointment. This unrepentant attitude made many former monarchists reverse the charge and blame Vittorio Emanuele as a scapegoat for fascism and military defeat.

Only when public opinion forced a referendum on the monarchy did the king grudgingly anticipate matters by abdication, hoping that the greater popularity of his son would tip the vote and save the dynasty. In May 1946 Umberto therefore became the legal sovereign for thirty-four days, and just had time to make a campaign tour of the country. The following month a referendum decided against him—twelve millions to ten millions. Enrico de Nicola became provisional head of a new republican state, at last realizing Mazzini's prophecy. Umberto, under protest, followed his father into exile, to continue from abroad a moderate but ineffective campaign for a monarchical restoration.

§●

Elections were held in June 1946 for a Constituent Assembly to choose a constitution which would replace that of 1848. In these elections, to which women were at last admitted, the Christian democrats obtained 35 per cent of the vote, the socialists 20 per cent, the communists 19 per cent. This first test of opinion for twenty-five years was a notable victory for De Gasperi and the Catholics, marking a fairly decisive reversal of *risorgimento* anticlericalism, and the women's vote was no doubt an important factor. Of the remaining fractions, the old liberals won only 6 per cent, a neo-fascist group 5 per cent, and the Party of Action just over 1 per cent. These results not only confirmed the defeat of the liberals who looked back to Giolitti and Cavour, but proved that a "third force" had little backing: the intellectuals of the Left Center were already reverting to type, breaking up into half a dozen doctrinaire factions more interested in splitting hairs with each other than finding a middle way between communism and clericalism.

The only threat to the Christian democrats was that communism and socialism might join to push Italy into the Russian camp; but this fear proved illusory. Indeed, the communists went out of their way to work with the conservatives, helping for instance to undermine Parri's Center-Left government in December 1945, supporting De Gasperi when even the socialists were reluctant to do so, and stressing that they meant to follow a parliamentary and not a revolutionary road to power. In return for their complaisance, however, De Gasperi decided that it was not safe to accept this change of heart as genuine; yielding to very strong pressure from America and the Vatican, he expelled the communists from his coalition in May 1947.

This was an important moment in the process by which Christian democracy acquired a conservative label and Italian politics were polarized into two irreconcilable, almost uncommunicating, extremes. The forces of the Left, not strong enough to form an alternative government coalition on their own, in any case disagreed with each other on almost everything, and this made De Gasperi's task much easier. Among the socialists, for instance, some were trying to be more proletarian and revolutionary than the communists themselves; on the other hand some were reformist, evolutionary, and more inclined to join De Gasperi in government than Togliatti in powerless opposition. Leading the former group was Nenni, who now decided to run a common electoral slate with the communists, but Saragat led a splinter faction of social democrats who maintained a noncommittal existence nearer the Center.

In 1947 the Constituent Assembly approved a new constitution by a remarkable majority of 453 to 62. The Left managed to insert in this fundamental law the statement that "sovereignty belongs to the people," and that there existed a constitutional right of citizens to a job, to a living wage, to free education and health treatment; also the *latifondi* were to be irrevocably abolished, and the right of workers to share in profits and management was guaranteed. To balance what turned out to be these vain and empty generalizations, the Christian democrats obtained what was most important to them, namely a renewal of Mussolini's concordat of 1929, with special privileges for the clergy and the repudiation of any kind of legal "divorce." The communists earned sharp criticism from socialists and *actionists* for voting to accept this illiberal concordat: Togliatti had agreed to it as an earnest of his determination to work with the Church in a world where democratic majorities must be accepted; but, in the atmosphere of the cold war, although De Gasperi gladly accepted the communist vote on this crucial point, he could not afford to yield anything substantial in return.

The constitution stated that the head of state should be a president elected for seven years, and chosen in joint session of both houses. Einaudi served a term in this post, followed by two Christian democrats, Gronchi and Segni, and then by a social democrat, Saragat. After bitter experience in the past, it was decided to keep the presidential office more honorific than powerful. Among other constitutional innovations, senators were to be elected instead of nominated. Legislation by decree would lapse if not sanctioned by parliament within sixty days, and the promotion and relegation of judges were subtracted from the purview of government or parliament. Italy was also to be divided into nineteen regions, each with a greater or lesser degree of administrative autonomy.

In January 1948 the constitution came into force, and elections for parliament were held in April, about a hundred parties presenting candidates. The recent communist coup in Czechoslovakia helped the Christian democrats on this occasion to obtain an absolute majority, with 48 per cent of the popular vote and 53 per cent of the seats in the Chamber, while socialism and communism together were supported by only 31 per cent of the electorate. This was an outstandingly large majority in the history of Italian party politics and represents the high watermark of Christian-democrat fortunes. It signified a further defeat for the "third force" represented by Parri, Sforza, and the radical *actionists,* as it also called a halt to their attempt to make Italy more secular, radical, and egalitarian. It was presumably a vote against authoritarianism and communism, but in favor of moderate, even conservative, reform. Unclouded by the confusing tactics of a Giolitti, or by the bludgeonings of Mussolini, Italian politics seemed to be shaking down into a roughly two-party system and a sharply uncompromising conflict between red and black. An absolute majority was, for the moment, accorded to the Center Right, moderately conservative, reasonably tolerant of everything which did not touch religion or property, but above all Catholic and sometimes clerical.

58 Christian Democracy and the Economic Miracle, 1948-1960

In May 1948, De Gasperi was confirmed in office by the first postwar legislature, and at once proved himself to be the most effective parliamentary leader since Cavour as well as one of the most high principled. Like Cavour, De Gasperi was something of an outsider in his relation to Italy, coming from the Trentino and having lived for almost forty years as an Austrian subject. He had been at the university of Innsbruck, and his parliamentary education had been in Vienna, not Rome. Unlike Cavour, he was a devout Catholic; yet Catholic Viennese politicians could have a more unclerical attitude to the Church than was common in Italy, and De Gasperi's fine political instinct therefore enabled him to resist the urgings of churchmen who wanted a one-party government. Realizing how important it was to heal the breach between Church and secular society which had caused such damage since 1861, he liked to include some non-Catholics inside his cabinet; and this sometimes made him greatly disliked in Vatican circles. The papacy had once hoped to prevent the creation of a liberal united Italy; it had subsequently forbidden Catholics to enter national politics, and then had thrown its weight to the fascists rather than the liberals. But in 1948, when a Catholic party at last achieved political power, De Gasperi was moderate and wise enough not to push his victory too far.

The Christian democrat party included different, even incongruous, elements. Many voters saw it mainly as a defense of Catholic prerogatives; many more as a guarantee against communism; hence at election time its left wing of advanced social reformers seemed more of an eccentric embarrassment than an effective force. To an outsider, the tensions inside such a broad political grouping were not always easy to decipher, though its center of gravity was obviously somewhere to the Right. Another difficulty for an outside observer was that much the same wide range of opinion could be found in the Liberal party and the Republican party, each of which subsequently split into two; the monarchists were also going to divide, though over a more metaphysical issue; the miniscule Party of Action split into many even tinier fractions as early as 1947; and the various socialist factions sometimes seemed in an almost incomprehensible state of flux. Even the apparently monolithic communists were to reveal internal divisions of their own.)

To an insider, especially one with De Gasperi's parliamentary skill, the multiplicity of parties, and the divisions between and inside them, made it possible to juggle advantageously with a series of coalition administrations and prevent the growth of a sizeable opposition: between 1945 and 1953 he presided over eight different governments. Being on most issues to the left of center in his own party, he distrusted attempts by the Confindustria and the Vatican to turn Italian politics into a simple conflict of Right against Left. Yet coalitions which, as well as Catholics, included liberals, republicans and the social-democrat *Saragattiani,* though they helped to preserve political stability and a rough consensus during a period of rapid social and economic change, inevitably meant sidetracking some controversial decisions which threatened cabinet solidarity. Powerful vested interests, for instance the higher echelons of the bureaucracy and the senior university professors, were all the more difficult to challenge: little could therefore be done about modernizing the civil service, without which indeed most reforms were almost bound to be fairly ineffective; nor could enough be done to improve the educational system so as to eliminate illiteracy and inaugurate an age of greater technological awareness. The privileged position of the Church was likewise quite beyond any constructive political debate, and this affected a number of important questions relating to education, divorce, censorship, and individual liberties.

The need to avoid or postpone decisions was an effect, but also a cause, of the Christian democrats remaining an essentially conservative force. True enough, they were not for the most part so conservative that they could willingly ally with the monarchists and fascists. This extreme anticonstitutional Right, whose reactionary politics could usually attract 10 per cent of the popular vote, just occasionally won a useful leverage on the main government party, but failed to produce a single leader of any ability. At the other extreme, the communists were far more of a problem, for they gradually grew to obtain over a quarter of the votes, and together with the revolutionary socialists could usually command a massive third of the parliamentary seats.

Active communist party membership was quite large. In addition, however, a considerable and growing number of people in every class, without being ideologically committed, supported them as the outlet for a disaffection and alienation that pervaded every layer of society;

they thus seemed a defense of secular society against clericalism, and the most obvious way to keep alive a meaningful political debate against the conservatism and *immobilismo* of coalition government. Communism never approached within measurable distance of becoming the majority party or even (after 1947) of belonging to a ruling coalition: to this extent Italy lacked any genuinely alternative government or even an effectively critical opposition, and this was not entirely healthy either for the Christian democrat party or for Italian politics as a whole. The communists and revolutionary socialists never managed to persuade enough people that they had genuinely accepted the democratic process; so they fell back on their residual function, which was to criticize unconstitutional actions by the government, and to keep issues of principle from being entirely swamped by transformist pragmatism. Herein they had a salutary, if not very effective, role to play.

Outside the area of national politics, the extreme Left had a clearer field of action, especially when the posthumous publication of Gramsci's prison writings in 1947–50, by offering a new and much less rigid version of Marxism, edged the conservative Croce out of his cultural monopoly over intellectual life. Many distinguished writers and artists stood on the extreme Left—Pasolini, Guttuso, Consagra, Visconti, De Sica, Levi, Quasimodo; many more, including Moravia, called themselves Marxists. Communism also made considerable inroads into local government, especially in Bologna and central Italy, but also in the big cities of Turin, Milan, Genoa, and Florence; and the Left once came close to capturing Rome itself. One important force they lacked was the support of a powerful Trade Union movement, for in 1949 the Confederation of Labor split along party lines and was replaced by four separate groups, Catholic, communist, social democrat, and fascist. It was as grave a disadvantage for industrial and agricultural workers as it was welcome to their employers that ideology thus kept the labor movement weak and divided.

§❦

An important moment arrived in Italy's economic revival when Luigi Einaudi in 1947 became governor of the Bank of Italy and then budget minister. This champion of economic freedom and financial orthodoxy risked popular opprobrium by placing monetary stability before economic expansion. By severely tightening credit, and at the cost of maintaining unemployment and restraining industrial development, he managed by 1948 to stem inflation and hold the lira. Approval of De Gasperi's expulsion of the communists from the government brought a continuance of massive financial grants from America, all of which helped to support the currency and minimize social unrest. Einaudi was obliged to retain Mussolini's huge public ownership of banks, shipyards, and steelworks, just because the market lacked sufficient resources to repurchase them from the Istituto per la Ricostruzione Industriale (I.R.I.), but the not very impressive experience of state planning under fascism made it easy for him to restore what was otherwise a fairly free market economy.

Now that Mussolini's grandiloquent rhetoric had been exposed as a sham, it could be seen that fascism had squandered resources in war and wastefully twisted the economy toward prestige—or rather an illusion of prestige. Hence there was general accord over replacing the excessive nationalism of economic self-sufficiency by an expansive confidence in freer international exchanges. Surviving fascists had, with surprise, to admit that a bellicose foreign policy was not an indispensable prerequisite of ranking with the other Great Powers, and indeed that a forceful foreign policy had resulted in positively diminishing Italian prestige and material success. De Gasperi's foreign minister, Carlo Sforza, who after the collapse of the Party of Action joined the tiny Republican party, was a man who had proved himself a good European before 1922 and became even more of an internationalist during years of exile. Together these two men ranged Italy firmly on the side of the Atlantic community and in favor of a common market for Europe.

Italian society still remained basically agricultural: in parts of Sardinia, Sicily, and the South it was even feudal. Poverty was such that great numbers still lived in caves and subterranean cellars or were crowded into a single room with their children and farm animals. Grisly slums continued to exist even on the outskirts of Rome itself. Nevertheless, an informed public opinion on problems of social welfare was beginning to emerge. Apart from denunciations by the political Left, consciences were stirred by activists whose views cut across strict ideological lines, as well as by the more liberal newspapers and publishing houses, and especially by the weekly *Mondo* and *Espresso*. Piero Calamandrei and Arturo Carlo Jemolo were names in this field which could stand comparison with any in public life since 1861, and their views at last reached down deeper than the surface levels of society. A strong educative force was exercised indirectly by nonconforming, eccentric individuals such as Adriano Olivetti, an enlightened industrialist; by Danilo Dolci, who set up a remarkable institute to encourage self-help in the poor villages of western Sicily; by Carlo Levi, who in his book *Christ Stopped at Eboli,* showed many northerners for the first time what southern Italy was like; and something, too, by Giorgio La Pira, the maverick mayor of Florence, a pious Catholic who defied religious superiors and current political shibboleths to create a colloquy with communism.

De Gasperi was among those who understood the need for a fairer deal between classes and regions so as to remove certain tensions which had hampered national life since 1900. No truly radical changes were possible without a risk of splitting Christian democracy, but some concessions to social reform were permitted by the conservatives of the party in their determination to attract mass support. De Gasperi was thus able to introduce greater welfare benefits and other social security measures, and many agricultural and industrial workers were given security of tenure for an emergency period until unemployment could be reduced. Furthermore, in perhaps the boldest attempt at agrarian reform in any noncommunist country, nearly two million acres of uncultivated land were compulsorily acquired from *latifondisti* in the early 1950's and distributed to create a larger class of smallholders. Against this policy, the argument was raised that it was not only an inefficient use of resources, but quite beyond the ability of the civil service to administer; nevertheless, its partial success helped to mitigate some hardships caused by the war and Einaudi's deflation, while in many places the *latifondo* system of cultivation gave way at long last to more intensive methods and more profitable crops.

§

Probably the most important single fact in postwar economic history was the discovery of natural gas in the Po Valley. This raised hopes of satisfying at least part of the need for a domestic source of power. Coal imports, on which Italy had always been obliged to lean heavily, were expensive and a great burden on the balance of payments; whereas gas could be easily transported and would almost certainly be much cheaper. Mussolini had done his level best to strike oil, but national arrogance made him averse to the use of foreign expertise; that success had to await the return of liberal government is a pertinent commentary on the self-justifying rodomontade of his regime.

This success was largely due to one man, Enrico Mattei, who in 1945 was given the task of dissolving Mussolini's Oil Exploration Agency. Disobeying repeated orders, Mattei persisted in drilling and found fair supplies of methane in 1946; large quantities were discovered three years later. In 1953 this find was usefully supplemented when an American company struck oil in eastern Sicily. By that time Mattei was producing two billion cubic meters of natural gas a year, and before he died in 1962 had raised this figure to nearly seven billion. A brilliant if unconventional and autocratic organizer, he was also an excellent publicist and an agile puller of political wires. By deliberately exaggerating the extent of his discovery, he stampeded parliament into taking action on incomplete evidence; and, despite strong political pressure from the United States, was therefore allowed a monopoly on further exploration in the most promising areas. Using this monopoly to charge a high price for his product, he was able to finance what became an enormous economic empire, covering chemicals, cement, textiles, tourism, nuclear energy, and including what some would call the best newspaper in Italy. He also purchased considerable political influence, in more parties than one, so that, although nominally a state corporation, this highly idiosyncratic empire was barely accountable to parliament or even to the government.

Mattei's career is one instance of how the removal of fascist controls led to an astonishing outburst of entrepreneurial activity. Another helpful factor for the economy was the many new industrial processes in other countries which had not been exploited in Italy under fascism or during the war. Yet another was that, with so many unemployed and a large surplus of agricultural workers, there was a vast labor reservoir for industry and hence little risk of wage increases that would make production uncompetitive. A long tradition of skilled craftsmanship was speedily converted to the needs of large-scale industry and advanced productive techniques. The traditional companies, Fiat, Pirelli, Montecatini, and Olivetti, made up lost ground and soon had few rivals in Europe. New firms also appeared to satisfy a strong home demand for such articles as scooters and espresso coffee machines, and from this basis the country developed for the first time into a major exporter of manufactured goods.

Industrial production was already up to prewar levels by 1948, and there then followed fifteen years of fairly sustained economic progress. This was on a scale that Italy had never known before. Alongside an annual growth rate of about 5.9 per cent, one of the highest anywhere in the world, and which even in relatively bad years such as 1953 and 1958 hardly fell below 5 per cent, there was an additional advantage that prices at first remained comparatively stable. No longer burdened by the heavy protectionism and military expenditures of fascism, Italy was ready to make full use of her economic potential when, in 1957–58, the Treaty of Rome inaugurated the European Economic Community, especially as she had more underdeveloped capacity and greater reserves of labor than her partners. Beyond Europe, too, scores of Italian civil engineering firms began to win substantial contracts all over the world.

Regional inequalities were inevitable in a country with the historical antecedents and geographical diverseness of Italy, but their reduction was agreed to be urgent, since provincial sentiment and local loyalties regularly took precedence over the sense of national identity and obligation. Especially in Sardinia and Sicily—not only cut off physically but with a historical background as much Spanish as Italian—a movement grew up in 1943 which aimed at autonomy and sometimes complete separation from Italy. Special situations also existed in the partly French-speaking Val d'Aosta, in the largely German-speaking Alto Adige, and in the Slav hinterland of Trieste.

So long as the Christian democrats had been an opposition party, for instance in 1919–25, they had strongly supported regional autonomy and had condemned centralization, but once in power they changed. It was rather their communist opponents who now stood for regional devolution and the letter of the 1947 constitution, whereas De Gasperi feared that, especially in the "red" areas of Tuscany, Umbria, and Emilia, regional autonomy would give the extreme Left power and the patronage that went with power. Although he was ready to create regional parliaments in the peripheral provinces of Sardinia, Sicily, Trentino–Alto Adige, and the Val d'Aosta (in none of which the Left had much chance of electoral victory), in practice he tried to restrict their autonomy within fairly narrow bounds, and he adamantly refused to create the rest of the nineteen regions.

In the few areas where local self-government was tried, the experiment did not prove wholly successful. This was notably so in Sicily. To a lesser degree it was true in the Trentino–Alto Adige, where a demand for an even greater degree of self-determination by the German-speaking element was sometimes backed by acts of terrorism. Undeniably there was a certain value in bringing the processes of government nearer to the ordinary citizen, as there was a good deal of point in training local politicians and a local civil service to deal with problems that did not have much impact on the nation at large; but the regional administrations proved to be overmanned, extremely costly, and not notably efficient, while the central bureaucracy was not correspondingly reduced. Since the regions raised little of their own revenue and depended on state grants, it was not hard for the government to restrict them. Moreover, the Constitutional Court, when finally it was set up in 1955 to resolve clashes in jurisdiction, did not like the untidiness of different legal systems, and usually favored centralized state authority.

Some people thought that this made the worst of two worlds. Italy retained the disadvantages of over-centralization, and, despite a succession of cabinet ministers appointed to reform the civil service, the central bureaucracy remained as complicated, as constricting, as dilatory, and in some respects as corrupt, as it had always been, while clientelism and boss rule received new vigor at a local level where regional bureaucracies provided luscious plums of patronage. Jobbery and pork-barrel handouts in the regional assemblies were sometimes employed to reinforce the local notables and create suspect enclaves of influence and financial immunity. Local deputies could vote themselves very large salaries; they occasionally passed special tax laws to favor certain interested parties and used their position to obtain credits for operations which brought local politics into disrepute.

The main regional disequilibrium was still, as it always had been, between North and South. The South, including the islands and the mainland south of Rome, contained some twenty million out of the fifty-three million population of Italy (1961 census figures). It was short on natural resources and possessed relatively little free capital. Geographically, it was as far as ever from the main industrial and agricultural markets, and this distance was all the greater in that communications often remained primitive. Overpopulation, a high birth rate, poor educational facilities, archaic agricultural techniques, and a primitive land tenure system, all helped to keep this large area backward, and in so doing delayed national economic unification. The bigger industries remained firmly in the much richer North—Fiat at Turin, Italsider and Ansaldo at Genoa, Olivetti in Ivrea, and at Milan the giants Pirelli, Edison, Montecatini, and Snia Viscosa.

The fairly consistent policy of successive governments in the past, whether intended or not, had hitherto been to preserve this dual system. In the first years of united Italy the government had largely been in the hands of northerners who identified the national welfare with their own: they had preferred, quite plausibly, to accumulate capital for an industrial take-off, and the agricultural South was therefore kept overtaxed and underinvested to provide the funds for northern industry. But northern interests subsequently used political power to reinforce this regional advantage even where it might mean reducing the national income and the rate of capital accumulation. Protection of steel suited northern industry, as well as discriminating against the South through the increased price of manufactures. Agricultural protection at the same time had kept alive in the South the inefficient and costly practices of the *latifondi*. Just as high steel prices acted as a drag on any expansion of engineering, so the artificial price of cereals had delayed the diversification of southern agriculture into more profitable channels: in other words, the political unification of Italy had not brought economic unification, but had tended to widen the gap between the capitalist North and the feudal, traditional, self-sufficient South; after 1922 Mussolini's armaments' policy and his uneconomic "battle for grain" increased the gap still further.

Postwar governments made a determined effort to reverse the process and integrate the backward South into Italian society. The potential danger of the situation was dramatically revealed when the 1946 referendum showed 76 per cent at Naples in favor of the monarchy, while the North voted heavily for a republic. Another index of the difference was that the Resistance movement in 1944–45 was confined to the North; hence, incidentally, the South missed out on a vital force for renovation which might otherwise have displaced some of the retrograde local élites. What was worse, the Americans in 1943 had deliberately reintroduced the Sicilian mafia as a *ruse de guerre,* and given it effective power over large areas of Sicilian society.

In De Gasperi's party there were many who, alarmed at the possible "southernization" of Italian political life, were anxious to extirpate this dual system of economics and morality. They were not allowed to touch the mafia, because the mafia's electoral support was soon found to be indispensable; but in 1950 the Cassa per il Mezzogiorno, a special investment board for the South, was set up with substantial sums for building roads, dams, aqueducts, and irrigation works. In 1954, a year when unemployment was especially bad, the "Vanoni plan" outlined a scheme by which direct public investment and incentives to private industry were expected to make some four million more jobs over ten years, with the avowed intention of creating a rate of real income growth which would be double in the South what it was in the North.

Much play was made with this plan, but it was not even presented to parliament: one can now see that it was little more than a vague statement of intent, for there was far too much prejudice among businessmen against any strong intervention by public authorities in the economy. Industrialists and landowners preferred the kind of state help which attracted private investment to the South by offering cheap credit, freight reductions, and tax incentives; but even these measures encountered the objection that, while good for the South and for some northern contracting firms, they merely diverted money from where the nation could most profitably use it, as well as being open to the temptation of helping to get votes at election time. The same arguments were raised when a special "Ministry of State Participations" was created in 1956, and when the large sector of publicly owned firms was instructed that 60 per cent of all new investments had to be located in the South.

This 60 per cent law was impossible to enforce, for no minister had enough authority to cut through the tangle of conflicting bureaucracies or even to obtain the basic statistical data on which he could act. There was still an insufficient theoretical basis on which could be developed a policy about depressed areas, and in practice a confusion arose between development projects and measures of social relief. For some time it was also assumed that "infrastructure" was all that was required, without any need for direct industrial incentives. Vast sums were certainly spent in the South: roads and proper water supplies were brought to some villages for the first time, and large sections of the rural population at last came within sight of a decent standard of living; but the experts nevertheless raised many objections to what was done and how it was done. It was said that reforms were tackled piecemeal, with far too little coordinated planning between the Cassa and other government agencies. Moreover, political considerations affected the allocation of money, with the result that development organizations were often staffed by second-rate politicians or clients of some notable who was ready to trade his electoral support. Whole villages were built in which no one ever came to live; dams were built from which the water trickled profitlessly into the sea. A fairly high percentage of the money— some said a good third—must thus have been completely wasted.

Private industry in the North did not in general enter with much enthusiasm into these schemes for southern development. Some of the larger firms contributed their share, as Olivetti set up an office machine factory near Naples, and Montecatini spent a great deal on petrochemicals and fertilizers in Sicily; but Fiat, arguing that the South lacked the market, the raw materials, the skills, and the requisite power supplies for an automobile industry, had good economic reasons for preferring to concentrate investment nearer home. On the whole it was state-controlled firms which moved south; it was also capital-intensive rather than labor-intensive industries, because skilled labor was lacking there, while officially sponsored credit made capital cheap; and the result was to leave southern unemployment little improved. Most private firms, even if they did not say so openly, preferred to rely on a continuance of southern unemployment from which they could draw labor as needed into their northern factories, and hence saw strong arguments for keeping the South dilapidated and poor.

For these reasons there now began another great period of emigration from the South, an emigration which eventually imposed a remedy of a much more drastic kind. Perhaps nearly two million people moved northward in the late 1950's and early 1960's, at a speed which increased along with the rate of development in Milan and Turin. Mussolini's law preventing labor moving out of agriculture, which at first had been unconstitutionally retained to protect northern trade unionists, was eventually repealed to assist this process. Vast new social problems were thus created in the North, for instance over houses, schools, and urban development. The emigrants did not mix easily in northern society, and they helped to create a fearful problem of violence in northern cities. Though unemployment fell in the South and wages increased there because of this emigration, nevertheless, by taking away men of working age, while leaving behind the old, the young, and the women, it solved one problem only to create another.

The South certainly made far more progress in the 1950's than ever before, though how far this was because of or irrespective of government action was in dispute. Everyone agreed, however, that progress was still disappointing in view of its formidable cost. Instead of catching up with the North, not even all this vast investment of thought and money had been able to prevent northerners increasing their lead in income and industrial development.

Another elusive problem in these postwar years was posed by the parliamentary system itself, for doubts remained whether the degree of authority required for decision and action could in practice be also accompanied by the give-and-take of free and effective criticism. The sweeping Christian-democrat victory of 1948 was not repeated, and evidently was due to casual factors which made it an inadequate test of public opinion. As the Left increased its strength, De Gasperi found it the more essential to try to keep other center parties in his coalition; yet the other components of his alliance were bound to have doubts when they found a compromise policy unreal, and the balance between authority and effective criticism became to that extent more difficult to preserve.

The Christian-democrat party in any case continued to be quite radically divided over such matters as land reform, tax reform, and economic planning. Also, over relations between Church and state, some good Catholics thought that clerical influence was far too intrusive in politics. To some a contradiction was growing up in practice between Article 7 of the Constitution, which recognized Catholicism as a privileged state religion, and Articles 8 and 19 which guaranteed freedom of conscience and the equality of all religions before the law; for, on

such issues as divorce and birth control, the law of the state imposed
Catholic penalties on Catholic and non-Catholic alike. Catholic Action,
an official body of laymen subordinate to the hierarchy, took a strongly
conservative line in politics, and its three million members wielded
great influence at election time. Also more directly, through episcopal
pronouncements, there was an insistence that obedience to ecclesiastical
authority, being a Christian virtue, could be used to make Christians
vote Christian democrat, or even to align the party with the monarchists
and fascists on the Right.

Pius XII, who reigned as Pope for the long period 1939–58, had
conservative political views like his predecessor, and made it clear that,
wherever politics touched on religion or morals, he had a right to pro-
nounce and to expect obedience. Withdrawal of the sacraments was
thus used as a highly effective weapon in the elections of 1948. In July
1949 Pius excommunicated all communists and forbade any believer
to vote for them. Subsequently, he added that socialism should be
regarded as having the same philosophy as communism and was also
irreconcilable with Christianity, while he guardedly expressed alarm
even over free education and free health services.

De Gasperi agreed with Pius at least to the point of rejecting
Togliatti's attempts to bring "atheistic communism" within the system
of democratic politics. Moreover, where various articles of the constitution were in conflict with each other, he was ready to give the
Church the benefit of any doubt, and if necessary would even allow the
bishops certain immunities from the ordinary laws. In private, nevertheless, he spoke strongly against clerical intervention in politics. When
informed of the Pope's personal wish that he desert the social democrats
and join the Right, he courageously but sensibly demurred, for, with the
existing balance of parties in parliament, this would simply have invited
defeat and given a gratuitous respectability to the communist opposition.

Yet he was not a completely free agent, or else his judgment
momentarily failed him in 1953, for he chose this moment to introduce
a new electoral law which, like Mussolini's law of 1923, was intended
to reduce the strength of the Left by guaranteeing his own coalition a
greatly increased majority if only they could win a clear 50 per cent of
the vote. This law was too provocative a method of compensating for
a fall-away in popular support. It led in the elections of 1953 to a much
higher Marxist vote, while some of the moderates in the Center abandoned him and so pushed support for his coalition below the required
50 per cent. Instead of winning the larger majority that he wanted, he
lost the fair majority he already possessed, and this brought his career
in parliament to a close.

§🐘

The 1953 elections dealt the four-party alliance a serious blow, and in the new parliament their reduced margin gave the Christian democrats much less freedom to maneuver. Out of 590 seats in the lower house, they now had 261 instead of 304, and furthermore they were disunited. Some kind of coalition support was more desirable than ever, even though it would be precarious and might spell ineffective government. Four Christian-democrat prime ministers formed governments in the next seven months to see if they could find a working formula, but there were personal differences between them, and the leaders of the other Center parties were reluctant to lend their names to anything so transient and inevitably noncommittal.

This second postwar legislature lasted until 1958, and it saw the emergence of no politician the equal of De Gasperi or Einaudi in ability and strength of character. In such an ambiguous political situation there was rather a premium on the accommodating type of parliamentary leader whose skill lay in mediating between different political groups and above all in avoiding radical action. Giuseppe Pella and Amintore Fanfani experimented with *monocolore* cabinets of Christian democrats only, with the tacit and conditional support of other parties. Then Mario Scelba and Antonio Segni managed to reassemble coalitions which once again included liberals and social democrats. But these successive cabinets hardly offered a truly alternative policy. The reality was one in which different notables inside this single party, each with his own individual group of followers, successively tried to find that nuance of policy or tactics which would mark them out from their rivals and create a new majority. Some of the group leaders, indeed, if like Bernardo Mattarella in western Sicily they represented a strong vested interest and could guarantee a bloc of parliamentary votes, remained almost permanently, and of right, in successive cabinets: Mattarella served in sixteen different governments over the space of twenty years, and Giulio Andreotti in nineteen.

Of the various groups inside this party, some had their own central office, their own funds, and an individual journal as their official mouthpiece. The most solid faction of the center was the Dorotei, among whose younger leaders were Emilio Colombo and Mariano Rumor; barely distinguishable were the Morotei, so called from their leader, Aldo Moro; to the Right were Scelba's Centrismo popolare and Andreotti's Primavera group; between Center and Left, Iniziativa democratica and the Nuove cronache which supported Fanfani, the Forze nuove, the Basisti and the Rinnovamento democratico, these were names of various currents which had a greater or lesser degree of durability and effectiveness. All had some claim to be represented in any cabinet, and a prospective prime minister would have to secure a broad balance among them before he looked to other parties for a wider coalition. The fact that his cabinet would also have to contain a rough balance between the various regions was a yet further restriction on his freedom of choice. Only when a real stalemate was reached would the party fall back on a noncompetitive, *monocolore* "administrator" to lead a nondescript government until the various factions could regroup themselves: such stopgap "administrative" cabinets were formed at intervals by Pella, Zoli, Tambroni, and Leone.

Among those who aspired to the premiership there could be keen rivalries, and these, in a sense, compensated for the lack of effective opposition from other parties. In 1955, for instance, when a new president had to be elected to succeed Einaudi, the official Christian-democrat candidate failed to get the required votes, because the ballot was secret and Fanfani was ambitious to secure the office for himself; but many of Fanfani's colleagues, with outside support on both the extreme Left and the extreme Right of parliament, managed to outmaneuver both of them and elect Giovanni Gronchi instead.

As the years went by, the perils inherent in these party factions became more apparent. When Segni lost the support of the republicans and social democrats in 1957, chiefly over questions arising out of agrarian reform, parliament had to accept another temporary *monocolore* administration under Adone Zoli; but Zoli found himself having to depend on the fascist vote, which to many of his colleagues was intolerable. Equally intolerable to others would have been an open alliance with socialism: indeed the suggestion received another public veto from the Vatican, and was strongly opposed by the conservative factions who ranged behind Scelba and Segni. Further elections in 1958 gave the party only 273 seats and it was still a minority, but they strengthened Fanfani's following in the party, so he once more became prime minister, this time with social-democrat support from the Left; he was followed soon afterward by Segni, who in turn was displaced, after further internal disagreements, by Fernando Tambroni.

The choice of Tambroni in 1960, though intended as an emollient stopgap, gave the whole system a jolt, for he turned out to have unexpected ideas of his own in favor of an "opening to the Right." One suggestion had already been mooted in some quarters that the whole form of parliamentary government might be changed in favor of a presidential regime, perhaps along *Gaulliste* lines. Some slight countenance was given to this by President Gronchi, who openly spoke of winning greater political initiative for the president's office and who publicly criticized the "dictatorship of the parties" as a threat to the freedom of parliament. It was Gronchi who chose Tambroni as prime minister, but the new government cannot have behaved quite as the president meant: for, by seeking support from monarchists and fascists, Tambroni offered the extreme Right a possible chance to recover political power. This aroused memories of Mussolini's civil war, and antifascist leaders of the wartime Resistance stirred up a mood of frenzied indignation against "clerical fascism," killing Tambroni's support among the noncommitted electorate and the left wing of Christian democracy. When severe rioting broke out, with a number of fatal casualties, it became more and more difficult to escape the conclusion that a new grouping of parties was urgently needed if parliamentary democracy was to survive.

59 Italy Shifts to the Left, 1960-1969

The election as Pope of the elderly John XXIII did not seem very significant in 1958; but by 1962, when the Second Vatican Council met, Catholicism could be seen to be moving toward greater changes than any in four hundred years. Pius IX, in the allocution *Jamdudum cernimus* of 1861, had formally repudiated "progress, liberalism, and modern civilization"; Pius X, in *Lamentabili sane* of 1907, gave a long list of further "modernistic" errors that the Inquisition had decided were more deadly than those of Luther; but now Pope John, in welcoming *aggiornamento,* went to what many churchmen would call the opposite extreme. Pius XI after 1922 had encouraged authoritarianism in Church and State, but John XXIII expressed a preference for the methods of liberal democracy and episcopal collegiality; in place of Pius XII's excommunication of the extreme Left in 1949, John was anxious to repair some of the bridges which had been so hastily burnt, and the hierarchy was even urged toward a hesitant acceptance of socialism as a possible partner in government. Freedom of conscience, once condemned in the Syllabus of Errors, was now praised as a

Christian virtue, and in the encyclical *Mater et Magistra* of 1961, as in that of *Pacem in Terris* of 1963, John showed how far the church could push its advocacy of progressive social ideas.

Another factor after 1960 which helped to change some of the old stereotypes was the rapid progress of an economic boom which brought a faster process of industrialization and urbanization than Italy had ever known before. One incidental result was to alter the framework of argument about state intervention and national economic planning. On the Right, the liberal party under Giovanni Malagodi now sloughed off its radical elements and received strong backing from the Confindustria in a delaying battle against *programmazione:* these liberals pointed out that prosperity was already being achieved without a national plan, even perhaps because there was no plan. The radicals demonstrated, on the contrary, that economic growth and laisser faire had eliminated neither unemployment nor the disparity between North and South; the implication being that government should go on providing those elements of the economic infrastructure which the private sector could not afford, as it should also terminate private monopolies and near monopolies such as existed in telephones and electricity. Even if government action were less efficient than private action, at least it would be more socially beneficent if it supplied antitrust legislation and intervened where ordinary criteria of free enterprise might be harmful. This could be proved by thirty years of experience with the I.R.I., where a public corporation had developed the technique of using normal market methods to raise money and run a great number of competitive industries in which the public interest was overriding.

By 1959–60 the main body of Christian democrats, under the uneasy joint leadership of Fanfani and Moro, was moving further away from doctrines of laisser faire. In the Piano Verde, for instance, a great deal of public expenditure was allocated to the modernization of agriculture and to the improvement of rural living conditions. Some economists and many industrialists wondered if enough investment opportunities still could be found for such a huge expenditure on agriculture, but tentative approval came from the Coltivatori diretti, a powerful and somewhat disreputable organization of small proprietors which was a right-wing pressure group inside Christian democracy. Certain basically conservative factions inside this party could thus accept greater government intervention in the economy when it suited them, as they also recognized that subsidies and cheap credit, especially when funneled through themselves, might provide useful patronage at the same time as they won votes away from communism.

§✿

As a result of the outburst of public anger which in July 1960 brought down the conservative Tambroni, the Christian-democrat notables were faced with a narrower range of options, since any alliance with the Right—even with Malagodi's liberals—might now be beyond the reach of any viable transformist coalition. It was abundantly clear at the same time that there was little to expect from the nonsocialist Left-Center. After the disintegration of the Party of Action, Parri and Calamandrei had fought the 1953 elections under the banner of Unità popolare but failed to win a single parliamentary seat, and their electoral list attracted fewer than a thousand votes in all southern Italy. Likewise in the 1958 elections, the Radicali, though notable for intellectual strength and behind-stage influence, could obtain not a single seat in the lower house. Another ingredient in the Left Center, the Republican party, now under the distinguished leadership of La Malfa, won seven seats in 1958, and La Malfa was eventually recruited by Fanfani as minister in charge of state enterprises. Together with the twenty-two social democrats who followed Saragat, this gave Christian democracy a bare majority, though it was an uncomfortable position because many conservatives in the party could be relied on to defect in any secret parliamentary vote.

One way out of this impasse would have been to push the alliance further leftward to include Nenni and his eighty-four independent socialists, because their adherence would lift the government majority to 387 against the 140 communists and the sixty-four deputies of the Right. Though a quarter of Nenni's party kept up an irreconcilable opposition against any "bourgeois" government, he himself had changed, and he had persuaded them in 1952–53 to drop their common slate with the communists; subsequently, Khrushchev's revelations about Stalinism and then the Russian invasion of Hungary still further weakened the cohesion of the Left, and improvement in living standards was continually helping to convert more socialists to a belief in gradualism. Meanwhile, in local government, a practical alliance was sometimes worked out which brought the Left into municipal administrations as the only means of providing a working majority. This happened at Milan and Genoa in 1961. Also, in Sicily the Christian democrats in the regional assembly defied repeated Vatican protests and accepted socialist, even communist, support. As Giolitti and Cavour had shown earlier, an alliance with the Left could be used to absorb or submerge a potentially dangerous opposition; but there was a price to pay, in that it might mean adopting a more frankly radical policy.

Everything depended on whether any Christian-democrat leader was skillful enough to carry out such an operation at national level without splitting his party or wrecking his own political future.

The first attempt was by Fanfani who followed Tambroni as prime minister in 1960. As secretary of the party since 1954, Fanfani had brought younger men to the forefront of politics and given them the backing of a reinforced party organization. These men set their mind to the only realignment of political alliances which offered much hope of success. At first they met renewed opposition from the hierarchy, but gradually Pope John prevailed against the conservative curia cardinals, until he was able to revoke Pius XII's prohibition against political alliance with Marxists. Though he must have known that this would increase the communist vote, his overriding aim was not to play politics, but to end the cold war and promote social justice.

Fanfani's fourth administration, in February 1962, was thus at last enabled to offer a left-oriented policy that the socialists might accept. He was ready to promise more government intervention in the economy, reform of the civil service, the abolition of share-cropping in agriculture, a program for building new schools, and another for controlling urban sprawl. He was even prepared to create the other fifteen regional governments promised in 1947. Higher pensions and social welfare were part of the package, and in foreign policy he persuaded the Americans to remove their missile bases from Italian soil.

The socialists supported this program, though they would not join the cabinet until they saw what, if anything, it meant in practice. But Fanfani had been too agile for his colleagues, and now discovered that he had vacated the center ground in his party which was a necessary basis for success. The Dorotei preferred Moro, party secretary since 1959, whose support for the Center Left was combined with greater political consistency, a less provocative ambition, and a positively Giolittian skill in avoiding rather than imposing solutions. Other right-wing Christian democrats also supported Moro as part of a deal whereby the conservative Segni was chosen as the official party candidate to succeed President Gronchi. Fanfani was finally displaced when, partly as a result of Pope John's more permissive attitude, the communists picked up a million extra votes in June 1963 and pushed down popular support for the Christian democrats from 42 per cent to 38 per cent. The obvious successor would have been Moro, but Fanfani's supporters made difficulties about serving under him, and so another caretaker government of *monocolore* Christian democracy was formed under Giovanni Leone. Only at the end of 1963 did the Nenni socialists at last agree to join a coalition, and, when the Dorotei admitted that there was no other alternative, Moro formed an administration, with Nenni as deputy prime minister. The "opening to the Left" was a reality.

୧◍

The first measure which in 1962 had been chosen to seal this alliance was the nationalization of electricity. Edison, the enormous electrical company, was rich enough to have acquired considerable political power, and had used that power to support the Right: that was one reason for nationalization. Another was the need to provide electricity as cheaply in southern Italy as in the North. The government simultaneously agreed that atomic power should be developed by the public not the private sector. It also agreed to meet socialist demands by taxing share dividends and speculation in real estate. Moreover, a withholding tax had the novel advantage of being hard to evade.

Most of the big industries in the Confindustria were, of course, strongly critical of such a program, insisting that it pointed the road to economic disaster, and suggesting that, before agreeing to more state intervention, civil service machinery would have to be thoroughly overhauled. Opposition was such that, to protect themselves against higher taxes and state controls, rich Italians illegally smuggled hundreds of billions of lire out of the country into Switzerland in a major flight of capital which helped to cause a collapse of the stock market. The Church, too, refused to declare or pay tax on its vast shareholdings, and in this case the government dared to override parliament and make a special exception by not claiming payment from the Vatican.

An economic recession, which began after 1962, had deeper origins than just this flight of capital. Another cause was the continuance of weak, compromise governments without a strong and agreed economic policy. More particularly, unemployment, which had continued high throughout the boom until 1959, then fell sharply, and the resultant shortages of skilled labor caused wage increases which at last made costs rise faster than production. On the Left it was said that these price rises were provoked by the economic Right as a protest against nationalization. In part the recession was a natural downturn after an excessive expansion of credit, but it was serious enough to cause a severe deficit in the balance of payments, and there was talk of possible devaluation. One political result, not entirely casual, was that the Center-Left alliance had to curtail its reform policy and use anti-inflationary measures to stop consumer demand. By the end of 1964 this deflation had largely succeeded in its object, but the socialists had not liked it, and a rift in the alliance could be discerned: any further program of radical reforms would evidently run the risk of a refusal by industry and the rich to cooperate.

Another minor blow to the coalition was the discovery of a mysterious plot in the summer of 1964, when certain right-wing elements, perhaps fearing what would happen if the recession became severe, were thought to have prepared a kind of military *coup*. Nothing came of it, and no doubt some of the attendant rumors were exaggerated; nevertheless, whatever the true explanation, enough information was subsequently made public to show that certain senior officers in the secret service (Sifar) had made contingent arrangements for the arrest of many people in public life. They apparently relied on the assumption that President Segni, whose election had received incidental fascist support, had no love for socialism or the Center Left. Segni was a sick man and was shortly to retire from office because of ill-health.

The Sifar episode, coupled with back-pedaling over the cabinet's reform program, came as a shock to many socialists, and suggested to them that Nenni had made a poor bargain in joining the government; they could think that, like Rattazzi, Depretis, and Crispi before him, he might have been disarmed by the insidious logic of transformism, or else was becoming *embourgeoisé* by the fact of political power. The conservatives, on the other hand, who had at first been outraged by the Moro-Nenni coalition, now realized that, contrary to their expectations, it had rendered socialism innocuous. Not for the first time in Italian history an alliance between radicals and conservatives had led to the putting off of reforms as unwelcome and divisive and had ultimately resulted in a further fragmentation of the Left.

A number of socialist deputies, led by Tullio Vecchietti, refused to follow Nenni along his chosen path and broke off to form a secessionist Party of Proletarian Unity. Others who stopped short of this, notably Riccardo Lombardi, did so with evident reluctance: while recognizing that socialism should remain free from the communists and not be intransigent on principle, they would not accept just a slow advance along the primrose capitalist path to the welfare state. At the socialist congress of 1965, Lombardi was not strong enough to force a withdrawal from the coalition, and Nenni was even empowered to accept back into the party those social-democrat Saragattiani who had left the main body of socialism in 1947; but many of his colleagues looked on this as a doubtful measure that could be justified only if it gave socialism more weight in deciding the government program.

For his part, Moro realized that lack of cohesion among the Christian democrats made it unwise to move too far or too fast to the Left; some of his colleagues, indeed, looked on Nenni's partial discomfiture and Vecchietti's secession with complacency. Their own internal feuds were again exposed when a new president was elected to succeed the ailing Segni in December 1964. Their official candidate, sprung on the party by the Dorotei, was Leone; other factions then rallied to push Fanfani; but party jealousies were such that, after twenty-one ballots, enough Christian-democrat votes deserted both candidates to decide the election in favor of the social-democrat Saragat. That this decision was openly supported by the communists was an additional embarrassment to the main government party.

The same wrangling and rivalries also affected substantial questions of policy. Moro's first cabinet collapsed in June 1964 over the issue of school reform, because party discipline failed, and the socialists, who had been especially nettled by the illegality of tax exemption for the Vatican, refused to vote for state support to private Catholic schools. His second cabinet fell in January 1966 over another issue affecting schools, as in a secret vote a number of Catholic deputies turned against him because he gave the appearance of weakening in defense of their religious rights. Moro in each case managed to assemble another Center-Left cabinet, but there were some notable defections at this sign of the Church's influence in politics, and it was feared that the Dorotei, perhaps also the Fanfaniani, were trying to win power by pushing the coalition program back in a conservative direction.

§❧

The fourth postwar legislature (1963–68), despite a large government majority for the Center-Left, drifted to a finish with few achievements to its credit, and so proved that the correct formula for a working government alliance had still not been found. Each year of this legislature had been hailed in turn as the great year for major legislative action, but nothing ever happened. Inability to liberalize and modernize the state universities was one of the failures of omission which weakened Moro's third government. Not only was there a ratio of nearly fifty students per teacher, but the fact that sixty parliamentarians were also "full-time" university professors (Moro and Fanfani among them) indicated a radical weakness in the educational system, and incidentally helped to explain why reform in this critical field was difficult.

Apart from education, Moro's projected law on the regions met consistent right-wing obstructionism. The regulations required to control urban development and speculation were not introduced, though the abuses under the existing system were officially acknowledged to be scandalous and dangerous. Nor was there any overhaul of the civil service or the social security system. No remedy was proposed for the great backlog of cases which jammed the law courts—there were stated to be over two million cases pending, and the average duration of a civil action was over six years. Tax reform, too, which for a long time had been promised as urgent and imminent, was too controversial an issue for the Center Left to settle. Parliament did succeed in agreeing to renegotiate those sections of the 1929 Concordat which conflicted with the 1947 Constitution, but this was a mere declaration of intent. A parliamentary commission was at long last meant to be looking into the mafia, but after nearly seven years of work there was no sign of any report, and evidently some people were dragging their feet.

The quinquennial election in May 1968 reflected the disappointment at these results, at the same time as it made a solution more remote than ever. In the new parliament the Right was weaker than before, and there was a significant move inside this Right away from the fascists to the more moderate liberals; but the Socialist party as a penalty for failure in government lost a quarter of its popular support, and so imperiled the coalition. The new opposition Party of Proletarian Unity obtained a remarkable million and a half votes, and the communists went up from seven and three-fourths to eight and a half million, so that noncooperators on the extreme Left once again held over a third of the parliamentary seats.

The Center-Left alliance could still be said to have 55 per cent of the vote after May 1968, and the elections showed that there was no clear alternative to it, but the socialist leaders recognized that to continue as allies of Christian democracy would even further erode their electoral support. Although Nenni still would have liked to remain in the government, four of his socialist colleagues—De Martino, Tanassi, Giolitti and Lombardi—were jockeying for power with four policies and factions which hardly differed much but which simply could not agree. All they would do was to retain party unity for the moment by a collective resignation, leaving another *monocolore* administration under Leone to continue on sufferance with an ostensibly Center-Left program. A more obvious candidate than Leone might have been Mariano Rumor, who since 1964 had held the commanding position of Christian-democrat party secretary; but he would not stake his reputation on a losing cause. Short of the Christian democrats accepting and enforcing a more radical program, it would not be easy to reassemble the one coalition which could command a real majority, and for the moment the party notables would not commit themselves. Once more there was an impasse in national and local politics, and a variety of problems continued to build up as government action had again to be postponed.

૭~

Many solid achievements had been registered in the economy by 1969. Standards of life for most people had greatly improved. Though terrible islands of poverty remained, the average income had risen perhaps twice as much in fifteen years as it had over the previous century; one index of greater affluence was that the number of television sets had doubled in four years to seven million, and the percentage of telephones to the population of Milan was greater than in London. The lira was one of the world's stronger currencies, and there was a substantial trade surplus. Italy was a heavy exporter of capital—some illegally, and much as a means of tax evasion. Workers in agriculture had declined by half in twenty years to little more than four million, and those who remained on the land were more prosperous than ever before. A traditional peasant and handicraft world was thus giving way to a consumer society with an altogether new demand for manufactured goods.

At long last Italy now experienced a real industrial revolution. Though the consumption of energy per head was still only half that in most north European countries, the steel industry, which before the war produced an average of only two and a half million tons a year from scrap, was producing 19 million, which was almost as much as France. Chemical engineering had grown on a similar scale. Zanussi, Ignis, Indesit were new names in a splendidly efficient refrigerator and washing machine industry which was way ahead of the rest of the Common Market, and Olivetti was the leading European manufacturer of office machinery. Foreign tourism, the largest source of foreign exchange, probably earned more money than anywhere else in the world, and almost every year brought still more visitors. Automobile production in 1938 had been 38,000 units, but topped 100,000 in 1953, 500,000 in 1960, a million in 1963, and reached over a million and a half by 1967. Russia in 1966 chose Fiat, now larger than Volkswagen, to build her first modern car factory, with a projected output of up to 2000 automobiles a day; other automobile plants were being planned for Poland and Romania; and Montecatini-Edison, who merged in 1966, had contracts for a dozen chemical factories in Russia alone.

Despite the claims made by Mattei, domestic supplies of oil provided only about 5 per cent of Italy's needs and were even beginning to fall. New sources of methane had been found in Sicily, Basilicata, and the Abruzzi, but increasing amounts of gas as well as oil had to be imported, especially from North Africa. Italy was very well placed for such imports and by 1969 had the largest oil refining industry in Europe, with a capacity between 100 and 130 million tons a year. Over four thousand miles of pipe had by then been laid for transporting gas supplies inside Italy. The National Hydrocarbons Institute continued to spend a great deal of money searching for new sources of supply in North Africa and the Middle East, with only fair results; it also found several promising sources near the Norfolk coast in the North Sea; and in 1968 it began a joint scheme with Shell Oil Co. to drill off-shore in the Adriatic, where a number of excellent discoveries were quickly made.

The promised expansion of the South, however, was a casualty of the 1962–65 recession. The so-called Pieraccini plan—presented in 1965 but interminably postponed—laid down once more the aim of eliminating the gap in living standards between North and South; but even when investment revived at the end of 1965 the planners were surprised to note that there was still a lag in the South. Whereas in 1951–54 the average income of southerners had been 47 per cent of that in the northwest, in 1963–66 the comparable figure was 43 per cent; in 1966 the increase in incomes was still lower south of Rome than in the northwest, and the amount spent on industrial investment in the South was falling. The year 1967 was better, but the rhythm of economic growth was still sluggish, and emigration continued through 1968. Not only were existing incentives evidently insufficient to attract private capital from northern investors, but government machinery was neither flexible nor powerful enough to act as a compensatory instrument of planning control. A great deal of the allocated funds thus continued to lie idle in credit with the Treasury just because decisions could not be taken on how to use them; and, for much the same sort of reason, nearly a year went by without adequate help arriving in Sicily after the worst earthquake disaster in half a century.

The result was that the aim of creating a self-propelling process of industrial growth seemed as remote as ever, and the gap between the two Italies, far from being eliminated, continued to widen. Some people again began to wonder if all the fine promises and statements of intent had not been mere electoral propaganda. At all events there were obviously more votes to be found in the preparation of a national plan than in its implementation, and officially inspired slogans about the South being "the California of Italy" can hardly have been intended seriously. An awkward fact was that no coalition could survive if it did not pay obeisance to the "southern lobby" and promise redress; at the same time the very nature of coalition government simultaneously forced it to pander to the even stronger "northern industrial lobby," whose solution to the southern problem was something far more ruthless. To this extent the South was a casualty not just of the recession but of the governmental system.

Even if the gap was growing, in absolute terms the level of life was better than before in southern Italy just as everywhere else. The old kind of *latifondo* had disappeared, unemployment and underemployment were greatly reduced, and the yield of agriculture was three times what it had been fifty years before. The world of welfare benefits, compulsory insurance, and television sets was gradually reaching out into the countryside. A splendid motorroad from the north was every year bringing Calabria closer to Milan, and at last the Cassa paid for a double-track railway down to the Straits of Messina; there was also a government plan for a university in Calabria to be organized on original lines. In Apulia the nine years after 1959 suddenly saw Taranto become an industrial city, and three weeks before the 1968 election Moro arrived at Naples to inaugurate the preliminary work on a vast new automobile plant for the government-controlled Alfa Romeo company. It may be true that the values found more readily in the North—not just materialist values, but respect for social equality, personal freedom, and mutual tolerance—were slow to permeate under the surface of southern life, but at least the cultural and ideological gap was lessening. Sardinian banditry was admittedly never so obtrusive and intractable as in 1967–68; and the Sicilian mafia, though less murderous, still managed to find protection in high places, giving up assassination for more lucrative operations; nevertheless, there was an outburst of local indignation against these twin scourges of the South, and this proved that a fundamental change must have begun.

Here was one way in which, despite regional tradition, the different elements in Italian society were gradually becoming more homogeneous, more harmonious, and at last able to accept a common national consciousness. The process was made easier as the disappearance of dictatorship left the way open to an invigorating cultural movement which spread from Milan, Turin, and Rome to affect every region of the peninsula. In some districts, it is true, there continued to be a serious problem of illiteracy: the 1951 figures showed 12.9 per cent of Italians over the age of six illiterate (in the South it was 24 per cent); in 1961 this figure had fallen to only 8.4 per cent, but still nearly a quarter of the population did not complete elementary school, and moreover the statistics were still bad for school attendance and newspaper readership. But the pace of change was increasing fast. Italian citizens, moreover, especially as the Common Market allowed so many to work abroad, were becoming much more conscious of events and ideas outside their own country.

In the same way the outside world admired the new movements in Italian painting and sculpture; there was an ever greater market for Italian fashion and industrial design; and, in film-making, the work of Antonioni, Pasolini, De Sica and Fellini became a familiar part of contemporary Western culture. Above all, perhaps for the first time since knowledge of the Italian language ceased to be the hallmark of a person's education, Italian literature became well known abroad. Moravia and Tomasi di Lampedusa were best sellers all over the world, while the ordinary reader in French-speaking and English-speaking countries began, through translation, to know the names of Betti, Svevo, Gadda, Calvino, Cassola, and a dozen other twentieth-century writers.

§

Compared with cultural and economic achievements, political success was elusive. By long and respected tradition, government was almost always by coalition between multiple parties, and yet the strength of clericalism and Marxism made an effective coalition very hard to find. Italy continued, just as in the years 1861–1922, to retain an unenviable primacy for unstable government, for there were twenty-nine different cabinets in these twenty-five years between 1943 and 1968. Admittedly, there was much more continuity than this annual succession of administrations might suggest, in that government remained basically in Christian-democrat hands; but this had its own disadvantages, for, while it did not prevent cabinet instability, it allowed vested interests and clienteles to continue undisturbed, and there was thus an almost built-in veto on many urgently needed reforms. Another result was that the parliamentary opposition, being permanently excluded from the responsibility of power, and realizing that even the most reasoned parliamentary criticism was a time-consuming ritual which would have no effect, resorted to the sterile and frustrating tactics of obstructionism.

Given time, it was possible to think that the extreme Left could one day be absorbed into the system. This had happened to other excluded minorities in the past, for example to Mazzini's republicans after 1861, and to the Catholics after 1900; likewise the ten million vote for the monarchy in 1946 dwindled to only one million in successive elections as the monarchists gradually accepted the constitution and distributed themselves over the political spectrum. The conservatives of the Confindustria had practical proof in the years 1963–68 that an alliance with socialism spelled neither red revolution nor toadying to Russia. Moreover, Catholicism, as a result of Pope John's initiative, was readier to accept reconciliation rather than exclusivism in politics. Even though some thought that this liberal interlude in the papacy would last no longer than similar interludes in 1846–48 and 1919–22, even despite Pope Paul's reversal to a more authoritarian concept of his office, at least the powerful spirit of accommodation unleashed by Vatican Council II was proving hard to check.

Some people were beginning to agree that communism might be changing in the same conciliatory direction. Until recently it had been fashionable to think that a strong, intransigent party on the extreme Left was the chief block in the path leading to a stable democracy; but in mid-1968 the communists could claim that, since the Center Left was in serious difficulties, one alternative was for themselves to be accepted as a constructive and not purely sterile ingredient in parliamentary politics. Possibly a popular front of communism and socialism might re-emerge as a coherent opposition and a conceivable alternative to Christian democracy. Alternatively, some Christian-democrat leader might see his chance for power (or his chance to foil his rivals in the party) in accepting some degree of communist support as a missing component in the system.

If this was improbable, it was by no means impossible. Communist support had already been welcomed by regional governments in Sicily and Aosta without causing a revolution, as well as by a number of municipal councils. Togliatti, before 1964, when he died in Russia, reached the point of declaring, like others before him, that the gradualist path of reforms might possibly be a road to the socialist society. One wing of his party, led by Giorgio Amendola, then took this attitude still further and began to envisage an altogether new party of the Left, neither communist nor social democrat, which might work with other parties on a more pragmatic and less dogmatically Marxist basis. This new-look communism, aided no doubt by the mass migration of peasants into the towns and the greater emancipation of women, evidently helped to win votes for the extreme Left in the 1968 elections. Many conservatives continued to think it insincere; nor was it entirely acceptable to Longo, Berlinguer, and the solid center of the communist party; nor was it helped by the Russian invasion of Czechoslovakia (an invasion which, incidentally, the Italian party condemned); but at least it indicated a relaxation of some rigidities and a possible, though slender, line of development for the future.

Toward the end of 1968, the major problem in Italy, without much doubt, was political. A slow leftward trend in Christian democracy had been confirmed in the May elections, but not enough to dictate the radicalization of policy which would whole-heartedly reactivate the alliance with socialism to provide an unassailable government majority. Possibly, Russian aggressiveness, if it continued, might supply what sweet reasonableness had failed to achieve. But though ideas, talent and good will abounded, the party system was too nicely balanced: the election of 1953 had upset one promising experiment by De Gasperi, as that of 1963 had upset a very different kind of political maneuver by Fanfani, and now that of 1968 upset another by Moro. The possibilities appeared to be narrowing once more as Leone's interregnum played out its term without any mandate for fundamental legislative action. The socialist congress in October came to physical blows, and nearly resulted in the complete disintegration of Nenni's party as his lieutenants fought each other for the succession to the party secretaryship. The Christian Democrats in November were in momentary disarray as Moro challenged Rumor's predominant position in the party, but he failed. Rumor became prime minister in December. He headed a coalition which, as well as for the Republican party, found place for four different "currents" of socialism and seven of Christian Democracy, and for representatives of the nineteen regions.

In January 1969 everyone was watching to see if Rumor could find a more effective formula of agreement which would enable him to modernize the structure of the state with support from the Left. Failure to do so, especially if further divisions inside socialism should coincide with another economic recession, might revive the failing fortunes of the extreme Right. Failure to reform the universities was already leading to student insurrections of a kind which had recently brought French society to its knees. There were still nearly a million unemployed. There were ominous strikes by teachers, by civil servants, by public transport officials, and even by the judges. In another sense there was a collective strike by the rich, for a huge flight of capital continued to suggest that the moneyed classes had lost confidence in the working of coalition government. Meanwhile, a long series of miscellaneous financial scandals reached an awe-inspiring peak as hundreds of public officials were sent to trial after revelations about the perversion of tax moneys for political purposes. Italy had weathered many worse storms than these in the past. But it would be a dangerous sign if she could not find a strong government just at a time when so many problems were urgently pressing for a solution, and when strong decisions had to be taken to avert a world monetary crisis. She could not afford another wasted year like 1968. After twenty years of the new republican constitution there was still no positive assurance that a solution could be found inside the traditional system of politics which derived from Cavour.

❧ PRIME MINISTERS OF ITALY

Camillo di Cavour	January 1860 to June 1861
Bettino Ricasoli	June 1861 to February 1862
Urbano Rattazzi	March 1862 to December 1862
Luigi Carlo Farini	December 1862 to March 1863
Marco Minghetti	March 1863 to September 1864
Alfonso Lamarmora	September 1864 to June 1866
Bettino Ricasoli	June 1866 to April 1867
Urbano Rattazzi	April 1867 to October 1867
Luigi Federico Menabrea	October 1867 to November 1869
Giovanni Lanza	December 1869 to July 1873
Marco Minghetti	July 1873 to March 1876
Agostino Depretis	March 1876 to March 1878
Benedetto Cairoli	March 1878 to December 1878
Agostino Depretis	December 1878 to July 1879
Benedetto Cairoli	July 1879 to May 1881
Agostino Depretis	May 1881 to July 1887
Francesco Crispi	August 1887 to February 1891
Antonio di Rudinì	February 1891 to May 1892
Giovanni Giolitti	May 1892 to November 1893
Francesco Crispi	December 1893 to March 1896
Antonio di Rudinì	March 1896 to June 1898
Luigi Pelloux	June 1898 to June 1900
Giuseppe Saracco	June 1900 to February 1901
Giuseppe Zanardelli	February 1901 to October 1903
Giovanni Giolitti	November 1903 to March 1905
Alessandro Fortis	March 1905 to February 1906
Sidney Sonnino	February 1906 to May 1906
Giovanni Giolitti	May 1906 to December 1909
Sidney Sonnino	December 1909 to March 1910
Luigi Luzzatti	March 1910 to March 1911
Giovanni Giolitti	March 1911 to March 1914
Antonio Salandra	March 1914 to June 1916
Paolo Boselli	June 1916 to October 1917
Vittorio Emanuele Orlando	October 1917 to June 1919
Francesco Nitti	June 1919 to June 1920
Giovanni Giolitti	June 1920 to July 1921

Ivanoe Bonomi	July 1921 to February 1922
Luigi Facta	February 1922 to October 1922
Benito Mussolini	October 1922 to July 1943
Pietro Badoglio	July 1943 to June 1944
Ivanoe Bonomi	June 1944 to June 1945
Ferrucio Parri	June 1945 to December 1945
Alcide de Gasperi	December 1945 to August 1953
Giuseppe Pella	August 1953 to January 1954
Amintore Fanfani	January 1954 to February 1954
Mario Scelba	February 1954 to June 1955
Antonio Segni	July 1955 to May 1957
Adone Zoli	May 1957 to June 1958
Amintore Fanfani	July 1958 to February 1959
Antonio Segni	February 1959 to March 1960
Fernando Tambroni	March 1960 to July 1960
Amintore Fanfani	July 1960 to June 1963
Giovanni Leone	June 1963 to December 1963
Aldo Moro	December 1963 to June 1968
Giovanni Leone	June 1968 to November 1968
Mariano Rumor	December 1968—

HEADS OF STATE

Vittorio Emanuele II, 1861–78
Umberto I, 1878–1900
Vittorio Emanuele III, 1900–46
Umberto II, 1946

Enrico de Nicola, 1946–48
Luigi Einaudi, 1948–55
Giovanni Gronchi 1955–62
Antonio Segni 1962–64
Giuseppe Saragat 1964—

POPES

Pius IX (Mastai-Ferretti) 1846–78
Leo XIII (Pecci) 1878–1903
St. Pius X (Sarto) 1903–14
Benedict XV (Della Chiesa) 1914–22
Pius XI (Ratti) 1922–39
Pius XII (Pacelli) 1939–58
John XXIII (Roncalli) 1958–63
Paul VI (Montini) 1963—

SUGGESTED READINGS

ACKNOWLEDGMENT is made to the following for permission to quote from the works listed: Pietro Nenni, for quotations from the books by him in the bibliography; Nazareno Padellaro, for *Libro della 111 classe elementare;* The Bodley Head, for *Mazzini's Letters to an English Family;* Hodder & Stoughton Ltd., for *The Memoirs of Francesco Crispi;* Weidenfeld & Nicholson Ltd., for *Mussolini's Memoirs, 1942–43,* ed. R. Klibansky; G. Bell & Sons Ltd., for *The Roman Journals of Ferdinand Gregorovius 1852–74,* ed. F. Althaus, tr. by Mrs. Gustavus Hamilton; Hutchinson, for *Benito Mussolini, My Autobiography,* tr. R. Washburn Child; G. Allen & Unwin Ltd., and also Little Brown & Co., and Franz J. Horch, for Emil Ludwig's *Talks with Mussolini,* tr. by Eden & Cedar Paul; Edward Arnold Ltd., for Salandra's *Italy and the Great War;* Deputazione subalpina di storia patria, for *Le carte di Giovanni Lanza;* Tom Antongini, for his biography of G. D'Annunzio; Arnoldo Mondadori, for quotations from D'Annunzio, Albertini, and C. Sforza; La Nuova Italia, for works of G. Fortunato; Rizzoli, for L. Albertini's *In difesa della libertà;* Edizioni scientifiche Italiane, for F. S. Nitti's *Rivelazioni,* and *Meditazioni dell'Esilio;* Licinio Cappelli, for G. Massari's *Diario 1858–60 sull'azione politica di Cavour;* G. C. Sansoni, for works of G. Gentile; Aldo Garzanti, for works of F. Crispi and G. Giolitti; E. Mariano, director of *Il Vittoriale,* for works of G. D'Annunzio; Istituto per gli studi di politica internazionale, Milan, for D. Farini's *Diario 1891–95;* La Fenice, for *Opera omnia di Benito Mussolini;* Giuseppe Laterza & Figli, for works of Benedetto Croce and Luigi Blanch; Doubleday & Co., Inc., for *Ciano's Diaries* ed. by Hugh Gibson, copyright 1945, 1946, by Doubleday & Co., Inc.; and also William Heinemann, Ltd., and Methuen and Co., Ltd., for *Ciano's Diaries.*

Full bibliographies may be found at the end of each chapter of *Nuove questioni di storia del Risorgimento e dell'unità d'Italia,* two vols. (Milan: Marzorati, 1961), and also in the *Enciclopedia italiana.*

ஃ GENERAL HISTORIES

Albrecht-Carrié, R. *Italy from Napoleon to Mussolini.* New York: Columbia University Press, 1950.

Bonomi, I. *La politica italiana da Porta Pia a Vittorio Veneto, 1870–1918.* Turin: Einaudi, 1944.

Chabod, F. *A History of Italian Fascism.* Translated by M. Grindrod. London: Weidenfeld & Nicolson, 1963.

Clough, Shepard B. *The Economic History of Modern Italy.* New York: Columbia University Press, 1964.

Colamarino, G. *Il fantasma liberale*. Milan: Bompiani, 1946.

Croce, B. *A History of Italy 1871–1915*. Translated by C. M. Ady. Oxford: Clarendon Press, 1929.

De Mauro, T. *Storia linguistica dell'Italia unita*. Bari: Laterza, 1965.

Falconi, C. *The Popes in the Twentieth Century*. Translated by M. Grindrod. London: Weidenfeld & Nicolson, 1967.

Halperin, S. William. *Mussolini and Italian Fascism*. Princeton: Van Nostrand, 1964.

Hentze, Margot. *Pre-fascist Italy. The Rise and Fall of the Parliamentary Régime*. London: Allen and Unwin, 1939.

Hughes, H. S. *The United States and Italy*. Revised edition. Cambridge, Mass.: Harvard University Press, 1965.

Hughes, Serge. *The Fall and Rise of Modern Italy*. New York: The Macmillan Company, 1967.

Jemolo, A. C. *Church and State in Italy, 1850–1950*. Translated by David Moore. Oxford: Blackwell, 1960.

King, Bolton. *A History of Italian Unity*. 2 vols. London: Nisbet, 1899.

Luzzatto, G. *L'economia italiana dal 1861 al 1914*, vol. I (1861–1894). Milan: Banca Commerciale Italiana, 1963.

Mack Smith, D. *Storia d'Italia dal 1861 al 1958, con documenti e testimonianze*. 2 vols. Milan: Edizioni Labor, 1968.

———. *Modern Sicily*. New York: Viking, 1968.

Maranini, G. *Storia del potere in Italia, 1848–1967*. Florence: Valecchi, 1967.

Mario, Jessie White. *The Birth of Modern Italy*. London: T. F. Unwin, 1909.

Meeks, Carroll L. V. *Italian Architecture, 1750–1914*. New Haven: Yale University Press, 1966.

Romeo, R. *Breve storia della grande industria in Italia*. Bologna: Cappelli, 1961.

Salvadori, Massimo L. *Il mito del buongoverno: la questione meridionale da Cavour a Gramsci*. Turin: Einaudi, 1960.

Seton-Watson, C. *Italy from Liberalism to Fascism, 1870–1925*. London: Methuen, 1967.

Thayer, J. A. *Italy and the Great War: Politics and Culture, 1870–1915*. Madison: University of Wisconsin Press, 1964.

Valeri, N. *La lotta politica in Italia dall'unità al 1925: idee e documenti*. Florence: Le Monnier, 1958.

Vöchting, F. *Die italienische Südfrage*. Berlin: Duncker & Humblot, 1951.

Volpe, G. *Italia moderna, 1815–1915*. 3 vols. Florence: Sansoni, 1943–52.

Webster, Richard A. *The Cross and the Fasces: Christian Democracy and Fascism in Italy*. Stanford: Stanford University Press, 1960.

♋ BEFORE 1870

Aquarone, A. *L'unificazione legislativa e i codici del 1865*. Milan: Giuffrè, 1960.

Aubert, A. *Le pontificat de Pie IX, 1846–1878*. Paris: Bloud et Gay, 1952.

Berselli, A. *La destra storica dopo l'unità*. Bologna: Il Mulino, 1963.

Brancato, F. *La Sicilia nel primo ventennio del regno d'italia*. Bologna: Zuffi, 1956.

Candeloro, G. *Storia dell'Italia moderna*. Vol. V (1860–71). Milan: Feltrinelli, 1968.

Case, L. M. *Franco-Italian Relations 1860–1865: the Roman Question and the Convention of September*. Philadelphia: University of Pennsylvania Press, 1932.

Cavour, Camillo di. *Il carteggio Cavour-Nigra dal 1858 al 1861*. Vols. III–IV. Bologna: Zanichelli, 1928–29.

Cobbe, F. P. *Italics: Brief Notes on Politics, People, and Places in Italy, in 1864*. London: Trübner, 1864.

Cusin, F. *L'Italia unita, 1860–1876*. Udine: Del Bianco, 1952.

D'Addio, M. *Politica e magistratura, 1848–76*. Milan: Giuffrè, 1966.

D'Amelio, G. *Stato e chiesa: la legislazione ecclesiastica fino al 1867*. Milan: Giuffrè, 1961.

De Cesare, R. *The Last Days of Papal Rome, 1850–1870*. Translated by Helen Zimmern. London: Constable, 1909.

De Ruggiero, G. *The History of European Liberalism*. Translated by R. G. Collingwood. London: Humphrey Milford, 1927.

Finali, G. *Memorie*. Edited by G. Maioli. Faenza: Fratelli Lega, 1955.

Ghiron, I. *Annali d'Italia, 1861–1870*. 3 vols. Milan: Hoepli, 1888–90.

Gramsci, A. *Il Risorgimento*. Turin: Einaudi, 1949.

Hales, E. E. Y. *Pio Nono: A Study in European Politics and Religion in the Nineteenth Century*. New York: Kenedy, 1954.

Halperin, S. W. *Diplomat under Stress: Visconti-Venosta and the Crisis of July 1870*. Chicago: University of Chicago Press, 1963.

Izzo, L. *La finanza pubblica nel primo decennio dell'unità italiana*. Milan: Giuffrè, 1962.

Luzio, A. *Aspromonte e Mentana*. Florence: Le Monnier, 1935.

Mack Smith, D. *Cavour and Garibaldi, 1860*. New York: Cambridge University Press, 1954.

———. *Garibaldi: A Great Life in Brief*. New York: Knopf, 1956.

———. *The Making of Italy, 1796–1870*. New York: Harper, 1968.

Massari, G. *Diario dalle cento voci 1858–1860*. Edited by E. Morelli, Bologna: Cappelli, 1959.

Maturi, W. (ed.) *Documenti diplomatici italiani*. 1st series. Vol. I. Rome: Libreria dello Stato, 1952.

———. *Interpretazioni del risorgimento, lezioni di storia della storiografia*. Turin: Einaudi, 1962.

Minghetti, M. *La convenzione di settembre, un capitolo dei miei ricordi*. Bologna: Zanichelli, 1899.

Molfese, F. *Storia del brigantaggio dopo l'unità*. Milan: Feltrinelli, 1964.

Mori, R. *La Questione Romana, 1861–1865*. Florence: Le Monnier, 1963.

———. *Il tramonto del potere temporale, 1866–70*. Rome: Edizioni di Storia, 1967.

Moscati, A. *I ministri del regno d'Italia*. 5 vols. Naples: Edizioni Comitato Napoletano, 1948–66.

Moscati, R. *Il ministero degli Affari Esteri, 1860–71*. Milan: Giuffrè, 1961.

Parravicini, G. *La politica fiscale e le entrate effettive del regno d'Italia, 1860–1890*. Turin: ILTE, 1958.

Pasolini, P. D. *Memoir of Count Giuseppe Pasolini*. Translated and abridged by the Countess of Dalhousie. London: Longmans, Green, 1885.

Pavone, C. *Amministrazione centrale e amministrazione periferica: da Rattazzi a Ricasoli (1859–1866)*. Milan: Giuffrè, 1964.

Pedìo, T. *Vita politica in Italia meridionale, 1860–1870*. Potenza: La Nuova Libreria, 1966.

Petruccelli della Gattina, F. *I moribondi del Palazzo Carignano*. Milan: Perelli, 1862.

Pieri, P. *Le forze armate nella età della Destra*. Milan: Giuffrè, 1962.

Pirri, P. Pietro. *La questione romana dalla convenzione di settembre alla caduta del potere temporale, 1864–1870*. 2 vols. Rome: Pontifica Università Gregoriana, 1961.

Ragionieri, E. *Politica e amministrazione nella storia dell'Italia unita*. Bari: Laterza, 1967.

Raponi, N. *Politica e amministrazione in Lombardia agli esordi dell'unità: il programma dei moderati*. Milan: Giuffrè, 1967.

Richards, E. F. (ed.) *Mazzini's Letters to an English Family*. 3 vols. London: John Lane, 1920.

Romeo, R. *Risorgimento e capitalismo*. Bari: Laterza, 1959.

Rosselli, N. *Mazzini e Bakounine, 1860–1872*. Turin: Bocca, 1927.

Rossi, Ernesto. *Il 'Sillabo'*. Florence: Parenti, 1957.

Salvatorelli, L. *Pensiero e azione del Risorgimento*. Turin: Einaudi, 1944.

———. *Il pensiero politico italiano dal 1700 al 1870*. Turin: Einaudi, 1941.

Salvemini, G. *Mazzini*. Translated by I. M. Rawson. Stanford, Calif.: Stanford University Press, 1956.

Salvestrini, A. *I moderati toscani e la classe dirigente italiana, 1859–1876*. Florence: Olschki, 1965.

Spadolini, G. *Firenze capitale*. Florence: Le Monnier, 1967.

Trevelyan, G. M. *Garibaldi and the Making of Italy*. New York: Longmans, Green, 1911.

Villari, P. *Le prime lettere meridionali*. Edited by G. Salvemini. Rome: La Voce, 1920.

Whyte, A. J. *The Political Life and Letters of Cavour, 1848–1861*. London: Humphrey Milford, 1930.

🦋 1870–1915

Albertini, L. *Venti anni di vita politica, 1898–1914.* 5 vols. Bologna: Zanichelli, 1950–52.

————. *The Origins of the War of 1914.* Translated and edited by I. M. Massey. 3 vols. Oxford: Oxford University Press, 1952–57.

Ansaldo, G. *Il ministro della buona vita.* Milan: Longanesi, 1950.

Aquarone, A. *Lo stato catechista.* Florence: Parenti, 1961.

Arcari, P. A. *Le elaborazioni della dottrina politica nazionale (1870–1914).* 3 vols. Florence: Marzocco, 1934–39.

Are, G. *I cattolici e la questione sociale in Italia, 1894–1904.* Milan: Feltrinelli, 1963.

Askew, W. C. *Europe and Italy's Acquisition of Libya, 1911–12.* Durham, N.C.: Duke University Press, 1942.

Billot, A. *La France et l'Italie, 1881–1899.* 2 vols. Paris: Plon, 1905.

Bissolati, L. *La politica estera dell'Italia dal 1897 al 1920.* Milan: Treves, 1923.

Borghi, A. *Mezzo secolo di anarchia (1898–1945).* Naples: Edizioni scientifiche italiane, 1954.

Bulferetti, L. *Le ideologie socialistiche in Italia (1870–1892).* Florence: Le Monnier, 1951.

Candeloro, G. *Il movimento cattolico in Italia.* Rome: Editori Riuniti, 1961.

Caracciolo, A. *L'inchiesta agraria Jacini.* Turin: Einaudi, 1958.

————. (ed.) *La formazione dell'Italia industriale.* Bari: Laterza, 1963.

Carocci, G. *Agostino Depretis e la politica interna italiana dal 1876 al 1887.* Turin: Einaudi, 1956.

————. *Giolitti e l'età giolittiana.* Turin: Einaudi, 1961.

Chabod, F. *Storia della politica estera italiana dal 1870 al 1896.* Bari: Laterza, 1951.

Chiala, L. *Pagine di storia contemporanea dal 1858 al 1892.* 3 vols. Turin: Roux, 1892–93.

Cilibrizzi, S. *Storia parlamentare politica e diplomatica d'Italia, 1848–1918.* 7 vols. Milan: Tosi, 1925.

Cingari, G. *Giustino Fortunato e il mezzogiorno d'Italia.* Florence: Parenti, 1954.

Colapietra, R. *Il novantotto: la crisi politica di fine secolo (1896–1900).* Milan: Edizioni Avanti, 1959.

Comandini, A. *L'Italia nei cento anni del secolo XIX, 1801–1900.* 5 vols. Milan: Vallardi, 1900.

Compendio delle statistiche elettorali italiane dal 1848 al 1934. 3 vols. Rome: Failli, 1946.

Corbino, E. *Annali dell'economia italiana.* 5 vols. Città di Castello: Società Leonardo da Vinci, 1931–38.

Corradini, E. *Il nazionalismo italiano.* Milan: Treves, 1914.

De Rosa, G. *L'azione cattolica: storia politica dal 1874 al 1919.* 2 vols. Bari: Laterza, 1953–54.

————. *Storia del movimento cattolico in Italia*. 2 vols. Bari: Laterza, 1966.

Ellena, V. *La statistica di alcune industrie italiane*. Rome: Botta, 1880.

Farini, D. *Diario di fine secolo*. Edited by Emilia Morelli. 2 vols. Rome: Bardi, 1961–62.

Foerster, R. F. *The Italian Emigration of Our Times*. Cambridge: Harvard University Press, 1919.

Fonzi, F. *Crispi e lo 'Stato di Milano'*. Milan: Giuffrè, 1965.

Fortunato, G. *Il mezzogiorno e lo stato italiano*. 2 vols. Vallecchi: Florence, 1926.

————. *Pagine e ricordi parlamentari*. 2 vols. Florence: Vallecchi, 1947.

Franchetti, L. *Mezzogiorno e colonie*. Florence: La nuova Italia, 1950.

————. and S. Sonnino. *La Sicilia nel 1876*. 2 vols. Florence: Barbèra, 1877.

Frassati, A. *Giolitti*. Florence: Parenti, 1959.

Frosini, V. *Breve storia della critica al marxismo in Italia*. Catania: Bonanno, 1965.

Gallavresi, G. *Italia e Austria, 1859–1914*. Milan: Treves, 1922.

Gerschenkron, A. 'Notes on the Rate of Industrial Growth in Italy, 1881–1913,' in *The Journal of Economic History*, 1955, vol. XV, pp. 360–75.

Giolitti, G. *Memoirs of My Life*. Translated by E. Storer. London: Chapman and Dodd, 1923.

————. *Quarant'anni di politica italiana: dalle carte di Giovanni Giolitti*. Edited by P. d'Angiolini. 3 vols. Milan: Feltrinelli, 1962.

Giovannetti, E. *Il tramonto del liberalismo*. Bari: Laterza, 1917.

Hilton-Young, W. *The Italian Left: A Short History of Political Socialism in Italy*. New York: Longmans, Green, 1949.

Hostetter, R. *The Italian Socialist Movement: Origins, 1860–1882*. Princeton: Van Nostrand, 1958.

Hughes, H. Stuart. *Consciousness and Society: The Reorientation of European Social Thought, 1890–1930*. New York: Knopf, 1958.

King, Bolton, and T. Okey. *Italy To-day*. London: Nisbet, 1901.

Lincei, Accademia dei (ed.). *Cinquanta anni di Storia Italiana*. 3 vols. Milan: Hoepli, 1911.

Manacorda, G. *Il movimento operaio italiano attraverso i suoi congressi, 1853–1892*. Rome: Edizioni Rinascita, 1953.

Manzotti, F. *La polemica sull'emigrazione nell'Italia unita fino alla prima guerra mondiale*. Città di Castello: Società Editrice Dante, 1962.

————. *Il socialismo riformista in Italia*. Florence: Le Monnier, 1965.

Martini, Ferdinando. *Diario: 1914–1918*. Edited by G. De Rosa. Milan: Mondadori, 1966.

Missiroli, M. *La monarchia socialista: estrema destra*. Bari: Laterza, 1914.

Mosca, G. *Partiti e sindacati nella crisi del regime parlamentare.* Bari: Laterza, 1949.

Musini, L. *Da Garibaldi al socialismo: memorie e cronache per gli anni dal 1858 al 1890.* Milan: Edizioni Avanti, 1961.

Natale, G. *Giolitti e gli Italiani.* Milan: Garzanti, 1949.

Nazionalismo italiano: atti del congresso di Firenze. Florence: Quattrini, 1911.

Nicolini, F. *Benedetto Croce.* Turin: Utet, 1962.

Novacco, D. *L'inchiesta Jacini;* and *Inchieste politiche.* Vols. 17 and 18 of *Storia del parlamento italiano,* edited by N. Rodolico. Palermo: Flaccovio, 1963–64.

Oriani, A. *La rivolta ideale.* Bologna: Gherardi, 1912.

————. *La lotta politica in Italia,* 5th ed. 3 vols. Bologna: Cappelli, 1925.

Palamenghi-Crispi, T. (ed.) *Carteggi politici inediti di Francesco Crispi (1860–1900).* Rome: L'Universelle, 1912.

————. *The Memoirs of Francesco Crispi.* Translated by M. Prichard-Agnetti. 3 vols. London: Hodder and Stoughton, 1922.

Papafava, F. *Dieci anni di vita italiana, 1899–1909.* 2 vols. Bari: Laterza, 1913.

Papini, G. *L'esperienza futurista (1913–1914).* Florence: Vallecchi, 1919.

Pinzani, C. *La crisi politica di fine secolo in Toscana.* Florence: Barbèra, 1963.

Quilici, N. *Banca Romana.* Rome: Mondadori, 1935.

Répaci, F. A. *La finanza pubblica italiana nel secolo 1861–1960.* Bologna: Zanichelli, 1962.

Romano, Aldo. *Storia del movimento socialista in Italia, 1861–1882.* 3 vols. Bari: Laterza, 1966–67.

Romanò, Angelo, and D. Frigessi (eds.). *La cultura italiana del '900 attraverso le riviste (La Voce,* and *Il Regno).* 2 vols. Turin: Einaudi, 1960.

Romano, S. F. *Storia dei fasci siciliani.* Bari: Laterza, 1959.

Salandra, A. *Italy and the Great War; from Neutrality to Intervention.* Shortened and translated by Kendrick Pyne. London: Arnold, 1932.

Salomone, A. *Italy in the Giolittian Era.* Revised edition. (Contains an important preface by G. Salvemini). Philadelphia: University of Pennsylvania Press, 1945.

Salvemini, G. *La politica estera dell'Italia dal 1871 al 1915,* 2d ed. Florence: Barbèra, 1950.

————. *Scritti sulla questione meridionale.* Bari: Laterza, 1955.

Sandonà, A. *L'irredentismo nelle lotte politiche (1866–1894).* 3 vols. Bologna: Zanichelli, 1932–38.

Sapori, A. "L'economia milanese dal 1860 al 1915," in *Storia di Milano,* vol. XV, edited by G. Treccani. Milan: Treccani, 1962.

Scoppola, P. *Crisi modernista e rinnovamento cattolico in Italia.* Bologna: Il Mulino, 1961.

Sereni, E. *Il capitalismo nelle campagne (1860–1900)*. Turin: Einaudi, 1948.

Sighele, S. *Il nazionalismo e i partiti politici*. Milan: Treves, 1911.

Spadolini, G. *L'opposizione cattolica da Porta Pia al '98*. Florence: Vallecchi, 1954.

Sprigge, C. J. S. *Benedetto Croce, Man and Thinker*. New Haven: Yale University Press, 1952.

Torre, A. (ed.) *Documenti diplomatici italiani*. 5th series, vol. I (1914–15). Rome: Istituto Poligrafico dello Stato, 1954.

Toscano, M. *Il Patto di Londra; storia diplomatica dell'intervento italiano, 1914–1915*. Bologna: Zanichelli, 1934.

Valiani, L. *Il partito socialista italiano nel periodo della neutralità, 1914–1915*. Milan: Feltrinelli, 1963.

Vigo, P. *Annali d'Italia, 1871–1900*. 7 vols. Milan: Treves, 1908–15.

Volpe, G. *Il popolo italiano tra la pace e la guerra, 1914–1915*. Milan: ISPI, 1946.

Zangheri, R. *Lotte agrarie in Italia: la federazione nazionale dei lavoratori della terra, 1901–1926*. Milan: Feltrinelli, 1960.

ॐ 1915–1940

Alatri, P. *Le origini del fascismo*. Rome: Editori riuniti, 1956.

———. *Nitti, D'Annunzio, e la questione adriatica, 1919–20*. Milan: Feltrinelli, 1959.

Albertini, A. *Vita di Luigi Albertini*. Milan: Mondadori, 1945.

Albertini, L. *In difesa della libertà*. Milan: Rizzoli, 1947.

Albrecht-Carrié, R. *Italy at the Paris Peace Conference*. New York: Columbia University Press, 1938.

Alfieri, Dino. *Dictators Face to Face*. Translated by David Moore. London: Elek, 1954.

Arfé, G. *Storia del socialismo italiano, 1892–1926*. Turin: Einaudi, 1965.

Baer, G. W. *The Coming of the Italian-Ethiopian War*. Cambridge: Harvard University Press, 1967.

Balabanoff, Angelica. *My Life as a Rebel*. London: Hamish Hamilton, 1938.

Balbo, I. *Diario, 1922*. Milan: Mondadori, 1932.

Barros, J. *The Corfu Incident of 1923: Mussolini and the League of Nations*. Princeton: Princeton University Press, 1965.

Binchy, D. A. *Church and State in Fascist Italy*. New York: Oxford University Press, 1941.

Bonomi, I. *From Socialism to Fascism: a Study of Contemporary Italy*. Translated by J. Murray. London: Hopkinson, 1924.

Borgese, G. A. *Goliath: the March of Fascism*. London: Gollancz, 1938.

Bottai, G. *Vent'anni e un giorno, 24 luglio 1943*. Milan: Garzanti, 1949.

Calogero, G. (ed.) *Conciliazione: un opuscolo clandestino del 1929*. Florence: Parenti, 1959.

Cammett, J. M. *Antonio Gramsci and the Origins of Italian Communism.* Stanford: Stanford University Press, 1967.

Cancogni, M. *Storia dello squadrismo.* Milan: Longanesi, 1959.

Capello, L. *Caporetto, perchè?* Edited by R. De Felice. Turin: Einaudi, 1967.

Carocci, G. *Giovanni Amendola nella crisi dello stato italiano, 1911–1925.* Milan: Feltrinelli, 1956.

Catalano, F. *Potere economico e fascismo: la crisi del dopoguerra, 1919–1921.* Milan: Lerici, 1964.

Caviglia, E. *La dodicesima battaglia (Caporetto).* Milan: Mondadori, 1933.

———. *Diario, 1925–1945.* Rome: Casini, 1952.

Chiurco, G. A. *Storia della rivoluzione fascista, 1919–1922.* 5 vols. Florence: Vallecchi, 1929.

Ciano, G. *Ciano's Diplomatic Papers.* Translated by Stuart Hood. London: Odhams, 1948.

———. *Ciano's Diary, 1937–1938.* Translated by A. Mayor. London: Methuen, 1952.

Ciasca, R. *Storia coloniale dell'Italia contemporanea.* Milan: Hoepli, 1938.

Craig, Gordon A., and Felix Gilbert. (eds.) *The Diplomats, 1919–1939.* Princeton: Princeton University Press, 1953.

D'Andrea, U. *La fine del regno; grandezza e decadenza di Vittorio Emanuele III.* Turin: Società editrice torinese, 1951.

De Begnac, Yvon. *Palazzo Venezia.* Rome: La Rocca, 1951.

De Bono, E. *Anno XIIII: the Conquest of an Empire.* Translated by Bernard Miall. London: Cresset Press, 1937.

De Felice, R. *Mussolini il rivoluzionario, 1883–1920;* and *Mussolini il fascista, 1921–1925.* Turin: Einaudi, 1965–66.

Di Nolfo, E. *Mussolini e la politica estera italiana (1919–33).* Padua: Cedam, 1960.

Dorso, G. *Mussolini alla conquista del potere.* Turin: Einaudi, 1949.

Edmonds, J. E. *Military Operations: Italy, 1915–1919.* London: HMSO, 1949.

Einaudi, L. *Cronache economiche e politiche di un trentennio.* 8 vols. Turin: Einaudi, 1959–65.

Faldella, E. *Caporetto, le vere cause di una tragedia.* Bologna: Cappelli, 1967.

Federzoni, L. *Italia di ieri per la storia di domani.* Milan: Mondadori, 1967.

Fermi, Laura. *Mussolini.* Chicago: University of Chicago Press, 1961.

Ferrari, F. L. *L'azione cattolica e il 'regime.'* Florence: Parenti, 1957.

Ferraris, E. *La marcia su Roma veduta dal Viminale.* Rome: Leonardo, 1946.

Finer, H. *Mussolini's Italy.* New York: Holt, 1935.

Fiori, G. *Vita di Antonio Gramsci.* Bari: Laterza, 1966.

Flora, F. *Stampa dell'era fascista.* Rome: Mondadori, 1945.

Garosci, A. *La vita di Carlo Rosselli.* 2 vols. Florence: Edizioni U., 1945.

————. *Storia dei fuorusciti*. Bari: Laterza, 1953.

Gentile, G. *Che cosa è il fascismo?* Florence: Vallecchi, 1924.

————. *Origini e dottrina del fascismo*. Rome: Libreria del Littorio, 1929.

Germino, D. L. *The Italian Fascist Party in Power*. Minneapolis: University of Minnesota Press, 1959.

Gobetti, P. *La rivoluzione liberale*. Turin: Einaudi, 1948.

Gramsci, A. *Lettere dal carcere*. Turin: Einaudi, 1947.

————. *L'ordine nuovo, 1919–1920*. Turin: Einaudi, 1955.

Guariglia, R. *Ricordi 1922–1946*. Naples: Edizioni scientifiche italiane, 1950.

Guarneri, F. *Battaglie economiche tra le due grandi guerre*. 2 vols. Milan: Garzanti, 1953.

Halperin, S. W. *Italy and the Vatican at War*. Chicago: University of Chicago Press, 1939.

Jacini, S. *Il regime fascista*. Cernusco: Garzanti, 1947.

————. *Storia del partito popolare italiano*. Cernusco: Garzanti, 1951.

Kirkpatrick, I. *Mussolini: a Study in Power*. New York: Hawthorne Books, 1964.

Leto, G. *Ovra*. Bologna: Cappelli, 1952.

Ludwig, E. *Talks with Mussolini*. Translated by E. and C. Paul. Boston: Little, Brown, 1933.

Lussu, E. *Enter Mussolini*. Translated by M. Rawson. London: Methuen, 1936.

Macartney, M. H. H., and P. Cremona. *Italy's Foreign and Colonial Policy, 1914–1937*. New York: Oxford University Press, 1938.

Mack Smith, D. *Da Cavour a Mussolini*. Catania: Bonanno, 1968.

Malagodi, O. *Conversazioni della guerra, 1914–1919*. 2 vols. Edited by B. Vigezzi. Milan: Ricciardi, 1960.

Matteotti, G. *The Fascisti Exposed: a Year of Fascist Domination*. Translated by E. W. Dickes. London: ILP, 1924.

Megaro, G. *Mussolini in the Making*. Boston: Houghton Mifflin, 1938.

Missiroli, M. *Cosa deve l'Italia a Mussolini*. Rome: Edizioni di Novissima, 1937.

Monelli, P. *Mussolini, an Intimate Life*. London: Thames and Hudson, 1953.

Montemaggiori, M. *Dizionario della dottrina fascista*. Turin: Paravia, 1934.

Morandi, C. *I partiti politici nella storia d'Italia*. Florence: Le Monnier, 1945.

Moscati, R. (ed.) *Documenti diplomatici italiani, 1922–1924*. 2 vols. Rome: Ist. poligrafico dello stato, 1954–55.

Mussolini, B. *My Autobiography*. Translated by Richard Washburn Child. New York: Scribner's, 1928.

————. *Fascism: Doctrine and Institutions*. Rome: Ardita, 1935.

————. *Opera omnia di Benito Mussolini*. Edited by Edoardo and Duilio Susmel. 36 vols. Florence: La Fenice, 1951–63.

Mussolini, Vittorio. *Voli sulle ambe*. Florence: Sansoni, 1937.

Nenni, P. *Storia di quattro anni, 1919–1922*. Rome: Einaudi, 1946.

———. *Pagine di diario*. Milan: Garzanti, 1947.

Nitti, F. *Meditazioni dell'esilio*. Naples: Edizioni scientifiche italiane, 1947.

———. *Rivelazioni: dramatis personae*. Naples: Edizioni scientifiche italiane, 1948.

Novacco, D. *Dalla proporzionale all'aventino (1919–24)*. Vol. 12 of *Storia del parlamento italiano*, ed. Rodolico. Palermo: Flaccovio, 1967.

Orano, P. (ed.) *Inchiesta sulla razza*. Rome: Pinciana, 1938.

Orlando, V. E. *Memorie (1915–1919)*. Edited by R. Mosca. Milan: Rizzoli, 1960.

Padellaro, N. *Il libro della terza classe elementare*. Rome, 1936.

Pantaleoni, M. *Bolcevismo italiano*. Bari: Laterza, 1922.

Papa, E. R. *Storia di due manifesti: il fascismo e la cultura italiana*. Milan: Feltrinelli, 1958.

Pieri, P. *L'Italia nella prima guerra mondiale, 1915–1918*. Turin: Einaudi, 1965.

Pini, G. *Filo diretto con Palazzo Venezia*. Rocca San Casciano: Cappelli, 1950.

———, and D. Susmel. *Mussolini, l'uomo e l'opera*. 4 vols. Florence: La Fenice, 1953–55.

Preti, L. *I miti dell'impero e della razza nell'Italia degli anni '30*. Rome: Opere Nuove, 1965.

Pugliese, E. *Io defendo l'esercito*. Naples: Rispoli, 1946.

Répaci, A. *La marcia su Roma*. 2 vols. Rome: Canesi, 1963.

Rossi, A. (Tasca, A.). *The Rise of Italian Fascism, 1918–1922*. Translated by P. and D. Wait. London: Methuen, 1938.

Rossi, E. *I padroni del vapore*. Bari: Laterza, 1955.

———. *Il manganello e l'aspersorio*. Florence: Parenti, 1958.

Salandra, A. *Memorie politiche, 1916–1925*. Milan: Garzanti, 1951.

Salvatorelli, L. *Nazionalfascismo*. Turin: Gobetti, 1923.

———, and G. Mira. *Storia del fascismo nel periodo fascista*. New edition. Turin: Einaudi, 1964.

Salvemini, G. *Mussolini diplomatico*. Rome: De Luigi, 1945.

———. *The Fascist Dictatorship in Italy*. New York: Oxford University Press, 1927.

———. *Under the Axe of Fascism*. New York: Viking Press, 1936.

———. *Prelude to World War II*. London: Gollancz, 1953.

Santarelli, E. *Storia del movimento e del regime fascista*. 2 vols. Rome: Editori Riuniti, 1967.

Sereni, E. *La questione agraria nella rinascita nazionale italiana*. Turin: Einaudi, 1946.

Seth, R. *Caporetto, the Scapegoat Battle*. London: Macdonald, 1965.

Sforza, C. *Pensiero e azione di una politica estera italiana*. Bari: Laterza, 1924.

———. *L'Italia dal 1914 al 1944 quale io la vidi*. Rome: Mondadori, 1944.

Soffici, A. *Battaglia fra due vittorie* (preface by C. Malaparte). Florence: La Voce, 1923.

Soleri, M. *Memorie.* Turin: Einaudi, 1949.

Spinetti, G. S. *Bibliografia degli esuli politici sotto il fascismo.* Rome: Edizioni di Solidarismo, 1959.

Spriano, P. *Storia del partito comunista italiano.* Vol. I, *Da Bordiga a Gramsci.* Turin: Einaudi, 1967.

Sturzo, L. *Italy and fascismo.* New York: Harcourt Brace, 1926.

Tagliacozzo, E. *Gaetano Salvemini nel cinquantennio liberale.* Florence: La Nuova Italia, 1959.

Tamaro, A. *Venti anni di storia, 1922–1943.* 3 vols. Rome: Tiber, 1954.

Toscano, M. *The Origins of the Pact of Steel.* Baltimore: Johns Hopkins Press, 1968.

————. *Pagine di storia diplomatica contemporanea.* 2 vols. Milan: Giuffrè, 1963.

Turati, F., and A. Kuliscioff. *Carteggio.* Vol. V, *Dopoguerra e fascismo (1919–22).* Turin: Einaudi, 1953.

Valeri, N. *Da Giolitti a Mussolini: momenti della crisi del liberalismo.* Florence: Parenti, 1956.

————. *D'Annunzio davanti al fascismo: con documenti inediti.* Florence: Le Monnier, 1963.

Vigezzi, B. *L'Italia di fronte alla prima guerra mondiale.* Milan: Ricciardi, 1966.

Villari, L. *The Fascist Experiment.* London: Faber & Gwyer, 1926.

Vivarelli, R. *Il dopoguerra in Italia e l'avvento del fascismo, 1918–1922.* Naples: Istituto Studi Storici, 1967.

Volpe, G. *Guerra, dopoguerra, fascismo.* Venice: La Nuova Italia, 1928.

————. *L'Italia in cammino, l'ultimo cinquantennio.* Milan: Treves, 1931.

————. *Storia del movimento fascista.* Milan: ISPI, 1939.

Welk, W. G. *Fascist Economic Policy.* Cambridge, Mass.: Harvard University Press, 1938.

Wiskemann, E. *The Rome-Berlin Axis, a History of the Relations Between Hitler and Mussolini.* Revised edition. London: Collins, 1966.

Zangrandi, R. *Il lungo viaggio attraverso il fascismo.* Milan: Feltrinelli, 1962.

Zingali, G. *Liberalismo e fascismo nel mezzogiorno d'Italia, 1860–1932.* Milan: Treves, 1933.

✎ 1940–1969

Adams, J. C., and P. Barile. *The Government of Republican Italy.* Boston: Houghton Mifflin, 1961.

Amé, C. *Guerra segreta in Italia, 1940–1943.* Rome: Casini, 1954.

Amicucci, E. *I 600 giorni di Mussolini: dal Gran Sasso a Dongo.* Rome: Editrice 'Faro', 1948.

Andreotti, G. *De Gasperi e il suo tempo.* Verona: Mondadori, 1956.

Anfuso, F. *Roma, Berlino, Salò (1936–1945)*. Cernusco: Garzanti, 1950.

Annuario Statistico Italiano. Milan: Etas Kompass, 1963–66.

Armellini, Q. *Diario di guerra*. Milan: Garzanti, 1946.

Badoglio, P. *Italy in the Second World War*. Translated by M. Currey. New York: Oxford University Press, 1948.

Banfield, E. C. *The Moral Basis of a Backward Society*. Glencoe: The Free Press, 1958.

Bartoli, D. *La fine della monarchia*. Milan: Mondadori, 1946.

Barzini, L. *The Italians*. New York: Atheneum, 1964.

Battaglia, R. *The Story of the Italian Resistance*. Translated and edited by P. D. Cummins. London: Odhams, 1957.

Bianchi, G. *25 luglio—crollo di un regime*. Milan: Mursia, 1964.

Bocca, G. *Storia dell'Italia partigiana*. Bari: Laterza, 1966.

Bolla, N. *Il segreto di due re*. Milan: Rizzoli, 1951.

Bonanni, M. (ed.) *La politica estera della repubblica Italiana*. 3 vols. Milan: Edizioni di Comunità, 1967.

Bragadin, M. *The Italian Navy in World War II*. Translated by G. Hoffman. Annapolis: U.S. Naval Institute, 1957.

Canevari, E. *Graziani mi ha detto*. Rome: Magi-Spinetti, 1947.

————. *La guerra italiana*. 2 vols. Rome: Tosi, 1949.

Carboni, G. *Memorie segrete, 1935–1948*. Florence: Parenti, 1955.

Carrillo, E. *De Gasperi: the Long Apprenticeship*. Notre Dame: Notre Dame University Press, 1965.

Catalano, F. *Storia del C.L.N.A.I.* Bari: Laterza, 1956.

————. *L'Italia dalla dittatura alla democrazia*. Milan: Lerici, 1962.

Cavallero, U. *Commando supremo; diario 1940–43 del capo di Stato Maggiore Generale*. Bologna: Cappelli, 1948.

Chassériaud, Jean-Paul. *Le parti Démocrate Chrétien en Italie*. Paris: Colin, 1965.

Chilanti, F. and M. Farinella. *Rapporto sulla mafia*. Palermo: Flaccovio, 1964.

Ciano, G. *Ciano's Diary: 1939–1943*. Introduction by Malcolm Muggeridge. London: Heinemann, 1947; New York: Doubleday, 1946.

Cione, E. *Storia della repubblica sociale italiana*. Caserta: Cenacolo, 1948.

Compagna, F. *La lotta politica italiana nel secondo dopoguerra e il mezzogiorno*. Bari: Laterza, 1950.

Croce, B. *Pagine politiche*. Bari: Laterza, 1945.

————. *Pensiero politico e poltica attuale*. Bari: Laterza, 1946.

————. *Due anni di vita politica italiana, 1946–47*. Bari: Laterza, 1948.

————. *Croce, the King and the Allies. Extracts from a Diary, July 1943–June 1944*. Translated by Sylvia Sprigge. New York: Norton, 1950.

Deakin, F. W. *The Brutal Friendship: Mussolini, Hitler and the Fall of Italian Fascism*. New Edition. New York: Doubleday, 1966.

De Gasperi, M. R. C. *De Gasperi, uomo solo*. Verona: Mondadori, 1964.

Delzell, C. F. *Mussolini's Enemies: the Italian Anti-Fascist Resistance.* Princeton: Princeton University Press, 1961.

Dieci Anni Dopo: saggi sulla vita democratica italiana. Bari: Laterza, 1955.

Dolci, Danilo. *Report from Palermo.* New York: Orion Press, 1959.
————. *The Outlaws of Partinico.* Translated by R. Munroe. London: Macgibbon and Key, 1960.

Einaudi, L. *Lo scrittoio del presidente, 1948–1955.* Turin: Einaudi, 1956.

Einaudi, M. and F. Goguel. *Christian Democracy in Italy and France.* Notre Dame: Notre Dame University Press, 1952.

Espinosa, A. degli. *Il regno del sud.* Florence: Parenti, 1955.

Falconi, C. *La chiesa e le organizzazioni cattoliche in Italia, 1944–55.* Turin: Einaudi, 1956.

Faldella, E. *L'Italia e la seconda guerra mondiale.* Rocca San Casciano: Cappelli, 1959.

Falzone, V. (ed.) *La costituzione della Repubblica Italiana, illustrata con i lavori preparatori.* Rome: Colombo, 1948.

Favagrossa, C. *Perchè perdemmo la guerra; Mussolini e la produzione bellica.* Milan: Rizzoli, 1946.

Frankel, H. *Mattei: Oil and Power Politics.* London: Faber, 1966.

Fenet, A. *La question du Tyrol du sud.* Paris: Pichon 1968.

Fried, R. C. *The Italian Prefects.* New Haven: Yale University Press, 1963.

Galli, G. *Il bipartitismo imperfetto.* Bologna: Il Mulino, 1966.

Garofalo, F. *Un anno al Quirinale.* Cernusco: Garzanti, 1947.

Godechot, T. *Le parti démocrate-chrétien italien.* Paris: Pichon, 1964.

Gorla, G. *L'Italia nella seconda guerra mondiale.* Milan: Baldini & Castoldi, 1959.

Grindrod, M. *The Rebuilding of Italy.* New York: Oxford University Press, 1955.

Hales, E. E. Y. *Pope John and His Revolution.* London: Eyre & Spottiswoode, 1965.

Hildebrand, G. H. *Growth and Structure in the Economy of Modern Italy.* Cambridge, Mass.: Harvard University Press, 1965.

Horowitz, D. L. *The Italian Labor Movement.* Cambridge, Mass.: Harvard University Press, 1963.

Italy Today. Rome: Information Service, Presidency Council of Ministers, 1962.

Kogan, N. *Italy and the Allies.* Cambridge, Mass.: Harvard University Press, 1956.
————. *The Politics of Italian Foreign Policy.* New York: Praeger, 1963.
————. *A Political History of Postwar Italy.* New York: Praeger, 1966.

LaPalombara, J. *The Italian Labor Movement: Problems and Prospects.* Ithaca: Cornell University Press, 1957.
————. *Interest Groups in Italian Politics.* Princeton: Princeton University Press, 1964.

————. *Italy: the Politics of Planning*. Syracuse: Syracuse University Press, 1966.

Leto, G. *Polizia segreta in Italia*. Rome: Vito Bianco, 1961.

Lombardini, G. *De Gasperi e i Cattolici*. Milan: Edizioni di Comunità, 1962.

Lussu, E. *Sul partito d'azione e gli altri: note critiche*. Milan: Mursia, 1968.

Lutz, V. *Italy: a Study in Economic Development*. London: Oxford University Press, 1962.

Mammarella, G. *Italy after Fascism: a Political History 1943–65*. Notre Dame: University of Notre Dame Press, 1966.

Monelli, P. *Roma 1943*. Rome: Migliaresi, 1946.

Morison, S. E. *Sicily-Salerno-Anzio: January 1943–June 1944*. Boston: Little, Brown, 1954.

Mussolini, B. *Memoirs, 1942–1943*. Edited by R. Klibansky. Translated by Frances Lobb. London: Weidenfeld and Nicolson, 1949.

Neufeld, M. F. *Italy: School for Awakening Countries: the Italian Labor Movement, 1800–1960*. Ithaca: Cornell University Press, 1961.

Novacco, D. *Inchiesta sulla mafia*. Milan: Feltrinelli, 1963.

Palazzoli, G. *Les régions italiennes*. Paris: Pichon, 1966.

Pantaleone, M. *Mafia and Politics*. London: Chatto & Windus, 1966.

Paulson, B. *The Searchers: Conflict and Communism in an Italian Town*. Chicago: Quadrangle Books, 1966.

Perticone, G. *La repubblica di Salò*. Rome: Edizioni Leonardo, 1947.

————. *La politica italiana dal primo al secondo dopoguerra*. Milan: Giuffrè, 1965.

Pini, G. *Itinerario tragico (1943–1945)*. Milan: Edizioni Omnia, 1950.

Ponce De Leon, A. M. *Guerra diplomatica a Salò*. Bologna: Cappelli, 1950.

Posner, M. V., and S. J. Woolf. *Italian Public Enterprise*. London: Duckworth, 1967.

Quazza, G. *La resistenza italiana: appunti e documenti*. Turin: Giappichelli, 1966.

Rossi-Doria, M. *Riforma agraria e azione meridionalista*. Bologna: Edizioni Agricole, 1948.

————. *Dieci anni di politica agraria nel mezzogiorno*. Bari: Laterza, 1958.

Saitta, A. *Dal fascismo alla resistenza*. Florence: La Nuova Italia, 1961.

Salvadori, M. *The Labour and the Wounds*. London: Pall Mall Press, 1958.

Sartori, G. (ed.) *Il parlamento italiano 1946–1963*. Naples: Edizioni Scientifiche, 1963.

Schachter, G. *The Italian South: Economic Development in Mediterranean Europe*. New York: Random House, 1965.

Senise, C. *Quando ero capo della polizia, 1940–1943*. Rome: Ruffolo, 1946.

Simoni, L. *Berlino: ambasciata d'Italia, 1939–1943*. Rome: Migliaresi, 1946.

Spreafico, A., and J. LaPalombara. (eds.) *Elezioni e comportamento politico in Italia*. Cremona: Edizioni di Comunità, 1963.

Stern, R. M. *Foreign Trade and Economic Growth in Italy*. Washington: Praeger, 1967.

Svimez. *Un secolo di statistiche italiane: nord e sud, 1861–1961*. Rome: Svimez, 1961.

Sylos-Labini, P. (ed.) *Problemi dell'economia siciliana*. Milan: Feltrinelli, 1966.

Tamaro, A. *Due anni di storia, 1943–1945*. 3 vols. Rome: Tosi, 1948–50.

Tarrow, S. G. *Peasant Communism in Southern Italy*. New Haven: Yale University Press, 1967.

Toscano, M. (ed.) *Documenti diplomatici italiani*. 9th series. Vols. IV–V (1940). Rome: Istituto Poligrafico dello Stato, 1960–65.

———. *Dal 25 luglio all' 8 settembre*. Florence: Le Monnier, 1966.

Tupini, G. *I Democratici Cristiani*. Milan: Garzanti, 1954.

Valiani, L. *Dall'antifascismo alla resistenza*. Milan: Feltrinelli, 1959.

Vaussard, M. *La conjuration du grand conseil fasciste contre Mussolini*. Paris: Editions Mondiales, 1965.

Votaw, D. *The Six-legged Dog: Mattei and ENI*. Berkeley: University of California Press, 1964.

Villari, L. *Affari esteri, 1943–1945*. Rome: Spinetti, 1948.

Zachariae, Georg. *Mussolini si confessa*. Cernusco: Garzanti, 1949.

Zincone, V. *Hitler e Mussolini: lettere e documenti*. Milan: Rizzoli, 1946.